Studies in Personnel and Industrial Psychology

THE DORSEY SERIES IN PSYCHOLOGY

EDITOR   HOWARD F. HUNT   *Columbia University*

Studies in Personnel and Industrial Psychology

Editors
EDWIN A. FLEISHMAN
American Institutes for Research
Washington, D.C.

ALAN R. BASS
Department of Psychology
Wayne State University

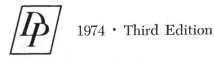 1974 · Third Edition

THE DORSEY PRESS Homewood, Illinois 60430
IRWIN-DORSEY INTERNATIONAL London, England WC2H 9NJ
IRWIN-DORSEY LIMITED Georgetown, Ontario L7G 4B3

Third Edition

First Printing, January 1974

ISBN 0-256-01085-4
Library of Congress Catalog Card No. 73–84299
Printed in the United States of America

To Pauline
and Janis

PREFACE

THERE HAVE BEEN a number of changes in the field of industrial psychology since the last edition of this book. Psychologists have become increasingly concerned with problems of unfair discrimination in employment and with the development of new techniques for personnel selection and appraisal. Important developments have occurred in understanding the bases of employee motivation, and new techniques have been proposed for making work more meaningful and satisfying. Increased emphasis is placed on understanding organizational characteristics and their impact on member behavior. Concern with methods for integrating so called unemployable or hard-core disadvantaged employees into the work force has also increased.

In this new edition, we have included recent articles that deal directly with many of these socially relevant issues. This volume, however, retains what we feel was a major value of the two previous editions—specifically, a *balanced* coverage of industrial psychology to include each of the major areas of concern to the field. Thus, we have chosen to retain coverage of the more traditional areas of industrial psychology (e.g., selection, criterion development, fatigue, accidents, working conditions) while continuing the intensive coverage of the currently popular topics of motivation, job satisfaction, leadership, and organizational psychology.

This book is designed for use in courses in personnel, industrial, and organizational psychology. It is particularly appropriate for introductory and survey courses in these fields, and does not presume extensive background in psychology, statistics, or research methodology. A number of articles were especially edited for this volume to make them more readable and understandable. We have tried to emphasize readings that provide an appreciation of the scientific aspects of industrial psychology as well as a critical regard for the methods and concepts used to investigate human behavior in organizational settings.

For each of the nine major sections of this volume we have written introductory text material showing the relevance of each article to the important issues in the field and to the theme of that section. We have tried to make this introductory material even more valuable to the student by providing summaries of important areas of research and methodology which may not be covered by articles in this volume.

The organization of the present edition is similar to that of the previous one, but the section "Criterion Development and Performance Appraisal" now appears first, since this seems to be one of the most pervasive problems the industrial psychologist faces and is relevant to virtually every other area in industrial and organizational psychology. The sections on "Personnel Selection" and "Training Employees and Managers" logically follow. We have combined the two sections on "Fatigue, Monotony and Working Conditions" and "Accidents and Safety," from the previous edition, into a shorter, single section called "Fatigue, Accidents, and Conditions of Work." We have retained the section on "Consumer Psychology," which was new in the last edition, although it too has been shortened.

Of the 56 articles in this volume, 25, or about 45 percent, are new to this edition. In revising the book since the last edition, we have attempted to include, wherever possible, more recent articles on particular topics. However, for a number of topics we found that no newer article was as well written, or as generally valuable, as the article previously included for that topic. We chose not to sacrifice quality for the sake of recency. Some excellent articles were not included to minimize overlap with included articles and to keep the book to manageable size.

In Section 1, "Criterion Development and Performance Appraisal," we have included a recent description of the logic and methods of functional job analysis, presented updated material on the problem of multiple v. composite criterion measures, and provided an example of the development of behaviorally-anchored rating scales. In Section 2, "Personnel Selection," we have provided a review of recent research on the employment interview, included an example of the use of "assessment centers" for personnel selection, and presented material on the problems involved in validating employment tests to avoid unfair discrimination. Section 3, "Training Employees and Managers," includes an up-dated review of the effectiveness of "sensitivity training" in industry and presents an example of a training program designed to orient "hard-core unemployed" job applicants to company policies and working procedures.

Section 4, "Motivation, Attitudes, and Job Satisfaction," includes a paper on employee motivation through job enrichment, and provides a theoretical discussion as well as a research study on "instrumentality-expectancy" motivation theory. In addition, we have provided an updated review of research and theory on the relationship between job satisfaction and employee performance. In Section 5, "Leadership and Supervision," we provide a general updating on current research on leader behavior and leadership effectiveness. Section 6, "Communication and Organizational Behavior," includes recent papers on organizational theory with emphasis on problems of organizational change and methods for assessing organizational effectiveness. In addition, we have included a paper illustrating the interrelationships of organizational and employee characteristics.

Section 7, "Fatigue, Accidents, and Conditions of Work," has been shortened from the previous edition, and has been updated to include a recent paper on the meaning and nature of industrial fatigue, and a research study on worker reactions to the four-day work week. Section 8, "Engineering Psychology," was shortened from the previous edition but in the articles retained we still attempt to cover the major topics that are most relevant to industrial psychology. Finally, Section 9, "Consumer Psychology," includes a new article on the use of operant conditioning techniques in assessing advertising effectiveness, as well as a "consumerism"-oriented paper dealing with methods for effectively presenting product information to consumers.

We have provided more supplementary references for the student's use in our introduction to each section. In addition, an innovation in the present edition is a section of suggested additional readings at the end of each section introduction. This selected bibliography, together with the supplementary references gives the student additional source materials which deal with the major topics covered in each section. In many cases, these materials include readings it was not possible to include because of space limitations, or suggest basic books which will allow the student to pursue a given area in more depth. These additional readings also provide the instructor added flexibility if he wishes to assign supplementary material.

As in the previous editions, we have done a good deal of editing here and there for which we hope the authors will forgive us. In a number of cases, complicated tabular material, analysis of variance tables, or involved descriptions of advanced statistical techniques were omitted or simplified. In no case did this seem to detract from the value of the article or to lose any essential information. Sometimes paragraphs or sentences were inserted to summarize the material omitted, especially in the case of elaborate tables and statistical tests. Similarly, some articles were shortened, discussion sections abbreviated, or exposition simplified. In all such cases we preferred this course to substituting less relevant articles for those considered more important.

We are indebted to the various publishers for providing permission to reprint or extract articles from their publications. In all cases, the original source of the individual articles is acknowledged on the title page of each article. Special permission to reprint was also obtained from each author and we are grateful to them. In some cases the authors prepared new material especially for this volume and we have acknowledged this in the text. We hope all the authors are pleased with the final product.

We are grateful to the following colleagues whose comments contributed in some manner to the shaping of this revision: Monroe P. Friedman, Milton D. Hakel, Thomas D. Hollmann, Cary Lichtman, Harvey Nussbaum, Hjalmar Rosen, Marshall Sashkin, Benjamin Schneider, Patricia C. Smith, Harry C. Triandis, and Myron M. Zajkowski. In addition, we are indebted to a number of industrial/organizational psychology students who made many helpful suggestions.

We are also indebted to Mrs. Pat Heald and Mr. Jerald Greenberg who provided valuable assistance in preparing the book for publication.

December 1973   EDWIN A. FLEISHMAN
                                                   ALAN R. BASS

CONTENTS

xi

SECTION NINE. CONSUMER PSYCHOLOGY

Section One

CRITERION
DEVELOPMENT AND
PERFORMANCE
APPRAISAL

INTRODUCTION

THE DEVELOPMENT OF ADEQUATE METHODS for measuring job proficiency is one of the most difficult problems facing the industrial and organizational psychologist. Such measures are essential, however, for many personnel decisions and for most of the research in industrial psychology. For example, one cannot investigate the relative effectiveness of various leadership styles on worker productivity unless an appropriate measure of productivity is available. Adequate criterion measures of job proficiency are also essential for validation of employment tests and other selection procedures such as those described in Section Two of this book. Further, criterion measures are necessary as a basis for promotion and transfer, evaluation of the need for and the results of training, estimating labor costs, determining wages, and many other purposes. Thus, the criterion problem is a pervasive problem in industrial psychology, and is really the first problem with which the industrial psychologist must be concerned. The articles in this section discuss some of the major issues involved in developing adequate job performance criteria.

In order to identify those aspects of job performance which are essential for success in a given job, a necessary first step is a job analysis. Also, job analyses are important sources of information about possible selection tests or devices which might be valid for screening job applicants, since a job analysis can identify necessary worker requirements as well as major job duties and responsibilities. The first article in this section, by Fine

1

and Wiley, entitled "An Introduction to Functional Job Analysis," describes one approach to the identification of major task activities and worker requirements in a job. This approach focuses on identifying exactly what a worker *does* on a job as well as on the result of the worker's behavior (that is, what gets done). Worker Function Scales are used to define a worker's task activities in relation to Data, People, and Things.[1]

A typical outcome of any job analysis is a list of several different aspects of performance which are considered to be important for job success. For example, one might find that speed, accuracy, dependability, good customer relations, and alertness to irregularities are all important criteria for success of bank tellers. Similarly, success on almost any job is probably best thought of as multidimensional, consisting of a number of differentiated components.[2] The next study, by Seashore, Indik, and Georgopoulos, "Relationships Among Criteria of Job Performance," reports empirical data indicating that different aspects of job performance often bear only small relationships to one another.

In view of the common observation of such "criterion multidimensionality," the question arises as to what to do about it. Should the various criterion measures be combined into an overall composite score, or should each be treated separately? And if they are to be combined, *how* should they be combined to arrive at an overall index of job success? Numerous authors have discussed these issues, and a controversy seems to have arisen between those proponents of the "single" or "composite" criterion and advocates of the use of multiple criterion measures. In the next article, "Composite vs. Multiple Criteria," Schmidt and Kaplan review the major arguments of the proponents of both sides of this controversy and suggest purposes for which a composite criterion index is appropriate and circumstances when it is more desirable to examine multiple criterion measures individually.

---

[1] Functional Job Analysis (FJA) was the method used to develop and classify job descriptions for the Dictionary of Occupational Titles used by the U.S. Employment Service (U.S. Department of Labor, *Dictionary of Occupational Titles.* 3rd Edition, Washington, D.C., U.S. Govt. Printing Office, 1965). Another approach to job and worker analysis, based on statistical analyses of ratings of worker-oriented and job-oriented requirements of positions in an organization, has been proposed by McCormick and his associates. (See E. J. McCormick, P. R. Jeanneret, and R. C. Mecham, "A Study of Job Characteristics and Job Dimensions as Based on the Position Analysis Questionnaire (PAQ)," *Journal of Applied Psychology* 56 (1972): 347–68; E. J. McCormick, J. W. Cunningham, and G. G. Gordon, "Job Dimensions Based on Factorial Analyses of Worker-oriented Variables," *Personnel Psychology* 20 (1967): 417–30; E. J. McCormick, J. W. Cunningham, and G. C. Thornton, "The Prediction of Job Requirements by a Structured Job Analysis Procedure," *Personnel Psychology* 20 (1967): 431–40.)

[2] See H. E. Brogden, and E. K. Taylor, "The Dollar Criterion—Applying the Cost Accounting Concept to Criterion Construction," *Personnel Psychology* 3 (1950): 133–54; E. E. Ghiselli, "Dimensional Problems of Criteria," *Journal of Applied Psychology* 16 (1961): 640–47; R. M. Guion, "Criterion Measurement and Personnel Judgments," *Personnel Psychology* 14 (1961): 141–49; M. D. Dunnette, "A Note on *the* Criterion," *Journal of Applied Psychology* 47 (1963): 251–54.

When obtaining measures of the various aspects of job success, it is always desirable, whenever possible, to obtain "objective" measures such as quantity of production, number of unauthorized absences, number of errors, accident frequency, and so forth. However, for most jobs it is not always possible to obtain objective criterion data, so that subjective judgments of job performance must be relied upon. The next four articles are concerned with problems involved in the use of subjective criteria, primarily performance ratings by supervisors.

There are many types of performance ratings which might be used. They can be divided into three main categories: (1) *Graphic rating scales.* These are the most well known and widely used rating methods, and consist of a graph or line segment divided into several parts, variously labeled with verbal or numerical anchors, on which the supervisor indicates his evaluation of the employee by checking the appropriate space on the scale. (2) *Ranking methods.* These consist of variations of the technique of rank-ordering employees from best to poorest on a particular rating dimension or on overall performance effectiveness. Besides straight rank ordering, variations such as alternation ranking (ranking the best employee and then the poorest, and then alternating between the top and bottom parts of the distribution), paired-comparisons (indicating which member of each of all possible pairs of employees is preferred); and forced-distributions (forcing the rater to place a certain percentage of his employees in each rating category from best to poorest) have been employed. (3) *Check-list methods.* These are methods in which the rater is asked to describe (rather than evaluate) the employee by checking which of a series of statements or phrases best characterize the employee. The best known variation of the check-list methods is the *forced-choice* procedure, in which the statements or phrases are grouped in sets of three or four, with the phrases in each set having been constructed to be of equal desirability or favorability to the rater, but to be of differing validity for differentiating between better and poorer employees. The rater is supposedly unaware of the differential validity of the phrases, and is asked to choose which of the phrases best describes the employee he is rating.

Graphic rating scales are subject to many methodological problems which make them of limited value as measures of job success. Several studies [3] have indicated that ratings show little relationship to more objective job performance criteria. Instead, it has been suggested that graphic ratings tend to reflect more the biases and response tendencies of the rater than true job performance of the ratee. They are frequently

---

[3] H. J. Hausmann, and H. H. Strupp, "Non-technical Factors in Supervisor's Ratings of Job Performance," *Personnel Psychology* 8 (1955): 201–17; R. H. Gaylord, E. Russell, C. Johnson and D. Severin, "The Relationship of Ratings to Production Records: An Empirical Study," *Personnel Psychology* 4 (1951): 363–71.

found to be contaminated with halo and leniency errors [4] and workers often refer to such ratings as being based primarily on "politics," general impressions or personality factors.

The article by Kipnis, "Some Determinants of Supervisory Esteem," deals directly with these problems involved in the use of graphic rating scales. Kipnis suggests that ratings are largely influenced by interpersonal relationships between rater and ratee and that favorable ratings are obtained to the extent to which the ratee shows supporting behaviors toward the rater. He further suggests that if ratings do indeed reflect these kinds of interpersonal variables that they ought not then be used as a substitute for actual job performance measures. Instead, objective performance indices or alternative rating methods need to be utilized as well.

Because of the problems with graphic rating scales, industrial psychologists and business managers have long sought alternative methods for evaluating employee performance. In fact, ranking methods and checklist methods were primarily developed as alternatives to graphic rating methods which, it was hoped, would be less subject to rater biases and interpersonal relationship considerations. Unfortunately, the available evidence has not shown these alternative rating methods to be a panacea for the problems involved in rating of employees. Instead, industrial psychologists have recently tended to concentrate on methods for improving graphic rating scales. One procedure has been to develop behaviorally anchored scales, so that the rater would have a clear idea of exactly what trait or job aspect he was supposed to be evaluating, and so that different raters would be likely to evaluate a particular ratee in the same way.

The next two articles illustrate two approaches to this objective of making rating scales more effective. The first article, by Kirchner and Dunnette, entitled "Using Critical Incidents to Measure Job Proficiency Factors," illustrates the use of the so-called critical incidents approach to the analysis of the job of salesman. Using this method, a job proficiency rating scheme was developed using as the rating stimuli specific behaviors of salesmen which had been previously determined to be critical behaviors for successful selling.

The next article, "Development of First-Level Behavioral Job Criteria," by Fogli, Hulin, and Blood, illustrates another current technique for constructing behaviorally anchored rating scales. This technique was originally proposed by Smith and Kendall [5] and involves the participation of the raters themselves in the development of the rating scale. In the article presented here, management personnel of a large grocery chain

---

[4] See J. P. Guilford, *Psychometric Methods*, 2d ed. (New York: McGraw-Hill Book Co., 1954), chap. 11.

[5] P. C. Smith and L. M. Kendall, "Retranslation of Expectations: An Approach to the Construction of Unambiguous Anchors for Rating Scales," *Journal of Applied Psychology* 47 (1963): 149–55.

participated in the development of rating scales for evaluating the behavior of supermarket checkers. This procedure has the advantage of using the rater's own vocabulary in constructing the rating scale, and of tending to increase the rater's motivation to use the scale effectively as a measure of job performance, since he participated in the design and construction of the scale.

Up to this point, we have emphasized the measurement and evaluation side of performance appraisal. Perhaps even more important is the problem of communicating the appraisal back to the employee so that: *(a)* he has "feedback" or "knowledge of results" of how his work is evaluated; *(b)* he develops some constructive approach to improving his performance; and *(c)* he is motivated to modify his behavior in the indicated directions. Thus, performance appraisal has a personnel development and goal-setting objective as well as an evaluation objective. The trouble is that these two objectives may work against each other. The final article in the section by Meyer, Kay, and French, entitled "Split Roles in Performance Appraisal," discusses and describes the very human problems involved in the superior-subordinate relationship of the appraisal interview. The authors describe some comprehensive research into the evaluation of an appraisal program which illuminates the relation between the supervisor's behavior, the subordinate's attitudes, and the success of the appraisal interview.[6]

SUGGESTED ADDITIONAL READINGS

Barrett, R. S. *Performance Rating.* Chicago: Science Research Associates, 1966.

Bittner, R. "Developing an Employee Merit Rating Procedure." *Personnel Psychology* 1 (1948): 403–32.

Flanagan, J. C. "The Critical Incident Technique." *Psychological Bulletin* 51 (1954): 327–58.

Lawler, E. E., III. "The Multitrait-multirater Approach to Measuring Managerial Job Performance." *Journal of Applied Psychology* 51 (1967): 369–81.

Miner, J. B. "Management Appraisal: A Capsule Review and Current References." *Business Horizons* 11 (1968): 5.

Ronan, W. W., and Prien, E. P., eds. *Perspectives on the Measurement of Human Performance.* New York: Appleton-Century-Crofts, 1971.

Whisler, T. L., and Harper, S. F., eds. *Performance Appraisal: Research and Practice.* New York: Holt, Rinehart, Winston, 1962.

Zavala, A. "Development of the Forced-choice Rating Scale Technique." *Psychological Bulletin* 58 (1965): 117–24.

---

[6] For another study comparing traditional supervisory performance appraisal with subordinate self appraisal, see G. A. Bassett and H. H. Meyer, "Performance Appraisal Based on Self-review," *Personnel Psychology* 21 (1968): 421–30.

1. AN INTRODUCTION TO FUNCTIONAL JOB ANALYSIS *

Sidney A. Fine and Wretha W. Wiley

THIS PAPER IS CONCERNED with the problem of how to arrive at a uniform and consistent understanding of what workers are expected to do on a job. Further, we are concerned with the problem of how to articulate such an understanding in a job description that can serve the needs of worker, supervisor, trainer, and recruiter.

A beginning can be made by analyzing the language of most ordinary descriptions of jobs. One quickly finds that the language of job descriptions has been used loosely and casually to serve a wide variety of purposes, but especially as a device for meeting individual and personal objectives such as justifying a desired status and/or pay level. In addition, job descriptions have tended to reflect management's emphasis on the results or outcome of a worker's performance with little attempt to delineate explicitly what the worker does.

When one begins to use explicit action verbs, rather than process names such as "interviewing and counseling," to describe worker behavior and, at the same time, makes an effort to distinguish between worker behavior (what the worker does) and the outcome of his behavior (the results expected to flow from the worker's action), a good deal of the confusion begins to disappear.

One is still faced, however, with the problem of how to state the worker action and its results and how to determine the limits of the statement. In effect, this problem raises the question: What are the fundamental units of work? A review of the areas of concern for personnel and management suggests that the basic unit which must be understood in order to describe jobs is the task.

- A job is made up of a series of *tasks*.
- Training is designed to enable a worker to perform a series of *tasks* in his job.
- Supervision of worker performance is based upon how well a worker performs assigned *tasks*.
- Recruitment and selection criteria are based upon the requirements or qualifications to perform specified *tasks*.

* Adapted and extracted from *An Introduction to Functional Job Analysis*, Methods for Manpower Analysis, Monograph no. 4 (Kalamazoo, Mich: W. E. Upjohn Institute, 1971).

- Classification of jobs is based upon an assessment of the complexity of the *level of tasks* which make up the job.

It may seem obvious to the reader that tasks are the fundamental modules or units of job design, job performance, and job management. But what is a task? What are its structure and form? And how does one go about writing a task statement?

What is a task? We define a task as an action or action sequence grouped through time designed to contribute a specified end result to the accomplishment of an objective and for which functional levels and orientation can be reliably assigned. The task action or action sequence may be primarily *physical,* such as operating an electric typewriter; or primarily *mental,* such as analyzing data; and/or primarily *interpersonal,* such as consulting with another person.

What are the structure and form of a task statement? The two most important elements of a task statement are:

1. The action the worker is expected to perform.
   Example: Asks questions, listens to responses, and writes answers on standard form.
2. The result expected of the worker action.
   Example: To record basic identifying information such as name, address, etc.

The worker action(s) phrase in the task statement describes as concretely as possible the worker's activity. The result phrase describes explicitly what his action is expected to produce or what gets done which identifies the worker's concrete contribution to a process or agency objective. While these two elements are the most critical in a task statement and can be thought of as the skeleton of a task, a task statement must include additional items of information to communicate clearly and consistently.

How does one go about writing a task statement? The following is a checklist of five questions which can be used in determining whether a task statement contains all the information needed and whether it can be consistently interpreted by operating people such as supervisors, trainers, and personnel officers.

1. Who? *(Subject)*
   The *subject* of a task statement is understood to be simply "worker." The task statement does not define what kind of worker.
   Example: A task statement contains no subject since it is always assumed to be "worker."
2. Performs what action? *(Action verb)*
   A task statement requires a concrete, explicit *action verb.* Verbs which point to a process (such as *develops, prepares, interviews, counsels, evaluates,* and *assesses*) should be avoided or used only to designate

broad processes, methods, or techniques which are then broken down into explicit, discrete action verbs.

Action: Asks client questions, *listens* to responses, and *writes* answers on standard intake form. . . .

3. To accomplish what immediate result?

   The purpose of the action performed must be explicit so that (1) its relation to the objective is clear and (2) performance standards for the worker can be set.

   Result: To record basic identifying information (items 1–8 on the intake form). The objective to which this result is directed is: To establish a client information system which enables workers to locate clients quickly and efficiently.

4. With what tools, equipment, or work aids?

   A task statement should identify the tangible instruments a worker uses as he performs a task; for example, telephone, typewriter, pencil/paper, checklists, written guides, and so forth.

   Tools: Form and pen.

5. Upon what instructions?

   A task statement should reflect the nature and source of instructions the worker receives. It should indicate what in the task is prescribed by a superior and what is left to the worker's discretion or choice.

   Prescribed content: Following standard intake form (items 1–8).

   Discretionary content: Exercising some leeway as to sequence of questions.

A completed, edited task statement, using the information generated and satisfying the five questions above, might read:

Asks client questions, listens to responses, and writes answers on standard intake form, exercising leeway as to sequence of questions, in order to record basic identifying information (items 1–8).

When a task statement contains all the information called for by these five questions, it becomes operationally useful; that is, it provides clear information which—

1. managers can use to assess the level of complexity of the task and compare its performance requirements with other tasks.
2. supervisors can use to give clear, accurate instructions to workers and develop criteria for assessing whether the worker's performance is satisfactory.
3. selection officers can use to infer worker qualifications needed to perform the task.
4. trainers can use to determine both classroom and on-the-job training needed by the worker to whom the task has been assigned.

GETTING CONTROL OF THE LANGUAGE OF WHAT WORKERS DO: THE WORKER FUNCTION SCALES

If an organization intends to employ workers with widely different levels of training, skill, and experience (or to plan for a differential use of staff), simply stating tasks to be performed is not enough. In addition to stating tasks, it is necessary to distinguish simpler (lower level) tasks from more complex (higher level) tasks. Job designers and managers must be able to identify levels of tasks so that they can delegate appropriate assignments to workers with no previous training and experience, to workers with some limited training and experience, and to workers with considerable specialized training, education, and experience.

Functional Job Analysis (FJA), which is both a conceptual system for defining the dimensions of worker activity and a method of measuring levels of worker activity, provides a set of tools for establishing the levels of tasks. It is concerned with *what a worker does,* and not with the results of the worker's action or *what gets done.* The reader will recall that in the task example the *worker action* (or what the worker does) is:

Asks client questions, listens to responses, and writes answers on standard intake form.

The *result* of his action (or what gets done) is:

To record basic identifying information (items 1–8).

What FJA does is provide (1) a standardized, controlled language to describe *what workers do* and (2) a means of assessing and measuring the *level* and *orientation* of what workers do. As a tool for controlling the language of tasks and measuring their complexity, FJA can be described in terms of the following principles:

1. What workers do as they perform the tasks that make up their jobs, they do in relation to Data, People, and Things. All jobs involve the workers, to some extent, with information or ideas (Data), with clients or co-workers (People), and with machines or equipment (Things). Workers function in unique ways in each of these areas. For example, when a worker's task involves him with machines or equipment (Things), the worker draws upon his physical resources (strength, dexterity, motor coordination, and so forth). When a worker's task involves him with information or ideas (Data), the worker calls his mental resources into play (knowledge, thought, intuition, insight, and so forth). When a worker's task involves him with clients, customers, and co-workers (People), the worker draws upon his interpersonal resources (empathy, courtesy, warmth, openness, guile, and so forth). All jobs require the worker to relate to each of these areas

and in doing so require him to draw upon his resources in each of these areas to some degree.

2. The concrete and specific actions workers perform in relation to Data, People, and Things as they execute different tasks can probably be described in an infinite number of ways; that is, there are as many specific ways of expressing what workers do in relation to Data, People, and Things as there are specific tasks to be performed or unique content and conditions to which to relate. While there may be an infinite number of ways of describing tasks, there is only a handful of significant patterns of behavior (functions) which describe how workers use themselves in relation to Data, People, and Things. Those patterns of behavior which can be articulated reliably have been defined in *Worker Function Scales*, (see Figure 1–1) the primary tools of

FIGURE 1–1

Summary Chart of Worker Function Scales

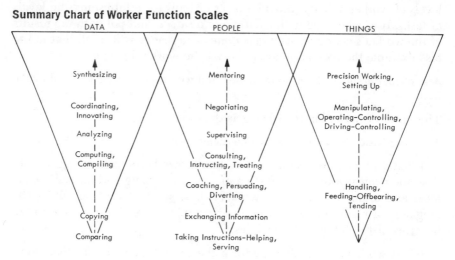

Note: Each successive function reading down usually or typically involves all those that follow it. The functions separated by a comma are separate functions on the same level separately defined. They are on the same level because empirical evidence does not make a hierarchical distinction clear.

The hyphenated functions: *Taking Instructions-Helping, Operating-Controlling, Driving-Controlling,* and *Feeding-Offbearing* are single functions.

Setting Up, Operating-Controlling, Driving-Controlling, Feeding-Offbearing, and *Tending* are special cases involving machines and equipment of *Precision Working, Manipulating,* and *Handling,* respectively, and hence are indented under them.

FJA, which provide a standardized, controlled language to describe what workers do in the entire universe of work.

For example, in relation to information and ideas, a worker functions to *compare, compile, compute,* or *analyze* data.

In interacting with clients, customers, and co-workers, workers *serve, exchange information, coach,* or *consult* with people.

In using equipment, workers *feed, tend, operate,* or *set up* machines and *drive/control* vehicles.

Although each of these worker functions is performed under widely varying conditions, occurs over a range of difficulty, and involves different specific content, each, within its scope, calls for similar kinds and degrees of worker characteristics to achieve effective performance.

3. The functions in each of the three areas of Data, People, and Things can be defined by a Worker Function Scale,[1] in which the performance requirements range from the simple to the complex in an ordinal scale. Because the scale is ordinal (that is, one in which any point on the scale includes lower levels and excludes higher levels), the selection of a specific function to reflect the requirements of a particular task indicates that the task includes the lower functions and excludes the higher ones. For example, on scanning the Worker Function Scale for Data, when one selects the *compiling* function as the appropriate worker behavior to describe the way a worker must relate to information in a given task, he is deciding two things: (1) that the worker's performance is more complex than *copying* and less complex than *analyzing;* and (2) that the worker must be able to perform all or at least comprehend all the data functions below *compiling,* but does not have to be able to perform or comprehend higher functions such as *analyzing* or *coordinating.*

4. The three hierarchies of Data, People, and Things functions provide two ways of systematically comparing and measuring the requirements of any task in any job. These two measures are *level* and *orientation.*

The *level* measure indicates the relative complexity or simplicity of a task when it is compared to other tasks. The level is expressed by selecting the function that best describes the pattern of behavior in which the worker engages to perform a given task effectively. The ordinal position of the function is the level measure. For example, to say that a worker in dealing with the Data content of a task is *compiling,* one has indicated that he is functioning at level 3B on the Data scale, which requires a higher level of functioning than is required in *copying* information (level 2) but is a lower level of functioning than *analyzing data* (level 4).

The *orientation* measure provided by FJA indicates the relative involvement of the worker with Data, People, and Things as he performs a given task. A basic concept of FJA is that the worker is not equally involved with all three in any task and that his relative involvement with any of the three may change from task to task. For example, in performing one task in his job, a worker may be involved almost exclusively with Data; that is, something like 75 percent of his

---

[1] See Appendix for an example of one of these scales, the Data Function Scale.

involvement, and the resources he draws upon to perform a task are related to Data at the *compiling* level; but in order to accomplish the task, he must also be involved interpersonally in *exchanging information* with co-workers (perhaps 15 percent) as well as in calling upon physical resources in *handling* various documents, paper, and pen (10 percent). The worker's total functional involvement with Data (75 percent), People (15 percent), and Things (10 percent) adds up to 100 percent.

The orientation measure, then, is expressed by assigning a percentage in units of five or ten to each of the three functions so that the total adds up to 100 percent. Note that these percentages are estimates. The reliability sought is in the pattern of the three estimates, not in the absolute amount of the estimates.

The orientation measure is a reflection of the performance requirements of a task. In the example above the estimates assigned must be in accord with the independent judgment that this task will be evaluated overwhelmingly on its data standards and quite lightly with regard to its people and things standards. The training the worker must have to perform the task should emphasize and build the mental skills required. The supervisor's instructions to the worker should emphasize and reflect the nature of the mental performance expected and the data standards by which the worker's results will be judged.

5. With the assignment to a given task of these two measures—level and orientation—the worker's total involvement with the specific content of his tasks—mentally, physically, and interpersonally—is obtained. Level and orientation are determined by selecting three functions, one from each of the three scales, most characteristic of the requirements of each task (yielding *level* measures). Each function is then weighted to show how much emphasis falls upon its requirements in the performance of the task (yielding *orientation* measures).

For the task example used previously,

Asks client questions, listens to responses, and writes answers on standard intake form, exercising leeway as to sequence of questions, in order to record basic identifying information (items 1–8),

the level and orientation would be:

Area	Functional Level	Orientation (percent)
Data	Copying (2)	50
People	Exchanging Information (2)	40
Things	Handling (1A)	10

6. Since the level and orientation measures can be applied to all tasks and, by integration, to all jobs, the Worker Function Scales provide a means

for comparing all tasks and all jobs on a common basis. This, of course, is a step forward from the situation where tasks cannot be compared because of the infinite number of ways of describing specific content.

APPENDIX

Complete Version of Data Function Scale

The arabic numbers assigned to definitions represent the successive levels of this ordinal scale. The *A* and *B* definitions are variations on the same level. There is no ordinal difference between *A* and *B* definitions on a given level.

Level	Definition
1	*Comparing*—Selects, sorts, or arranges data, people, or things, judging whether their readily observable functional, structural, or compositional characteristics are similar to or different from prescribed standards.
2	*Copying*—Transcribes, enters, and/or posts data, following a schema or plan to assemble or make things and using a variety of work aids.
3A	*Computing*—Performs arithmetic operations and makes reports and/or carries out a prescribed action in relation to them.
3B	*Compiling*—Gathers, collates, or classifies information about data, people, or things, following a schema or system but using discretion in application.
4	*Analyzing*—Examines and evaluates data (about things, data, or people) with reference to the criteria, standards, and/or requirements of a particular discipline, art, technique, or craft to determine interaction effects (consequences) and to consider alternatives.
5A	*Innovating*—Modifies, alters, and/or adapts existing designs, procedures, or methods to meet unique specifications, unusual conditions, or specific standards of effectiveness within the overall framework of operating theories, principles, and/or organizational contexts.
5B	*Coordinating*—Decides time, place, and sequence of operations of a process, system, or organization, and/or the need for revision of goals, policies (boundary conditions), or procedures on the basis of analysis of data and of performance review of pertinent objectives and requirements. Includes overseeing and/or executing decisions and/or reporting on events.
6	*Synthesizing*—*Takes off in new directions* on the basis of personal intuitions, feelings, and ideas (with or without regard for tradition, experience, and existing parameters) *to conceive new approaches* to or statements of problems and the development of system, operational, or aesthetic "solutions" or "resolutions" of them, typically outside of existing theoretical, stylistic, or organizational context.

2. RELATIONSHIPS AMONG CRITERIA OF JOB PERFORMANCE *

*Stanley E. Seashore, Bernard P. Indik,
and Basil S. Georgopoulos*

THIS PAPER REPORTS an empirical exploration of the generality of relationships among criteria of job performance in an industrial situation. We are concerned with the question whether a set of intercorrelations among job performance criteria is likely to be unique to the population and situation studied, or whether, instead, it can be considered to be an approximation of some generally valid system of criterion relationships.

THE PROBLEM

While the use of multiple criteria in studies of individual and organizational job performance is becoming more common, it is still rare. It is even more rare that multiple criteria are chosen or treated in terms of some theory of the composition of job performance, or in terms of some rational basis for choosing among, combining, or treating separately the various measures of performance. The few studies of multiple criteria have without exception raised new and serious problems, as well as doubts about assumptions that are commonly made.[1] The study by Kelly of the performance of medical students is an example.[2] From an analysis of 32 criterion variables, he concluded that the criterion relationships are variable in size and sign, and that most of the common variance is accounted for by five factors, of which four are relatively independent of one another. It is clearly not reasonable, in the case of these medical students, to take one measure as representing total performance, or to combine the measures in any simple way.

One approach to the solution of multiple criterion problems lies in postulating a unidimensional construct representing "overall job performance" or "net performance," and to treat various separate measures as

---

* Adapted from "Relationships among Criteria of Job Performance," *Journal of Applied Psychology* 44, no. 3 (1960): 195–202. Copyright 1960 by the American Psychological Association. Reprinted by permission.
[1] See E. L. Gaier, "The Criterion Problem in the Prediction of Medical School Success," *Journal of Applied Psychology* 36 (1952): 316–22; C. H. Rush, Jr., "A Factorial Study of Sales Criteria," *Personnel Psychology* 6 (1953): 9–24.
[2] E. L. Kelly, "Multiple Criteria of Medical Education and Their Implications for Selection," in *The Appraisal of Applicants to Medical Schools* (Evanston, Ill.: Association of American Medical Colleges, 1957).

independent estimates of such a single variable. This approach leads to attempts to combine the elemental criteria through techniques which maximize a common factor, maximize the predictability of the joint elements, or weight the elements in accordance with their reliability or predictability.[3] The logical problems here arise from the common finding that the elements of performance may be negatively correlated, that the elements interact, and that the resulting single measure does not reflect well the values implied by the initial choice of elemental measures.

Progress in the conceptualization and measurement of work performance is likely to lie in the direction of creating some theory (or several theories) of performance comparable in nature and complexity to those which have been developed in other areas of human behavior, for example, "intelligence" and "personality." However, to move in such a direction requires that we first do some exploration of the range and incidence of the relational phenomena with which we are concerned. In this paper we will deal with only three issues: (a) whether "job performance" reasonably can be treated as an unidimensional construct, (b) whether the relationships among a set of criterion measures are constant within error limits, in similar organizations rather than being unique in each organization, and (c) whether the relationships among a set of job performances are the same when treated as referring to a population of individuals as they are when treated as referring to a population of sets of individuals comprising separate organizations.

SOURCE AND NATURE OF DATA

For the present analysis we have confined our attention to five job performance variables, four of which are "objective" and one judgmental. The variables are called (a) overall effectiveness, (b) productivity, (c) chargeable accidents, (d) unexcused absences, and (e) errors. It is not proposed that these five variables represent all aspects of performance. They were selected from a larger roster of measures because of their face validity with reference to the purpose of the firm, their objectivity, their measured or estimated high reliability, and their relevance to both individual and organizational performance.

The data concern a delivery service firm having operations in several metropolitan areas in different parts of the country. Each area is organized as a "plant" with two or more major divisions, and each division has several operating units called "stations." A typical station has a supervisor, an assistant supervisor, several "night men" or "leaders," and about

---

[3] See H. E. Brogden and E. K. Taylor, "The Dollar Criterion: Applying the Cost Accounting Concept to Criterion Construction," *Personnel Psychology* 3 (1950): 133–54; B. F. Nagle, "Criterion Development," *Personnel Psychology* 6 (1953): 271–89; and G. H. Thompson, "Weighting for Battery Reliability and Prediction," *British Journal of Psychology* 30 (1940): 357–66.

25 drivers or deliverymen who work days delivering packages on their respective routes. The stations are geographically separated from one another, and somewhat variable in size but otherwise remarkably alike. They perform the same kind of activity, employ uniformly standard equipment and procedures, draw upon the same organizational and financial resources, employ the same system for establishing work standards, observe the same managerial and personnel policies, and maintain uniform records. Twenty-seven such stations, and their 975 nonsupervisory employees, comprise the populations for this report.

The data allow the computation of relationships among the five criteria for different populations as follows: *(a)* for all individuals $(N = 975)$, *(b)* for all stations $(N = 27)$, and *(c)* for individuals in each of the separate stations (Ns ranging from 13 to 54).

DESCRIPTION OF VARIABLES

Productivity. This measure was derived from individual worker records showing "allowed" and "actual" hours for an assigned daily task. Allowed times are synthetic standard times computed from locally established elemental times, or else direct standards derived from time study of the particular job in question. The data were reduced to the number of man-hours over or under "allowed" for a given period of time. Productivity data were available for all members of each station except those few assigned to jobs for which there are no time standards. Data for a one-month period were used. The productivity of a station was derived by averaging the productivity of the members. These data have interval scale properties, and for individuals range from 30 to 70. Individual performance in terms of this productivity measure is remarkably reliable, giving a correlation of about .91 for successive two-week periods.[4]

Effectiveness: Individual. Each station manager was asked to rank-order all of his men on the basis of his judgment of the overall quality of their job performance, taking into account any special circumstances relevant to each individual's assignment. Rankings were sent directly to the research team as confidential data. Within each station, the rank-orders were normalized and reduced to a scale with a range of 1 to 7.

Effectiveness: Station.[5] Independent judgments were obtained from a group of operating and staff managers concerning the relative effective-

---

[4] For a more detailed description of this variable see B. S. Georgopoulos and A. S. Tannenbaum, "A Study of Organizational Effectiveness," *American Sociological Review* 22 (1957): 534–40.

[5] Both individual and station effectiveness ratings are, no doubt, somewhat contaminated by the rater's knowledge of past performance records. For example, they have common variance with measured productivity of 10 percent and 55 percent respectively.

ness of the various stations. The raters had first-hand knowledge of the stations they rated, but were not directly involved in the operation of the stations. Judgments were obtained in the form of ratings on a five-point scale of the overall performance of the station as a whole during the prior six months. Raters were given instructions intended to assure that they would take into account any unique circumstances in each station, and take into account all aspects of station performance. The ratings were sent directly to the research team as confidential information, in order to maximize the independence of judgments. This measure was actually obtained before collection of other data, and was a basis for selection of stations for study. Stations on which there was disagreement among raters were eliminated from the study. Consistency among raters exceeded expectations; reliability cannot be known but is probably high.

Accidents. Since the firm operates trucks on public roads and streets, accident hazards and costs tend to be high. Each accident is investigated, and if it involves any degree of negligence or improper performance on the part of the employee, it is considered a "chargeable accident." The number of chargeable accidents during the two years preceding the study was used as a measure of performance. The range for individuals is from 0 to 9+. Station performance is represented by the mean of individual scores, and ranges from 0 to 3.81 chargeable accidents. These measures have ratio scale properties, and in the case of the individual data, scores are bunched at the low end of the scale.

Absences. Since the work of a station is highly coordinated and tied to a daily schedule, an unanticipated absence may sometimes be costly and disruptive. Individual scores on absence represent the actual number of instances of "unexcused absence" during a two-year period, with individual scores ranging from 0 to 9+. Station performance on absences is represented by the mean of individual member scores, and ranges from 0 to 1.51. These data have ratio scale properties.

Errors. This variable is intended to represent the quality of work performed by a driver, and is based on his performance in making delivery in difficult cases. For each driver, there is a daily count of "C.O.D.'s" and "send agains," these being instances of nondelivery. Return of a package to the station may, of course, occur for reasons beyond the control of the driver, but there are also differences in performance arising out of the driver's familiarity with the habits of people on his route and out of the driver's ingenuity, effort, and judgment in making delivery through neighbors and in other ways. To an extent, these all reflect "quality" of performance. For present purposes, individual scores are based on a count of nondeliveries over a one-month period. The reliability of this variable is $r = .76$ for successive two-week periods for individuals. Station performance on this variable is based on the mean of member scores, and ranges from 1.85 to 4.69 instances of nondelivery.

PLAN OF ANALYSIS

Pearson *r* correlations were computed for all pairs of variables for all types of analyses. The data were then analyzed in a manner that allows assessment of the hypotheses stated below.

It is a common practice to assume that any one of several relevant criteria of job performance may be taken to represent the totality of job performance. This is the case in all studies in which a single variable (such as productivity, length of tenure, or accident rate) is used as a basis for evaluation of predictor variables (for example, selection tests, training methods, and so forth). The implicit model of "overall job performance" is one of multiple elements having additive or multiplicative relationships such that the elemental measures may be used separately as estimates of "true" performance or that the elements may be combined to reduce measurement error or bias. This conception is tenable only if it is generally true that job performance criteria are significantly related in consistent ways, and if the relations, with due allowance for measurement errors and unreliability, are high. HYPOTHESIS: *Intercorrelations among a set of job performance measures for a given homogeneous population of individuals or organizations will be consistent (in terms of positive or negative association) and relatively high.* It is our expectation that this hypothesis will be found invalid, and that the lack of validity of the model from which it derives will be demonstrated.

Few investigators have concerned themselves with the question of comparability between job performance at the level of the individual and job performance at the level of the organization. This neglect probably arises out of the practical difficulty of getting performance measures for a homogeneous set of organizations, and measures that are comparable at both individual and organizational levels. We propose here, as a basis for analysis, the simplest conception of the matter, namely, that there exists some generally valid system of relationships among a given set of performance variables such that the same relationships hold whether the performances are those of an individual or those of a set of individuals who share the work of an organization. HYPOTHESIS: *The pattern of intercorrelations among a set of job performance variables, with allowance for measurement errors, will be similar in size and sign as between the individual and organizational levels of analysis.* A confirmation of this hypothesis will lend support to the view that there may exist some widely generalizable system of relationships among the several components of job performance. A denial of the hypothesis will suggest that the conceptual meaning of the job performance variables changes when one shifts the referent from individual to organization. It would suggest also the possibility that there is a still different set of relationships among the variables which applies to other units of analysis, for example, each of the subtasks comprising an individual's job as compared with the individual's total job or the organization's job.

Another common assumption about job performance measures relates to the presumed invariance of relationships across a set of similar organizations. The limited available published data show wide variations in relationships among aspects of job performance for unlike occupations and unlike organizations. However, it is customary to generalize findings from one situation to a class of apparently similar situations. It is possible that such generalizations are valid. It is also possible that each situation is unique and that there does not exist a "pattern" of criterion relationships which holds for all members of a set of similar organizations. Our hypothesis, however, is stated positively, as follows: *The relationships among job performance criteria for the individuals in any one organization are, within limits of measurement error, representative of the relationships which hold across a homogeneous set of such organizations.* Our expectation is that there will be more variance in criterion relationships than can be attributed to the random effects of measurement error and sampling.

RESULTS

Hypothesis I

Results relevant to Hypothesis I are presented in Table 2–1. Table 2–1 (col. A) shows interrelationships among the five criteria for the population of 27 organizations (stations). Of the ten correlations only five have a sign consistent with the hypothesis that "good" performance on any one variable will be related to "good" performance on others. Four of the ten correlations are statistically significant at the .05 level or lower, and the sizes of correlations bear no apparent relationship to the known or estimated reliability of the component variables. It appears that three of the five criteria—effectiveness, productivity, and errors—constitute a set of internally consistent criteria, while accidents and absences are inconsistent with that set and unrelated to each other. For example, good performance with respect to accidents (that is, low accident rate) is associated with poor performance with respect to productivity (that is, low productivity); low accident rates are associated with high error rates. It appears that "job performance" as measured by these variables at the organizational level does not constitute a unidimensional construct and may even be differently constituted, in terms of direction of relationships, than might be expected. That is, the five variables are not all significantly related to one another, nor do all the variables appear to belong to a common cluster.

Table 2–1 (col. B) replicates Table 2–1 (col. A) but shows the interrelationships for the population of 975 individuals. Of the ten correla-

TABLE 2–1

Intercorrelations among Five Job Performance Criterion Variables in 27 Operating Stations of a Delivery Service Firm (Decimals Omitted)

Criteria	Population A (Station)				Population B (Individuals)				Population C (Individuals Within Stations)			
	2	3	4	5	2	3	4	5	2	3	4	5
Effectiveness	74*	25	–10	–46*	28*	–02	–08	–32*	36*	–05	–17*	–42*
Productivity.	–	30	08	–39*	–	12*	–01	–26*	–	–01	02	–23*
Chargeable accidents		–	02	–65*		–	03	–18*		–	09	04
Unexcused absences			–	–11			–	15*			–	17*
Errors (nondeliveries) . . .				–				–				–

* Significantly different from zero at .05 level or better. Population A: 27 stations. Intercorrelations based on means of member scores. Population B: 975 individuals. Nonsupervisory employees in all stations. Population C: Approximately 975 individuals. Intercorrelations shown are weighted average within-group correlations for individuals grouped according to station membership. Zero correlations arising from instances of within-station invariance are omitted from data. Station Ns range from 13 to 54, with a mean of 36.

tions, nine have signs consistent with Hypothesis I, but the reversed one is statistically significant. In addition, the correlations are all small in absolute magnitude, indicating that there is little common variance among the five variables. Considering both sign and size of correlations, there is general confirmation of the conclusion reached on the basis of Table 2–1 (col. A) namely, that there appears to be an internally consistent set of three variables, and two other variables independent of that set.

Table 2–1 (col. C) is an alternative representation of the intercorrelations of the five variables at the individual level but, in this case, the data show the weighted average intraclass correlation computed separately for each of the 27 organizations. This treatment removes any effects, whether spurious or valid, arising from the clustering of our 975 individuals into 27 organizational sets. The findings in this table more nearly conform to Hypothesis I than do the results in Table 2–1 (cols. A and B), as there is now only one insignificant reversal of sign, and the pattern differentiating the accident and absence variables from the remaining three is less apparent. However, the correlations remain low, and there is little common variance in our set of five performance measures.

Hypothesis II

This hypothesis proposed that the intercorrelations among the five criteria will be similar in size and sign at the individual and organizational levels of analysis. Comparing Table 2–1 (col. A) to Table 2–1 (col. B), it can be seen that the correlations tend to be higher in the case of the organizational level of analysis, and substantially higher in some cases. For example, effectiveness versus productivity shifts from +.28 to +.74, and accidents versus errors shifts from −.18 to −.65. There is one rather large shift involving a reversal of sign, from +.15 to −.11 in the case of absences versus errors. These results do not permit any conclusive interpretation as the obtained differences in correlation size are variable and not subject to statistical test of significance. The differences in pattern of correlations between individual and group levels are also rather modest and possibly insignificant.

Hypothesis III

Hypothesis III proposed that there is an invariance of criteria interrelationships across a set of similar organizations. To test this hypothesis, the intercorrelations among our five variables were computed separately for individuals in each of the 27 stations.

According to the operational hypothesis, we should expect the correlations between any pair of variables to be the same for all stations, within limits of measurement and sampling error. We should further expect that the average within-groups correlation for each pair of variables should, within error limits, be representative of the obtained distribution of correlations. These expectations are met with a high level of confidence only in the case of two pairs of variables—productivity versus accidents, and absences versus errors. With reference to the other eight pairs, one cannot with confidence say that there exists for this set of organizations any correlation which is "representative" or "typical" of the relationships between a given pair of job performance variables.

The absolute size of the obtained differences in correlation is quite striking for some of the pairs of variables. For example, a station chosen at random from this firm could produce a correlation between accidents and errors anywhere from about −.50 to about +.50. For effectiveness versus accidents, the range is from −.41 to +.44. For effectiveness versus productivity, the range is from −.56 to +.83. The variation is so great that even the pair of variables with highest average correlation produced two reversals of sign.

One must conclude from this evidence that the relationships among various aspects of job performance are highly variable, even within a set of unusually similar organizations. For organizations of lesser homogeneity, one should expect even greater variation in criterion interrelationships. The hypothesis that there exists some generalizable set of relationships between various aspects of job performance is not supported.

DISCUSSION

These results indicate that relationships among certain different aspects of job performance are generally small, and that the size and direction of relationships are to a large degree unique to each population and situation, and somewhat different for organizations as contrasted to individuals. There is little support for the notion that there may exist some generalizable pattern, or set of patterns, describing the composition of job performance and the relationships among the components of job performance. The evidence, however, does not warrant the serious consideration of an extremely opposite view, namely, that criterion interrelationships are indeterminate or random. The following discussion presents some reasons for discounting this view and possible ways of finding the elusive organizing principles which will reveal the orderliness of otherwise random-appearing phenomena.

Choice of Criterion Variables. The present study deals with only five job performance variables, chosen because they have face validity, objectivity, and either measured or estimated high reliability. It is unlikely that these measures are all independent of one another. It is likely that there is some interaction among them. It is unlikely that they adequately represent any true factor structure of job performance that may exist. A proper test of our hypotheses would require the use of variables that are factorially pure and cover a wider range of on-the-job behavior. One clue to the relevance of this criticism of the results is to be seen by post facto interpretation of the data itself. Had we used only three variables—effectiveness, productivity, and errors—the results would have conformed much more closely to our hypotheses in most (but not all) tests.

Choice of Firm. The study was done in a firm in which the operating units (stations) are unusually similar in structure and function. This was considered an advantage, as this high degree of homogeneity can maximize the possibility of finding uniformities in criteria interrelationships of a kind that would confirm our hypotheses. However, it is also true that a high degree of population homogeneity can allow an undetected conditioning variable to maximize its effect. This is an improbable but possible defect in the study.

Range of Variation. The obtained correlation between a pair of criterion variables depends in part upon the "range of talent" or absolute range of variation on the two measures. It may be that our populations of individuals and organizations are so uniform that only small correlations could be generated, and that the size of these depended more on range than on "true" covariation. This would account for some of the apparent randomness of obtained correlations. Although plausible, this argument appears to have little merit, as the absolute variations in productivity, error rates, and accident rates, for example, seem relatively large rather than relatively small in comparison with the ranges commonly reported from other kinds of firms. A specific test of this possibility was made in the case of Hypothesis III, as the several organizations differed considerably in the absolute range of performance on some of the five variables. However, there proved to be no significant connection between absolute range and the obtained size or direction of criterion inter-relationships, except in the case of accident rates. Even in this case, removing from the population of organizations those which were relatively invariant on one or more variables had no significant effect on the overall results.

If we assume that the results are generally valid, in spite of these defects, there remains the problem of speculating about the modifications and elaborations of theory that will be necessary in order to measure and assess uniformities that we assume to exist in the relationships among elements of job performance. Three possibilities are here proposed.

Patterning. It is possible that an individual or an organization has a limited number of "choices" among alternative patterns of criterion relationships. One could speculate, for example, that if one aspect of job performance (for example, safety, or productivity) is given priority in job performance, then a given pattern of relationships among other performance variables may necessarily follow. The patterning of performance variables may also follow from individual or organizational preferences among certain nonperformance values, personnel policies, and the like. The presence of several such "patterns," each uniform across a subset of a population of organizations, could produce a superficial appearance of randomness in criterion relationships. An inspection of the data for our 27 organizations, however, did not reveal any patterns which recurred frequently enough to encourage more precise analysis along this line.

Conditioning Variables. It is possible that there are some conditioning variables, operating like catalysts in a chemical system, which need to be taken into account in order to discern uniformities in the relationships among job performance variables. For example, it is plausible that productivity and accident rates may have a positive relationship under conditions of low hazard and a negative relationship under conditions of high hazard, and that both conditions could occur in the same organization.

Independent Causal Variables. Each of a set of job performance variables may well be dependent upon different causal variables, or differently weighted common determinants. There is considerable evidence already that different aspects of job performance may be to some extent independently determined.[6] Under these conditions it cannot be expected that criterion measures will be highly correlated, and it is possible also for fluctuations in intercorrelations to arise from differential weighting of casual elements in each situation. If, for example:

$$Criterion\ Variable\ V_1 = f(ax_1 + bx_2 + cx_3\ \ldots)$$

---

[6] A. H. Brayfield and W. H. Crockett, "Employee Attitudes and Performance," *Psychological Bulletin* 52 (1955): 396–424; E. E. Ghiselli, "Dimensional Problems of Criteria," *Journal of Applied Psychology* 40 (1956): 1–4; and V. H. Vroom, "Employee Attitudes," in *The Expanding Frontiers of Industrial Relations* (1959).

then in different organizations the values of the coefficients, a, b, c, and so forth, could be different in such a way that Variable V_1 would have a different composition from situation to situation. Such a condition would lead to criterion intercorrelations of great variability as each criterion may be a product of a different causal system.

In any case, it seems clear that it is risky to make any simple assumptions about the elements which comprise "job performance," and about the probable relationships among them in any given situation. The weight of the evidence favors more emphasis on the use of multiple criteria and, at least for the present, the separate treatment of each criterion. The practice of combining criteria is likely, in many cases, to simply randomize out real differences in quality of performance or, at best, to maximize a unitary construct of "job performance" which is unique to the population which originally provided the raw data.

SUMMARY AND CONCLUSIONS

Intercorrelations among five job performance variables for 27 organizations and for their respective and combined members show that the relationships are generally small, and that the size and direction of relationships are generally more variable than can be accounted for on the basis of measurement and sampling errors.

These data are interpreted as contradicting the validity of "overall job performance" as a unidimensional construct, and as a basis for combining job performance variables into a single measure having general validity. The data also indicate that the use of a single job performance variable as a "sample" of a set of job performances is not justified without prior determination of interrelations among the different aspects of performance.

It is proposed that the measurement and use of job performance criterion variables will remain at a primitive and empirical level until there is created some complex theory of job performance which takes into account systems of causal and conditioning variables.

3. COMPOSITE VS. MULTIPLE CRITERIA *

Frank L. Schmidt and Leon B. Kaplan

THERE HAS BEEN A CONTROVERSY of long standing in industrial psychology between the advocates of the single composite criterion and those favoring multiple criteria. Earlier writers on this problem tended to favor the composite criterion concept,[1] and this doctrine remained essentially unchallenged until the second half of the 50s. Then, starting in 1956, a series of statements by a number of well-known industrial psychologists appeared seriously questioning the utility of this concept and concluded that, in most cases, the use of multiple criteria was to be preferred to the use of the traditional composite.[2] To date, this controversy has not been satisfactorily resolved, as is obvious from the cautious and rather indecisive treatment the question receives in most standard texts in industrial psychology.[3] The purpose of this paper is to set forth the basic arguments advanced for each position, to explore the assumptions underlying these arguments, and, finally, to offer a practical and conceptual resolution of the controversy.

ARGUMENTS FOR THE COMPOSITE CRITERION

The basic contention of the advocates of the composite criterion is that the criterion should provide a measure of the overall "success" or "value-to-the-organization" of the individual—because such an index is needed to compare and make decisions about individuals.[4] They maintain that, even if the criterion elements are used separately in validation, they must

---

* Adapted from "Composite vs. Multiple Criteria: A Review and Resolution of the Controversy," *Personnel Psychology* 24 (1971): 419–34.
[1] See H. A. Toops, "The Criterion," *Educational and Psychological Measurement* 4 (1944): 271–97; H. E. Brogden and E. K. Taylor, "The Dollar Criterion—Applying the Cost Accounting Concept to Criterion Construction," *Personnel Psychology* 3 (1950): 133–67; and B. F. Nagle, "Criterion Development," ibid. 6 (1953): 271–89.
[2] See E. E. Ghiselli, "Dimensional Problems of Criteria," *Journal of Applied Psychology* 40 (1956): 1–4; R. M. Guion, "Criterion Measurement and Personnel Judgement," *Personnel Psychology* 14 (1961): 141–49; idem, *Personnel Testing* (New York: McGraw-Hill Book Co., 1965), pp. 114–19; M. D. Dunnette, "A Note on the Criterion," *Journal of Applied Psychology* 47 (1963): 251–54; and idem, "A Modified Model for Test Validation and Selection Research," ibid., pp. 317–23.
[3] See J. Tiffin and E. J. McCormick, *Industrial Psychology*, 5th ed. (Englewood Cliffs, N.J.: Prentice-Hall, 1965), pp. 47–54; M. L. Blum and J. C. Naylor, *Industrial Psychology* (New York: Harper & Row, 1968), pp. 184–93.
[4] See Toops, "Criterion"; R. L. Thorndike, *Personnel Selection* (New York: John Wiley & Sons, 1948), p. 125; Brogden and Taylor, "The Dollar Criterion"; and Nagle, "Criterion Development."

be combined in some way when decisions are made about individuals.[5] If, adopting the multiple criteria approach and following Ghiselli's suggestion,[6] the decision-maker conceptualizes each individual's performance as a point in multidimensional space, where the dimensions represent criterion elements, it is maintained that he has no basis for preferring one individual over another—unless he somehow collapses the various criterion scores onto one dimension. This he usually does subjectively, thus obscuring the relative sizes of the weights placed on the criterion elements. A formal weighting into a composite makes known the absolute and relative sizes of the weights used and, in addition, insures that they will be stable across occasions and decision-makers. It is also contended that the formal solution makes explicit the basis of decisions as to the relative importance of the criterion elements.[7] It can thus be seen that the advocates of the composite criterion view the multiple criteria approach as evading rather than solving the weighting problem.

ARGUMENTS FOR MULTIPLE CRITERIA

The basic contention of those favoring multiple criteria is that measures of different variables should not be combined. Cattell puts it thus: "ten men and two bottles of beer cannot be added to give the same total as two men and ten bottles of beer." [8] If criterion elements display low positive, zero, or low negative correlations with one another, then they are obviously measuring different variables, and weighting them into a composite result in scores that are so ambiguous as to be uninterpretable. Very different patterns of scores on the criterion elements can result in the same composite score. The worker who is slow and accurate in assembly work, for example, may achieve the same composite criterion score as another worker who works fast but makes more errors. It is maintained that since these two patterns of work behavior are so different in nature, it makes no sense to assign them the same composite score.[9] The ambiguity of composite scores is much reduced, of course, by high intercorrelations among the criterion elements, but the advocates of multiple criteria cite many studies [10] which indicate very strongly that, even in the

[5] Compare particularly Toops, "The Criterion"; Tiffin and McCormick, *Industrial Psychology*, p. 52; also H. E. Brogden, personal communication, 1967.

[6] Ghiselli, "Dimensional Problems."

[7] See Brogden and Taylor, "The Dollar Criterion."

[8] R. B. Cattell, *Personality and Motivation: Structure and Measurement* (New York: Harcourt, Brace and World, 1957), p. 11.

[9] See Ghiselli, "Dimensional Problems"; Dunnette, "Note on the Criterion"; and Guion, *Personnel Testing*, p. 113–14.

[10] See S. E. Seashore, B. P. Indik, and B. S. Georgopoulos, "Relationships among Criteria of Job Performance," *Journal of Applied Psychology* 44 (1960): 195–202; S. H. Peres, "Performance Dimensions of Supervisory Positions," *Personnel Psychology* 15 (1962): 405–10; and Ghiselli, "Dimensional Problems."

case of relatively low-level jobs, performance is often, if not typically, multidimensional.[11] For higher level jobs, such as that of scientist or college professor, there is evidence that performance is even more complex, with up to 15 relatively independent factors emerging.[12] On such jobs, it would appear that there would be a very large number of performance patterns that could result in the same composite criterion score.

Those favoring multiple criteria view the composite criterion as not only virtually uninterpretable in most cases, but also as an impediment to progress in practical prediction. Dunnette suggests [13] that the use of composite criteria may go far in explaining the failure of industrial psychology to break through the ceiling of about .50 on validity coefficients pointed out by Hull over 50 years ago.[14] Ghiselli makes the same implication,[15] and even Tiffin and McCormick, who identify with neither side in this controversy, suggest that one cannot "reasonably expect" to identify, for a given ambiguous composite criterion score, a common set of personal characteristics associated with that score.[16]

ASSUMPTIONS UNDERLYING THE TWO POSITIONS

The Nature of the Construct Represented by the Criterion Measure

Underlying the arguments for a composite criterion is the assumption, often unarticulated, that the criterion should represent an economic, rather than a behavioral, construct. The economic nature of this dimension is often obscured by the use of such terms as "overall success," [17] "perform-

---

[11] Performance on some jobs has also been shown to be "dynamic," that is, to change in apparent factorial composition over time. See E. E. Ghiselli and M. Haire, "The Validation of Selection Tests in the Light of the Dynamic Characteristics of Criteria," *Personnel Psychology* 13 (1960): 225–31; E. A. Fleishman and B. Fruchter, "Factor Structure and Predictability of Successive Stages of Learning Morse Code," *Journal of Applied Psychology* 44 (1960): 97–101; and B. Bass, "Further Evidence on the Dynamic Character of Criteria," *Personnel Psychology* 15 (1962): 93–97. In addition, see E. P. Prien, "Dynamic Character of Criteria: Organizational Change," *Journal of Applied Psychology* 50 (1966): 501–4. Prien has pointed out that changes in organizational needs and goals can change the nature of the criteria of success in individual jobs within the organization. Criterial dynamism is an important problem in industrial psychology, meriting much more research than has been devoted to it to date. However, our concern here is with what Ghiselli refers to as "static dimensionality"—dimensionality without respect to time. See Ghiselli, "Dimensional Problems."

[12] See C. W. Taylor et al., "Explorations in the Measurement and Prediction of Contributions of One Sample of Scientists," ASD-TR-61-96, Personnel Laboratory (Lackland Air Force Base, Texas, 1961); C. W. Taylor et al., "An Investigation of the Criterion Problem for a Medical School Faculty," *Journal of Applied Psychology* 48 (1964): 294–301.

[13] Dunnette, "Modified Model for Test Validation."

[14] C. L. Hull, *Aptitude Testing* (New York: World Book Co., 1928).

[15] Ghiselli, "Dimensional Problems."

[16] Tiffin and McCormick, *Industrial Psychology*, p. 51.

[17] See Toops, "The Criterion."

ance on the task," [18] "overall contribution," [19] and "overall value of the individual in the job." [20] The basic criterion of "relevancy," discussed by these writers, is defined in a number of superficially different ways, all of which ultimately relate the criterion measure to an underlying economic dimension. Thus Nagle defines relevancy as "the extent to which an index of success (criterion) is related to the true order of success in the given activity." [21] Thorndike states that a criterion measure is relevant "as far as the knowledge, skills, and basic aptitudes required for success on it are the same as those required for performance of the ultimate goal." [22] Tiffin and McCormick define relevance as "the extent to which criterion measures of different individuals are meaningful in terms of the objectives for which such measures are derived." [23] In most organizations, the objectives or "ultimate goals" are economic in nature. Certainly this is true for industrial firms, whose general objective is to make money. Even in the case of nonprofit organizations and governmental agencies, the general objective is to deliver services as efficiently as possible, all other things equal—and efficiency is measured in terms of economic units. Brogden and Taylor are most explicit in advocating that criteria be economic in nature, stating that "the criterion should measure the contribution of the individual to the overall efficiency of the organization." [24] They recommend that such contributions be measured, whenever possible, in dollars and cents—by means of the application of cost accounting concepts and procedures to the individual job behaviors of the employee. They are quite definite in stating that it is the economic end products of job behaviors, and not the behaviors themselves, that the criterion measure should assess:

In job analysis for criterion purposes we believe that a clear-cut distinction must be made between the end products of a given job and the job processes that lead to these end products. It may be pertinent to such other legitimate objectives of job analysis as training or position classification to study the exact sequence of operations in the production of the finished product. The skills needed, the tools used, and the methods employed may all be needed for this purpose. Such information does not, however, give a direct answer to the major question, "How much does the employee produce and how good is it?" [25]

By contrast, the assumption, often implicit, that the criterion should represent a behavioral or psychological construct is the basis of all the arguments in favor of multiple criteria. This assumption is rather clear in the following statement:

---

[18] See Thorndike, *Personnel Selection,* p. 125.
[19] See Nagle, "Criterion Development."
[20] See R. H. Gaylord and H. E. Brogden, "Optimal Weighting of Unreliable Criterion Elements," *Educational and Psychological Measurement* 24 (1964): 529–33.
[21] Nagle, "Criterion Development," p. 274.
[22] Thorndike, *Personnel Selection,* p. 125.
[23] Tiffin and McCormick, *Industrial Psychology,* p. 44.
[24] Brogden and Taylor, "Dollar Criterion."
[25] Ibid., p. 141.

Even a very low level of aspiration in prediction requires that the *behavior* on our scale be operationally defined to have some homogeneity, and defined in such a way which will not permit its confusion with an essentially different kind of behavior.[26]

Ghiselli states that attempts to justify combining criterion elements into a composite rest on the assumption of a general factor in job performance.[27] Since this general factor can be shown not to exist in many, if not most cases, he advises that criterion elements be used separately rather than combined. The general factor to which he refers is certainly behavioral or psychological in nature. Otherwise, he would be putting himself in the position of denying the ubiquity of the economic factor in "relevant" criterion elements. Similarly, Dunnette states that high intercorrelations among criterion elements can be taken as justification for a composite criterion, and, conversely, lack of correlation among elements argues for multiple criterion.[28] Again, the common variance represented by the intercorrelations must reflect a unitary behavioral factor. Guion writes that if the criterion elements to be combined are "essentially similar," the resultant composite is "psychologically sensible." [29] A "psychologically sensible" criterion composite is, it seems obvious, one that is behaviorally homogenous, or nearly so. Haire states that criterion measures should represent behavioral and psychological variables, suggesting that lack of progress in the improvement of validities may be due to the use of criterion measures representing business or economic constructs.[30]

Primary Goals of the Validation Process

The partisans of these two positions differ in their basic assumptions as to the primary purpose of the validation process itself. Those favoring the composite criterion are assuming, usually implicitly, that the validation process is initiated and carried out only for practical and economic reasons. While some are rather vague on this point,[31] Brogden and Taylor could hardly be more explicit:

. . . the only functions of the criterion are (*a*) to establish the basis for choosing the "best" battery from the experimental predictors, and (*b*) to provide an estimate of the validity of that battery.[32]

None of those favoring composite criteria mention the attainment of increased understanding of the psychological and behavioral processes involved in various tasks as a goal of the validation process.

---

[26] Cattell, *Personality and Motivation*, p. 11 (italics added).
[27] Ghiselli, "Dimensional Problems."
[28] Dunnette, "Note on the Criterion."
[29] Guion, *Personnel Testing*, p. 114.
[30] M. Haire, "Business Is Too Important to Be Studied Only by Economists," *American Psychologist* 15 (1960): 271–72.
[31] Toops, "Criterion"; Nagle, "Criterion Development."
[32] Brogden and Taylor, "Dollar Criterion," p. 138.

By contrast, the advocates of multiple criteria view increased understanding as an important goal of the validation process, perhaps co-equal with the practical and economic goals. Dunnette, for example, postulates that validation goals should include increased understanding both of what the test scores measure and of the behaviors involved in each criterion element.[33] Using the term "description" rather than understanding, Ghiselli makes a similar appeal.[34] This emphasis on understanding is undoubtedly the factor which has led to the concept of the criterion as a measure of a behavioral and/or psychological construct. The goal of the search for understanding is a theory (or theories) of work behavior; theories of human behavior are cast in terms of psychological and behavioral, not economic, constructs.

Both Dunnette and Guion advance validation models designed to aid in the attainment of understanding.[35] For purposes of the present discussion, the important thing about these models is the fact that they both depict predictors as predicting a number of intermediate criterion measures which are behavioral and homogenous in nature. These behavioral measures are then, in effect, used in turn to predict the practical, economic outcomes, referred to by Dunnette as "consequences to the organization" and by Guion as "the observable consequence."

EVALUATION OF THE ARGUMENTS

The Composite as Necessary for Decisions

What can be said of the contention that an overall criterion of some sort is necessary in order to make decisions about individuals? Apparently only two of the advocates of multiple criteria have addressed themselves to this problem; neither has satisfactorily answered the argument. As noted earlier, Ghiselli suggests that each individual be conceptualized as a point in N-dimensional space, where the N dimensions are the criterion elements.[36] He further indicates that perhaps the space should be divided into parts. But he admits that the problem of deciding which [parts] are relatively more desirable is unsolved. It can easily be seen that the process of rank ordering the various portions of the criterion space in overall desirability is identical with the process of combining the criterion elements into an overall composite. Thus Ghiselli's solution to the problem of the practical use of multiple criteria takes him back to a composite.

Guion argues that the criterion elements are best kept separate during

---

[33] Dunnette, "Note on the Criterion"; idem, "Modified Model for Test Validation."
[34] Ghiselli, "Dimensional Problems."
[35] Dunnette, "Note on the Criterion"; Guion, *Personnel Testing*, pp. 115–16.
[36] Ghiselli, "Dimensional Problems."

the validation process and then, during the actual selection process, sub-jectively weighted into a composite for each individual when decisions are made.[37] This procedure, he contends, moves the reliance on judgment to a "more sensible place" in the employment procedure. The decision-maker can then make his decisions about the relative importance of the criterion elements for each individual at the time of selection or rejection. As pointed out by those favoring the composite criterion, there are a number of shortcomings inherent in approaches of this general nature: (a) neither the basis for the assignment of the weights nor the actual weights are made explicit; (b) the relative sizes of the weights are un-known; and (c) the reliability of the weights is unknown. In addition, use of subjective weights means that the efficacy of the selection program can not be evaluated independently of the individual making these judgments. The adequacy of the selection program depends heavily on the adequacy of the decision-maker in assigning subjective criterion weights. If the pro-gram is evaluated with this judge included as an element of the system, the evaluation can not be generalized to other judges.

The Combining of Uncorrelated Variables

Next, consider the argument that the weighting of uncorrelated varia-bles into a composite results in an ambiguous, essentially meaningless score. This argument asserts, in effect, that such composite criteria do not represent meaningful behavioral or psychological constructs. Combining into a single composite implies that there is a single underlying dimen-sion in job performance, but it does not, in itself, imply that this single underlying dimension is behavioral or psychological in nature. A com-posite criterion may represent very well an underlying economic dimen-sion, while at the same time being virtually meaningless from a behavioral point of view. Now, as Brogden and Taylor point out, when the criterion elements are all "relevant" measures of economic variables, they can be combined into a composite without regard to their intercorrelations.[38] Even if these intercorrelations are zero and/or negative, the criterion ele-ments are, by definition, positively related to the underlying economic construct and hence are measures of the same variable. Thus, assuming equal units in the criterion elements, if two employees have the same composite criterion score but have achieved this score by means of dif-ferent patterns of scores on the various criterion elements, there is no construct ambiguity. Both composite scores represent the same point along a unidimensional economic scale. The problem arises from the fact that those discussing the question of criterion element intercorrelations have failed to distinguish explicitly between criterion measures that rep-

---

[37] Guion, "Criterion Measurement."
[38] Brogden and Taylor, "Dollar Criterion."

resent economic constructs and criterion measures that represent behavioral or psychological constructs.[39] As a result, the advocates of multiple criteria have, in general, failed to recognize the possibility that, in certain contexts, behaviorally meaningless composite criteria can be quite useful from a practical point of view. In these contexts, it may make economic sense to use psychological predictors to predict economic measures, even though there is no basis in psychological theory for doing so. Such a procedure can be seen to be well within the American tradition of empiricism in the behavioral sciences, especially as this tradition is found in the applied behavioral sciences [40] and, as such, should not be viewed as in any way illegitimate. Furthermore, there is even a rationale, in terms of factor theory, that can be offered for such a procedure, as we shall see below.

The Argument to Validity

What is to be said of the argument that the factorial complexity of most composite criteria leads to lower validity coefficients? Discussions of factorial heterogeneity and resultant ambiguity seem to be limited to the criterion. None of the advocates of multiple criteria, in discussing this question, address themselves to the problem of factorial complexity in the predictors, despite the fact that most tests are, in fact, far from factorially unitary.[41] It is difficult to see how increased factorial purity in the criterion can lead to higher correlations with heterogenous tests. In fact, psychometric considerations predict exactly the opposite outcome.

It can readily be shown that the contention that the factorial complexity and resultant ambiguity that characterizes many composite criterion measures acts to depress the size of obtained validity coefficients has little conceptual justification. Thus, there is, apparently, no real basis for the hope that the use of factorially pure or homogenous criteria will, per se, lead to increases in the magnitudes of validity coefficients.

The controversy over heterogeneity in the criterion is analogous to the controversy of long standing between the advocates of "rationally" constructed, homogenous predictors and those who prefer "empirically" constructed, heterogenous predictors. Some writers have disparaged the use of multifactor predictors, constructed by item analysis against an external

---

[39] Guion distinguishes between "behavioral data" and "result-of-behavior data" as criterion measures, and Dunnette distinguishes between "behavior" and "consequences of behavior," but neither recognizes or develops this distinction as one between the measurement of behavioral constructs, on the one hand, and the measurement of economic constructs, on the other. See Guion, "Criterion Measurement"; Dunnette, "Modified Model for Test Validation."

[40] See L. E. Tyler, *The Psychology of Human Differences* (New York: Appleton-Century-Crofts, 1965), pp. 129–33.

[41] See J. P. Guilford, *Psychometric Methods* (New York: McGraw-Hill Book Co., 1954), p. 356.

criterion, as lacking in rationale and as incapable of leading to "progress in prediction." [42] Others have preferred this approach as more practical and useful than the construction and use of homogenous predictors.[43] In general, the literature indicates a certain degree of superiority in size of validity coefficients for the heterogenous, empirically constructed predictors.[44]

The Argument to Understanding

The contention that composite criteria, unlike multiple criteria, do not and cannot lead to understanding of psychological and behavioral processes is probably the most persuasive of the arguments for multiple criteria; indeed, it may be the only persuasive argument. But despite this fact, the multiple criteria advocates have failed to develop this line of reasoning fully. They have not, in general, explicitly recognized the fact that the degree of understanding attainable is a function of the predictor as well as the criterion end of the prediction equation.[45] The understanding that can be attained from homogenous criteria when the predictor or predictors are heterogenous is limited. In such a situation, the ambiguity and uninterpretability of the criterion scores have been eliminated or much reduced, but the predictor scores remain psychologically ambiguous. To illustrate, if the correlation of a given test with a given unifactor criterion element is, say, 30, then one knows that one of the psychological factors measured by the test corresponds, at least to some extent, to the behavioral factor measured by the homogenous criterion element. The knowledge that a certain portion of the variance of the test reflects a given, known behavioral factor represents a degree of understanding. But it is not possible, given the heterogeneity of the test, to ascertain which set of items within the test is measuring this factor. The fuller understanding and insight that could result from a careful examination of this subset of items is not possible. Dunnette's position with respect to this problem

---

[42] See R. M. W. Travers, "Rational Hypotheses in the Construction of Tests," *Educational and Psychological Measurement* 11 (1951): 128–37; Guion, *Personnel Testing*, pp. 201–2; Guilford, *Psychometric Methods*, p. 356; and J. C. Nunnally, *Psychometric Theory* (New York: McGraw-Hill Book Co., 1967), pp. 245–50.

[43] See E. K. Strong, *Vocational Interests of Men and Women* (Stanford, Calif.: Stanford University Press, 1943), p. 73; Dunnette, *Personnel Selection and Placement* (Belmont, Calif.: Wadsworth, 1966), pp. 43–46; and L. E. Albright, J. R. Glennon, and W. J. Smith, *The Use of Psychological Tests in Industry* (Cleveland: Howard Allen, 1963).

[44] Compare S. R. Wallace, "Criteria for What?" *American Psychologist* 20 (1965): 411–17; K. E. Clark, *The Vocational Interests of Nonprofessional Men* (Minneapolis: University of Minnesota Press, 1966), pp. 69–112; and D. P. Campbell et al., "A Set of Basic Interest Scales for the Strong Vocational Interest Blank for Men," *Journal of Applied Psychology Monograph* 52 (1968).

[45] See Guion, "Criterion Measurement"; idem, *Personnel Testing*, pp. 114–16; Dunnette, "Note on the Criterion"; idem, "Modified Model for Test Validation"; and Ghiselli, "Dimensional Problems."

is especially curious. On the one hand, he advocates the use of homogenous multiple criteria as a method of gaining "understanding of the meaning of our test scores"; [46] on the other hand, he is one of the most enthusiastic advocates of heterogenous, empirically constructed tests.[47] Guion, by contrast, takes a strong position in favor of the use of homogenous predictor tests, but he does not discuss the relation between this question and the question of the use of multiple, homogenous criteria as a method of increasing understanding of work behavior.[48] Nunnally vigorously condemns the use of heterogenous, empirically constructed tests in criterion prediction as not leading to understanding, but he does not suggest that factorially complex criteria be subdivided into homogenous criterion elements to further enhance the possibilities for understanding.[49] In short, those psychologists concerned with conditions necessary for the attainment of understanding in the validation process have concentrated on either the predictor or the criterion end of the prediction equation, but none have attempted to integrate simultaneously into their treatment of this problem the factorial compositions of the variables on both ends of the equation.

To sum up, it would appear that the use of both homogenous criteria and homogenous predictors holds the most promise as a method of attaining some degree of insight into the nature of job behaviors. If the unambiguous scores of a unifactor test correlate with a unifactor criterion measure, the size of this correlation indicates the extent to which the psychological trait measured by the test is associated with a specific kind of job behavior. It is clearly interpretable and can potentially be employed in the construction of a theory of job behavior.

Goals of the Validation Process

As discussed earlier, those favoring composite criterion measures have generally assumed that the goals of the validation process are essentially limited to the practical and economic. This assumption appears difficult to defend. It seems to mean asking far too little of the validation process; it seems to mean asking too little of industrial psychology as a discipline. It is interesting to note that the advocates of the composite criterion, that is, the criterion as representing an economic dimension, wrote, for the most part, during the 1940s and early 1950s, before industrial psychology was as established and accepted in the industrial and governmental sectors as it is today.[50] They wrote for a young and somewhat insecure profession, anxious to prove its value in the "real," that is, economic, world.

---

[46] Dunnette, "Note on the Criterion."
[47] Idem, *Personnel Selection*, pp. 43–46.
[48] Guion, *Personnel Testing*, pp. 202–3.
[49] Nunnally, *Psychometric Theory*, pp. 245–50.
[50] Toops, "Criterion"; Nagle, "Criterion Development"; and Brogden and Taylor, "Dollar Criterion."

By contrast, the advocates of multiple criteria, that is, criteria as representing behavioral constructs, emerged more recently, most within the last 10 to 15 years, a period during which the profession has enjoyed rather wide acceptance.[51] The quest for understanding, once perhaps an unaffordable luxury, is coming to be viewed more and more as a basic necessity for the survival and advancement of the field.[52] The essential question seems to be whether industrial psychology shall be conceived of as a technology seeking application or as a science seeking to delineate general principles of human behavior in the economic sector of life.[53] The growing consensus seems to be that the discipline should definitely not limit itself to the former and that the latter concept should become an important part of the definition of our area. Pugh states that the traditional tendency of industrial psychology to define its concerns and problems in terms of "economic and management problems" rather than in terms of psychological problems has hindered the development of the discipline.[54] Guion criticized the "narrow view" of industrial psychology as a "management tool" employed mostly for industrial "fire-fighting." [55] He recommends that the success or failure of industrial psychology be "measured on the scales of psychology, not those of industry." Haire makes a similar appeal.[56] Wallace calls for the construction and use of criteria with construct validity as a means of achieving understanding and urges the use of such criterion measures even when they are not relevant to "management's ultimate goals," that is, economic goals.[57] Criterion measures with theoretical relevance should not replace the economically relevant measures, he suggests, but rather should be used along with them. Wallace's recommendations are especially significant in that he has long been identified with the purely empirical, practical approach to test validation, an orientation which he has come to feel is "approaching the end of its tether" [58] Along with Blum and Naylor,[59] Wallace suggests that industrial psychologists loosen somewhat their grip on the specific empirical criterion measure and begin to theorize in terms of behavioral constructs. Later, he says, operational definitions can be constructed for the constructs.

---

[51] See Ghiselli, "Dimensional Problems"; Dunnette, "Note on the Criterion"; Guion, "Criterion Measurement"; and idem, *Personnel Testing*, pp. 113–15.

[52] See Wallace, "Criteria for What?"; M. L. Blum and J. C. Naylor, *Industrial Psychology* (New York: Harper & Row, 1968), pp. 193–94; Dunnette, "Modified Model for Test Validation"; Guion, "Criterion Measurement"; and idem, "Industrial Psychology as an Academic Discipline," *American Psychologist* 20 (1965): 815–21.

[53] Ibid.; D. S. Pugh, "Modern Organizational Theory: A Psychological and Sociological Study," *Psychological Bulletin* 66 (1966): 235–37.

[54] Ibid.

[55] Guion, "Industrial Psychology."

[56] Haire, "Business Is Too Important."

[57] See Wallace, "Criteria for What?"

[58] Ibid.

[59] See Blum and Naylor, *Industrial Psychology,* pp. 193–94.

Thus it seems obvious that understanding is today viewed in industrial psychology as a legitimate goal of the validation process and that this goal is intimately bound up with the question of the nature of the criterion measure. As Wallace sums up: ". . . the answer to the question 'Criteria for what?' must always include—for understanding!" [60]

RESOLUTION

It would appear that two very different conceptions of the validation process—both legitimate for their own purposes—emerge from the discussion up to this point. The first is applicable to situations in which goals are limited to the practical and economic. This conception allows for factorial complexity in both the predictors and the criteria. The goal is the largest possible validity coefficient, and as we have seen, heterogeneity on both ends of the prediction equation does not impair the attainment of this goal. Criterion elements can be, and, in fact, at some point must be, weighted into a composite irrespective of their intercorrelations. If all criterion elements are considered to be measures of a single underlying economic construct, the resulting composite unambiguously represents the economic construct and is interpretable as such. If the criterion elements are conceived of as measures of essentially uncorrelated behavior variables, then the factor theory of validity provides a model to account for the resulting validity coefficients. This approach, stemming from the American tradition of empiricism in applied social science, might be referred to as the "test validation" concept of the validation process.

The other concept of the validation process which this discussion has brought to light might be referred to as the "validation research" approach. This conception of the validation process is applicable to situations in which increased understanding is the primary or only goal. This model, in its ideal form, calls for homogeneity in both predictors and criterion measures, these being the circumstances under which the potentialities for contribution to understanding are maximal. In practice, this concept must be flexible enough to include situations in which relative homogeniety exists on one end of the prediction equation but not on both.[61] As we have seen, this approach is capable of yielding some degree of understanding. Other methods and techniques for the attainment of understanding, such as the subgrouping approaches recommended by Dunnette and Owens, are easily integrated into this concept of the validation process.[62] Since the resulting predictions are not to be employed in

---

[60] Wallace, "Criteria for What?"

[61] Under these conditions, when it is the predictors that are univocal, it can be seen that the criterion need not be multiple. In composite form, it is viewed as an initially uninterpretable, factorially complex behavioral measure which is to be clarified somewhat by examination of its correlations with the unifactor predictor or predictors.

[62] See Dunnette. "Modified Model for Test Validation"; W. A. Owens, "Toward One Discipline of Scientific Psychology," *American Psychologist* 23 (1968): 782–85.

the making of practical decisions about individuals, there is no necessity for weighting the criterion elements into a composite.

The majority of industrial psychologists will probably not find either of these models entirely satisfactory, and, indeed, they are introduced here for heuristic purposes rather than as normative standards. The typical practicing industrial psychologist probably seeks both economic and psychological ends in the validation process. From the point of view of the criterion end of the prediction equation, the implication of this fact is that he should, ideally, weight criterion elements, regardless of their intercorrelations, into a composite representing an economic construct in order to achieve his practical goals, and, at the same time, he should analyze the relationships between predictors and separate criterion elements in order to achieve his psychological goals. It is this sort of approach, and this sort of concept of the validation process, that embodies the ideal that we have set up for ourselves as applied psychologists—the ideal of the scientist-professional.

4. SOME DETERMINANTS OF SUPERVISORY ESTEEM *

David Kipnis

FEW TOPICS IN INDUSTRIAL PSYCHOLOGY have received more attention than the use of supervisory evaluations of performance as a source of criterion data. The simple and still appealing notion that supervisors are in the best position to evaluate various aspects of the subordinate's performance has been made suspect by the prevalence of errors of halo and leniency as well as the lack of equivalence often found between supervisory ratings and other estimates of production efficiency.[1] In general, research on supervisory evaluations of performance, rather than resolving problems of criteria, have pointed out their complexities. This lack of clarification remains a major stumbling block to progress in selection and classification.[2]

It is often profitable when one is stalled on some problem to attempt to

* From *Personnel Psychology* 13 (1960): 377–91.

[1] See, for example, R. H. Gaylord et al., "The Relationship of Ratings to Production Records: An Empirical Study," *Personnel Psychology* 4 (1951): 363–71; R. R. Mackie, C. L. Wilson, and D. N. Buckner, *Research on the Development of Shipboard Performance Measures,* 4 vols. ONR Contracts Nonr 7001 and Nonr 1241 (00) (Los Angeles: Management and Marketing Research Corp., 1954); and D. Severin, "The Predictability of Various Kinds of Criteria," *Personnel Psychology* 5 (1952): 93–103.

[2] See M. Haire, "Psychological Problems Relevant to Business and Industry," *Psychological Bulletin,* 56 (1959): 169–94.

approach it from a different point of view. For the most part, research on supervisory ratings has concentrated on the practical problem of developing procedures and instruments to objectify raters' judgments and to eliminate sources of errors from their ratings. Not as much attention has been paid to the *processes* by which supervisors arrive at their judgments of performance. Here an attempt will be made to specify such processes by relating supervisory ratings to the broader area of research on interpersonal perception. Since supervisory ratings are basically the impressions that one person has of another, it is reasonable that these areas should overlap. And since research on interpersonal perceptions has been specifically concerned with the processes by which we build up information about and form relationships with others, many of the findings may be directly applicable to ratings.

Specifically, two problems of concern in both industrial ratings and the larger area of interpersonal perception are reviewed.[3] The first deals with factors external to the behavior of the person evaluated which may be expected to promote rater leniency. The second presents some suggestions as to what kinds of subordinate behaviors may promote favorable supervisory evaluations.

EXTERNAL FACTORS

Glickman notes reasons for a supervisor to rate leniently.[4] By and large, these concern the rater's appraisal of the consequence to himself and the ratee of giving harsh ratings. In addition to such considerations as these, the following three sources of influence upon the promotion of leniency have been noted—although not specifically in terms of merit

---

[3] While not covered in the paper, it may be noted that the works of S. E. Asch, "Forming Impressions of Personality," *Journal of Abnormal and Social Psychology* 41 (1946): 258–90 and N. Kogan and R. Tagiuri, "Interpersonal Preference and Cognitive Organization," ibid. 56 (1958): 113–16 on processes by which impressions of individuals are formed, as well as the works of J. Bieri, "Cognitive Complexity-Simplicity and Predictive Behavior," ibid. 51 (1955): 263–68; E. S. Gollins and S. Rosenberg, "Concept Formation and Impressions of Personality," ibid. 56 (1956): 39–42; M. Haire and W. Grunes, "Perceptual Defenses: Processes Protecting an Organized Perception of Another Personality," *Human Relations* 3 (1950): 403–12; G. A. Kelly, *The Psychology of Personal Constructs*, vol. 1, *A Theory of Personality* (New York: W. W. Norton, 1955); H. Leventhal, "Cognitive Processes and Interpersonal Predictions," *Journal of Abnormal and Social Psychology* 55 (1957): 176–80; A. Pepitone and R. G. Hayden, "Some Evidence for Conflict Resolution in Impression Formation," ibid. 51 (1955): 302–7; and I. D. Steiner, "Ethnocentrism and Tolerance of Trait Inconsistency," ibid. 49 (1954): 349–54 on the conditions under which complex or discrepant behaviors of an individual are perceived and reported, have direct implications for problems usually associated with halo in ratings. These studies, in addition to their general implications, suggest that the extent of halo in ratings may be conditioned in part, at least, by identifiable and measurable individual differences among raters.

[4] A. S. Glickman, "Effects of Negatively Skewed Ratings on Motivation of the Rated," *Personnel Psychology* 8 (1955): 39–47.

rating. However, to the extent that the variables have promoted liking between persons in other situations, they may be suspected of operating in the rating situation.

Propinquity. Sheer physical proximity between two persons will affect the probability of friendship developing between them. The pervasiveness of propinquity in promoting friendships has caused Caplow and Forman to speak of the "mechanical effects of accessibility upon intimacy."[5] For example, Byrne and Buehler found that friendships made in a classroom were strongly conditioned by whether or not students sat next to each other.[6] Festinger, Schachter, and Back in a study of friendship formations in a veterans' housing project found that such details as the floor on which one lived, and the way one's door faced on a court, affected the likelihood of friendship formation.[7]

The studies cited have been done mostly among relatively homogeneous groups where no formal barriers to the establishment of friendship existed. Within industrial settings, however, interaction between supervisors and subordinates is monitored by formal status differentials which might well militate against propinquity affecting liking. On the other hand, such factors as the arrangement of working space and duty assignments, which require the supervisor to spend more time with some employees than with others, suggest that different opportunities for contact may lead to differences in leniency. This point was tangentially investigated by Dorothy Kipnis in a study of the prediction of sociometric choices of B-29 Bomber crews, which found that officers' evaluations of enlisted men were clearly affected by the physical distance that separated them in the aircraft.[8] More lenient ratings were given to men who worked nearest the officers.

While length of acquaintance is usually thought of as causing leniency in ratings,[9] it is suspected that the time period per se is not an important factor—to the extent it does not facilitate increased interaction between rater and ratee. For instance, given two subordinates, the first employed ten years but seeing his supervisor only once a week, and the second employed for five years but in constant interaction with the supervisor, it would be guessed that the supervisor might evaluate higher the latter employee, all other factors between the two employees being equal.

Social Setting. A second set of conditions which may affect leniency is the "social setting" under which the ratings are made. In general, a setting

---

[5] T. Caplow and R. Forman, "Neighborhood Interaction in a Homogeneous Community," *American Sociological Review* 15 (1950): 357–66.

[6] D. Byrne and J. A. Buehler, "A Note on the Influence of Propinquity upon Acquaintanceship," *Journal of Abnormal and Social Psychology* 51 (1955): 147–48.

[7] L. Festinger, S. Schachter, and K. Back, *Social Pressures in Informal Groups* (New York: Harper and Brothers, 1950).

[8] Dorothy M. Kipnis, "Interaction Between Members of Bomber Crews as a Determinant of Sociometric Choice," *Human Relations* 10 (1957): 263–70.

[9] See J. P. Guilford, *Psychometric Methods* (New York: McGraw-Hill Book Co., 1954), p. 295.

which encourages cooperation,[10] participation,[11] or is free from arbitrary sanctions,[12] may be expected to result in more congenial interpersonal relationships and the promotion of greater liking among participants. These findings are based upon ratings of co-equals or of subordinates rating superiors, and they cannot be expected to apply directly to the supervisor rating subordinates. However, the significant point of these studies with reference to ratings is that changes in social structural variables can affect interpersonal liking.

Along these lines, a variable which probably has great consequences for rater leniency is the degree of pressure from the social structure that is placed upon the rater. It is assumed that such pressure increases stress. Among others, Murray [13] and Feshbach and Singer [14] have studied the effects of stress upon the perception of other people. The main results indicate that the arousal of stress produces significant changes in the liking of others. Concomitant with stress is greater projection of maliciousness and aggression by the perceiver onto those he was rating. In industry, departments and work units vary widely in the degree of pressure under which employees are working. This pressure may be short term or an inherent aspect of the work. A shortage of work personnel with no corresponding decrease in the necessity for work output will increase the degree of pressure placed upon subordinates and supervisors. A sudden increase in the work load, or work where the consequences of error are costly, are other examples of situations involving heightened pressure. As pressure increases, less leniency in ratings is to be expected—due not only to projective factors, but also because as work load demands increase there will be a greater likelihood of errors and mistakes being made by subordinates.

Expression of Criticism. A third variable which may affect rater leniency has to do with the finding that expressions of criticism are found to have a cathartic effect which reduces interpersonal hostility. Thibaut and Coules [15] and Pepitone and Kleiner [16] report that, when individuals

---

[10] See M. Deutsch, "An Experimental Study of the Effects of Cooperation and Competition upon Group Process," *Human Relations* 2 (1949): 199–231.

[11] See E. W. Bovard, Jr., "The Experimental Production of Interpersonal Affect," *Journal of Abnormal and Social Psychology* 46 (1951): 521–28; N. C. Morse and E. Reimer, "The Experimental Change of a Major Organizational Variable," ibid. 56 (1956): 120–29.

[12] See K. Lewin, R. Lippitt, and R. T. White, "Patterns of Aggressive Behavior in Experimentally Created 'Social Climates'," *Journal of Social Psychology* 10 (1939): 271–99.

[13] H. A. Murray, "The Effects of Fear upon Estimates of Maliciousness of Other Personalities," ibid. 4 (1933): 310–29.

[14] S. Feshbach and R. D. Singer, "The Effects of Fear Arousal and Suppression of Fear upon Social Perception," *Journal of Abnormal and Social Psychology* 55 (1957): 283–88.

[15] J. Thibaut and J. Coules, "The Role of Communication in the Reduction of Interpersonal Hostility," ibid. 47 (1952): 770–77.

[16] A. Pepitone and R. Kleiner, "The Effects of Threat and Frustration on Group Cohesiveness," ibid. 54 (1957): 192–99.

are restrained from directly criticizing others, they retain less friendly feelings toward these individuals. Since supervisory duties usually involve the criticism of subordinates' work, it may prove that inhibition of this criticism on the part of the rater is reflected in harder ratings at some later date. The findings of Spector in this area most closely approximate the industrial rating situation.[17] He directly investigated the effects of blocking rater criticism of an individual's performance on later evaluations of this performance. The most lenient ratings were given by raters who were allowed to criticize the ratee, and this criticism was accepted by the ratee as being helpful. The most severe ratings of performance were assigned by raters who were given no chance to express criticism of the performance. For the most part, personal qualities of the rater may determine the extent to which he will openly criticize subordinates. However, blockages to direct criticism may inadvertently occur through "human relations" training wherein supervisors are cautioned to temper criticism of subordinates with understanding of the motivations underlying their behavior, or through assigning this function to the personnel department.

BEHAVIORS OF SUBORDINATES AFFECTING RATINGS

To this point, sources external to the behavior of subordinates which may influence ratings have been discussed. Of course it has long been recognized that ratings are sensitive to such external influences, if not specifically to the foregoing. The conversion of ratings to rankings, for instance, to eliminate between-rater variations is one method used to control these factors.

Less recognition has been given, however, to the possibility that some subordinate behaviors may be more influential than others in determining supervisors' evaluations. This lack of recognition is primarily due to the current conceptualization of the rating process. As ordinarily stated, the rating problem centers around means of objectifying ratings. It is expected that, given guidance, the rater can evaluate impartially, if imperfectly, the more important aspects of a subordinate's job proficiency. As such, no special subordinate behaviors are expected to be more influential than others. The facts of halo, leniency, lack of equivalence between ratings, and other measures are considered errors to be minimized by the development of scales and procedures which will objectify and guide the supervisor's observations toward those aspects of performance which he logically should see. The lack of success achieved to date through this approach suggests that a reexamination of the nature of these ratings may prove profitable.

---

[17] A. J. Spector, "Influences on Merit Ratings," *Journal of Applied Psychology* 38 (1954): 393–96.

One possibility is that the content of ratings is mainly determined by a restricted class of subordinate behaviors. To the extent that the subordinate successfully carries out this class of behavior, perceptions and judgments of other aspects of his work are distorted in the direction of greater leniency. It follows that the remaining aspects of work are not measured as validly as the class of subordinate behavior which primarily influenced the supervisor's judgment.

There is evidence from various sources to support the proposition that a restricted class of behaviors can determine evaluations of other aspects of an individual's performance. Asch [18] and Haire and Grunes,[19] studying processes by which impressions and opinions of other persons are formed, have found that the total impression of another person is frequently based upon limited aspects of the other person's behavior. Less central behaviors are distorted to make them consistent with the core behaviors around which impressions have been formed. Barrett, investigating the processes by which psychologists were able to integrate information about an industrial applicant into one overall appraisal, found that total impressions were based upon only a limited portion of the information available.[20] Interviews and a clinical rating of the applicant were the main determinants of overall ratings. Objective test data, which presumably gave new and independent information about the candidate, were not influential in determining opinions.

Mackie, Wilson, and Buckner [21] and Sherif, White, and Harvey [22] have also presented data which illustrate how perceptions of directly observed behavior are distorted to conform to previous notions. Judges in Mackie's study were supervisors of Navy-enlisted submariners; in Sherif's study groups of boys judged each other's performance. In both instances, negligible correlations were found between judges' ratings of subjects' performance on tasks (job sample tests for submariners, target throw for boys) and actual performance on these tasks (correlations from .01 to .18). On the other hand, correlations ranging from .42 to .74 were found between ratings of task performance and the overall ratings or status accorded the subjects by the judges. The higher the status, the more performance was overestimated. The lower the status, the more performance was underestimated. In addition, Sherif and his co-workers found that the longer a group had been organized, the more judges' estimates of performance were distorted towards overall status.

---

[18] Asch, "Forming Impressions of Personality."
[19] Haire and Grunes, "Perceptual Defenses."
[20] R. S. Barrett, "The Process of Predicting Job Performance," *Personnel Psychology* 11 (1958): 39–58.
[21] Mackie, Wilson, and Buckner, *Shipboard Performance Measures.*
[22] M. Sherif, J. B. White, and O. J. Harvey, "Status in Experimentally Produced Groups," *American Journal of Sociology* 60 (1955): 370–79.

What subordinate behaviors, then, may be most influential in determining status in the eyes of supervisors?[23] Some guide to this problem may be found by considering the role of the supervisor. Haire,[24] Steiner,[25] and others[26] have shown that a judge will pay attention to different aspects of an individual's behavior depending upon the judge's own role, and the goals of his position, at the time he makes his observations. Within the military, Moore found that superiors of noncommissioned officers based their evaluations of them upon their ability to get out the work.[27] Conversely, the subordinates of these noncommissioned officers based their evaluations of them primarily in terms of their human relations ability. Clearly, markedly different bases for the evaluation of the same person may be found depending upon the position of the evaluator. In general, given knowledge of the perceiver's role, predictions can be made concerning the salient behaviors of the object person that will most influence the perceiver.

It is fairly well agreed that the supervisor's role is a difficult one. Balma, Maloney, and Lawshe have indicated some of the problems faced by the supervisor as a result of scientific management and the growth of unions.[28] In his role the supervisor is subjected to a variety of pressures from his superiors to maintain production and efficiency; at the same time he has responsibilities to his subordinates which are often in conflict with these pressures from above. While these pressures may vary in intensity, they are present in most hierarchical structures. Mann, in referring to these

---

[23] While, logically, technical proficiency should be high on the list of behaviors that promote lenient ratings, this is not often found to be the case. One possible reason for this may be that most employees can do their work, at least at the minimum level of technical competence demanded by the job. In addition, attrition of the most incompetent from the job, as well as raising of the general proficiency level of those who remain on the job through training and previous experience, may serve to reduce noticeable differences among men. Finally, the observations of L. J. Cronbach, "The Two Disciplines of Scientific Psychology," *American Psychologist* 12 (1957): 671–85, that applied technology is constantly striving to reduce individual differences among men through introduction of improved machinery, would also lead to reduced variance associated with technical proficiency.

[24] M. Haire, "Interpersonal Relations in Collective Bargaining," in *Research in Industrial Human Relations: a Critical Appraisal*, eds. C. M. Arensberg et al. (New York: Harper and Brothers, 1957), chap. 12.

[25] Steiner, "Ethnocentrism and Tolerance"; idem, "Interpersonal Behavior as Influenced by Accuracy of Social Perception," *Psychological Review* 62 (1955): 268–74.

[26] E. E. Jones and R. deCharms, "The Organizing Function of Interaction Roles in Person Perception," *Journal of Abnormal and Social Psychology* 57 (1958): 155–64; Kelley, cited in J. S. Bruner and R. Tagiuri, "The Perception of People," in *Handbook of Social Psychology* ed. G. Lindzey (Cambridge, Mass.: Addison Wesley, 1954), p. 642.

[27] J. V. Moore, *Factor Analytic Comparison of Superior and Subordinate Ratings of the Same NCO Supervisors*, Technical Report 53–29 (Washington, D.C.: Human Resources Research Center, 1953).

[28] M. J. Balma, J. C. Maloney, and C. H. Lawshe, "The Role of the Foreman in Modern Industry," *Personnel Psychology* 11 (1958): 195–206.

conflicting obligations, has aptly termed the supervisor a "member of two families."[29]

If the supervisor had no personal stake in the outcome of these conflicting elements, it could still be argued that he could maintain the necessary objectivity to evaluate performance. However, a final element which contributes to "subjectivity" in ratings is the fact that the supervisor's own reputation and chances for success are primarily dependent upon the work of his subordinates. Subordinate delinquencies mean that the supervisor's work schedules and goals have been delayed, and they reflect upon his effectiveness to his superiors. Under these conditions the supervisor may be described as highly involved with those he is reporting upon, and evaluations of their work may be strongly conditioned by the nature of the interaction between himself and subordinates.

Returning to the question of what subordinate behaviors may be most likely to promote supervisory esteem, as a first approximation the author suggests that supervisors may be most influenced by behaviors in subordinates that show support for himself and his goals. By supportive behaviors are meant behaviors that reflect a willingness to accept the supervisor's influence or which promote confidence in the subordinate's ability to carry out the work.

In themselves, of course, such behaviors are an important component of job performance. Subordinates who are lazy, insolent, forgetful or argumentative, or misinterpret the range of their responsibilities, for instance, tend to be disruptive and impede the flow of work.[30] However, to the extent that these behaviors become the basis for the interpretation of other behaviors of the subordinate, limits are placed on the range of behaviors which we may expect the supervisor to reliably evaluate. This is because evaluations may be more affected by the diligence with which the subordinate supports the supervisor than by the subordinate's technical knowledge. For instance, the oft-noted, but little investigated, success of "yes-man" behavior in winning supervisory esteem is an example of supportive behavior which serves to alleviate supervisory anxiety rather than promote production.

Whether the specific behaviors designated here as the content of ratings are correct is a matter of empirical research. Beyond this question, further discussion is in order concerning the general question of implications for rating research brought about by postulating that supervisory evaluations are mainly determined by a limited number of subordinate behaviors.

---

[29] F. Mann and J. Dent, "The Supervisor: Member of Two Organizational Families," *Harvard Business Review* 32 (1954): 103–12.

[30] See C. H. Lawshe, "Of Management and Measurement," *American Psychologist* 14 (1959): 290–94.

1. Assumptions and Data of Ratings

One useful standard for the evaluation of theory is the necessity for it to be consistent with existing data.[31] Applying this standard, it may be seen that the proposition, that overall evaluations are determined by a specific class of subordinate behaviors, can accommodate rather well two important findings of rating research. It describes the conditions giving rise to halo and, secondly, it does not require that the supervisor's description of subordinate behaviors be congruent with more objective measures. In fact, it predicts little relationship insofar as the supervisor is not describing the central class of subordinate behaviors which primarily determined the rating. From this point of view, significant problems of rating research are the identification of the specific class of subordinate behaviors determining ratings, as well as the conditions under which these behaviors will be most influential. Two such conditions may be (a) the extent the supervisor is dependent upon the work of subordinates to maintain his own reputation as against only nominal supervision without involvement and (b) the length of time the supervisor has led the group he is rating. The longer the time, the higher the probability that perceptions of specific behaviors will be distorted.[32]

Finally, this assumption can be readily coordinated with current research in interpersonal perception. As findings accumulate in that area, it seems more and more likely that ratings cannot be excepted from general uniformities of interpersonal perception. Similar factors may determine ratings in the case of the supervisor evaluating subordinates and in the case of the college sophomore rating his friends on maturity. As this point becomes recognized, the interaction between the two areas should provide two beneficial effects. First, an important industrial field setting for research in interpersonal perceptions will be provided. Second, the results of such studies in turn may clarify many problems currently associated with supervisors' ratings.

2. Measurement of Performance

Ghiselli has recently pointed out that performance on any given job may be best described in terms of at least several independent dimensions.[33] As a corollary, it can be added that no one measure of performance may be adequate to describe these independent dimensions. While we recognize this, our efforts to measure performance are usually limited

---

[31] See F. H. Allport, *Theories of Perception and the Concept of Structure* (New York: John Wiley & Sons, 1955), chap. 1.

[32] See Sherif, White, and Harvey, "Status in Experimentally Produced Groups."

[33] E. E. Ghiselli, "Dimensional Problems of Criteria," *Journal of Applied Psychology* 40 (1956): 1–4.

to the use of one measuring instrument. In part, dissatisfaction with ratings as a criterion measure stems from this practice of expecting them to measure total job performance. For instance, Taylor, Parker, and Ford concluded,[34] after an unsuccessful attempt to cross-validate a rating scale format found less subject to "bias" in a prior methodological research project:

We rather question the ability of the average supervisor in industrial management to provide an appraisal of his subordinates adequate to the needs of predictor validation. From this, it necessarily follows that ordinary appraisals by superiors are probably even less adequate to provide a basis for personnel action, particularly those of promotion or transfer.[35]

If the proposition is valid that supervisor's ratings are measuring only an aspect of job performance, then some progress toward salvaging ratings as a measure of performance can be made. This more modest definition allows room for the development of other measures of job performance without expectation that the measures should correlate with each other, or more importantly, correlate with supervisors' ratings. If technical knowledge is an important component of the criterion, then job knowledge tests might be used. If willingness and diligence are important, supervisors' ratings could be included (assuming for the moment that the guess as to the class of behaviors is correct). If human relations skills are to be measured, the opinions of peers or subordinates might be solicited. Certainly the gathering of these data is no easy task. The identification and measurement of the various dimensions of performance in itself presents many challenging and difficult problems. Beyond that problem, the monumental task of combining the various sources of information into an overall description of subordinate performance must be solved.[36] These problems are, of course, beyond the scope of this paper. Ghiselli has addressed himself to the logical and methodological considerations involved here.[37]

3. Prediction of Performance

A third consequence of distinguishing between performance as perceived by the supervisor, and performance as estimated by other measures, may be noted in terms of the development and validation of selection tests. Such tests are, of course, constructed from an analysis of the abilities and temperamental qualities needed on the job. While the specific nature of the tests may vary according to the orientation or insightfulness of the test constructor, the focus is usually on the job elements.

---

[34] E. K. Taylor, J. W. Parker, and G. L. Ford, "Rating Scale Content. IV. Predictability of Structured and Unstructured Scales," *Personnel Psychology* 12 (1959): 247–266.

[35] Ibid., p. 266.

[36] Editors' note: See the article by Schmidt and Kaplan in this Section for a discussion of the problems involved here.

[37] Ghiselli, "Dimensional Problems."

In validating these tests, however, the most frequent criterion is supervisory ratings of performance. The disappointing validities so often obtained with this criterion may stem from the dubious assumption that supervisors' ratings are equivalent with the performance the investigator is attempting to predict. To the extent that ratings are used as criterion measures, it may be more appropriate to develop tests to measure how the subordinate accommodates his actions to the supervisor. Kipnis and Glickman have attempted to do this in developing a battery of tests to predict Navy sailors performance evaluations.[38] Tests to measure such hypothesized "support" behaviors as insolence (lack of), decisiveness, and willingness to work beyond minimum standards on tiring jobs were developed. In two small pilot studies multiple correlations with supervisors' ratings of over .40 were obtained. Larger scale studies with these tests are now in progress.

In general, greater flexibility of choice of criteria for test validation follows from the assumption that supervisors' evaluations cover only an aspect of job performance. Balancing this gain, however, is the fact that many of the problems, discussed in the previous section on the measurement of performance, apply as well to its prediction. As Ghiselli has indicated, the prediction of any one dimension of job performance cannot be taken as synonymous with the prediction of job performance in its entirety.[39] At best more limited statements about validity are required. The multidimensionality of job performance is not likely to be completely described by either single tests and/or single criterion measures.

5. USING CRITICAL INCIDENTS
TO MEASURE JOB
PROFICIENCY FACTORS *

Wayne K. Kirchner and Marvin D. Dunnette

WHILE NEARLY EVERY NEWSPAPER, magazine, or professional journal is bemoaning the current shortage of engineers and offering sage advice as to what should be done about it, there is another manpower problem, less publicized but nonetheless crucial—the shortage of salesmen. Large and

---

[38] D. Kipnis and A. S. Glickman, *The Development of a Non-Cognitive Battery to Predict Enlisted Performance,* Technical Bulletin 58–9 (Washington, D.C.: U.S. Naval Personnel Research Field Activity, 1958); idem, *The Development of a Non-Cognitive Battery: Prediction of Radioman Performance,* Technical Bulletin 59–11, ibid. (1959).

[39] Ghiselli, "Dimensional Problems."

* From "Identifying the Critical Factors in Successful Salesmanship," *Personnel* 34 (1957): 54–59.

small companies alike are "beating the bushes" hoping to flush reasonably competent males to handle their selling jobs. It has been estimated that over 400,000 new salesmen are needed in 1957 alone. As matters stand now, the basic question in hiring a salesman is not *can he sell* but *will he try*.

To increase the flow of applicants, recruiting programs have been stepped up by many companies and emphasis has been placed on making selling a more prestigeful job. Both these approaches have produced results. Generally speaking, however, not enough emphasis has been placed on the most important question at all: *What are the critical factors in successful selling?* If these can be identified, certainly the selection and placement of applicants, as well as the utilization of the current sales force, can be greatly improved.

Determining the "critical" factors is a tough job, however. There is no shortage of *opinions* about what constitutes salesmanship, but *facts* are harder to come by. The reason is that it is difficult to define in any objective form the actual behavior that characterizes the successful salesman. Such indicators as volume of sales, number of calls made, or number of orders taken certainly provide some measures of the overall effectiveness of a salesman, but they do not tell *why* he is or is not successful. Nor do they yield any clues, in most cases, as to why one salesman is better than another. Here again there is no dearth of personal opinions— "he looks like a good boy," or "he's not too sharp"—but these are of little help in actually defining the elements that go to make up "good" or "poor" sales behavior.

A real need exists, therefore, for measures of sales effectiveness based on the actual behavior of salesmen on the job. With such data, the training of new sales people, the appraisal of selling performance, and the selection of candidates can be undertaken with greater accuracy and assurance.

While many approaches are available for studying behavior on the job, the technique of critical incidents seems ideally suited to our purposes. Originally developed by Flanagan,[1] this method has been used by many firms to obtain information about behavior in various kinds of jobs. The major purpose of this article is to describe certain critical incidents in selling behavior that actually occurred among salesmen in one company and to show how such incidents may be categorized into meaningful factors or functions in effective selling.

The Critical Incidents Approach

The rationale of this technique is simple enough. Critical incidents are just what the name implies—occurrences that have proved to be the key

---

[1] John C. Flanagan, "A New Approach to Evaluating Personnel," *Personnel* 26 (1949): 35–42.

to effective performance on the job. They involve not routine activities but rather those essentials in job performance which make the difference between success and failure. In applying the technique, critical incidents are recorded in the form of stories or anecdotes about how a person handles certain situations, and from these data a composite picture of job behavior is built up.

EXHIBIT 5–1

Critical Incident Record Form (Type I) *

Think back over a period of time (six months or so) long enough for you to have observed the activities of all your salesmen. Focus your attention on any one thing that one of your salesmen may have done which made you think of him as an outstandingly *good* or *very effective* salesman. In other words, think of a *critical incident* which had added materially to the overall success of your sales group. *Please do not record any names of persons involved in the following incident.*

What were the general circumstances leading up to this incident?

Tell exactly what your salesman did that was so *effective* at that time.

How did this particular incident contribute to the overall effectiveness of your sales group?

When did this incident happen?

How long has this salesman been on his present territory?

How long has this salesman been with 3M?

---

* Type II is designed for incidents involving ineffective performance and is similar in form.

The study reported here was carried out in the Minnesota Mining and Manufacturing Company, which employs over 1,000 salesmen. Critical incident forms were printed and sent to 85 sales managers in four separate product divisions (see Exhibit 5–1). Each manager was asked to report as many critical incidents as possible illustrating both effective and noneffective behavior among his own group of salesmen. It was felt that sales managers would be acquainted with many such incidents because of their day-to-day contact with the problems of their salesmen, and this belief was amply confirmed. A total of 135 incidents was reported, of which 96 could be classified as "usable." Sixty-one of these 96 were instances of effective performance while 35 concerned noneffective performance. Each incident was reviewed and summarized.

To illustrate the type of information contained in these reports, five of the incidents reported are given below in summary form:

1. A salesman received a complaint from a customer about the quality of a particular type of tape. He failed to look into the matter or write up a formal complaint. The defective tape was returned to the jobber and no credit was issued to the jobber or to the retailer involved. While the account was not lost, the customer was dissatisfied for a long time.
2. A large customer complained about our tape and decided to try out a competitor's tape. The complaint was justified and a substitution run was recommended. The salesman told the customer about this new run and said it would come in the next order. He did not tie this down with the jobber, however, and the jobber shipped more of the old run when the customer's order came through. As a result, the customer felt that the salesman could not be trusted and withdrew his business.
3. A salesman driving down the street saw a truck containing equipment for which company products might be used. He followed the truck to find the delivery point, made a call on this account, which was a new one, and obtained an order.
4. A jobber account had been lost. The salesman made it a point to contact the account once a month for over a year, explaining company policy and showing that our products would be easier to sell. After a year, the jobber returned to the company.
5. A large plant working on a defense project suddenly discovered that they were out of belts of a certain length which had to be made to order. The salesman borrowed utility rolls of the correct width and grit from a jobber, took them to a woodworking plant which made endless belts, and had enough belts made to keep the defense project going.

Critical Factors in Selling

Since many of the incidents reported were overlapping, they could be grouped into broad and more meaningful categories. For example, a number of incidents concerned failures or successes in following up various types of requests, orders, and leads; hence it was a fairly simple matter to group these under the general head of "Following-up." Similar groupings were made for other related incidents, and this procedure yielded the following categories of critical functions or factors in selling:

1. Following-up:
   a. Complaints.

    b. Requests.
    c. Orders.
    d. Leads.
 2. Planning ahead.
 3. Communicating all necessary information to sales managers.
 4. Communicating truthful information to managers and customers.
 5. Carrying out promises.
 6. Persisting on tough accounts.
 7. Pointing out uses for other company products besides the salesman's
    own line.
 8. Using new sales techniques and methods.
 9. Preventing price-cutting by dealers and customers.
10. Initiating new selling ideas.
11. Knowing customer requirements.
12. Defending company policies.
13. Calling on all accounts.
14. Helping customers with equipment and displays.
15. Showing nonpassive attitude.

These 15 factors derive from the actual job behavior of salesmen. A good salesman had to handle all or most of them well in order to succeed, and failure on any one count could lead to failure on the entire job.

As might be expected, however, these factors were not of equal weight in terms of the number of incidents reported for each category. The factor most often cited was that of "Following-up." Another was persistence on the part of the salesman. It seems that good salesmen do not give up easily; they tend to keep after tough accounts. In addition, they plan their activities well, as indicated by the number of incidents related to planning or the lack of it.

All 15 factors, however, seemed to characterize the behavior of the best salesmen in the company. Different items might be added to the list from studies made at other companies, of course, but these 15 seem to be the core of effective selling behavior.

The practical uses of critical incident data are evident. With information of this kind at hand, it becomes possible to pinpoint areas of strength or weakness in selling behavior. Checklists, appraisals by supervisors, self-appraisal, and similar methods can be used to compare the actual behavior of salesmen with the "model" and to institute improvements where needed.

One example of these methods is the sales behavior rating sheet derived from critical incidents, shown in Exhibit 5–2. Each item on the questionnaire represents a summary of a particular incident or group of incidents reported by sales managers. This questionnaire is now being used in further research to establish criteria of sales effectiveness that will aid in validating tests of applicants for sales positions.

EXHIBIT 5–2

A Behavior Rating Sheet Derived from Critical Selling Incidents

Name of person being described _____

Below are listed several statements about selling behavior. Consider each statement in terms of the person named above. Would you agree or disagree with the statement if you heard it used to describe that person? How strongly would you agree or disagree?

For each statement, please check the category which most accurately reflects your agreement or disagreement. Remember to base each answer on how well or how poorly the statement describes the person named above.

Thanks a great deal for your help.

1. Allows too much credit to doubtful customers.
   __Strongly Agree   __Agree   __Undecided   __Disagree   __Strongly Disagree
2. Gossips about customer's confidential information.
   __Strongly Agree   __Agree   __Undecided   __Disagree   __Strongly Disagree
3. Writes poor sales reports.
   __Strongly Agree   __Agree   __Undecided   __Disagree   __Strongly Disagree
4. Assists fellow salesmen with displays, and so forth, when needed.
   __Strongly Disagree   __Disagree   __Undecided   __Agree   __Strongly Agree
5. Apt to be late in passing along price changes to customers.
   __Strongly Disagree   __Disagree   __Undecided   __Agree   __Strongly Agree
6. Shows lackadaisical attitude.
   __Strongly Disagree   __Disagree   __Undecided   __Agree   __Strongly Agree
7. Follows up quickly on requests from customers.
   __Strongly Disagree   __Disagree   __Undecided   __Agree   __Strongly Agree

                          *   *   *

21. Promises too much to customers.
   __Strongly Agree   __Agree   __Undecided   __Disagree   __Strongly Disagree
22. Is familiar with competitive products and sales methods.
   __Strongly Disagree   __Disagree   __Undecided   __Agree   __Strongly Agree

Another possibility is the use of the questionnaire in setting up criteria of sales effectiveness focused on the company's actual job requirements. Here, obviously, is a major advantage of the critical incident method. It is "tailor-made." Whatever the company, its needs can be served most directly by data based on the performance of its own employees.

Inasmuch as this kind of information gives clues to the type of person needed on sales jobs, it is also valuable, of course, in the actual selection of sales candidates.

6. DEVELOPMENT OF FIRST-LEVEL BEHAVIORAL JOB CRITERIA *

Lawrence Fogli, Charles L. Hulin, and Milton R. Blood

THE TASK OF DEVELOPING reliable and valid job criteria is one of the most challenging and desired objectives in contemporary industrial psychology. Dunnette has emphasized the need for developing job-behavior descriptions in order to establish relationships between specific job behaviors and global dimensions of success.[1] At the same time, predictor batteries can be developed which are aimed at predicting these specific behaviors rather than global measures (which are normally predicted with a consistent, albeit discouraging, lack of success). The relevance of the specific behaviors to more global criterion measures and predictors should be determined empirically. The present study systematically develops criteria for observing and evaluating the behavior of grocery checkers.

Smith and Kendall's development of criteria of nursing performance provides a procedure for obtaining dimensions and specific aspects of job behavior based on descriptions of actual behavior.[2] The objective for those authors was to develop rating scales that are equivalent from rater to rater and from occasion to occasion in terms of dimensions and levels of job performance, even though the task was complex and varied. The present study strives to establish criteria scales with high interrater reliability that can be used by raters to judge the magnitudes of attributes of workers.

The goal of such research is to develop synthetic criteria which may be substituted for actual specific behavior with little loss of information. Scales and items must indicate the same quality of performance among raters and among divisions of a company. If a sample of potential raters judged the relative quality of performance indicated by each of a set of items, we would expect that the rank order, the location, and the spread of the items would be highly similar to the same statistics computed for the set of items from another sample of potential raters.

---

* Adapted from "Development of First-Level Behavioral Job Criteria," *Journal of Applied Psychology* 55, no. 1 (1971): 3–8. Copyright 1971 by the American Psychological Association. Reprinted by permission.

[1] M. D. Dunnette, *Personnel Selection and Placement* (Belmont, Calif.: Wadsworth, 1966).

[2] P. C. Smith and L. M. Kendall, "Retranslation of Expectations: An Approach to the Construction of Unambiguous Anchors for Rating Scales," *Journal of Applied Psychology* 47 (1963): 149–55.

METHODS

The initial step was to conduct interviews with staff personnel of a grocery chain concerning the purpose of a grocery checker's job at the same time critical incidents of good–poor behavior of checkers were obtained. The most frequent behaviors were selected and the grocer's terminology was retained.

Three groups of managers, assistant managers, and department heads were selected from three districts of a large grocery store chain in the San Francisco Bay area. The three groups consisted of staff personnel from ten stores in each district, which differed on the basis of geographical location, as designated by company districts—A, B, C. The content of the items and job description is limited to behavior performed in the checkstand.

One hundred and twenty staff personnel were available for participation in the procedures for the development of rating-scale criteria. Interviewing was terminated after a total of 43 interviews for obtaining behavioral examples and critical incidents of checkstand behavior because of redundancy in behavioral incidents in the job domain.

The interviews were structured so that the interviewer recorded the verbatim responses to the structured questions. The questionnaire commenced with the following discussion designed to convince the interviewees of the importance of the study and their cooperation:

We are making a study of grocery checking and trying to learn in detail just what successful work as a grocery clerk includes. In order to facilitate the performance of grocery clerks for checkout stand procedures, we need to know what aspects of checking performance make an especially effective or ineffective clerk. Managers, assistant managers, and department heads such as yourselves are constantly observing and evaluating the work of the clerk. Therefore, you are in an unusually good position to report effectiveness.

Participation in the study was further assured by convincing the respondents of the usefulness of both the expected results and procedures of the study. Interviewees were informed that the incidents reported would serve as characteristic levels of different dimensions of the job, and that later they would be asked to allocate those behavioral incidents to different dimensions.

Questions about primary and specific aspects of job behavior were similar to the critical incident method of Flanagan.[3] Many respondents gave general behavioral examples, even to such statements as "describe specifically the behavior you would expect from the best checker you have ever known." Global descriptions of "he is an accurate checker," "he is friendly," and "he is a fast checker" are too general and are unaccept-

---

[3] J. C. Flanagan, "The Critical Incident Technique," *Psychological Bulletin* 51 (1954): 327–55.

able for behaviorally anchored scales. The respondents were able to provide more definite and well thought out examples when the generality of their responses was indicated to them.

Among the questions designed to obtain specific behaviors were:

1. Please describe the critical characteristics of the behavior of a grocery checker that make him effective—be specific.
2. Similarly describe the specific behavior of an extremely ineffective checker. Remember incidents in your store that displayed vividly poor performance. It might help you to describe the behavior you would expect from the worst checker you have ever known.
3. Now, think of the last time you saw one of the checkers do something that was very significant in displaying effective performance in the checkstand. How did this action result in increasing the effectiveness of the clerk's overall performance?

After analyzing the verbatim responses to the structured questionnaire, the first two authors categorized the behavioral incidents into eight functional dimensions. Store personnel were not asked to define the job dimensions so that demands on their working time would not be excessive.

Staff personnel were presented with dimensions defined by the researchers and instructed to place each behavioral incident into the dimension for which it was an example. Each behavioral incident was judged by 15 independent raters. An incident was eliminated if there was not majority agreement as to the dimension to which it belonged.

A final rating format composed of all of the items that were maintained in the eight dimensions was sent to all 120 Ss, and 97 Ss completed it. Judges rated the degree to which each item indicated good–poor performance on a 7-point scale. Large standard deviations indicated a lack of agreement on the meaning of the behavior, and items were arbitrarily eliminated if their standard deviations were 1.5 or greater. If items had similar mean values, the item with the smallest standard deviation was retained. Items were selected for each categorical scale by these criteria. The mean scale positions of each item assigned by personnel in districts A, B, and C were intercorrelated to give estimates of scale reliabilities. This procedure assumes that the rater can make inferences from observations about the interrelations of behaviors and that a group of managers, assistant managers, and department heads will have well-differentiated and standardized judgments about checking performance.

The behavioral examples that were used in the final rating format were reworded as expected behaviors rather than actual behaviors. This restatement of the items followed the procedures of the Smith and Kendall study.[4] Instead of statements like "When everybody is checking, this checker leaves the checkstand to get the customer an item," statements

----

[4] Smith and Kendall, "Retranslation of Expectations."

consisted of expectations such as "If everybody is checking, this checker can be expected to leave the checkstand to get the customer an item." According to Smith and Kendall, the expected-behavior format will improve the final ratings by making the predictions:

(a) so concrete that, in view of previous agreement by the peer group, central tendency or judging effects will be minimized; and *(b)* so verifiable that insight, judgment, values, etc. of the rater are potentially challenged if later behavior of the ratee would fail to confirm the prediction.[5]

RESULTS

The dimensions that proved to be meaningful after the judges allocated items to dimensions are listed in Table 6–1. Even though the researchers, rather than job incumbents, defined the dimensions of the job, the total number of items (211) in the high agreement column of Table 6–1 is indicative of the usefulness of those dimensions. The rating questionnaire was composed of items of at least 60 percent agreement except for categories 1, 6, and 8. These categories contained some items with only 50 percent agreement.

TABLE 6–1

Agreement of Allocation of Items to Characteristics

Characteristic	High Agreement (above 60%)	Lower Agreement (40%–59%)
Conscientiousness.	10	5
Knowledge and judgment	37	13
Skill in human relations	36	5
Skill in operation of register	34	3
Skill in bagging	36	1
Organizational ability of checkstand work	13	11
Skill in monetary transactions	34	0
Observational ability	11	2
Total no. of items.	211	40

Table 6–2 shows scale reliabilities of items retained in the final rating format. The mean score of each of the retained items for the three districts was intercorrelated to obtain scale reliabilities.[6] The lowest scale

[5] Ibid., p. 151.

[6] The reader should be aware that pooling item scores leads to more accurate estimates of scale values in this assessment of scale reliability. With 30 Ss per sample, this is the empirical equivalent of adjusting the average interrater correlation by the Spearman–Brown formula with a multiplicative factor of 30. For a discussion of such scale reliability estimation see C. E. Noble, "Scale Reliability and the Spearman–Brown Equation," *Educational Psychological Measurement* 15 (1955): 195–205.

TABLE 6–2

Intercorrelations, Standard Deviations, and Regression Data of Mean Scale Positions Assigned by Three Districts for Seven Scales

Characteristic	No. items	District	Correlations A	Correlations B	$\bar{X}$	σ	Reg. Coef. A	Reg. Coef. B	Reg. Coef. C	Intercept A	Intercept B	Intercept C
Conscientiousness	13	A			5.89	1.08		1.14	1.03		-.33	.01
		B	.98		5.46	.93	.89		.84	-.37		.50
		C	.97	.97	5.71	1.01	.92	1.06		-.28	-.08	
Knowledge and judgment	24	A			4.75	1.74		.97	.90		.30	.66
		B	.98		4.59	1.76	.99		.92	-.11		.43
		C	.99	.99	4.55	1.90	1.08	1.07		-.58	-.36	
Skill in human relations	16	A			4.88	1.57		1.04	.97		.09	.33
		B	.98		4.61	1.48	.93		.90	.08		.35
		C	.99	.98	4.72	1.61	1.01	1.07		-.21	-.21	
Skill in operation of register	26	A			5.04	1.49		1.13	1.04		-.29	.25
		B	.98		4.71	1.32	.86		.92	.36		.30
		C	.98	.98	4.78	1.41	.93	1.05		.12	-.17	
Skill in bagging	21	A			4.27	1.93		1.07	1.01		-.10	-.10
		B	.99		4.09	1.78	.91		.93	.02		.24
		C	.99	.99	4.14	1.90	.98	1.05		-.03	-.14	
Organizational ability of checkstand work	30	A			4.79	1.79		1.07	.95		-.18	.39
		B	.99		4.64	1.65	.92		.88	.25		.22
		C	.99	.99	4.62	1.86	1.03	1.11		-.31	-.53	
Skill in monetary transactions	32	A			4.36	1.72		1.07	.95		-.02	.41
		B	.99		4.09	1.58	1.03		.91	-.40		.31
		C	.98	.99	4.16	1.78	1.01	1.01		-.24	.03	

* Regression coefficients and intercepts are given for predicting the variable designated by the row by the variable designated by the column.

FIGURE 6–1

An Example Scale for the Knowledge and Judgment Decision

Extremely good performance	7	
	6	By knowing the price of items, this checker would be expected to look for mismarked and unmarked items.
Good performance		You can expect this checker to be aware of items that constantly fluctuate in price.
	5	You can expect this checker to know the various sizes of cans—No. 303, No. 2, No. 2½.
Slightly good performance		When in doubt, this checker would ask the other clerk if the item is taxable.
		This checker can be expected to verify with another checker a discrepancy between the shelf and the marked price before ringing up that item.
Neither poor nor good performance	4	
		When operating the quick check, the lights are flashing, this checker can be expected to check out a customer with 15 items.
Slightly poor performance	3	
		You could expect this checker to ask the customer the price of an item that he does not know.
Poor performance		In the daily course of personal relationships, may be expected to linger in long conversations with a customer or another checker.
	2	In order to take a break, this checker can be expected to block off the checkstand with people in line.
Extremely poor performance	1	

reliability was .97. Means, standard deviations, and regression information are also given for each district in Table 6–2. An examination of these data substantiate the similarity of rating between districts on each scale. The regression coefficient and intercept which are required to indicate perfect agreement among districts are a coefficient of 1.00 and an intercept of .00. The observed coefficients range from .84 to 1.14 with a median of .99. The observed intercepts range from −.58 to .66 with a median of .05.

Figures 6–1 and 6–2 present example scales made from items which represent two of the dimensions—knowledge and judgment, and organiza-

FIGURE 6–2

An Example Scale for the Organizational Ability of Checkstand Work Dimension

Extremely good performance	7	
		This checker would organize the order when checking it out by placing all soft goods like bread, cake, etc. to one side of counter; all meats, produce, frozen foods, to the other side, thereby leaving the center of the counter for can foods, boxed goods, and so forth.
Good performance	6	
Slightly good performance		When checking, this checker would separate strawberries, bananas, cookies, cakes, and breads, and so forth.
	5	You can expect this checker to grab more than one item at a time from the cart to the counter.
	4	
Neither poor nor good performance		After bagging the order and customer is still writing a check, you can expect this checker to proceed to the next order if it is a small order.
	3	
Slightly poor performance		This checker may be expected to put wet merchandise on the top of the counter.
		This checker can be expected to lay milk and by-product cartons on their sides on the counter top.
Poor performance	2	
		This checker can be expected to damage fragile merchandise like soft goods, eggs, and light bulbs on the counter top.
Extremely poor performance	1	

tional ability of checkstand work.[7] Category 8, observational ability, was eliminated as a useful scale because of poor dispersion of behavioral items along the good–poor continuum.

CONCLUSIONS

The method of criterion-scale development reported in this article, which involves staff members in each step of the development, provides

---

[7] A complete list of items retained for each of the seven scales and the scale values of the items has been deposited with the National Auxiliary Publications Service. Order Document No. 01257 from the National Auxiliary Publications Service of the American Society for Information Science, c/o CCM Information Sciences, Inc., 909 3rd Avenue, New York, New York 10022. Remit in advance $5.00 for photocopies or $2.00 for microfiche and make checks payable to Research and Microfilm Publications, Inc.

behavioral scales that are specific and apparently nonambiguous. In the case of the specific job studied, seven major and discriminable dimensions were obtained: *(a)* conscientiousness, *(b)* knowledge and judgment, *(c)* skill in human relations, *(d)* skill in operation of register, *(e)* skill in bagging, *(f)* organizational ability of checkstand work, and *(g)* skill in monetary transactions. The procedure provides carefully designated behavioral incidents for each scale. The examples of behavior are in the grocer's terminology, and there is excellent agreement of the allocation of incidents, discrimination, and high scale reliability. The degree of colinearity among these scales, when used as rating devices, remains to be determined.

This method eliminates ambiguity by having those who will eventually use the rating criteria develop the scales with their own observations about behavior. Furthermore, the staff allocates incidents to dimensions and makes final judgments about the level of performance each behavior indicates. Since high agreement is obtained in the three samples, the scales may serve as standards to evaluate specific behaviors that can be expected in the checkstand. The reliability of ratings of performance may increase since the dimensions and incidents are easily and accurately distinguished from one another. Because there are multiple ratings, raters are not restricted to the gross generalizations which are necessary when global performance evaluations are made. The success of a job incumbent can be evaluated in terms of specific behaviors and dimensions. This behavioral information should prove more useful to both the worker and his immediate supervisor than general statements of overall performance level.

There are many items with standard deviations less than 1.5 which were eliminated from the scales because their mean scores were similar to other items on the same dimension. These items still provide reliable job criteria. This company could use these items plus the behavioral scales for development of a training program for checkers. A training program based upon the behavioral incidents and dimensions would inform checkers about the expected behaviors for their job. Since the level of the behaviors is highly agreed upon from store to store, a uniform training program could be developed for all of the stores.

An additional use of the behavioral items would be to ask trainees and/or incumbent checkers to rate the items on the 7-point good–poor scale. Their ratings of items could be compared to the ratings made by managers. Discrepancies could be discussed to teach the checker what he should do. Training programs could be modified to take account of the results of such item ratings.

Another benefit of this procedure is that it provides information about specific behaviors that are not highly agreed upon among staff personnel. Items with very large variances can be investigated by the organization to change or develop policy about such behavior. The following are examples of behavioral incidents which had large variances on the good–poor continuum in this study: (a) When customer feels that the total bill was too high, you can expect this checker to rering the order ($S^2 = 3.20$). (b) When dealing with an overring, this checker would subtract over-charged items from another item in the same department—a grocery item from a grocery item ($S^2 = 3.02$). (c) You can expect this checker not to separate wet produce from other merchandise on the table top ($S^2 = 2.53$). (d) You can expect this checker to check items without looking at the prices because of memorizing prices ($S^2 = 3.50$). (e) This checker can be expected not to bother to change departmental sales ring-up error but would ignore the mistake ($S^2 = 2.43$). For these behaviors and others with large variances, the organization may wish to enunciate or communicate its policy more clearly.

7. SPLIT ROLES IN PERFORMANCE APPRAISAL *

Herbert H. Meyer, Emanuel Kay, and John R. P. French, Jr.

IN MANAGEMENT CIRCLES, performance appraisal is a highly interesting and provocative topic. And in business literature, too, knowledgeable people write emphatically, pro and con, on the performance appraisal question.[1] In fact, one might almost say that everybody talks and writes about it, but nobody has done any real scientific testing of it.

At the General Electric Company we felt it was important that a truly scientific study be done to test the effectiveness of our traditional per-formance appraisal program. Why? Simply because our own experience with performance appraisal programs had been both positive and nega-tive. For example:

Surveys generally show that most people think the idea of performance appraisal is good. They feel that a man should know where he stands and, therefore, the manager should discuss an appraisal of his performance with him periodically.

In actual practice, however, it is the extremely rare operating manager

* From *Harvard Business Review* 43 (1964): 124–29. © 1964 by the President and Fellows of Harvard College; all rights reserved.

[1] Douglas McGregor, "An Uneasy Look at Performance Appraisal," *Harvard Business Review*, May–June 1957, p. 89; Harold Mayfield, "In Defense of Performance Appraisal," ibid., March–April 1960, p. 81; and Alva F. Kindall and James Gatza, "Positive Program for Performance Appraisal," ibid., November–December 1963, p. 153.

who will employ such a program on his own initiative. Personnel specialists report that most managers carry out performance appraisal interviews only when strong control procedures are established to ensure that they do so. This is surprising because the managers have been told repeatedly that the system is intended to help them obtain improved performance from their subordinates.

We also found from interviews with employees who have had a good deal of experience with traditional performance appraisal programs that few indeed can cite examples of constructive action taken—or significant improvement achieved—which stem from suggestions received in a performance appraisal interview with their boss.

TRADITIONAL PROGRAM

Faced with such contradictory evidence, we undertook a study several years ago to determine the effectiveness of our comprehensive performance appraisal process. Special attention was focused on the interview between the subordinate and his manager, because this is the discussion which is supposed to motivate the man to improve his performance. And we found out some very interesting things—among them the following:

a) Criticism has a negative effect on achievement of goals.
b) Praise has little effect one way or the other.
c) Performance improves most when specific goals are established.
d) Defensiveness resulting from critical appraisal produces inferior performance.
e) Coaching should be a day-to-day, not a once-a-year, activity.
f) Mutual goal setting, not criticism, improves performance.
g) Interviews designed primarily to improve a man's performance should not at the same time weigh his salary or promotion in the balance.
h) Participation by the employee in the goal-setting procedure helps produce favorable results.

As you can see, the results of this original study indicated that a detailed and comprehensive annual appraisal of a subordinate's performance by his manager is decidedly of questionable value. Furthermore, as is certainly the case when the major objective of such a discussion is to motivate the subordinate to improve his performance, the traditional appraisal interview does not do the job.

In the first part of this article, we will offer readers more than this bird's-eye view of our research into performance appraisal. We will also describe the one-year follow-up experiment General Electric conducted to validate the conclusions derived from our original study. Here the traditional annual performance appraisal method was tested against a new method we developed, which we called Work Planning and Review (WP&R). As you will see, this approach produced, under actual plant conditions, results which were decidedly superior to those afforded by the traditional performance appraisal method. Finally, we will offer evidence to support our contention that some form of WP&R might well be incorporated into other industrial personnel programs to achieve improvement in work performance.

APPRAISING APPRAISAL

In order to assure a fair test of the effectiveness of the traditional performance appraisal method, which had been widely used throughout General Electric, we conducted an intensive study of the process at a large GE plant where the performance appraisal program was judged to be good; that is, in this plant—

. . . appraisals had been based on job responsibilities, rather than on personal characteristics of the individuals involved;

. . . an intensive training program had been carried out for managers in the use of the traditional appraisal method and techniques for conducting appraisal interviews;

. . . the program had been given strong backing by the plant manager and had been policed diligently by the personnel staff so that over 90 percent of the exempt employees had been appraised and interviewed annually.

This comprehensive annual performance appraisal program, as is typical, was designed to serve two major purposes. The first was to justify recommended salary action. The second, which was motivational in character, was intended to present an opportunity for the manager to review a subordinate's performance and promote discussion on needed improvements. For the latter purpose, the manager was required to draw up a specific program of plans and goals for the subordinate which would help him to improve his job performance and to qualify, hopefully, for future promotion.

Interview Modifications

Preliminary interviews with key managers and subordinates revealed the salary action issue had so dominated the annual comprehensive performance appraisal interview that neither party had been in the right frame of mind to discuss plans for improved performance. To straighten this out, we asked managers to split the traditional appraisal interview into two sessions—discussing appraisal of performance and salary action in one interview and performance improvement plans in another to be held about two weeks later. This split provided us with a better opportunity to conduct our experiment on the effects of participation in goal planning.

To enable us to test the effects of participation, we instructed half the managers to use a *high participation* approach and the other half to use a *low participation* technique.

Each of the "high" managers was instructed to ask his appraisee to prepare a set of goals for achieving improved job performance and to submit them for the manager's review and approval. The manager also was encouraged to permit the subordinate to exert as much influence as possible on the formulation of the final list of job goals agreed on in the performance improvement discussion.

The "low" managers operated in much the same way they had in our traditional appraisal program. They formulated a set of goals for the subordinate, and these goals were then reviewed in the performance improvement session. The manager was instructed to conduct this interview in such a way that his influence in the forming of the final list of job goals would be greater than the subordinate's.

Conducting the Research

There were 92 appraisees in the experimental group, representing a cross section of the exempt salaried employees in the plant. This group included engineers; engineering support technicians; foremen; and specialists in manufacturing, customer service, marketing, finance, and purchasing functions. None of the exempt men who participated as appraisees in the experiment had other exempt persons reporting to them; thus they did not serve in conflicting manager-subordinate roles.

The entire group was interviewed and asked to complete questionnaires (*a*) before and after the salary action interview, and (*b*) after the delayed second discussion with their managers about performance improvement. These interviews and questionnaires were designed to achieve three objectives:

1. Assess changes in the attitudes of individuals toward their managers and toward the appraisal system after each of the discussions.
2. Get an estimate from the appraisee of the degree to which he usually participated in decisions that affected him. (This was done in order to determine whether or not previous lack of participation affected his response to participation in the experiment.)
3. Obtain a self-appraisal from each subordinate before and after he met with his manager. (This was done in order to determine how discrepancies in these self-appraisals might affect his reaction to the appraisal interview.)

Moreover, each salary action and performance improvement discussion was observed by outsiders trained to record essentially what transpired. (Managers preferred to use neither tape recorders nor unseen observers, feeling that observers unaffiliated with the company—in this case, graduate students in applied psychological disciplines—afforded the best way of obtaining a reasonably close approximation of the normal discussions.) In the appraisal for salary action interviews, for example, the observers recorded the amount of criticism and praise employed by the manager, as well as the reactions of the appraisee to the manager's comments. In the performance improvement discussions, the observers recorded the participation of the subordinate, as well as the amount of influence he seemed to exert in establishing his future success goals.

Criticism and Defensiveness

In general, the managers completed the performance appraisal forms in a thorough and conscientious manner. Their appraisals were discussed with subordinates in interviews ranging from approximately 30 to 90 minutes in length. On the average, managers covered 32 specific performance items which, when broken down, showed positive (praise) appraisals on 19 items, and negative (criticism) on 13. Typically, praise was more often related to *general* performance characteristics, while criticism was usually focused on *specific* performance items.

The average subordinate reacted defensively to seven of the manager's criticisms during the appraisal interview (that is, he reacted defensively about 54 percent of the time when criticized). Denial of shortcomings cited by the manager, blaming others, and various other forms of excuses were recorded by the observers as defensive reactions.

Constructive responses to criticism were *rarely* observed. In fact, the average was less than one per interview. Not too surprising, along with this, was the finding that the more criticism a man received in the performance appraisal discussion, the more defensively he reacted. Men who received an above-average number of criticisms showed more than five times as much defensive behavior as those who received a below-average number of criticisms. Subordinates who received a below-average number of criticisms, for example, reacted defensively only about one time out of three. But those who received an above-average number reacted defensively almost two times out of three.

One explanation for this defensiveness is that it seems to stem from the overrating each man tended to give to his own performance. The average employee's self-estimate of performance *before* appraisal placed him at the 77 percentile. (Only 2 of the 92 participants estimated their performance to be below the average point on the scale.) But when the same men were asked *after* their performance appraisal discussions how they thought their bosses had rated them, the average figure given was at the 65 percentile. The great majority (75 out of 92) saw their manager's evaluation as being less favorable than their self-estimates. Obviously, to these men, the performance appraisal discussion with the manager was a deflating experience. Thus, it was not surprising that the subordinates reacted defensively in their interviews.

Criticism and Goal Achievement

Even more important is the fact that men who received an above-average number of criticisms in their performance appraisal discussions generally showed *less* goal achievement 10 to 12 weeks later than those who had received fewer criticisms. At first, we thought that this difference might be accounted for by the fact that the subordinates who received more criticisms were probably poorer performers in general. But there was little factual evidence found to support this suspicion.

It was true that those who received an above-average number of criticisms in their appraisal discussions did receive slightly lower summary ratings on over-all performance from their managers. But they did not receive proportionally lower salary increases. And the salary increases granted were *supposed* to reflect differences in job performance, according to the salary plan traditionally used in this plant. This argument, admittedly, is something less than perfect.

But it does appear clear that frequent criticism constitutes so strong a threat to self-esteem that it disrupts rather than improves subsequent performance. We expected such a disruptive threat to operate more strongly on those individuals who were already low on self-esteem, just as we expected a man who had confidence in his ability to do his job to react more constructively to criticism. Our group experiment proved these expectations to be correct.

Still further evidence that criticism has a negative effect on performance was found when we investigated areas which had been given special emphasis by the manager in his criticism. Following the appraisal discussion with the manager, each employee was asked to indicate which one aspect of his performance had been most criticized by the manager. Then, when we conducted our follow-up investigation 10 to 12 weeks later, it revealed that improvement in the most-criticized aspects of performance cited was considerably *less* than improvement realized in other areas!

Participation Effects

As our original research study had indicated, the effects of a high participation level were also favorable in our group experiment. In general, here is what we found:

Subordinates who received a high participation level in the performance interview reacted more favorably than did those who received a low participation level. The "highs" also, in most cases, achieved a greater percentage of their improvement goals than did their "low" counterparts. For the former, the high participation level was associated with greater mutual understanding between them and their managers, greater acceptance of job goals, a more favorable attitude toward the appraisal system, and a feeling of greater self-realization on the job.

But employees who had traditionally been accustomed to low partici-pation in their daily relationship with the manager did not necessarily perform better under the high participation treatment. In fact, those men who had received a high level of criticism in their appraisal interviews actually performed better when their managers set goals for them than they did when they set theeir own goals, as permitted under the high participation treatment.

In general, our experiment showed that the men who usually worked under high participation levels performed best on goals they set for themselves. Those who indicated that they usually worked under low levels performed best on goals that the managers set for them. Evidently, the man who usually does not participate in work-planning decisions considers job goals set by the manager to be more important than goals he sets for himself. The man accustomed to a high participation level, on the other hand, may have stronger motivation to achieve goals he sets for himself than to achieve those set by his manager.

Goal-Setting Importance

While subordinate participation in the goal-setting process had some effect on improved performance, a much more powerful influence was whether goals were set at all. Many times in appraisal discussions, man-agers mentioned areas of performance where improvement was needed. Quite often these were translated into specific work plans and goals. But this was not always the case. In fact, when we looked at the one perform-ance area which each manager had emphasized in the appraisal interview as most in need of improvement, we found that these items actually were translated into specific work plans and goals for only about 60 percent of our experiment participants.

When performance was being measured 10 to 12 weeks after the goal-planning sessions, managers were asked to describe what results they hoped for in the way of subordinate on-the-job improvement. They did this for those important performance items that had been mentioned in the interview. Each manager was then asked to estimate on a percentage scale the degree to which his hoped-for changes had actually been ob-served. The average percent accomplishment estimate for those perform-ance items that *did* get translated into goals was 65, while the percent estimate for those items that *did* not get translated into goals was about 27! Establishing specific plans and goals seemed to ensure that attention would be given to that aspect of job performance.

Summation of Findings

At the end of this experiment, we were able to draw certain tentative conclusions. These conclusions were the basis of a future research study which we will describe later. In general, we learned that:

Comprehensive annual performance appraisals are of questionable value. Certainly a major objective of the manager in traditional appraisal discussions is motivating the subordinate to improve his performance. But the evidence we gathered indicated clearly that praise tended to have no effect, perhaps because it was regarded as the sandwich which surrounded the raw meat of criticism.[2] And criticism itself brought on defensive reactions that were essentially denials of responsibility for a poor performance.

Coaching should be a day-to-day, not a once-a-year, activity. There are two main reasons for this:

1. Employees seem to accept suggestions for improved performance if they are given in a less concentrated form than is the case in comprehensive annual appraisals. As our experiment showed, employees become clearly more prone to reject criticisms as the number of criticisms mount. This indicates that an "overload phenomenon" may be operating. In other words, each individual seems to have a tolerance level for the amount of criticism he can take. And, as this level is approached or passed, it becomes increasingly difficult for him to accept responsibility for the shortcomings pointed out.
2. Some managers reported that the traditional performance appraisal program tended to cause them to save up items where improvement was needed in order to have enough material to conduct a comprehensive discussion of performance in the annual review. This short-circuited one of the primary purposes of the appraisal program—that of giving feedback to the subordinates as to their performance. Studies of the learning process point out that feedback is less effective if much time is allowed to elapse between the performance and the feedback. This fact alone argues for more frequent dicussions between the manager and the subordinate.

Goal setting, not criticism, should be used to improve performance. One of the most significant findings in our experiment was the fact that far superior results were observed when the manager and the man *together* set specific goals to be achieved, rather than merely discussed needed improvement. Frequent reviews of progress provide natural opportunities for discussing means of improving performance *as needs occur,* and these reviews are far less threatening than the annual appraisal and salary review discussions.

Separate appraisals should be held for different purposes. Our work demonstrated that it was unrealistic to expect a single performance appraisal program to achieve every conceivable need. It seems foolish to

---

[2] See Richard E. Farson, "Praise Reappraised," *Harvard Business Review,* September–October 1963, p. 61.

have a manager serving in the self-conflicting roles as a counselor (helping a man to improve his performance) when, at the same time, he is presiding as a judge over the same employee's salary action case.

NEW WP&R METHOD

This intensive year-long test of the performance appraisal program indicated clearly that work-planning-and-review discussions between a man and his manager appeared to be a far more effective approach in improving job performance than was the concentrated annual performance appraisal program.

For this reason, after the findings had been announced, many GE managers adopted some form of the new WP&R program to motivate performance improvement in employees, especially those at the professional and administrative levels. Briefly described, the WP&R approach calls for periodic meetings between the manager and his subordinate. During these meetings, progress on past goals is reviewed, solutions are sought for job-related problems, and new goals are established. The intent of the method is to create a situation in which manager and subordinate can discuss job performance and needed improvements in detail without the subordinate becoming defensive.

Basic Features

The WP&R approach differs from the traditional performance appraisal program in that:

1. There are more frequent discussions of performance.
2. There are no summary judgments or ratings made.
3. Salary action discussions are held separately.
4. The emphasis is on mutual goal planning and problem solving.

As far as frequency is concerned, these WP&R discussions are held more often than traditional performance appraisal interviews, but are not scheduled at rigidly fixed intervals. Usually at the conclusion of one work planning session the man and manager set an approximate date for the next review. Frequency depends both on the nature of the job and on the manager's style of operating. Sometimes these WP&R discussions are held as often as once a month, whereas for other jobs and/or individuals, once every six months is more appropriate.

In these WP&R discussions, the manager and his subordinate do not deal in generalities. They consider specific, objectively defined work goals and establish the yardstick for measuring performance. These goals stem, of course, from broader departmental objectives and are defined in relation to the individual's position in the department.

Comparison Setting

After the findings of our experiment were communicated by means of reports and group meetings in the plant where the research was carried out, about half the key managers decided they would abandon the comprehensive annual performance appraisal method and adopt the new WP&R program instead. The other half were hesitant to make such a major change at the time. They decided, consequently, to continue with the traditional performance appraisal program and to try to make it more effective. This provided a natural setting for us to compare the effectiveness of the two approaches. We decided that the comparison should be made in the light of the objectives usually stated for the comprehensive annual performance appraisal program. These objectives were (a) to provide knowledge of results to employees, (b) to justify reasons for salary action, and (c) to motivate and help employees do a better job.

The study design was simple. Before any changes were made, the exempt employees who would be affected by these programs were surveyed to provide base-line data. The WP&R program was then implemented in about half of the exempt group, with the other half continuing to use a modified version of the traditional performance appraisal program. One year later, the identical survey questionnaire was again administered in order to compare the changes that had occurred.

Attitudes and Actions

The results of this research study were quite convincing. The group that continued on the traditional performance appraisal showed no change in *any* of the areas measured. The WP&R group, by contrast, expressed significantly more favorable attitudes on almost all questionnaire items. Specifically, their attitudes changed in a favorable direction over the year that they participated in the new WP&R program with regard to the—

. . . amount of help the manager was giving them in improving performance on the job;
. . . degree to which the manager was receptive to new ideas and suggestions;
. . . ability of the manager to plan;
. . . extent to which the manager made use of their abilities and experience;
. . . degree to which they felt the goals they were shooting for were what they *should* be;
. . . extent to which they received help from the manager in planning for *future* job opportunities;
. . . value of the performance discussions they had with their managers.

In addition to these changes in attitudes, evidence was also found which showed clearly that the members of the WP&R group were much more likely to have taken specific actions to improve performance than were those who continued with the traditional performance appraisal approach.

CURRENT OBSERVATIONS

Recently we undertook still another intensive study of the WP&R program in order to learn more about the nature of these discussions and how they can be made most effective. While these observations have not been completed, some interesting findings have already come to light— especially in relation to differences between WP&R and traditional performance appraisal discussions.

Perceived Differences

For one thing, WP&R interviews are strictly man-to-man in character, rather than having a father-and-son flavor, as did so many of the traditional performance appraisals. This seems to be due to the fact that it is much more natural under the WP&R program for the subordinate to take the initiative when his performance on past goals is being reviewed. Thus, in listening to the subordinate's review of performance, problems, and failings, the manager is automatically cast in the role of *counselor*. This role for the manager, in turn, results naturally in a problem-solving discussion.

In the traditional performance appraisal interview, on the other hand, the manager is automatically cast in the role of *judge*. The subordinate's natural reaction is to assume a defensive posture, and thus all the necessary ingredients for an argument are present.

Since the WP&R approach focuses mainly on immediate, short-term goals, some managers are concerned that longer range, broader plans and goals might be neglected. Our data show that this concern is unfounded. In almost every case, the discussion of specific work plans and goals seems to lead naturally into a consideration of broader, longer range plans. In fact, in a substantial percentage of these sessions, even the career plans of the subordinates are reviewed.

In general, the WP&R approach appears to be a better way of defining what is expected of an individual and how he is doing on the job. Whereas the traditional performance appraisal often results in resistance to the manager's attempts to help the subordinate, the WP&R approach brings about acceptance of such attempts.

CONCLUSION

Multiple studies conducted by the Behavioral Research Service at GE reveal that the traditional performance appraisal method contains a number of problems:

1. Appraisal interviews attempt to accomplish the two objectives of providing a written justification for salary action and motivating the employee to improve his work performance.
2. The two purposes are in conflict, with the result that the traditional appraisal system essentially becomes a salary discussion in which the manager justifies the action taken.
3. The appraisal discussion has little influence on future job performance.
4. Appreciable improvement is realized only when specified goals and deadlines are mutually established and agreed on by the subordinate and his manager in an interview split away from the appraisal interview.

This evidence, coupled with other principles relating to employee motivation, gave rise to the new WP&R program, which is proving to be far more effective in improving job performance than the traditional performance appraisal method. Thus, it appears likely that companies which are currently relying on the comprehensive annual performance appraisal process to achieve improvement in work performance might well consider the advisability of switching to some form of work-planning-and-review in their industrial personnel programs.

Section Two
PERSONNEL SELECTION

INTRODUCTION

THIS SECTION DESCRIBES the application of scientific methods in the selection of employee and management personnel. The basic problem is that of improving decisions made at the hiring stage. Essentially, the person doing the hiring is making a prediction of an applicant's probable success on a particular job. Put another way, he is trying to match individual differences in people to differences in the requirements of particular jobs. The adequacy with which he can do this depends on his knowledge of how to assess the relevant individual differences, on the accuracy of his information regarding the requirements of the jobs in question, and on the validity of the assessment procedures used.

Many tools may be used to assist the personnel department in making hiring decisions. These include job descriptions, application blank information, interviews, psychological-test data, and employment references. Often these are used unsystematically and without knowledge of their actual usefulness in particular job situations. The readings in this section include descriptions of specific research studies aimed at developing, evaluating, or improving such procedures.

The first step in setting up a personnel selection program involves a thorough job analysis and, based upon this analysis, the development of appropriate job-performance criteria against which selection procedures can be validated. The problems of job analysis and criterion development were discussed in Section One of this book. Once adequate job descriptions and criterion measures are available, specific personnel selection techniques can then be evaluated by investigating their relationships to job performance criteria.

Perhaps the most widely used (and misused) personnel selection technique is the employment interview. It is here that the applicant may have his first personal contact with the company. Thus, the employment interview has a public relations function. It also has the function of informing the applicant about the company. But its principal function is to allow the interviewer to seek information about the interviewee from which he can make a prediction about future job success. Despite its widespread use, how valid are these predictions? What does research show about what can and cannot be accomplished in the employment interview? The first article in this section, by Carlson, Thayer, Mayfield, and Peterson, entitled "Research on the Selection Interview," discusses some of the major problems with the selection interview and describes an extensive series of research studies designed to investigate some of the factors which affect the decisions made in the interview. Although most research has suggested relatively poor reliability and validity of the selection interview, studies such as those described here have as their objective an attempt to find out *why* the interview has fared so poorly as a selection device, with the hope of developing improved interviewing techniques and methods for training interviewers so as to improve the overall effectiveness of the interview as a selection tool.

Practically every organizaiton uses an application blank in its employment procedure. Essentially, this is an attempt to make use of the applicant's personal history in placing him on the job.[1] The report by Fleishman and Berniger, "Using the Application Blank to Reduce Office Turnover," demonstrates the kind of improvement which can be made through a statistical, follow-up approach to application blank data.

Letters of recommendation from previous acquaintances, employers, teachers, co-workers, and so forth are also frequently used as employment tools. The validity of these, however, is difficult to evaluate since such reports are typically in narrative form and vary from one person to the next.[2]

---

[1] Some organizations utilize more objectively scored Biographical Information Blanks (BIBs) as part of their selection procedures. The validity of these procedures has been described by W. A. Owens and E. R. Henry, *Biographical Data in Industrial Psychology: A Review and Evaluation*, (Greensboro, N.C.: Creativity Research Institute, Richardson Foundation, 1966); more recently, J. J. Asher, "The Biographical Item: Can It Be Improved?" *Personnel Psychology* 25 (1972): 251–69.

[2] An exception is described in J. N. Mosel and H. W. Goheen, "The Validity of the Employment Recommendation Questionnaire in Personnel Selection," *Personnel Psychology* 11 (1958): 481–90. However, validities reported by these authors range from zero to very low. More recently, similarly disappointing results for the validity of employment references were reported by R. C. Browning, "Validity of Reference Ratings from Previous Employers," *Personnel Psychology* 21 (1968): 389–93. He found low validity of employment references for predicting job performance of school teachers.

The next two articles deal with the use of psychological tests in personnel selection and placement. The use of psychological tests for employment purposes has recently come under considerable attack, especially with regard to such issues as invasion of privacy and potential ethnic group discrimination in the use of tests. Recently, two federal government agencies, the Office of Federal Contract Compliance (OFCC) and the Equal Employment Opportunity Commission (EEOC) have issued guidelines concerning the use of employment selection procedures. In essence, these guidelines require that, where the use of tests has an adverse impact on the hiring of minority group members, the employer must demonstrate that the tests are job related. Recently, the U.S. Supreme Court, in effect, upheld the legality of these guidelines by ruling against the use of tests by an employer who had not been able to demonstrate the job-relatedness of his tests (Griggs vs. Duke Power Company, U.S. Supreme Court, March 8, 1971). Thus, public policy now requires that employers use the kinds of procedures for validating tests which industrial psychologists have been advocating for over 50 years.

In his article "Guide to Using Psychological Tests," Barrett indicates some of the pitfalls often encountered in using tests, clarifies many of the issues concerning the appropriate use of psychological tests in industry and answers some criticisms of the role of such tests in personnel selection. The next article, by Gael and Grant, "Employment Test Validation for Minority and Nonminority Telephone Service Company Representatives" is a validation study in which the validity of certain employment tests were systematically investigated, separately for minority and nonminority employees, as currently required by EEOC and OFCC testing guidelines, wherever feasible. This study clearly demonstrated the job-relatedness of certain of the tests for these employees, and indicated that common test standards could be used, in this case, to evaluate both minority and nonminority job applicants. Also, this study illustrates the major steps involved in validation of employment tests, including criterion development, test selection, determination of prediction equations, and development and use of expectancy tables for personnel selection.

A number of recent publications have attempted to clarify some of the issues involved in the problem of possible minority group discrimination in employment testing. Bartlett and O'Leary [3] discuss the various possible test-criterion relationships that might occur when one looks at test validity separately for minority and nonminority employees. Einhorn and Bass [4] discuss the methodological problems involved in test discrimination and suggest a general strategy for using tests which avoids

---

[3] C. J. Bartlett and B. S. O'Leary, "A Differential Prediction Model to Moderate the Effects of Heterogeneous Groups in Personnel Selection and Classification," *Personnel Psychology* 22 (1969): 1–18.

[4] H. J. Einhorn and A. R. Bass, "Methodological Considerations Relevant to Discrimination in Employment Testing," *Psychological Bulletin* 75 (1971): 261–69.

unfair discrimination against minority group members while at the same time selecting the most qualified job applicants. Boehm [5], who reviewed studies which have compared the validity of employment tests for members of different ethnic groups, concluded that different validities are the exception rather than the typical pattern. When different validities do occur, for different ethnic groups, it may be due to the use of poor job-performance criteria (that is, global performance *ratings* by supervisors are more likely to show differential validity than more objective performance criteria).[6] Byham and Spitzer [7] present a general discussion of the legal problems involved in personnel testing and make recommendations regarding appropriate testing policies and practices that companies should maintain in order to comply with current testing regulations and guidelines.

One area in which the use of tests for selection purposes has proved particularly troublesome has been the area of personality testing.[8] While there seems little doubt that personality and motivational factors play an important role in job performance of many employees, especially managerial and sales personnel, personality tests have simply not been found to be as effective as tests of abilities and skills for personnel selection. As a result, psychologists have sought for new methods for assessing important personality and motivational factors for employees such as managers, salesmen, and other professional personnel for whom personality variables may play a large role in job effectiveness.

A currently prominent technique of this type is the so-called assessment center for assessing job applicants for managerial and sales positions. The study by Bray and Campbell, "Selecting Salesmen by Means of an Assessment Center," describes some of the elements of an assessment center and provides evidence of the validity of the assessment center for predicting job performance of sales representatives.[9]

The final article by Dunnette describes "A Modified Model for Test Validation and Selection Research." In this presentation, Dunnette pro-

---

[5] W. R. Boehm, "Negro-white Differences in Validity of Employment and Training Selection Procedures: Summary of Research Evidence," *Journal of Applied Psychology* 56 (1972): 33–39.

[6] A recent study (A. R. Bass and J. N. Turner, "Ethnic Group Differences in Relationships Among Criteria of Job Performance," *Journal of Applied Psychology* 57 (1973): 101–09) found that supervisors' ratings of job performance were based on objective performance data to a greater extent for black employees than for white employees.

[7] W. C. Byham and M. E. Spitzer, *The Law and Personnel Testing* (New York: American Management Association, 1971).

[8] R. Guion and R. F. Gottier, "Validity of Personality Measures in Personnel Selection," *Personnel Psychology* 18 (1965): 49–65.

[9] For an extensive review of the research literature on validity of assessment centers for identifying managerial talent, see J. R. Huck, "Assessment Centers: A Review of the External and Internal Validities," *Personnel Psychology* 26 (1973): 191–212.

vides a more comprehensive examination of some of the variables that need to be considered in research on personnel selection.[10]

SUGGESTED ADDITIONAL READINGS

Bass, A. R. "Personnel Selection and Evaluation," in *Management of the Urban Crisis*, ed. S. E. Seashore and R. J. McNeill (New York: Free Press, 1971), chap. 11.

Crooks, L. A., ed. *An Investigation of Sources of Bias in the Prediction of Job Performance: A Six-year Study*. Proceedings of Invitational Conference, Princeton, N. J.: Educational Testing Service, 1972.

Dunnette, M. D. *Personnel Selection and Placement*, Belmont, Calif.: Wadsworth, 1966.

Ghiselli, E. E. *The Validity of Occupational Aptitude Tests*, New York: John Wiley & Sons, 1966.

Guion, R. M. *Personnel Testing*. New York: McGraw-Hill Book Co., 1965.

————. "Synthetic Validity in a Small Company." *Personnel Psychology* 18 (1965): 49–65.

Mayfield, E. C. "The Selection Interview—a Re-evaluation of Published Research." *Personnel Psychology* 17 (1964): 239–60.

Webster, E. C. *Decision Making in the Employment Interview*. Montreal: Industrial Relations Center, McGill University, 1964.

8. RESEARCH ON THE SELECTION INTERVIEW *

Robert E. Carlson, Paul W. Thayer,
Eugene C. Mayfield, and Donald A. Peterson

THE EFFECTIVENESS and utility of the selection interview has again been seriously questioned as a result of several comprehensive reviews of the research literature.[1] Not one of these classic summary reviews of the

---

[10] For an especially advanced treatment of personnel selection and placement within the framework of statistical decision theory, the reader is referred to L. J. Cronbach and G. C. Gleser, *Psychological Tests and Personnel Decisions* (Urbana: University of Illinois Press, 1965).

* Extracted from "Improvements in The Selection Interview," *Personnel Journal* 50, no. 4 (April 1971): 268–75.

[1] See, for example, R. Wagner, "The Employment Interview: A Critical Summary," *Personnel Psychology* 2 (1949): 17–46; G. W. England and D. G. Paterson, "Selection and Placement—The Past Ten Years," in *Employment Relations Research: A Summary and Appraisal*, ed. H. G. Henneman, Jr. et al. (New York: Harper & Row, 1960),

interview research literature arrived at conclusions that could be classed as optimistic when viewed from an applied standpoint. Yet none of this is new information. As early as 1915, the validity of the selection interview was empirically questioned.[2] Despite the fact that it is common knowledge that the selection interview probably contributes little in the way of validity to the selection decision, it continues to be used. It is clear that no amount of additional evidence on the lack of validity will alter the role of the interview in selection. Future research should obviously be directed at understanding the mechanism of the interview and improving interview technology. As Schwab has stated, "Companies are not likely to abandon the use of the employment interview, nor is it necessarily desirable that they do so. But it is grossly premautre to sit back comfortably and assume that employment interviews are satisfactory. It is even too early to dash off unsupported recommendations for their improvement. A great deal of research work remains, research which companies must be willing to sponsor before we can count the interview as a prime weapon in our selection arsenal."[3] This was essentially the conclusion that the Life Insurance Agency Management Association (LIAMA) reached some six years ago. In addition, the life insurance industry, through LIAMA, took action and sponsored basic research on the selection interview.

The research reported here is an attempt to improve the use of the selection interview in the life insurance industry. The role of the interview in selection presented a particularly difficult problem for the life insurance industry where each agency manager is responsible for many of the traditional personnel management functions. In addition, these agencies are scattered across the United States and Canada and make centralizing the selection process difficult. In order to strengthen the role of the selection interview in each manager's selection system, LIAMA has been doing basic research on the selection interview for the past six years.

The research reported here is part of a long-run research program concerned with how interviewers make employment decisions. Its purpose is to try to determine the limits of an interviewer's capability in extending his judgment into the future. This summary covers the early studies in a program of research to develop interim tools and the training necessary to make the selection interview a useful selection instrument.

The first step in the interview research program was to observe and record numerous interviews, to interview in depth the interviewers on their decision process, to conduct group-decision conferences where the

---

pp. 43–72; E. C. Mayfield, "The Selection Interview: A Reevaluation of Published Research," *Personnel Psychology* 17 (1964): 239–60; and L. Ulrich and D. Trumbo, "The Selection Interview since 1949," *Psychological Bulletin* 63 (1965): 100–16.

[2] W. D. Scott, "The Scientific Selection of Salesmen," *Advertising and Selling* 25 (1915): 5–6, 94–96.

[3] D. P. Schwab, "Why Interview? A Critique," *Personnel Journal* 48, no. 2 (1969): 129.

interviewers discussed their perception of their decision process for a given taped interview, and to examine the published research on the selection interview. Based upon this information, a model of the selection interview was constructed that specified as many of the influences operating during the interview as could be determined. Initially, there appeared to be four main classes of influences operating to affect/limit the decision of the interviewer. They were:

- the physical and psychological properties of the interviewee.
- the physical and psychological properties of the interviewer.
- the situation/environment in which the interviewer works.
- the task or type of judgment the interviewer must make.

The research strategy has been to systematically manipulate and control the variables specified in the model, trying to eliminate variables that do not have any influence, trying to assess the magnitude of those variables that have an influence, and adding variables that other research has shown to be promising. This article will describe some of these research findings.

WHAT ARE SOME FINDINGS?

Structured versus Unstructured Interviews

One question that has often been asked is, "What kind of interview is best?" What interview style—structured, where the interviewer follows a set procedure; or unstructured, where the interviewer has no set procedure and where he follows the interviewee's lead—results in more effective decisions? In this study, live interviews were used. Each interviewee was interviewed three times. Interviewers used the following three types of interviewing strategies: structured, where the interviewer asked questions only from an interview guide; semistructured, where the interviewer followed an interview guide, but could ask questions about any other areas he wished; and unstructured, where the interviewer had no interview guide and could do as he wished. The basic question involved was the consistency with which people interviewing the same interviewee could agree with each other. If the interviewers' judgments were not consistent—one interviewer saying the applicant was good and the other saying he was bad—no valid prediction of job performance could be made from interview data. Agreement among interviewers is essential if one is to say that the procedure used has the potential for validity.

The results indicated that only the structured interview generated information that enabled interviewers to agree with each other. Under structured conditions, the interviewer knew what to ask and what to do with the information he received. Moreover, the interviewer applied the same frame of reference to each applicant, since he covered the same areas for each. In the less-structured interviews, the managers received additional information, but it seemed to be unorganized and made their evaluation task more difficult. Thus, a highly structured interview has the greatest potential for valid selection.[4]

Effect of Interviewer Experience

In the past it had been assumed that one way to become an effective interviewer was through experience. In fact, it has been hypothesized that interviewers who have had the same amount of experience would evaluate a job applicant similarly.[5] To determine whether this was indeed the case, a study was done that involved managers who had conducted differing numbers of interviews over the same time period. Managers were then compared who had similar as well as differing concentrations of interviewing experience. It was found that when evaluating the same recruits, interviewers with similar experiences did not agree with each other to any greater degree than did interviewers with differing experiences. It was concluded that interviewers benefit very little from day-to-day interviewing experience and apparently the conditions necessary for learning are not present in the day-to-day interviewer's job situation.[6] This implied that systematic training is needed, with some feedback mechanism built into the selection procedure, to enable interviewers to learn from their experiences; the job performance predictions made by the interviewer must be compared with how the recruit actually performs on the job.

Situational Pressures

One of the situational variables studied was how pressure for results affected the evaluation of a new recruit. One large group of managers was told to assume that they were behind their recruiting quota, that it was October, and that the home office had just called. Another group was ahead of quota; for a third group, no quota situation existed. All three groups of managers evaluated descriptions of the same job applicants. It was found that being behind recruiting quota impaired the judgment of those managers. They evaluated the same recruits as actually

---

[4] R. E. Carlson; D. P. Schwab; and H. G. Henneman III, "Agreement Among Selection Interview Styles," *Journal of Industrial Psychology* 5, no. 1 (1970): 8–17.

[5] P. M. Rowe, "Individual Differences in Assessment Decisions," (Ph.D. diss., McGill University, 1960).

[6] R. E. Carlson, "Selection Interview Decisions: The Effect of Interviewer Experience, Relative Quota Situation, and Applicant Sample on Interviewer Decisions," *Personnel Psychology* 20 (1967): 259–80.

having greater potential and said they would hire more of them than did the other two groups of managers.[7]

One more highly significant question was raised: Are all managers, regardless of experience, equally vulnerable to this kind of pressure? Managers were asked how frequently they conducted interviews. Regardless of how long the person had been a manager, those who had had a high rate of interviewing experience—many interviews in a given period of time—were less susceptible to pressures than were those with a low interviewing rate. The interviewers with less interviewing experience relied more on subjective information and reached a decision with less information. It was concluded that one way to overcome this problem of lack of concentrated interviewing experience was through the general use of a standardized interview procedure and intensive training in its use.

Standard of Comparison

Another condition studied was the standards managers applied in evaluating recruits. It was found, for example, that if a manager evaluated a candidate who was just average after evaluating three or four very unfavorable candidates in a row, the average one would be evaluated very favorably.[8] When managers were evaluating more than one recruit at a time, they used other recruits as a standard.[9] Each recruit was compared to all other recruits. Thus, managers did not have an absolute standard —who they thought looked good was partly determined by the persons with whom they were comparing the recruit. This indicated that some system was necessary to aid a manager in evaluating a recruit. The same system should be applicable to each recruit. This implied that some standardized evaluation system was necessary to reduce the large amount of information developed from an interview to a manageable number of constant dimensions.

Effect of Appearance

Some of the early studies utilized photographs to try to determine how much of an effect appearance had on the manager's decision. A favorably rated photograph was paired with a favorably rated personal history description and also with an unfavorably rated personal history. It was found that appearance had its greatest effect on the interviewer's

---

[7] Ibid.

[8] R. E. Carlson, "Effects of Applicant Sample on Ratings of Valid Information in an Employment Setting," *Journal of Applied Psychology* 54 (1970): 217–22.

[9] R. E. Carlson, "Selection Interview Decisions: The Effect of Mode of Applicant Presentation on Some Outcome Measures," *Personnel Psychology* 21 (1968): 193–207.

final rating when it complemented the personal history information.[10] Even when appearance and personal history information were the same (both favorable or both unfavorable), the personal history information was given twice as much weight as appearance. However, the relationship is not a simple one and only emphasized the need for a more complete system to aid the manager in selection decision-making.

Effect of Interview Information on Valid Test Results

In many selection situations, valid selection tests are used in conjunction with the interview data in arriving at a selection decision. Two recent studies have investigated how the emphasis placed on valid test results (*Aptitude Index Battery*) is altered by the more subjective interview data. Managers do place great emphasis on the AIB knowing that the score does generate a valid prediction.

However, how much weight is given to the score depends on other conditions; that is, a low-scoring applicant is judged better if preceded by a number of poor applicants, unfavorable information is given much greater weight if it is uncovered just prior to ending the interview, and so forth. This finding suggested that what is needed is some system that places the interview information and other selection information in their proper perspective.[11]

Interview Accuracy

A recent study tried to determine how accurately managers can recall what an applicant says during an interview. Prior to the interview the managers were given the interview guide, pencils, and paper, and were told to perform as if *they* were conducting the interview. A 20-minute video tape of a selection interview was played for a group of 40 managers. Following the video tape presentation, the managers were given a 20-question test. All questions were straightforward and factual. Some managers missed none, while some missed as many as 15 out of 20 items. The average number was 10 wrong. In a short 20-minute interview, half the managers could not report accurately on the information produced during the interview! On the other hand, those managers who had been following the interview guide and taking notes were quite accurate on the test; note-taking in conjunction with a guide appears to be essential.

Given that interviewers differed in the accuracy with which they were able to report what they heard, the next question appeared to be "How

---

[10] R. E. Carlson, "The Relative Influence of Appearance and Factual Written Information on an Interviewer's Final Rating," *Journal of Applied Psychology* 51 (1967): 461–68.

[11] R. E. Carlson, "Effect of Interview Information in Altering Valid Impressions," *Journal of Applied Psychology* 55 (1971): 66–72.

does this affect their evaluation?" In general it was found that those inter-viewers who were least accurate in their recollections rated the interviewee higher and with less variability, while the more accurate interviewers rated the interviewee average or lower and with greater variability. Thus, those interviewers who did not have the factual information at their disposal assumed that the interview was generally favorable and rated the interviewee more favorable in all areas. Those interviewers who were able to reproduce more of the factual information rated the inter-viewee lower and recognized his intra-individual differences by using more of the rating scale. This implied that the less accurate interview-ers selected a "halo strategy" when evaluating the interviewee, while the more accurate interviewers used an individual differences strategy. Whether this is peculiar to the individual interviewer or due to the fact that the interviewer did or didn't have accurate information at his dis-posal is, of course, unanswerable from this data.

Can Interviewers Predict?

The ultimate purpose of the selection interview is to collect factual and attitudinal information that will enable the interviewer to make accurate and valid job behavior predictions for the interviewee. The interviewer does this by recording the factual information for an applicant, evaluating the meaning of the information in terms of what the interviewee will be able to do on the job in question, and extending these evaluations into the future in the form of job behavior predictions. The question is, "How reliably can a group of interviewers make predictions for a given inter-viewee?" Without high inter-interviewer agreement, the potential for interview validity is limited to a few interviewers and cannot be found in the interview process itself.

In this study, a combination of movies and audio tapes were played simulating an interview. In addition, each of the 42 manager-interviewers was given a detailed written summary of the interview. The total inter-view lasted almost three hours and covered the interviewee's work his-tory, work experience, education and military experience, life insurance holdings, attitude toward the life insurance career, family life, financial soundness, social life and social mobility, and future goals and aspirations. After hearing and seeing the interview and after studying a 20-page written summary, each interviewer was asked to make a decision either to continue the selection process or to terminate negotiations. In addition, each interviewer was asked to make a list of all the factual information he considered while making his decision. Also, the interviewer was to rate the interviewee in 31 different areas. The ratings were descriptive of the interviewee's past accomplishments, such as his job success pat-tern, the quantity and quality of his education, his family situation, finan-cial knowledge and soundness, and so forth. Finally, the interviewers were asked to make job-behavior predictions in 28 different job-specific activities such as, Could he use the telephone for business purposes? Could he make cold calls? Would he keep records? Would he take direction? What about his market?

The interviewers agreed quite well with each other on which facts they reportedly considered in making their employment decision. Almost 70 percent of the factual statements were recorded by all the interviewers. The remaining 30 percent of the factual statements were specific to interviewers. This tended to confirm a hypothesis of Mayfield and Carlson where they postulate that the stereotypes held by interviewers consist of general as well as specific content.[12] It was concluded that interviewers do record and use similar factual information with agreement.

The interviewers agreed less well with each other on the evaluation or value placed on the facts. The median inter-interviewer correlation was .62, with a low of .07 and a high of .82. This means that the interviewers still agreed reasonably well on the evaluation—good versus bad—quality of the information they received. They would make similar selection–rejection decisions.

The job behavior predictions of the interviewers, however, were not nearly as high in agreement. The median inter-interviewer correlation was .33 with a low of −.21 and a high of .67. This means that the interviewers do not agree with each other on how well the interviewee will perform the job of a life insurance agent in 28 different areas. In addition, those predictions that required the interviewer to extend his judgment further into the future had significantly greater inter-interviewer variability than did those predictions that could be verified in a shorter period of time. Thus, interviewers can agree more with each other's predictions if the job behavior is of a more immediate nature.

These findings imply that although interviewers probably use much the same information in making a decision, they will evaluate it somewhat differently. Furthermore, the interviewers are not able to agree on how well the individual will perform on the job.

Thus, it was concluded that interviewers evaluate essentially similar things in an applicant; they agree reasonably well whether an applicant's past record is good or bad, but they cannot agree on good or bad for what. Yet here, and only here, is where the clinical function of the interviewer is difficult to replace with a scoring system. In being able to make accurate and valid job behavior predictions, the interview can pay for itself in terms of planning an applicant's early job training and as a mechanism whereby a supervisor can learn early how to manage an applicant. In order for the interviewer to be able to make accurate and valid job-behavior predictions, it follows that he must have a feedback system

---

[12] E. C. Mayfield and R. E. Carlson, "Selection Interview Decisions: First Results from a Long-Term Research Project," *Personnel Psychology* 19 (1966): 41–53.

whereby he can learn from his past experiences. Only through accurate feedback in language similar to the behavior predictions can the interviewer learn to make job behavior predictions. The results further imply that the interviewer must be equipped with a complete selection system that coordinates all the selection steps and provides the interviewer with as relevant and complete information as possible when he makes job behavior predictions.

CONCLUSIONS

These early studies in LIAMA's interview-research program provided little in the way of optimism for the traditional approach to the selection interview. However, this research did indicate specific areas where improvements in selection and interview technology could be made. It did indicate where interim improvements could be tried and evaluated while the long-term research on the interview continued.

Two major applied implications may be derived from the interview research to date. First, the selection interview should be made an integral part of an overall selection procedure, and to accomplish this, new and additional materials are needed. The new materials should include a broad-gauge, comprehensive, structured interview guide; standardized evaluation and prediction forms that aid the interviewer in summarizing information from all steps in the selection process; and an evaluation system that provides feedback to the interviewer in language similar to the preemployment job behavior predictions he must make. The second major applied implication is that an intensive training program for interviewers is necessary if interviewers are to initially learn enough in common to increase the probability of obtaining general validity from the selection interview. Thus, the early studies have provided specific information that has been used to change the way selection is carried out in the insurance industry.

9. USING THE APPLICATION BLANK TO REDUCE OFFICE TURNOVER *

Edwin A. Fleishman and Joseph Berniger

THOUGH THE APPLICATION BLANK, in one form or another, is omnipresent in business and industry, all too often it is used in a superficial and unsystematic manner. In many employment siutations, for example, the personnel interviewer either merely scans the blank for items he considers pertinent or uses the information only as a point of departure for the employment interview. As a result, much of the wealth of information in the application blank is going to waste, or worse, is often improperly used. In actual fact, however, there is sufficient evidence to indicate that, properly validated and used, the application blank can markedly increase the efficiency of the company's selection procedures.

The rationale for using the application blank (though this is seldom verbalized explicitly) is that the applicant's personal history, such as his previous experience and interests, is predictive of his future success on the job. And, indeed, it does seem reasonable to assume that such data as previous employment history, specific skills, education, financial status, marital record, and so forth, reflect a person's motives, abilities, skills, level of aspiration, and adjustment to working situations.

A number of assumptions can be made from such information. For example, the fact that an applicant has held a similar job indicates the likelihood of his transferring some of his training to the new job. Similarly, what he has done successfully before is likely to reflect his basic abilities in that area, as well as his interest in and satisfaction derived from these activities. Such personal-history items as age, number of dependents, years of education, previous earnings, and amount of insurance have also been found to correlate with later proficiency on the job, earnings, length of tenure, or other criteria of job success. It should be emphasized, however, that the items found to be predictive of success in one job may not be the same for another, similar job—even in the same company. Furthermore, even for the same job, some items on the application blank may be more predictive of one particular aspect of job performance than of other aspects (for example, turnover, accidents, or earnings).

Hand in hand with this consideration is the fact that, in personnel selection, the application blank is usually reviewed as a whole by an

---

* From "One Way to Reduce Office Turnover," *Personnel* 37 (1960): 63–69.

employment interviewer, a procedure that obviously involves a great deal of subjective judgment on his part. Consequently, the success of the form in predicting job performance depends not only upon the accuracy of the job description used as a reference, but also upon the skill of the interviewer and, most importantly, on his knowledge of the validity of individual items in relation to certain jobs and criteria. Unfortunately, however, it is this last critical point that most organizations fail to check out with empirical data. In this article, we shall endeavor to point out that such data are not difficult to obtain and may materially help the employment interviewer in arriving at better hiring decisions.

Design of Study

The study outlined here describes the way in which the potential value of the routine application blank used at Yale University was enhanced through appropriate research methods. The purpose of the study was to develop a way of scoring the application blank to select clerical and secretarial employees who were most likely to remain on the job. In other words, it was designed to explore the possibility of using the blank as part of a selection program aimed at reducing turnover.

The first step in the study was to find out which items in the application blank actually differentiated between short-tenure and long-tenure employees who had been hired at about the same time. For this purpose, 120 women office employees, all of whom had been hired between 1954 and 1956, were studied. Half of these, designated the "long-tenure" group, were women whose tenure was from two to four years and who were still on the job. The other 60 employees had terminated within two years and accordingly were designated the short-tenure group. Of this group, 20 percent had terminated within six months and 67 percent within the first year. The sample excluded known "temporaries" and summer employees. The women studied had all been hired as "permanent" employees, and all who had left had done so voluntarily.

The application blank in question is similar to those used in most organizations. It takes up four pages and includes approximately 40 items—personal data, work history, education, interests, office skills, and the like. The original application blanks of the employees in both the short- and long-tenure groups were examined and the responses to the individual items were then compared to determine which, if any, differentiated the employees who terminated from those who stayed and, if so, which items were the best predictors of tenure.

A preliminary review suggested the ways in which to classify the answers to the various items. The next step was to tally the responses for each group and then convert them to percentages to facilitate comparisons. Some examples of items that did and did not differentiate between the two groups are shown in Table 9–1. As the table shows, local address,

TABLE 9–1

How Item-Responses by Long- and Short-Tenure Office Employees Compared

| Application Blank Items | Percentage of | | Weight Assigned to Response |
	Short-Tenure Group	Long-Tenure Group	
Local address			
Within city.	39	62	+2
Outlying suburbs	50	36	−2
Age			
Under 20.	35	8	−3
21–25	38	32	−1
26–30	8	2	−1
31–35	7	10	0
35 and over	11	48	+3
Previous salary			
Under $2,000	31	30	0
$2,000–3,000	41	38	0
$3,000–4,000	13	12	0
Over $4,000	4	4	0
Age of children			
Preschool	12	4	−3
Public school	53	33	−3
High school or older	35	63	+3

for instance, was a good differentiator, but previous salary was not. Certain responses to the question of age also distinguished between the two groups, as did "reason for leaving last employment," "occupation of husband," and "number of children."

Weighting the Items

Since some items were found to be better predictors of tenure than others, it seemed reasonable to assign them more weight in the actual hiring procedure—the next step in our study. Thus, items that did not discriminate were weighted zero (that is, they were not counted). Others were weighted negatively (they counted against the applicant), and still others, positively (in favor of the applicant). For example, an address in the suburbs was more characteristic of short-tenure employees, and so this response was scored negatively. An address in the city, on the other hand, was scored positively. Similarly, "age over 35" received a positive weight, but "under 30" received a negative weight.

Next, the size of the weight was determined. Items that showed a bigger percentage difference between the long- and short-tenure groups were given a higher weight. For example, "age under 20" was weighted −3, whereas "age 26–30" was weighted only −1. (Though there are more precise methods for assigning weights;[1] we found that the simple but systematic procedure described above yielded comparable results.)

An applicant's total score is, of course, obtained by adding or subtracting the weights scored on each item on the application blank. In our first sample, we found that total scores ranged from −17 to 27, the average score for the short-tenure group being −2.3, while that for the long-tenure group was 8.9—a difference of 11.2, which is highly significant statistically. The correlation between the total scores made by these employees and their subsequent tenure was .77.

This correlation was, of course, misleading and spuriously high since we had calculated it from the very sample from which we had determined the weights for the individual items in the first place. To obtain an unbiased estimate of the validity of our scoring procedure, we had to try it out, therefore, on an independent sample of employees.

The Cross-Validation Study

Accordingly, the application blanks of a second random sample of short- and long-tenure women, hired during the same period, were drawn from the files. Again, the short-tenure group consisted of women who had left within two years and the long-tenure group was composed of those who were still on the job after two years or more. The scoring system developed on the first sample was then applied to the application blanks of this second group (85 clerical and secretarial employees).

The range of scores for this sample was −10 to 21, and the correlation with subsequent tenure was .57. This confirmed that the weighted blank did possess a high degree of validity for predicting tenure. The average score for the short-tenure group was −0.7, while that of the long-tenure group was 6.3. Again, this was a statistically significant difference. A recheck was also made on the individual items, which showed, in general, that those items which differentiated in the first sample did so in the second sample as well.

We had, then, a selection instrument that indicated the probability of an applicant's staying with the organization or not, but the question of how to use it in reaching the actual hiring decision still remained. Of course, such factors as the relative importance of turnover in the organization, the number of available applicants during a hiring period, and other selection procedures in use have to be taken into account here. It is desirable, nonetheless, to set a score on the application blank that does the best job of differentiating between "long-" and "short-" tenure risks at the time of employment. In other words, what is needed is a cut-off score that will maximize correct hiring decisions; or—to put it another

---

[1] See, for example, W. H. Stead and C. L. Shartle, *Occupational Counseling Techniques* (New York: American Book Company, 1940).

TABLE 9–2

Obtaining a Cutting Score by Using "Maximum Differentiation"

		Percentage of Subjects at or above a Given Score		
	Total Score	*A Percentage of Long-Tenure Employees*	*B Percentage of Short-Tenure Employees*	*Index of Differentiation (A Minus B)*
	21	4	0	4
	20	4	0	4
	19	4	0	4
	18	12	0	12
	17	16	0	16
	16	20	0	20
	15	20	0	20
	14	24	0	24
	13	24	3	21
	12	28	3	25
	11	32	5	27
	10	36	8	28
	9	40	10	30
	8	40	14	26
	7	44	15	29
	6	48	17	31
Cutting	5	60	20	40
Score	4	68	22	46 — *Point of Greatest Differentiation*
	3	72	27	45
	2	72	32	40
	1	72	39	33
	0	80	42	38
	−1	80	46	34
	−2	80	54	26
	−3	84	66	18
	−4	92	68	24
	−5	92	76	16
	−6	92	85	7
	−7	96	90	6
	−8	96	94	2
	−9	100	98	2
	−10	100	100	0

way—a score that will minimize both the number of people hired who will turn out to be short-tenure employees and the number rejected who would have actually remained on the job.

To establish our cut-off score, we used the method of "maximum differentiation." In other words, we tabulated the percentage of employees reaching or exceeding each score point in the range, −10 to 21. We then calculated the differences between the percentages obtained in the two groups at each score point to find the point of greatest differentiation.

The result is shown in Table 9–2, from which it will be seen that in our case the difference between the two groups reached its maximum at a

FIGURE 9–1

Percentages of Correct Hiring Decisions That Would Have Been Obtained through Using Cutting Score

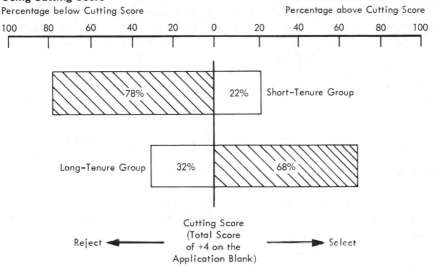

score of +4. This told us that applicants scoring 4 points or more were most likely to stay on the job two years or more, whereas those scoring less than 4 could be considered potential short-tenure employees.

Figure 9–1 shows the degree of success that would have been achieved if this cutting score of +4 had been used on our second sample of 85 employees. The shaded areas represent the percentage of correct hiring decisions, and the unshaded areas, the percentage of incorrect hiring decisions. As may be seen, the personnel interviewer would have hired two out of three of the employees who stayed more than two years and rejected approximately four out of five of those who had left before that time.

Finally, to facilitate routine scoring, we constructed a cardboard template for each page of the application blank.[2] In the template are windows, which expose only the responses to be scored. The weights for each response are printed on the template next to the appropriate window.

An interesting offshoot of our study was the picture it yielded of the woman office worker most likely to be the best long-tenure risk at Yale University. We arrived at it by using the application blank items that differentiated between long- and short-tenure employees in both our original and our cross-validation samples. Here is a profile of the typical long-tenure woman office employee at Yale:

---

[2] W. F. Wood, "A New Method for Reading the Employment Questionnaire," *Journal of Applied Psychology* 31 (1947): 9–15.

She is 30 years old or over, has a local address rather than a suburban one, is married (but not to a student), or is a widow. Her husband is most likely to be an executive or a professional man. She may have one or two children, but if she does they are of high school age or over. At least one member of her family has been employed at Yale. She herself is not employed at the time of application. She has had a business, secretarial school, or college education, and can often speak more than one language. If she can type, she does so at a speed of 50–60 words per minute. Usually, she cannot take shorthand—but if she does, it is at a relatively high rate of speed. She does not list more than one outside interest aside from work, and that one indicates that she is most interested in organizations and people. Finally, she spent at least two years at her last job.

The findings of our study bear out those obtained in previous studies at the Prudential Life Insurance Company [3] and the Minnesota Mining and Manufacturing Company,[4] both of which showed that a high degree of predictability of turnover among female office employees was achieved from a weighted application blank. Our study extends the generality of these findings from two diverse companies to a university organization. However, an examination of all three studies underscores the fact that the specific biographical items contributing to prediction of turnover vary from one organizational setting to the next. Thus, while the validity of the general technique for predicting turnover has been established for clerical employees, the weighted application blank that will work best for a particular company must be tailor-made for that organization.

Another consideration worth mentioning, perhaps, is that though the biographical data used here have been found to be most useful in predicting turnover, other studies have indicated that such data are also of value in predicting accidents and proficiency. (They have been found especially useful in predicting proficiency in the sales field.) [5] Of course, turnover and proficiency are not unrelated—it is well known that many girls leave because of low proficiency. However, the company that uses other selection instruments to predict proficiency can combine them with the weighted application blank scores and thereby select employees who will be the best risks in terms of both proficiency *and* tenure.

One final point: The research described in this article is relatively inexpensive. Indeed most companies have file drawers literally bulging with application blank data that are well suited to the kind of analysis described here.

---

[3] P. H. Kreidt and M. S. Gadel, "Prediction of Turnover among Clerical Workers," *Journal of Applied Psychology* 37 (1953): 338–40.

[4] W. K. Kirchner and M. D. Dunnette, "Applying the Weighted Application Blank Technique to a Variety of Office Jobs," *Journal of Applied Psychology* 41 (1957): 206–8.

[5] "The AI-4-48 in Use: A Selection Study" (Hartford, Conn.: Life Insurance Agency Management Association, 1951).

10. GUIDE TO USING PSYCHOLOGICAL TESTS *

Richard S. Barrett

THE OBJECTIVE of the psychologist who works in employment is simple. He wants to reduce the errors made by industry in hiring, placing, and promoting personnel—so that the more qualified people will be put in responsible positions and the less qualified will be placed in jobs they can handle.

This is a complex, often controversial field, and one which is little known and less understood by the general public. What follows are some guidelines to the possible help which psychological tests may provide.

Do Tests Work?

No one can tell whether a given test works in a particular situation unless he conducts an impartial research study and bases his conclusions on a careful weighing of all the evidence. Among the most intensive such investigations conducted to date are two carried out by psychologists at Standard Oil (New Jersey):

Here a test battery was developed which predicts long-term success with the company so well that an executive who scores in the top 20 percent on the tests is nine times as likely to do better than average on the job as one who scores in the bottom 20 percent.

In 1959 the psychologists took a look at the predictions made in 1949 concerning the potential of men who were then supervisors. Many were no longer associated with the company, but of those who were, the tests had predicted their long-term achievement within the company well, better even than had the ratings made by their managers in 1949. Since the managers had worked for some time with the men whom they were rating, they obviously were in a better position to evaluate their capabilities than they would have been if their entire knowledge had been gained in a brief preemployment interview.

Standard Oil's results are not unique. Psychological tests have been found valuable, for example, for selecting physicians for psychiatric training, Saudi Arabians to operate an oil refinery, and enlisted men for training in technical schools.

Nevertheless, such evidence by itself is not an adequate answer to the

---

* Extracted from *Harvard Business Review*, September–October 1963, pp. 138–46.

charge that tests do not work, because there are so many different kinds of tests or other procedures, not all of which are equally effective.

Background Questionnaire.   The greatest success to date has been with the personal background questionnaire, which asks question about hobbies, school performance, attitudes toward past experiences, and the like. But instead of the applicant's answering in his own words (as he would in an interview), he checks one of the several alternative answers provided in the questionnaire. What is lost by the restriction of freedom to answer is more than offset by the value of a permanent record. The record may then be studied in the light of later success or failure in order to identify those answers which separate the potentially good performers from those who will not do so well. By using this technique, researchers of the Life Insurance Agency Management Association have shown that 40 percent of applicants for insurance sales positions who fall in the top quarter on the questionnaire are successful; only 11 percent of those in the bottom quarter meet the same standards.

Intelligence Tests.   There are mixed results from intelligence tests. In present-day society, intelligence, and educational achievement (which itself depends heavily on intelligence) are used to eliminate many candidates from consideration before they arrive at the employment office. Most of the intellectually unqualified never have a chance to apply for an engineering job, for example, because they are already eliminated by their inability to cope with the complex material presented to them in college. Therefore, since the bulk of those applying for engineering jobs are qualified intellectually, their success depends on qualities other than the relatively small differences in intelligence which exist among them. On the other hand, wherever broad ranges of people must be considered for jobs (such as in the armed services), intelligence tests are most useful. In fact, they save millions of dollars each year by predicting how well recruits can be expected to learn the more technical jobs.

Personality Tests.   A dismal history has been recorded by personality tests. There have been a few scattered successes with some modern techniques, but on the whole the typical personality questionnaire, test, or inventory has not proved to be useful. In many of them, the "right" answers (which exist despite the usual naive disclaimer that there are no right answers) are so obvious that everyone comes out a model of healthy adjustment. But even if all applicants were to answer each question with complete candor, the value of their answers for predicting success would still be in doubt because the complexities of human personality are as yet poorly understood. Nevertheless, psychologists, convinced that "there's gold in them thar hills," continue to devise new theories of personality and more sophisticated paper-and-pencil tests. Perhaps some day a test will be devised that *will* work.

In their efforts to obtain measurements of personality which could not easily be distorted by the job applicants, and to uncover information not tapped by the questionnaires, industrial psychologists have turned also to the projective techniques of the clinicians. In this type of test, the applicant tells what he sees in inkblots, tells stories about pictures, and so forth. A highly trained psychologist analyzes the results, working from the assumption that the differences in what people say under these circumstances reflect differences in their personalities. The best known of these tests, the Rorschach inkblot test, has been studied the most thoroughly and has accumulated such a long record of failure as a selection test that, unless someone develops and verifies a new approach to analyzing it, it is, in my opinion, a complete waste of time.

Other personality tests have fared little better. At best they work only after a long-term research project, followed by special intensive training of the psychologists who use them; but adequate predictions are difficult and expensive to accomplish.

Deciding to Test

Now let us consider some of the troublesome questions which have to be answered before management can decide how far it ought to go with psychological selection procedures.

Privacy invaded? Unfortunately there exist in this world many busybodies, some of whom become psychologists and write questionnaires and conduct pre-employment interviews. Instead of sticking to information bearing directly on the job (such as training, experience, skills, and attitudes toward work), some psychologists delve into the applicant's married life, the state of his digestive tract, and his attitudes toward his mother. Such questions are not only in bad taste, but are also of doubtful validity. I believe that the job applicant has the right to keep his troubles to himself without penalty. Executives, by asking that reports be confined to job-relevant issues, can help to safeguard the applicant's privacy.

Conformists Selected? The continued use of tests, it is alleged, would lead to an organization in which everyone exhibits the same dull, unimaginative personality; there would be no room for a Franklin, a Steinmetz, or an Einstein. And such might be the case if the company relied on the patent-medicine test because, in an effort to build a test which is all things to all men, the psychologist must often fall back on truisms such as these:

An emotionally stable person is better to have around than one who is erratic.
All managers must be "leaders."
A sales applicant will do well if he knows the same things that successful salesmen of an older generation know.

Without an opportunity to find out what is really required on a job, or how well his predictions are working, the psychologist is unable to take into account the differences existing between companies and individual jobs.

But the psychologist who studies jobs so that he can match candidates and requirements soon learns that the simple clichés about job requirements do not stand up under scrutiny. He finds that many useful citizens do not fit into the gray flannel straitjacket with which the psychologist is reputed to clothe his victims.

Contrary to popular belief, even a battery of tests does not select a single type of employee:

Take, for example, a simple battery of two tests, one of intelligence and the other of motivation, which yields a total score simply by adding the scores on the two tests. Since no one expects that a passing score will be reserved only for those who score perfectly on both tests, some range of acceptable total scores must be determined. A person could pass by scoring high on intelligence and low on motivation, high on motivation and low on intelligence, or moderately high on both.

As the number of tests increases, the number of different combinations which lead to an acceptable score increases.

Thus the testing procedure reflects the commonsense idea of compensating skills. If management has to settle on less than a paragon (and it generally does), then the best that can be done is to find someone whose strengths balance his weaknesses.

Also contrary to the popular belief, the right answers as shown on the scoring key do not necessarily favor the conventional. Some psychologists, in writing items, word their questions so that only a few will pick a given response, with the prediction (later verified) that these people will be the more successful ones. Other psychologists are actively searching out how to measure creativity, and are actually testing the tests, questionnaires, and other procedures developed to measure this factor in industrial situations.

Still others have found that the successful businessman turns out on the tests to be described as "intelligent," as an "innovator" or an "experimenter," who "shows signs of early independence without rebellion," and who is "aggressive" to boot. The less successful all too often are the ones who fit more nearly into the mold of the conformist.

But the issue of conformity is not disposed of simply by showing that no one set of standards is, in fact, applied by the psychologists or that they often do favor nonconforming attitudes. What about that large number of people who are conformists? Our pluralistic society permits many routes to success for the individual, depending on his particular constellation of abilities, attitudes, and so on. Does it not leave room for the man who will quietly and competently do a routine job? There are certainly plenty of routine jobs. Should we fill them only with the restless rebel who will make himself and everyone around him miserable?

It is easy to beat the drum for the uncommon man, but it is the proper business of a society to make the best use of the talents of all our citizens (common or uncommon), even when their personalities do not live up to what one idealizes.

Some Unfairly Rejected? So long as any reliance is placed on the psychologist's tests, some qualified people will be turned down solely because of their inability to take tests. But does this mean that the tests should be abandoned? *Certainly,* if there is a better procedure available; *certainly not,* if they help to reduce the number of errors which exist after all the other screening and evaluation devices have been used.

The psychologist's work is governed by this simple creed, "There is no prediction without error" (and its corollary, "The less error, the better"). Therefore, he directs his attention not only on any capable candidates turned down by the tests, but also on the good people turned down by other procedures who nevertheless are accepted because of the influence of the tests.

Objective measures, even their critics will admit, give a break to the person who does not make a good impression otherwise. Those who are not particularly attractive, who lack social sparkle, or who find it difficult to warm up quickly in the interview have a chance to show what they can do. Furthermore, the tests do not care about a person's religious beliefs or his parents' homeland. They do not indulge in the petty idiosyncrasies so dear to the less competent chief clerk—the cut of a man's jib, the firmness of his grasp, or the steadiness of his gaze.

Only Management's Interest? In a sense, tests do serve management's interest. If the tests work well in selecting the best people, of course the company benefits. That is why the tests were installed in the first place. But the allegation that they are detrimental to the applicant's interest is reminiscent of the Marxian notion of constant class struggle.

In the long run the employees will benefit if each open position is filled by the best available candidate. Those who possess talent will be rewarded by positions which challenge them. Consequently, they will cease to feel the frustration which occurs when a more able person has been passed over in favor of his less able, but somehow more impressive, competitor. At the same time, fewer people will be shoved forward into positions beyond their talents. They will be spared anxieties and an ultimate feeling of inadequacy when they fail. In short, the only people who really benefit from an inaccurate selection procedure are those whose one talent is to cover up their lack of talent. And these are not the people who have built the economy we know today.

Selecting a Psychologist

The following provide a checklist of questions which, when fully answered, will give the executive a better basis for evaluating psychological services when they are offered to him.

Is He Qualified? Psychological services are satisfactorily performed only by psychologists or under their supervision. The untrained test salesman or the personnel assistant (who majored in psychology back in 1952) cannot be expcted to know which tests fit a given situation. Nor does he know how they should be administered, scored, and interpreted. Legislatures of more and more states are enacting laws requiring that a person who calls himself a psychologist (or who renders services which he calls psychological) must be certified or licensed. Possession of a license is, of course, a minimum qualification, and even this is not required in many states. A license shows only that the holder is adequately trained and that he has sufficient knowledge of psychology, but it does not prove that he is an expert in selection.

The executive may next check the psychologist's membership in the American Psychological Association or his status as a Diplomate in Industrial Psychology of the American Board of Examiners in Professional Psychology. Neither, however, is an infallible guide. Membership requirements in the American Psychological Association are minimal, and any representation to the effect that status as a Member or a Fellow in the Association carries with it the Association's endorsement is expressly forbidden by its rules. Diplomate status is another matter, since the purpose of the board's extensive tests and interviews and the recommendations of other psychologists is to determine the candidate's competence. Even so, possession of the diploma alone is a slender reed on which to lean. There are many Diplomates whose talents and interests lie in areas other than selection, and, on the other hand, there are many competent psychologists who have never taken Board examinations, even though they could ceratinly pass them if they wanted to.

The best thing for an executive to do is to ask the opinion of other industrial psychologists, preferably those employed by some friendly members of the business community or a university. Industrial psychology is a small, relatively closely knit profession; with a little inquiry a reasonably accurate impression of a practitioner's reputation may be obtained.

Does He Understand? It is not realistic for executives to tell a psychologist merely that the company wants to hire better salesmen or clerks who will be on the payroll two years hence, and then expect him to choose some tests, recommend a passing score, develop an interview, train interviewers, and integrate the whole procedure with the rest of the selection process. Before he is allowed to open his test catalog, the tester should have been told the answers to two questions: "What are the company's objectives?" and "What are the job duties?"

There are no stock answers to these questions. The selection procedure recommended for one company differs in many respects from that recommended for its neighbor. Thus:

A few years ago I worked with a company to update its selection procedure for office workers. Exploration of the company's objectives led to the conclusion that management wanted to hire people who were capable of making a satisfactory career. All other considerations were secondary.

Three years later I went across the street to do the same kind of work for another organization. The primary concern here was to hire office workers who could be counted on to give a few years' satisfactory service.

If I had usd the same techniques on both jobs, I would have ended up dissatisfying one of them.

What Is He Doing? The profession of psychology is a technical one, and the psychologist cannot explain everything he does to businessmen, regardless of their talents, if they do not have an adequate background. But part of the business of a psychologist working in industry is to communicate to those who do not have his training. If he does not explain what he is doing and why he is doing it, something is wrong. Either he has difficulty in rephrasing his technical terms into conversational English or he is, wittingly or unwittingly, creating an air of mystery which may impress the uninitiated.

Communication is a two-way street, and can be successful only if the executive asks for clarification of difficult points, studies the tests and the rest of the procedure, observes the psychologist in action, or in some other way takes the necessary time to participate actively in an exchange of ideas.

Oscar K. Buros has for years compiled opinions on published tests in the *Mental Measurements Yearbook,* the latest of which (the *Sixth*) was published in 1965 by the Gryphon Press. Each published test of consequence is reviewed by one or more experts in the field; these reviewers are frank, often blunt, in their criticisms. The recommended procedure for the executive who wants to learn about a test is to look it up first in the latest edition, and then work his way back through earlier editions until he has found out what he wants to know.

Did He Get Results? Here is the all-important question. If a test, questionnaire, or other technique has been used in the past, the company which is contemplating its use has a right to know how it turned out; and, if it is going to be used or installed, current information on its value is even more pertinent.

Determining how well a test has worked is a tricky business. There are so many possible sources of error that an evaluation can only be safely accomplished by someone who is appropriately trained. Nevertheless, a report or a test manual can provide much useful information to the businessman if he knows what to look for.

In judging technical reports supplied by prospective testing agencies, I have found it useful to make two assumptions: (1) everything that is presented is true, and (2) the author is presenting all the supporting information he can.

The first assumption is necessary if there is any point in reading the report in the first place (and it is a reasonable one to make since very few people deliberately manufacture data).

The second is more critical and subtle since it requires that a report be read for what is not there. If the author fails to present information which would help make his case stronger, he does so for one of three reasons: (*a*) he does not have the information which he should have; (*b*) he has it, but it didn't work out the way he wanted it to, so he buried it; or (*c*) he has it, but doesn't know if he should report it. No matter what the reason, the omission of pertinent material makes the entire report suspect. Here are a few of the questions which the reader might want to apply to a report or sales presentation.

What was the psychologist trying to accomplish, and for what kinds of jobs? I have already described how one company might select people on the basis of their potential for a good career, and another might look for short-term proficiency. And I pointed out the importance of knowing what jobs are being studied. A good report gives sufficient detail so that the reader can tell if the results apply to his problem.

What sample was studied? Were they applicants or current employees? It does not make much difference when a person takes an intelligence test whether he is an employee or an applicant; his scores will be about the same. But the responses to many questionnaires are so sensitive to motivation that results obtained on current employees may be quite different from those on applicants who know that their employment depends on what they say. Were the people tested the same age as the applicants? If age or experience influences test scores, results obtained from older employees may be misleading. Most stenographers lose speed when they leave school; many typists improve.

If only certain members of a larger group were studied, how were they selected? Was the selection random, or was it done on some other basis? If some refused to take part in a volunteer study, how many were they, and how did they compare with the participants? It is important to know how the subjects were chosen, because it is easy to be misled if the sample is not truly representative of the whole group.

What were the standards against which the tests were measured? A good report describes how the psychologist came to believe that some employees were better than others. If ratings were used, who did them, and under what circumstances? If net sales, parts produced, or other objective standards were used, are they realistic? The number of reasons why performance measures may be suspect is too large to permit discussion here. Suffice it to say that it is essential for the reader of a report to have enough information on how results were obtained so that he may have an opportunity to detect any sources of error.

How does it work? We can finally return to the original question. With the background I have just outlined, the executive is in a position to decide how closely the results bear on the selection problem which faces him; but, even so, he may need some help in interpreting the more abstruse statistics.

SUMMARY

To underscore the points I have just made I have four aphorisms which readers may want to carry away with them:

1. *Need distorts perception.* Among the best substantiated psychological truths is that what we think we see differs, sometimes dramatically, from what is really there, as we remold it nearer to our heart's desire. I once disputed with a successful executive his statement that a mediocre test battery he used always worked. According to him, not only did his pet tests predict, without exception, the success that people would have if they were employed by his company, but, whenever he followed up on people his tests rejected, the prediction also worked out. I explained to him that perfection is not for this world, and that even the best selection techniques are certain to go wrong—even if for reasons such as some unforeseeable change occurring in an employee's health or a distressing but temporary family situation which would depress his performance. But I was never able to convince my friend, so I suppose that he is still using the second-rate battery.

2. *One swallow never makes a summer.* Nor do three, or four, Anyone who looks far enough can find a few cases to support his prejudices, even if he has to ignore dozens of contradictory instances. This is why I am so concerned that, if the total group is not tested, a sample be chosen in a way which does not distort the results. If conclusions about a selection program are based on a small number of "typical" cases, they are—and I mean this statement to be as dogmatic as it sounds—worthless.

3. *Testimonials are not evidence.* Some of the more aggressive psychologists attempt to persuade a prospective client to use their services or to buy their tests by the use of "testimonials from satisfied customers"—a practice which the American Psychological Association labels unacceptable. For if these testimonials were actually based on soundly gathered evidence, we could be sure that the salesman would present the evidence instead and let it speak eloquently for itself. When he must rely on the unsupported work of a few hand-picked friends, this fact alone is sufficient reason to doubt the value of their testimony.

4. *Psychology is arcane.* "Arcane" is an arcane word meaning, according to Webster, "hidden, secret." It figures in the legal definition of a profession and the rationale for licensing and certification. It means, in this context, that sufficient specific knowledge and training is required to evaluate a professional's performance. It means, also, that a person who is not trained in the field is likely to be unable to tell good work from bad.

Therefore, if an executive who is called on to make the decision to use a psychological technique is not sure of the distinction between content, construct, concurrent and predictive validity, is not familiar with sources of criterion bias, or does not know the appropriate use of product moment, rank order, biserial, point biserial, or tetrachoric correlations, I recommend that he ask someone who does.

11. EMPLOYMENT TEST VALIDATION FOR MINORITY AND NONMINORITY TELEPHONE COMPANY SERVICE REPRESENTATIVES *

Sidney Gael and Donald L. Grant

EMPLOYMENT TEST BIAS, as is the case with test utility, cannot be gauged unless the tests are related to meaningful job standards. The position that employment tests are biased against minority group members because they usually score lower than white applicants is untenable unless accompanied by a statement regarding job performance. Invariably, definitions and discussions of employment test bias or unfair discrimination refer to the important relationship between tests and job performance.[1]

Unfortunately, studies of test bias have not paved the way for clear-cut conclusions. In most cases white applicants averaged better on employment tests than their minority counterparts, but the ethnic groups did not necessarily attain different criterion levels.[2] Differential validity was obtained in several studies,[3] and equal validity in others.[4] Bray and Moses point out ". . . as a general rule most studies showing lack of differential validity have used better than average criterion measures, while most of

* From *Journal of Applied Psychology* 56, no. 2 (1972): 135–39. Copyright 1972 by the American Psychological Association. Reprinted by permission.
[1] See, for example, R. M. Guion, "Employment Tests and Discriminatory Hiring," *Industrial Relations* 5 (1966): 20–37.
[2] See, for example, J. J. Kirkpatrick et al., *Testing and Fair Employment* (New York: New York University Press, 1968).
[3] See, for example, B. S. O'Leary, J. L. Farr, and C. J. Bartlett, *Ethnic Group Membership as a Moderator of Job Performance* (Washington, D.C.: American Institutes for Research, 1970).
[4] See Gael and D. L. Grant, "Validation of a General Learning Ability Test for Selecting Telephone Operators," *Experimental Publication System*, 1971, no. 10; D. L. Grant and D. W. Bray, "Validation of Employment Tests for Telephone Company Installation and Repair Occupations," *Journal of Applied Psychology* 54 (1970): 7–14.

the studies supporting differential validity rely on subjective, poorly determined rating criteria." [5]

The objectives of the present test validation study were to (a) determine which combination of tests already in use contribute significantly to the selection of job applicants with appropriate service representative (SR) potential, (b) ascertain the fairness of the selected tests to minority (black) as well as nonminority job applicants, and (c) formulate employment test standards for SRs that will be used nationwide.

METHOD

Job

A brief description of the SR job is contained in the *Dictionary of Occupational Titles* under Code 249.368.[6] The SR is required to integrate a wide variety of customer contact, clerical, computational, and filing activities under the pace imposed by a steady influx of calls. Examples of the work performed are (a) taking orders for new telephone services, (b) explaining and adjusting telephone bills, (c) recording the details associated with equipment malfunctions and reporting problems to the maintenance organization, and (d) notifying customers that their payments are due and making payment arrangements. Throughout, the SR prepares, handles, and files a large amount of paperwork.

Sample

Applicants were first screened for the study in April 1968, and data collection continued until December 1969. Performance evaluations were obtained upon the conclusion of training for 107 minority and 193 nonminority SRs. The age range for the total sample was 18–47 years, the average being 23 years. Only 1 percent of the sample did not graduate from high school, while most had some education beyond high school, and 10 percent were college graduates. Two percent of the sample had no prior work experience, whereas the majority had worked for 2 or more years prior to accepting the SR job. Incidentally, the biographical items mentioned above were not related to performance as measured.

Predictors

A general learning ability test, five clerical aptitude tests, and a specially developed role-play interview were administered to study participants during the employment process. Specifically, the tests were:

---

[5] D. W. Bray and J. L. Moses, "Personnel Selection," *Annual Review of Psychology* 23 (1972): 545–76.

[6] United States Department of Labor, *Dictionary of Occupational Titles* (Washington, D.C.: United States Government Printing Office, 1965).

1. Bell System Qualification Test I (BSQT 1) Short Form—an adaptation of the School and College Ability Test, Level 2, published by Educational Testing Service
2. Spelling—40 multiple-choice items with one of three spellings correct
3. Number Comparison—100 pairs of four- to nine-digit numbers
4. Arithmetic—100 simple addition and subtraction examples
5. Number Transcription—25 randomly arranged numbers and 25 names to be paired with the numbers
6. Filing—15 randomly listed names to be interfiled with 44 alphabetically arranged names
7. SR Aptitude (SRAT)—a role-playing interview modeled after tasks performed by SRs in telephone contacts with customers

Unlike the BSQT I and the SRAT which require 30 and 45 minutes, respectively, the clerical tests are highly speeded with time limits ranging from 1½ minutes, for the Spelling test to 3½ minutes, for the Number Transcription test. Exclusive of directions, 87.5 minutes were required to test each job applicant.

Employment offices were requested regarding the assignment of applicants to the study to obtain broad and comparable BSQT I score ranges for both ethnic groups.

Criteria

The guidelines followed in designing and developing the criterion instruments were to (a) measure both the acquisition and application of job knowledge as objectively as possible, and (b) obtain direct measures of task proficiency in a standardized situation. Accordingly, a pencil and paper achievement test, the Job Knowledge Review (JKR) and an individually administered work sample test, the Job Performance Review (JPR) were developed specifically for the study by a team of SR supervisors, SR trainers, and a psychologist. The JKR was composed of approximately 70 completion and 40 multiple-choice items covering every major aspect of the 8 weeks of training and was aimed at determining comprehension and retention of company policies and job procedures and practices. The JPR required about 75–90 minutes for each administration and was composed of typical calls in which SRs engage, plus the concomitant clerical work.

When a class of SRs completed the JKR, one SR at a time was oriented to the JPR, a replica of the SR work position. The scene was set by a specially trained administrator who reviewed instructions and encouraged questions about the expected performance. Prior to leaving the SR on her own, the administrator set the wall clock at 8:55 A.M., and told the SR to get ready to begin a typical work day (the starting time, the date, and several other conditions were constant throughout to agree with the available records, and so forth). The administrator then proceeded to an adjoining room where telephone calls to the SR originated. One administrator initiated the calls and acted as a customer while a second specially trained administrator listened to each customer contact and evaluated the SR's oral performance on a specially prepared rating form. Examples of oral behavior rated are the way the SR opened the contact with the customer, determined the primary reason the customer called, sold new equipment and services, quoted charges for different types of equipment, obtained credit information, and closed the contact.

Proficiency measures resulting from the JPR were: (a) record preparation (RP), the sum of the points accorded each part of a record prepared or completed (points were determined by comparing the records to a model set with points already assigned), (b) verbal contact (VC), the sum of the ratings of the verbal interaction with the "customer", and (c) filing (F), the number of records *not* in the designated location when the JPR was terminated.

Criterion scores were standardized by city, and standard scores were combined to form a composite performance index (CPI) by the formula

$$CPI = Z_{JKR} + Z_{RP} + 2Z_{VC} - Z_F.$$

The Z_{VC} was doubled because of its judged importance to overall performance, and the Z_F was subtracted because the raw score was an error score.

Separate analyses were conducted for the black, white, and combined samples by city and across cities. Means and standard deviations were computed for each variable. All variables intercorrelated, and statistics for the ethnic groups compared. A multiple correlation between the employment tests and the CPI was calculated in accordance with the Wherry test selection method.[7] The two most predictive tests were combined by simply adding the raw scores. Regression equations were obtained for the combined white and black samples, and the regression equations compared using a procedure outlined by Potthoff.[8] Finally, expectancy tables were prepared and employment standards derived.

RESULTS

The predictor and criterion means; standard deviations; sample sizes for the combined, nonminority, and the minority samples; and the results of the comparisons between the nonminority and minority sample means are presented in Table 11–1. It was not possible within the data collection period to obtain the desired correspondence between the nonminority and minority sample BSQT I distributions. Though the BSQT I score ranges for the ethnic groups are comparable, the difference between the means is statistically significant, as are the differences between the arithmetic,

---

[7] See W. H. Stead et al., *Occupational Counseling Techniques* (New York: American Book Co., 1940).

[8] R. F. Potthoff, "Statistical Aspects of the Problem of Biases in Psychological Tests," mimeographed, no. 479 (Chapel Hill, N.C.: University of North Carolina, 1966).

TABLE 11–1

Employment Test and Criteria Means and Standard Deviations

Variable	Nonminority Sample			Minority Sample			Minority vs. Nonminority
	$\bar{X}$	SD	N	$\bar{X}$	SD	N	
Employment tests							
BSQT I.	307.3	11.3	193	299.4	11.0	106	5.88***
Arithmetic.	57.3	18.1	186	53.1	15.7	103	2.06*
No. Comparison	49.7	17.2	186	51.2	11.0	103	.90
Filing.	12.3	2.6	186	11.0	2.9	103	3.79***
No. Transcription.	29.1	6.0	184	27.2	6.1	97	2.50*
Spelling .	37.5	7.0	186	38.8	6.8	103	1.54
SR Aptitude.	2.0	.51	184	2.0	.44	101	–
Composite.	336.4	13.52	184	326.6	13.15	97	5.88***
Criteria							
JKR	.14	1.02	193	–.24	.91	107	3.33***
JPR							
F.	–.08	1.02	193	.17	.93	107	2.17*
VC.	.07	1.02	193	–.12	.94	107	1.63
RP.	.08	1.02	193	–.13	1.07	107	1.66
CPI.	.44	3.64	193	–.78	3.32	107	2.95**

Note: Abbreviations: BSQT = Bell System Qualification Test, SR = service representative, JKR = Job Knowledge Review, JPR = Job Performance Review, F = filing, VC = verbal contact, RP = record preparation, CPI = composite performance index.

* $p < .05$.
** $p < .01$.
*** $p < .001$.

TABLE 1-2
Validity Coefficients

Employment Tests	JKR			JPR-F			JPR-RP			JPR-VC			CPI		
	Total	Non-minority	Minority	Total	Non-minority	Minority	Total	Non-minority	Minority	Total	Non-minority	Minority	Total	Non-minority	Minority
BSQT I	40**	39**	31**	11	11	02	23**	18**	28**	22**	27**	09	33**	33**	23*
Arithmetic	18**	18*	11	08	13	-09	11	10	10	17**	17*	16	19**	20**	13
No. Comparison	02	03	01	04	03	08	05	02	16	01	02	08	04	02	13
Filing	23**	22**	15	12	09	10	10	09	07	10	09	06	18*	16*	13
No. Transcription	09	04	11	19**	19**	15	21**	22**	16	17**	18*	12	23**	22**	20*
Spelling	13*	24*	-04	16**	26**	00	09	12	05	12*	18*	03	17**	27**	02
SR Aptitude	13*	13	14	09	05	20*	13*	19**	00	18*	15*	22*	20**	18*	24*

Note: The sample size for each correlation is a smaller n in Table 1 for the pair. Decimal points have been omitted, and the JPR-F score was reflected. Abbreviations: BSQT = Bell System Qualification Test, SR = service representative, JKR = Job Knowledge Review, JPR = Job Performance Review, F = filing, VC = verbal contact, RP = record preparation, CPI = composite performance index.

* p < .05.
** p < .01.

filing, and number transcription test means. Criterion mean differences are significant for the JKR and the JPR-F but not for the RP and the VC. The difference in overall performance as represented by the CPI is significant with the nonminority sample attaining higher scores than the minority sample.

Validity coefficients are shown in Table 11–2. Six of the seven employment tests are significantly related to the CPI for the total and the nonminority samples, and three tests are significantly related for the minority sample. The BSQT I, Number Transcription, and SRAT are significantly related to the CPI for both ethnic samples. The differences between the validity coefficients for the minority and nonminority samples, except for the Spelling test, are not statistically significant.

The best single predictor of overall performance for the total sample is the BSQT I. The Number Transcription and the SRAT were identified by the Wherry test selection method as the second and third tests to combine with the BSQT I. The respective shrunken multiple correlations are .37 and .40. None of the remaining tests contribute to the multiple correlation despite the fact that three of the four tests are individually predictive. The three employment tests selected by the Wherry method are the same three tests that are significantly related to the CPI for the total, minority, and nonminority samples. The SRAT, however, was not recommended for employment office use because its contribution to test variance and predictability were outweighed by practical administering and scoring considerations.

Test fairness or bias, a primary concern, was examined by comparing the slopes and intercepts of the minority and nonminority sample regression lines.[9] The results of the comparisons, along with the composite test and criterion statistics, and the regression equations appear in Table 11–3. Regression line slopes and intercepts for the nonminority and minority samples are not significantly different, indicating that the composite predictor is unbiased.

Test standards were established by first selecting a proficiency level that distinguished the more from the less effective performers. Several managers responsible for SR performance concluded that the total sample CPI average was a reasonable point at which to make the distinction. Composite predictor distributions were plotted separately for the more effective and less effective SRs, and the intersection of the distributions was used to determine the test cutting score that would minimize employment decision errors.[10]

Inasmuch as the lower limit of the second quarter coincided with the previously determined cutting score, the top two composite test-score quarters were combined to form a test-qualified category. The third

---

[9] Ibid.

[10] M. L. Blum and J. C. Naylor, *Industrial Psychology: Its Theoretical and Social Foundations* (New York: Harper & Row, 1968).

TABLE 11–3

Composite Predictor and Criterion Means and Standard Deviations, Regression Equations, and Comparison of Regression Lines

Sample	Composite Test		Composite Criterion			Regression Equation	Significance Test	
	$\bar{X}$	S_x	$\bar{Y}$	S_y	r		Slope F	Intercept F
Total.........	333.0	14.08	.00	3.57	.375	$\hat{Y} = .0950X - 31.6350$		
Nonminority...	336.4	13.52	.44	3.64	.386	$\hat{Y} = .1039X - 34.5119$	1.04	1.67
Minority......	326.6	13.15	-.78	3.32	.283	$\hat{Y} = .0714X - 24.0992$		

TABLE 11–4

Expectancy Table for the Composite Predictor and Composite Criterion

Test Category	Total Sample[a] Predictor Composite Range	% Average & Above	Minority Sample[b] % Average & Above	Nonminority Sample[c] % Average & Above
Qualified.	332 & above	63	59	64
Intermediate.	323–331	40	25	48
Unqualified	322 & below	32	29	36
Total.		50	38	56

[a] $N = 281$.
[b] $N = 97$.
[c] $N = 194$.

quarter is offered as an intermediate range from which applicants can be selected only under extended tight-labor market conditions. Finally, the bottom quarter is the test unqualified range. Table 11–4 contains the test standards recommended for employment office use and the associated expectancies.

Though the validity coefficients with the CPI range from zero to moderate (.02–.33) and the shrunken multiple correlation (.37) is not especially high, the expectancies indicate that the composite predictor differentiated the more from the less effective performers for the minority, nonminority, and total samples. As expected, the largest percentages of more effective performers are found in the test-qualified range, and as the test score ranges decline so do the percentages, except for a slight reversal for the minority sample. Additionally, the percentages of more effective performers in the test-qualified range differ sharply from those in the intermediate and test-unqualified ranges. Nearly two thirds of the test qualified SRs for the total sample were more effective performers, but only a little more than one third of the SRs in the intermediate and unqualified ranges were more effective performers. Of the 140 SRs obtaining average and above average CPIs, 26 percent are minority SRs and 74 percent are nonminority SRs. Below average CPIs were obtained by 43 percent minority and fifty-seven percent nonminority SRs. When minority and nonminority samples are considered separately, the percentages obtaining average and above average CPIs are 38 percent and 56 percent, respectively.

DISCUSSION

Tests, singly or in combination, can be said to be biased with respect to a population (specified by ethnic background, sex, age.) if they are not predictive of performance for the population or inaccurately estimate performance of its members. The purpose of designing a test validation study in which the results are separately determined for identified populations is, therefore, to determine whether the tests involved are biased with respect to the populations studied.

The study described resulted in the selection of a combination of two tests which are reasonably free of the undesired bias for two ethnic populations, that is, minority (black) and nonminority applicants for SR positions in Bell System telephone companies. For both populations, scores on the combined tests are predictive of performance, as measured, and estimate performance with relatively the same degree of accuracy. Generalizing the results to other populations (for example, Spanish-surnamed Americans), to other performance criteria (for example, supervisory ratings), and to other occupations would, of course, be questionable. The results, however, do correspond with those achieved for other telephone company occupations (that is, installation and repair [11] and toll operators.[12]

A major effort was devoted to the development of instruments that provide measures of directly relevant job proficiency. Although the overall correlations with performance are not as high as might be desired, probably due to restrictions in range on the predictors and on the criterion, it was shown that the selected test combination identifies SRs who, on the average, will be able to learn and perform the work.

12. SELECTION OF SALESMEN BY MEANS OF AN ASSESSMENT CENTER *

Douglas W. Bray and Richard J. Campbell

THE ASSESSMENT CENTER [1] received its first industrial application when it was introduced into the Bell System in 1956 as a major research method of the Management Progress Study.[2] Two years later, in 1958, an assessment center was opened in the Michigan Bell Telephone Company for

---

[11] Grant and Bray, "Validation of Employment Tests."

[12] Gael and Grant, "Validation of a General Learning Ability Test."

* Adapted from *Journal of Applied Psychology* 52, no. 1 (1968): 36–41. Copyright 1968 by the American Psychological Association. Reprinted by permission.

[1] See R. Taft, "Multiple Methods of Personality Assessment," *Psychological Bulletin* 56 (1959): 333–52.

[2] D. W. Bray, "The Management Progress Study," *American Psychologist* 19 (1964): 419–20.

the appraisal of candidates for promotion to management from vocational occupations. The results of this first operational assessment center were deemed so useful by line managers that the assessment-center method spread widely through the Bell System until over 50 assessment centers were established in the Bell System Companies processing approximately 8,000 men and women each year who are candidates for management positions.

Follow-up investigations in the Management Progress Study demonstrated considerable predictive power for the assessment-center method both for young noncollege management men who had emerged from the ranks at an early age and for college recruits assessed very shortly after employment.[3] In addition, a study of 500 men recently appointed to management, some of whom had not been assessed and some of whom had received various ratings at the assessment center, further demonstrated the usefulness of the method.[4]

The above assessment centers were designed to assess the ability to function successfully as a supervisory line manager. The present article describes the application of the assessment-center method to a quite different problem—the selection of prospective communications consultants. The job of the communications consultant is to work with business customers to determine their objectives, uncover inconsistencies in methods of reaching these objectives, and suggest improved communications, where appropriate, for improved operations.

A first step in devising an assessment center is a statement of the qualities relevant to success in the job for which assessment is planned. In order to arrive at this list of qualities, a psychologist experienced in the assessment-center approach due to his work on the Management Progress Study, David Berlew, spent several weeks interviewing sales personnel, observing sales training, and making numerous customer visits with experienced communications consultants. When a preliminary list of qualities had been isolated, assessment techniques designed to reveal these qualities were selected or developed. A group of experienced assessors, under the direction of the senior author, then applied these methods to a trial group of six successful salesmen.

This pretest resulted in some redefinition of the assessment qualities and some revision of the assessment-center techniques. The list of qualities was reduced to 20 and included such characteristics as resistance to premature judgment, oral presentation, oral defense, behavior flexibility, and persistence. The major assessment techniques were three simulations.

Leaderless Group Discussion—This technique involves six assessees.

[3] D. W. Bray and D. L. Grant, "The Assessment Center in the Measurement of Potential for Business Management," *Psychological Monographs* 80, no. 625 (1966).

[4] R. J. Campbell and D. W. Bray, "Assessment Centers: An Aid in Management Selection," *Personnel Administration* 30, no. 2 (1967): 6–13.

They are told to assume that they are attending a meeting with five of their peers to discuss candidates for promotion from among their fictitious subordinates. Each is given a description of a subordinate whom the assessee is to present as his candidate. Each assessee is given up to 5 minutes to present his man, followed by a 1-hour group discussion which must result in a rank ordering of the six candidates.

Oral Fact-Finding Exercise—This is an individual technique in which the assessee is told that he is an arbitrator in a labor-management dispute. He is given a short outline of the dispute and the opportunity to question a staff member to determine additional facts and issues. He then presents his decision and its rationale orally to the staff member and is questioned intensively about it.

Consulting Case—This is an individual technique in which the assessee is given written material—textual, graphic, and tabular—concerning the operation and problems of a business concern. His task is to study this material and prepare recommendations for the company. He presents his recommendations orally to two staff members who role play the two controlling partners of the enterprise and discusses his recommendations with them. He then prepares a final written recommendation.

In addition to these simulations, the assessees completed a biographical data blank, underwent a lengthy interview, and took four tests, all cognitive in nature. These tests were the School and College Ability Test, a Critical Thinking Test, an Abstract Reasoning Test, and a Test of Knowledge of Contemporary Affairs.

A trial of the assessment-center methods outlined above was conducted by setting up a Sales Assessment Center in Cleveland, Ohio, to which some 14 participating Bell Telephone Companies sent candidates with little or no Bell System sales experience. This assessment center was staffed by a seven-man team, including a fourth-level director and six third-level sales managers from various telephone company sales departments. This staff received 3-weeks' training by the authors and others before beginning the actual assessment of the trial Ss.

Assessees were processed by the assessment center in groups of six, and it required 2 full days for each group of six to undergo the various assessment techniques. Only one group of six was processed per week, however —the remaining days of each week being used by the assessment staff in preparing reports of the behavior of each candidate in each exercise and for holding staff sessions to hear these reports for each candidate, to rate him on the 20 sales-assessment qualities, and to make a final recommendation as to his suitability as a communications consultant.

In all, some 142 men from the 14 participating telephone companies were assessed, but various factors reduced the sample of men for the present report to 78. This sizable reduction was due to the fact that not all of the men sent to the assessment center met the standards which had been set up for the study. Some had had previous Bell System sales experience, others were on a special training program for college recruits, and some were not assigned to communications consultant work after assessment. In addition, a few resigned from the company before on-the-job criteria were collected.

Great care was taken that the results of the man's performance at the assessment center did not affect his assignment or appraisal on the job. All of the men in the study were Bell System employees at the time of their assessment and there was no feedback to their trainers, their supervisors, or to the men themselves on their performance at the assessment center. It was anticipated that if the assessment center proved a valuable screening method, it would be used as a preemployment screen, but since the individual results of the trial assessments were not to be fed back to the supervisors immediately concerned with the man's training or assignments, all Ss were employed. In fact, the participating companies were urged to keep as many as possible on the payroll so that criterion data could be collected after they had had sales training and were on the job for several months.

Before proceeding to a discussion of the criterion against which the assessment judgments were compared, it may be of interest to examine the final judgments of the candidates made by the assessment staff. After the reports on each candidate were read at the weekly staff meeting and the 20 sales qualities rated on a 5-point scale, the assessment staff made a final judgment as to each candidate's acceptability as a potential communications consultant. The 78 assessees were put into four groups—one group was called "more than acceptable," another "acceptable," a third group was considered "less than acceptable," and the final and lowest group was considered "unacceptable." Table 12–1 shows the distribution of assessment-staff judgments. It will be seen that only 9 of the 78 men performed outstandingly at the assessment center while 21 men did very poorly. The top two groups—the acceptable groups—totaled 41 men, or 53 percent of the sample, while 47 percent were considered unacceptable in varying degrees.

This finding itself is of interest. It indicates that even though the 78 assessees had met all employment standards and had been screened by their local companies as qualified for the job of communications consultant, experienced sales managers judged that from what they could see at the assessment center, only about half possessed good potential for their proposed job. This result is in keeping with other assessment findings in the Bell System, both of the college recruits of the late 1950s and the male and female candidates for management in the various telephone companies. Assessment staffs characteristically reject one-half or more, usually more, of the candidates.

The distribution of assessment-staff judgments was not significantly

TABLE 12–1

**Assessment-Staff Judgments of Acceptability
for Sales Employment**

Assessment Judgment	No. Men	Percentage of Group
More than acceptable.	9	12%
Acceptable.	32	41%
Less than acceptable	16	20%
Unacceptable	21	27%
Total.	78	100%

different for the 64 men who were eliminated from the study. Forty-seven percent of that group "passed" the center as compared to 53 percent of those retained in the sample.

The primary criterion against which assessment-center judgments were compared was first-hand observation of actual behavior in sales contacts 6 months, on the average, after assessment. By that time each of the candidates had had sales training and had been working in the field for several months. This criterion had been decided upon before the assessment study was even begun. It was considered more pertinent than "sales results" which are influenced by many factors other than the behavior of the salesman. Company sales executives had, in any case, indicated that because of differences in market characteristics in the many areas across the United States to which these candidates were assigned, no statistic or group of statistics would accurately reflect individual performance.

The performance observations were carried out by a field-review team working out of American Telephone and Telegraph headquarters in New York. This group's regular work involved such field reviews, and it was an entirely experienced team that went out on these special criterion reviews. A reviewer accompanied each S on as many visits as necessary to determine whether he did or did not meet established standards in conducting his sales activities. These standards included preparation, usage prospecting, recommendations, closing, and implementation. As a result of the observations, each man's performance was classified as meeting standards or failing to meet standards. The reviewers were, of course, entirely unaware of any judgments or observations made of the candidate at the assessment center.

Of the 78 men, 37 men or 47 percent met review standards. Table 12–2 shows the relationship between the assessment-center judgments and whether or not the salesmen met the standards. It will be seen that all of the 9 men deemed more than acceptable at the assessment center met review standards, while only 2 of the 21 men deemed completely unacceptable at the assessment center passed the field review.

TABLE 12–2

Assessment Judgments and Field-Performance Ratings

Assessment Judgment	No. Men	No. Meeting Review Standards	Percentage Meeting Review Standards
More than acceptable.	9	9	100%
Acceptable.	32	19	60%
Less than acceptable	16	7	44%
Unacceptable	21	2	10%
Total	78	37	47%

Note: $x^2 = 24.19$; $p < .001$.

A supplementary investigation looked into the ratings of the Ss given by their sales supervisors and by the trainers who had had each man in sales training.[5] A preliminary letter was sent to each supervisor indicating that he would be asked to rate each salesman reporting to him. He was asked to prepare himself to do this and, when ready, to telephone either of a two-man team in the sales staff in A.T.&T. in New York. The New York staff member verified that he and the supervisor each had the same list of salesmen, and the supervisor was then asked to rank all of the men reporting to him in terms of their excellence as a communications consultant. After the ranking was recorded, the supervisor was then asked to rate each man on a graphic rating scale, the upper end of which was labeled "highest—I wish I had many more like him" and the lower end labeled "lowest—He's in the wrong job." The supervisor was then asked whether he knew if any of the men had been assessed and, if he did, he was asked whether he knew how the man had come out at the assessment center. In most cases, the supervisors did not know the men had been assessed and in no case did the supervisor have any accurate information about the outcome of the man's assessment. The same procedure was carried on with trainers, who rated and ranked all men in each training group in which an assessee had been trained.

In order to maximize differentiation for purposes of comparison, the average rating given by the supervisors and by the trainers was determined. The study group was then divided at about the midpoint of each set of ratings. In the following tables, those men who scored above the midpoint are described as having received higher ratings and those who scored below the midpoint are described as having received lower ratings. It should be noted, however, that the ratings were biased in an upward direction, so some of the men counted as receiving lower ratings were not, in an absolute sense, rated below average.

---

[5] This approach was devised by Ira Cisin of George Washington University.

TABLE 12–3

Assessment Judgments and Supervisors Ratings

Supervisors' Rating	No. Men	Met Review Standards	Did Not Meet Review Standards
Higher	41	47%	53%
Lower	37	44%	56%

Note: Differences not statistically significant.

Table 12–3 shows the relationship between the assessment-center judgments and the supervisors' ratings. It can be seen that there was not a strong relationship—57 percent of those who received acceptable assessment-center judgments received higher ratings by the supervisors, as compared to 47 percent of those who had received unacceptable assessment-center ratings. This difference is not statistically significant.

These results immediately raised the question of to what extent the supervisor's ratings were related to the field-performance ratings. Table 12–4 shows the results. It will be seen that there was very little or no relationship between supervisory ratings and ratings of performance on the sales job by the field-review team. Such a result has, of course, considerable import for questions of appraisal. Of considerable methodological importance, however, is the observation that the assessment center might have been considered not sufficiently accurate for use if supervisory judgment had been relied upon as the sole criterion.

Table 12–5 shows shows the relationship between the assessment-center judgments and the trainers' ratings. Here the relationship is very slight and negative, if indeed there is a relationship. There is somewhat more of a suggestion that trainers might be able to predict field performance, as Table 12–6 shows. Fifty-six percent of the men who received higher training ratings met review standards as compared to 40 percent of those who had received lower ratings. This difference is, however, not statistically significant. In addition, eighty-five percent of the Ss had been given above-average training ratings—not a very fine screen.

TABLE 12–4

Supervisors' Ratings and Field-Performance Ratings

Assessment Judgment	No. Men	Supervisors' Rating	
		Higher	Lower
Acceptable.	41	57%	43%
Less than acceptable	37	47%	53%

Note: Differences not statistically significant.

TABLE 12–5

Assessment Judgments and Trainers' Ratings

		Trainers' Rating	
Assessment Judgment	No. Men	Higher	Lower
Acceptable.	41	51%	49%
Less than acceptable	37	55%	45%

Note: Differences not statistically significant.

TABLE 12–6

Trainers' Rating and Field-Performance Rating

Trainers' Rating	No. Men	Met Review Standards	Did Not Meet Review Standards
Higher	41	56%	44%
Lower	37	40%	60%

Note: Differences not statistically significant.

TABLE 12–7

Trainers' Rating and Field-Performance Rating (men judged acceptable or better at assessment center only)

Trainers' Rating	No. Men	Met Review Standards	Did Not Meet Review Standards
Higher	21	71%	29%
Lower	20	65%	35%

Note: Differences not statistically significant.

In spite of this lack of strong evidence for the usefulness of trainers' ratings, there remained the possibility that such ratings could make a further selection of those who were deemed acceptable (or better) by the assessment center. Table 12–7 shows the relationship between trainers' ratings and field performance for the 41 men who were judged acceptable (or better) by the assessment staff. There is only a very slight, and insignificant, relationship between trainers' ratings and performance, and almost two-thirds of those who get lower ratings show good performance. It does not appear that the trainers' ratings, as they were made in this study, would be of practical use as a selection device. There remains, of

TABLE 12–8

Correlations of Assessment Prediction and Paper-and-Pencil Tests with Field-Performance Ratings

Assessment Judgment	*.51*
SCAT	.25
Critical Thinking Test	.26
Contemporary Affairs Test	.28
Abstract Reasoning Test	.02
Multiple R—Four Tests	.33

course, the possibility that trainers' observational and rating methods could be improved.

It may be of interest to compare the degree of prediction obtained from the assessment-center staff judgment and that from the four paper-and-pencil tests. Table 12–8 shows the data in correlation form. It will be seen that the highest correlation of any of the tests with the criterion is .28. The multiple correlation using all four tests is .33 (not corrected for shrinkage). These, of course, are considerably below the .51 correlation of the assessment judgment with the field-performance ratings.

DISCUSSION

The assessment-center method of evaluating potential for various occupations has had a spotty history.[6] Conclusions about its effectiveness have been difficult to draw because the number of applications of the method has been small, techniques and procedures have varied markedly from one application to the next, and criterion problems are formidable. Studies of Bell System assessment centers for the prediction of success in management positions have, however, uniformly shown that the method has substantial validity. This has been true whether the assessment staff consisted primarily of professional psychologists or of specially trained management personnel. The present study demonstrates that an assessment center staffed by sales managers instructed in assessment techniques can afford a valuable aid in the selection of prospective salesmen.

---

[6] Taft, "Multiple Methods."

13. A MODIFIED MODEL FOR TEST
VALIDATION AND SELECTION
RESEARCH *

Marvin D. Dunnette

OVER 35 YEARS AGO, Clark Hull discussed the level of forecasting efficiency shown by the so-called modern tests of the time.[1] He noted that the upper limit for tests was represented by validity coefficients of about .50. We should be somewhat dismayed by the fact that today our tests have still not penetrated the region of inaccessibility defined so long ago by Hull. Ghiselli's[2] comprehensive review of both published and unpublished studies showed average validities ranging in the .30s and low .40s; an average validity of .50 or above was a distinct rarity.

It seems wise, therefore, to discuss the possibility of improving our batting average in test validation and selection research. I believe we now have the capability for increasing our validities above .50.

First, let us examine the classic validation or prediction model. This model has sought simply to link predictors, on the one hand, with criteria, on the other, through a simple index of relationship, the correlation coefficient. Such a simple linkage of predictors and criteria is grossly oversimplified in comparison with the complexities actually involved in predicting human behavior. Most competent investigators readily recognize this fact and design their validation studies to take account of the possible complexities—job differences, criterion differences, and so forth—present in the prediction situation. Even so, the appealing simplicity of the classic model has led many researchers to be satisfied with a correspondingly simplified design for conducting selection research. Thus, the usual validation effort has ignored the events—on the job behavior, situational differences, dynamic factors influencing definitions of success, and so forth—intervening between predictor and criterion behavior. I believe that the lure of this seemingly simple model is, to a great extent, responsible for the low order of validities reported in the Ghiselli[3] review.

Guetzkow and Forehand have suggested a modification of the classic validation model which provides a richer schematization for prediction

* Extracted from *Journal of Applied Psychology* 47 (1963): 317–23. Copyright 1963 by the American Psychological Association. Reprinted by permission.
    [1] Clark L. Hull, *Aptitude Testing* (Yonkers, N.Y.: World Book Co., 1928).
    [2] E. E. Ghiselli, *The Measurement of Occupational Aptitude* (Berkeley: University of California Press, 1955).
    [3] Ibid.

FIGURE 13–1

A Modified Model for Test Validation and Selection Research

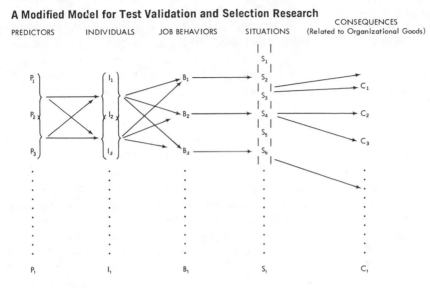

research and which offers important implications for the direction of future research.[4] Their model along with certain additional modifications is shown in Figure 13–1. Note that the modified prediction model takes account of the complex interactions which may occur between predictors and various predictor combinations, different groups (or types) of individuals, different behaviors on the job, and the consequences of these behaviors relative to the goals of the organization. The model permits the possibility of predictors being differentially useful for predicting the behaviors of different subsets of individuals. Further, it shows that similar job behaviors may be predictable by quite different patterns of interaction between groupings of predictors and individuals or even that the same level of performance on predictors can lead to substantially different patterns of job behavior for different individuals. Finally, the model recognizes the annoying reality that the same or similar job behaviors can, after passing through the situational filter, lead to quite different organizational consequences.

This modified and more complex prediction model leads to a number of important considerations involving the emphases to be followed by future validation research:

First, we must be willing to back off a step or two from global measures of occupational effectiveness—ratings, volume of output, and other so-called criteria of organizational worth, and do a more careful job of study-

---

[4] H. Guetzkow and G. A. Forehand, "A Research Strategy for Partial Knowledge Useful in the Selection of Executives," in *Research Needs in Executive Selection,* ed. R. Taguiri (Boston: Harvard Graduate School of Business Administration, 1961).

ing actual job behavior—with particular focus on behavioral or stylistic variations among different individuals with the same jobs. Most previous validation research has been overly concerned with predicting organizational consequences without first determining the nature of possible linkages between such consequences and differences in actual job behavior. It is true that industrial psychologists should continue to be concerned about predicting organizational consequences. Certainly, the modified model implies no lessening of such an interest. What is hoped, however, is that the more careful analysis of the behavioral correlates of differences in organizational consequences will lead to broader understanding of them and, eventually, to their more accurate prediction.

Secondly, as implied by the point just made, the modified model demands that we give up our worship of *the* criterion.[5] I believe that our concept of *the* criterion has suggested the existence of some single, all encompassing measure of occupational success against which predictors must be compared. Our modified model demands that we work with multiple measures of individual behavior and organizational consequences. I suggest therefore that we cease talking about *the* criterion problem and that we discard the notion of a so-called ultimate criterion. Such action should result in a research emphasis which will be more aware of the necessity of analyzing and predicting the many facets of occupational success.

Thirdly, the modified model implies nothing concerning the form of the relationships to be expected. One of the unfortunate consequences of utilizing the classic validation model was its overemphasis on the correlation coefficient as almost the sole statistic of validation research. The notion of a simple linkage between predictor and criterion led easily to the equally simple assumption of the applicability of the linear, homoscedastic model for expressing the magnitude of relationships. Kahneman and Ghiselli, in investigating relationships between 60 aptitude variables and various criteria, showed that 40 percent of the scatter diagrams departed significantly from the linear, homoscedastic model, and 90 percent of these departures held up on cross-validation.[6] This is an important finding for it points up the necessity in future validation research of adopting a methodology taking account of the very great likelihood of nonlinear, heteroscedastic models. Our more complex prediction model, focusing as it does on the complex linkages between predictors and consequences, implies also the necessity of adopting more complex and sophisticated tools of analysis in studying these linkages.

Fourth, and most obviously, our modified model demands that we develop a sort of typology for classifying people, tests, job situations, and

---

[5] M. D. Dunnette, "A Note on *the* Criterion," *Journal of Applied Psychology* 47 (1963): 251–54.

[6] D. Kahneman and E. E. Ghiselli, "Validity and Nonlinear Heteroscedastic Models," *Personnel Psychology* 15 (1962): 1–11.

behaviors according to their relative predictability. Future validation research must define the unique conditions under which certain predictors may be used for certain jobs and for certain purposes. Research studies should, therefore, be devoted to the definition of homogeneous subsets within which appropriate prediction equations may be developed and cross-validated. This idea is not particularly startling nor even new. But it has *not* been applied widely in the conduct of selection research. The modified model rather explicitly directs us to carry out such subgrouping studies in order to learn more about the complex linkages between predictors and consequences. Fortunately several studies already are available which confirm the advantages of studying differential patterns of validity for various subgroups. A brief review of some of these research approaches should illustrate the utility of applying our more complicated model to validation research.

With respect to job groupings, Dunnette and Kirchner have studied the different patterns of validities obtained when careful techniques of job analysis are used to discover groupings of jobs which relatively are homogeneous in terms of actual responsibilities.[7] Substantially different validities were obtained for engineers grouped according to functional similarities (research, development, production, and sales), salesmen (industrial and retail), and clerical employees (stenographers and clerk typists). These studies highlight the necessity of studying job differences and the differential predictability of effectiveness in various job groupings.

Everyone recognizes the possibility of situational effects on the validity of psychological predictions, but there is a paucity of research designed to estimate systematically the magnitude of such effects. Perhaps the best example of such research is provided by Vroom.[8] He showed that various aptitude tests (verbal and nonverbal reasoning, arithmetic reasoning) predicted ratings of job success most effectively for persons who were highly motivated. Job effectiveness in nonmotivating situations showed either no relationship or negative relationships with tested abilities. In a second study with Mann, it was shown that the size of work groups strongly influenced employee attitudes toward their supervisors.[9] Employees in small groups preferred democratic or equalitarian supervisors; employees in large work groups preferred authoritarian supervisors. In a significant series of studies, Porter is also investigating situational factors such as hierarchical level, firm size, and job function

---

[7] M. D. Dunnette, "Validity of Interviewer's Ratings and Psychological Tests for Predicting the Job Effectiveness of Engineers" mimeographed (St. Paul: Minnesota Mining & Manufacturing Co., 1958; M. D. Dunnette and W. K. Kirchner, "Validation of Psychological Tests in Industry," *Personnel Administration* 21 (1958): 20–27.

[8] V. H. Vroom, *Some Personality Determinants of the Effects of Participation* (Englewood Cliffs, N.J.: Prentice-Hall, 1960).

[9] V. H. Vroom and F. C. Mann, "Leader Authoritarianism and Employee Attitudes," *Personnel Psychology* 13 (1960): 125–39.

as they affect managerial perceptions of their jobs.[10] More emphasis needs to be given to these and other situational factors in validation studies, particularly as they serve to operate as moderating variables in behavioral predictions.[11]

Many studies have shown different validities for different subgroups of individuals. For example, Seashore summarized a vast number of scholastic success studies which show almost uniformly that the grades of women (in both high school and college) are significantly more predictable than those of men.[12] It is also well established that differing patterns of validity are typically obtained for subgroups differing in amounts of education and/or years of job experience. It may seem obvious that such factors as sex, education, and experience provide useful moderating variables in validation research. However, researchers also have identified variables which are much less *obvious* but which *do* make substantial differences in the patterns and magnitudes of validities obtained. For example, Grooms and Endler showed that the grades of anxious college students were much more predictable ($r = .63$) with aptitude and achievement measures than were the grades of nonanxious students ($r = .19$) [13]; and Frederiksen, Melville, and Gilbert have shown that interest in engineering (as measured by the Strong test) has a higher validity for predicting grades for noncompulsive engineers than for compulsive ones.[14] Berdie showed that the grades of engineering students with relatively consistent scores on an algebra test were more predictable from the total test score than were the grades of students with less consistent scores.[15] Ghiselli has developed a method of dividing persons, on the basis of a screening test, into more and less predictable subgroups.[16]

These studies and methods mark the bare beginnings of efforts to take account of complexities which have been ignored by the oversimplified prediction model of the past. It appears that subgrouping of tests, people, jobs, situations, and consequences is necessary to a thorough understand-

---

[10] L. W. Porter, "Some Recent Explorations in the Study of Management Attitudes" (Paper read at the American Psychological Association, St. Louis, September 1962).

[11] D. R. Saunders, "Moderator Variables in Prediction," *Educational and Psychological Measurement* 16 (1956): 209–22.

[12] H. G. Seashore, "Women Are More Predictable than Men" (Presidential address, Division 17, American Psychological Association, New York, September 1961).

[13] R. R. Grooms and N. S. Endler, "The Effect of Anxiety on Academic Achievement," *Journal of Educational Psychology* 51 (1960): 299–304.

[14] N. Frederiksen and A. C. Gilbert, "Replication of a Study of Differential Predictability," *Educational and Psychological Measurement* 20 (1960): 759–67; N. Frederiksen and S. D. Melville, "Differential Predictability in the Use of Test Scores," *Educational and Psychological Measurement* 14 (1954): 647–56.

[15] R. F. Berdie, "Intra-Individual Variability and Predictability," *Educational and Psychological Measurement* 21 (1961): 663–76.

[16] E. E. Ghiselli, "Differentiation of Tests in Terms of the Accuracy with Which They Predict for a Given Individual," *Educational and Psychological Measurement* 20 (1960): 675–84; E. E. Ghiselli, "The Prediction of Predictability and the Predictability of Prediction" (Paper read at the American Psychological Association, St. Louis, September 1962).

ing of what is going on in a prediction situation. The widespread acceptance of the modified model which we have been discussing should lead to
a new and refreshing series of questions about problems of selection and
placement. Instead of asking whether or not a particular selection technique (test, interview, or what have you) is any good, we will ask under
what circumstances different techniques may be useful. What sorts of
persons should be screened with each of the methods available, and how
may the various subgroups of persons be identified and assigned to
optimal screening devices? [17] Finally, what job behaviors may be expected
of various people and how may these behaviors be expected to aid or to
detract from accomplishing different organizational objectives which
may, in turn, vary according to different value systems and preferred
outcomes?

What are the implications of these trends for the selection function in
industry? Primarily, I believe they suggest the possibility of a new kind
of selection process in the firm of the future. The selection expert of
tomorrow will no longer be attempting to utilize the same procedure for
all his selection problems. Instead, he will be armed with an array of
prediction equations. He will have developed, through research, a wealth
of evidence showing the patterns of validities for different linkages in the
modified prediction model—for different predictors, candidates, jobs, and
criteria. He will be a flexible operator, attentive always to the accumulating information on any given candidate, and ready to apply, at each
stage, the tests and procedures shown to be optimal.

---

[17] [Editors' note: An excellent example of this is provided by D. Kipnis, "A Non-
cognitive Correlate of Performance among Lower Aptitude Men," *Journal of Applied
Psychology* 46 (1962): 76–80.]

Section Three

TRAINING EMPLOYEES
AND MANAGERS

INTRODUCTION

THE TRAINING OF EMPLOYEES AND MANAGERS represents one of the most extensive personnel activities in modern organizations. This section describes some representative contributions of psychologists to principles and developments in this area.

We must point out that a recent trend in training has been to broaden its scope in industry, with particular current emphasis on *management* training and development. Companies are becoming more concerned with developing the individual in more ways than in his immediate job behavior. Thus, many companies offer employees courses ranging from public speaking and blueprint reading to psychology and mathematics. Or executives may participate in programs to improve their reading speed or to become "more sensitive" to interpersonal relations. In one company, some managers are sent back to college for a year of "liberal arts," which, it is hoped, may broaden their approach to complex decisions and policy-making problems. However, we must not lose sight of the fact that much training activity is still concerned with specific job skills.

There is much experimentation in training today with new methods and procedures. Many procedures which represented innovations just a few years ago are now seen as established practice in many industrial training programs. This section will examine a number of these developments (for example, programmed learning, sensitivity training, management games). The precise value of many of these programs is not yet known, but many

127

of these developments and ideas are exciting and present a challenge to educators and researchers in this field. These new developments underscore the need for careful research to evaluate their value in achieving the objectives of improved on-the-job performance.

This section on training is intimately linked with the previous two sections. Specifically, the need to determine training objectives in advance seems obvious, but is too frequently overlooked. This cannot really be done adequately without the detailed job analysis information about the tasks involved and the skill requirements of the job. And the kinds of performance criteria described in Section One are critical for proper evaluation of training in terms of meaningful indices of job performance.

Training might be thought of as the applied psychology of learning.[1] Studies of learning from basic psychology should presumably be of help in determining the optimum conditions of training. Knowledge about principles of motivation, reinforcement, transfer of training, knowledge of results, and so forth, would seem to have application here. The first article, by Gagné, "Training and Principles of Learning," discusses some of the issues and problems in applying such principles in the industrial training environment and shows that principles of training need to be developed from a more detailed task analysis of the job to be performed.

One well-known training principle is that without some kind of "feedback" or "knowledge of results" the learner cannot improve very much. Yet, in industry this principle is too often ignored. This is especially true of on-the-job training where the worker is often "turned loose." He may actually learn poor working habits and methods. Even when knowledge of results is provided, there is still the question of the kind of "feedback" that would be most effective, and the best method for presenting this feedback to the learner. Feeding back knowledge of results is much more complicated than might appear at first glance, since there are "motivational" as well as "informational" aspects to this variable. A good deal of research has been conducted in this area, and the results of these studies along with implications for the most effective methods for presenting feedback to trainees may be found in Mosel,[2] Bass and Vaughn,[3] and Blum and Naylor.[4]

One training technique in which the principles of feedback to the learner are systematically applied is programmed learning, an aspect of which is the concern with teaching machines. It is interesting to note that in recent years there has been increased attention to problems of effective

---

[1] For a comprehensive discussion of this, see W. McGehee and P. W. Thayer, *Training in Business and Industry* (New York: John Wiley & Sons, 1961).

[2] J. N. Mosel, "How to Feed Back Performance Results to Trainees." *Journal of American Society of Training Directors* 12, no. 2 (1958): 37–46.

[3] B. M. Bass and J. A. Vaughn, *Training in Industry: The Management of Learning* (Belmont, Calif.: Wadsworth, 1966), chap. 4.

[4] M. L. Blum and J. C. Naylor, *Industrial Psychology* (New York: Harper & Row, 1968), chap. 8.

programming of material to be taught and less emphasis on the particular "hardware" or machine to be used. The machine is less important than the program. The need to "program" courses has forced those who design training to take a more "task analysis" approach to training. The programmer must think through the kinds of behavior he wants the student to perform and the sequences that will produce this most effectively. By now there have been many industrial applications of programmed learning for a wide variety of jobs and it seems likely that this trend will continue.[5] The next article by Abma, "Programmed Instruction—Past, Present, and Future," summarizes some of the major approaches in this area. The appendix which follows gives some additional examples. We should add that some recent extensions in this field are linking computers with programmed learning. Many new companies have been organized to develop such systems. It seems that "Computer Assisted Instruction" is beginning to have important and far-reaching educational consequences.[6]

A considerable number of techniques have been developed and have become popular in the area of management training and development.[7] Two primary management skills for which training methods have been developed involve "administrative decision making" and "interpersonal relations." The next two articles describe training methods in these areas. Dill's article, "Management Games for Training Decision-Makers," illustrates the use of "management games" which allow a simulation of "real-life" industrial problems. With the assistance of high-speed computers, management trainees make business decisions and get feedback on the consequences of these decisions.

[5] For specific examples of industrial applications, see G. Ofiesh, *Programmed Instruction* (New York: American Management Association, 1967). For more general sources, see A. Lumsdaine and R. Glaser, eds., *Teaching Machines and Programmed Learning* (Washington, D.C.: National Education Association, 1960); R. Glaser, ed., *Teaching Machines and Programmed Learning, Part II* (Washington, D.C.: National Education Association, 1965). For a recent review of the use and effectiveness of programmed learning in industry, see A. N. Nash, J. P. Muczyk, and F. L. Vettori, "The Relative Practical Effectiveness of Programmed Instruction," *Personnel Psychology* 24 (1971): 397–418.

[6] For a general presentation of the major issues and techniques involved in computer-assisted instruction, see R. C. Atkinson and H. A. Wilson, *Computer-Assisted Instruction: A Book of Readings* (New York: Academic Press, 1969); P. Suppes and M. Morningstar, "Computer-Assisted Instruction," *Science* 166 (1969): 343–50. For a discussion of computer-*managed* instruction, in which the computer is used to provide appropriate educational materials to the student, as well as to monitor his progress, see J. C. Flanagan, "Functional Education for the Seventies," *Phi Delta Kappan,* September 1967, pp. 27, 33; J. Coulson, *Computer-Assisted Instructional Management* (System Development Corporation Document SP-3300, 1969).

[7] For a general discussion of management training methods, see J. P. Campbell, M. D. Dunnette, E. E. Lawler III, and K. E. Weick, *Managerial Behavior, Performance, and Effectiveness* (New York: McGraw-Hill Book Co., 1970), especially chap. 10, 11, 12, and 13. Also see J. P. Campbell, "Personnel Training and Development," *Annual Review of Psychology* 22 (1971): 565–602.

In recent years, there has been increasing involvement of organizations and individuals in T-groups (T for Training), sensitivity training, laboratory education, or some variant.[8] These methods have frequently been used by business organizations for the purpose of improving interpersonal relations skills of managers and executives. Since these methods often involve a deeper involvement of the individual's personality and feelings, they have been the object of some controversy. The article by Dunnette and Campbell, "Laboratory Education: Impact on People and Organizations," points out some of the major objectives of T-groups and reviews a number of research studies which were designed to evaluate the effectiveness of this training procedure.

Overall, these authors suggest that the evidence to date does not lead to any clear conclusion that laboratory education methods are very effective in accomplishing their objectives for management training. At the same time, however, we should point out that other reviews of the T-group literature [9] are somewhat more favorable as to the effectiveness of these methods for management training, so that, while laboratory education appears to be a currently popular management training procedure, the overall value of this technique is not yet known.

In recent years, organizational psychologists have gone beyond traditional concepts of training specific groups of employees or managers in an organization and have increasingly concentrated on "organization development," which might involve development of relatively large, autonomous subunits of the organization or even development of the organization as a whole. In effect, the organizational psychologist acts as a consultant to the entire organization in helping it to find ways of coping with both its internal and external environment. While this obviously goes beyond the conventional notions of training or management development, such training notions and techniques as we have discussed here, as well as many other approaches, might all be part of an overall organization development program.[10]

As we have seen, a major problem with regard to employee training involves the evaluation of the effectiveness of the training. The next article, by Fleishman, describes the evaluation of a particular supervisory train-

---

[8] For reviews of these developments, see L. P. Bradford, J. R. Gibb, and K. D. Benne, eds., *T-Group Theory and Laboratory Method* (New York: John Wiley & Sons, 1964); E. H. Schein and W. G. Bennis, *Personal and Organizational Change Through Group Methods* (New York: John Wiley & Sons, 1965).

[9] For example, P. C. Buchanan, "Laboratory Training and Organization Development," *Administrative Science Quarterly* 14 (1969): 466–79; C. L. Cooper and I. L. Mangham, "T-Group Training: Before and After," *Journal of Management Studies* 7 (1970): 224–39; I. L. Mangham and C. L. Cooper, "The Impact of T-Groups on Managerial Behavior," *Journal of Management Studies* 6, no. 2 (1969): 53–72.

[10] For an overview of the concepts and methods of organization development programs, see W. Bennis, *Organization Development: Its Nature, Origins, and Prospects* (Reading, Mass.: Addison-Wesley, 1969); R. Beckhard, *Organization Development: Strategies and Models* (Reading, Mass.: Addison-Wesley, 1969).

ing program. "Leadership Climate, Human Relations Training, and Supervisory Behavior" shows the importance of evaluating such training in terms of effects back on the job. The study illustrates that the particular effects of such courses may depend on the individual and the situation in which he finds himself.

The study also emphasizes that the role of the immediate supervisor in training should not be overlooked. We tend to stress the importance of formal programs and courses. However, the supervisor is really "training" his men every day in the types of feedback he supplies to them and in the kinds of behavior he rewards on the job.

The final article in this section describes an employee training problem which is currently of considerable concern in our society. Rosen and Turner, in "Effectiveness of Two Orientation Approaches in Hard-Core Unemployed Turnover and Absenteeism" describe two different training approaches to training the hard-core unemployed and suggest that in-house training programs are likely to be more effective with this type of employee population than sessions conducted by outside professionals. Clearly this is an area which needs further study, in order to find the best ways of providing job training to a segment of our population which has been too often neglected in the past.

SUGGESTED ADDITIONAL READINGS

Cooper, C. L., and Mangham, I. L.   *T-Groups: A Survey of Research*. London: Wiley–Interscience, 1971.

Craig, R. T., and Bittel, L. R. eds.   *Training and Development Handbook*. New York: McGraw-Hill Book Co., 1967.

Lynton, R. P., and Pareek, U.   *Training for Development*, Homewood, Ill.: Richard D. Irwin, Inc., 1967.

Rundquist, E. A.   "Designing and Improving Job-Training Courses." *Personnel Psychology* 25 (1972): 41–52.

Wohlking, W.   "Management Training: Where Has It Gone Wrong?" *Training and Development Journal* 25, no. 12 (1971): 2–8.

14. TRAINING AND PRINCIPLES OF LEARNING *

Robert M. Gagné

Suppose that I were a learning psychologist, fresh out of an academic laboratory, who was to take a new job in charge of a program of research on some type of training. What principles of learning would I look for to bring to bear on training problems?

SOME REPRESENTATIVE TASKS

First, we need to have in mind certain representative tasks for which training either is or has been given, in order that we can consider in detail the kinds of learning principles that are applicable. Here are three military tasks which will serve well as examples: (1) flexible gunnery, (2) putting a radar set into operation, (3) finding malfunctions in an electronic system.

Flexible gunnery. The gunner of a now obsolete type of bomber aircraft was typically located in the waist or the tail of the plane, and aimed and fired a gun at fighter aircraft attacking on what was called a "pursuit course." To do this he looked at the attacking fighter through a reticle containing a central dot, which he lined up with the target by rotating his gunsight horizontally and vertically. At the same time, he had to "frame" the aircraft within a set of dots arranged in a circle whose circumference could be varied by rotating the round hand-grip by means of which he grasped the gunsight. This is the kind of task the psychologist calls "tracking," on which a great many laboratory studies have been carried out. It was, of course, tracking simultaneously in the three dimensions of azimuth, elevation, and range. To perform this task, the individual had to learn a motor skill.

Putting a radar set in operation. This kind of task is typically what is called a "fixed procedure." That is, the individual is required to push buttons, turn switches, and so on, in a particular sequence. Here, for example, is a set of steps in a procedure used by radar operators to check the transmitter power and frequency of an airborne radar: [1]

---

* Extracted from "Military Training and Principles of Learning," *American Psychologist* 17 (1962): 83–91. Copyright 1962 by the American Psychological Association. Reprinted by permission.

[1] L. J. Briggs and E. J. Morrison, "An Assessment of the Performance Capabiilties of Fire Control System Mechanics," USAF Personnel Training Research Center Technical Memo no. ML–56–19, 1956.

1. Turn the radar set to "Stand-by" operation
2. Connect power cord of the TS-147
3. Turn power switch on
4. Turn the test switch to transmit position
5. Turn DBM dial fully counter-clockwise
6. Connect an RF cable to the RF jack on the TS-147

There are 14 more steps in this procedure. Notice that each of the steps by itself is easy enough; the individual is quite capable of turning a switch or connecting a cable. What he must learn to do, however, is to perform each step in the proper sequence. The sequence is important, and doing step 5 before step 4 may be not only an error, it may be dangerous. What must be learned, then, is a sequence of acts in the proper order.

Finding malfunctions in complex equipment. This is in many respects a most complex kind of behavior. There are of course some very simple kinds of equipment in which this activity can be reduced to a procedure; and when this is true, the task is one that can be learned from that point of view. But the major job, for complex equipment, is one of troubleshooting, a problem-solving activity that has considerable formal resemblance to medical as well as other kinds of diagnosis. Suppose this a radar set, again, and that the initial difficulty (symptom) is that no "range sweep" appears on the oscilloscope tube face. Beginning at this point, the trouble-shooter must track down a malfunctioning component. He does this first by making a decision as to how he will check the operation of subordinate parts of the system, next by carrying out the check and noting the information it yields, next by making another decision about a next check, and so on through a whole series of stages until he finds the malfunctioning unit. In each of these stages, he presumably must be formulating hypotheses which affect his actions at the next stage, in the typical and classically described manner of problem solving. What does the individual have to learn in order to solve such problems? This is indeed a difficult question to answer, but the best guess seems to be that he must acquire concepts, principles, rules, or something of that nature which he can arouse within himself at the proper moment and which guide his behavior in diagnosing malfunctions.

Here are, then, three types of activities that are not untypical of military jobs. Each of these tasks can be shown to represent a rather broad class of tasks, in its formal characteristics, which cuts across particular content or occupational areas. For example, flexible gunnery is a tracking skill, which formally resembles many others, like maneuvering an airplane, sewing a seam on a sewing machine, hovering a helicopter, and many others. As for procedures, these are common indeed, and may be found in jobs such as that of a clerk in filling in or filing forms, a cook preparing food, or a pilot preflighting an airplane. Diagnosing difficulties is certainly a widely occurring kind of activity, which may be engaged in by the leader of a group who detects the symptom of low morale, as well as by a variety of mechanics who "fix" equipment of all sorts. Accordingly, one should probably not consider these particular examples as peculiar ones; instead, they appear to be representative of a wide variety of human activities.

WHAT IS APPLICABLE TO THE DESIGN OF TRAINING?

Here are the psychological principles that seem to me to be useful in training for such jobs.

1. Any human task may be analyzed into a set of component tasks which are quite distinct from each other in terms of the experimental operations needed to produce them.
2. These task components are mediators of the final task performance; that is, their presence insures positive transfer to a final performance, and their absence reduces such transfer to near zero.
3. The basic principles of training design consist of (a) identifying the component tasks of a final performance, (b) insuring that each of these component tasks is fully achieved, and (c) arranging the total learning situation in a sequence which will insure optimal mediational effects from one component to another.

These statements certainly imply a set of principles which would have very different names from those we are now most familiar with. They are concerned with such things as *task analysis, intra-task transfer, component task achievement,* and *sequencing* as important variables in learning and consequently in training. These principles are not set in opposition to the traditional principles of learning, such as reinforcement, differentiation of task elements, familiarity, and so on, and do not deny their relevance, only their *relative importance.* They are, however, in complete opposition to the assumption "the best way to learn a task is to practice the task."

It should also be pointed out here that I am unable to refer to any well-organized body of experimental evidence for these newly proposed principles. They come instead by inference and generalization from a wide variety of instances of learning and military training. I do not claim more for them than this. But they have to be stated before any systematic experimental work can be done on them.

Let me try now to illustrate a definite meaning for these principles with some examples. Consider first the procedural task of putting a radar set into operation described previously: "(1) Turn radar set to 'standby' operation; (2) Connect power cord of the TS-147; (3) Turn power switch on; (4) Turn test switch to transmit position; etc." The first step to be undertaken here is to analyze the task; and (with certain minor assumptions on our part) this is seen to be, first, the learning of an order series of responses to things; and second and subordinate to this, the locating of these things. These two *component tasks* have a hierarchial relationship to each other, and immediately suggest the proper *sequencing* for the arrangement of the learning (or training) situation. That is to say, what must first be undertaken is that the learner learn what and where the "things" are (the "standby operation" switch, the "TS-147," the power switch, the test switch, and so forth). This is a matter of identification learning, which has considerable resemblance to the paired-associate learning of the psychological laboratory. Having achieved this subordinate task, it is then possible for the learner to undertake the second, or "serial order of things" task. According to the principle proposed here, maximal positive transfer to this task would be predicted following completely adequate performance on the subordinate task of identifying the "things."

Laboratory experiments which have undertaken to test such a hypothesis seem to be scarce. It is possible, however, to make reference to two studies [2] which have some suggestive findings. Generally speaking, when one learns a set of paired associates first, and then undertakes the learning of these units serially, there is high positive transfer; but when one learns units serially first, the amount of transfer to paired associate learning is very low indeed. These results strongly suggest that there is a *more efficient* and a *less efficient* sequence which can be arranged for the learning of a procedural task, and that this sequence involves learning one subtask before the total task is undertaken. A procedure is a task that can be analyzed into at least two component tasks, one of identification, and the other of serial ordering. The first is subordinate to the second in the sense that it mediates positive transfer to the second, provided it is first completely mastered.

Can this kind of analysis be applied to a more complex task like troubleshooting? Indeed it can, and those psychologists who thought about the problem of training troubleshooters came close to the kind of analysis I have suggested. Generally speaking, they recognized that troubleshooting some particular equipment as a final performance was supported by two broad classes of subordinate tasks. First, there was knowledge of the rules of signal flow in the system, and second, the proper use of test instruments in making checks. The rules of signal flow themselves constitute an elaborate hierarchy of subordinate tasks, if one wants to look at it that way. For example, if the signal with which the mechanic is concerned is the output of an amplifier, then it may be necessary that he know some of the rules about data flow through an amplifier. Thus the task may be progressively analyzed into subordinate components

---

[2] E. Primoff, "Backward and Forward Association as an Organizing Act in Serial and in Paired Associate Learning," *Journal of Psychology* 5 (1958): 375–95; R. K. Young, "A Comparison of Two Methods of Learning Serial Associations," *American Journal of Psychology* 72 (1959): 554–59.

which support each other in the sense that they are predicted to mediate positive transfer.

The task of using test instruments in making checks provides an even clearer example, perhaps. Obviously, one subordinate task is "choosing the proper check to make" (presumably a matter of knowing some "rules"); another is "selecting the proper test instrument" (an identification task); still another is "setting up the test instrument" (a procedural task, which in its turn has components like those previously described); and another is "interpreting the instrument reading" (another task involving a "rule"). Even identifying these component tasks brings to troubleshooting a vast clarification of the requirements for training. If one is able to take another step of arranging the proper sequencing of these tasks in a training program, the difference which results is remarkable. This is the interpretation I should be inclined to make of the studies which have demonstrated significant improvements in troubleshooting training, such as those of Briggs and Besnard;[3] of Highland, Newman and Waller;[4] and of French, Crowder, and Tucker.[5] In providing training which was demonstrably successful, these investigators were given instruction on a carefully analyzed set of subordinate tasks, arranged in a sequence which, so far as they could tell, would best insure positive transfer to the variety of problem situations encountered in troubleshooting. It was *the identification of these tasks and this sequence* which I believe was the key to training improvement.

A good deal of other work also proceeded along these lines, although not always with a terminal phase of measured training effectiveness. For example, a whole series of studies by Miller and Folley, and their associates, were concerned with what was called *task analysis.* They had such titles as these: Line Maintenance of the A-3A Fire Control System: III. Training Characteristics;[6] Job Anticipation Procedures Applied to the K-1 System;[7] A Comparison of Job Requirements for the Line Mainte-

---

[3] L. J. Briggs and G. G. Besnard, "Experimental Procedures for Increasing Reinforced Practice in Training Air Force Mechanics for an Electric System," in *Research Symposium on Air Force Human Engineering, Personnel, and Training Research,* ed. G. Finch and F. Cameron (Washington, D.C.: National Academy of Sciences–National Research Council, 1956), pp. 48–58.

[4] R. W. Highland, S. E. Newman, and H. S. Waller, "A Descriptive Study of Electronic Troubleshooting," in *Research Symposium on Air Force Human Engineering, Personnel, and Training Research,* ed. G. Finch and F. Cameron (Washington, D.C.: National Academy of Sciences–National Research Council, 1956), pp. 48–58.

[5] R. S. French, N. A. Crowder, and J. A. Tucker, Jr., "The K-System MAC-1 Troubleshooting Trainer: II. Effectiveness in an Experimental Training Course," USAF Personnel Training Research Center Technical Note no. 56–120, 1956.

[6] J. D. Folley, Jr. and R. B. Miller, "Line Maintenance of the A-3A Fire Control System: III. Training Characteristics," USAF Personnel Training Research Center Technical Note no. 57–71, 1957.

[7] R. B. Miller, J. D. Folley, Jr., and P. R. Smith, "Job Anticipation Procedures Applied to the K-1 System," USAF Human Resources Research Center Technical Report no. 53–20, 1953.

nance of Two Sets of Electronic Equipment.[8] What was all this talk about task analysis? Did it have anything to do with training? My answer is that it had to do with training more than with anything else. These were thoroughgoing and highly successful attempts to identify the variety of tasks contained in a job, and the variety of subtasks which contributed to each task. There was in fact explicit recognition of the idea that successful final performance must be a matter of attaining competence on these subtasks. So here again was the notion that effective training somehow depended on the identification of these subordinate tasks, as well as on their arrangement into a suitable sequence to insure positive transfer to the final performance.

A third source of these ideas in military training research should be mentioned. This was the development of training devices applicable to such jobs as electronic maintenance. It came to be recognized that these devices were in some respects very different from the traditional trainers such as those for developing skill in aircraft maneuvers. They were called "concept trainers," and this, as Briggs'[9] discussion of them implies, was another name for "teaching machines." As such, they were developed independently of Skinner's ideas, and they were in fact based upon an entirely different set of principles, as is clear from the accounts provided by Briggs,[10] Crowder,[11] and French.[12] Each of these training devices (or teaching machines), aside from its hardware engineering, was developed on the basis of a painstaking task analysis, which identified the subordinate tasks involved in a total task like troubleshooting a particular electronic system. The subordinate tasks thus identified were then incorporated into a sequence designed to insure maximal positive transfer to the final task. There were certainly some programming principles, but they bore little resemblance to those which are most frequently mentioned in recent literature; in my opinion, they were much more important than these.

Still a fourth area of effort in training research was related to these ideas. This was the development of techniques to provide behavioral guides, or "jobs aids" in support of performance in various technical

[8] R. B. Miller, J. D. Folley, Jr., and P. R. Smith, "A Comparison of Job Requirements for Line Maintenance of Two Sets of Electronics Equipment," USAF Personnel Training Research Center Technical Report no. 54–83, 1954.

[9] L. J. Briggs, "Teaching Machines for Training of Military Personnel in Maintenance of Electronic Equipment," in *Automatic Teaching: The State of the Art,* ed. E. Galanter (New York: John Wiley & Sons, 1959), chap. 12.

[10] L. J. Briggs, "A Troubleshooting Trainer for the E-4 Fire Control System," USAF Personnel Training Research Center Technical Note no. 56–94, 1956.

[11] N. A. Crowder, "A Part-Task Trainer for Troubleshooting," USAF Personnel Training Research Center Technical Note no. 57–71, 1957.

[12] R. S. French, "The K-System MAC-1 Troubleshooting Trainer: I. Development, Design, and Use," USAF Personnel Training Research Center Technical Note no. 56–119, 1956.

jobs.[13] In order to do this, it was found necessary to distinguish between those kinds of capabilities which could best be established by thorough training, and those kinds which could be established by minimal training plus the provision of a check list or handbook. Obviously, here again there had to be a detailed task analysis. Subordinate tasks had to be identified which would mediate transfer either to the kind of performance required without a handbook, or the kind required with a handbook. Besides the initial task analysis, it is again evident that this line of work was making use of ideas about component task achievement and intra-task transfer.

SUMMARY

Now that I have conveyed the message, my summary can be quite brief. If I were faced with the problem of improving training, I should not look for much help from the well-known learning principles like reinforcement, distribution of practice, response familiarity, and so on. I should look instead at the technique of task analysis, and at the principles of component task achievement, intratask transfer, and the sequencing of subtask learning to find those ideas of greatest usefulness in the design of effective training. Someday, I hope, even the laboratory learning psychologist will know more about these principles.

15. PROGRAMMED INSTRUCTION— PAST, PRESENT, FUTURE *

John S. Abma

Introduction

AN IDEAL EDUCATIONAL OR TRAINING SYSTEM would be one in which every student could be instructed by an expert tutor. This is the technique we actually use for some difficult, specialized skills, as in pilot training, the training of astronauts, musical performance, sports and athletics, and advanced studies of some kinds at the college level. In all of these cases, an instructor spends time working with individual students. However, there are not enough instructors to go around for this kind of teaching when large numbers of students are involved. Here is where pro-

---

[13] A. J. Hoehn, S. E. Newman, E. Saltz, and J. J. Wulff, "A Program for Providing Maintenance Capability," USAF Personnel Training Research Center Technical Memo no. ML–57–10, 1957.
* From *RTD Technology Briefs* 10, no. 10 (October 1964), pp. 3–9.

grammed instruction can play a role. Programmed instruction is one way to make the advantages of private tutoring available to large groups of students being trained in routine topics or skills. The key idea of programmed instruction is that the material is taught in the same way a tutor would teach it, except that the material is presented in printed form, and sometimes by a "teaching machine."

As in tutoring, the major features of programmed instruction are (1) each student can proceed at his own pace, not being held back by slower students nor rushed by the faster ones; (2) each student is kept informed of how he is progressing at every step of the course; (3) the system offers rewards or encouragement as the student tackles difficult subjects; and (4) the emphasis is upon student involvement and activity—not passive reading or listening. In some types of programmed instruction, the content of the course can be altered to meet the needs of each individual student.

Programmed instruction is not new. It has been with us at least ten years, reckoning from B. F. Skinner's 1954 article in the *Harvard Educational Review*.[1] Other calculations, based on the work of S. L. Pressey in the 1920s [2] or the invention of educational drill machines starting in the 1870s [3] would reveal an even longer history. Indeed, some writers compare programmed instruction with the method employed by Socrates in his instructional dialogues.[4] But in 1954, all the major current approaches to programmed instruction had been enunciated. In this article we will examine these various approaches and assess the present status of programmed instruction in the light of current research. We shall also attempt to predict what influence programmed instruction will have on future educational and training methods.

PAST

Early terms used to describe this area were "Teaching Machines," "Automated Instruction," "Self-Tutoring," and "Programmed Learning." These terms suggest the concern with automation, self-instruction and

[1] B. F. Skinner, "The Science of Learning and the Art of Teaching, *Harvard Educational Review* 24 (1954): 86–97. Also in A. A. Lumsdaine and R. Glaser eds., *Teaching Machines and Programmed Learning: A Source Book* (Washington, D.C.: National Education Association, 1960).

[2] S. L. Pressey, "A Simple Apparatus Which Gives Tests and Scores—and Teaches," *School and Society* 23 (1926): 373–76. Also in A. A. Lumsdaine and R. Glaser eds., *Teaching Machines and Programmed Learning: A Source Book* (Washington, D.C.: National Education Association, 1960).

[3] I. Mellan, "Teaching and Educational Inventions," *Journal of Experimental Education* 4 (1936): 291–300. Also in A. A. Lumsdaine and R. Glaser eds., *Teaching Machines and Programmed Learning: A Source Book,* (Washington, D.C.: National Education Association, 1960).

[4] Ira S. Cohen, "Programmed Learning and the Socratic Dialogue," *American Psychologist* 17 (1962): 772–75.

individual tutoring methods that should improve our educational and training activities. Today, there is a distinction between automation and programmed instruction. Automation can be applied to any educational technique. It includes televised lectures, automatic test scoring and complex audio-visual aids, including language laboratories. Although programmed instruction usually does reduce the role of the human instructor, it does not necessarily rely upon complex machinery and it may retain the human instructor for some of the tutorial functions. In this article we will deal with programmed instruction, not automation.

Just as there are different ideas about what a good human tutor should do to teach effectively, there are different ideas about how programmed instruction should be implemented. One approach we will consider is that of Sidney L. Pressey, starting in the 1920s. Dr. Pressey was originally concerned with automating the testing process and developed machines that provided automatic scoring of multiple-choice tests.[5] Inasmuch as his machines gave feedback to the student indicating the correctness of each answer, they could also be used to teach drill material. Later, Pressey integrated the devices into courses of instruction that included the usual methods of lecture and text study. In this application, the devices provided "Adjunct Autoinstruction"—something new added to the usual methods of instruction. Pressey continues to recommend multiple-choice test items, never essay or short-answer tests. He believes more can be learned by distinguishing right answers from among wrong possibilities than from constructed answers.

Two distinct possibilities are presented by the self-testing idea. First, it is possible for the student to learn from the test itself. Second, it is possible for self-testing to make other sources of instruction more effective by showing the student where he is weak. For example, Figure 15–1 indicates both uses of self-testing.

Box A. shows that a student or group of students would be exposed to classroom lectures and demonstrations, or text book assignments, or both. After an hour or more of such study, the students would leave that activity (arrow 1). Students would then take multiple-choice tests (box B), finding out immediately what items they missed. Such a test might indicate that they needed more study or another lecture on the topic, or the test might indicate that the student had learned the material. In either case, he would return (arrow 2) for more conventional instruction. The dashed line (3) around box B shows that some learning can take place when self-tests are used in isolation from conventional instruction. Students can repeat the self-tests often enough to discover correct answers by "trial and error." This is sufficient for the learning of some material.

In recent articles Pressey urges reconsideration of "Adjunct Auto-

---

[5] [Editors' note: See Figure 1 in the appendix added to this article for a photo of such a device.]

FIGURE 15–1

Adjunct Autoinstruction

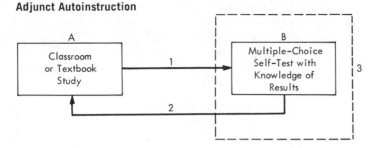

instruction." [6] He cites as one of its advantages that it employs conventional materials and approaches. We can retain our courses and materials as they are, and simply add multiple-choice self-testing. This certainly is easier to implement than other systems of programmed instruction, and experiments have shown that gains can be made from this procedure. [7] However, some educators and psychologists are quite concerned about the teaching effectiveness of lectures and ordinary texts. Group lectures, for example, may leave some students behind and, at the same time, be too easy for others. When the progress of an individual is tied to that of the group, we are confronted with a "lock step" in education and training. Also, the ever-increasing size of lecture groups makes any personal interaction between student and instructor most unlikely. With regard to textbooks, it is possible that their logical organization, sometimes amounting to a catalogue of facts, is not the best organization for teaching purposes. Even though self-testing adds to the effectiveness of orthodox methods in some cases, many feel that greater improvement may be expected from the design of better teaching procedures.

Intrinsic programming, a development of Norman A. Crowder, also relies upon text study as the main source of information. However, the texts are specially written to provide for different student needs. After each page of text, a single multiple-choice test item appears. A different page number is printed by each alternative answer. After a student selects the answer he thinks is correct, he turns to the page number given with that alternative. On that page he finds out if his choice was correct. If it was not, he has reached a "wrong answer" page which tells him he was wrong and gives additional explanation. He is then usually told to return to the page he just left and try the same item again. When his answer is correct, he reaches a "right answer" page which says "You are correct,"

---

[6] S. L. Pressey, "Teaching Machine (and Learning Theory) Crisis," *Journal of Applied Psychology* 47 (1963): 1–6; idem, "A Puncture of the Huge 'Programming' Boom," *Teachers College Record* 65 (1964), 413–18.

[7] J. K. Little, "Results of Use of Machines for Testing and for Drill upon Learning in Educational Psychology," *Journal of Experimental Education* 3 (1934): 45–49.

FIGURE 15–2

Intrinsic Programming

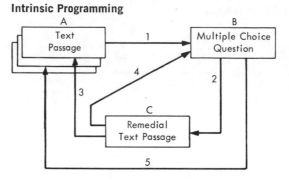

and continues with new material.[8] Figure 15–2 represents an intrinsic programming system.

Each student starts with box A which contains one or two paragraphs of text instruction. As arrow 1 indicates, students then go to a multiple-choice test question (box B). (This question is usually printed on the same page as the text instruction, but, since their functions are different, we show them in separate boxes.) At this point, students can branch out on their own, since they may choose different answers from the 2 to 5 alternatives usually given. (For this reason, intrinsic programs are also called branching programs.) Students who choose a wrong answer reach a page with remedial or corrective instruction, (arrow 2 to box C). They are then usually returned (arrow 3) to the same page they started with for restudy. However, they may simply be told to try the multiple-choice questions again (arrow 4). In either case, they eventually pick the right answer to the multiple-choice question. When this happens, they reach another page (arrow 5) which gives new material. Obviously, the branching procedure can be made complex. For example, remedial instruction might be followed by a test question which would be the occasion for more branching, and, conceivably, some branches could even advise a student to take a different course as a needed prerequisite. What we have diagramed here is both the simplest and most common form of intrinsic programming.

The largest evaluation of intrinsic programming was conducted by the Air Force at Keesler Air Force Base from 1960 to 1962. The subject matter was electronics, and programs were presented both in booklets and on a special film viewer. Results of the study were equivocal, with no improvement in amount learned, but some indication that time was saved over orthodox methods.

The system requires clear writing in text portions and the very greatest

---

[8] [Editors' note: See Figure 15–6 in the appendix to the article.]

FIGURE 15–3

A Linear Programming Frame

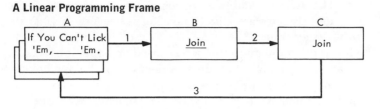

skill in construction of multiple-choice questions. Possible student mis-understanding must be anticipated by the alternatives presented and no correct answers must be "give-aways." If they are easy, students will get right answers even though they might not comprehend the material they have just read.

The last approach we will consider is called "Linear Programming," and is a development of B. F. Skinner. This represents the most ambitious attempt to overhaul orthodox means of instruction. Whereas lectures and texts have in the past concentrated on mere presentation, Skinner's approach concentrates on what the student is doing as well as on clear presentation. Active student responding and participation, in contrast to a passive manner of listening or reading, may be the key to improved educational efficiency.

A linear program looks like a series of incomplete sentences. Each sentence, along with the blank usually found at the end of it, is called a "frame." The sentences are so written that students can usually figure out what word should be used to complete the sentence. After writing in the word the student thinks should go in the blank, he turns the page or moves a masking device to reveal the right answer. When he sees that he has written the correct answer, that answer is said to be "reinforced." In the future, he will be likely to give the same answer under similar questioning conditions. Figure 15–3 is a diagram of a single linear frame. Thousands of such frames may be used in a complete program.

The incomplete sentence is found in box A. After considering what word to put in the blank, the student follows arrow 1 to box B where he writes out the word. (He may write directly in the sentence portion, or, in other cases, on a separate answer sheet, as diagramed here.) Then, as indicated by arrow 2, the student reaches box C where the correct answer is printed. He notes that he was correct and goes to the next frame (arrow 3). If his answer was wrong, he could correct it and go on. It is called a linear program because each student proceeds in a straight-line fashion; everyone takes the same frames in the same order. Students may differ, however, in the speed with which they work, and some may finish in half the time required by the slowest students. Although the first frames in a program would be easy for anyone to get right, later frames would be practically impossible unless the student had gone through the program. The frames gradually become more and more technical or "difficult," and students are able to take them because of what they have learned in earlier frames.[9]

The linear programming approach is based on, or, at least, analogous to, effective animal-training procedures worked out in the psychology laboratory. This has caused critics to be skeptical because people, of course, do differ from animals—most obviously in language skills. But this hardly constitutes proof that similar learning procedures will not work for different species, if properly adapted and applied.

In the next section we will examine some current research findings, especially for linear programming.

PRESENT

Research on learning and training methods presents special problems. The first requirement is to specify the goals of training. If these are not spelled out, then an advocate of one method or another can always say that some other goal was met by this method that was not sufficiently well measured in the experiment. Once all the goals have been defined, measurement techniques are necessary. It is not sufficient to specify "understanding" of a particular area because understanding cannot be measured directly. Instead, the exact performances and test items to be mastered are needed. Then the relative skill of students taught by different methods can be observed and measured. Developing that kind of test is time consuming.

In addition to these difficulties, there are two unsolved problems in educational research. First, student motivation over a short period may make any method look good. Related to motivation is the novelty effect, which may also mask real differences among methods. The second unsolved problem is that of control when human instructors are involved. During an experiment, instructors may act differently than they do day in and day out.

Perhaps for these reasons, most of the experiments done to compare various types of programmed instruction have shown "no significant differences." That is, even though the methods were varied systematically from group to group, the amount learned was so similar that statistical tests revealed no above-chance variations. Notwithstanding these problems, research does give valuable indications of training effectiveness, especially when pursued over extended periods. Brief experiments have their place, too. One of their purposes is to suggest the possible success of larger evaluations of the same approaches.

---

[9] [Editors' note: Figures 3 and 4 in the appendix illustrate a teaching machine and a linear program for use with this approach.]

By far most of the programs that have been written have been linear programs and most of the research on programmed instruction has centered on linear programming. Questions are raised about the efficiency of the approach. Current programs often take more time to complete than other means. To be balanced against this finding, however, are some of the inherent advantages of programmed instruction. Students can work individually, they can schedule themselves, and they can study at remote sites where other training would be impossible.

Textbooks can also be used in this manner, of course. However, they provide little structure for the study activity, and some students simply cannot learn well from ordinary printed matter. In other cases the text itself may be too difficult or confusing. A program tells the student just how to proceed, and the program is revised until it is clear. It is usually possible to guarantee a given level of learning if a program is used as directed.

Research results call into question some features of linear programming. The requirement for students to write out their responses has been shown unnecessary time and again. Students apparently learn just as much if they only "think" their answers, and they learn in much less time. There is an interesting exception, however. Cummings and Goldstein found that students actually had to draw complex diagrams rather than just think about how they would draw them.[10] The point is that written responses are necessary whenever the response itself is something new to be learned, like making accurate technical drawings. In addition, if the response is complex, the student needs to have written record to compare accurately with the given right answer. (During program development, there is no question that written responses are necessary because the programmer needs these to assess the clarity of each frame. The question relates only to routine use of fully developed programs.)

About 350 programs of all types are available. Costs vary from $2 to over $17, and lengths vary from under 50 to over 10,000 frames. Typical cost is $5 for a 1,000-frame program. These figures correspond to study times of under one hour to over 100 hours. The most common length is 1,000 frames, requiring ten hours of study. Mathematics is the most frequently programmed topic, with science subjects running second. Business education, economics, grammar, and social studies are also programmed. Catalogues of programs are available.[11] It is difficult to estimate how widespread is the use of programmed instruction. Most use, in public schools and colleges, is on an experimental basis so far. In-

---

[10] A. Cummings, and L. S. Goldstein, *The Effect of Overt and Covert Responding on Two Kinds of Learning Tasks* (New York: The Center for Programmed Instruction, 1962).

[11] C. H. Hendershot, *Programmed Learning—A Bibliography of Programs and Presentation Devices* (Copyright 1964 by Carl H. Hendershot, 4114 Ridgewood Drive, Bay City, Michigan 48707.)

dustry uses many programmed courses, and private individuals also use them for self-improvement. The Air Training Command of the US Air Force has trained a large number of programmers and is using programs in many locations.

Perhaps Pressey's adjunct autoinstruction has not attracted more research because it is so closely bound up with conventional lecture-text means. Investigators are content to believe that, even though adjunct autoinstruction has benefits in some situations, its value will always be affected by the conventional means employed. Improvement of the conventional means will be necessary to get the most out of Pressey's approach. In addition, the exclusive use of multiple-choice questioning seems arbitrary. Short-answer, constructed response items are valuable for some kinds of learning.[12]

An experiment on Crowder's intrinsic programming has been completed at the Behavioral Sciences Laboratory of the US Air Force. For the particular program studied, the branching feature did not improve its effectiveness. College students did just as well when all the branches were removed from a program on computer arithmetic.[13]

FUTURE

Programmed instruction, especially of the linear type, is causing many educators to view learning as a closed-loop system. The system output (learning) is fed back into the instructional materials so that deficiencies can be corrected. This is in contrast to a lecture series, for example, where student learning is measured infrequently, and deficiencies may not bring about changes in the lectures. Figure 15–4 shows how the instructional process may be viewed as a system.

The educator or manager (box A) realizes that certain training goals must be met for the effective functioning of society, or business, or a military organization. Therefore, he contacts a designer of instructional materials and procedures, who is often an author of programmed instruction (box B). The author considers the objectives presented by the manager, (arrow 1) and, interacting with the manager, (arrow 2) transforms them into measurable specifications. Typically, a criterion test is developed at this time that will indicate the extent to which goals of training will be met by the materials yet to be developed. The author then selects one or two students (box C) to try out short portions of his materials. He administers the materials (arrow 3) and receives immediate knowledge of their effectiveness (arrow 4). Through this process, he re-

---

[12] J. P. Williams, "The Effectiveness of Constructed Response and Multiple-Choice Programming Modes as a Function of Test Mode," submitted for publication, 1964.

[13] R. J. Senter et al., "An Evaluation of Branching and Motivational Phrases in a Scrambled Book," Tech. Doc. Rep. no. AMRL-TRD-63-122, 6570th Aerospace Medical Research Laboratories, Wright-Patterson AFB, Ohio, November 1963.

FIGURE 15–4

A System View of Instruction

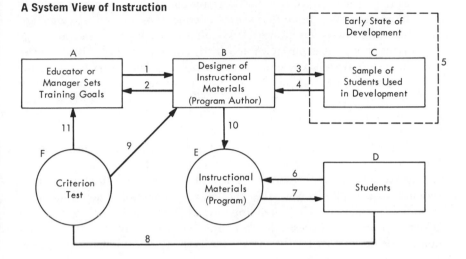

vises materials until a potentially effective course has been designed. Typically, this process is used early in development, and then eliminated, as indicated by dashed line 5. Once the program or other material is written, it is used by students (box D) in a routine manner. They write, or perhaps just "think" their responses to the program (arrow 6). They find out from the program whether their responses are correct (arrow 7). After finishing the entire program (circle E) the students, following arrow 8, take the criterion test (circle F). Results of this test are fed (arrow 9) to the author. If results are unsatisfactory, he will revise the program (arrow 10) to make it more effective. In some cases the author may revert to the use of sample students as in box C. Program revisions can be continued until the criterion test is passed by a required proportion of qualified students. At this stage we can refer to the program as "validated instruction." The educator or manager may receive criterion test results from the programmer, or he may prefer to look for himself (arrow 11). The many feedback loops in this system make it possible for effective materials and procedures to be developed.

The fields of education and training are undergoing many changes. The most significant of these are the press of increasing student enrollments, and the increasing levels of skill required of graduates to cope with the problems of our technological age. Programmed instruction will help alleviate these problems to some extent. The future will probably see greater use on a routine basis of well-designed programs in all subject-matter areas. Such use can reduce classroom burdens of instructors and make high-quality training available on an individual basis to students at home or during leisure hours. But training methods will also benefit from the side effects, or implications, of programmed instruction. These are better specifications of the goals of any course, with a corresponding drop in nonessential content; better assessment of the effectiveness of any educational procedure; and the system's concept of education.

Valuable though it is, programmed instruction does not by itself represent a final solution to many educational problems. There is still a need for student contact with teachers, especially in discussions. There is still a need for student contacts with other students for formal and informal discussions and mutual help. There is still a need for excellent reference books, texts, films, recordings, libraries and laboratories.

One possibility being considered for the future is called "independent study," or "self-directed study." In this situation the teacher becomes a manager of instructional resources, and provides enough direction so that students can capitalize on the materials presented, (including programmed instruction). Class meetings are reduced, but small group discussions are increased. In cases where this has been explored, it has been found to work not only for the most intelligent students, but to be feasible also for the average or less qualified students.[14]

Perhaps the future will reveal that a far-reaching consequence of programmed instruction is the insistence upon proof that a given method or course really works. It makes good sense that procedures should be tried often enough and revised frequently enough to insure course effectiveness. Significantly, it is only through student responses that we can judge whether any given training procedure has been effective. These same responses are also important for the student's efficient progress through a course. The basic philosophy of programmed instruction is certainly a permanent contribution which will have an important effect upon future educational and training methods.

---

[14] S. Baskins, "Experiment in Independent Study (1956–1960)," *Antioch College Reports* (Antioch College, Yellow Springs, Ohio, 1961).

APPENDIX *

Some Illustrations of Teaching Machines and Programmed Materials

FIGURE 15–5

Pressey's self-testing machine. The device directs the student to a particular item in a multiple-choice test. The student presses the key corresponding to his choice of answer. If his choice is correct, the device advances to the next item. Errors are totaled.

Source: B. F. Skinner, "Teaching Machines," *Science* 128 (1958): 769–77.

---

* This appendix has been added by the Editors.

FIGURE 15–6

An example from an intrinsic branching program in mathematics. The student first reads a passage and then attempts to answer the multiple-choice question at the bottom of the page. Each different answer has an associated page number which directs the student to another page. Incorrect answers branch him to remedial sequences. The correct answer directs the student to a page which confirms his answer, and presents the next step in the program.

Page 101:

Now, you recall that we had just defined

$$b^0 = 1$$

for any b except where $b = 0$. We had reached this definition by noting that our division rule,

$$\frac{b^m}{b^n} = b^{(m-n)}$$

will give b^0 as a result if we apply it to the case of dividing a number by itself. Thus,

$$\frac{b^3}{b^3} = b^{(3-3)} = b^0$$

but

$$\frac{b^3}{b^3}, \text{ or any number (except 0),}$$

divided by itself equals 1, so we defined $b^0 = 1$.

We used a division process to find a meaning to attach to the exponent 0. Very well, let's see what other interesting results we can get with this division process. Let's apply our division rule to the case of $\frac{b^2}{b^3}$. What result do we get?

ANSWER	PAGE
$\frac{b^2}{b^3} = b^1$	94
$\frac{b^2}{b^3} = b^{(-1)}$	115
The rule won't work in this case	119

Source: N. A. Crowder, "Automatic Tutoring by Means of Intrinsic Programming," in *Teaching Machines and Programmed Learning*, ed. A. L. Lumsdaine and R. Glaser (Washington, D.C.: National Education Association, 1960): 286–98.

FIGURE 15–6 (Continued)

The student who elects page 94 will find:

Page 94:

YOUR ANSWER: $\dfrac{b^2}{b^3} = b^1$

Come, come, now. The rule is

$$\frac{b^m}{b^n} = b^{(m-n)}.$$

Now, in the case of

$$\frac{b^2}{b^3},$$

we have $m = 2$ and $n = 3$, so we are going to get

$$\frac{b^2}{b^3} = b^{(2-3)}.$$

So, $2 - 3$ isn't 1, is it? It's –1.

Return to Page 101, now, and quit fighting the problem.

The student who elects page 119 will find:

Page 119:

YOUR ANSWER: The rule won't work in this case.

Courage! The division rule got us through b^0, where $m = n$, and it will get us through the case where m is smaller than n. In this case we have

$$\frac{b^2}{b^3} = ?$$

and applying the rule

$$\frac{b^m}{b^n} = b^{(m-n)}$$

we get

$$\frac{b^2}{b^3} = b^{(2-3)}.$$

So the exponent of our quotient is $(2 - 3)$ which is –1, isn't it? So just write

$$\frac{b^2}{b^3} = b^{(2-3)} = b^{(-1)}$$

as if you knew what it meant.

Now return to Page 101 and choose the right answer.

FIGURE 15–6 (Continued)

And the student who chooses the right answer will find:

Page 115:

YOUR ANSWER: $\dfrac{b^2}{b^3} = b^{(-1)}$

You are correct. Using our rule for division

$$\frac{b^m}{b^n} = b^{(m-n)}$$

in the case of

$$\frac{b^2}{b^3}$$

we get

$$\frac{b^2}{b^3} = b^{(2-3)} = b^{(-1)}.$$

Now, by ordinary arithmetic, we can see that

$$\frac{b^2}{b^3} = \frac{b \times b}{b \times b \times b} = \frac{\cancel{b} \times \cancel{b}}{\cancel{b} \times \cancel{b} \times b} = ?$$

So how shall we define $b^{(-1)}$?

ANSWER	PAGE
$b^{(-1)} = \dfrac{0}{b}$	95
$b^{(-1)} = \dfrac{1}{b}$	104

FIGURE 15–7

A teaching machine using a linear program. One frame of material is partly visible in the left-hand window. The student writes his response on a strip of paper exposed at the right. He then lifts a lever with his left hand, advancing his written response under a transparent cover and uncovering the correct response in the upper corner of the frame. If he is right, he moves the lever to the right, punching a hole alongside the response he has called right thus altering the machine so that that frame will not appear again when he goes through the series a second time. A new frame appears when the lever is returned to its starting position.

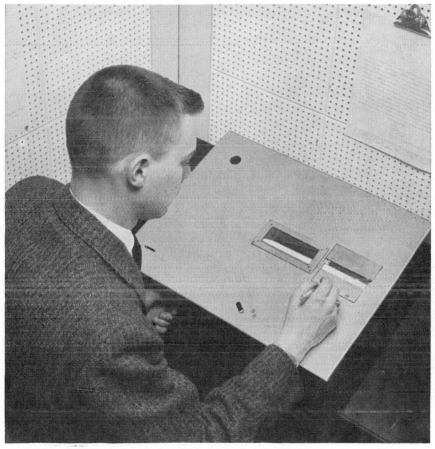

Source: B. F. Skinner, "Teaching Machines," *Science* 128 (1958): 769–77.

FIGURE 15-8

Part of a Linear Program in High-School Physics

The machine in Figure 15–7 presents one item at a time. The student completes the item and then uncovers the corresponding word or phrase shown at the right.

Sentence to Be Completed	*Word to Be Supplied*
1. The important parts of a flashlight are the battery and the bulb. When we "turn on" a flashlight, we close a switch which connects the battery with the ——.	bulb
2. When we turn on a flashlight, an electric current flows through the fine wire in the ——and causes it to grow hot.	bulb
3. When the hot wire glows brightly, we say that it gives off or sends out heat and ——.	light
4. The fine wire in the bulb is called a filament. The bulb "lights up" when the filament is heated by the passage of a(n) —— current.	electric
5. When a weak battery produces little current, the fine wire, or ——, does not get very hot.	filament
6. A filament which is *less* hot sends out or gives off —— light.	less
7. "Emit" means "send out." The amount of light sent out, or "emitted," by a filament depends on how —— the filament is.	hot
8. The higher the temperature of the filament the —— the light emitted by it.	brighter, stronger
9. If a flashlight battery is weak, the —— in the bulb may still glow, but with only a dull red color.	filament
10. The light from a very hot filament is colored yellow or white. The light from a filament which is not very hot is colored ——.	red
11. A blacksmith or other metal worker sometimes makes sure that a bar of iron is heated to a "cherry red" before hammering it into shape. He uses the —— of the light emitted by the bar to tell how hot it is.	color
12. Both the color and the amount of light depend on the —— of the emitting filament or bar.	temperature
13. An object which emits light because it is hot is called "incandescent." A flashlight bulb is an incandescent source of ——.	light
14. A neon tube emits light but remains cool. It is, therefore, not an incandescent —— of light.	source
15. A candle flame is hot. It is a(n) —— source of light.	incandescent
16. The hot wick of a candle gives off small pieces or particles of carbon which burn in the flame. Before or while burning, the hot particles send out, or ——, light.	emit
17. A long candlewick produces a flame in which oxygen does not reach all the carbon particles. Without oxygen the particles cannot burn. Particles which do not burn rise above the flame as ——.	smoke
18. We can show that there are particles of carbon in a candle flame, even when it is not smoking, by holding a piece of metal in the flame. The metal cools some of the particles before they burn, and the unburned carbon —— collect on the metal as soot.	particles
19. The particles of carbon in soot or smoke no longer emit light because they are —— than when they were in the flame.	cooler, colder
20. The reddish part of a candle flame has the same color as the filament in a flashlight with a weak battery. We might guess that the yellow or white parts of a candle flame are —— than the reddish part.	hotter
21. "Putting out" an incandescent electric light means turning off the current so that the filament grows too —— to emit light.	cold, cool
22. Setting fire to the wick of an oil lamp is called —— the lamp.	lighting
23. The sun is our principal —— of light, as well as of heat.	source

Source: B. F. Skinner, "Teaching Machines," *Science* 128 (1958): 769–77.

FIGURE 15–8 (Continued)

Sentence to Be Completed	*Word to Be Supplied*
24. The sun is not only very bright but very hot. It is a powerful ―― source of light.	incandescent
25. Light is a form of energy. In "emitting light" an object changes, or "converts," one form of ―― into another.	energy
26. The electrical energy supplied by the battery in a flashlight is converted to ―― and ――.	heat, light; light, heat
27. If we leave a flashlight on, all the energy stored in the battery will finally be changed or ―― into heat and light.	converted
28. The light from a candle flame comes from the ―― released by chemical changes as the candle burns.	energy
29. A nearly "dead" battery may make a flashlight bulb warm to the touch, but the filament may still not be hot enough to emit light―in other words, the filament will not be ―― at that temperature.	incandescent
30. Objects, such as a filament, carbon particles, or iron bars, become incandescent when heated to about 800 degrees Celsius. At that temperature they begin to ―― ――.	emit light
31. When raised to any temperature above 800 degrees Celsius, an object such as an iron bar will emit light. Although the bar may melt or vaporize, its particles will be ―― no matter how hot they get.	incandescent
32. About 800 degrees Celsius is the lower limit of the temperature at which particles emit light. There is no upper limit of the ―― at which emission of light occurs.	temperature
33. Sunlight is ―― by very hot gases near the surface of the sun.	emitted
34. Complex changes similar to an atomic explosion generate the great heat which explains the ―― of light by the sun.	emission
35. Below about ―― degrees Celsius an object is not an incandescent source of light.	800

FIGURE 15–9

A "Programmed Envelope." Steps (or "frames") of the program were typed on 8½ by 11 inch sheets, with 10 or 12 frames on each page. The pages were inserted into the envelope, with a flap extending to conceal the correct answers. After the student makes his response, he pulls the page further out of the envelope to reveal both the correct answer to that frame and the next frame to be read. This particular program is for training salesgirls for a large department store. The results of an evaluation study found that, in terms of salesgirl performance scores, this method of presenting the program was just as good as use of the same program in a more elaborate teaching machine; and both methods of programmed instruction were superior to a lecture-demonstration method.

Source: Summarized by the Editors from J. S. Abma, "The Development and Evaluation of a Programmed Training Course for Sales Personnel," *Journal of the American Society of Training Directors* 16 (1962): 20–29.

16. MANAGEMENT GAMES FOR TRAINING DECISION-MAKERS *

William R. Dill

MANAGEMENT GAMES are a recent innovation in business school teaching and research programs. The excitement and confusion that they have generated is evident in recent articles in *Business Week*,[1] and a symposium held at the University of Kansas in December, 1958.[2] It already seems apparent that when the dust settles, gaming will bring the same kind of basic changes to our methods for training managers that the "case method" and renewed emphasis on fundamental subjects like economics, statistics and the behavioral sciences have brought.

THE CONCEPT OF "GAMING"

Gaming is not a new concept. Management games are close cousins to the "war games" that military groups pioneered many years ago. Businesses and business schools cannot even claim credit for the first games that involved the use of electronic computers to simulate the actions of the environment. Here the Air Force had a head start in setting up elaborate man-machine simulations of the military environment to design logistics organizations and to train personnel for air defense work.[3]

The concept of a management decision game is simple. One or more teams, each representing a "firm," make a series of decisions governing their firms' operations during the next period of play. Then a "model" of how the industry or the economy operates is used to figure out for each team the outcomes of their decisions. If the "model" is simple, calculations can be made by a human referee; otherwise, they are made by computer. The teams get partial or complete information about the results of their decisions and then make new decisions for the next period. A period of play in the different games that are now available represents

* From "A New Environment for Training Decision Makers—The Carnegie Management Game" (Carnegie Institute of Technology, Graduate School of Industrial Administration, 1960).
    [1] "The Gentle Art of Simulation," *Business Week*, 29 November 1958; "In Business Education, the Game's the Thing," *Business Week*, 25 July 1959.
    [2] *Proceedings of the First National Symposium on Management Games* (Lawrence: University of Kansas, Bureau of Business Research, December 1958).
    [3] R. M. Bauner, "Laboratory Evaluation of Supply and Procurement Procedures," Rand Paper R-323, July 1958; S. Enke, "On the Economic Management of Large Organizations," *Journal of Business*, October 1958.

FIGURE 16–1

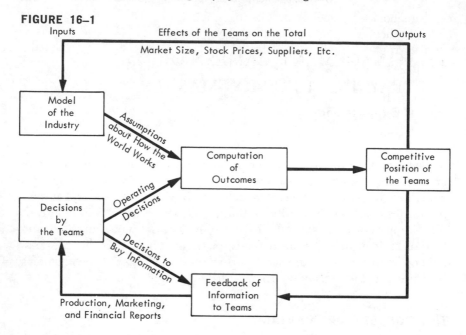

anything from a week to a year of "real time" in the life of the industry. The process is diagrammed in Figure 16–1.

The early business games were relatively simple in structure. The first was developed by the American Management Association for their executive training seminars.[4] Similar games were devised by James R. Jackson at UCLA,[5] Truman Hunter at IBM, and Albert Schrieber at the University of Washington.[6] Andlinger of McKinsey and Company has published a simpler game that does not require a computer.[7] All these games ask teams of four or five players to make about a dozen decisions every "quarter" about price; gross production rates; and overall expenditures for things like research, sales promotion, and plant investment. Players have 15–30 minutes to make each set of decisions, and they need wait only a few minutes before they know the results. In one day of play, teams can simulate several years of actual business operations.

These games are labeled as general management training devices because the teams must make decisions concerning all three basic manage-

---

[4] L. A. Appley, "Executive Decision-Making: A New Strategy," *Think,* December 1957; J. McDonald and F. Ricciardi, "The Business Decision Game," *Fortune,* March 1958.

[5] J. R. Jackson, "Learning from Experience in Business Decision Games," *California Management Review,* Winter 1959.

[6] A. N. Schrieber, "Gaming—A New Way to Teach Business Decision Making," *University of Washington Business Review,* April 1958.

[7] G. R. Andlinger, "Business Games—Play One!" *Harvard Business Review,* March–April 1958.

ment functions—production, marketing, and finance. The total number of decisions they must make and the amounts of information they have about what goes on within each functional area, however, are very small.

Emphasis in these simple games is placed on making good judgments under time pressure, more than on the analysis of complex problem situations. It does not take many moves or large amounts of skill to deduce effective strategies for playing the simple games because the models of the environment from which outcomes are computed are relatively simple. Players have found the games challenging, and they claim to have gained some insight into the problems of general management. They are not likely to see the relation between these and the problems of specialized areas of production or finance, though, because the latter are not built into the early games with sufficient detail.

Even the simplest games have proved challenging and exciting to play —in part because of their novelty appeal, but to a large extent because they give players a chance to experiment with different kinds of decisions and to get first hand feedback about their results. It is easier in a game than in a discussion of "case problems" to give students or managers an indication of the cumulative influence of their decisions on company performance.

The limits of simple games, though, are readily apparent. Managing a company involves more than making a small number of general policy decisions under time pressure. An executive has hundreds of decisions he can make in a month or a quarter; his skill, to a large extent, lies in knowing which ones he should make.

An effective manager must be able to abstract information from a complex environment under time pressure. He must decide which problems are worth attention, and he must continually evaluate how well his organization is doing. He is expected to develop alternative courses of action and to make decisions that will benefit the organization under conditions where it is hard to predict what the outcome of a decision will be. He has to translate his general decisions into programs of action that specialized units of the organization can—and will—carry through.

THE CARNEGIE MANAGEMENT GAME

The Carnegie management game has been developed to mirror more realistically the problems of running a company. We have deliberately made our game slower to play in order to make it more complex and more challenging for players.

For example, in earlier games, if players choose a specific production level, they get that much output. To get a desired level of output, players in the Carnegie game must do more than request it. They have to worry about maintenance, overtime policies, hiring policies, raw materials purchasing, and other variables that affect the extent to which scheduled production and actual output coincide. Instead of making a dozen decisions every "quarter," players in the Carnegie game have to record between 100 and 300 decisions for every "month" of simulated time. To make these decisions, they get on a regular basis or through special purchase several hundred pieces of information about their own performance and about their relations with competitors, suppliers, customers, and financial institutions.

The easiest way to describe the Carnegie game is to present it as it appears to the players. Three teams of players form the "industry" in the Carnegie game. Each set of decisions covers a month of operating time.

Each team has one factory, located in the Central Region. At the factory, there is a raw materials warehouse and a warehouse for finished goods. Factory facilities can be used interchangeably to produce different mixes of product. In each of the four marketing regions, a team leases a district warehouse for finished goods, from which deliveries are made to the wholesalers and retailers who are the customers in the game.

All products which the teams can make can be manufactured from a basic set of seven raw materials which must be ordered from suppliers one to three months before they are delivered to the factory. Raw material prices fluctuate, and discounts are available for prompt payment of bills to suppliers.

The players schedule production; but to get what they schedule, they must make sensible decisions about raw materials, maintenance, changes in plant capacity, overtime, hiring, and firing. Finished goods can be consigned to any of the five warehouses; and within cost and time constraints on transshipments, can be moved from one warehouse to another. Inventory run-outs at a warehouse carry penalties for future sales.

Products are not available for delivery to customers until the month following their manufacture. Sales in any one month depend on the total market for detergents; on consumers' reactions to product characteristics such as "sudsiness"; and on the teams' decisions about advertising, price, and outlays for sales promotion. Consumer behavior may not be the same in the four market regions.

By spending money for product research, teams can generate new products. Not all new products will be worth marketing, though, and laboratory reports on their characteristics will be only partially reliable. A team must buy market surveys to get better, but still not perfect, estimates of consumer reactions to new products. A team must also spend for market research to get information about what consumers think of their current products and to get estimates of competitors' prices and expenditures by product and region for advertising and sales promotion.

The teams can expand production facilities and the central warehouses by building new facilities, but new construction takes six months to complete. Additional space in the district warehouses can be leased as needed. Expenditures for maintenance must be large enough to cover repair and renovation of existing facilities.

To finance their operations, players will start the game with a reserve of cash and government bonds. If they need additional funds, they can defer the payment of bills and negotiate bank loans in the short run (30–60 days). By making application four to six months in advance, they can obtain funds by issuing debentures or common stock. Funds from outside sources are available only if the company's financial position satisfies a number of realistic constraints.

Teams must plan and budget carefully to survive. For some sequences of action, plans must be made 12 to 15 months ahead to achieve desired results. In addition to the regular obligations for raw materials, production, marketing, and research, the teams must deal with such other financial variables as depreciation, income taxes, dividends, and investments in new construction.

The information that players receive and the decisions they must make are summarized in Figure 16–2.

The game is mutually being played at the rate of one or two moves a week with graduate student teams during the regular school year. Because we believe that organizing to make decisions and to plan for effective long-run performance is an important element in the game, we are using teams of seven to ten players to represent each company. A great deal of emphasis is put on discussing results with the teams. They review their moves with faculty members during class sessions of courses like Marketing or Business Policy that can contribute to playing the game. Periodically, players must report on their performance and their plans to a faculty board of directors. Faculty reactions to the reports are one of the factors that determine the going price for each company's stock.

The complexity of the Carnegie game makes it slow and expensive to play. Making a set of decisions takes two to three hours, not 15 minutes; and teams need to play 30 or 50 moves in order to experience the long-run consequences of their decisions. The computation of results for each move ties up an IBM 650 computer (with a RAMAC memory unit) for about 45 minutes. Faculty guidance and supervision takes a great deal of time.

THE REASONS FOR COMPLEXITY

Why, then, is the Carnegie game so complex? We believe, first of all, that complexity is an essential ingredient in training good "problem solvers"—men who can succeed as innovators and managers in a diverse and rapidly changing industrial environment.

Simpler games tend to fall in two categories: those which are challenging because in time it is possible to develop something close to an optimal strategy for playing the game and those which are challenging because

FIGURE 16–2

Information Received and Decisions Made in the Carnegie Game

Information

At Start of Game	Monthly	As Requested or Required
Historical data on operations.	Balance sheet.	Statement of construction obligations.
Constraints on policy and operations.	Income statements.	Statement on loans and securities.
Instructions for organizations and play.	Statement of inventory position.	Availability of financing.
Hints about strategy.	Status of plant and equipment.	Inventory losses.
	Receipts and disbursements.	Product preference tests.
	Financial commitments.	New product descriptions.
	Report on money market.	Market survey data.
	Cost of raw materials.	
Quarterly	Cost of goods sold.	
	Raw materials usage and inventory.	
Balance sheets, income statements for competitors.	Warehouse stocks and shipments.	
	Finished product inventories.	
	Work force and equipment down time data.	
	Deliveries to customers.	

Decisions

Monthly	As Desired
Advertising, distributions expenditures.	Applications for financing.
Price levels.	Market and product research expenditures.
Sales forecasts.	New construction.
Raw material orders.	
Payment of current obligations.	
Amount of production.	
Allocation of products to regions.	
Number of workers.	
Overtime authorized.	
Maintenance expenditures.	

they involve making a small number of critical, risky decisions under time pressure. Through its complexity, the Carnegie game gives players more information than they can easily use in making decisions and presents them with important problems of codifying and evaluating information to interpret the environment and understand the results of their decisions. The players learn, if they have not already learned, that different indices of performance (like profit and rate of growth) do not always correlate. They find that decisions faced in any one month are closely related to events in past and future months.

A spokesman for one of the early games says that his game teaches mainly that the world is complicated, and that company decisions are interdependent. We accomplish this, but by challenging players with a complex set of problems and by spending lots of time discussing the results, we hope to help them learn ways to beat complexity by systematic analysis. There is no simple analytic method that will guarantee success in the game, but there are many ways that players can profitably apply basic problem-solving concepts to help arrive at a good strategy. The basic ideas of marginal analysis from economics, for example, can furnish a framework for evaluating the effects of advertising expenditures or price changes, but the complexity of the market and the inherent limits to the reliability of market information soon force the players to recognize the dangers of overreliance on simple economic models. Similarly, players who understand statistical sampling theory can use this knowledge to estimate how much they need to spend on market research to get information with a given degree of precision from competitors. Those who do not know elementary concepts of statistical sampling can learn them in the context of the game.

A second reason for building a complex game is that it permits an organization with differentiated roles. We believe that there are very few executives who are concerned only with overall company decisions, to the exclusion of detailed problems in production, finance, or marketing. Even in large companies, the top vice presidents are generally vice presidents over a function or a group of functions. The executive, in our view, must be both generalist and specialist; and some of his most difficult moments come when he must compromise his ideas as a specialist to satisfy the requirements of other functions in the organization.

In the Carnegie game, players have the dual role of specialist and generalist. Each of the three major functional areas of the game—production, marketing, or finance—presents problems as complex as those presented by the simpler general management games. Yet, in the Carnegie game, there is a genuine interdependence among functions at several levels that makes the effective coordination of production, financial, and marketing operations vital to success in the game.

A third reason for complexity is to provide players with organizational as well as analytical experience. One shortcoming of the simpler games is that they are played by small, homogeneous teams. Efforts to use larger teams or to impose hierarchical patterns of organization seldom work out because the task does not warrant such steps. In the Carnegie game, we believe we have an environment that can keep teams of seven to ten men busy planning, deciding on moves, and evaluating earlier performance. With teams of this size, whose members have differentiated functions to perform, we can expect (and by control of external conditions, can help induce) some of the symptoms of bureaucracy and some of the problems of rank and status that men have to deal with in real organizations.

By complexity, then, we hope to achieve a game which fits with

Carnegie's emphasis on the importance of systematic analysis and problem-solving strategies in the mastery of managerial problems. We hope to make players aware of the problems of overall coordination at the top management level in business, but we also hope to fit them for the role they will play for most of their careers—the role of the functional specialist in interaction with other specialists at his own level on problems that involve conflict and compromise. We hope, finally, to provide experience in interpersonal interaction that involves not only the kinds of relations we find in small face-to-face groups, but in formalized organizational situations.

Complexity, we might also argue, is necessary if the game is to be realistic. We have placed considerable value on making our game like the detergent industry, but it would obscure the issue to say that this was a major objective. A truly realistic game might take a lifetime to play. The kind of realism we have tried to achieve is a realism in the behavioral demands that we make on players, not a realism in the model we use to represent the world. The job of the players is to diagnose the model that we have used and to develop effective strategies for working against it and their competitors. If the model requires the kinds of approaches to diagnosis and decision-making that the players will use in later life, it does not really matter whether the model is a mirror image of a real industry.

We do not insist, for example, in teaching mathematics to engineers that all the practice problems be drawn from engineering. They can be phrased in other terms so long as the basic methods of solution are taught and practiced.

THE VALUE OF DEVELOPING GAMES

We are only beginning to assess the potential of management games in general, and of the Carnegie game in particular. An important dividend of gaming—and one not often mentioned—is its effect on the men who develop it. It has taken a year and a half to get the Carnegie game ready for trial runs. As a first step, those of us who worked on the game had to agree on its basic structure. In doing this, we raised fundamental questions about what we were trying to teach and about the nature of the industry we had decided to simulate. It is one thing to say that the sale of detergents in a given month depends on advertising expenditures, on price, and on product characteristics; it is quite another to specify *how* sales depends on these variables in a way that makes sense both to an experienced soap salesman and to an electronic computer. Hundreds of questions of this kind had to be answered.

The final computer program which governs the play of the game contains about 20,000 separate instructions and several thousand "words" of data.

We have gained almost as much in the process of developing the game as we will in playing it. The men who planned the game had a variety of special interests in fields like marketing, finance, production, organization theory, and information processing. Simply to design the game and to carry through the designs to an operating computer program and a set of instructions for players, we have faced basic questions of how to educate our students, how a real industry operates from month to month in a complex environment, and how we simulate industrial operations on the computer. Our efforts to answer these questions will not only help us design better decision games, but will also help us do a better job with many other aspects of our task of training managers.

THE CARNEGIE GAME AS A WAY OF LEARNING HOW TO MANAGE

The educational benefits for ourselves of developing a management game seem obvious. What, though, are the benefits of playing a game like the Carnegie game? Some of these have already been suggested, but it will be worthwhile to summarize them here.

Games are an important innovation in management training because they are the only means, short of real on-the-job experience, of putting trainees—whether students or executives—up against an environment which responds definitely and consistently to all the different strategies that the trainees may try and of forcing trainees to make and "live with" sequences of decisions over time. Even at current levels, the computational capacities of the electronic computer make it a better and more reliable source of estimates about how the world will react to certain kinds of decisions than discussion leaders who have only limited, second-hand information about the effects that decisions will create.

Games are also effective for teaching men to deal with a changing world. Case problems, drawn from actual company experiences, tend to focus on the world as it was; games, with careful development, can present the world as it *may be* five, ten, or twenty years ahead, when the men who are now trainees become managers.

Simple games are useful as "ice-breakers"—as ways of raising questions for exploration and discussion in other parts of a training program. Complex games, like the Carnegie game, though, seem to have real promise for posing trainees with problems like those that managers face. Players must be able to separate the important from the trivial in the large masses of information that they receive, that they can buy, or that they can produce for themselevs. They must decide which of the decisions that they might make are worth making. They must plan and coordinate because decisions cannot be taken in isolation. To make better decisions, they can apply many of the concepts and tools they learn in courses or in their work experience; but analytic prowess alone will not guarantee good results.

We already have some evidence from trial runs that these effects are achieved in the Carnegie game and that, in addition, organizing as a team to play the game is a challenging experience for participants.

To be successful as a means for learning how to manage, though, any game requires large amounts of time for the discussion and analysis of results. In playing the Carnegie game with graduate students and executives, we are not only making teams report to boards of directors; we are also working with them on various aspects of their performance in other kinds of courses. The game is meant to supplement, not to replace other sorts of training.

Enthusiasm for games as *the* method for teaching management should be tempered by these observations:

1. Playing games will not produce the "complete manager." No games yet conceived really incorporate the problems that managers have in interacting with subordinates in the organization to explain, introduce, and implement decisions. In fact, one real danger of the game for naive players is that they will become accustomed to getting all the information they need from a computer. In industry, though, they will need also to know how to get information and ideas from workers, clerks, engineers, salesmen, and the like. Organizational and labor problems can be built into the game; but so far only in a way which de-emphasizes the importance of skillful person-to-person dealings with other individuals and groups outside the top management group.

2. Particularly if we succeed at making games realistic, we may accentuate the problem that some bright young men already have when they go into industry. Now instead of "thinking" they know how to run a company, they may really "believe" from their experience with a game that they can run a company better than its present managers. A manager is judged in the final analysis, not by the amount he knows about performing well in his previous environment, but by his agility to adapt to new environmental demands.

3. It is not appropriate to try to create games simply on the principle of duplicating existing or anticipated conditions in industry. Our job is to train men to learn and develop in the face of constantly changing problems, not to train them to solve some particular set of problems that have been important or typical in the past. Games are only effective if they prepare men to look ahead and to continue learning from their experiences. We cannot hope to anticipate accurately many of the problems they are going to be called on to solve.

The Carnegie game is being used initially with graduate students and executives as a "laboratory" assignment which supplements the regular courses. It presents an opportunity for students to integrate, to apply, and to evaluate the things they have learned in more traditional ways. If early experiences are borne out, it also feeds back on courses such as economics, production, or administration by stimulating players to seek knowledge and strategies which they can use in the game.

USES OF THE CARNEGIE GAME IN RESEARCH

In addition to helping to educate business school faculty members and young men who want to become managers, we hope that the Carnegie game, and others like it, will become valuable settings for research. At the most obvious level, we need research that will tell us more precisely what we are accomplishing when we use the game as part of our educational programs. Our confidence in the educational value of the simpler management games rests more heavily than it should on the testimony of men who have played them. Players enjoy the experience, and they are sure that they learned a great deal from it. But, when pressed, as one industrial training expert has reported, players have a hard time saying what they learned.

We need comparative analysis of the educational effects of the Carnegie game, of simpler and more specialized games, and of alternative patterns of teaching (such as the "case method" or "role playing").

In addition to doing research *on* the Carnegie game, though, it is important that we do research *with* it. Two of the many research possibilities are of immediate interest to managers. The first is the possibility that something like the Carnegie game, which lies midway between the simplicity of the behavioral science laboratory and the complexity of the real world, can serve as a bridge between the two. Concerning leadership, for example, we have many findings that stem from psychological and sociological experiments involving small groups and simple task assignments. The applicability of such findings to real life situations may be explored at an intermediate level among groups of seven to ten people playing the Carnegie game.

Conversely, much of the businessman's "folklore" about leadership can be evaluated more effectively in the game environment than in real life because, in the game, it is possible to eliminate or to control the effects of many extraneous variables. To the extent that the Carnegie game provides a realistic simulation of industrial conditions, we can plan and carry through experiments that will compare the gains and costs associated with different policies for action or with different styles of organization.

More basically, the Carnegie game will permit the exploration of fundamental questions in organization theory and in the theory of the firm. Field research that involves observation of on-going organizational processes and decisions is expensive to conduct; and in the field situation, experimental controls are difficult to impose. We plan to use the Carnegie game partly as a substitute for field studies and partly as a preparation for doing field research more effectively. Among the questions we plan to explore are these:

1. What effects do time constraints, initial job assignments, and restrictions on communication among players have on the speed with which teams organize, on the kinds of organization that they develop, and on the amount of long-range planning and budgeting that they do?

2. Under conditions where players do not have time to reconsider all possible decisions every month, how do they decide which problems deserve attention? How does the choice of problems that a team will work on affect its performance against competition?

3. By varying the number and size of firms in an industry, what changes do we observe in competitive patterns (decisions on price, advertising, product research, and so forth).

4. In what ways does a team's pattern of organization affect its short- and long-run performance? Does a team which is allowed to develop its own organization structure, for example, perform better or worse against competition than a team whose organization has been imposed by the Board of Directors?

17. LABORATORY EDUCATION: IMPACT ON PEOPLE AND ORGANIZATIONS *

Marvin D. Dunnette and John P. Campbell

By LABORATORY EDUCATION we mean those personnel and organizational development and training courses which combine traditional training features—such as lectures, group problem-solving sessions, and role-planning—with T-group or sensitivity training techniques.[1] Laboratory education is being used more and more by industry. No national statistics are available on total volume or frequency of use, but it is clear that consumer demand is high.[2] The National Training Laboratories and the Western Training Laboratories conduct programs for hundreds of industrial man-

---

* Adapted and extracted from *Industrial Relations* 8 (1968): 1–27.

[1] For detailed accounts of the basic T-group method, see descriptions given by S. Klaw, "Two Weeks in a T-Group," *Fortune* 64 (1961): 114–17; A. H. Kuriloff and S. Atkins, "T-Group for a Work Team," *Journal of Applied Behavioral Science* 2 (1966): 63–94; R. Tannenbaum, I. R. Weschler, and F. Massarik, *Leadership and Organization: A Behavioral Science Approach* (New York: McGraw-Hill Book Co., 1961); and I. R. Weschler and J. Reisel, *Inside a Sensitivity Training Group* (Los Angeles: Institute of Industrial Relations, University of California, 1959).

[2] For example, see R. J. House, "T-Group Education and Leadership Effectiveness: A Review of Empirical Literature and a Critical Evaluation," *Personnel Psychology* 20 (1967): 1–32; or the latest *Information Brochure* (1967) describing the 21st Annual Summer Laboratories sponsored by the National Training Laboratories.

agers each year. Many consulting firms now offer such training as a standard part of their bill of fare; many colleges and universities incorporate T-groups into their business, public administration, education, and psychology curricula; and a number of university institutes (for example, Boston University's Human Relations Center and UCLA's Institute of Industrial Relations) conduct T-groups for business people. Moreover, psychologists working in companies have developed laboratory education programs for internal use by managers, and a substantial number of line managers have been trained to conduct such programs as an ongoing feature of their firms' management development efforts. It is apparent that laboratory education (or a T-group) is now within easy reach of almost any manager.

There is a widespread need in today's organizations for teaching business managers to be more analytical, more aware of how they affect others, develop better interpersonal skills, and use constructive approaches for resolving conflict.

Does laboratory education accomplish these goals? Certainly, most of the advocates of the method would argue that it does. For example, the following list—drawn from many sources—is a distillation of the desirable outcomes sought by and advocated, either implicitly or explicitly, by most T-group and/or laboratory education practitioners:

1. Increased self-insight or self-awareness concerning one's own behavior and its meaning in a social context—this refers to the process of learning how others see and interpret one's behavior, as well as insight about one's reasons for behaving in various ways in different interpersonal situations.
2. Increased sensitivity to the behavior of others—this outcome is closely linked to the first. It refers, first, to the development of an increased awareness of the full range of communicative stimuli emitted by other persons (voice inflections, facial expressions, body positions, and other contextual factors, in addition to the actual choice of words); and, second, to developing the ability to infer accurately the emotional or noncognitive bases for interpersonal communications. This goal is very similar to the concept of empathy as it is used by clinical and counseling psychologists; that is, the ability to infer correctly what another person is feeling.
3. Increased awareness and understanding of the types of processes that facilitate or inhibit group functioning and the interactions between different groups—specifically, why do some members participate actively, while others retire to the background? Why do subgroups form and wage war against each other? How and why are pecking orders established? Why do different groups, who may actually share the same goals, sometimes create seemingly insoluble conflict situations?

4. Heightened diagnostic skill in social, interpersonal, and intergroup situations—achievement of the first three objectives should provide an individual with a set of concepts to be used in his analysis of conflict situations. Moreover, he should be equipped to work constructively with others to resolve interpersonal and/or intergroup conflict.
5. Increased action skill—the ability to intervene successfully in inter- or intragroup situations in order to increase member satisfactions, effectiveness, or productivity.[3] The major thrust of increased action skill is toward intervention at the *interpersonal* instead of merely the technological level, thereby enhancing the likelihood that coordinated, instead of alienated and disputative efforts will be brought to bear in solving technological problems.
6. Learning how to learn—this refers not simply to an individual's cognitive approach to the world, but instead, and far more importantly, to his ability to analyze continually his own interpersonal behavior in order to help himself and others achieve more effective and satisfying interpersonal relationships.[4]

Obviously, these outcomes fulfill organizational needs for behavioral reeducation. It should now be asked: Are these behavioral outcomes really accomplished? If they are, by whom—everyone undergoing such training or just a few? And, if a few, who, and under what conditions? Can sick organizations be "cured" through T-group training and laboratory education? In short, what research evidence can be offered either to support or to question whether this relatively new training strategy accomplishes the aims claimed for it?

THE EVIDENCE

We turn now to a review and evaluation of published research studies done to assess the effects of laboratory education. We have classified the investigations into five groups roughly located at various points along a continuum extending from private (not publicly verifiable), individual perceptions to very broad organizational outcomes. The primary changes measured by studies in each of the groups are: (1) self-reports of changes

---

[3] Although very similar to point 4 this is mentioned separately in M. B. Miles, "Research Notes From Here and There—Human Relations Training: Process and Outcomes," *Journal of Counseling Psychology* 7 (1960): 301–6.

[4] The sources for the above listing of T-group goals include C. Argyris, "T-Groups for Organizational Effectiveness," *Harvard Business Review* 42 (1964): 60–74; P. C. Buchanan, "Evaluating the Effectiveness of Laboratory Training in Industry," in *Explorations in Human Relations Training and Research*, no. 1 (Washington, D.C.: National Training Laboratories, National Education Association, 1965); L. P. Bradford, J. R. Gibb, and K. D. Benne, *T-Group Theory and Laboratory Method* (New York: John Wiley & Sons, 1964); E. H. Schein and W. G. Bennis, *Personal and Organizational Changes through Group Methods: The Laboratory Approach* (New York: John Wiley & Sons, 1965); Tannenbaum et al., *Leadership and Organizations;* and Miles, "Research Notes," pp. 301–6.

in the work setting; (2) changes in attitudes, outlooks, perceptions of others, or orientations toward others; (3) changes in self-awareness or interpersonal sensitivity; (4) observed changes in behavior on the job; and (5) changes in organizational outcomes.

The major results shown by studies in each of these areas are summarized below.

SELF-PERCEPTIONS AND SELF-REPORTS

There is an overwhelming amount of anecdotal evidence on the presumed effects of laboratory education. Most, however, involves introspection, free association, or testimonies collected in an uncontrolled and nonsystematic way. Here is a greatly abbreviated excerpt from one such report:

The leadership laboratory was a marvelous experience. I was in it a month ago, and I am still awestruck. I might be able to give you a glimmer or two about what happened in relaxed conversation, oiled by a martini or two, but a letter is bound to miss, but I'll give it a try anyway. The process is like the dropping of Salome's seven veils. Eventually the group comes to a condition of complete trust, and communications become so acute that they seem metaphysical. Not that the group gets this way without strain. It was fascinating to see how the group came to respect the need for time for an idea to sink in. When an important point was made to a member, the group often fell silent while the point perked, even if it took 30 seconds. The silence wasn't oppressive or embarrassing; it served a purpose. After the last day's session, each group ate at a long table by itself. You never saw such uninhibited, free people. The next morning, my group had a final session and then we walked around the place like a bunch of bananas, we felt so close.[5]

The above account is highly favorable about what happened in the group, but it also is highly subjective, introspective, and nonbehavioral. Because of this, we chose *not* to attempt a review of such reports. As a consequence, we found only two studies using structured or systematic measures for assessing self report of behavior changes. Neither of the studies used pretraining measures. In both studies, supervisors who had been in intraorganizational laboratory training groups reported (after three to seven months back on the job) changes in the effectiveness of their units or critical job incidents they believed were due to the laboratory training. Buchanan and Brunstetter found that the 224 managers reported relatively more examples of effective changes than a comparison (control) group of 133 untrained managers. Morton and Bass used no control group, but 359 incidents were reported by 97 trainees, and nearly

---

[5] Drawn from a letter from one of the first author's close friends, who prefers to remain anonymous.

all of them were judged by the authors to be favorable influences relating to improved working relationships.[6]

Obviously, self-reports of the type obtained in these two studies—even though elicited in a systematic way and focused on job behaviors—are subject to a wide variety of biases. The trainees knew that their training was intended to produce certain behavioral effects; thus, they probably tended to note and report many occurrences which would otherwise go unnoticed and unreported. In a sense, one might argue that the trainees had been committed by their company to enumerate instances of the worth or return on the training investment. Thus, self-imposed internalized organizational expectations and response-set biases seem to us an equally viable explanation for the results obtained.

ATTITUDES, OUTLOOKS, AND ORIENTATIONS

Several studies have examined possible effects of laboratory education on trainees' attitudes and outlooks. Discovering attitudinal effects of laboratory education is important because several of the goals of such training (that is, better understanding of intergroup processes, improved interpersonal diagnostic skills, increased interest and skill in interpersonal intervention, and stronger drive toward personal learning or improvement) strongly imply the necessity of marked attitudinal changes. We found nine studies in this area [7] and we conclude from these studies that there is little firm evidence of any significant change in attitude, outlook, orientation, or view of others as a result of T-group training. This statement is based on the following three observations.

1. Control groups were not included in five of the nine studies. Because of this, interpretation of the results in terms of T-group training per se

---

[6] R. B. Morton and B. M. Bass, "The Organizational Training Laboratory," *Journal of the American Society of Training Directors* 18 (1964): 2–15; P.C. Buchanan and P. H. Brunstetter, "A Research Approach to Management Development: Part II," *Journal of the American Society of Training Directors* 13 (1959): 18–27.

[7] B. M. Bass, "Reactions to *Twelve Angry Men* as a Measure of Sensitivity Training," *Journal of Applied Psychology* 46 (1962): 361–64; R. R. Blake and Jane S. Mouton, "Some Effects of Managerial Grid Seminar Training on Union and Management Attitudes Toward Supervision," *Journal of Applied Behavioral Science* 2 (1966): 387–400; H. Baumgartel and J. W. Goldstein, "Need and Value Shifts in College Training Groups," *Journal of Applied Behavioral Science* 3 (1967): 87–101; R. Harrison, "Cognitive Change and Participation in a Sensitivity Training Laboratory," *Journal of Consulting Psychology* 30 (1966): 517–20; H. H. Kassarjian, "Social Character and Sensitivity Training," *Journal of Applied Behavioral Science* 1 (1965): 433–40; J. P. Kernan, "Laboratory Human Relations Training: Its Effect on the Personality of Supervisory Engineers," *Dissertation Abstracts* 24 (1964): 665–66; B. I. Oshry and R. Harrison, "Transfer from Here-and-Now to There-and-Then: Changes in Organizational Problem Diagnosis Stemming from T-Group Training," *Journal of Applied Behavioral Science* 2 (1966): 185–98; W. C. Schutz and V. L. Allen, "The Effects of a T-Group Laboratory on Interpersonal Behavior," *Journal of Applied Behaviorial Science* 2 (1966): 265–86; and P. B. Smith, "Attitude Changes Associated with Training in Human Relations," *British Journal of Social and Clinical Psychology* 3 (1964): 104–13.

is strained, at best. The changes occurring in the trained groups could easily be attributable to the passage of time or to the mere act of taking the same test a second time. Two of the four studies using control groups report no significant differences between the trained and untrained individuals; in the two where differences were obtained (Smith; Schutz and Allen), the nature of the changes is only sketchily described, offering little basis for speculation or further hypothesis formulation.

2. Eight of the nine studies failed to collect data about possible interaction effects between the evaluation questionnaires or tests and the training program. This is serious when the effort is directed toward evaluating changes via such self-report measures as attitude or orientation inventories because the results from such instruments very often are made available to trainees and actually become a part of the feedback process during training. The result is that trainees, in effect, are either explicitly or implicitly "coached" on the instruments to be used later in evaluating the presumed effects of training. None of the studies we reviewed mention whether or not such strategies were used as part of the training "package," but even if they were not, merely taking the instruments in the pretest session often serves as kind of an alerting mechanism for trainees to alter their responses to the questionnaires when they take them again later.

At least two quasi-control approaches can be suggested for learning more about the possibility and nature of such instrument-interaction effects. First, a group might take the questionnaires, get feedback on their results, and then retake them after an intervening period of no training. Results would provide an estimate of the possible magnitude of response changes (independent of training content) due to learning more about what the questionnaires are "getting at." Second, an additional trained group might take the evaluation instruments only after training. This is the approach used by Bass. If the "after-only" trained group scores like the trained group with both "before" and "after" measures, the possibility of interpreting changes as due only to artifactual interaction effects is greatly lessened.

3. Finally, the actual magnitudes of changes obtained in these studies (even when control groups weren't used and interaction effects weren't checked) are small, and it would be unwise to argue that these minor attitudinal changes indicate, in any substantial way, the accomplishment of the broad behavioral goals and objectives of laboratory education.

Thus, it seems clear that research has not yet demonstrated that T-group training and/or laboratory education has any marked effect on one's "scores" on objective measures of attitude, orientation, outlook, or style.

SELF-AWARENESS AND INTERPERSONAL SENSITIVITY

Our listing of the goals of laboratory education placed self-insight or self-awareness (that is, the ability to perceive one's self as others see one) and interpersonal sensitivity (that is, broader awareness of interpersonal stimuli and increased accuracy in inferring others' feelings) in a position central to accomplishing the other goals. In a way, it is unfortunate that the practitioners of T-group or sensitivity training have claimed improved self-awareness and interpersonal sensitivity as goals, for measurement problems in the area of interpersonal perception are among the most difficult the behavioral scientist has ever faced.[8] Still we agree that methodological difficulties, no matter how great, should not deter investigators from considering the area, for we believe that T-group advocates rightly emphasize the crucial role of interpersonal perception in getting to know, and learning to work constructively with, other people.

We located a total of only seven studies related to the effects of laboratory education on self-awareness or interpersonal sensitivity.[9] Examination of these studies reveals that most failed to use control groups, possible interaction effects between the questionnaires and the training programs were not examined, and (with the exception of the Dunnette study) no precautions were taken to assess the nature of possible differences in the prediction strategies used by subjects in the studies designed to get at possible changes in "interpersonal sensitivity." In terms of self-awareness, the studies by Burke and Bennis and by Gassner, Gold, and Snadowsky deserve special mention. With no control group, Burke and Bennis apparently showed that T-group training has the effect of reducing discrepancies in subjects' descriptions of real and ideal selves.

---

[8] Recent articles summarizing the difficulties are M. D. Dunnette, "People Feeling: Joy, More Joy and the Slough of Despond," *Journal of Applied Behavioral Science* 5 (1969): 25–44; J. P. Campbell and M. D. Dunnette, "The Effectiveness of T-Group Experience in Managerial Training and Development," *Psychological Bulletin* 70 (1968): 73–104. Earlier, more technical statements, include L. J. Cronbach, "Processes Affecting Scores on 'Understanding of Others' and 'Assumed Similarity,'" *Psychological Bulletin* 52 (1955): 177–93; N. L. Gage and L. J. Cronbach, "Conceptual and Methodological Problems in Interpersonal Perception," *Psychological Review* 62 (1955): 411–22.

[9] B. M. Bass, "Mood Changes During a Management Training Laboratory," *Journal of Applied Psychology* 46 (1962): 361–64; W. Bennis et al., "A Note on Some Problems of Measurement and Prediction in a Training Group," *Group Psychotherapy* 10 (1957): 328–41; R. L. Burke and W. G. Bennis, "Changes in Perception of Self and Others during Human Relations Training," *Human Relations* 14 (1961): 165–82; Suzanne Gassner, J. Gold, and A. M. Snadowsky, "Changes in the Phenomenal Field as a Result of Human Relations Training," *Journal of Psychology* 58 (1964): 33–41; K. Lohman, J. H. Zenger, and I. R. Weschler, "Some Perceptual Changes during Sensitivity Training," *Journal of Educational Research* 53 (1959): 28–31; N. L. Gage and R. V. Exline, "Social Perception and Effectiveness in Discussion Groups," *Human Relations* 6 (1953): 381–69; M. D. Dunnette, "People Feeling: Joy, More Joy and the Slough of Despond."

But Gassner, Gold, and Snadowsky obtained the same results for *both* T-group trained and control group subjects, thereby substantially weakening the tenability of any assertions about the *unique* effects of T-group training on the nature of one's self-perception or its relative accuracy.

The study by Dunnette is the only one in this group showing any evidence that T-groups may result in increased interpersonal sensitivity. The methodology was designed to reduce substantially the likelihood of accurate predictions due to stereotypy or assumed similarity strategies. Therefore, accuracy, when it occurred, was much more likely to be the result of truly individualized patterns of interpersonal perception. Moreover, the T-group and control group meetings were recorded and rated according to the quality of interpersonal interaction. Members of the more interactive groups were more accurate in their designations of whom they knew best (as measured by the empathy inventories) than members of the less interactive groups. This is the only direct evidence we know of that the interpersonal interaction of a "good" T-group has the effect of developing greater and more accurate social differentiation among the group's members.

Thus, from this group of studies, we must conclude that evidence in favor of any claims that laboratory education can increase or change interpersonal awareness, "self insight," or interpersonal sensitivity is very nearly nonexistent. Dunnette's is the only study offering much hope to the practitioners of T-group training, and the conclusions from it must be carefully qualified because the subjects were not industrial employees and no measures of interpersonal sensitivity outside the immediate confines of the T-groups were obtained. As in the other two areas already discussed, we must conclude that much additional research needs to be done; the final answers are still far in the future.

OBSERVED CHANGES IN JOB BEHAVIOR

So far, we have reviewed studies bearing quite directly on whether or not T-groups actually accomplish their stated goals. Now, we move to those studies using more global (and, perhaps, more meaningful) measures of training outcomes. We suggest that individual behavior change is desirable in at least four broad areas for ["sick"] organizations to overcome their "sickness" and regain operating effectiveness.[10] We now ask about possible evidence in favor of laboratory education's bringing about behavior changes in any or all of these areas.

---

[10] The four areas are to teach managers (1) to be more analytical in their study of people and problems, (2) to be less self-centered and more aware of how they affect others, (3) to face up to and to encourage conflict as an important basis for problem-solving, and (4) to develop both the skill and desire to work interpersonally with others.

We located five studies bearing directly on this question.[11] Although carefully designed and conducted, they all suffer from the possibility of bias in the behavior change reports. This is because control groups and job behavior observers were chosen by the trained subjects. Thus, reports of behavior change for trained and nontrained subjects are subject to the contaminating effects of the observers' prior knowledge of the training histories of the persons being described and to whatever selective bias may have affected the trainees' designations of people for inclusion in the control groups. Even so, since these studies did actually focus on independent observations of job behaviors and behavioral changes rather than merely subjects' self-reports or questionnaire responses, they come much closer than other investigations to giving us direct information about possible behavioral effects of laboratory education. Their results constitute the backbone of favorable evidence usually offered by T-group practitioners and advocates.

The central approach used in each of the five investigations was to ask associates of trained and untrained subjects to describe changes they may have observed in the subjects' job behaviors during the previous year (which included the training experience). Efforts were made to match the control group with experimental subjects on such dimensions as type of job, organization (or department), and age.

What may be concluded from an analysis of the results of these five investigations? Primarily, we can say that associates of most persons who have received T-group training report observable changes in their (the trainees') behavior back on the job. Whether or not these reported changes are based on actual changes in job behavior is difficult to know because of many possible sources of contamination and bias common to the studies. For example:

1. Asking the trained subjects to name persons for control group subjects very likely tipped the hand of the investigators. Trained subjects, knowing they were to be compared in some way with their control mates, might alter their behavior accordingly. Moreover, their selection of possible control persons might be biased in the direction of naming persons who had a history of less effective interpersonal behavior, who had shown fewer recent changes in their job behavior, or both. It is impossible to estimate whether or not these biases occurred or what their relative magnitude may have been. Only Miles, by choosing a

---

[11] J. B. Boyd and J. D. Elliss, *Findings of Research into Senior Management Seminars* (Toronto: Hydro-Electric Power Commission of Ontario, 1962); D. R. Bunker, "Individual Applications of Laboratory Training," *Journal of Applied Behavioral Science* 1 (1965): 131–48; M. B. Miles, "Changes During and Following Laboratory Training: A Clinical-Experimental Study," *Journal of Applied Behavioral Science* (1965): 215–42; I. M. Valiquet, *Contribution to the Evaluation of a Management Development Program* (Boston: MIT, 1965); W. J. Underwood, "Evaluation of Laboratory Method Training," *Training Directors Journal* 19 (1965): 34–40.

random control group in addition to a nominated control group, guarded against such biasing components. It is encouraging, therefore, that his results were similar to those reported by other researchers.

2. Many sources of potential bias are related to the subjects' nomination of observers. First, the original designation would be more likely to include friendly co-workers, who would tend to say "good" rather than unfriendly things. Second, subjects—particularly the trained ones—would have the opportunity to "brief" the observers before they responded to the questionnaires. Third, most observers—especially those from the intraorganizational studies—would be aware of which subjects had been through the T-groups and which had not, and such knowledge could easily result in either conscious or unconscious perceptual distortions of "changes" in subjects' behavior. Finally, since several observers were usually chosen for each subject, they would probably have ample opportunity to talk with one another and compare notes before completing and returning their questionnaires. Only Boyd and Elliss, by personally designating the observers ahead of time and by interviewing them instead of depending on questionnaire responses, probably avoided most of these biases.

3. Judgments about the extent and nature of the behavior changes reported were undoubtedly subject to biases of interpretation, based as they were on analyses of anecdotal responses to open-ended questions. Miles and Boyd and Elliss asked observers to supplement their subjective descriptions with more objective behavior descriptions. Since no differences between trained and untrained subjects were obtained on the objective instruments, it is difficult to know just what factors contributed most to the differences obtained on the subjective material. The probability is great that a major determinant of the differences may be the various biasing sources we have outlined here.

4. The studies are rendered even more difficult to interpret because all but Underwood relied on retrospective accounts. No observations of job behavior were made before training. Even Underwood used no before measures, but he did ask observers to be alert to and to record instances of behavior change as they occurred rather than relying on their memories and faulty perceptions of possible changes.

5. Finally, even if it is granted that the reported changes do indeed reflect actual changes in trainees' job behavior, we must note that the changes are restricted almost entirely to the domain of greater openness, better understanding, more consideration, and interpersonal warmth. Few, if any, of the reported changes were in the equally important areas of analytical problem-solving attitudes and skills, encouragement of and increased skill in resolving conflict, or decreased self-centeredness and greater self-awareness. Moreover, none of the studies except Underwood's attempted to estimate the possible effects of any observed

changes on overall job effectiveness. Unfortunately, his yielded results opposite to those we should expect.

Based on these observations, we conclude that the evidence of training-produced changes in job behavior, though present, is severely limited by the two major considerations we have mentioned. First, the many sources of bias constitute competing explanations for the results obtained. Second, none of the studies yields any evidence that the changes in job behavior have any favorable effect on actual performance effectiveness. Thus, there is little to support a claim that T-group or laboratory education effects any substantial behavioral change back on the job for any large proportion of trainees. Whatever change does occur seems quite limited in scope and may not contribute in any important way to changes in overall job effectiveness.

CHANGES IN ORGANIZATIONAL OUTCOMES

When a "company doctor" undertakes diagnosis and therapy on a "sick" organization, his ultimate aim must certainly be to turn the functioning of that organization around, to do whatever is necessary to get it on the move again, to restore it to efficient operation. Thus, the ultimate practical payoff for any training or personnel development program is not apt to be changes in trainee attitudes, levels of self-awareness, or even job behavior, but instead, the possibility of a "turnaround" in the overall functioning of the organizational unit. Obviously, this is the broadest, most global level that one may use in undertaking a training evaluation study, and it is rare to find such studies reported. Nonetheless, we have located five (varying *greatly* in quality) which seem to qualify at this level.[12]

The studies by Blansfield and Buchanan are reported so sketchily that they deserve only brief mention. Both involved lengthy laboratory programs within large organizational units. Blansfield's report is devoted exclusively to an anecdotal account of organizational changes presumably due to and reflecting favorably upon the program. Buchanan's report is centered on descriptive material showing changes toward decentralization in decision-making, greater cooperation among work units, and a substantial increase in organizational profits after the organization experienced widespread personnel retrenchment following the 1957 recession.

Blake, Mouton, Barnes, and Greiner presented the first phases of the Management Grid program to all 800 supervisors and managers of a large

---

[12] See M. G. Blansfield, "Depth Analysis of Organizational Life," *California Management Review* 5 (1962): 29–42; P. D. Buchanan, "Organizational Development Following Major Retrenchment" (mimeographed, 1964); R. R. Blake et al., "Breakthrough in Organizational Development," *Harvard Business Review* 42 (1964): 133–55; B. M. Bass, "The Anarchist Movement and the T-Group," *Journal of Applied Behavioral Science* 3 (1967): 211–26; and S. T. White, *Evaluation of an Analytic Trouble Shooting Program: A Preliminary Report* (research memorandum, Kepner-Tregoe and Associates, 28 July 1967), 14 pp.

organizational unit (4,000 employees) of a petroleum corporation.[13] A number of measures were made before and after training and others only after the program had been completed. The former included organizational outcome indicators such as net profit, controllable operating costs, unit production per employee, and relative success in solving such problems as high maintenance and utility costs, plant safety, and management communication. The information about solving problems was, of course, mostly anecdotal and largely subjective. No comparable organizational unit was used as a control group. During the training program, profits increased substantially and costs decreased. Although a substantial portion of the profit increase was due to economic and other noncontrollable factors and to manpower reduction, the authors estimate that 13 percent (amounting to several million dollars) was due to improved operating procedures and higher productivity per man-hour.

What were these improved operating procedures? According to other indexes, they apparently included such things as more meetings, more efficient use of manpower skills as shown by more job transfers and a higher rate of promotion for young line managers (as opposed to highly tenured staff men), greater success in solving cost, safety, and communication problems, and increased use of the 9, 9 management style (as indicated by posttraining responses to attitude measures).

It seems apparent from the report that this organizational unit did indeed accomplish a "turnaround" during the time the supervisors were exposed to the Management Grid program. What is far less apparent is the exact cause of the turnaround. Would *any* total push emphasis pointing up organizational problems, emphasizing the need for more cost consciousness, and calling for greater team effort among the 800 supervisors and managers have worked as well? Or was the specific technology of the T-group-like early phases of the grid program specifically responsible for the changes in organizational outcomes? Might the changes in profits not have occurred without any training at all—merely as a consequence of widespread cost emphasis and extensive manpower reductions? Unfortunately, it is impossible to answer these important questions from the data of this particular investigation.

Both Bass and White used control groups to assess effects of training on organizational outcomes. White's study involved training nonmanagerial employees in a real work setting, whereas Bass's study involved

---

[13] For a thorough description of the Management Grid program, see R. R. Blake and Jane Mouton, *The Management Grid* (Houston: Gulf, 1964). The program involves several stages. Initially a series of T-group-like (but more heavily instrumented) sessions are used to explore peer relationships and the managerial styles of the participants. An important aim is to change individuals' styles in the direction of so-called 9, 9 management, a style giving heavy emphasis to *both* people and production. Over a year's time, other phases explore authority relationships among management levels, provide practice in resolving intergroup conflict, and offer aids to developing more collaborative problem-solving methods.

training business students and observing how they did in "running" computer-simulated organizations. Unfortunately, White's research was an evaluation of a variant of the Kepner-Tregoe decision-making program and does not, therefore, relate to T-grouping or laboratory education. Still, the study serves as a model of careful research and deserves mention for that reason, if for no other. The study was conducted on two widely separated production lines—both producing doors—in a large automobile assembly plant. Production measures (readily translatable into dollar costs) were gathered for one month for both lines.[14] During the ensuing three weeks, 31 of the 44 troubleshooters on the experimental line received training in the Kepner-Tregoe Analytic Trouble Shooting program.[15] The 39 troubleshooters on the control line received no training; in fact, they were unaware of the training received by the men on the experimental line. Production measures were gathered again during the month immediately following the training program. Production measures gathered after training were lower (reflecting poorer efficiency) than those gathered before training for *both* lines because preparations were begun during the month for the model change-over. However, the loss in efficiency was negligible for the trained line and substantial for the untrained line.

Bass used the Carnegie Institute of Technology Management Game in an experimental setting to study transfer effects from the T-group setting to a new group.[16] The Carnegie Tech game is extremely complex, simulating the activities of several firms in a multiproduct industry. Several students make up each firm, and they must interact effectively if the company is to prosper. Nine student T-groups (without trainers) met for 15 weeks. At the end of the 15 weeks, three of the groups were divided into thirds and reformed into three new groups, three were split in half and reassembled, and three remained intact. The nine teams then competed with one another in the game. The splintered groups broke even or made a profit, but the intact groups lost an average of 5.37 million dollars over the 15-week trial period, even though the intact groups gave the most positive descriptions of their openness, communication, and cooperation. On the basis of his observations, Bass attributed the lower performance of the intact groups to a general neglect of the control function.

---

[14] Three measures were used: (1) manned downtime, (2) scrap, and (3) off-standard percent (an index of production efficiency).

[15] The program has two main objectives: to develop ability to anticipate and prevent trouble from occurring and to find and fix trouble more efficiently when it does occur. The program presents no technical knowledge, but teaches a method of production problem analysis. The program used in this experiment was five days long. Half of each day was spent in the classroom with the instructor, and the other half day was spent practicing the analytic method on actual production problems. The emphasis was entirely on increasing analytical skills and *not* on interpersonal or human relations skills.

[16] For a description of the Carnegie Tech game, see K. J. Cohen and E. Rhenman, "The Role of Management Games in Education and Research," *Management Science* 7 (1961): 131–66.

Apparently, the members of the intact groups never bothered to check on each other to see if assignments were being completed.

What may we conclude from these studies about the effect of laboratory education on organizational outcomes? Not much, actually. Of the five studies, three were purely descriptive, offering no experimental evidence about possible organizational effects due to the training technology specific to T-groups or laboratory education. It seems safe to say that concurrent T-group training is at least not incompatible with organizational "turnarounds" in profits and overall operating efficiency, but this is a far cry from stating that laboratory education is *the* prescription for an organization's ills. Of the two experimental studies, only one utilized T-group training methodology and that in a simulated rather than real organization setting. The best of the lot (White's study) does yield solid, experimental evidence that a particular training approach, tailor-made to accomplish specific behavioral and organizational outcomes, apparently did so successfully. As such, the study may serve the important function of alerting T-group advocates to the old training dictum that the first step in training program development should be a checklist of training needs. Training and development programs might be tailored to accomplish changes in line with such needs, rather than being directed toward the broad and rather amorphous goals (such as increased sensitivity, interpersonal awareness, and social diagnostic skills) usually claimed for their programs by the advocates of laboratory education.

REPRISE, APPRAISAL, AND FORECAST

We have recounted many problems wrought by organizational malaise and reviewed research evidence about individual organizational effects of laboratory education. What may we conclude?

Laboratory education has not been shown to bring about any marked change in one's standing on objective measures of attitudes, values, outlooks, interpersonal perceptions, self-awareness, or interpersonal sensitivity. In spite of these essentially negative results on objective measures, individuals who have been trained by laboratory education methods are more likely to be seen as changing their job behavior than are individuals in similar job settings who have not been trained. These reported changes are in the direction of more openness, better self- and interpersonal understanding, and improved communications and leadership skills. Unfortunately, these behavior reports suffer from many possible sources of bias and must, therefore, be taken with a grain of salt. Moreover, we have practically no evidence about possible effects of laboratory education on individuals' skills in analyzing problem situations, synthesizing information, facing up to and resolving interpersonal conflict, and deriving and implementing solutions to organizational problems. Most research has been restricted to "demonstrating" the so-called human relations effects of

T-groups and has given little attention to other equally important areas in the total process of recognizing, diagnosing, and solving problems in an organizational setting. Finally, we do know (from the large-scale study by Blake, Mouton, Barnes, and Greiner) that laboratory education conducted extensively among supervisors can occur concomitantly with a "turnaround" in an organization's overall functioning.

Overall, then, we must recognize that certain "truths" of medical diagnosis and treatment apply equally to the diagnosis and treatment of organization ills. It is easier to describe symptoms than to identify causal agents. It is easier to prescribe broad spectrum treatments than to specify the exact therapeutic effects of any one. And, cures often occur without any clear indication of which therapeutic agent may have been most effective.

We sincerely hope that this review of research evidence will not be viewed as irrevocably damaging to laboratory education. It is true, unfortunately, that few if any individual or organizational behavioral outcomes can be specified as due strictly to laboratory education. But this is not unusual. The same can be said for most present training procedures in industry.

Primarily then, our review has brought out weaknesses and gaps in the research related to the effects of laboratory education. We believe that research in the area of interpersonal behavior is too important to suffer a demise based on results from the studies done so far. We hope, therefore, that we have provided impetus for an expanded rather than a diminished emphasis on the behavioral effects of laboratory education.

We need to know the behavioral prescriptions—according to different individuals and different organizational situations—that may be attached to laboratory education and T-group training. We need to know the causal agents underlying the symptoms of organizational ill health described earlier. We need, in particular, to know not only the effects on interpersonal skills but also the cognitive, analytical, and information-processing effects of laboratory education. All this must be studied with more sophisticated measures of interpersonal perception and problem solving procedures, more frequent use of control groups, greater attention to possible interaction effects between measures and training content, application of behavioral observations and reports before as well as after training, and increased care to assure the absence of biasing factors in behavioral observations.

We predict that industrial practice is about to witness a revolution in training and training evaluation research. Excellent research investigations will become the rule rather than the exception. Fifteen years from now, we expect that a review article should be able to outline specific behavioral outcomes to be expected from different learners after exposure to particular training programs in response to carefully diagnosed organizational needs. Manpower development in the firm of the future will

be centered on no single method or technique. Instead, industrial education will make flexible use of many approaches—carefully researched, programmed, and sequenced to instill in *all* learners the desired repetoire of
knowledges, attitudes, and job and interpersonal skills.

18. LEADERSHIP CLIMATE,
HUMAN RELATIONS TRAINING,
AND SUPERVISORY BEHAVIOR *

Edwin A. Fleishman

INDUSTRIAL ORGANIZATIONS are becoming more deeply concerned with the
interpersonal relations of their members. They seem increasingly anxious
to reduce conflict and to promote harmonious working relationships. They
are searching for policies and programs which can be used to promote
greater satisfaction. Evidence of this can be seen in recent business and
industrial literature which has given considerable emphasis to problems
of human relations. Other evidence can be seen in the increasing number
of leadership training programs which have been instituted in various
industries. These industries want their supervisors to understand and be
able to use certain techniques which will develop and sustain mutually
satisfying human relations in the industrial situation. Implicit in these
programs is the assumption that such relationships will result in increased
organizational effectiveness.

The crucial role of leadership in this complex area of human relations
has long been recognized but significant research in this area is a fairly
recent development. The present paper represents a summary of research
that was undertaken to throw at least some light on certain complex
factors which might affect the leadership role of the foreman in industry.

PURPOSE OF THE STUDY

The study consisted of several major phases.[1] The first phase was concerned with the development of dependable research instruments for

---

* From *Personnel Psychology* 6 (1953): 205–22. This paper represents a summary
of research carried out with the cooperation of the International Harvester Company.
    [1] More detailed descriptions of this work have been presented in E. A. Fleishman,
E. F. Harris, and H. E. Burtt, *Leadership and Supervision in Industry* (Columbus:
Ohio State University, Bureau of Educational Research, 1955); "The Description of
Supervisory Behavior," *Journal of Applied Psychology* 37 (1953): 1–6; "The Measurement of Leadership Attitudes in Industry," *Journal of Applied Psychology* 37 (1953):
153–58.

measuring different aspects of leadership behavior, attitudes, and expectations. The present paper will discuss this developmental work only briefly.

The second phase, with which this paper is primarily concerned, consisted in using these instruments to investigate some specific industrial leadership problems. An investigation was made of the relationship between how the foreman leads his group and the attitudes and behavior of those above him in the organization. The study also investigated the extent to which certain leadership attitudes and behavior were maintained by foremen over periods of time elapsed since leadership training, when foremen returned to different kinds of supervisors in the industrial situation.

FIRST PHASE—DEVELOPING MEASURES OF LEADERSHIP BEHAVIOR AND ATTITUDES

One hundred foremen, representing 17 company plants, participated in this phase of the research. They filled out three questionnaires. On a Leadership Opinion Questionnaire containing 110 items, they described their own *attitudes* about how to lead their work groups. Next, they filled out a 136 item Supervisory Behavior Description questionnaire [2] in which they described their own supervisor's leadership *behavior*. In a third 110 item questionnaire they described how they felt their own supervisor *expected* them to lead their work groups.

In each questionnaire, the foremen checked one of five frequency alternatives which followed each item (for example, always, often, occasionally, seldom, never). In the case of the Supervisory Behavior Description, the foreman indicated for each item how frequently his own supervisor did what the item described. Examples of items in this questionnaire are:

- He plans each day's activities in detail.
- He insists that everything be done his way.
- He helps his men with their personal problems.

A similar procedure was used with the other two questionnaires. Thus, on the Leadership Opinion Questionnaire, the foremen were asked to indicate how frequently they felt they should do what each item described. Examples of such items are:

- Speak in a manner not to be questioned.
- Follow to the letter standard procedures handed down to you.
- Treat people in the work group as your equals.

---

[2] The Supervisory Behavior Description developed in this study is based on earlier work by J. K. Hemphill, *Leader Behavior Description* (Columbus, Ohio: Personnel Research Board, Ohio State University, 1950) and subsequent work reported by A. W. Halpin and B. J. Winer, "Studies in Aircrew Composition III: The Leadership Behavior of the Airplane Commander," Technical Report no. 3 (HRRL contract) (Columbus, Ohio: Personnel Research Board, Ohio State University, 1952).

Extensive statistical analysis was then made of the scores and answers given by these foremen on the questionnaires. Response distributions among the five choices for each item, tetrachoric correlations of the items with total scores on the questionnaires, and factor analysis data were utilized. On the basis of these analyses revised forms were developed which were shortened considerably and contained only items found most applicable to the industrial situation.

Items on each revised questionnaire were scored into one or the other of two leadership "dimensions" identified by factor analysis procedures. One dimension, called "Consideration," reflected the extent to which the leader has established rapport, two-way communication, mutual respect, and consideration of the feelings of those under him. It comes closest to the "human relations" aspects of group leadership. The other dimension, called "Initiating Structure," contained items reflecting the extent to which the supervisor defines or facilitates group interactions toward *goal attainment*. He does this by planning, scheduling, criticizing, initiating ideas, organizing the work, and so forth. It was found in subsequent analyses of these revised forms that these two behavior (or attitude) patterns were *independent* of each other and that they had adequate reliabilities.[3]

SECOND PHASE—THE MAIN STUDY IN A SINGLE PLANT

Samples. Various forms of these revised questionnaires were used in a research design within one of the Company's plants. Four groups of foremen, totaling 122 foremen in a motor truck plant, constituted the primary sample in the study. One group of 32 foremen had not received leadership training at the Company's Central School.[4] The three remaining groups of foremen had received training 2 to 10 (30 foremen), 11 to 19 (31 foremen), and 20 to 39 (29 foremen) months previous to the study. No biasing factors which determined the order in which foremen were sent to training could be found. Differences between the four groups of foremen in average age, years with the company, years as a supervisor, education, and number of men supervised were not statistically significant.

All 122 foremen, 60 supervisors above these foremen, and 394 workers drawn randomly from the foremen's work groups filled out the questionnaires.

---

[3] E. A. Fleishman, *Leadership Climate and Supervisory Behavior* (Columbus, Ohio: Personnel Research Board, Ohio State University, 1951); idem, "The Description of Supervisory Behavior," *Leadership Climate;* idem, "The Measurement of Leadership Attitudes in Industry," *Leadership Climate.*

[4] The School has been in operation several years. Each plant has a regular quota of foremen which it sends to the School every two weeks. The course involves eight hours a day for two weeks. A summary of the purpose, scope, and workings of the School has been published by C. L. Walker, Jr., "Education and Training at International Harvester," *Harvard Business Review* 27 (1949): 542–58.

The Information Obtained. Each *foreman* in the study filled out the following three generally parallel questionnaires:

1. A 40-item *Foreman's Leadership Opinion Questionnaire:* A description of how the foreman thinks he should lead his own work group.
2. A 48-item *Supervisory Behavior Description:* A description of the leadership behavior toward the foreman of the foreman's own boss.
3. A 40-item questionnaire entitled *What Your Boss Expects of You:* A description of how the foreman feels his own boss wants him to lead the work group.

Representatives of each foreman's *work group* filled out the following two questionnaires:

1. A 48-item *Foreman Behavior Description:* A description of the leadership behavior of the foreman with his work group.
2. A 40-item questionnaire entitled *How You Expect an Ideal Foreman to Act:* A description of worker expectations regarding leadership behavior.

Each foreman's boss filled out the following two questionnaires:

1. A 40-item *Leadership Opinion Questionnaire:* A description of how the boss thinks he should lead the foreman under him.
2. A 40-item questionnaire entitled *What You Expect of Your Foremen:* A description of how the boss wants his foremen to lead their workers.

All these forms were variations of the questionnaires revised on the basis of the pilot study. Each questionnaire yielded a score for "Consideration" and a score for "Initiating Structure."

Background data such as age, education, years with the company, years as a supervisor, and number of men supervised also were collected for each foreman.

How the Data Were Analyzed. The foreman's description of his own boss' behavior, the foreman's perception of what his boss expected of him, what the boss said he expected, and the boss' own leadership attitudes about leading foremen were considered aspects of "leadership climate" under which different foremen operate. We then examined the behavior and attitudes of foremen who operated under different kinds of bosses ("leadership climates") in the industrial situation. This was done by dividing the foreman groups (as close to the median score on the "climate" measures as possible) into those operating under "climates" high and low on either "Consideration" or "Initiating Structure." Also, by comparing the four groups of foremen (with different amounts of time elapsed since training) we could get some indication of how the attitudes and behavior of these foremen had changed when they returned from training to different kinds of "leadership climates" in the work situation.

Some evaluation also was made of changes occurring *during* the training course. This was done by administering the attitude questionnaires immediately before and immediately after training. A comparison was then made of the leadership attitudes held immediately after training and attitudes held in the actual industrial environment by foremen who had been trained some time before.

RESULTS AND DISCUSSION

Background Factors Related to the Foreman's Leadership Attitudes and Behavior.   No significant relationships were found between personal data items and scores on the questionnaires measuring the attitudes and behavior of the foremen. Age, education, years with the company, years as a supervisor, and number of men supervised did not seem to make a difference in how the foremen behaved leadershipwise with their workers. These data do not support the popular stereotype of the dominating, driving old-line foreman as typical of older foremen. For example, age and years as a supervisor seem to have no relationship with how "considerate" the foreman is or how much he pushes for production, plans, criticizes, and so forth.

The data of this study do tend to emphasize again that the nature of leadership depends more on certain factors in the particular situation than on these background characteristics of the leader.

The Foreman's Leadership Attitudes and Behavior as Related to the Kind of Boss He Works Under.   What did seem to make a difference in how different foremen led their work groups was the kind of boss under whom the foremen themselves had to operate. Those foremen who operated under a supervisor who was "considerate" toward them tended to express more "considerate" attitudes toward their own workers. Moreover, these same foremen were described by their own work groups as behaving more "considerately" toward the workers. For example, the foremen operating under supervisors high in "consideration" received a mean score of 76.5 on "consideration" when described by their workers, while foremen under supervisors low in "consideration" received a mean score of 70.6 (difference significant beyond the .01 level).

The same "chain-reaction" effect was observed when we examined the "initiating structure" attitudes of different foremen. Those foremen who were under bosses who planned a great deal, stressed deadlines, assigned people to particular tasks, and so forth, tended themselves to score higher in their "structuring" attitudes. Although differences in "structuring" behavior between groups of foremen operating under "climates" high and low in "structuring" were not statistically significant, the trends were in the same direction.

Changes in the Attitudes and Behavior of the Foremen Produced by the Leadership Training Course.   By giving our attitude questionnaires to foremen the first day and again the last day of training we could get some indication of changes produced during the training course. The results of this before and after evaluation indicated a general increase in "consideration" attitudes (significant beyond the .05 level) and a decrease in "initiating structure" attitudes (significant beyond the .01 level) during the course. The correlations between "consideration" and "initiating structure" before and after training presented a check on whether some functional relationship was "learned" between the two dimensions during training. In each case the correlations did not differ significantly from zero. This presents further evidence of the independence on these leadership patterns and indicates that the decrease in "initiating structure" was not necessarily a function of the increase in "consideration." The increase in "consideration" and decrease in "structure" are fairly independent phenomena. Figure 18–1 shows this shift graphically.

The objectives of the training, however, are to produce a lasting change in the trainee's behavior. A comparison of this before and after evaluation with what happened in the actual plant situation revealed an obvious discrepancy. Figure 18–2 presents the results of this "back-in-the-plant" evaluation. Differences in the leadership behavior as well as differences in leadership attitudes for the four groups of foremen (at different stages since training) are presented.

Although the effects of the training generally appear minimal, back in the plant the behavior of the most recently trained group of foremen was significantly lower in "consideration" ($P < .01$) than that of the untrained group of foremen. In the case of "consideration" *attitudes* this initial drop does not reach statistical significance although the trend is in the same direction. Moreover, there appeared to be a trend in the direction of increased "initiating structure" attitudes and behavior in certain of the trained groups at the plant. Confidence in these results is increased when we observe the close correspondence between the attitudes expressed by the foremen and our independent reports of their behavior made by their workers (especially in the case of the "structure" curves and the initial drop in "consideration").

Since "leadership climate" was found related to the attitudes and behavior of the foremen, a check was made to see if our four primary groups of foremen (trained at different times) were matched on the "climate" measures. This analysis showed that the four groups did not differ significantly with respect to our measures of "leadership climate" under which they operated. Hence, this drop in "consideration" and rise in "structuring" in the overall comparison of the trained and untrained groups is not attributable to differences between these groups in overall "leadership climate."

These results seem puzzling because in the course the "human relations" approach is stressed. It may be that being sent to supervisory training made the foremen more aware of their leadership role. Perhaps they really felt more "membership character" (as "one of the boys") in the work groups before training, and being selected for training made them feel "separate" from their work groups. Although "human relations"

FIGURE 18–1

Distributions * of Foreman's Leadership Opinion Questionnaire Scores Before and After Training (N = 46)

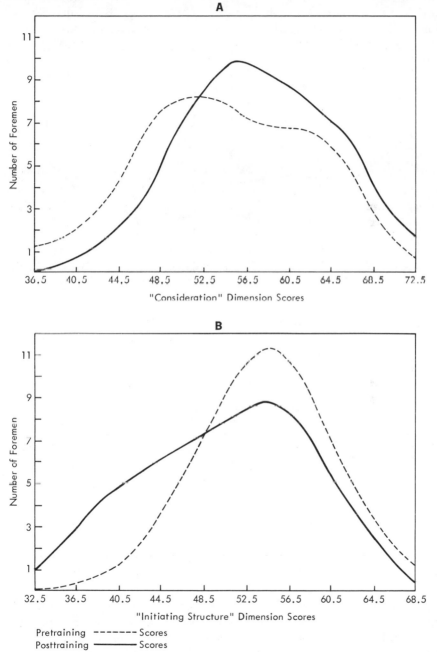

A

B

Pretraining ------- Scores
Posttraining ——— Scores

* The distributions have been smoothed arithmetically by the method suggested by J. P. Guilford, *Psychometric Methods* (New York: McGraw-Hill Book Co., 1936).

FIGURE 18–2

Comparison of the Leadership Attitudes and Behavior of Untrained and Trained Groups of Foremen Back in the Plant

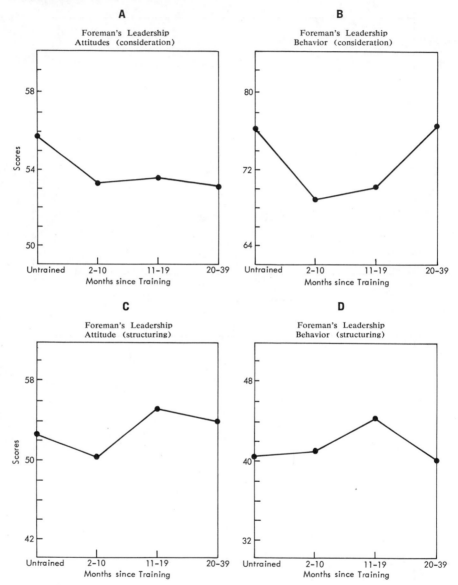

are stressed in the course, the foreman is certainly made more aware of his part as a member of management. The human relations aspect may persist only briefly, whereas what he actually takes back to the plant is a tendency to assume more of a leadership role; that is, do more "structuring" and behave less "considerately."

FIGURE 18–3

Comparison of the Leadership Attitudes and Behavior of Foremen Operating under Different "Leadership Climates" Back in the Plant

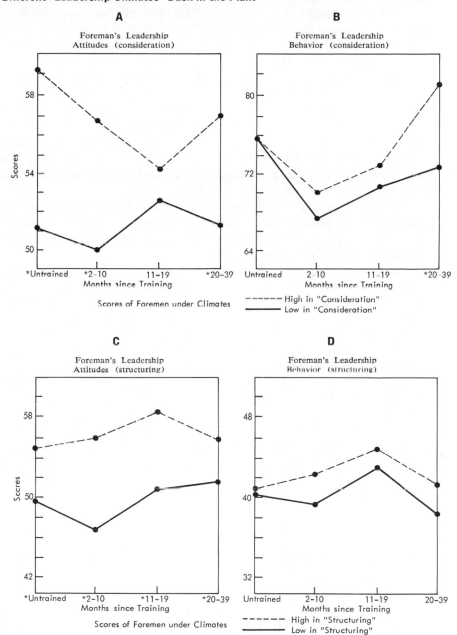

* Indicates difference between the curves statistically significant at these points.

The discrepancy between our results at the School and at the plant points up the danger of evaluating training outcomes immediately after training. The classroom atmosphere is quite different from that in the actual work situation. Our results suggest that the foreman may learn different attitudes for each situation. The attitude that is "right" in the training situation may be very different from the one that "pays off" in the industrial environment.

The Interaction of the Training Effects with the Industrial Environment. The kind of supervisor ("leadership climate") under whom the foreman operated seemed more related to the attitudes and behavior of the foremen in the plant than did the fact that they had or had not received the leadership training course. In the untrained group and at each stage since training, the behavior and attitudes of the foremen were generally related to the "leadership climate" under which they operated. Figure 18–3 presents some of these results.

It can be seen in Figure 18–3 that the attitude and behavior curves of the foremen operating under "climates" high in "consideration" and high in "structuring" are generally above the curves of foremen under "climates" low on each of these leadership patterns.

An implication of these results seems to be that if the old way of doing things in the plant situation is still the shortest path to approval by the boss, then this is what the foreman really learns. Existing behavior patterns are part of, and are moulded by, the culture of the work situation. In order effectively to produce changes in the foreman's behavior some changes in his "back-home-in-the-plant" environment would also seem to be necessary. The training course alone cannot do it.

Comparison of the Degree of "Conflict" among Trained and Untrained Foremen. Further evidence along these lines is furnished by the degree of conflict within trained foremen who return to different kinds of bosses. A "conflict index" was computed between "what the foremen thought they *should* do" and what they were reported as "actually *doing*" in the plant situation. This index was derived from the absolute discrepancy between scores on the Foreman's Leadership Opinion Questionnaire and the Foreman Behavior Description. It was found that whenever our differences were statistically significant these were in favor of more "conflict" within trained foremen when they returned to supervisors higher in "structuring" and lower in "consideration." As indicated previously, the foremen apparently learned to do less "structuring" and to show more "consideration" in the training course.

Comparison of the "Leadership Adequacy" of Trained and Untrained Foremen. It will be recalled that the workers filled out the Foreman Behavior Description and a questionnaire entitled "How You Expect an Ideal Foreman to Act." The absolute discrepancy between scores on these questionnaires present measures of "leadership adequacy" for each foreman with respect to his own work group's expectations. The lower the discrepancy, the higher the "adequacy" from the group's point of view. Our results showed that with respect to "consideration" behavior there was no significant improvement in "leadership adequacy" for the trained foremen who returned to "climates" low in "consideration," but there was significant improvement among foremen who returned to "climates" higher in "consideration." The foremen who returned to supervisors high in "consideration" seemed now to conform more closely to their group's leadership ideal, but no such change occurred in the case of foremen who returned to supervisors lower in "consideration." These results present still further evidence of the interaction of the training effects with the "back in the plant" environment. Differences in "leadership adequacy" along the "initiating structure" dimension, however, were generally not significant.

Comparison of the Leadership Attitudes of the Foremen, Their Workers, and Their Own Supervisors. It was possible to compare the leadership attitudes about how work groups should be led at four clear-cut levels in the plant. The results of this comparison showed no significant differences between the attitudes of the foremen and their supervisors, but highly significant differences between the attitudes of the foremen and their workers. The workers preferred more "consideration" and less "structuring." It also appeared that the higher up people were in the plant hierarchy, the less "consideration" they felt the workers should get. Moreover, the higher the level, the more "structuring" the people felt should be initiated with the work groups. The tendency was for the foreman's attitudes to fall somewhere between what the workers expect and what people higher up in the organization expect.

IMPLICATIONS OF THE RESULTS FOR LEADERSHIP TRAINING IN INDUSTRY

Final evaluation of such training must depend on some kind of intensive criterion study relating supervisory behavior to group effectiveness. This criterion study would be aimed at finding out what kinds of leadership behavior make for higher productivity and/or morale. On the basis of this kind of study recommendations about "What to teach?" could be made. The present research made little attempt to investigate this problem. Some limited evidence was obtained which showed some relationship between labor grievance rates and certain kinds of leadership attitudes and behavior. For example, based on a very small sample of 23 departments, correlations as high as .53 were found between grievance rates in these departments and scores made by supervisors on these questionnaires. The trend was for high grievance departments to be those whose supervisors were lower in "consideration" and tended to do more "structuring."

These results are regarded as merely suggestive and certainly no substitute for a well-controlled criterion study.[5] Ideally such a criterion study would take into consideration the situational nature of leadership. For example, comparative studies of effective leadership in production, maintenance, and administrative departments could be made. It is possible that different combinations of "consideration" and "initiating structure" may be found desirable for different kinds of departments. This might suggest setting up separate leadership training courses for supervisors in these different kinds of departments. An important contribution of the present study in this regard was the development of instruments to measure relatively independent dimensions of leadership which in a later study could be related to criteria of group effectiveness. If important relationships with external criteria are found, some interesting implications would be pointed up. For example, a combination of such things as group characteristics, needs and expectations, leadership attitudes, behaviors, and perceptions, pressures from supervisors, and so forth, might yield more successful predictions where ordinary testing procedures have failed in the field of leadership. With larger samples and adequate criteria it may be possible to predict group effectiveness given measures of several aspects of the social situation.

The present study presents evidence of what changes occurred in the attitudes and behavior of foremen after training. There is no implication, however, as to whether these changes are desirable or undesirable. Pending the availability of more ultimate criteria, training can be evaluated with respect to the major objectives set for such courses. The objective of this particular course was to make the foremen more "human relations" oriented. This corresponds to a desired increase on the "consideration" dimension of the instruments used in this study. Although training objectives with regard to the "initiating structure" dimension were not defined, changes along this dimension were also investigated.

In terms of changes in "consideration" attitudes, this course met this objective partially. When the leadership attitude scales were administered immediately before and immediately after training, there was an average increase in "consideration" scores during the course. "Initiating structure" attitudes showed a general decrease for the foremen during the course. A limitation of this pre-post training evaluation was the fact that it was not feasible to use a control group in this phase of the study and these same men could not be followed back to their plants.

The training, however, did not produce any kind of permanent change in either the attitudes or behavior of the trained foremen. Evaluation of the training back in the actual work situation yielded results quite different from the pre-post training evaluation. In fact, there were trends

---

[5] [Editors' note: This study subsequently was carried out and is described in E. A. Fleishman, E. F. Harris, and H. E. Burtt, *Leadership and Supervision*. See Section 5 for a summary of some of these later findings.]

in the direction of more "structuring" and less "consideration" in those foremen who returned to the industrial environment. Further study is needed to determine how to make the intended effects of such courses more permanent. Indications from this study are that the back home "leadership climate" is an important variable related to the behavior and attitudes of foremen in the work situation. Although the effects of training were minimal among foremen working under either of the kinds of "leadership climates" investigated, those foremen who operated under bosses higher in "consideration" tended themselves to be more "considerate" with their workers. This was also generally true of the foreman's "structuring" attitudes and behavior under "climates" higher in "structuring." Further evidence along this line was furnished by the comparison of the attitudes of the foremen in the plant with those of their bosses and workers. No significant differences were found between the attitudes of the foremen and their bosses, but there were highly significant differences between the attitudes of the foremen and their workers. In addition, there was greater conflict between the attitudes and actual behavior of the trained foremen who returned to "climates" at variance with what the foremen learned in training than among those who returned to "climates" consistent with what they learned. It was also found that the behavior of foremen who returned to "climates" consistent with what was taught in training conformed more closely to the leadership expectations of their work groups. No such improvement was found among foremen who returned to "climates" at variance with the training course.

These results suggest that leadership training cannot be considered in isolation from the social environment in which the foremen must actually function. In this sense leadership training must be viewed as an attempt at *social change* which involves the reorganization of a complex perceptual field. It is difficult to produce in an individual a behavior change that violates the culture in which this behavior is imbedded. When foremen are trained and sent back to the factory, it is unrealistic to expect much change when so many factors in the social situation remain constant. The implication seems to be that certain aspects of the foreman's environment may have to be reorganized if training is to be effective in modifying his behavior. It would appear, then, that more intensive training of supervisors above the level of foreman in the organization might be more effective in making the training effects more permanent among the foremen. If he could return to an environment where the boss behaved in a way consistent with what the foreman was taught in the training course, where these new modes of behavior were now the shortest path to approval, we might expect a more permanent effect of such training.

On the basis of the data of this study some reexamination of course *content* might be made. For example, what is in such courses that might account for the increase in "structuring" and the decrease in "consideration" when the foremen get back to the plant? Do such courses make the foreman too aware of his role as a member of management and how does he interpret this when he goes back? Does the foreman tend to lose his "membership character" in the work group after he has returned from training? In terms of the "human relations" objective, is there anything in the course content or in the attitudes fostered there which defeats this purpose? Research in training *methods* is another possibility. Would a more therapeutic or individualistic approach produce greater or more permanent effects? At least it would seem that something more than classroom training is probably needed if real changes in the attitudes or behavior of supervisors is to be expected.

Similar evaluations of the training in the plant situation need to be made in other plants and in other industries. This drop in "consideration" and the trend in increased "structuring" may not occur in other industrial situations. It may be, for example, that the overall "leadership climate" in this plant was lower in "consideration" than the overall "climate" in some other plant. This study afforded no opportunity for comparing this plant on the whole with some other plant.

In general, interest in the course among foremen is very high. Enthusiasm at the verbal level is almost universal. A frequent comment made by the foremen during the course was "I certainly wish my own boss would get this course." Favorable comments about the course also are expressed by people at all levels in the organization. The writer sat through the course and was very favorably impressed with the teaching methods and the participation of the foremen. Before any reorganization of the course, criterion research revealing what to teach and further research on how to make the effects of what is taught more permanent should be undertaken.

19. EFFECTIVENESS OF TWO ORIENTATION APPROACHES IN HARD-CORE UNEMPLOYED TURNOVER AND ABSENTEEISM *

Hjalmar Rosen and John Turner

INDUSTRY AND BUSINESS in the United States are increasingly engaging in employment programs for the hard-core unemployed—particularly minority group members from inner city locations of large, industrial urban centers. A good deal of time, money, and effort are being expended to successfully integrate the hard core into the world of work.

Programs have had, for the most part, one of two emphases: skill training, to compensate for lack of work experience and to develop job competence, and work orientation programs that have focused on developing techniques to aid the hard-core in making an easier and more successful transition from the culture of poverty to the culture of work. The research reported here focuses on the latter type of effort.

As is too often the case when significant policy and practice transitions occur in industry, the pressure to become actively involved minimizes thoughtful and organized preplanning of procedures and strategies. Many companies rushed into such programs on, literally, a trial-and-error basis. As the programs became more popular, however, packaged programs were developed and promoted that implicitly claim to provide the answers to achieving an effective transition for the hard core.[1] Unfortunately, there are few, if any, systematic evaluations of the success and/or failure of any of the many orientation efforts. Although many hard-core hiring programs have been given extensive popular coverage in the news media, well-documented statements of program success are almost impossible to find.

The research to be reported is one attempt to provide the needed evaluation of hard-core hiring effectiveness. It should be pointed out, however, that the problems involved in designing and implementing a well-controlled, quasiexperimental design in a field setting are manifest and significantly influence both the results obtained and the interpretations that can be made. Before engaging in a formal presentation of the results

---

* From *Journal of Applied Psychology* 55, no. 4 (1971): 296–301. Copyright 1971 by the American Psychological Association. Reprinted by permission.
[1] "How to Succeed in Hard-Core Hiring," *Business Week,* 24 August 1968, pp. 65–66.

of this study, a brief discussion of problems encountered and their impact is necessary.

One of the most critical problems encountered was related to the matter of implementing the controls demanded by the design in an on-going, industrial organization. In this study, the intention was to test the relative utility of a quasitherapeutic approach to job orientation of the hard core. This university-conducted orientation was to be contrasted to the impact of an equally extensive, passive, information-centered orientation carried out by company training personnel. Only after the program was well underway was there a realization that the informational orientation had become far more than intended: Discussion was encouraged using the information presentation as a springboard. Individual counseling of problem employees, designated as such by line supervision, occurred frequently. And, in many cases, training personnel interceded on the behalf of the employee in the relationship between first-line supervision and the hard-core employee. What had been designated as a passive placebo appeared to have become a dynamic, personalized treatment condition. As a consequence, this study became less a test of the impact of quasitherapeutic style orientation per se and more a study of how effective a company-run orientation could be, given commitment, latitude, and innovation on the part of the training staff.

Another critical problem encountered, and one characteristic of many research efforts where intervention is used,[2] relates to the fact that any modification of an organizational environment has the potential for being reactive. Bringing hard core into a plant as special employees, requiring extensive off-the-job support time for them and their supervisors, well may have communicated to first-line supervision the company's commitment to "make the program work at any cost." Absenteeism data (presented in Tables 19–2, 19–3, and 19–4 suggests that a leniency occurred regarding absences for the hard-core in comparison to the normal hire. Consequently, differences between hard-core and normal hires probably underrepresents the true magnitude of the difference—particularly with regard to turnover via termination.

One final limitation should be noted. This study focused on job-stability characteristics of hard core. Any attempt to generalize from these findings to results of other studies and programs is hazardous. Not only would generalization be limited by lack of comparability in intervention strategies imposed, but it also would be limited by lack of comparability among the local groups. Unfortunately, in many programs, the hard-core designation refers to urban, minority group members—usually black—unemployed at the time of hire, that is, persons that company personnel officers privately confide are not really different from the general run of new hires in a tight labor market. Hard core in this study refers to persons having

---

[2] E. J. Webb et al., *Unobtrusive Measures* (Chicago: Rand McNally, 1966).

long histories of unemployment for a variety of reasons (some of which relate to being black), and therefore represent a difficult group to retain in employment. To compensate for this lack of comparability, job stability was compared not only between the two intervention groups of hard core but between those groups and normal hires employed during approximately the same period and assigned to similar, unskilled positions.

METHOD

Subjects.   Forty-nine Negro Ss (males), who had been residents of the urban community in which the sponsoring company was located for at least 1 year, made up the hard-core sample. Hard-core unemployment was defined essentially in terms of work history. To be permitted to enter the program, the applicants could not have held any single job for more than 3 months and had to have total employment of less than 6 months during the 2-year period prior to hiring. Educational level, selection test data, and criminal record (except for crimes of extreme violence) were ignored. The Ss did, however, have to be evaluated as physically able to work by the estimation of the company medical staff. The Ss were obtained from welfare roles, supportive agencies, and from day-labor lines. Normal hires were defined as walk in applicants who met the typical hiring standards of the company. This second group happened to be one-third black and, like the hard-core, were assigned to manual, unskilled level jobs.

Setting.   The employing company was a public utility. The company was located in a large, Midwest urban center that, during the year prior to the study, had experienced severe race riots. A large proportion of company employees were technicians rather than unskilled workers. Most new nonprofessional or clerical employees, however, were assigned to an unskilled labor pool. The company, as a matter of policy, viewed the labor pool as a reservoir for future technical personnel rather than as a stable, unskilled work force. It actively encouraged job bidding and training for higher skill positions. At the time of the study approximately 10 percent of the work force was black.

Procedure.   The hard-core sample was divided into two groups. Group designation was determined by matching in terms of demographic variables obtained during the hiring interview.[3] Orientation for both groups consisted of 21 hours of exposure in 14 sessions over a 12-week period.[4]

---

[3] Critical variables included age, education, number of dependents, and criminal record. As far as possible, job assignments were balanced so that any given supervisor would have an S from each type of orientation group assigned to him.

[4] For the first 4 weeks, two 1½-hour sessions were held. For the next 4 weeks, there was one session per week. During the final four weeks, a session was held every other week. All sessions were conducted on company time and the employees were paid their normal hourly rate.

University-developed training was conducted with three groups of eight Ss each. The training style used a quasitherapeutic approach. Although the direction was in terms of job-related problems, complete freedom was permitted in group meetings. The groups were led by a white, clinical psychologist who had had considerable experience in group psychotherapy with mixed racial groups.

The company-developed training was directed by a white member of the personnel division of the company. The program content was developed by the training division of the company from existing orientation materials and primarily stressed job-related information. The company-trained hard-core met as a single group of 25 Ss. Although it was intended that company orientation be a passive treatment—that is, essentially a lecture, tour, and film series—it was discovered that considerable free discussion was permitted during the group sessions. Moreover, toward the end of the training sessions, the group leader used this time to talk to Ss who were having job-related problems. Neither modification was planned in the study design.

As noted earlier, three types of criterion data were collected. After the tenth week of the program, immediate supervision was requested to evaluate hard-core employees in terms of recommendations for a wage increment.[5] At the end of 6 months, turnover data and absenteeism data (both authorized and unauthorized) were collected from company personnel records and tabulated for both the hard-core and the normal-hire groups.

RESULTS

At the tenth week after hiring, 44 hard core remained employed. In terms of supervisor evaluation for a pay increment, 57 percent of the hard core were considered worthy of the merit raise. The company-trained group had 65 percent within this category and the university-trained group had 48 percent. Although the advantage was not statistically significant, it was the first indication in the study of the possible superiority of the company-sponsored training over that offered by the university.

At the end of 6 months, 34 Ss, or 69 percent of the original hard-core hires, remained on the company employment rolls. At this point, turnover data for the two hard-core training groups and the normal-hire sample were compared. From Table 19–1, it can be noted that the hard-core as a composite had a turnover rate, which, although higher, was not significantly different from that of the normal-hire group. The university-trained group had a significantly higher $(p = .01)$ turnover rate

---

[5] The company had a policy that permitted a small merit increment for employees who were considered to have good potential on the basis of recommendations from their immediate supervisors.

TABLE 19-1

Turnover Rate and Average Length of Employment before Termination for Normal Hires and University- and Company-Trained Hard Core

Measure	Normal	Hard-core	Univer-sity Hard-core	Company Hard-core
Original N	49	49	24	25
No. terminations	12	16	11	5
% Terminations	24.49	32.7	45.83	20.0
Average no. days before termination (5-day week)	59.15		65.45	56.25

than did either the company-trained group or the regular hires. Termination time, approximately 12 weeks, did not differentiate among the three groups.

In comparing the three groups on 6 months authorized and unauthorized absence rate (computed in terms of percentage of lost time to total time worked), no significant differences were found in terms of authorized absence (see Table 19-2). The university-trained group had the highest rate. In terms of unauthorized absence rate, however, significant differences occurred. Both hard-core groups had a significantly higher rate ($p = .01$) than did normal hires. Moreover, the university-trained group had a significantly higher ($p = .05$) rate than did the company-trained group.

Breaking down the absenteeism data in terms of stays and leaves for the three groups, Table 19-3 presents the data for the stays, that is, for those remaining employed after 6 months. The rates of authorized and unauthorized absences were higher for the university-trained group than for the company-trained group, although not significantly so. Both hard-core trained groups had significantly higher ($p = .01$) unauthorized

TABLE 19-2

Comparison of Authorized and Unauthorized Absenteeism Rate for Total Samples of Normal Hires, University-Trained Hard Core, and Company-Trained Hard Core

Measure	Normal Hires[a]	University Trained[b]	Company Trained[c]
% Authorized	3.52	6.67	4.43
% Unauthorized	2.20	11.83	6.48

Note: Comparison in terms of percentage of time lost.
[a] $N = 49$.
[b] $N = 24$.
[c] $N = 25$.

TABLE 19–3

Comparison of Authorized and Unauthorized Absenteeism Rate for Those Remaining Employed after Six Months

Measure	Normal Hires[a]	University Trained[b]	Company Trained[c]
% Authorized 71		7.93	4.85
% Unauthorized 1.95		6.79	4.44

Note: Comparison is in terms of percentage of time lost.
[a] $N = 37$.
[b] $N = 13$.
[c] $N = 20$.

absence than did the normal hires, and both were higher, but not significantly so in authorized absence.

The trends were much the same for the terminated employees, although the absenteeism rate was considerably higher than for the non-terminated employees (see Table 19–4). University-trained and company-trained hard-core were not significantly differentiated from one another, either in terms of authorized or unauthorized absence. In terms of these variables, however, the hard-core groups did have significantly higher ($p = .01$) unauthorized rates than did the normal hires. No significant differences were found among the three groups regarding authorized absence.

To estimate whether or not absenteeism played a role in termination,[6] the rate of absenteeism for stays versus leaves in the three groups were analyzed (see Table 19–5). For all groups, unauthorized absenteeism was

TABLE 19–4

Comparison of Authorized and Unauthorized Absenteeism Rate for Those Terminated during the First Six Months

Measure	Normal Hires[a]	University Trained[b]	Company Trained[c]
% Authorized 7.88		6.53	3.80
% Unauthorized 6.33		16.44	12.99

Note: Comparison is in terms of percentage of time lost.
[a] $N = 12$.
[b] $N = 11$.
[c] $N = 5$.

---

[6] From other data in the study, that is, exit interviews and foreman training session tapes, it appeared that absenteeism was a significant variable in termination. Company records indicating formal reasons for termination supported this conclusion.

TABLE 19–5

Comparison of Unauthorized and Authorized Absenteeism Rate for Stays Versus Leaves in Normal Hires, University-Trained, and Company-Trained Groups

Measure	Normal Hires		Total Hardcore		University Trained		Company Trained	
	Stays	Leaves	Stays	Leaves	Stays	Leaves	Stays	Leaves
% Unauthorized	.71	6.33*	6.44	15.36*	7.93	16.44*	4.85	12.99*
% Authorized	.95	7.88*	5.62	5.67	6.79	6.53	4.44	3.80

Note: Comparison in terms of time lost.
* $p = .01$.

significantly higher for the leaves than the stays $(p = .01)$. For the terminated employees in the hard-core training groups, the rate of unauthorized absence was significantly higher $(p = .01)$ than authorized absence.

DISCUSSION

Keeping in mind the variance from the intended design, particularly with regard to the company-sponsored orientation, two important aspects of the results stand out. The first relates to the comparability between the hard-core (taken as a totality) and regular hires in terms of turnover, in spite of the significantly higher absenteeism rates for the hard core. The second is the clear advantage in terms of all of the criteria used of the company-trained versus the university-trained hard-core hires.

In terms of the hard-core versus the normal-hire findings, one could summarize the implications of the results in the following manner: If hard-core unemployed are given extensive orientation training, particularly if such training is job oriented in content and directed by company personnel, and if company standards regarding absenteeism are loosened during the early employment period, the hard core will turn out to be as stable a work force as men hired via normal hiring channels.

The key to developing job stability among hard-core employees, then, seems to be a matter of modifying poor work habits and developing an acceptance (and understanding) of the rigorous and systematic attendance demands made by a large business organization on its work force. Habit patterns developed in extended periods of unemployment, particularly related to time, apparently have to be extinguished before the hard-core hire can effectively operate within the constraints a steady job imposes on his personal freedom. This change, for many, will not occur spontaneously, and must be carefully nurtured over a considerable period of time. The comparisons of the two hard-core orientation approaches shed additional light on how this adaptation might best be brought about.

The only apparent advantage the university orientation had, as compared to company-directed orientation as it actually was carried out, related to the professional stature and experience of the orientation leader in using quasitherapeutic, participative group techniques. The quasitherapeutic approach, in and of itself, could not a priori be evaluated as a superior acculturation strategy over the free discussion, personal counseling, and intervention with supervision used in the company-orientation procedures.

On the other hand, the company strategy as it was implemented had some obvious advantages over the university approach. First, the subject matter covered in the sessions was job oriented and crucial to acceptable work behavior. Benefits derived from working for the company were spelled out and relevant rules and penalties for their infraction were emphasized time and again. The rationale for the rules and penalties also was discussed at length. In contrast, the university trainees established their own content, much of which was not directly related to their jobs—or, for that matter, to work in general—but rather to a protest against white establishments and life in general. Work problems tended to be brushed aside with the most cursory discussion in spite of the efforts of the trainer. Only in terminal sessions did the groups begin to focus on job problems.

A second accrual of the company trainees was the direct access the training supervisor had to the organization and the fact that he represented the company. He knew the rules and could assess them realistically, particularly in terms of the supervisors that would be implementing them. Given a problem employee, he not only could call him aside after the meeting and give him a clear picture of the consequences related to rule breaking, but could and did intercede with the employee's supervisor on the employee's behalf. In a sense, company training included a liaison function that was absent from the university-orientation training and may have played a critical role.

The poor showing of the university-sponsored, quasitherapeutic group orientation raises several critical questions. First, is it advisable to have orientation initiated by a source outside the company organization? Second, is there utility in using a clinically derived adjustment technique for hard-core employees in terms of the critical job-behavior criteria used, that is, supervisor ratings, turnover, and absenteeism?

Assuming for the moment the need for special intervention in the form of orientation, the outsider is at a distinct disadvantage regardless of his professional stature and experience. He is not apt to be well-versed in company practices and policies. Without elaborate exposure and probing, the most he will obtain is a set of formal statements undifferentiated in terms of importance and enforcement. Second, he is not in a position to intercede for the employee either to clarify rule-enforcement standards of supervision with regard to a given infraction or to request a temporary, less rigorous rule enforcement.

On the basis of such logic, there is also a very real question as to the merit of using a quasitherapeutic group approach. The goals of such a strategy, on one level, make a good deal of conceptual sense. Sharing of common problems should not only be supportive but should lead to a more realistic group-derived solution. In turn, assuming that the problems are job related—even if indirectly so—the trainee should benefit by being able to cope with his adjustment problems more successfully. Theoretically, he should be less likely to quit because of the group support and should learn to modify his behavior and thereby reduce punitive action from the organization.

A critical assumption, however, is that job-related problems will be salient ones for him and will be the problems he and his group will discuss. This assumption did not hold true for the group studied. Job-related problems were lost in a mosaic of problems induced by being black and living in the ghetto.

Although, ideally, personal adjustment may be desirable for job success, its development may be too amorphous and gradual to help in coping with ongoing, job-related problems. To remain employed, the employee, hard-core or not, must conform to avoid dismissal and must accept to minimize self-termination. These adjustments must be achieved in a relatively short period of time regardless of his overall personal adjustment. The quasipsychotherapeutic group treatment, as implemented, did not seem to achieve these ends.

SUMMARY AND CONCLUSION

In terms of the findings of this study and the conditions under which they were generated, there is little doubt that hard-core orientation can be advantageously accomplished, in terms of the criteria used by—(a) introducing a content structure in orientation that focuses on work-related materials, (b) having the program administered and conducted by members of the hiring organization who are not only knowledgeable about company practices and policies but who can intervene between hard-core and first-line supervision in problem areas, and (c) using a part of the orientation period to cope with and counsel problem employees. Extra-organizational intervention, particularly using a quasitherapeutic group strategy, does not seem to be an optimal or viable alternative.

Section Four

MOTIVATION
ATTITUDES, AND
JOB SATISFACTION

INTRODUCTION

WHY DO PEOPLE ACT as they do? Why does one group of workers restrict their production while others produce at high levels? What do people want out of their jobs? What are their needs? What goals do they seek to satisfy these needs? What factors make for satisfying work relationships and job satisfaction? How are the incentives provided in industry related to the motivations of organization members? In this section we examine some principles and research bearing on these questions.

Perhaps at the outset we should recognize that research interest in such questions was, to a great extent, stimulated by the classic Western Electric Company studies carried out in the Hawthorne plant beginning in the late 1920s.[1] These studies did not start out to examine questions of attitudes and group processes; the initial objective was to determine the effect of different intensities of illumination on worker output. The main finding of this initial work was that production varied without any direct relationship to amount of illumination. In many cases, productivity went up when the bulbs were changed—without change in actual intensity—and, in other cases, productivity was maintained even when illumination was

---

[1] For a comprehensive summary, see F. J. Roethlisberger and W. Dickson, *Management and the Worker* (Cambridge, Mass.: Harvard University Press, 1946); E. Mayo, *The Human Problems of an Industrial Civilization* (New York: Viking Press, 1960).

207

reduced to low levels. What accounted for these puzzling results? In order to gain more insight and better control over variables that might affect productivity, a second series of studies was initiated concerned with such factors as working conditions, fatigue, length of working day, number and length of rest pauses. Six girls who assembled telephone equipment (relays) were placed in an experimental room under supervision and observed over a period of five years. It was found that with variations in conditions of work substantial increases in production continued to occur, even if working hours were shortened. And when the girls were returned to their original, more poorly lighted work benches, for a longer work day without rest pauses, the researchers were astonished to find output rising again to even higher levels. This forced the researchers to look for other factors to account for this. It became evident that the girls had become motivated to work harder. Some of the reasons seemed to be: (a) many felt special in being singled out for study, (b) since they had more freedom in pacing their work and in dividing it they had developed good relations with one another and with their supervisor, and (c) the social contact made the work more generally pleasant. The chief result of this research was to emphasize the importance of employee attitudes and to stimulate further research on employee attitudes and motivation.

A third phase of this program involved a mass-interviewing program which showed that such items as wages, hours of work, and so forth, varied according to an individual's position in his group and the group's attitude toward the item. Out of this stage of the research a new hypothesis was formulated—that motivation to work and productivity were related to the nature of the social relations on the job.

To investigate this further, a group of 14 men were studied over a 6½-month period in a special "bank wiring room." One of the first things observed was the formation of cliques, each with their own special games, habits, and norms, and with competition between them. The group as a whole had norms about the proper way to behave; for example, there were norms for a fair day's production. If a worker produced too much above this he was a "rate buster"; if he produced too low he was a "chiseler." Those who deviated too far in either direction were subjected to social pressures to get back in line. The norm to produce less than capacity has been called "restriction of output." The big finding was that social membership in the cliques was the key to output rates. Some cliques produced higher than others, but the highest and lowest producers were the social isolates who did not belong to either group.

This study, coupled with those from the earlier study of girl relay assemblers, suggested that social processes can restrict as well as facilitate productivity. There were many other findings of this research, but the major implication of this work was to bring home to the industrial psychologist the importance of social, motivational, and attitudinal factors in the work situation, and the need for more definitive research on these questions.[2] The issues raised have proven to be among the most complex in industrial psychology. The articles in this section, as well as those in the two sections which follow, amply demonstrate this.

The first article, by McGregor, "The Human Side of Enterprise," introduces us to the central role of motivation in the social-industrial milieu and questions many of the assumptions reflected in traditional organization structures and managerial policies. The article provides a framework for describing the complexities of human motivation. The organizing principle is the "need hierarchy," and McGregor shows how this principle relates to the motivation of human effort in organizations.

The second article, "How Do You Motivate Employees?" by Herzberg, continues this discussion of the motivational basis of behavior in the industrial environment. Herzberg's research led him to conclude that the factors which serve to make people satisfied with their jobs are not the same factors which make people unhappy or dissatisfied with their jobs. The first set of factors, which lead to job satisfaction, were labeled "motivators" by Herzberg and generally consisted of characteristics of the work *content*, such as achievement, responsibility, and so forth. The second set of factors, which lead to job dissatisfaction, were labeled "hygiene" factors and primarily relate to aspects of the work environment or the job *context*, such as working conditions, company policies, and so forth. Herzberg concludes that the most effective method of motivating employees is to enrich the content of the job by providing greater opportunities for the employee's psychological growth. The article suggests some basic concepts of job enrichment and gives examples of how job enrichment might best be implemented.[3]

A major value of Herzberg's two-factor theory is that it has stimulated a great deal of research, since it was possible to test the formulation in a variety of organizations and cultures. While many confirmations of the two-factor theory have been obtained using the same methods,[4] many

---

[2] For critical evaluations of the Hawthorne studies, see H. A. Landsberger, *Hawthorne Revisited* (Ithaca, N.Y.: Humphrey Press, 1958); A. Carey, "The Hawthorne Studies: A Radical Criticism," *American Sociological Review* 33 (1968): 403–16.

[3] For a description of an actual job-enrichment program at AT&T, see R. Ford, *Motivation through the Work Itself* (New York: American Management Association, 1969). General discussions of job enrichment are presented in J. R. Maher, *New Perspectives in Job Enrichment* (New York: Van Nostrand, Reinhold, 1971); W. J. Roche and N. L. MacKinnon, "Motivating People with Meaningful Work," *Harvard Business Review* 48 (1970): 3, 97–110; R. Janson, "Job Enrichment: Challenge of the 70s," *Training and Development Journal* 24 (1970): 6, 7–9. For an excellent research study on the effectiveness of job enrichment for different types of employees, see J. R. Hackman and E. E. Lawler, "Employee Reactions to Job Characteristics," *Journal of Applied Psychology* 55 (1971): 259–86. Another approach to the problem of job enrichment and redesigning jobs to increase efficiency as well as motivation is presented by L. E. Davis, "Job Design and Productivity," *Personnel* 33 (1957): 418–30; idem, "The Design of Jobs," *Industrial Relations* 6 (1967): 21–45.

[4] See, for example, B. S. Grigaliunas and F. Herzberg, "Relevancy in the Test of Motivator-Hygiene Theory," *Journal of Applied Psychology* 55 (1971): 73–79; D. P. Schwab and H. G. Henemann, "Aggregate and Individual Predictability of the Two-

studies reveal only limited or partial support.[5] It appears that the methods used in asking workers to recall instances of satisfaction and dissatisfaction may influence whether one can confirm the two factors or not. An alternative explanation is that job satisfaction has several components with each component able to contribute to both satisfaction and dissatisfaction. Nevertheless, a finding which seems to persist in many of these studies is the potency or importance of the "motivators" (for example, achievement, responsibility) relative to the potency of the "hygienes" in accounting for overall job satisfaction.

The preceding two papers (by McGregor and Herzberg) are concerned with attempting to understand the kinds of factors which are important in satisfying and motivating employees. Other theories of motivation are more concerned with the behavioral dynamics involved in the motivation process. Rather than focusing on the specific factors in the work setting which are important to employees, these theories focus instead on explaining the general principles underlying the initiation and maintenance of on-the-job behavior. One of the most prominent motivational theories of this type in the industrial psychology literature is what has been called "expectancy-instrumentality" theory of motivation. Essentially, this theory maintains that individuals are motivated to engage in behavior to the extent that the behavior is perceived as resulting in (being instrumental for) rewards or outcomes that are desired by the individual.[6] The next two articles deal specifically with this theoretical framework for explaining motivation of organization members.

In the article "Job Attitudes, Effort, and Performance: A Theoretical Model," Lawler and Porter present their version of expectancy-instrumentality theory. They distinguish between effort (motivation to work) and performance, and they suggest that effort is determined by the value of rewards expected to accrue from exerting effort and the expectancy

---

Factor Theory of Job Satisfaction," *Personnel Psychology* 23 (1970): 55–66; M. S. Myers, "Who Are Your Motivated Workers?" *Harvard Business Review* 42 (1964): 73–88.

[5] For reviews of the numerous studies concerning the Herzberg theory, see R. J. House and L. A. Wigdor, "Herzberg's Dual-Factor Theory of Job Satisfaction and Motivation: A Review of the Evidence and a Criticism," *Personnel Psychology* 20 (1967): 369–90; D. A. Whitsett and E. K. Winslow, "An Analysis of Studies Critical of the Motivator-Hygiene Theory," *Personnel Psychology* 20 (1967): 391–416; V. M. Bockman, "The Herzberg Controversy," *Personnel Psychology* 24 (1971): 155–90.

[6] For a statement of the basic premises and postulates of expectancy theory as applied to industrial motivation, see V. Vroom, *Work and Motivation* (New York: John Wiley and Sons, 1964). Subsequent versions of the theory have been presented by G. Graen, "Instrumentality Theory of Work Motivation: Some Experimental Results and Suggested Modifications," *Journal of Applied Psychology* 53 (1969), 2; pt. 2, pp. 1–25; L. W. Porter and E. E. Lawler, *Managerial Attitudes and Performance* (Homewood, Ill.: Irwin-Dorsey, 1968). For recent reviews of the research on expectancy-instrumentality theory, see T. R. Mitchell and A. Biglan, "Instrumentality Theories: Current Uses in Psychology," *Psychological Bulletin* 76 (1971): 432–54; H. G. Henemann and D. P. Schwab, "An Evaluation of Research on Expectancy Theory Predictions of Employee Performance," *Psychological Bulletin* 78 (1972): 1–9.

that a given level of effort will indeed result in these rewards. They further point out that actual performance depends, in addition to effort, on abilities and role perceptions.

The next article, "Expectancy Theory Predictions of Work Effectiveness," by Hackman and Porter, is a research study which attempted to test the basic concepts of expectancy-instrumentality theory using a sample of telephone company service representatives. These investigators found that an index derived from employee expectations of the consequences of working hard on the job, and the employee's values attached to these consequences, did indeed predict the employee's effort and work effectiveness, as evaluated by supervisors.

In spite of motivational theories such as those of McGregor, Herzberg, Lawler, and Porter, and others, which emphasize the complexity of human motivation and the variety of human needs, management has too often taken an oversimplified view of employee motivation, placing the emphasis on economic needs. While pay certainly *is* an important incentive used in industry, it has often been found not to have the motivational properties which management has attributed to it. The next article, "Motivational Aspects of Pay," by Opsahl and Dunnette, takes a closer look at various pay plans which have been tried in industry and reviews the research evidence on the motivational effects of money. Of particular interest in this article is the discussion of "equity theory" as a basis for understanding the motivational effects of pay. Based on the notions of cognitive dissonance,[7] equity theory maintains that individuals are motivated to reduce perceived states of inequity in their environments. With reference to industrial motivation, equity theory focuses on employee's perceptions of the "fairness" of their pay, and suggests that perceptions of either underpayment or overpayment will result in attempts by the employee to adjust the quality or quantity of his output. A considerable amount of research has now been conducted to test the basic premises of equity theory, and most of this research has provided support for the theory.[8]

Besides pay, of course, there are many other incentives that manage-

---

[7] Festinger, *A Theory of Cognitive Dissonance* (Evanston, Ill.: Row, Peterson, 1957).

[8] Fairly strong support for equity-theory predictions of employee satisfaction and job performance in a simulated industrial setting are found in the recent comprehensive study by R. D. Pritchard, M. D. Dunnette, and D. O. Jorgenson, "Effects of Perceptions of Equity and Inequity on Worker Performance and Satisfaction," *Journal of Applied Psychology* 56 (1972): 75–94. For reviews of the research on equity theory as it applies to workers' job performance and satisfaction, see E. E. Lawler, "Equity Theory as a Predictor of Productivity and Work Quality," *Psychological Bulletin* 70 (1968): 596–610; R. D. Pritchard, "Equity Theory: A Review and Critique," *Organizational Behavior and Human Performance* 4 (1969): 176–211; P. Goodman and A. Friedman, "An Examination of Adams' Theory of Inequity," *Administrative Science Quarterly* 16 (1971): 271–88. For a recent general discussion of the role of pay in employee performance, see E. E. Lawler, *Pay and Organizational Effectiveness: A Psychological View* (New York: McGraw-Hill Book Co., 1971).

ment might use to motivate employee performance. As we have seen, there is considerable evidence that the most effective incentives are those intrinsic to the job itself. One approach to developing intrinsic satisfactions on the job has been the use of employee *participation* in decisions (for example, setting production goals, changing work methods) which heretofore had been imposed on him by management, time-study engineers, or other "specialists." There has now been a considerable amount of research on employee participation, and the evidence suggests that such participation often results in greater job satisfaction as well as increased productivity,[9] although it seems that the effectiveness of such participation may vary with the personality and needs of the individual.[10] A number of papers in the present volume deal with the issue of employee participation in one form or another (see the papers by Likert, and by Maier and Sashkin in Section Five and the papers by Argyris; Likert and Bowers; and Seashore and Bowers in Section Six).

Basic to many of the problems already discussed in this section is the problem of *measurement* of attitudes toward the job. The development of quantitative measures of job satisfaction allows us to compare the attitudes of different individuals, to detect changes in attitudes, and to relate attitudes to other conditions. One of the most comprehensive programs concerned with the development of improved methods of measuring job satisfaction is described in "The Development of a Method of Measuring Job Satisfaction: The Cornell Studies," by Smith. The article discusses the issues in such measurement, outlines the rationale and procedures developed, and presents evidence on the utility of the questionnaire developed. The method developed is based on considerable research which emphasizes the need to measure a number of separate dimensions of satisfaction.

An assumption frequently encountered in dealing with questions of motivation in industry is that the satisfied worker is always the productive worker. There is now considerable evidence that this represents a greatly oversimplified view. Satisfaction with one's work does *not necessarily* provide strong motivation to high levels of production. More consistent positive relationships have been found between job satisfaction and other criteria such as absences, turnover, conflicts in the organization—all of which also involve costs to management. Although job satisfaction may sometimes be associated with high productivity, both varia-

---

[9] See, for example, A. Marrow, D. Bowers, and S. Seashore, *Management by Participation: Creating a Climate for Personal and Organizational Development* (New York: Harper & Row, 1967); M. S. Myers, "Every Employee a Manager," *California Management Review* 10 (1968): 3, 9–20; G. Farris, "Organizational Factors and Individual Performance: A Longitudinal Study," *Journal of Applied Psychology* 53 (1969): 87–91.

[10] V. Vroom, *Some Personality Determinants of the Effects of Participation* (Englewood Cliffs, N.J.: Prentice-Hall, 1960); R. C. Albrook, "Participative Management: Time for a Second Look," *Fortune,* May 1967; pp. 167ff; A. Lowin, "Participative Decision-Making: A Model, Literature Critique, and Prescriptions for Research," *Organizational Behavior and Human Performance* 3 (1968): 68–106.

bles are likely to be part of a more complex set of relationships. And in many cases it is possible that performance on the job is the *cause* of satisfaction rather than the effect of it. One of the difficulties here is the need to distinguish between satisfaction and motivation. Insofar as his needs are met, a person may be satisfied with his job. But his overall satisfaction does not necessarily indicate his motivation to work, particularly when his satisfaction does not depend on the effort he puts into his work.

The final article in this section, "The Effect of Performance on Job Satisfaction," by Lawler and Porter reviews the evidence on these questions and presents a theoretical model which indicates conditions under which job satisfaction is (or is not) likely to be related to productivity. Lawler and Porter suggest that satisfaction is likely to result from job performance when effective performance results in rewards which are desired by and perceived as equitable by the employee. Under these conditions satisfaction and job performance will be found to be positively related, and Lawler and Porter present research evidence which indicates just such a relationship between job satisfaction and performance. The conclusion is that high productivity and satisfaction can be expected to occur together when productivity is perceived as a means to the achievement of certain of the individual's goals. It is particularly interesting to note Lawler and Porter's finding that those areas of satisfaction intrinsic to the job (for example, opportunity for advancement) are more highly related to increased job performance than are other areas of satisfaction (for example, satisfaction with job security). This is very much consistent with the views of other articles presented in this section, such as those of McGregor and Herzberg, that intrinsic job factors are most important for employee satisfaction and motivation.

SUGGESTED ADDITIONAL READINGS

Campbell, J. P.; Dunnette, M. D.; Lawler, E. E.; and Weick, K. E. *Managerial Behavior, Performance, and Effectiveness.* New York: McGraw-Hill Book Co., 1970, especially chap. 15.

Herzberg, F.; Mausner, B.; Peterson, R. O.; and Capwell, D. F. *Job Attitudes: A Review of Research and Opinion.* Pittsburgh: Psychological Service of Pittsburgh, 1957.

Herzberg, F.; Mausner, B.; and Snyderman, B. *The Motivation to Work.* 2d rev. ed. New York: John Wiley & Sons, 1959.

Lawler, E. E. III, *Motivation in Work Organizations.* Monterey, Calif.: Brooks/ Cole, 1973.

Locke, E. A. "Job Satisfaction and Job Performance: A Theoretical Analysis." *Organizational Behavior and Human Performance* 5 (1970): 484–500.

Locke, E. A.; Cartledge, N.; and Knerr, C. S. "Studies of the Relationship between Satisfaction, Goal-Setting, and Performance." *Organizational Behavior and Human Performance* 5 (1970): 135–58.

20. THE HUMAN SIDE OF ENTERPRISE *

Douglas M. McGregor

IT HAS BECOME trite to say that the most significant developments of the next quarter century will take place not in the physical but in the social sciences, that industry—the economic organ of society—has the fundamental know-how to utilize physical science and technology for the material benefit of mankind, and that we must now learn how to utilize the social sciences to make our human organizations truly effective.

Many people agree in principle with such statements; but so far they represent a pious hope—and little else. Consider with me, if you will, something of what may be involved when we attempt to transform the hope into reality.

I.

Let me begin with an analogy. A quarter century ago basic conceptions of the nature of matter and energy had changed profoundly from what they had been since Newton's time. The physical scientists were persuaded that under proper conditions new and hitherto unimagined sources of energy could be made available to mankind.

We know what has happened since then. First came the bomb. Then, during the past decade, have come many other attempts to exploit these scientific discoveries—some successful, some not.

The point of my analogy, however, is that the application of theory in this field is a slow and costly matter. We expect it always to be thus. No one is impatient with the scientist because he cannot tell industry how to build a simple, cheap, all-purpose source of atomic energy today. That it will take at least another decade and the investment of billions of dollars to achieve results which are economically competitive with present sources of power is understood and accepted.

It is transparently pretentious to suggest any *direct* similarity between the developments in the physical sciences leading to the harnessing of atomic energy and potential developments in the social sciences. Nevertheless, the analogy is not as absurd as it might appear to be at first glance.

---

* From "Adventure in Thought and Action," *Proceedings of the Fifth Anniversary Convocation of the School of Industrial Management, Massachusetts Institute of Technology* (Cambridge, Mass.: Massachusetts Institute of Technology, June 1957).

To a lesser degree, and in a much more tentative fashion, we are in a position in the social sciences today like that of the physical sciences with respect to atomic energy in the 30s. We know that past conceptions of the nature of man are inadequate and in many ways incorrect. We are becoming quite certain that, under proper conditions, unimagined resources of creative human energy could become available within the organizational setting.

We cannot tell industrial management how to apply this new knowledge in simple, economic ways. We know it will require years of exploration, much costly development research, and a substantial amount of creative imagination on the part of management to discover how to apply this growing knowledge to the organization of human effort in industry.

May I ask that you keep this analogy in mind—overdrawn and pretentious though it may be—as a framework for what I have to say.

Management's Task: Conventional View

The conventional conception of management's task in harnessing human energy to organizational requirements can be stated broadly in terms of three propositions. In order to avoid the complications introduced by a label, I shall call this set of propositions "Theory X":

1. Management is responsible for organizing the elements of productive enterprise—money, materials, equipment, people—in the interest of economic ends.
2. With respect to people, this is a process of directing their efforts, motivating them, controlling their actions, modifying their behavior to fit the needs of the organization.
3. Without this active intervention by management, people would be passive—even resistant—to organizational needs. They must therefore be persuaded, rewarded, punished, controlled—their activities must be directed. This is management's task in managing subordinate managers or workers. We often sum it up by saying that management consists of getting things done through other people.

Behind this conventional theory there are several additional beliefs—less explicit, but widespread:

4. The average man is by nature indolent—he works as little as possible.
5. He lacks ambition, dislikes responsibility, prefers to be led.
6. He is inherently self-centered, indifferent to organizational needs.
7. He is by nature resistant to change.
8. He is gullible, not very bright, the ready dupe of the charlatan and the demagogue.

The human side of economic enterprise today is fashioned from propositions and beliefs such as these. Conventional organization structures, managerial policies, practices, and programs reflect these assumptions.

In accomplishing its task—with these assumptions as guides—management has conceived of a range of possibilities between two extremes.

The Hard or the Soft Approach?

At one extreme, management can be "hard" or "strong." The methods for directing behavior involve coercion and threat (usually disguised), close supervision, tight controls over behavior. At the other extreme, management can be "soft" or "weak." The methods for directing behavior involve being permissive, satisfying people's demands, achieving harmony. Then they will be tractable, accept direction.

This range has been fairly completely explored during the past half century, and management has learned some things from the exploration. There are difficulties in the "hard" approach. Force breeds counterforces: restriction of output, antagonism, militant unionism, subtle but effective sabotage of management objectives. This approach is especially difficult during times of full employment.

There are also difficulties in the "soft" approach. It leads frequently to the abdication of management—to harmony, perhaps, but to indifferent performance. People take advantage of the soft approach. They continually expect more, but they give less and less.

Currently, the popular theme is "firm but fair." This is an attempt to gain the advantages of both the hard and the soft approaches. It is reminiscent of Teddy Roosevelt's "speak softly and carry a big stick."

Is the Conventional View Correct?

The findings which are beginning to emerge from the social sciences challenge this whole set of beliefs about man and human nature and about the task of management. The evidence is far from conclusive, certainly, but it is suggestive. It comes from the laboratory, the clinic, the schoolroom, the home, and even to a limited extent from industry itself.

The social scientist does not deny that human behavior in industrial organization today is approximately what management perceives it to be. He has, in fact, observed it and studied it fairly extensively. But he is pretty sure that this behavior is *not* a consequence of man's inherent nature. It is a consequence rather of the nature of industrial organizations, of management philosophy, policy, and practice. The conventional approach of Theory X is based on mistaken notions of what is cause and what is effect.

"Well," you ask," what then is the *true* nature of man? What evidence leads the social scientist to deny what is obvious?" And, if I am not mistaken, you are also thinking, "Tell me—simply, and without a lot of scientific verbiage—what you think you know that is so unusual. Give me—without a lot of intellectual claptrap and theoretical nonsense—some practical ideas which will enable me to improve the situation in my organization. And remember, I'm faced with increasing costs and narrowing profit margins. I want proof that such ideas won't result simply in new and costly human relations frills. I want practical results, and I want them now."

If these are your wishes, you are going to be disappointed. Such requests can no more be met by the social scientist today than could comparable ones with respect to atomic energy be met by the physicist fifteen years ago. I can, however, indicate a few of the reasons for asserting that conventional assumptions about the human side of enterprise are inadequate. And I can suggest—tentatively—some of the propositions that will comprise a more adequate theory of the management of people. The magnitude of the task that confronts us will then, I think, be apparent.

II.

Perhaps the best way to indicate why the conventional approach of management is inadequate is to consider the subject of motivation. In discussing this subject I will draw heavily on the work of my colleague, Abraham Maslow of Brandeis University. His is the most fruitful approach I know. Naturally, what I have to say will be over-generalized and will ignore important qualifications. In the time at our disposal, this is inevitable.

Physiological and Safety Needs

Man is a wanting animal—as soon as one of his needs is satisfied, another appears in its place. This process is unending. It continues from birth to death.

Man's needs are organized in a series of levels—a hierarchy of importance. At the lowest level, but preeminent in importance when they are thwarted, are his physiological needs. Man lives by bread alone, when there is no bread. Unless the circumstances are unusual, his needs for love, for status, for recognition are inoperative when his stomach has been empty for a while. But when he eats regularly and adequately, hunger ceases to be an important need. The sated man has hunger only in the sense that a full bottle has emptiness. The same is true of the other physiological needs of man—for rest, exercise, shelter, protection from the elements.

A satisfied need is not a motivator of behavior! This is a fact of profound significance. It is a fact which is regularly ignored in the conventional approach to the management of people. I shall return to it later. For the moment, one example will make my point. Consider your own need for air. Except as you are deprived of it, it has no appreciable motivating effect upon your behavior.

When the physiological needs are reasonably satisfied, needs at the next higher level begin to dominate man's behavior—to motivate him. These are called safety needs. They are needs for protection against danger, threat, deprivation. Some people mistakenly refer to these as needs for security. However, unless man is in a dependent relationship where he fears arbitrary deprivation, he does not demand security. The need is for the "fairest possible break." When he is confident of this, he is more than willing to take risks. But when he feels threatened or dependent, his greatest need is for guarantees, for protection, for security.

The fact needs little emphasis that since every industrial employee is in a dependent relationship, safety needs may assume considerable importance. Arbitrary management actions, behavior which arouses uncertainty with respect to continued employment or which reflects favoritism or discrimination, unpredictable administration of policy—these can be powerful motivators of the safety needs in the employment relationship *at every level* from worker to vice president.

Social Needs

When man's physiological needs are satisfied and he is no longer fearful about his physical welfare, his social needs become important motivators of his behavior—for belonging, for association, for acceptance by his fellows, for giving and receiving friendship and love.

Management knows today of the existence of these needs, but it often assumes quite wrongly that they represent a threat to the organization. Many studies have demonstrated that the tightly knit, cohesive work group may, under proper conditions, be far more effective than an equal number of separate individuals in achieving organizational goals.

Yet management, fearing group hostility to its own objectives, often goes to considerable lengths to control and direct human efforts in ways that are inimical to the natural "groupiness" of human beings. When man's social needs—and perhaps his safety needs, too—are thus thwarted, he behaves in ways which tend to defeat organizational objectives. He becomes resistant, antagonistic, uncooperative. But this behavior is a consequence, not a cause.

Ego Needs

Above the social needs—in the sense that they do not become motivators until lower needs are reasonably satisfied—are the needs of greatest significance to management and to man himself. They are the egoistic needs, and they are of two kinds:

1. Those needs that relate to one's self-esteem—needs for self-confidence, for independence, for achievement. for competence, for knowledge.

2. Those needs that relate to one's reputation—needs for status, for recognition, for appreciation, for the deserved respect of one's fellows.

Unlike the lower needs, these are rarely satisfied; man seeks indefinitely for more satisfaction of these needs once they have become important to him. But they do not appear in any significant way until physiological, safety, and social needs are all reasonably satisfied.

The typical industrial organization offers few opportunities for the satisfaction of these egoistic needs to people at lower levels in the hierarchy. The conventional methods of organizing work, particularly in mass-production industries, give little heed to these aspects of human motivation. If the practices of scientific management were deliberately calculated to thwart these needs—which, of course, they are not—they could hardly accomplish this purpose better than they do.

Self-Fulfillment Needs

Finally—a capstone, as it were, on the hierarchy of man's needs—there are what we may call the needs for self-fulfillment. These are the needs for realizing one's own potentialities, for continued self-development, for being creative in the broadest sense of that term.

It is clear that the conditions of modern life give only limited opportunity for these relatively weak needs to obtain expression. The deprivation most people experience with respect to other lower-level needs diverts their energies into the struggle to satisfy *those* needs, and the needs for self-fulfillment remain dormant.

III.

Now, briefly, a few general comments about motivation:

We recognize readily enough that a man suffering from a severe dietary deficiency is sick. The deprivation of physiological needs has behavioral consequences. The same is true—although less well recognized—of deprivation of higher-level needs. The man whose needs for safety, association, independence, or status are thwarted is sick just as surely as is he who has rickets. And his sickness will have behavioral consequences. We will be mistaken if we attribute his resultant passivity, his hostility, his refusal to accept responsibility to his inherent "human nature." These forms of behavior are *symptoms* of illness—of deprivation of his social and egoistic needs.

The man whose lower-level needs are satisfied is not motivated to satisfy those needs any longer. For practical purposes they exist no longer. (Remember my point about your need for air.) Management often asks, "Why aren't people more productive? We pay good wages, provide good working conditions, have excellent fringe benefits and steady employment. Yet people do not seem to be willing to put forth more than minimum effort."

The fact that management has provided for these physiological and safety needs has shifted the motivational emphasis to the social and perhaps to the egoistic needs. Unless there are opportunities *at work* to satisfy these higher-level needs, people will be deprived; and their behavior will reflect this deprivation. Under such conditions, if management continues to focus its attention on physiological needs, its efforts are bound to be ineffective.

People *will* make insistent demands for more money under these conditions. It becomes more important than ever to buy the material goods and services which can provide limited satisfaction of the thwarted needs. Although money has only limited value in satisfying many higher-level needs, it can become the focus of interest if it is the *only means available.*

The Carrot and Stick Approach

The carrot and stick theory of motivation (like Newtonian physical theory) works reasonably well under certain circumstances. The *means* for satisfying man's physiological and (within limits) his safety needs can be provided or withheld by management. Employment itself is such a means, and so are wages, working conditions, and benefits. By these means the individual can be controlled so long as he is struggling for subsistence. Man lives for bread alone when there is no bread.

But the carrot and stick theory does not work at all once man has reached an adequate subsistence level and is motivated primarily by higher needs. Management cannot provide a man with self-respect, or with the respect of his fellows, or with the satisfaction of needs for self-fulfillment. It can create conditions such that he is encouraged and enabled to seek such satisfactions *for himself,* or it can thwart him by failing to create those conditions.

But this creation of conditions is not "control." It is not a good device for directing behavior. And so management finds itself in an odd position. The high standard of living created by our modern technological know-how provides quite adequately for the satisfaction of physiological and safety needs. The only significant exception is where management practices have not created confidence in a "fair break"—and thus where safety needs are thwarted. But by making possible the satisfaction of low-level needs, management has deprived itself of the ability to use as motivators the devices on which conventional theory has taught it to rely—rewards, promises, incentives, or threats and other coercive devices.

Neither Hard nor Soft

The philosophy of management by direction and control—*regardless of whether it is hard or soft*—is inadequate to motivate because the human needs on which this approach relies are today unimportant motivators of behavior. Direction and control are essentially useless in motivating people whose important needs are social and egoistic. Both the hard and the soft approach fail today because they are simply irrelevant to the situation.

People, deprived of opportunities to satisfy at work the needs which are now important to them, behave exactly as we might predict—with indolence, passivity, resistance to change, lack of responsibility, willingness to follow the demagogue, unreasonable demands for economic benefits. It would seem that we are caught in a web of our own weaving.

In summary, then, of these comments about motivation: management by direction and control—whether implemented with the hard, the soft, or the firm but fair approach—fails under today's conditions to provide effective motivation of human effort toward organizational objectives. It fails because direction and control are useless methods of motivating people whose physiological and safety needs are reasonably satisfied and whose social, egoistic, and self-fulfillment needs are predominant.

IV.

For these and many other reasons, we require a different theory of the task of managing people based on more adequate assumptions about human nature and human motivation. I am going to be so bold as to suggest the broad dimensions of such a theory. Call it "Theory Y," if you will.

1. Management is responsible for organizing the elements of productive enterprise—money, materials, equipment, people—in the interest of economic ends.
2. People are *not* by nature passive or resistant to organizational needs. They have become so as a result of experience in organizations.
3. The motivation, the potential for development, the capacity for assuming responsibility, the readiness to direct behavior toward organizational goals are all present in people. Management does not put them there. It is a responsibility of management to make it possible for people to recognize and develop these human characteristics for themselves.
4. The essential task of management is to arrange organizational conditions and methods of operation so that people can achieve their own goals *best* by directing *their own* efforts toward organizational objectives.

This is a process primarily of creating opportunities, releasing potential, removing obstacles, encouraging growth, providing guidance. It is what Peter Drucker has called "management by objectives" in contrast to "management by control."

And I hasten to add that it does *not* involve the abdication of management, the absence of leadership, the lowering of standards, or the other characteristics usually associated with the "soft" approach under Theory X. Much on the contrary. It is no more possible to create an organization today which will be a fully effective application of this theory than it was to build an atomic power plant in 1945. There are many formidable obstacles to overcome.

Some Difficulties

The conditions imposed by conventional organization theory and by the approach of scientific management for the past half century have tied men to limited jobs which do not utilize their capabilities, have discouraged the acceptance of responsibility, have encouraged passivity, have eliminated meaning from work. Man's habits, attitudes, expectations—his whole conception of membership in an industrial organization—have been conditioned by his experience under these circumstances. Change in the direction of Theory Y will be slow, and it will require extensive modification of the attitudes of management and workers alike.

People today are accustomed to being directed, manipulated, controlled in industrial organizations and to finding satisfaction for their social, egoistic, and self-fulfillment needs away from the job. This is true of much of management as well as of workers. Genuine "industrial citizenship"—to borrow again a term from Drucker—is a remote and unrealistic idea, the meaning of which has not even been considered by most members of industrial organizations.

Another way of saying this is that Theory X places exclusive reliance upon external control of human behavior, while Theory Y relies heavily on self-control and self-direction. It is worth noting that this difference is the difference between treating people as children and treating them as mature adults. After generations of the former, we cannot expect to shift to the latter overnight.

V.

Before we are overwhelmed by the obstacles, let us remember that the application of theory is always slow. Progress is usually achieved in small steps.

Consider with me a few innovative ideas which are entirely consistent with Theory Y and which are today being applied with some success.

Decentralization and Delegation

There are ways of freeing people from the too-close control of conventional organization, giving them a degree of freedom to direct their own activities, to assume responsibility, and, importantly, to satisfy their egoistic needs. In this connection, the flat organization of Sears, Roebuck and Company provides an interesting example. It forces "management by objectives" since it enlarges the number of people reporting to a manager until he cannot direct and control them in the conventional manner.

Job Enlargement

This concept, pioneered by IBM and Detroit Edison, is quite consistent with Theory Y. It encourages the acceptance of responsibility at the bottom of the organization; it provides opportunities for satisfying social and egoistic needs. In fact, the reorganization of work at the factory level offers one of the more challenging opportunities for innovation consistent with Theory Y. The studies by A. T. M. Wilson and his associates of British coal mining and Indian textile manufacture have added appreciably to our understanding of work organization. Moreover, the economic and psychological results achieved by this work have been substantial.

Participation and Consultative Management

Under proper conditions these results provide encouragement to people to direct their creative energies toward organizational objectives, give them some voice in decisions that affect them, provide significant opportunities for the satisfaction of social and egoistic needs. I need only mention the Scanlon Plan as the outstanding embodiment of these ideas in practice.[1]

The not infrequent failure of such ideas as these to work as well as expected is often attributable to the fact that a management has "bought the idea" but applied it within the framework of Theory X and its assumptions.

Delegation is not an effective way of exercising management by control. Participation becomes a farce when it is applied as a sales gimmick or a device for kidding people into thinking they are important. Only the management that has confidence in human capacities and is itself directed toward organizational objectives rather than toward the preservation of personal power can grasp the implications of this emerging theory. Such management will find and apply successfully other innovative ideas as we move slowly toward the full implementation of a theory like Y.

---

[1] [Editors' note: See, for example, F. G. Lesieur and E. S. Puckett, "The Scanlon Plan Has Proved Itself," *Harvard Business Review* 47 (1969: 107–118.]

Performance Appraisal

Before I stop, let me mention one other practical application of Theory Y which—while still highly tentative—may well have important consequences. This has to do with performance appraisal within the ranks of management. Even a cursory examination of conventional programs of performance appraisal will reveal how completely consistent they are with Theory X. In fact, most such programs tend to treat the individual as though he were a product under inspection on the assembly line.

Take the typical plan: substitute "product" for "subordinate being appraised," substitute "inspector" for "superior making the appraisal," substitute "rework" for "training or development," and, except for the attributes being judged, the human appraisal process will be virtually indisguishable from the product inspection process.

A few companies—among them General Mills, Ansul Chemical, and General Electric—have been experimenting with approaches which involve the individual in setting "targets" or objectives *for himself* and in a *self*-evaluation of performance semi-annually or annually.[2] Of course, the superior plays an important leadership role in this process—one, in fact, which demands substantially more competence than the conventional approach. The role is, however, considerably more congenial to many managers than the role of "judge" or "inspector" which is forced upon them by conventional performance. Above all, the individual is encouraged to take a greater responsibility for planning and appraising his own contribution to organizational objectives; and the accompanying effects on egoistic and self-fulfillment needs are substantial. This approach to performance appraisal represents one more innovative idea being explored by a few managements who are moving toward the implementation of Theory·Y.

VI.

And now I am back where I began. I share the belief that we could realize substantial improvements in the effectiveness of industrial organizations during the next decade or two. Moreover, I believe the social sciences can contribute much to such developments. We are only beginning to grasp the implications of the growing body of knowledge in these fields. But if this conviction is to become a reality instead of a pious hope, we will need to view the process much as we view the process of releasing the energy of the atom for constructive human ends—as a slow, costly, sometimes discouraging approach toward a goal which would seem to many to be quite unrealistic.

---

[2] [Editors' note: See Section 1, Article 7.]

The ingenuity and the perseverance of industrial management in the pursuit of economic ends have changed many scientific and technological dreams into commonplace realities. It is now becoming clear that the application of these same talents to the human side of enterprise will not only enhance substantially these materialistic achievements but will bring us one step closer to "the good society." Shall we get on with the job?

21. HOW DO YOU MOTIVATE EMPLOYEES? *

Frederick Herzberg

How MANY ARTICLES, BOOKS, SPEECHES, AND WORKSHOPS have pleaded plaintively, "How do I get an employee to do what I want him to do?"

The psychology of motivation is tremendously complex, and what has been unraveled with any degree of assurance is small indeed. But the dismal ratio of knowledge to speculation has not dampened the enthusiasm for new forms of snake oil that are constantly coming on the market, many of them with academic testimonials. Doubtless this article will have no depressing impact on the market for snake oil, but since the ideas expressed in it have been tested in many corporations and other organizations, it will help I hope—to redress the imbalance in the aforementioned ratio.

'MOTIVATING' WITH KITA

In lectures to industry on the problem, I have found that the audiences are anxious for quick and practical answers, so I will begin with a straightforward, practical formula for moving people.

What is the simplest, surest, and most direct way of getting someone to do something? Ask him? But if he responds that he does not want to do it, then that calls for a psychological consultation to determine the reason for his obstinacy. Tell him? His response shows that he does not understand you, and now an expert in communication methods has to be brought in to show you how to get through to him. Give him a monetary incentive? I do not need to remind the reader of the complexity and difficulty involved in setting up and administering an incentive system. Show him? This means a costly training program. We need a simple way.

---

* From "One More Time: How Do You Motivate Employees?" *Harvard Business Review* 46 (January–February 1968): 53–62. © 1968 by the President and Fellows of Harvard College; all rights reserved.

Every audience contains the "direct action" manager who shouts, "Kick him!" And this type of manager is right. The surest and least circumlocuted way of getting someone to do something is to kick him in the pants—give him what might be called the KITA.

There are various forms of KITA, and here are some of them:

Negative physical KITA. This is a literal application of the term and was frequently used in the past. It has, however, three major drawbacks: (1) it is inelegant, (2) it contradicts the precious image of benevolence that most organizations cherish, and (3) since it is a physical attack, it directly stimulates the autonomic nervous system, and this often results in negative feedback—the employee may just kick you in return. These factors give rise to certain taboos against negative physical KITA.

The psychologist has come to the rescue of those who are no longer permitted to use negative physical KITA. He has uncovered infinite sources of psychological vulnerabilities and the appropriate methods to play tunes on them. "He took my rug away"; "I wonder what he meant by that"; "The boss is always going around me"—these symptomatic expressions of ego sores that have been rubbed raw are the result of application of:

Negative Psychological KITA. This has several advantages over negative physical KITA. First, the cruelty is not visible, the bleeding is internal and comes much later. Second, since it affects the higher cortical centers of the brain with its inhibitory powers, it reduces the possibility of physical backlash. Third, since the number of psychological pains that a person can feel is almost infinite, the direction and site possibilities of the KITA are increased many times. Fourth, the person administering the kick can manage to be above it all and let the system accomplish the dirty work. Fifth, those who practice it receive some ego satisfaction (one-upmanship), whereas they would find drawing blood abhorrent. Finally, if the employee does complain, he can always be accused of being paranoid, since there is no tangible evidence of an actual attack.

Now, what does negative KITA accomplish? If I kick you in the rear (physically or psychologically), who is motivated? *I* am motivated; you move! Negative KITA does not lead to motivation, but to movement. So:

Positive KITA. Let us consider motivation. If I say to you, "Do this for me or the company, and in return I will give you a reward, an incentive, more status, a promotion, all the quid pro quos that exist in the industrial organization," am I motivating you? The overwhelming opinion I receive from management people is, "Yes, this is motivation."

I have a year-old Schnauzer. When it was a small puppy and I wanted it to move, I kicked it in the rear and it moved. Now that I have finished obedience training. I hold up a dog biscuit when I want the Schnauzer to move. In this instance, who is motivated—I or the dog? The dog wants the biscuit, but it is I who want it to move. Again, I am the one who is motivated, and the dog is the one who moves. In this instance all I did was apply KITA frontally; I exerted a pull instead of a push. When industry wishes to use such positive KITAs, it has available an incredible number and variety of dog biscuits (jelly beans for humans) to wave in front of the employee to get him to jump.

Why is it that managerial audiences are quick to see that negative KITA is *not* motivation, while they are almost unanimous in their judgment that positive KITA *is* motivation? It is because negative KITA is rape, and positive KITA is seduction. But it is infinitely worse to be seduced than to be raped; the latter is an unfortunate occurrence, while the former signifies that you were a party to your own downfall. This is why positive KITA is so popular: it is a tradiiton; it is in the American way. The organization does not have to kick you; you kick yourself.

Myths about Motivation

Why is KITA not motivation? If I kick my dog (from the front or the back), he will move. And when I want him to move again, what must I do? I must kick him again. Similarly. I can charge a man's battery, and then recharge it, and recharge it again. But it is only when he has his own generator that we can talk about motivation. He then needs no outside stimulation. He wants to do it.

With this in mind, we can review some positive KITA personnel practices that were developed as attempts to instill "motivation":

1. *Reducing time spent at work*—This represents a marvelous way of motivating people to work—getting them off the job! We have reduced (formally and informally) the time spent on the job over the last 50 or 60 years until we are finally on the way to the "6½-day weekend." An interesting variant of this approach is the development of off-hour recreation programs. The philosophy here seems to be that those who play together, work together. The fact is that motivated people seek more hours of work, not fewer.

2. *Spiraling wages*—Have these motivated people? Yes, to seek the next wage increase. Some medievalists still can be heard to say that a good depression will get employees moving. They feel that if rising wages don't or won't do the job, perhaps reducing them will.

3. *Fringe benefits*—Industry has outdone the most welfare-minded of welfare states in dispensing cradle-to-the-grave succor. One company I know of had an informal "fringe benefit of the month club" going for a while. The cost of fringe benefits in this country has reached approximately 25 percent of the wage dollar, and we still cry for motivation.

People spend less time working for more money and more security than ever before, and the trend cannot be reversed. These benefits are no longer rewards; they are rights. A 6-day week is inhuman, a 10-hour day is exploitation, extended medical coverage is a basic decency, and stock options are the salvation of American initiative. Unless the ante is continuously raised, the psychological reaction of employees is that the company is turning back the clock.

When industry began to realize that both the economic nerve and the lazy nerve of their employees had insatiable appetites, it started to listen to the behavioral scientists who, more out of a humanist tradition than from scientific study, criticized management for not knowing how to deal with people. The next KITA easily followed.

4. *Human relations training*—Over 30 years of teaching and, in many instances, of practicing psychological approaches to handling people have resulted in costly human relations programs and, in the end, the same question: How do you motivate workers? Here, too, escalations have taken place. Thirty years ago it was necessary to request, "Please don't spit on the floor." Today the same admonition requires three "please"s before the employee feels that his superior has demonstrated the psychologically proper attitudes toward him.

The failure of human relations training to produce motivation led to the conclusion that the supervisor or manager himself was not psychologically true to himself in his practice of interpersonal decency. So an advanced form of human relations KITA, sensitivity training, was unfolded.

5. *Sensitivity training*—Do you really, really understand yourself? Do you really, really, really trust the other man? Do you really, really, really, really cooperate? The failure of sensitivity training is now being explained, by those who have become opportunistic exploiters of the technique, as a failure to really (five times) conduct proper sensitivity-training courses.

With the realization that there are only temporary gains from comfort and economic and interpersonal KITA, personnel managers concluded that the fault lay not in what they were doing, but in the employee's failure to appreciate what they were doing. This opened up the field of communications, a whole new area of "scientifically" sanctioned KITA.

6. *Communications*—The professor of communications was invited to join the faculty of management training programs and help in making employees understand what management was doing for them. House organs, briefing sessions, supervisory instruction on the importance of communication, and all sorts of propaganda have proliferated until today there is even an International Council of Industrial Editors. But no motivation resulted, and the obvious thought occurred that perhaps management was not hearing what the employees were saying. That led to the next KITA.

7. *Two-way communication*—Management ordered morale surveys, suggestion plans, and group participation programs. Then both employees and management were communicating and listening to each other more than ever, but without much improvement in motivation.

The behavioral scientists began to take another look at their conceptions and their data, and they took human relations one step further. A glimmer of truth was beginning to show through in the writings of the so-called higher-order-need psychologists. People, so they said, want to actualize themselves. Unfortunately, the "actualizing" psychologists got mixed up with the human relations psychologists, and a new KITA emerged.

8. *Job participation*—Though it may not have been the theoretical intention, job participation often became a "give them the big picture" approach. For example, if a man is tightening 10,000 nuts a day on an assembly line with a torque wrench, tell him he is building a Chevrolet. Another approach had the goal of giving the employee a *feeling* that he is determining, in some measure, what he does on his job. The goal was to provide a *sense* of achievement rather than a substantive achievement in his task. Real achievement, of course, requires a task that makes it possible.

But still there was no motivation. This led to the inevitable conclusion that the employees must be sick, and therefore to the next KITA.

9. *Employee counseling*—The initial use of this form of KITA in a systematic fashion can be credited to the Hawthorne experiment of the Western Electric Company during the early 1930s. At that time, it was found that the employees harbored irrational feelings that were interfering with the rational operation of the factory. Counseling in this instance was a means of letting the employees unburden themselves by talking to someone about their problems. Although the counseling techniques were primitive, the program was large indeed.

The counseling approach suffered as a result of experiences during World War II, when the programs themselves were found to be interfering with the operation of the organizations; the counselors had forgotten their role of benevolent listeners and were attempting to do something about the problems that they heard about. Psychological counseling, however, has managed to survive the negative impact of World War II experiences and today is beginning to flourish with renewed sophistication. But, alas, many of these programs, like all the others, do not seem to have lessened the pressure of demands to find out how to motivate workers.

Since KITA results only in short-term movement, it is safe to predict that the cost of these programs will increase steadily and new varieties will be developed as old positive KITAs reach their satiation points.

HYGIENE VERSUS MOTIVATORS

Let me rephrase the perennial question this way: How do you install a generator in an employee? A brief review of my motivation-hygiene theory of job attitudes is required before theoretical and practical suggestions can be offered. The theory was first drawn from an examination of events in the lives of engineers and accountants. At least 16 other investigations, using a wide variety of populations (including some in the

Communist countries), have since been completed, making the original research one of the most replicated studies in the field of job attitudes.

The findings of these studies, along with corroboration from many other investigations using different procedures, suggest that the factors involved in producing job satisfaction (and motivation) are separate and distinct from the factors that lead to job dissatisfaction. Since separate factors need to be considered, depending on whether job satisfaction or job dissatisfaction is being examined, it follows that these two feelings are not opposites of each other. The opposite of job satisfaction is not job dissatisfaction but, rather, no job satisfaction; and, similarly, the opposite of job dissatisfaction is not job satisfaction, but no job dissatisfaction.

Stating the concept presents a problem in semantics, for we normally think of satisfaction and dissatisfaction as opposites—that is, what is not satisfying must be dissatisfying, and vice versa. But when it comes to understanding the behavior of people in their jobs, more than a play on words is involved.

Two different needs of man are involved here. One set of needs can be thought of as stemming from his animal nature—the built-in drive to avoid pain from the environment, plus all the learned drives which become conditioned to the basic biological needs. For example, hunger, a basic biological drive, makes it necessary to earn money, and then money becomes a specific drive. The other set of needs relates to that unique human characteristic, the ability to achieve and, through achievement, to experience psychological growth. The stimuli for the growth needs are tasks that induce growth; in the industrial setting, they are the *job content*. Contrariwise, the stimuli inducing pain-avoidance behavior are found in the *job environment*.

The growth or *motivator* factors that are intrinsic to the job are: achievement, recognition for achievement, the work itself, responsibility, and growth or advancement. The dissatisfaction-avoidance or *hygiene* (KITA) factors that are extrinsic to the job include: company policy and administration, supervision, interpersonal relationships, working conditions, salary, status, and security.

A composite of the factors that are involved in causing job satisfaction and job dissatisfaction, drawn from samples of 1,685 employees, is shown in Exhibit 21–1. The results indicate that motivators were the primary cause of satisfaction, and hygiene factors the primary cause of unhappiness on the job. The employees, studied in 12 different investigations, included lower-level supervisors, professional women, agricultural administrators, men about to retire from management positions, hospital maintenance personnel, manufacturing supervisors, nurses, food handlers, military officers, engineers, scientists, housekeepers, teachers, technicians, female assemblers, accountants, Finnish foremen, and Hungarian engineers.

EXHIBIT 21–1

Factors Affecting Job Attitudes (as reported in 12 investigations)

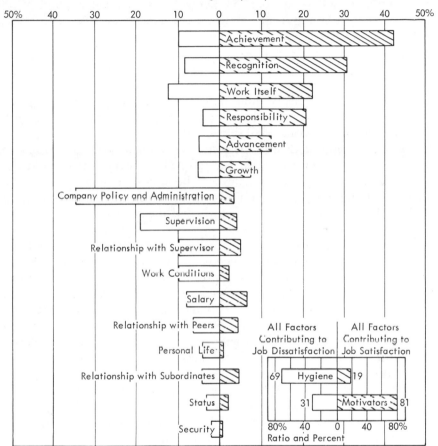

Factors Characterizing 1,844 Events on the Job that Led to Extreme Dissatisfaction | Factors Characterizing 1,753 Events on the Job that Led to Extreme Satisfaction

Percentage Frequency

They were asked what job events had occurred in their work that had led to extreme satisfaction or extreme dissatisfaction on their part. Their responses are broken down in the exhibit into percentages of total "positive" job events and of total "negative" job events. (The figures total more than 100 percent on both the "hygiene" and "motivators" sides because often at least two factors can be attributed to a single event; advancement, for instance, often accompanies assumption of responsibility.)

To illustrate, a typical response involving achievement that had a negative effect for the employee was, "I was unhappy because I didn't do the job successfully." A typical response in the small number of positive job events in the Company Policy and Administration grouping was, "I was happy because the company reorganized the section so that I didn't report any longer to the guy I didn't get along with."

As the lower right-hand part of the exhibit shows, of all the factors contributing to job satisfaction, 81 percent were motivators. And of all the factors contributing to the employees' dissatisfaction over their work, 69 percent involved hygiene elements.

Eternal Triangle

There are three general philosophies of personnel management. The first is based on organizational theory, the second on industrial engineering, and the third on behavioral science.

The organizational theorist believes that human needs are either so irrational or so varied and adjustable to specific situations that the major function of personnel management is to be as pragmatic as the occasion demands. If jobs are organized in a proper manner, he reasons, the result will be the most efficient job structure, and the most favorable job attitudes will follow as a matter of course.

The industrial engineer holds that man is mechanistically oriented and economically motivated and his needs are best met by attuning the individual to the most efficient work process. The goal of personnel management therefore should be to concoct the most appropriate incentive system and to design the specific working conditions in a way that facilitates the most efficient use of the human machine. By structuring jobs in a manner that leads to the most efficient operation, the engineer believes that he can obtain the optimal organization of work and the proper work attitudes.

The behavioral scientist focuses on group sentiments, attitudes of individual employees, and the organization's social and psychological climate. According to his persuasion, he emphasizes one or more of the various hygiene and motivator needs. His approach to personnel management generally emphasizes some form of human relations education, in the hope of instilling healthy employee attitudes and an organizational climate which he considers to be felicitous to human values. He believes that proper attitudes will lead to efficient job and organizational structure.

There is always a lively debate as to the overall effectiveness of the approaches of the organizational theorist and the industrial engineer. Manifestly they have achieved much. But the nagging question for the behavioral scientist has been: What is the cost in human problems that eventually cause more expense to the organization—for instance, turnover, absenteeism, errors, violation of safety rules, strikes, restriction of output, higher wages, and greater fringe benefits? On the other hand, the behavioral scientist is hard put to document much manifest improvement in personnel management, using his approach.

EXHIBIT 21–2

'Triangle' of Philosophies of Personnel Management

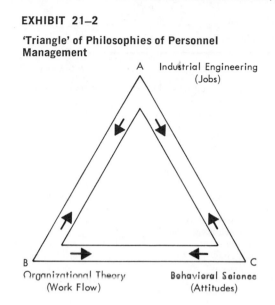

The three philosophies can be depicted as a triangle, as is done in Exhibit 21–2, with each persuasion claiming the apex angle. The motivation-hygiene theory claims the same angle as industrial engineering, but for opposite goals. Rather than rationalizing the work to increase efficiency, the theory suggests that work be *enriched* to bring about effective utilization of personnel. Such a systematic attempt to motivate employees by manipulating the motivator factors is just beginning.

The term *job enrichment* describes this embryonic movement. An older term, job enlargement, should be avoided because it is associated with past failures stemming from a misunderstanding of the problem. Job enrichment provides the opportunity for the employee's psychological growth, while job enlargement merely makes a job structurally bigger. Since scientific job enrichment is very new, this article only suggests the principles and practical steps that have recently emerged from several successful experiments in industry.

Job Loading

In attempting to enrich an employee's job, management often succeeds in reducing the man's personal contribution, rather than giving him an opportunity for growth in his accustomed job. Such an endeavor, which I shall call horizontal job loading (as opposed to vertical loading, or providing motivator factors), has been the problem of earlier job-enlargement programs. This activity merely enlarges the meaninglessness of the job. Some examples of this approach, and their effect, are:

EXHIBIT 21–3

Principles of Vertical Job Loading

Principle	Motivators Involved
A. Removing some controls while retaining accountability	Responsibility and personal achievement
B. Increasing the accountability of individuals for own work	Responsibility and recognition
C. Giving a person a complete natural unit of work (module, division, area, and so on)	Responsibility, achievement, and recognition
D. Granting additional authority to an employee in his activity; job freedom	Responsibility, achievement, and recognition
E. Making periodic reports directly available to the worker himself rather than to the supervisor	Internal recognition
F. Introducing new and more difficult tasks not previously handled	Growth and learning
G. Assigning individuals specific or specialized tasks, enabling them to become experts	Responsibility, growth, and advancement

1. Challenging the employee by increasing the amount of production expected of him. If he tightens 10,000 bolts a day, see if he can tighten 20,000 bolts a day. The arithmetic involved shows that multiplying zero by zero still equals zero.
2. Adding another meaningless task to the existing one, usually some routine clerical activity. The arithmetic here is adding zero to zero.
3. Rotating the assignments of a number of jobs that need to be enriched. This means washing dishes for a while, then washing silverware. The arithmetic is substituting one zero for another zero.
4. Removing the most difficult parts of the assignment in order to free the worker to accomplish more of the less challenging assignments. This traditional industrial engineering approach amounts to subtraction in the hope of accomplishing addition.

These are common forms of horizontal loading that frequently come up in preliminary brainstorming sessions on job enrichment. The principles of vertical loading have not all been worked out as yet, and they remain rather general, but I have furnished seven useful starting points for consideration in Exhibit 21–3.

A Successful Application

An example from a highly successful job enrichment experiment can illustrate the distinction between horizontal and vertical loading of a job.

The subjects of this study were the stockholder correspondents employed by a very large corporation. Seemingly, the task required of these carefully selected and highly trained correspondents was quite complex and challenging. But almost all indexes of performance and job attitudes were low, and exit interviewing confirmed that the challenge of the job existed merely as words.

A job-enrichment project was initiated in the form of an experiment with one group, designated as an achieving unit, having its job enriched by the principles described in Exhibit 21–3. A control group continued to do its job in the traditional way. (There were also two "uncommitted" groups of correspondents formed to measure the so-called Hawthorne Effect—that is, to gauge whether productivity and attitudes toward the job changed artificially merely because employees sensed that the company was paying more attention to them in doing something different or novel. The results for these groups were substantially the same as for the control group, and for the sake of simplicity I do not deal with them in this summary.) No changes in hygiene were introduced for either group other than those that would have been made anyway, such as normal pay increases.

The changes for the achieving unit were introduced in the first two months, averaging one per week of the seven motivators listed in Exhibit 21–3. At the end of six months the members of the achieving unit were found to be outperforming their counterparts in the control group, and in addition indicated a marked increase in their liking for their jobs. Other results showed that the achieving group had lower absenteeism and, subsequently, a much higher rate of promotion.

Exhibit 21–4 illustrates the changes in performance, measured in February and March, before the study period began, and at the end of each month of the study period. The shareholder service index represents quality of letters, including accuracy of information, and speed of response to stockholders' letters of inquiry. The index of a current month was averaged into the average of the two prior months, which means that improvement was harder to obtain if the indexes of the previous months were low. The "achievers" were performing less well before the 6-month period started, and their performance service index continued to decline after the introduction of the motivators, evidently because of uncertainty over their newly granted responsibilities. In the third month, however, performance improved, and soon the members of this group had reached a high level of accomplishment.

Exhibit 21–5 shows the two groups' attitudes toward their job, measured at the end of March, just before the first motivator was introduced. and again at the end of September. The correspondents were asked 16 questions, all involving motivation. A typical one was, "As you see it, how many opportunities do you feel that you have in your job for making worthwhile contributions?" The answers were scaled from 1 to 5, with 80

EXHIBIT 21–4

Shareholder Service Index in Company Experiment (three-month cumulative average)

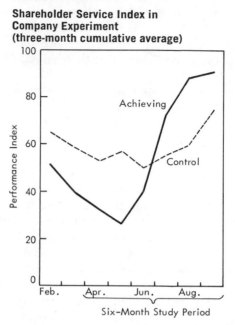

EXHIBIT 21–5

Changes in Attitudes toward Tasks in Company Experiment (changes in means scores over six-month period)

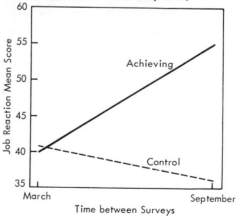

as the maximum possible score. The achievers became much more positive about their job, while the attitude of the control unit remained about the same (the drop is not statistically significant).

How was the job of these correspondents restructured? Exhibit 21–6 lists the suggestions made that were deemed to be horizontal loading, and

EXHIBIT 21–6

Enlargement versus Enrichment of Correspondents' Tasks in Company Experiment

Horizontal-loading suggestions (rejected)	Vertical-loading suggestions (adopted)	Principle
Firm quotas could be set for letters to be answered each day, using a rate which would be hard to reach.	Subject matter experts were appointed within each unit for other members of the unit to consult with before seeking supervisory-help. (The supervisor had been answering all specialized and difficult questions.)	G
The women could type the letters themselves, as well as compose them, or take on any other clerical functions.	Correspondents signed their own names on letters. (The supervisor had been signing all letters.)	B
All difficult or complex inquiries could be channeled to a few women so that the remainder could achieve high rates of output. These jobs could be exchanged from time to time.	The work of the more experienced correspondents was proofread less frequently by supervisors and was done at the correspondents' desks, dropping verification from 100 percent to 10 percent. (Previously, all correspondents' letters had been checked by the supervisor.)	A
The women could be rotated through units handling different customers, and then sent back to their own units.	Production was discussed, but only in terms such as "a full day's work is expected." As time went on, this was no longer mentioned. (Before, the group had been constantly reminded of the number of letters that needed to be answered.)	D
	Outgoing mail went directly to the mailroom without going over supervisors' desks. (The letters had always been routed through the supervisors.)	A
	Correspondents were encouraged to answer letters in a more personalized way. (Reliance on the form-letter approach had been standard practice.)	C
	Each correspondent was held personally responsible for the quality and accuracy of letters. (This responsibility had been the province of the supervisor and the verifier.)	B, E

the actual vertical-loading changes that were incorporated in the job of the achieving unit. The capital letters under "Principle" after "Vertical loading" refer to the corresponding letters in Exhibit 21–3. The reader will note that the rejected forms of horizontal loading correspond closely to the list of common manifestations of the phenomenon shown in the left column of Exhibit 21–3.

STEPS TO JOB ENRICHMENT

Now that the motivator idea has been described in practice, here are the steps that managers should take in instituting the principle with their employees:

1. Select those jobs in which (a) the investment in industrial engineering does not make changes too costly, (b) attitudes are poor, (c) hygiene is becoming very costly, and (d) motivation will make a difference in performance.
2. Approach these jobs with the conviction that they can be changed. Years of tradition have led managers to believe that the content of the jobs is sacrosanct and the only scope of action that they have is in ways of stimulating people.
3. Brainstorm a list of changes that may enrich the jobs, without concern for their practicality.
4. Screen the list to eliminate suggestions that involve hygiene, rather than actual motivation.
5. Screen the list for generalities, such as "give them more responsibility," that are rarely followed in practice. This might seem obvious, but the motivator words have never left industry; the substance has just been rationalized and organized out. Words like "responsibility," "growth," "achievement," and "challenge," for example, have been elevated to the lyrics of the patriotic anthem for all organizations. It is the old problem typified by the pledge of allegiance to the flag being more important than contributions to the country—of following the form, rather than the substance.
6. Screen the list to eliminate any *horizontal*-loading suggestions.
7. Avoid direct participation by the employees whose jobs are to be enriched. Ideas they have expressed previously certainly constitute a valuable source for recommended changes, but their direct involvement contaminates the process with human relations *hygiene* and, more specifically, gives them only a *sense* of making a contribution. The job is to be changed, and it is the content that will produce the motivation, not attitudes about being involved or the challenge inherent in setting up a job. That process will be over shortly, and it is what the employees will be doing from then on that will determine their motivation. A sense of participation will result only in short-term movement.

8. In the initial attempts at job enrichment, set up a controlled experiment. At least two equivalent groups should be chosen, one an experimental unit in which the motivators are systematically introduced over a period of time, and the other one a control group in which no changes are made. For both groups, hygiene should be allowed to follow its natural course for the duration of the experiment. Pre- and post-installation tests of performance and job attitudes are necessary to evaluate the effectiveness of the job-enrichment program. The attitude test must be limited to motivator items in order to divorce the employee's view of the job he is given from all the surrounding hygiene feelings that he might have.

9. Be prepared for a drop in performance in the experimental group the first few weeks. The changeover to a new job may lead to a temporary reduction in efficiency.

10. Expect your first-line supervisors to experience some anxiety and hostility over the changes you are making. The anxiety comes from their fear that the changes will result in poorer performance for their unit. Hostility will arise when the employees start assuming what the supervisors regard as their own responsibility for performance. The supervisor without checking duties to perform may then be left with little to do.

After a successful experiment, however, the supervisor usually discovers the supervisory and managerial functions he has neglected, or which were never his because all his time was given over to checking the work of his subordinates. For example, in the R&D division of one large chemical company I know of, the supervisors of the laboratory assistants were theoretically responsible for their training and evaluation. These functions, however, had come to be performed in a routine, unsubstantial fashion. After the job-enrichment program, during which the supervisors were not merely passive observers of the assistants' performance, the supervisors actually were devoting their time to reviewing performance and administering thorough training.

What has been called an employee-centered style of supervision will come about not through education of supervisors, but by changing the jobs that they do.

CONCLUDING NOTE

Job enrichment will not be a one-time proposition, but a continuous management function. The initial changes, however, should last for a very long period of time. There are a number of reasons for this:

1. The changes should bring the job up to the level of challenge commensurate with the skill that was hired.

2. Those who have still more ability eventually will be able to demonstrate it better and win promotion to higher-level jobs.
3. The very nature of motivators, as opposed to hygiene factors, is that they have a much longer-term effect on employees' attitudes. Perhaps the job will have to be enriched again, but this will not occur as frequently as the need for hygiene.

Not all jobs can be enriched, nor do all jobs need to be enriched. If only a small percentage of the time and money that is now devoted to hygiene, however, were given to job enrichment-efforts, the return in human satisfaction and economic gain would be one of the largest dividends that industry and society have ever reaped through their efforts at better personnel management.

The argument for job enrichment can be summed up quite simply: If you have someone on a job, use him. If you can't use him on the job, get rid of him, either via automation or by selecting someone with lesser ability. If you can't use him and you can't get rid of him, you will have a motivation problem.

22. JOB ATTITUDES, EFFORT, AND PERFORMANCE: A THEORETICAL MODEL *

Edward E. Lawler III and Lyman W. Porter

THE PURPOSE OF THIS ARTICLE is to explore some of the attitudes of managers that are presumed to be related to effective job performance, . . . by presenting a conceptual model that attempts to tie these attitude variables to task performance.

We shall refer to the attitudes we are about to discuss as "antecedent" attitudes because we believe they help to determine job performance rather than being the result of such performance. At the outset, however, let us note that this set of antecedent attitudes does *not* include the type of attitude most frequently studied in investigations of the attitudes—performance relationship in industrial psychology, namely, job satisfaction. For too long, in our opinion, psychologists interested in work behavior have acted as if job satisfaction were the only type of attitude that has any theoretical significance in the understanding of individual differences in job performance. Our position is that attitudes that can be classified

---

* Adapted and extracted from "Antecedent Attitudes of Effective Managerial Performance," *Organizational Behavior and Human Performance* 2 (1967): 122–42.

under the satisfaction label are only one type (and perhaps not the most important type) of attitudes that are in some way associated with behavior in the job situation. More importantly, we would hypothesize that job satisfaction is primarily a dependent variable in relation to job performance, and that other types of attitudes may have a much more crucial role in determining task behavior. Therefore, in this article, which is addressed to the attitudinal antecedents of managerial job performance, we shall focus on types of job attitudes other than that of satisfaction with the job.

THE THEORETICAL MODEL

That part of our conceptual model that we will deal with in this article is addressed to two basic questions: (1) What factors determine the *effort* a person puts into his job, and (2) What factors affect the relationship between effort and *performance?* To answer these two questions, we have diagramed our view of the relationships involved among six relevant variables (see Figure 22–1). We will proceed to define each variable and try to indicate how they interact in determining task-relevant performance.

As can be seen from Figure 22–1, we propose that there are two variables that must be considered in answering the question: "What factors determine the *effort* a person puts into his job?" These two variables are (1) value of rewards, and (2) probability that rewards depend upon effort. We define the first of these variables—value of rewards—as the attractiveness of possible rewards or outcomes to the individual. We are here not particularly concerned about how different rewards come to be thought of as differentially desirable by a given individual, although this is an important theoretical question in itself. All that is hypothesized is that, for any given individual at any particular point in time, there is a variety of possible outcomes that he differentially desires. Although, as Vroom has pointed out,[1] some outcomes may have aversive qualities which lead them to have negative values, the focus in the present paper will be upon positively valued outcomes or rewards. Specifically, the emphasis will be upon rewards that are relevant to the list of needs suggested by Maslow with the modifications of Porter.[2] The expectation is that rewards will be valued by an individual to the extent in which he believes they will provide satisfaction of his needs for security, social, esteem, autonomy and self-actualization. Although there is a certain degree of stability to the value of rewards over time for a given person, it is also clear that the values can and do change, depending upon various circumstances in the

---

[1] V. H. Vroom, *Work and Motivation* (New York: John Wiley & Sons, 1964).

[2] A. H. Maslow, *Motivation and Personality* (New York: Harper, 1954); L. W. Porter, "A Study of Perceived Need Satisfactions in Bottom and Middle Management Jobs," *Journal of Applied Psychology* 45 (1961): 1–10.

FIGURE 22–1

Diagram of the Theoretical Model

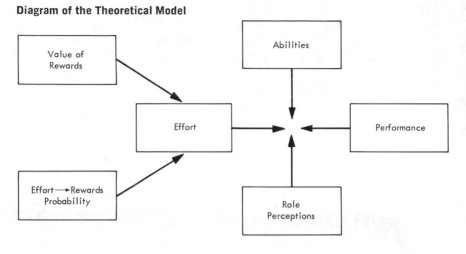

environment. This concept is similar to the subjective utility concept used in behavioral decision theories.[3]

In our model the second variable hypothesized to affect effort is the probability that rewards depend upon effort. This variable refers to an individual's subjective expectance concerning the likelihood that the rewards he desires will follow from putting forth certain levels of effort, and is similar to the concept of subjective probability. Such an expectation can be thought of as representing the combination of two separate subsidiary expectancies, namely: (*a*) the probability that rewards depend upon performance, and (*b*) the probability that performance depends upon effort. Let us use an example to clarify these points.

Suppose that a manager in charge of a manufacturing unit in a large plant desires a promotion to a higher-level job. (Such a promotion would be considered as having a high "value of reward" in our terms, since it appears to satisfy several needs.) The manager may believe that obtaining the promotion does not depend upon his performance (that is, the output and efficiency of his unit). He may feel that the promotion will more likely be made on the basis of straight seniority. Or, he may feel that, no matter how well his unit performs, he will not be promoted (in the reasonable future) because there are no openings above him to which he could be promoted even if the company desired to do so. In such instances, if the manager reports that this is how he sees the situation, we would say he has a low perceived probability that rewards depend upon performance, and therefore his perceived probability that rewards depend upon effort

---

[3] For example, W. Edwards, "Behavioral Decision Theory," *Annual Review of Psychology* 12 (1961): 473–98; D. Davidson, P. Suppes, and S. Siegel, *Decision-Making: an Experimental Approach* (Stanford, Calif.: Stanford University Press, 1957).

is also low. However, let us suppose the manager does feel that rewards do depend upon performance and that the next promotion will go to the manager whose unit is performing most effectively. Even in this case, his expectations that rewards depend upon effort may still be low. The reason for this is that, although he feels that promotions are made on the basis of performance in his company, he may feel that no amount of additional effort on his part will improve the performance of his group. He may feel this, for example, simply because of his belief that the situational factors governing the performance of his unit are beyond his control, or because he does not think he has the necessary abilities to perform the job well enough to deserve a reward. He is saying, in effect, "No matter how much effort I put into the job, I probably won't get that promotion."

A possible further complication arising with respect to the probability dimension is that of the manager's feeling that effort may result in rewards even though it does not necessarily result in unit performance. This would be the case where an organization pays off for trying—with or without concommitant performance. Where this is true, the probability that effort can be converted into performance will be irrelevant in determining how much effort an individual will put forth on the job. In this case the prediction is that the individual would put forth effort but that it would be rather diffuse and not necessarily productive.

It is necessary to keep in mind that, when we are referring to this second variable in our model (the probability that rewards depend upon effort), we are talking about the *perceived* probability or subjective expectancy, not about actual probabilities. In our example, even though the manager might think the promotion will be based strictly on seniority, he may be incorrect in that higher officials are actually planning to make it totally on the basis of whose unit is performing best. In such a circumstance the manager's perceived probability is low and this will have a deleterious effect on his effort, even though his perceptions are, in fact, wrong. It is clear, then, that to measure this variable we need to obtain an estimation from the individual himself as to his beliefs concerning probabilities or expectancies—that is, perceptions of path (effort)-goal (rewards) relationships. Such perceptions regarding the effort–reward probabilities can be obtained directly, or by combining the two separate subsidiary probabilities, namely, performance–reward, and effort–performance. In the latter case, we would advise that such probabilities be combined in a multiplicative way to obtain the overall effort–reward probability that is specified in the diagram of the model.

We are now faced with the question of how the first two variables— value of rewards and probability that rewards depend upon effort—combine to determine effort. To do this, we first need to define effort. In our model, effort refers to the amount of energy an individual expends in a given situation. In nonpsychological terms it refers to how hard the person is trying to perform a task. Effort, of course, is to be distinguished from performance (the amount of task accomplishment). A student may put in great effort (that is, review his notes and assigned readings for many hours) in studying for a test, but his achievement on the test may be low. Effort is the variable in our model that most closely corresponds to the motivational component in typical discussions of the motivation of performance.

Effort can be measured in several different ways. For certain limited types of tasks, especially in laboratory-type settings, objective physical measurements can be obtained. In typical managerial jobs, of course, such measurements are essentially irrelevant. Here we must rely either on self-reports or the judgments of qualified observers. The problem is that in many instances the two kinds of reports may not agree, and the investigator is left with the dilemma of determining which is *the* measure of effort. (We do not pretend to have a solution to this problem. For the moment, we are willing to use either or both measures to indicate "effort" in our model.)

Returning now to the question of how value of reward and probability that rewards depend upon effort determine effort, we can state the basic hypothesis: *The greater the value of a set of rewards and the higher the probability that receiving each of these rewards depends upon effort, the greater the effort that will be put forth in a given situation.* Stating the hypothesis in this form still leaves unknown the exact nature of the interaction between reward value and probability in determining effort. Although there is little previous research relevant to the question, we hypothesize that the interaction is essentially a multiplicative one. Thus, for each reward it is necessary to multiply its value by the perceived probability that receiving it depends on effort. In other words, either variable alone is a necessary but not sufficient condition for effort. If an individual highly values a reward potentially available in the situation, and if he believes that its attainment in no way at all depends upon his level of effort, he will put forth minimum effort. Likewise, if a reward is provided and the person feels its attainment does depend strongly upon his level of effort, he may still put in a minimum of effort if the reward has very low value for him.

The hypothesis emphasizes the point that the amount of effort put forth is determined by a number of different rewards. Thus, in order to determine how much effort will be put forth, it is necessary to consider the products obtained from multiplying each reward value by the probability that such reward is dependent upon effort. Here we hypothesize that the best way to combine the products obtained from multiplying the reward values and probabilities is by addition. It is necessary to consider all rewards because, in a given situation, individuals may be putting forth the same amount of effort in order to obtain entirely different rewards. It may also be that an individual sees only one reward as related to effort, while another sees one reward plus several others as related to effort, and therefore works harder. In summary, then, it has been argued that the amount of anticipated effort to be expended is a function of the sum of (reward value × perceived probability that effort leads to the reward), where all rewards relevant to the list of needs suggested by Maslow are considered.[4]

FACTORS AFFECTING THE RELATIONSHIP BETWEEN EFFORT AND PERFORMANCE

As we have pointed out, effort is not synonymous with performance. This is another way of saying that other variables, in addition to effort, affect task achievement. With this in mind, let us now turn to the second of the two major questions addressed in our model: "What factors affect the relationship between effort and performance?" As can be seen in Figure 22–1, our model points to two major categories of variables that combine with effort in determining performance. These two variables are abilities (including personality traits) and role perceptions.

For our purposes in the model, we have defined ability as the individual's currently developed power to perform. The set of variables encompassed under the term "ability" refers to such characteristics of the individual as intelligence, manual skills, personality traits, and so forth. To a certain extent it is a sort of catch-all category of individual difference variables with the important common feature of being relatively stable and long-term characteristics of the individual. They can be modified, but they typically do not change very much over the short run. In this sense, then, abilities are relatively independent of immediate environmental circumstances. Measurement of abilities depends upon the specific ability being considered, but typically such measurements involve tests of some sort—intelligence tests, aptitude tests, personality inventories, and the like. Also, of course, it is possible for other individuals to estimate a given person's abilities in a particular area, although it is obvious that frequently such estimates might be quite at variance with supposedly more valid test data.

In contrast to abilities and their long-term nature, the variable of role perceptions in our model refers to a more situationally modified variable, namely, the kinds of activities and behaviors in which the individual feels he should engage so as to perform his job successfully. In other words, role perceptions determine the *direction* in which the individual applies his effort. Since they can be affected by immediate cues coming from the environment, they are much more dynamic in their character than are relatively static abilities. There are many important situational factors, other than role perceptions, which can and do influence performance. For example, the production-line worker is frequently limited in terms of the

---

[4] Maslow, *Motivation and Personality.*

variability of his performance regardless of how much effort he puts forth.[5] Thus, there are many situational factors influencing performance, and which could potentially be included along with role perceptions as moderators of the relationship between effort and performance. Argyris has recently discussed many of the relevant situational factors such as job design and managerial controls.[6] However, we have decided to focus here on only one kind of situational factor—role perceptions—because they are a psychological or human variable rather than an environmental one, and because it is relatively easy to study them empirically.

An individual's role perceptions can be termed accurate ("good") if his views concerning the placement of his effort correspond closely with the views of those who will be evaluating his performance. If the individual's role perceptions are inaccurate, he may expend a great deal of effort without performing at a high level, even though his abilities are more than adequate for superior performance. To measure role perceptions involves, by definition, acquiring information as to how the individual himself views the requirements of a particular job. Thus, some sort of report must be obtained from the individual. This can be in several forms: narrative descriptions of the job, answers to open-ended questions concerning the job, or answers to directive-type, closed-end questions.

As we have previously noted, the sixth and final term in the theoretical model presented here is performance, defined as the amount of successful role achievement. Broadly considered, the model does appear to be potentially applicable with respect to explaining the amount of successful role achievement an individual will obtain in any number of behavioral situations. Thus, the model presumably can explain an individual's performance on the golf course as well as his job performance. In the present study, however, the focus is upon job performance, which traditionally has been measured in three ways: (1) objective indices (rate of output of a manufacturing unit, amount of sales, amount of profits, and so forth); (2) appraisals and ratings by individuals other than the person whose performance is being evaluated; and (3) self-appraisals and self-ratings. Although objective measures of performance are usually considered the most advantageous for the researcher, we can note that in many instances (for example, management jobs), ratings—especially ratings of the person by other individuals—often have greater overall relevance for the goals of the organization than do certain objective measures covering, perhaps, only minor or peripheral aspects of the job.

Now, how do traits and role perceptions modify the relationship between effort and performance? We hypothesize that higher effort will lead to higher performance, the greater extent to which the individual

---

[5] C. R. Walker and R. H. Guest, *The Man on the Assembly Line* (Cambridge, Mass.: Harvard University Press, 1952).

[6] C. Argyris, *Integrating the Individual and the Organization* (New York: John Wiley & Sons, 1964).

possesses task-relevant abilities, and the greater extent to which his role perceptions are congruent with those who will be evaluating his performance.

More specifically, we hypothesize that both abilities and role perceptions interact multiplicatively with effort to produce performance. The evidence (not extensive, but nonetheless convincing) for the multiplicative interaction of effort and abilities has been reviewed in detail by Vroom and by Lawler.[7] Evidence for the interactive nature of effort and role perceptions is essentially nonexistent, but it is our thesis that the degree of accuracy of role perceptions determines the proportion of effort relevant for task achievement.

If we were going to put the above ideas into a purely hypothetical example, we could consider the following: Assume the amount of possible effort that can be expended runs from 0 (no effort) to 10 (maximum effort) units, the amount of a particular ability in a given situation runs from 0 (no ability) to 10 (maximum ability) units, and that accuracy of role perceptions runs from 0 percent (completely inaccurate) to 100 percent (completely accurate). Then, hypothetically, these values could be combined multiplicatively in an equation to derive the task achievement that would be expected from a given individual in a given situation: for example,

> 8 units of effort × 6 units of ability × 80 percent role-perception accuracy = 38.4 units of task performance (out of a theoretical maximum of 100 units).

The important point to keep in mind in the above hypothetical equation is that attitudes are involved in affecting performance primarily through only two of the three antecedent variables, namely effort and role perceptions. Two types of attitudes—value of rewards and probability that rewards depend on effort—are involved in determining effort, and role perceptions are themselves a particular type of attitude. Thus, according to our model, if it is desired to modify performance through changing attitudes, the three specific types of attitudes just mentioned are the ones we consider to be the most crucial antecedent attitudes of effective managerial performance.

---

[7] Vroom, *Work and Motivation;* E. E. Lawler, "Ability as a Moderator of the Relationship between Job Attitudes and Job Performance," *Personnel Psychology* 19 (1966): 153–64.

23. EXPECTANCY THEORY PREDICTIONS OF WORK EFFECTIVENESS *

J. Richard Hackman and Lyman W. Porter

WHILE EXPECTANCY THEORY has enjoyed considerable currency among psychologists since its beginnings in the work of Tolman and Lewin,[1] until recently there have been relatively few studies testing the predictions of the theory in "real-world" performance situations. In recent years, the relevance and usefulness of the theory for understanding work behavior in organizations has been demonstrated by Georgopoulos, Mahoney, and Jones; Vroom; Galbraith and Cummings; and Lawler and Porter.[2]

This study utilizes measurement techniques adapted from the attitude theory of Fishbein to generate expectancy theory predictions of effort and performance in an on-going work situation.[3] Since this methodology makes the *components* of the expectancy theory predictions operationally explicit, it has the potential for considerably facilitating efforts to diagnose and change individuals' motivation. Thus, the present research has the dual purpose of assessing the usefulness of the Fishbein methodology for generating expectancy theory predictions, and of providing additional data on the relationship between these predictions and performance effectiveness in a field setting.

METHOD

The Measurement Strategy

Expectancy theory states that the strength of the tendency for an individual to perform a particular act is a function of (*a*) the strength

---

* From *Organizational Behavior and Human Performance* 3 (1968): 417–26.

[1] E. C. Tolman, *Purposive Behavior in Animals and Men* (New York: Century, 1932); K. Lewin, *The Conceptual Representation and Measurement of Psychological Forces* (Durham, N.C.: Duke University Press, 1938).

[2] B. S. Georgopoulos, G. M. Mahoney, and N. W. Jones, Jr., "A Path-Goal Approach to Productivity," *Journal of Applied Psychology* 41 (1957): 345–53; V. Vroom, *Work and Motivation* (New York: John Wiley & Sons, 1964); J. Galbraith and L. L. Cummings, "An Empirical Investigation of the Motivational Determinants of Task Performance: Interactive Effects between Instrumentality-Valence and Motivation-Ability," *Organizational Behavior and Human Performance* 2 (1967): 237–57; and E. E. Lawler, III and L. W. Porter, "Antecedent Attitudes of Effective Managerial Performance." *Organizational Behavior and Human Performance* 2 (1967): 122–42.

[3] M. Fishbein, "An Investigation of the Relationships between Beliefs about an Object and the Attitude toward That Object" *Human Relations* 16 (1963): 233–39.

with which he expects certain outcomes to be obtained from the act, times
(b) the attractiveness to him of the expected outcomes. Thus, the theory
frequently is summarized by the phrase "Force equals expectancy times
valence" ($F = E \times V$). Since there usually are several different outcomes
potentially associated with any given action, most expectancy theorists
sum the $E \times V$ component across the total number of possible or relevant
outcomes (n) to obtain an overall estimate of motivation or "force" to act,
yielding

$$F = \sum_{i=1}^{n} E_i \times V_i$$

In this study, expectancy theory is used to generate predictions of how
hard employees work on their jobs, and how effective their performance
is. Thus, three kinds of information must be obtained from the employees:
(a) a list of outcomes which they expect to obtain as a result of "working
hard" on the job, (b) an estimate of the level of certainty they have that
the outcomes will in fact be obtained as a result of working hard (E_i), and
(c) an estimate of the degree to which they like or dislike the outcomes
(V_i).

Procedures developed for applications of Fishbein's attitude theory
offer an appropriate and relatively refined means of obtaining these data,
since the Fishbein theory parallels expectancy theory closely in form and
content.[4] In brief, Fishbein specifies that an individual's attitude toward
an object equals

$$\sum_{i=1}^{n} B_i \times a_i$$

Where B_i is the strength of a particular belief about the object (analogous
to E_i in expectancy theory), a_i is the evaluation associated with that
belief (analogous to V_i in expectancy theory) and n is the number of
beliefs held by the individual about the object (analogous to the number
of outcomes in expectancy theory). The means by which the Fishbein
procedures were applied to obtain expectancy theory predictions are
presented below.

The Research Setting

The study was conducted at three comparably sized offices of a telephone company. Subjects were 82 female service representatives working
at these offices who had been on the job for more than three months, and
for whom it was possible to obtain complete predictor and criterion

---

[4] Ibid.

data. Service representatives are responsible for most aspects of customers' telephone service, including arranging new or changed service, handling complaints and special requests, maintaining records of customer services and charges, and servicing overdue accounts. The job involves both customer contact and clerical activities, and is generally described by the representatives as having considerable variety and responsibility. Although part of the "pace" of the work is determined by the rate of incoming calls from customers, the representatives reported that they had control over the pace and scheduling of a significant portion of their activities.

Predictor Scores

The expectancy theory formula was used to generate a single predictor score for each subject. The means by which the information required to compute these scores was obtained is presented below.

Obtaining a List of Expected Outcomes. In its most elegant form, expectancy theory requires that the outcomes which are utilized in the prediction equation be obtained from the particular individual whose behavior is to be predicted. A similar requirement exists for the Fishbein attitude theory; in order to best predict an individual's attitude, only those beliefs which are idiosyncratic to him should be employed. However, recent research by Hackman and Anderson and Kaplan and Fishbein has shown predictions of attitudes are not attenuated when beliefs are obtained on a group basis.[5] That is, when only those beliefs which generally are held *in common* by subjects are used in prediction, the level of prediction is just as high as when idiosyncratic beliefs are used for each subject. Thus, to the extent that these findings about "beliefs about an object" also are relevant to "beliefs about outcomes" (as is reasonable to assume, given the strong parallels between the Fishbein attitude theory and expectancy theory), only those outcomes which are held in common by most of the service representatives need to be identified for use in the prediction equation. This procedure, of course, renders studies such as this one much more feasible to conduct, and, more importantly, allows direct comparison of the responses of different subjects, since all respondents deal with identically the same set of beliefs about outcomes.

A list of common outcomes or consequences of working hard on the job was obtained in the present study by interviewing 24 service representatives, 8 from each of the three research sites. A frequency distribution was computed and 14 outcomes which were mentioned by three or more interviewees were selected for use in computing predictions. Probably

---

[5] J. R. Hackman and L. R. Anderson, "The Strength, Relevance, and Source of Beliefs about an Object in Fishbein's Attitude Theory," *Journal of Social Psychology* 76 (1968): 55–67; K. J. Kaplan and M. Fishbein, "The Source of Beliefs, Their Saliency, and Prediction of Attitude," *Journal of Social Psychology* 78 (1969): 63–74.

TABLE 23–1

Beliefs about the Consequences of Working Hard Used in Predicting Work Behavior

---

If a person works especially hard on this job:
1. Time will seem to go faster.
2. She is likely to be of more help to her customers.
3. She is more likely to feel tired and fatigued at the end of the day.
4. She is more likely to feel a sense of completion and accomplishment at the end of the day.
5. She is more likely to receive thanks and gratitude from her customers.
6. She is not as likely to need the help of other girls to catch up on her work.
7. Her supervisor will expect it from her all the time.[a]
8. It is more likely that her office will win contests with other offices.[b]
9. She is more likely to gain admiration and respect from her fellow workers.
10. She is likely to receive more compliments and praise from her supervisor.
11. She is more likely to win individual contests.[b]
12. Her supervisor is likely to check up on her work less frequently.
13. Her customers are likely to buy more service.
14. She is likely to receive a promotion more quickly.
15. She will simply get more work assigned to her.[a]
16. She is likely to receive a raise more quickly.
17. She will set too high a standard for other girls in the office.[a]
18. Her customers are more likely to get annoyed.[a]

Note: Beliefs are listed in order of decreasing mean strength; that is, the first belief listed was held most strongly by the subjects and the last one listed was held least strongly.
[a] "Moderately negative" beliefs supplied by the experimenters.
[b] The reference to contests has to do with company-initiated sales competitions.

because of the generally high morale of the service representatives, there were very few *negative* consequences included in the set of outcomes. Therefore, 4 possible outcomes of moderately negative tone (for example, "If a person works especially hard on this job, she will set too high a standard for other girls in the office") were added to the list to allow for as wide a range of response as possible. It was expected these negative items would turn out to have relatively low-expectancy strengths for most representatives, and this was in fact the case. A complete list of outcomes used in the study, arranged in order of decreasing strength of expectancy, is presented in Table 23–1. (The questionnaire with which the expectancy measures were obtained is described below.)

Obtaining Indices of Expectancy and Valence. A questionnaire was constructed to obtain measures of how strongly the representatives believed that each of the outcomes would in fact result from working hard on the job (E_i), and how positively (or negatively) the representatives evaluated each of the outcomes (V_i). In the first half of the questionnaire, designed to measure strength of expectancy, subjects responded to items of the following format:

If a person works especially hard on this job, *she is more likely to feel a sense of completion and accomplishment at the end of the day.* A

7-point scale was used, ranging from "not at all true" (meaning that the employee did not expect to obtain this outcome as a result of working hard) to "very true."

In the second half of the questionnaire the subjects used a 7-point scale to react evaluatively to the outcomes themselves, as a means of obtaining estimates of valence. This scale ranged from "very bad" to "very good" with "neither good nor bad" at the midpoint, and the items were the outcomes themselves, namely, "feeling a sense of completion and accomplishment." Thus, the responses of the subjects indicated the value which they placed on each of the outcomes.

The questionnaire emphasized that the researchers were university-connected (and not company-connected), and that the subjects' responses would be seen only by the researchers. The questionnaires were administered to all service representatives at the three sites (not just those who had been interviewed). The subjects took the questionnaire in small groups, and the researchers reemphasized the anonymity of the questionnaires as they were administered.

Criteria

Five criteria were utilized to test the adequacy of the expectancy theory predictions. These were:

1. *Job Involvement and Effort.* Ratings by the representatives' supervisors of the involvement of each representative in her job. Each representative was rated by two supervisors on four scales: *(a)* enthusiasm about the job itself, *(b)* effort and energy expended in doing her job, *(c)* personal involvement in the job itself, and *(d)* feelings of concern about the job. Ratings were made on a 9-point continuum for each scale, and a total score was obtained by summing across the four scales. Median intercorrelation among the four scales was .83. Inter-rater reliability for the judgments was .60; Spearman-Brown projected reliability for the summed judgments (across the four scales) was .86.
2. *Employee Appraisal Form.* Periodically each representative is assessed by her supervisor on seven scales as part of the company's regular appraisal process. These scales are quality of work, quantity of work, cooperativeness, judgment, dependability, initiative, and ability to learn. Appraisals were obtained from company records for each representative in the sample.
3. *Error Rate.* The company maintains complete records of errors made by the representatives in processing customer orders, and these data were obtained for all subjects.
4. *Sales Data.* The company also maintains data on each representative's sales effectiveness, and these data were obtained for all subjects. Error rate and sales data were converted to standard scores within

each of the three research sites before analysis, to compensate for minor differences in the way in which these data were compiled at the three locations.

5. *Composite Criterion.* The job involvement, error rate, and sales data were converted to standard scores and combined to yield one "overall" index of work effectiveness.

RESULTS

The expectancy theory predictor of how hard the subjects would work on the job

$$\left(\sum_{i=1}^{n} E_i \times V_i \right)$$

correlated .40 with the composite criterion of work effectiveness. In addition, the predictor was significantly related to supervisors' ratings of effort, to sales, to error rate (negatively), and to five of the seven scales of the Employee Appraisal Form. These results are summarized in Table 23-2.[6]

DISCUSSION

Magnitude of the Results

The relationships between the expectancy theory predictions and the performance criteria, while statistically significant, are not strikingly large. Yet there are reasons for optimism about them. First, as is noted in reviews by Brayfield and Crockett, Vroom, and others, attitude measures have been notoriously poor predictors of performance in work situations.[7] The present relationships, in which (following Fishbein) the expectancy

---

[6] Expectancy theory, as can be seen from the $\Sigma E_i \times V_i$ formula, implies that it is the *interaction* between expectancy and valence which will yield the best predictions of behavior. To check this, other combinations of the data were correlated with the criteria, and these relationships compared to those presented in Table 23-2. In particular, the two components of the predictor (ΣE_i and ΣV_i) and the sum of the components ($\Sigma E_i + \Sigma V_i$) each were correlated with the criteria. The results supported the multiplicative model in each case. The correlations between the ΣE_i term and the eleven criteria (reversing the sign of the correlation with error rate) ranged from −.08 to .23, with a median of .11; for the ΣV_i term the correlations ranged from .08 to .33, with a median of .16; and for the $\Sigma E_i + \Sigma V_i$ term the correlations ranged from −.01 to .27, with a median of .17. All three sets of correlations are lower than those obtained using the $\Sigma E_i \times V_i$ predictor, which ranged from .08 to .40, with a median of .27.

[7] A. H. Brayfield and W. H. Crockett, "Employee Attitudes and Employee Performance," *Psychological Bulletin* 52 (1955): 396–424; Vroom, *Work and Motivation.*

TABLE 23–2

Correlations between Expectancy Theory Predictions and Criteria

Criterion Measure	Correlation with $\Sigma E_i \times V_i$ Predictor
Supervisor Ratings of Involvement and Effort	.27**
Employee Appraisal Form	
Quality of work	.06
Quantity of work	.37**
Cooperativeness	.13
Judgment	.25**
Dependability	.36**
Initiative	.28**
Ability to learn	.25**
Error rate	−.23*
Sales Data	.31**
Composite Criterion	.40**

* $p \leq .05$.
** $p \leq .01$.

theory predictions can be viewed as *attitudes toward actions,* appear quite strong in this context. Further, the present results serve to emphasize the contention of Porter and Lawler that specific attitudes about expectancies (or "path-goal relationships") and outcomes are a more appropriate basis for making predictions about performance effectiveness than are general attitudes toward the task or the performance setting.[8]

Secondly, the present results were obtained using *only* the subjects' perceptions of the consequences of working hard as the basis of prediction. There obviously are other factors which have substantial impacts on performance as well, such as ability and personality predispositions. If measures of individual differences on dimensions such as these had been included, the magnitude of the results might have been substantially increased.

Prediction of Work Quality

The relationship between the predictor scores and supervisors' appraisals of work quality (primarily assessments of thoroughness, neatness, and accuracy) was near zero. This finding is not unexpected, since the predictor was derived on the basis of outcomes which were expected to result from "working especially hard" (not working especially *well*.)

The differentiation between "hard work" and "high-quality work" also was evident in the interviews which were conducted early in the study. When the representatives discussed "hard work" on the job, they frequently would inquire "What do you mean by 'hard work'?" When the

---

[8] L. W. Porter and E. E. Lawler III, *Managerial Attitudes and Performance* (Homewood, Ill.: Irwin-Dorsey, Ltd., 1968).

question was returned by asking the interviewee what *she* meant by "hard work" the answer invariably was something about "doing a lot" in a day —often because of an especially heavy load of incoming calls on a particular day, or because of a decision, say, to try to get all the paperwork cleared up before going home. Thus, the conception of hard work held by the service representatives seemed generally to have more to do with quantity than with quality, and they tended to perceive quantity and quality as independent aspects of their performance. (This perceived independence also was borne out in supervisors' appraisals, in which judgments of quantity and quality correlated only .07.)

Thus, it is not surprising to find that the questionnaire-derived predictions were much more closely associated with quantity of work than with work quality. Nevertheless, the predictions were not entirely irrelevant to work quality, since there was a significant negative relationship between the predictor and one objective measure of work quality, namely, error rate.

Implications of the Findings

The results and the methodology of the study have considerable relevance to the problem of *diagnosing* a performance situation in motivational terms, and for effectively *changing* aspects of the situation so as to obtain higher levels of effort from the performers. According to expectancy theory as it has been applied in this research, there are three factors which affect the level of effort an individual exerts in a performance situation: (*a*) the particular outcomes which the performer perceives as occurring as a result of working hard on the job; (*b*) the strength of expectancy, that is, the level of certainty which the performer has that he actually will obtain particular outcomes by working hard; and (*c*) the valence of the outcomes, that is, the evaluations which the performer makes of the perceived outcomes.

Use of a methodology (such as that of the present study) which makes explicit these three components allows an investigator to identify those aspects of a performer's perceptions and evaluations which tend to enhance his motivation to work hard, and those which tend to detract from it. For example, outcomes which have high expectancies and high positive valences will, according to the results of this study, enhance a performer's motivation to work hard. Outcomes with high expectancies and high negative valences will detract from his motivation. Outcomes with relatively low expectancies or with neutral valences will have no substantial impact on the performer's motivation. By examining the expectancies and valences associated with a performer's perceived outcomes of hard work, an investigator can identify the motivational problems and opportunities which are inherent in the performance situation.

Once a diagnosis of the situation is made (as suggested above), changes can be instituted to improve the performer's motivation to work hard. Such changes can involve (a) instituting new outcomes which will be valued by the performer and which will be seen by him as resulting from hard work, (b) changing the expectancies of existing outcomes so that the link between hard work and positively valued outcomes is strengthened and that between hard work and negatively valued outcomes is weakened, or (c) changing the valences of existing outcomes. The first two alternatives probably are much more amenable to external change than is the last one; it should be much easier to change aspects of the situation so that the performer will perceive it differently than it would be to change the evaluations which a performer makes of various outcomes.

The discussion above has focussed only on the use of expectancy theory in understanding and changing the level of effort which performers put into their work. The same kinds of analyses and similar suggestions could be made as well for other performance and decision-making situations. To the extent that the findings are generalizable to these other situations, the present study suggests that expectancy can be a broadly useful tool in understanding behavior in "real world" settings.

24. MOTIVATIONAL ASPECTS OF PAY *

Robert L. Opsahl and Marvin D. Dunnette

WIDESPREAD INTEREST in money as a motivational tool for spurring production was first stimulated in this country by Frederick Taylor. Some years before the turn of the century, Taylor observed an energetic steelworker who, after putting in a twelve-hour day of lifting pigs of iron, would run 12 miles up a mountainside to work on his cabin. If this excess energy could be used to produce more on the job, thought Taylor, higher profits from lower fixed costs could be used to pay the worker significantly more for his increased efforts. Such was the beginning of *scientific management*, which was based essentially on the assumption that workers will put forth extra effort on the job in order to maximize their economic gains. This became a guiding principle in pay practices until the late 1920s, when the *human-relations movement* in industrial psychology was ushered in with the Western Electric studies directed by Elton Mayo. As a result of these studies, recognition of man's ego and social needs became widespread, and job factors other than pay came to be emphasized as the major reasons why men work. To a large extent, these later ideas are still with us. Yet few would disagree that money has

* Extracted from "The Role of Financial Compensation in Industrial Motivation," *Psychological Bulletin* 63 (1966): 94–118. Copyright 1966 by the American Psychological Association. Reprinted by permission.

been and continues to be the primary means of rewarding and modifying human behavior in industry.

Strangely, however, in spite of the large amounts of money spent and the obvious relevance of behavioral theory for industrial compensation practices, there is probably less solid research in this area than in almost any other field related to worker performance. The major research problem in industrial compensation is to determine exactly what effects monetary rewards have for motivating various behaviors. More specifically, we need to understand more precisely how money can be used to induce employees to perform at high levels.

Our assumption is that the manner in which financial compensation is administered undoubtedly has potential for accounting for a large amount of the variation in job behavior. The particular schedule of payment, the degree of secrecy surrounding the amount of pay one receives, how the level of salary or pay is determined, and the individual's long-term or career pay history all have important potential effects on how the employee responds to any specific amount of money.

Schedules of Pay

In this review we shall be concerned solely with "incentive" payment systems [1] which are based on behavioral criteria (usually amount of output) rather than on biographical factors such as education, seniority, and experience. Incentive pay schemes of various sorts are believed to function primarily to "increase or maintain some already initiated activity or . . . to encourage some new form of activity." [2]

There is considerable evidence that installation of such plans usually results in greater output per man hour, lower unit costs, and higher wages in comparison with outcomes associated with straight payment systems.[3] However, the installation of an incentive plan is not and can never be an isolated event. Frequently, changes in work methods, management policies, and organization accompany the changeover, and it is difficult to determine the amount of behavioral variance that each of these other events may contribute.

Incentive plans can be based on either the worker's own output or on the total output of his working group. The relative efficiency of the two methods are dependent upon such factors as the nature of the task

---

[1] We shall not attempt to evaluate all the evidence on incentive plans. For an excellent review and evaluation of these, see R. Marriott, *Incentive Payment Systems: A Review of Research and Opinion* (London: Staples Press, 1957).

[2] Ibid., p. 12.

[3] J. Dale, "Increase Productivity 50 Percent in One Year with Sound Wage Incentives," *Management Methods* 16 (1959): 5–18; A. A. Rath, "The Case for Individual Incentives," *Personnel Journal* 39 (1960): 172–75; M. S. Viteles, *Motivation and Morale in Industry* (New York: W. W. Norton, 1953).

performed,[4] the size of the working group,[5] the social environment,[6] and the particular group or individual plan employed. The chief disadvantage with group incentives is the likelihood of a low correlation between a worker's own individual performance and his pay in large groups. There is also evidence [7] that individual output decreases as the size of the work group increases, and this apparently is due to workers' perceiving a decreased probability that their efforts will yield increased outcomes, (that is, the workers have less knowledge of the relationships between effort and earnings). Of course, both of these effects run counter to the main principle of incentive plans—immediate reward for desired job behaviors.

Not only do financial incentives operate with different efficacy in different situations, but often they do not even lead to increased production. Group standards and social pressures frequently induce workers to perform considerably below their potential. Most of the data on such rate restriction are either observational [8] or in the form of verbal responses to surveys.[9] The results of these studies suggest that changes in the monetary consequences of performance are usually accompanied by changes in other expected consequences of performance. Thus, instituting an incentive plan may alter not only the expected consequences in terms of amount of money received, but also expected consequences related to

---

[4] N. Babchuk and W. J. Goode, "Work Incentives in a Self-Determined Group," *American Sociological Review* 16 (1951): 679–87; Marriott, *Incentive Payment Systems.*

[5] H. Campbell, "Group Incentive Payment Schemes: The Effects of Lack of Understanding and Group Size," *Occupational Psychology* 26 (1952): 15–21; R. Marriott, "Size of Working Group and Output," *Occupational Psychology* 25 (1949); idem, "Socio-Psychological Factors in Productivity," ibid. 25 (1951): 15–24; Marriott and R. A. Denerley, "A Method of Interviewing Used in Studies of Workers' Attitudes: II. Validity of the Method and Discussion of the Results," *Occupational Psychology* 29 (1955): 69–81; and S. Shimmin, J. Williams, and L. Buck, "'Studies of Some Factors in Incentive Payment Systems" (Industrial Psychology Research Group report to Medical Research Council, 1956).

[6] B. M. Selekman, "Living with Collective Bargaining," *Harvard Business Review* 22 (1941): 21–23.

[7] Campbell, "Group Incentive."

[8] M. Dalton, O. Collins, and D. Roy, "Restriction of Output and Social Cleavage in Industry," *Applied Anthropology* 5, no. 3 (1946): 1–14; Dalton "The Industrial 'Rate-Buster': A Characterization," *Applied Anthropology* 7 (1948): 5–18; B. H. Dyson, "Whether Direct Individual Incentive Systems Based on Time-Study, However Accurately Computed, Tend over a Period to Limitation of Output" (Paper read at British Institute of Management, London, Spring Conference, 1956); S. B. Mathewson, *Restriction of Output among Unorganized Workers* (New York: Viking Press, 1951); C. S. Myers, *Mind and Work* (London: University of London Press, 1920); F. J. Roethlisberger and W. J. Dickson, *Management and the Worker* (Cambridge, Mass.: Harvard University Press, 1939); D. Roy, "Quota Restriction and Goldbricking in a Machine Shop," *American Journal of Sociology* 57 (1952): 427–42; and W. F. Whyte, *Money and Motivation: An Analysis of Incentives in Industry* (New York: Harper, 1955).

[9] Opinion Research Corporation, *Productivity from the Workers' Standpoint* (Princeton, 1949); Viteles, *Motivation and Morale.*

possible loss of esteem in the eyes of one's co-workers or the presumed bad connotations of "selling out" or accepting the goals of management.

Hickson has divided the causes of rate restriction into five categories.[10] Three of the causes are essentially negative or avoidance reasons; uncertainty about the continuance of the existing "effort-bargain" between the workers and management, uncertainty about the continuance of employment, and uncertainty about the continuance of existing social relationships. The other two causes are positive or approach-type factors —the desire to continue social satisfactions derived from the practice of restriction, and a desire for at least a minimal area of external control over one's own behavior.

Perhaps the most intensive analysis of rate restriction has been undertaken by Whyte.[11] It is the thesis of Whyte and his co-workers that many piece-rate incentive situations actually resemble the condition of experimentally induced neurosis. He reasons that most incentive "packages" do not provide the employee with sufficient cues to allow him to discriminate effectively between stimuli signaling the onset of punishing circumstances (loss of co-worker respect, and so forth) and stimuli signaling the onset of rewarding circumstances (more pay, higher job success, and so forth).[12] Thus, money itself is only *one* of many possible rewards and punishments that invariably accompany any incentive situation. We believe Whyte's effort to show similarity between piece-rate incentive systems and the conditions accompanying experimental neurosis is misleading. The discriminative stimuli for the rewards and punishments administered by the work group and by management seem to us to be clearly differentiable. A double approach-avoidance conflict between the rewards and punishments of management and the work group is more descriptive of the situation. If this is the case, our job should be to study more thoroughly the conditions necessary for maintaining the group as an effective reinforcing agent even in the face of an incentive piece-rate plan. Variables for study would include group cohesiveness; interaction patterns within the group; amount of intergroup competition; identification of individuals with the group; uniformity of group opinion; group control over the environment; and the extent to which group pressures support rather than subvert organizational goals and demands.[13]

Thus, although "everyone knows" that incentive pay schemes work very effectively some of the time, it is painfully apparent that they are far from uniformly effective. As we have said, the emphasis in research should now turn to more controlled observations of the effects of money

---

[10] D. J. Hickson, "Motives of Work of People Who Restrict Their Output," *Occupational Psychology* 35 (1961): 110–21.

[11] W. F. Whyte, "Economic Incentives and Human Relations," *Harvard Business Review* 30 (1952): 73–80; Whyte, *Money and Motivation.*

[12] Whyte, "Economic Incentives and Human Relations."

[13] J. G. March and H. A. Simon, *Organizations* (New York: John Wiley & Sons, 1958), pp. 59–61.

in the context of the many other sources of reward and punishment in the work setting. So far, we have only a wealth of field observations. It is necessary now to learn more exactly just what employees will or will not give up for money or, more importantly, to learn how incentive payments may be made without engendering the painful and onerous circumstances which so often seem to accompany such payments.

Secret Pay Policies

In addition to the particular kind of pay plan, the secrecy surrounding the amount of money given an employee may have motivational implications. Lawler's recent study indicates that secret pay policies may contribute to dissatisfaction with pay and to the possibility of lowered job performance.[14] He found that managers overestimate the pay of subordinates and peers, and underestimate their superiors' pay; they see their own pay as being too low by comparison with all three groups. Moreover, they also underestimate the financial rewards associated with promotion. Lawler argues that these two results of pay secrecy probably reduce the motivation of managers both to perform well on their present jobs and to seek higher level jobs. Another disadvantage of secrecy is that it lowers money's effectiveness as a knowledge-of-results device to let the manager know how well he is doing with respect to others. Lawler advocates the abandonment of secrecy policies. According to him, "there is no reason why organizations cannot make salaries public information." [15]

Lawler's assertion seems to have a good deal of merit; his results are impressive and his arguments sound. It would be very useful, at this stage, to conduct "before-after" studies of the effects on employees' perceptions of relationships between pay and job performance of instituting policies of openness concerning wage and salary payments. At the very least, Lawler's data suggest that useful effects would be produced by informing employees (particularly managers) more about how their salaries are derived; the logical next step would be to provide normative data (for example, percentile distributions of employee pay levels); and, finally, salary administrators might even work up the courage to publicize actual salary levels of persons in the firm.

This is not to say, of course, that there might not be negative outcomes from the sudden implementation of such policies. For example, one rather obvious possibility is that such action might crystallize present hierarchical "pecking orders"; group cohesiveness could be disrupted by the sudden awareness of substantial intra-work-group differences. But most such fears stem, we believe, from the prevalence in many firms of actual pay inequities related to inadequate job-performance appraisal systems and

---

[14] E. E. Lawler, III, "Managerial Perceptions of Compensation" (Paper presented at the Midwestern Psychological Association convention, Chicago, April 30, 1965).

[15] Ibid., p. 8.

current weaknesses in administering salary payments in such a way as to reflect valid relationships with job performance. We believe, with Lawler, that present policies of secrecy are undoubtedly due, in part, to fear on the part of most salary administrators that they would have a tough time mustering convincing arguments in favor of many of their present practices. Thus, it is true that until greater rationality is introduced into the basis for determining salaries and until money becomes more firmly accepted as a way of rewarding outstanding job behavior, public disclosure of salary arrangements may probably not have the desirable consequences suggested by Lawler. Perhaps his results are merely symptomatic of present unsuccessful efforts to use pay effectively for motivating employees. If this is true, it seems all the more important and timely to undertake thorough studies of the effects of relaxing present policies of pay secrecy.

Pay Curves

An employee's periodic pay increases, as he progresses in his career with a company, constitutes another job or task variable with the potential for differentially motivating effects. Wittingly or not, every company "assigns" each employee a "pay curve" which is the result of successive alterations in compensation and compensation policies through the years. One way of doing this (the usual way) is with little or no advanced planning; increments in this instance are given haphazardly on a year-to-year basis and the resulting career pay curve simply "grows" somewhat akin to Topsy. Another alternative is to plan the future compensation program shortly after the individual enters the organization and then to modify it subsequently on the basis of his job behavior as his career unfolds. No matter which pay policy is adopted, the results will most likely affect the employee's job behavior, his aspirations and anticipations of future earnings, and his feelings of fairness with respect to his career-pay "program."

Most companies administer pay increments on a periodic (for example, year-to-year) basis. The rationale for this is quite simple, the usual idea being that differential pay increments may be given for differential results produced by employees on their jobs. Over a span of many years, then, we might expect a consistent pattern of positive correlations for the salary increments received by the individuals comprising any particular group of employees. This expectation would be based on two rather reasonable and closely related assumptions: first, that the acquisition of job skills is a predictable process; and second, that the effectiveness of a person's job performance in any given period is predictable from his own past patterns of job performance.

In fact, however, career-pay histories for employee groups do *not* usually show such patterns of consistently positive relationships between year-to-year salary gains. Haire mapped the correlations between salary levels at the end of each year and raises over 5- and 10-year periods in two large national companies.[16] In one company the correlations decreased over the 5-year span from +.38 to −.06 for one executive group (median salary $41,600) and from +.36 to −.25 for a second group (median salary $18,000). In the second firm, the correlations between salaries and raises for adjacent years over the 10-year period varied between −.33 and +.83 with no consistent pattern discernible. Haire believes that his results constitute damning evidence that these two companies had no consistent policies with respect to the incentive use of salary increases; he suggests that the trend in the first company reflects a shift from a policy of distributing raises under the assumption that good performance is related to past excellence to the assumption that it is either not related at all or that it is negatively related. He also asserts that a pattern showing extremely low correlations between present salary levels and salary increments indicates that wage increases might just as well be distributed by lottery—that the incentive character of a raise is thereby nullified and that consistent striving for job excellence would seem futile under such circumstances. Haire's assertions are provocative and they may indeed follow from his results, but we believe that other explanations may be equally compatible with his findings. For example, low correlations could just as reasonably be viewed as reflecting a successfully administered wage policy allowing for greater rather than less flexibility in using money to reward top job performance. Such a policy might suggest, in effect, an employee who has done well in the past cannot rest on his laurels in expectation of future "rewards" and that a lower salaried employee (with presumably a history of less effective performance) still has rich opportunities to be recognized and appropriately rewarded for improved job performance in the future.

The idea of specifying individual career pay curves has received extensive attention by Jaques, through his "standard payment and progression method." [17] By analyzing the pay histories of 250 male workers, Jaques derived a family of negatively accelerated pay curves extending from ages 20 to 65. It should be noted, however, that his curves are plotted with a log scale for the ordinate (salary). If actual dollar values were plotted, the data very likely would yield positively rather than negatively accelerated curves. However, as plotted by Jaques, the curves rise rapidly in the younger age groups, slow down at older ages, and show a greater rate of progression at the higher earning levels. According to Jaques, these smoothed curves (called standard earnings progressions) follow "the sigmoidal progression characteristic of biological growth," [18]

---

[16] M. Haire, "The Incentive Character of Pay," in *Managerial Compensation*, ed. R. Andrews (Ann Arbor: Foundation for Research on Human Behavior, 1965), pp. 13–17.

[17] E. Jaques, *Equitable Payment* (New York: John Wiley & Sons, 1961).

[18] Ibid., p. 185.

and are the basis for his payment theory. Jaques believes that the standard earning progression curves represent a close approximation to the lines of growth of "time span of discretion" in individuals. This time span of discretion is the period of time during which the work assigned by a manager requires his subordinate to exercise discretion, judgment, or initiative in his job without that discretion being subject to review by the manager. This is an objective yardstick that supposedly can be used for direct comparison of work levels between any two jobs, regardless of content. The major significance of the time span, according to Jaques, is that workers in jobs having different contents but the same time span of discretion privately perceive the same wage or salary bracket to be equitable for the work they are doing.

Assuming that individuals seek an equitable level of payment for the level of work consistent with their capacity, an employee's future pay curve can be determined by: (1) determining the employee's present time span of discretion along with the equitable payment for that time span, (2) plotting the employee's achieved earning progression to date, (3) allowing the manager once removed to determine the employee's potential progress assessment (that is, the manager's assessment of the level of work a person is likely to achieve), which can be expressed in terms of the earning progression that he would likely achieve if it is assumed that he receives equitable payment for his work, (4) letting the immediate manager assess the employee's performance, and altering the employee's wage or salary according to this performance, (5) having the once-removed manager revise the potential progress assessment if performance continues above or below the original potential progress assessment.

The above is only a brief sketch of Jaques' theory of payment. It is a highly interesting one, but until further data concerning its motivational consequences are compiled, it must be regarded as highly tentative.

The "sigmodial biological growth" pay curves that Jaques describes are not the only possible ones; Ghiselli has pointed out other possibilities and has attempted to provide the rationale behind them.[19] For instance, one possibility is having average increments in pay increase from year to year. The result would be a positively accelerated pay curve consonant with the philosophy of paying an employee a substantial amount only after he becomes highly effective to the organization, instead of when he is in the early stages of his career and easily tempted to move to another organization. If the organization wished to budget a fixed amount for pay increases each year, linear pay curves would result. If, on the other hand, one assumed an employee is unlikely to leave a firm after he has been with it a long time and has a huge personal investment in it (such as retirement benefits, stock options, and so forth), it might

---

[19] E. E. Ghiselli, "The Effects on Career Pay of Policies with Respect to Increases in Pay," *Managerial Compensation*, ed. R. Andrews (Ann Arbor: Foundation for Research on Human Behavior, 1965), pp. 21–34.

be advantageous to reward him generously when he first starts his job to help ensure that he will not go to another firm (that is, assign him a negatively accelerated curve). To our knowledge, no empirical studies on the relative effectiveness of different possible pay curves have been undertaken.

Although it would appear that pay curves have a significant influence on job behavior, parametric experiments in this area are practically non-existent. Several aspects of pay curves need to be studied before we are in a position to construct or use these curves with even a moderate degree of effectiveness.

First and most important, we must find out how a given pay curve differentially affects employees' motivation and job behaviors. It is not at all plausible to assume that we can find one best curve for *all* employees, or even for a subgroup of employees at a given job level or with common job duties. Some evidence of this was revealed by Festinger [20] when he found that promotions (with related pay increases, presumably) *increased* the aspired-to job level and perceived importance of pay for about 30 percent of the cases. It is not known why these groups reacted so differently to promotions. The overall level of aspiration of the employees certainly would be a prime variable; *need achievement* might be another. But we know little about the stability of these two variables, and therefore assessment of them early in an employee's career may not be a valid index of later expectations or the effectiveness of career pay-curve policies. It is necessary to conduct longitudinal studies over extended periods of time—studies which, by the way, are all too infrequent in the area of compensation. Some, although by no means all, of the data necessary for this type of study are already on file in computer memory banks in the larger companies and need only to be retrieved and analyzed.

Since pay curves do not operate within a vacuum, the effect of one employee's pay curve on another employee must not be overlooked. Ghiselli's rationale for positively and negatively accelerated curves, for instance, may not prove effective in the context of the total industrial situation.[21] Since pay is on a competitive basis across companies, a negatively accelerated curve in one company might well lead to feelings of inequity and possible job termination for a young employee if other companies offered linear or positively accelerated pay increments in a similar situation. We are not saying that the effectiveness of the different curves should not be studied. They should; but the concept of equity applies to pay-curve comparisons as well as to wage comparisons, and this is an important area for potential investigation.

Several methods of deriving pay curves deserve further investigation.

---

[20] L. Festinger, "How Attitudes toward Compensation Change with Promotion," in *Managerial Compensation,* ed. R. Andrews (Ann Arbor: Foundation for Research on Human Behavior, 1965), pp. 19–20.

[21] Ghiselli, "The Effects on Career Pay."

One option would be to inform the employee of the tentative curve agreed upon for him. This could be done piecemeal, by setting monetary goals for him to shoot at within a specific time period. An interesting variation of this procedure that to our knowledge has not been studied would be to include pay goals in the goal-setting interviews given high-level managers in some companies. The behavioral goals set in these interviews could have monetary rewards attached to them, thereby providing further incentive for their attainment. Informing an employee of his progress along his proposed pay curve might also serve a valuable feedback function for helping him evaluate his progress to date.

Other relevant research problems are almost too numerous to mention. Important ones include determining how to alter an employee's subsequent curve on the basis of under- or overachievement; discovering valid criteria for constructing a tentative curve; and determining which variables influence the perception of pay increments and *how* they influence it. With expanded knowledge in these areas, pay curves and their determination may come to play a central role in industrial compensation practices of the future.

Perceived Relations between Performance and Pay

According to Vroom's theory of work motivation, the valence of effective performance increases as the instrumentality of effective performance for the attainment of money increases, assuming that the valence of money is positive.[22] Vroom cited supporting evidence from experiments by Atkinson and Reitman, Atkinson, and Kaufman showing a higher level of performance by subjects who were told that their earnings were contingent on the effectiveness of their performance.[23] Georgopoulos, Mahoney, and Jones' Path-Goal Approach theory similarly states that if a worker has a desire for a given goal and perceives a given path leading to that goal, he will utilize that path if he has freedom to do so.[24] Georgopoulos and others found that workers who perceived higher personal productivity as a means to increased earnings performed more effectively than workers who did not perceive this relationship.

The effectiveness of incentive plans in general depends upon the worker's knowledge of the relation between performance and earnings. The lack of this knowledge is one cause of failure in incentive schemes.

22 V. H. Vroom, *Work and Motivation* (New York: John Wiley & Sons, 1964).

23 J. W. Atkinson and W. R. Reitman, "Performance as a Function of Motive Strength and Expectancy of Goal Attainment," *Journal of Abnormal and Social Psychology* 53 (1956): 361–66; Atkinson, ed., *Motives in Fantasy, Action, and Society* (Princeton: Van Nostrand, 1958); and H. Kaufman, "Task Performance, Expected Performance, and Responses to Failure as Functions of Imbalance in the Self-Concept" (Ph.D. diss., University of Pennsylvania, 1962).

24 B. S. Georgopoulos, G. M. Mahoney, and N. W. Jones, "A Path-Goal Approach to Productivity," *Journal of Applied Psychology* 41 (1957): 345–53.

As already mentioned, Campbell's study showed that one of the major reasons for lower productivity in large groups under group incentive plans is that the workers often do not perceive the relation between pay and productivity as well as they do in smaller groups.[25] In the Georgopoulos et al. study, only 38 percent of the workers perceived increased performance as leading to increased earnings.[26] More amazingly, 35 percent perceived *low* productivity as an aid to higher earnings in the long run. Lawler recently found that 600 managers perceived their training and experience to be the most important factors in determining their pay—not how well or how poorly they performed their jobs.[27] Since Lawler found that the relation between their pay and their rated job performance also was low, their perceptions were probably quite accurate. A separate analysis of the most highly motivated managers, however, indicated that they attached greater importance to pay and felt that good job performance would lead to higher pay.

These studies confirm the importance of knowing how job performance and pay are related. The relation between performing certain desired behaviors and attainment of the pay incentive must be explicitly specified. The foregoing statement seems so obvious as hardly to warrant mentioning. Unfortunately, as we have seen, the number of times in industry that the above *rule* is ignored is surprising. Future research must determine how goals or incentives may best be presented in association with desired behaviors. Practically nothing has been done in this area—especially for managers. In fact, programs for the recognition of individual merit are notoriously poor. Methods for tying financial compensation in with management-by-results [28] or with systematic efforts to set job goals and methods of unambiguously outlining what the end result of various job behaviors will be should be developed and studied.

Concept of Equitable Payment

Several theories have been independently advanced proposing that employees seek a just or equitable return for what they have contributed to the job.[29] A common feature of these theories is the assumption that

---

[25] Campbell, "Group Incentive."

[26] Georgopoulos, Mahoney, and Jones, "A Path-Goal Approach."

[27] E. E. Lawler, III, "Managers' Job Performance and Their Attitudes Toward Their Pay" (Ph.D. diss., University of California, Berkeley, 1964).

[28] E. C. Schleh, *Management by Results: The Dynamics of Profitable Management* (New York: McGraw-Hill Book Co., 1961).

[29] J. S. Adams, "Toward an Understanding of Inequity," *Journal of Abnormal and Social Psychology* 67 (1963): 422–36; idem, "Injustice in Social Change," in *Advances in Experimental Social Psychology*, ed. L. Berkowitz (New York: Academic Press, 1965), 2: 267–99; G. C. Homans, *Social Behavior: Its Elementary Forms* (New York: Harcourt, Brace & World, 1961); Jaques, *Equitable Payment*; M. Patchen, *The Choice of Wage Comparisons* (Englewood Cliffs, N.J.: Prentice-Hall, 1961); L. R. Sayles, *Behavior of Industrial Work Groups: Prediction and Control* (New York: John Wiley &

compensation either above or below that which is perceived by the employee to be "equitable" results in tension and dissatisfaction due to dissonant cognitions. The tension, in turn, causes the employee to attempt to restore consonance by a variety of behavioral or cognitive methods.

The most rigorous and best researched theory of equity is that of Adams.[30] His theory is derived mostly from the postulates of Festinger's cognitive dissonance theory[31] but was influenced also by Stouffer and others earlier work on relative deprivation[32] and by Homan's research on distributive justice.[33] Adams' definition of inequity states that

inequity exists for Person[34] whenever he perceives that the ratio of his outcomes to inputs and the ratio of Other's outcomes to Other's inputs are unequal, either (a) when he and Other are in a direct exchange or (b) when both are in an exchange relationship with a third party and Person compares himself to Other.[35]

This implies, as do all the above-mentioned theories, that an inequitable relation occurs not only when the exchange is not in Person's favor, but when it is to his advantage as well. Adams, like Homans, hypothesized that the thresholds for underreward and overreward differ. Thus, a certain amount of overreward may be written off as "good luck," whereas similar deviations in the direction of underreward will not be so easily tolerated.

Inputs mentioned in the definition are anything a worker perceives as constituting his contribution to the job—age, skill, education, experience, and amount of effort expended on the job. Outcomes, or rewards from the job, are also dependent upon the worker's perception and would normally include pay, status symbols, intrinsic job satisfaction, and fringe benefits, to mention a few examples.

The existence of equity or inequity is not an all-or-none phenomenon. Many degrees of inequity can be distinguished, and the magnitude of the inequity is assumed to be some increasing monotonic function of the size of the difference between the ratios of outcomes to inputs. Thus, it is not the absolute magnitudes of perceived inputs and outcomes that are important, but rather the discrepancy between the two ratios. In-

---

Sons, 1958); and A. Zaleznik, C. R. Christenson, and F. J. Roethlisberger, *The Motivation, Productivity, and Satisfaction of Workers: A Prediction Study* (Boston: Harvard University, Graduate School of Business Administration, 1958).

[30] Adams, "Toward an Understanding of Inequity"; idem, "Injustice in Social Change."

[31] L. A. Festinger, *A Theory of Cognitive Dissonance* (Evanston, Ill.: Row, Peterson, 1957).

[32] S. A. Stouffer et al., *The American Soldier: Adjustment during Army Life,* vol. 1 (Princeton: Princeton University Press, 1949).

[33] Homans, *Social Behavior.*

[34] Person is anyone for whom equity or inequity exists. Other is any individual or group used by Person as a referent in social comparisons of what he contributes to and what he receives from an exchange.

[35] Adams, "Injustice in Social Change," p. 22.

equity may exist for both Person and Other, so long as each perceives discrepant ratios. The greatest inequity exists when both inputs and outcomes are discrepant.

The presence of inequity creates tension within a person in an amount proportional to the magnitude of the inequity. This tension creates a drive to reduce the inequity feelings, the strength of the drive being proportional to the tension created. Adams suggested several possible avenues of achieving an equitable state.[36] A person may increase or decrease his inputs (for example, by increasing or decreasing either the quality or quantity of his work); he may increase or decrease his outcomes (by asking for a raise, or by giving part of his pay to charity, for example); he may change his comparison group or cognitively alter its inputs or outcomes, or force it out of the field; he may leave the field himself (by quitting, transferring, or being absent); or he may cognitively distort his own inputs and outcomes. It is not yet clear what principles govern the choice of method for inequity reduction, although Lawler and O'Gara have recently obtained evidence that the choice is related to such personality "traits" as self-esteem and responsibility.[37]

A series of experiments to test this theory have been undertaken.[38] These studies have all been directed toward the effects of overcompensation on behavior. In the first of these, the hypothesis that workers who felt they were overpaid would reduce their feelings of inequity by increasing the amount of work performed was tested.[39] Twenty-two college students were hired to conduct interviews at $3.50 per hour; half of them were made to feel qualified and equitably paid, and the other half were made to feel unqualified and thus overpaid. As predicted, the overpaid group conducted significantly more interviews within the allotted time than did the control group.

It could reasonably be hypothesized that the group made to feel overpaid for the job worked harder because they felt insecure and were afraid of being fired. Another experiment was performed by Arrowood, reported in Adams, with the same design—but with the addition of a

---

[36] Adams, "Toward an Understanding of Inequity"; idem, "Injustice in Social Change."

[37] E. E. Lawler, III and P. W. O'Gara, "Effects of Inequity Produced by Underpayment on Work Output, Work Quality, and Attitudes toward the Work," *Journal of Applied Psychology* 51 (1967): 403–10.

[38] Adams, "Toward an Understanding of Inequity"; idem, "Injustice in Social Change"; idem, "Wage Inequities, Productivity, and Work Quality," *Industrial Relations* 3 (1963): 9–16; Adams and P. Jacobson, "Effects of Wage Inequities on Work Quality," *Journal of Abnormal and Social Psychology* 69 (1964): 19–25; Adams and W. B. Rosenbaum, "The Relationship of Worker Productivity to Cognitive Dissonance about Wage Inequities," *Journal of Applied Psychology* 46 (1962): 161–64; and A. J. Arrowood, "Some Effects of Productivity of Justified and Unjustified Levels of Reward under Public and Private Conditions" (Ph.D. diss., University of Minnesota, 1961).

[39] Adams and Rosenbaum, "The Relationship of Worker Productivity."

"private" group that was under the impression that their employer would never see their work.[40] Within this private group, the students who felt overcompensated also conducted significantly more interviews than the students who felt equitably compensated, thus showing the predicted effect is still obtained when pains are taken to remove the insecurity motive.

Although it is predicted from the theory that workers overpaid on an hourly basis will increase the quantity of their work, workers overpaid on a piecework basis would actually increase feelings of inequity if they produced more since they would be increasing the amount of their over-payment. Therefore, it was hypothesized that these workers would reduce inequity by reducing the quantity of their output—a procedure which increases inputs and decreases outcomes. Adams and Jacobsen tested this hypothesis on students hired for a proofreading task.[41] Persons in the overpaid, experimental group were told they were not qualified but would be paid the usual rate of 30 cents per page anyway. Persons in one equitably paid control group were made to feel qualified and were also paid 30 cents per page. Persons in a second equitably paid control group were made to feel unqualified but were paid the more equitable rate of only 20 cents per page. Adams also sought to assess any possible effects due to differing feelings of job security by manipulating the perceived possibility of future employment. This was done because it was reasoned that subjects made to feel overpaid and unqualified might perceive an implication that their tenure was in jeopardy unless they showed they were good workers. Thus, for half the subjects in each group, Adams created a condition in which they perceived that there was something to lose (that is, insecurity) and for the other half a condition in which they perceived that there was nothing to lose (that is, relative security). Adams reasoned that if job security were important, the overpaid secure subjects would work fast but carelessly whereas the overpaid insecure subjects ought to work with much greater care.

The index of quantity was the number of pages proofread, and the index of quality was the number of implanted errors detected (each page, averaging 450 words, had an average of 12 errors implanted in the text, such as misspellings or grammatical, punctuational, and typographical errors).

At first glance, the results substantiate the hypothesis. They show that the overpaid, experimental group proofed significantly fewer pages and detected significantly more implanted errors per page than the two equitably paid groups. The job security manipulation had no significant

---

[40] Arrowood, "Some Effects of Productivity"; Adams, "Toward an Understanding of Inequity"; and idem, "Injustice in Social Change."
[41] Adams and Jacobsen, "Effects of Wage Inequities."

effect, which was in keeping with the hypothesis that quality and productivity should vary with feelings of equity and not as a function of
perceived job security.

It should be noted, however, that quality was not entirely adequately
measured in the experiment. Detecting implanted errors is only one
possible evidence of quality in proofreading. Another aspect of quality
not included in Adams' quality score is the number of words detected
as errors, but which were actually correctly spelled or punctuated. If a
proofreader detected all of the real errors in a text, but also claimed
several words or punctuation marks to be in error when they actually
were correct, his stay on the job probably would be shortlived. Yet, in
the experiment just described, he would get a perfect quality score
because the specification of detecting nonerrors as errors was ignored.
Significantly more of these nonerrors were falsely called errors by the
overpaid group. If these "errors" had been taken into account, their
quality scores would have been considerably lower. It can be argued, of
course, that such nonerror detection simply illustrates effort and conscientiousness that these subjects were devoting to the task, and this
would then be further evidence in favor of the theory and of the effectiveness of the experimental manipulation. Even so, the net effect of
"correcting" nonerrors is to reduce the job effectiveness of a proofreader;
and it is not entirely clear whether this aspect of ineffectiveness was due
to the equity manipulation, the different emphasis on detecting errors
in two sets of direction, or some interaction of the two.

Recent research indicates that predictions derived from equity theory
in cases of underreward may require modification.[42] All of the above
studies showed that underpaid persons work harder, and also like the
task more than persons who are overpaid or equitably paid.

Weick hypothesized that high effort for insufficient pay represents an
attempt to raise outcomes, and suggested that proponents of equity
theory give greater consideration to the proposition that persons may
control their outcomes to reduce inequity.[43] Thus, in the above-mentioned
studies, increased satisfaction gained from performing the task may
heighten outcomes and bring them more in line with the person's inputs.

One of the major problems with which equity theory must cope is the
obvious fact of the large number of variables, the complexities of their
interaction, and the inadequacy of the operational definitions. Vroom

---

[42] For example, see J. L. Freedman, "Attitudinal Effects of Inadequate Justifica-
tion," *Journal of Personality* 31 (1963): 371–85; G. S. Leventhal, "Reward Magnitude
and Liking for Instrumental Activity: Further Test of a Two-Process Model" (Yale
University, 1964); K. E. Weick and D. D. Penner, "Comparison of Two Sources of
Inadequate and Excessive Justification" (Purdue University, 1965); Weick, "The Con-
cept of Equity in the Perception of Pay" (Paper read at Midwestern Psychological
Association, April 1965); and D. E. Linder, "Some Psychological Processes Which
Mediate Task Liking" (Ph.D. diss., University of Minnesota, 1965).

[43] Weick, "The Concept of Equity."

pointed out that, according to the theory, a worker's satisfaction with his pay is a function of—

1. his beliefs concerning the degree to which he possesses various characteristics;

2. his convictions concerning the degree to which these characteristics should result in the attainment of rewarding outcomes from his job, i.e., their value as inputs;

3. his beliefs concerning the degree to which he receives these rewarding outcomes from his job;

4. his beliefs concerning the degree to which others possess these characteristics;

5. his beliefs concerning the degree to which others receive rewarding outcomes from their jobs; and

6. the extent to which he compares himself with these others.[44]

We agree with Vroom's conclusion that the complexity of equity theory makes conclusive tests difficult, and that "a great deal of theoretical and methodological refinement remains to be carried out before this approach can be properly evaluated." [45]

As research on the role of financial compensation in industrial motivation becomes more and more prevalent, answers to many questions (such as those discussed in this paper) should be forthcoming. Increased knowledge should be accompanied by more effective use of money in industry. It is hoped that the firm of the future will be able to establish compensation policies and practices based on empirical evidence about the behavioral effects of money as an incentive rather than on the non-tested assumptions, hunches, and time worn "rules-of-thumb" so common in industry today.

---

[44] Vroom, *Work and Motivation*, p. 171.
[45] Ibid., p. 172.

25. THE DEVELOPMENT OF A METHOD OF MEASURING JOB SATISFACTION: THE CORNELL STUDIES *

Patricia Cain Smith

THE CORNELL STUDIES OF JOB SATISFACTION were initiated in 1959 with the purpose of studying job satisfaction among a representative cross section of workers in the United States. One specific goal of these studies was to relate job satisfaction to measurable company and community characteristics and to characteristics of the individual worker. Since the success of the entire study hinged on the nature and quality of the instrument to be used to measure job satisfaction, a considerable amount of time and effort went into constructing this device. This paper summarizes the rationale behind the approach to measurement and the particular characteristics of the measure finally adopted. Before turning to this, however, a brief description of what job satisfaction is and why it should be measured at all would seem to be in order.

WHAT IS JOB SATISFACTION?

We define job satisfaction as an affective response of the worker to his job. It is viewed as a result or consequence of the worker's experience on the job in relation to his own values, that is, to what he wants or expects from it. Satisfaction can be viewed as similar in meaning to pleasure.

WHY MEASURE JOB SATISFACTION?

Job satisfaction was originally thought to be a cause or at least a concomitant of high productivity: "The satisfied worker is the productive worker" was the implicit assumption of many early studies of job satisfaction. Unfortunately, subsequent research has not borne out this assumption; a large number of studies have testified to the fact that there is no *necessary* connection between productivity and satisfaction. Satisfied workers may be high producers or low producers and high producers may

* This article has been prepared specially for this volume. The project described, which was under the direction of Dr. Smith, was carried out under a grant from the Ford Foundation. The contributions of Drs. Charles L. Hulin, Lorne M. Kendall and Edwin A. Locke are gratefully acknowledged. A comprehensive review of the entire program appears in P. C. Smith, L. M. Kendall, and C. L. Hulin, *Measurement of Satisfaction in Work and Retirement* (Chicago: Rand McNally, 1969).

or may not like their jobs. Satisfaction and dissatisfaction may or may not result in overt behavior (changes in productivity, grievances, absences, turnover, and so forth), depending upon the individual's personality (whether he acts on or controls or represses his emotions), the opportunities for self-expression on the job (closeness of supervision, company rules and regulations, and so forth), and the other job alternatives open to him (labor market for his particular skill, his financial condition, and so forth). To repeat, job satisfaction is viewed primarily as a consequence of job experience (and, in fact, high productivity may produce satisfaction as much as the other way around). The causal efficacy of job satisfaction is, then, problematic, rather than something to be assumed.

However, there are still valid reasons for wanting to study job satisfaction. Most obviously it can be viewed as an end in itself. In fact, it is not really meaningful to ask why pleasure or satisfaction are good or desirable. They are desirable by nature.

Secondly, *under certain circumstances* job satisfaction and particularly job dissatisfaction may lead to overt behavior which is of interest to organizations. For instance, there is evidence that dissatisfied workers have a higher turnover and absence rate than satisfied workers. Since training new employees and lost time can cost a company large sums of money, both directly and in terms of poor quality of production and lost business, it is to its self-interest to have satisfied workers.

WHAT CAN MEASURES OF JOB SATISFACTION BE USED FOR?

If job satisfaction is taken to be a desirable goal of management practices, then measures of employee satisfaction can be taken as one of the criteria or standards by which to judge the success of management policies and practices, for example, job enlargement, supervisory training, participative management, group decision-making, employee welfare programs, bonus or incentive-payment systems, and so forth.

Such measures might also be used to predict future absences or turnover among personnel (providing factors such as the job market are taken into consideration).

Thirdly, such measures are a precondition for the testing of various general theories of attitudes and motivation and theories specifically concerned with the factors which produce satisfaction and the factors correlated with it—community, company, and individual characteristics. Such investigations may not have immediate practical utility, but such findings may be of current theoretical interest and of long-term practical value.

Finally, one might simply be interested in knowing what percent of the population are satisfied and what percent dissatisfied with their jobs, either as something of interest in itself, or for purposes of group or cross-cultural comparisons, or to plot trends over time.

REQUIREMENTS OF A USEFUL MEASURE OF JOB SATISFACTION

A useful measure of job satisfaction should be capable of being used over a wide range of job classifications and with people of varying job levels. In other words, its content should be such that the meanings of the words used are common to workers on many different kinds of jobs, and the verbal level should be low enough so that poorly educated as well as well-educated workers can understand the questions.

Practical considerations would demand that the measure be short, easily administered (in groups), and easily scorable. Long, involved measures with complicated scoring systems would be precluded in a large-scale study due to time and financial considerations.

The measure should generate scores indicative of satisfaction with a number of discriminably different aspects of the work situation (pay, work, supervision, co-workers, and so forth). A measure of overall (global) job satisfaction may be sufficient for some purposes but would be inadequate for an intensive study aimed at identifying the relationships between different aspects of the job situation and individual and company characteristics. The same variables may be related quite differently to satisfaction with different aspects of the job, but these relationships would be diluted if only a global measure of satisfaction were used.

The scale should be free from obvious biases, such as acquiescence—the tendency to "agree" with an item independent of item content—so that people who agree with everything will not get artificially high scores.

The worker's frame of reference, his standard of judgment, when responding to the items either should be taken into consideration when constructing and scoring the measure or should be demonstrated not to affect the answers markedly. To cite an obvious example, if the word "simple" meant "good" to one worker but was interpreted as meaning "bad" by another worker, the item would not yield useful results.

The measure should demonstrate reliability: both internal consistency (agreement among items intended to measure the same thing) and stability over time in the same individual.

Finally, the measure should be valid—it should measure what it is intended to measure.

THE CORNELL JOB DESCRIPTIVE INDEX (JDI)

Areas Measured

To fulfill the criteria set out above, a number of different types of measures were tried. The one finally settled upon measured five areas of job satisfaction: satisfaction with work, satisfaction with pay, satisfaction with opportunities for promotion, satisfaction with supervision. and satsfaction with co-workers. These categories were arrived at after considerable review of the factor-analysis literature on job satisfaction, and after an extensive analysis of our own preliminary categories.

For each area there is a list of adjectives or short phrases, each with a blank space beside it. The respondent is instructed to show how well each word or phrase describes the aspect of his job in question (for instance, his pay). If a word describes the pay on his present job (or his supervision, and so forth), he is instructed to write the letter "Y" for "Yes" beside that word or phrase. If the word does not describe his present pay (or supervision, and so forth), he is asked to write "N" for "No" beside that word or phrase. If he cannot decide, he is asked to place a "?" in the blank for "Cannot decide." The scales for each of the five job areas are shown in Table 25–1.

Developing the Scoring Procedure

To investigate the best scoring procedures to use, in our early studies these scales were administered to each person a second and a third time. The second time each person was asked to describe the "best" job he could think of or the "best" job he had ever had. The third time the individual was asked to describe the "worst" previous job he had had or could think of. This made it possible to score the questionnaires in four different ways:

1. Satisfaction could be inferred from the similarity of his responses when describing his present job to his responses when describing his "best" job; that is, if he described his best and present jobs in the same way, one could infer that he was satisfied with the job.

2. Satisfaction could be inferred from the dissimilarity of his responses when describing his present job to his responses when describing his "worst" job; that is, if he described his present and worst jobs completely differently, it could be inferred that the individual was satisfied with his job.

3. Satisfaction could be inferred simultaneously from the similarity of his present job responses to his "best" job responses and their dissimilarity to his "worst" job responses. For instance, if a person described his best and present jobs as "challenging," whereas he described his worst job as not challenging, it could be inferred that he was satisfied with his job in that respect. On the other hand, if he described his present, best, *and* worst jobs as "challenging," satisfaction would not be inferred from that item; in fact, the item would not be used in scoring at all, because it would indicate that for him that characteristic was not important.

4. Satisfaction could be inferred from direct, a priori scoring of the items under the assumption that most individuals would interpret the items in the same way and would see the same things as desirable and un-

desirable on a job; that is, it would be assumed that all people would see a "challenging" job as desirable.

The rationale behind the first three scoring methods was to eliminate the possible effects of different frames of reference of different individuals in answering the items; that is, to control for the fact that some people might not see "challenging" work as a good thing. The question then became how to decide which of these scoring methods was the best. Since there are no behavioral or performance criteria of job satisfaction (recall that our definition of satisfaction indicated that it was a *response* to the work situation, not a determinant or cause of performance), other methods of comparing the validity of the various scales had to be used.

An alternative method of validation in a situation like this is to choose the method that *(a)* is most representative of all the methods used, that most consistently agrees with the other methods, and *(b)* shows the best discrimination among the different job areas. For instance, if a method yielded scores on the five areas of job satisfaction (work, pay, promotions, supervision, and co-workers) and all these scores correlated very highly with each other, but did not correlate at all with scores on the same areas as measured by other methods, we would conclude that this particular measure of satisfaction contained some special bias and was not very useful.

Using these criteria, it was found that the a priori scoring of the JDI scales gave the best results; that is, it yielded scores that agreed most highly with scores derived from other scoring methods and yielded the clearest discrimination or independence among the five job-area scales. The direct JDI measures also correlated highly with several entirely different sets of measures which asked the individual to rate his job satisfaction directly, which gave added credence to its validity.

Thus, the JDI yields five scores, one for each scale. These scores are obtained by adding up the number of responses within each scale, according to the keys provided in Table 25–1.

Selection of Items

The items for the JDI were selected by a three-stage process. First, items were selected from other inventories and by common sense which seemed to be relevant to each of the five area scales. This original search yielded from 30 to 40 items per scale. Next we looked at how frequently each item was used to describe "best" and "worst" jobs. Items which were used equally frequently to describe "best" and "worst" jobs were discarded on the grounds that they probably were not important in determining job satisfaction. Finally, the scales were administered to several samples of employees and the subjects were divided (on each scale) into a "satisfied" half and a "dissatisfied" half on the basis of their total scores on each scale. Proportional differences in item responses between high

TABLE 25-1

Items in Final Version of JDI *

Each of the five scales was presented on a separate page.

The instructions for each scale asked the subject to put "Y" beside an item if the item described the particular aspect of his job (work, pay, and so forth), "N" if the item did not describe that aspect, or "?" if he could not decide.

The response shown beside each item is the one scored in the "satisfied" direction for each scale.

	Work		*Supervision*		*People*
Y	Fascinating	Y	Asks my advice	Y	Stimulating
N	Routine	N	Hard to please	N	Boring
Y	Satisfying	N	Impolite	N	Slow
N	Boring	Y	Praises good work	Y	Ambitious
Y	Good	Y	Tactful	N	Stupid
Y	Creative	Y	Influential	Y	Responsible
Y	Respected	Y	Up-to-date	Y	Fast
N	Hot		Doesn't supervise	Y	Intelligent
Y	Pleasant	N	enough		Easy to make
Y	Useful	N	Quick-tempered	N	enemies
N	Tiresome		Tells me where I	N	Talk too much
Y	Healthful	Y	stand	Y	Smart
Y	Challenging	N	Annoying	N	Lazy
N	On your feet	N	Stubborn	N	Unpleasant
N	Frustrating	Y	Knows job well	N	No privacy
N	Simple	N	Bad	Y	Active
N	Endless	Y	Intelligent	N	Narrow interests
	Gives sense of		Leaves me on my	Y	Loyal
Y	accomplishment	Y	own	N	Hard to meet
			Around when		
		Y	needed		
		N	Lazy		

	Pay		*Promotions*
	Income adequate for normal		Good opportunity for advance-
Y	expenses	Y	ment
Y	Satisfactory profit sharing	N	Opportunity somewhat limited
N	Barely live on income	Y	Promotion on ability
N	Bad	N	Dead-end job
Y	Income provides luxuries	Y	Good chance for promotion
N	Insecure	N	Unfair promotion policy
N	Less than I deserve	N	Infrequent promotions
Y	Highly paid	Y	Regular promotions
N	Underpaid·	Y	Fairly good chance for promotion

* Permission to use these scales should be obtained from Dr. Patricia C. Smith, Dept. of Psychology, Bowling Green State University, Bowling Green, Ohio, 43403.

and low halves in each sample were computed for each item. Only items were retained which showed a clear differentiation between satisfied and dissatisfied workers. This process was repeated over five different samples of workers and only those items which showed consistent discrimination were retained.

The final pay and promotion scales included nine items each and the work, supervision, and co-workers scales included eighteen items each. About half the items chosen for each scale are positive, so that a "Y" response would indicate satisfaction, and about half are negative, so that an "N" response would indicate satisfaction. Thus a person who put a "Y" before every item would not get a high (satisfied) score simply because of a tendency to say yes.

Reliability and Validity of the JDI

The internal consistency reliabilities of the five JDI scales range from .80 to .88, as determined by corrected split-half correlations based on the responses of eighty male employees from two different electronic plants.

There is no single general criterion measure which can be used to validate a measure of job satisfaction. What is needed is evidence that the scales relate to other independent meaningful indices of satisfaction in the situation. The approach used was to study (a) relations of the various JDI scales to other measures of job satisfaction, (b) the influence of situational characteristics on these scales, and (c) the relations between the scales and individual differences thought to be related to job satisfaction. These studies have been reported elsewhere.[1] Briefly these studies indicate that the JDI yields measures of satisfaction with five different aspects of jobs which are discriminably different from each other; the average correlation between the different scales is approximately .37 which is low enough to indicate a great deal of discrimination among the five areas. The scales correlate highly with other measures of satisfaction (average $r = .70$) and are affected in the expected directions by worker, job, and situational differences. In this sense the JDI has validity as a measure of job satisfaction.

In sum, the JDI, using the direct a priori scoring method, appears to meet the criteria set out initially. The JDI appears to be valid in the sense that it is representative of other types of measures of satisfaction and discriminates well among the various job areas. It demonstrates adequate internal reliability (although no test-retest studies have been

---

[1] C. L. Hulin and Patricia C. Smith, "Sex Differences in Job Satisfaction," *Journal of Applied Psychology* 48 (1964): 88–92; idem, "A Linear Model of Job Satisfaction," ibid. 49 (1965): 209–16; L. M. Kendall, "Canonical Analysis of Job Satisfaction and Behavioral, Personal Background, and Situational Data," (Ph.D. diss., Cornell University, 1963); E. A. Locke et al., "Convergent and Discriminant Validity for Areas and Methods of Rating Job Satisfaction," *Journal of Applied Psychology* 48 (1964): 313–19.

done as yet) and is relatively free from obvious response biases such as acquiescence. It yields scores on five different areas of job satisfaction and it is short, easily administered, and easily scored.

There is another interesting characteristic of the JDI that should be noted. It does not ask the employee to indicate directly how satisfied he is, but rather asks him to describe his job (that is, his pay, his work) by putting the appropriate symbol (Y, N, or ?) in the blank beside each item (for example, "boring"). It was felt that such a task would be easier, particularly for more poorly educated workers, than describing internal feeling states. Satisfaction is thus inferred from these job descriptions; for instance, if an individual describes his work as "boring," "frustrating," and not "pleasant," dissatisfaction with the work is inferred on those items. Actually, as indicated above, scores on the JDI scales agree well with more direct measures of job satisfaction.

All told, over nine hundred people in seven different organizations were used in the development of the JDI. Thus far, the JDI has been administered to over two thousand employees in more than twenty different companies in a number of different types of communities and geographical locations in the United States. The JDI scales have shown substantial relationships to individual, company, and community characteristics.[2] Although the data analyses are not complete as yet, it appears that the JDI has adequately fulfilled the purposes for which it was designed.

26. THE EFFECT OF PERFORMANCE ON JOB SATISFACTION [*]

Edward E. Lawler III and Lyman W. Porter

THE HUMAN RELATIONS MOVEMENT with its emphasis on good interpersonal relations, job satisfaction, and the importance of informal groups provided an important initial stimulant for the study of job attitudes and their relationship to human behavior in organizations. Through the 30s and 40s, many studies were carried out to determine the correlates of high and low job satisfaction. Such studies related job satisfaction to seniority, age, sex, education, occupation, and income, to mention a few. Why this great interest in job satisfaction? Undoubtedly some of it stemmed from a simple desire on the part of scientists to learn more about job satisfaction, but much of the interest in job satisfaction seems

---

[2] C. L. Hulin, "The Effects of Community Characteristics on Measures of Job Satisfaction," *Journal of Applied Psychology* 50 (1966): 185–92; idem, "Job Satisfaction and Turnover in a Female Clerical Population," ibid., pp. 280–85.

[*] From *Industrial Relations* 7 (1967): 20–28.

to have come about because of its presumed relationship to job perfor- mance. As Brayfield and Crockett have pointed out, a common assumption that employee satisfaction directly affects performance permeates most of the writings about the topic that appeared during this period of two decades.[1] Statements such as the following characterized the literature· "Morale is not an abstraction; rather it is concrete in the sense that it directly affects the quality and quantity of an individual's output," and "Employee morale—reduces turnover—cuts down absenteeism and tardi- ness; lifts production." [2]

It is not hard to see how the assumption that high job satisfaction leads to high performance came to be popularly accepted. Not only did it fit into the value system of the human relations movement but there also appeared to be some research data to support this point. In the Western Electric studies, the evidence from the Relay Assembly Test Room showed a dramatic tendency for increased employee productivity to be associated with an increase in job satisfaction. Also, who could deny that in the Bank Wiring Room there was both production restric- tion and mediocre employee morale. With this background it is easy to see why both social scientists and managers believed that if job dissatis- faction could be reduced, the human brake on production could be re- moved and turned into a force that would increase performance.

PREVIOUS RESEARCH

But does the available evidence support the belief that high satis- faction will lead to high performance? Since an initial study, in 1932, by Kornhauser and Sharp, more than 30 studies have considered the relation- ship between these two variables.[3] Many of the earlier studies seemed to have assumed implicitly that a positive relationship existed and that it was important to demonstrate that it in fact did exist. Little attention was given to trying to understand *why* job satisfaction should lead to higher performance; instead, researchers contented themselves with routinely studying the relationship between satisfaction and performance in a num- ber of industrial situations.

The typical reader of the literature in the early 50s was probably aware of the fact that some studies had failed to find a significant satis- faction-performance relationship. Indeed, the very first study of the prob- lem obtained an insignificant relationship.[4] However, judging from the impact of the first review of the literature on the topic, by Brayfield and

---

[1] A. H. Brayfield and W. H. Crockett, "Employee Attitudes and Employee Perfor- mance," *Psychological Bulletin* 52 (September 1955): 396–424.

[2] Ibid.

[3] A. Kornhauser and A. Sharp, "Employee Attitudes: Suggestions From a Study in a Factory," *Personnel Journal* 10 (1932): 393–401.

[4] Ibid.

Crockett, many social scientists, let alone practicing managers, were unaware that the evidence indicated how little relationship exists between satisfaction and performance.[5] The key conclusion that emerged from the review was that "there is little evidence in the available literature that employee attitudes bear any simple—or, for that matter, appreciable—relationship to performance on the job." (The review, however, pointed out that job satisfaction did seem to be positively related, as expected, to two other kinds of employee behavior—absenteeism and turnover.)

The review had a major impact on the field of industrial psychology and helped shatter the kind of naive thinking that characterized the earlier years of the Human Relations movement. Perhaps it also discouraged additional research, since few post-1955 studies of the relationship between satisfaction and performance have been reported in scientific journals.

Another review, covering much of the same literature, was completed about the same time.[6] This review took a more optimistic view of the evidence: ". . . there is frequent evidence for the often suggested opinion that positive job attitudes are favorable to increased productivity. The relationship is not absolute, but there are enough data to justify attention to attitudes as a factor in improving the worker's output. However, the correlations obtained in many of the positive studies were low."[7] This review also pointed out, as did Brayfield and Crockett, that there was a definite trend for attitudes to be related to absenteeism and turnover. Perhaps the chief reasons for the somewhat divergent conclusions reached by the two reviews were that they did not cover exactly the same literature and that Brayfield and Crockett were less influenced by suggestive findings that did reach statistical significance. In any event, the one conclusion that was obvious from both reviews was that there was not the *strong, pervasive* relationship between job satisfaction and productivity that had been suggested by many of the early proponents of the Human Relations movement and so casually accepted by personnel specialists.

A more recent review of the literature by Vroom has received less attention than did the two earlier reviews,[8] perhaps because it is now rather generally accepted that satisfaction is not related to performance. However, before we too glibly accept the view that satisfaction and performance are unrelated, let us look carefully at the data from studies reviewed by Vroom. These studies show a median correlation of +.14 between satisfaction and performance. Although this correlation is not large, the consistency of the direction of the correlation is quite impres-

---

[5] Brayfield and Crockett, "Employee Attitudes and Employee Performance."
[6] Frederick Herzberg et al., *Job Attitudes: Review of Research and Opinion* (Pittsburgh: Psychological Service, 1957).
[7] Ibid., p. 103.
[8] V. H. Vroom, *Work and Motivation* (New York: John Wiley & Sons, 1964).

sive. Twenty of the 23 correlations cited by Vroom are positive. By a statistical test such consistency would occur by chance less than once in a hundred times.

In summary, the evidence indicates that a low but consistent relationship exists between satisfaction and performance, but it is not at all clear *why* this relationship exists. The questions that need to be answered at this time, therefore, concern the place of job satisfaction both in theories of employee motivation and in everyday organizational practice. For example, should an organization systematically measure the level of employee satisfaction? Is it important for an organization to try to improve employee job satisfaction? Is there theoretical reason for believing that job satisfaction shuold be related to job behavior and if so, can it explain why this relationship exists?

WHY STUDY JOB SATISFACTION?

There are really two bases upon which to argue that job satisfaction is important. Interestingly, both are different from the original reason for studying job satisfaction, that is, the assumed ability of satisfaction to influence performance. The first. and undoubtedly the most straightforward reason, rests on the fact that strong correlations between absenteeism and satisfaction, as well as between turnover and satisfaction, appear in the previous studies. Accordingly, job satisfaction would seem to be an important focus of organizations which wish to reduce absenteeism and turnover.

Perhaps the best explanation of the fact that satisfaction is related to absenteeism and turnover comes from the kind of path-goal theory of motivation that has been stated by Georgopoulos, Mahoney and Jones; Vroom; and Lawler and Porter.[9] According to this view, people are motivated to do things which they feel have a high probability of leading to rewards which they value. When a worker says he is satisfied with his job, he is in effect saying that his needs are satisfied as a result of having his job. Thus, path-goal theory would predict that high satisfaction will lead to low turnover and absenteeism because the satisfied individual is motivated to go to work where his important needs are satisfied.

A second reason for interest in job satisfaction stems from its low but consistent *association* with job performance. Let us speculate for a moment on why this association exists. One possibility is that, as assumed by many, the satisfaction *caused* the performance. However, there is little theoretical reason for believing that satisfaction can cause performance.

[9] B. S. Georgopoulos, G. M. Mahoney, and N. W. Jones, "A Path-Goal Approach to Productivity," *Journal of Applied Psychology* 41 (1957): 345–53; Vroom, *Work and Motivation;* E. Lawler III and L. W. Porter, "Antecedent Attitudes of Effective Managerial Performance," *Organizational Behavior and Human Performance* 2 (May 1967): 122–43. See also idem, *Managerial Attitudes and Performance* (Homewood, Ill.: Irwin–Dorsey, Ltd., 1968).

Vroom, using a path-goal theory of motivation, has pointed out that job satisfaction and job performance are caused by quite different things: ". . . job satisfaction is closely affected by the amount of rewards that people derive from their jobs and . . . level of performance is closely affected by the basis of attainment of rewards. Individuals are satisfied with their jobs to the extent to which their jobs provide them with what they desire, and they perform effectively in them to the extent that effective performance leads to the attainment of what they desire." [10]

RELATIONSHIP BETWEEN SATISFACTION AND PERFORMANCE

Vroom's statement contains a hint of why, despite the fact that satisfaction and performance are caused by different things, they do bear some relationship to each other. If we assume, as seems to be reasonable in terms of motivation theory, that rewards cause satisfaction, and that in some cases performance produces rewards, then it is possible that the relationship found between satisfaction and performance comes about through the action of a third variable rewards. Briefly stated, good performance may lead to rewards, which in turn lead to satisfaction; this formulation then would say that satisfaction, rather than causing performance, as was previously assumed, is caused by it. Figure 26–1 presents this thinking in a diagrammatic form.

This model first shows that performance leads to rewards, and it distinguishes between two kinds of rewards and their connection to performance. A wavy line between performance and extrinsic rewards indicates that such rewards are likely to be imperfectly related to performance. By extrinsic rewards is meant such organizationally controlled rewards as pay, promotion, status, and security—rewards that are often referred to as satisfying mainly lower level needs.[11] The connection is relatively weak because of the difficulty of tying extrinsic rewards directly to performance. Even though an organization may have a policy of rewarding merit, performance is difficult to measure, and in dispensing rewards like pay, many other factors are frequently taken into consideration. Lawler, for example, found a low correlation between amount of salary and superiors' evaluation for a number of middle- and lower-level managers.[12]

Quite the opposite is likely to be true for intrinsic rewards, however, since they are given to the individual by himself for good performance. Intrinsic or internally mediated rewards are subject to fewer disturbing

---

[10] Vroom, *Work and Motivation*, p. 246.

[11] A. H. Maslow, *Motivation and Personality* (New York: Harper, 1954). According to Maslow, needs are arranged in a hierarchy with physiological and security needs being the lowest level needs, social and esteem needs next, and autonomy and self-actualization needs the highest level.

[12] E. E. Lawler, "Managers' Attitudes toward How Their Pay Is and Should Be Determined," *Journal of Applied Psychology* 50 (August 1966): 273–79.

FIGURE 26–1

The Theoretical Model

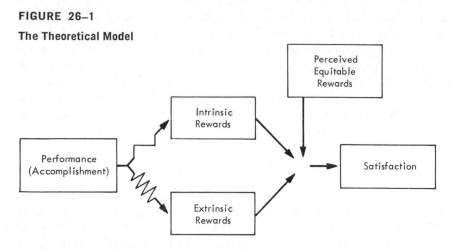

influences and thus are likely to be more directly related to good perform-ance. This connection is indicated in the model by a semiwavy line. Probably the best example of an intrinsic reward is the feeling of having accomplished something worthwhile. For that matter, any of the rewards that satisfy self-actualization needs or higher order growth needs are good examples of intrinsic rewards.

The model also shows that intrinsic and extrinsic rewards are not directly related to job satisfaction since the relationship is moderated by expected equitable rewards. This variable refers to the level or amount of rewards that an individual feels he *should* receive as the result of his job performance. Thus, an individual's satisfaction is a function both of the number and amount of the rewards he receives as well as what he considers to be a fair level of reward. An individual can be satisfied with a small amount of reward if he feels that it is a fair amount of reward for his job.[13]

This model would seem to predict that because of the imperfect rela-tionship between performance and rewards and the importance of ex-pected equitable rewards there would be a low but positive relationship between job satisfaction and job performance. The model also leads to a number of other predictions about the relationship between satisfaction and performance. If it turns out that, as this model predicts, satisfaction is dependent on performance, then it can be argued that satisfaction is an important variable from both a theoretical and a practical point of view despite its low relationship to performance. However, when satisfaction is viewed in this way, the reasons for considering it to be important are quite different from those that are proposed when satisfaction is consid-

[13] L. W. Porter, "A Study of Perceived Need Satisfactions in Bottom and Middle Management Jobs," *Journal of Applied Psychology* 45 (January 1961): 1–10.

ered to cause performance. But first, let us look at some of the predictions that are derivable from the model and at some data that were collected in order to test the predictions.

RESEARCH DATA

Usable data were collected from 148 middle and lower level managers in five organizations. One of the organizations was a large manufacturing company; the others were small social service and welfare agencies. As determined from the demographic data collected from each manager, the sample was typical of other samples of middle- and lower-level managers, with one exception—31 of the managers were female.

Two kinds of data were collected for each manager. Superior and peer rankings were obtained on two factors: (1) how hard the manager worked, and (2) how well the manager performed his job. Since a number of peers ranked each manager, the average peer's rankings were used for data-analysis purposes. The rankings by the superiors and peers were in general agreement with each other, so the rankings met the requirements for convergent and discriminant validity. In addition to the superior and peer rankings, each manager filled out an attitude questionnaire designed to measure his degree of satisfaction in five needed areas. This part of the questionnaire was identical to the one used in earlier studies by Porter.[14] It consists of 13 items in the following form:

The opportunity for independent thought and action in my management position:
(a) How much is there now?
        (min)   1   2   3   4   5   6   7   (max)
(b) How much should there be?
        (min)   1   2   3   4   5   6   7   (max)

The answers to the first of these questions (a) for each of the 13 items was taken as the measure of need fulfillment or rewards received. The answer to the second of the questions (b) was taken as a measure of the individual's expected equitable level of rewards. The difference in answers between the second and first of these questions was taken as the operational measure of need satisfaction. That is, the larger the difference between "should" and "is now" in our findings, the greater the dissatisfaction.[15]

The 13 items, though presented in random order in the questionnaire, had been preclassified into five types of needs that have been described by Maslow: security, social, esteem, autonomy, and self-actualization.

---

[14] Ibid.
[15] A third question about the importance of the various types of needs was also included, but the results based on it are not reported in the findings presented in this article.

PREDICTIONS AND RESEARCH RESULTS

Let us now consider two specific predictions that our model suggests. The first is that an individual's degree of need satisfaction is related to his job performance as rated by his peers and by his superior. A second prediction is that this relationship is stronger for managers than for non-managers.

The basis for this second prediction can be found in the assumed connection between rewards and performance. It seems apparent that most organizations have considerably more freedom to reward their managers differentially than they do their often unionized rank-and-file employees (unless the latter are on incentive pay plans). Even in a nonunionized organization (such as a governmental unit), management jobs generally offer the possibility of greater flexibility in differential rewards, especially in terms of prestige and autonomy in decision-making. Management jobs also typically provide greater opportunities to satisfy higher-order intrinsic needs. As the model shows, satisfaction of these higher-order needs is more closely tied to performance.

Satisfaction and Performance. Data collected from our sample of managers generally support the first two predictions. Job satisfaction (the sum of the difference scores for all 13 items) correlates significantly with both the superiors' rankings (r = .32, p < .01) and peers' rankings (r = .30, p < .01) of performance. Although the correlations are not large, they are substantially larger than the median correlation between satisfaction and performance at the level of rank-and-file workers (r = .14 as given in Vroom's review). It is possible that this higher relationship came about because we used a different measure of need satisfaction than has been typically used before or because we used a better performance measure. However, our belief is that it came about because the study was done at the management level in contrast to the previous studies which mainly involved nonmanagement employees. Neither our measure of job performance nor our measure of satisfaction would seem to be so unique that either could account for the higher relationship found between satisfaction and performance. However, future studies that use the same measure for both managers and nonmanagers are needed if this point is to be firmly established.

Satisfaction and effort. An additional prediction from the model is that satisfaction should be more closely related to the rankings obtained on performance than to the rankings obtained on effort. The prediction is an important one for the model and stems from the fact that satisfaction is seen as a variable that is more directly dependent on performance than on effort. Others have pointed out that effort is only one of the factors that determines how effective an individual's performance will be. Ability factors and situational constraints are other obviously relevant

TABLE 26–1

Pearson Correlations between Performance and Satisfaction in Five Need Areas

Needs	Rankings by	
	Superiors	*Peers*
Security	.21[a]	.17[b]
Social	.23[a]	.26[a]
Esteem	.24[a]	.16[b]
Autonomy	.18[b]	.23[a]
Self-actualization	.30[a]	.28[a]

[a] $p < .01$
[b] $p < .05$

determinants. It is also important to note that if we assume, as many previous writers have, that satisfaction causes performance then it would seem logical that satisfaction should be more closely related to effort than to performance. Satisfaction should influence an individual's performance by affecting his motivation to perform effectively, and this presumably is better reflected by effort than by job performance.

The results of the present study show, in fact, a stronger relationship between the superiors' rankings of performance and satisfaction ($r = .32$). than between the superiors' rankings of effort and satisfaction ($r = .23$). Similarly, for the peer rankings there is a stronger relationship between performance and satisfaction ($r = .30$), than between effort and satisfaction ($r = .20$).

Intrinsic and extrinsic rewards. The model suggests that intrinsic rewards that satisfy needs such as self-actualization are more likely to be related to performance than are extrinsic rewards, which have to be given by someone else and therefore have a weaker relationship between their reception and performance. Thus, the satisfaction should be more closely related to performance for higher than for lower order needs. Table 26–1 presents the data relevant to this point. There is a slight tendency for satisfaction of the higher-order needs to show higher correlations with performance than does satisfaction with lower-order needs. In particular, the highest correlations appear for self-actualization which is, of course, the highest-order need, in the Maslow need hierarchy.

Overall, the data from the present study are in general agreement with the predictions based on the model. Significant relationships did appear between performance and job satisfaction. Perhaps even more important for our point of view, the relationship between satisfaction and performance was stronger than that typically found among blue-collar employees. Also in agreement with our model was the finding that satisfaction was more closely related to performance than to effort. The final prediction, which was supported by the data, was that the satisfaction of higher-order needs would be the most closely related to performance. Taken together then, the data offer encouraging support for our model and in particular for the assertion of the model that satisfaction can best be thought of as depending on performance rather than causing it.

IMPLICATIONS OF THE FINDINGS

At this point we can ask the following question: what does the strength of the satisfaction-performance relationship tell us about an organization? For example, if a strong positive relationship exists we would assume that the organization is effectively distributing differential extrinsic rewards based on performance. In addition, it is providing jobs that allow for the satisfaction of higher-order needs. Finally, the poorer performers rather than the better ones are quitting and showing high absenteeism, since, as we knew, satisfaction, turnover, and absenteeism are closely related.

Now let us consider an organization where no relationship exists between satisfaction and performance. In this organization, presumably, rewards are not being effectively related to performance, and absenteeism and turnover in the organization are likely to be equally distributed among both the good and poor performers. Finally, let us consider the organization where satisfaction and performance bear a negative relationship to each other. Here, absenteeism and turnover will be greatest among the best performers. Furthermore, the poor performers would be getting more rewards than the good performers.

Clearly, most organization theorists would feel that organizational effectiveness is encouraged by rewarding good performers and by restricting turnover to poorer performers. Thus, it may be desirable for organizations to develop a strong relationship between satisfaction and performance. In effect, the argument is that the less positive relationship between satisfaction and performance in an organization, the less effective the organization will be *ceteris paribus*. If this hypothesis were shown to be true, it would mean that a measure of the relationship between satisfaction and performance would be a helpful diagnostic tool for examining organizations. It is hardly necessary to note that this approach is quite different from the usual human relations one of trying to maximize satisfaction, since here we are suggesting trying to maximize the relationship between satisfaction and performance, rather than satisfaction itself.

One further implication of the model appears to warrant comment. It may well be that a high general level of satisfaction of needs like self-actualization may be a sign of organization effectiveness. Such a level of satisfaction would indicate, for instance, that most employees have interesting and involving jobs and that they probably are performing them well. One of the obvious advantages of providing employees with intrinsically interesting jobs is that good performance is rewarding in and of itself. Furthermore, being rewarded for good performance is likely to encourage further good performance. Thus, measures of higher-order need satisfaction may provide good evidence of how effective organizations have been in creating interesting and rewarding jobs and, therefore, indirect evidence of how motivating the jobs themselves are. This discussion of the role of intrinsic rewards and satisfaction serves to highlight the importance of including measures of higher-order need satisfaction in attitude surveys. Too often attitude surveys have focused only on satisfaction with extrinsic rewards, such as pay and promotion, and on the social relations which were originally stressed by the human relations movement.

In summary, we have argued that it is important to consider the satisfaction level that exists in organizations. For one thing, satisfaction is important because it has the power to influence both absenteeism and turnover. In addition, in the area of job performance we have emphasized that rather than being a cause of performance, satisfaction is caused by it. If this is true, and we have presented some evidence to support the view that it is, then it becomes appropriate to be more concerned about which people and what kind of needs are satisfied in the organization, rather than about how to maximize satisfaction generally. In short, we suggest new ways of interpreting job-satisfaction data.

Section Five
LEADERSHIP AND SUPERVISION

INTRODUCTION

LEADERSHIP ONCE WAS THOUGHT OF AS A PERSONALITY TRAIT that some people had and others didn't. However, research has indicated that no dependable traits could be isolated which consistently identified effective leaders or which differentiated leaders from nonleaders in all situations. It takes only a little reflection to realize this when one considers the diversity of people in history, politics, religion, athletics, as well as in industry, who would be considered "effective leaders." A more fruitful approach is to think of leadership in terms of "activities which influence others." By this definition leadership cannot be separated from the activities of groups. The leader is effective only to the extent that his group is influenced by his behavior to move toward certain shared goals. By this definition people in supervisory positions may or may not be leaders. Conversely, other individuals in the group not officially designated as supervisors may turn out to be leaders. We can evaluate leadership only in terms of its effects on the behavior of individuals in the group.

There still remains the question of identifying those patterns of leader behavior which are effective with certain kinds of groups. In this section we will focus on leadership patterns and practices in industrial settings. We will examine what these patterns are, the situational forces that influence them, and their relation to group effectiveness.

It is immediately apparent that two basic problems in this area are *(a)* the identification of meaningful leadership patterns and *(b)* the development of methods to measure these patterns. The Ohio State University Leadership Studies made these problems major research objectives. Focusing on the kinds of behavior engaged in by people in leadership roles, these investigators developed over eighteen hundred items (for example, he calls the group together to talk things over; he knows about it when something goes wrong) descriptive of what supervisors do in their leadership roles. These items were then classified into ten broad categories of leader behavior (for example, initiation, domination, evaluation, communication). Questionnaires were developed by means of which leader behavior could be described and scored on these ten dimensions. Each supervisor was described in terms of how frequently (for example, always, often, . . . never) he did what each item stated. Repeated use of these questionnaires in a variety of leader-group situations (foreman-worker, executive-subordinate, school principal-teacher, university department head-professor, aircraft commander-crew, submarine officer-crew) showed that these ten categories overlapped with one another and that the items could be grouped into two more basic dimensions of leader behavior. These were labeled *Consideration* and *Initiating Structure*. We have already met these dimensions in the Fleishman article on human relations training in Section Three, Article 18. The important point is that the research identified and defined these dimensions and showed that the two dimensions are uncorrelated; supervisors may be high on Consideration and still be either high or low on the Structure dimension. Thus, these attributes are more usefully considered as separate dimensions and not as opposite poles of the same dimension.

The earlier article by Fleishman, in Section Three, described how measures of these patterns were developed and used in a complex industrial setting. The article focused on some situational variables that influence the particular leadership patterns used by supervisors. It was shown that the organizational value system, particularly the "leadership climate," influences the supervisor's leader behavior, and may even negate the intended effects of management training.

As a follow-up to this study, it was later found that management in this plant actually *rated* as "most proficient" those foremen who turned out (on independent measurement) to be low in Consideration and high in Structure. In other words, the supervisor was rewarded in the plant for behavior patterns different from that intended by the training. It was also found that foremen with these patterns most often had work groups with higher grievance rates, accidents, turnover, and absences.[1] It appeared, then, that management was responding more to a "stereotype" of effective leadership and was not focusing on leadership acts which actually "influenced group members toward shared goals."

---

[1] These findings also underscore a theme found in Sections One and Two, which stressed the need to examine not one, but many criteria of on-the-job performance.

The first article in this section, by Fleishman and Harris, "Leadership Behavior Related to Employee Grievances and Turnover," carries this research one step further. It takes a closer look at how Consideration and Structure, singly and in combination, are related to the behavior of work-group members. These later results in this same plant indicated that the foremen who are higher in Consideration could also be higher in Structure with no necessary increase in grievances, turnover, or other negative behavior of the work group.

Evidence to date on these patterns suggests that supervisors who emphasize one pattern at the expense of the other are apt to be less effective, but that some balance between them is needed to satisfy organizational as well as individual needs. Supervisors who are low in both patterns are not even seen as "leaders" by their groups—they are frequently by-passed by their own work groups.[2]

One of the most extensive research programs on supervision was carried out at the University of Michigan's Institute for Social Research. In the article "Patterns in Management," Likert summarizes some management concepts and reviews many of the early findings of this program.[3] Likert uses the terms "employee-centered" and "production-centered" supervision, but it will be recognized that these seem similar to the Consideration and Structure patterns just described. The studies described focus on the complex relations of supervisory behavior, morale, and productivity. It is important to note Likert's conclusion that "those employee-centered supervisors who get the best results tend to recognize that getting production is also one of their major responsibilities." This, of course, fits our previous discussion regarding the proper balance between Consideration and Structure.

Besides supervisory styles such as Consideration and Structure or employee-centered and production-centered, there are, of course, a number of other factors that may be important in determining effective leadership. Specifically, these include other aspects of the leader's behavior, his subordinates' perceptions of his competence and influence, and factors in the situation.

The next article, "Specific Leadership Behaviors That Promote Problem Solving," by Maier and Sashkin, indicates that training leaders of problem-solving groups in certain leadership behaviors leads to higher quality problem solutions by members of the group. Specifically, Maier and Sashkin found that training the leader to present the problem and to share

---

[2] For a recent review of research on Initiation of Structure and Consideration, see E. A. Fleishman, "Twenty Years of Consideration and Structure," in *Contemporary Developments in the Study of Leadership,* edited by E. A. Fleishman and J. G. Hunt (Carbondale, Ill.: Southern Illinois University Press, 1973).

[3] For a more comprehensive and more recent treatment of this program, as well as a presentation of Likert's theories of leadership and organizational effectiveness, see R. Likert, *New Patterns of Management* (New York: McGraw-Hill Book Co., 1961); Idem, *The Human Organization* (New York: McGraw-Hill Book Co., 1967).

relevant factual information with the group members was superior to other leadership approaches such as attempting to persuade the group on a particular solution to the problem.

Another potentially important characteristic for effective leadership is the leader's perceived expertise or technical competence in the eyes of his subordinates. Even though a leader may behave in a considerate and structuring way, showing concern for his employees as well as emphasizing task performance, he still may not be influential with his group if he is not seen to possess appropriate technical competence. The next article, "Leader Influence and Performance," by Ivancevich and Donnelly, reports a research study concerned with this particular aspect of leadership. They found that the higher the degree to which a leader was respected by his subordinates, especially with regard to his experience, training, and judgment, the more effective was the performance of his work group (in this case, retail food salesmen).

Most current conceptions of leadership generally agree that in order to understand leadership it is necessary to understand not only the leader and his personal characteristics, behaviors, leadership styles, and so forth, but also the *situation* in which leadership occurs. Situational variables include such factors as the personalities, attitudes, needs, and problems of subordinates; the nature of the group task; interpersonal relationships between the leader and the group members; and various aspects of the larger organization or context in which leadership occurs. The next two articles take a closer look at some situational factors which may condition the behavior and effectiveness of individuals in supervisory roles. The identification of those situational factors which make a difference in the kinds of leadership behavior which turn out to be effective has posed a difficult research problem. However, much progress has been made and a number of critical factors can now be specified.

The .article by Kipnis and Cosentino, "Use of Leadership Powers in Industry," investigates the use of specific leadership powers (such as reprimands, persuasion, instruction, and so forth) in correcting subordinate behavior. They found several situational factors, such as number of employees supervised, nature of the problem, and type of organization (military versus industrial) to be influential in determining the supervisor's choice of corrective powers.

For many years, Fiedler has been studying the relationship between leadership patterns and group effectiveness in a variety of types of groups, tasks, and situations. The leadership measure which Fiedler developed seems to emphasize the tendency of leaders either to be primarily concerned with task accomplishment or with maintaining good interpersonal relations within the group. As we have pointed out earlier, other research has considered consideration and task orientation as representing two independent leadership dimensions, where different supervisors can emphasize different combinations of them. However, there is nothing inconsistent between this view and a single measure which emphasizes the tendency of a supervisor to be most concerned with one pattern or the other. In "Situational Factors Related to Leadership," Fiedler reviews his research and develops a model to integrate his findings in terms of the group-task situation or "job environment" within which leaders have to operate. The factors he considers are leader-member relations, task structure, and position power of the leader. The findings lead to the provocative view that knowledge of these situational factors may provide some basis for modifying supervisory jobs to fit an individual's leadership pattern.[4]

Since the research evidence suggests that the effective supervisor must often keep a balance between Consideration and Structure (or between satisfying individual and organizational needs), some writers have suggested that the successful leader must be able to *vary* his leadership style and must be able to emphasize different leadership patterns at different times. Thus, in a widely cited article, Tannenbaum and Schmidt[5] have suggested that the successful manager must be sensitive to different forces which might be relevant to his behavior at any given time. These include forces in the leader himself, forces in his subordinates, and forces in the situation. They suggest that the effective leader must accurately understand and perceive himself, the individuals with whom he interacts, and the organizational environment in which he operates. Further, the leader must then be able to behave appropriately in the light of these perceptions. He must exercise direct control when direction is called for and he must allow participation and decision-making by subordinates when such a leadership style is appropriate. Thus, rather than training leaders to adopt a particular leadership style, or engineering environments to fit a particular leader's orientation, Tannenbaum and Schmidt emphasize the notion of leadership flexibility in adapting to different circumstances.

In a recent research study, Hill[6] investigated subordinate's perceptions of the flexibility of the leadership styles of their superiors. Hill found that a good deal of flexibility of leadership style was perceived by these subordinates, and that most leaders were seen to be capable of be-

---

[4] For later reviews of research on Fiedler's contingency theory of leadership effectiveness, see F. E. Fiedler, *A Theory of Leadership Effectiveness* (New York: McGraw-Hill Book Co., 1967); idem, "Validation and Extension of the Contingency Model of Leadership: A Review of Empirical Findings," *Psychological Bulletin* 76 (1971): 128–48. For a critical review of Fiedler's contingency model, see G. Graen, K. Alvares, J. B. Orris, and J. Martella, "Contingency Model of Leadership Effectiveness: Antecedent and Evidential Results," *Psychological Bulletin* 74 (1970): 285–96; G. Graen, J. B. Orris, and K. Alvares, "Contingency Model of Leadership Effectiveness: Some Experimental Results," *Journal of Applied Psychology* 55 (1971): 196–201. Also see replies by Fiedler, "Validation and Extension of the Contingency Model of Leadership," and idem, "Note on the Methodology of the Graen, Orris, and Alvares Studies Testing the Contingency Model," *Journal of Applied Psychology* 55 (1971): 202–04.

[5] R. Tannenbaum and W. H. Schmidt, "How to Choose a Leadership Pattern," *Harvard Business Review* 36 (1958): 95–101.

[6] W. A. Hill, "Leadership Style: Rigid or Flexible?" *Organizational Behavior and Human Performance* 9 (1973): 35–47.

having flexibly enough to cope with different kinds of leadership situations. Thus, it would appear that an organization has a number of options which might be considered for achieving effective supervision, including leadership training, job engineering, and identification of leaders who are able to adapt to environmental demands.

SUGGESTED ADDITIONAL READINGS

Gibb, C. A. "Leadership." In *The Handbook of Social Psychology*, 2d ed., vol. 4, edited by G. Lindzey and E. Aronson. Reading, Mass.: Addison-Wesley, 1969.

Hollander, E. P., and Julian, J. W. "Contemporary Trends in the Analysis of Leadership Processes." *Psychological Bulletin* 71 (1969): 387–97.

House, R. "Path-Goal Theory of Leadership Effectiveness." *Administrative Science Quarterly* 16 (1971): 321–38.

Yukl, G. "Toward a Behavioral Theory of Leadership." *Organizational Behavior and Human Performance* 6 (1971): 414–40.

27. LEADERSHIP BEHAVIOR RELATED TO EMPLOYEE GRIEVANCES AND TURNOVER *

Edwin A. Fleishman and Edwin F. Harris

THIS STUDY INVESTIGATES SOME RELATIONSHIPS between the leader behavior of industrial supervisors and the behavior of their group members. It represents an extension of earlier studies carried out at the International Harvester Company, while the authors were with the Ohio State University Leadership Studies.

Briefly, these previous studies involved three primary phases which have been described elsewhere.[1] In the initial phase, independent leader-

---

* From "Patterns of Leadership Behavior Related to Employee Grievances and Turnover," *Personnel Psychology* 15 (Spring 1962): 43–56.

[1] E. A. Fleishman, *"Leadership Climate" and Supervisory Behavior* (Columbus, Ohio: Personnel Research Board, Ohio State University, 1951); idem, "Leadership Climate, Human Relations Training, and Supervisory Behavior," *Personnel Psychology* 6 (1953): 205–22; idem, "The Description of Supervisory Behavior," *Journal of Applied Psychology* 37 (1953): 1–6; "The Measurement of Leadership Attitudes in Industry," *Journal of Applied Psychology* 37 (1953): 153–58; E. A. Fleishman, E. F. Harris, and H. E. Burtt, *Leadership and Supervision in Industry* (Columbus, Ohio: Bureau of Educational Research, Ohio State University, 1955); Harris and Fleischman, "Human Relations Training and the Stability of Leadership Patterns," *Journal of Applied Psychology* 39 (1955): 20–25.

ship patterns were defined and a variety of behavioral and attitude instruments were developed to measure them. This phase confirmed the usefulness of the constructs "Consideration" and "Structure" for describing leader behavior in industry.

Since the present study, as well as the previous work, focused on these two leadership patterns, it may be well to redefine them here·

Consideration includes behavior indicating mutual trust, respect, and a certain warmth and rapport between the supervisor and his group. This does not mean that this dimension reflects a superficial "pat-on-the-back, first name calling" kind of human relations behavior. This dimension appears to emphasize a deeper concern for group members' needs and includes such behavior as allowing subordinates more participation in decision-making and encouraging more two-way communication.

Structure includes behavior in which the supervisor organizes and defines group activities and his relation to the group. Thus, he defines the role he expects each member to assume, assigns tasks, plans ahead, establishes ways of getting things done, and pushes for production. This dimension seems to emphasize overt attempts to achieve organizational goals.

Since the dimensions are independent, a supervisor may score high on both dimensions, low on both, or high on one and low on the other.

The second phase of the original Harvester research utilized measures of these patterns to evaluate changes in foreman leadership attitudes and behavior resulting from a management training program. The amount of change was evaluated at three different times—once while the foremen were still in the training setting, again after they had returned to the plant environment, and still later in a "refresher" training course. The results showed that while still in the training situation there was a distinct increase in Consideration and an unexpected decrease in Structure attitudes. It was also found that leadership attitudes became more *dissimilar* rather than similar, despite the fact that all foremen had received the same training. Furthermore, when behavior and attitudes were evaluated back in the plant, the effects of the training largely disappeared. This pointed to the main finding, that is, the overriding importance of the interaction of the training effects with certain aspects of the social setting in which the foremen had to operate in the plant. Most critical was the "leadership climate" supplied by the behavior and attitudes of the foreman's own boss. This was more related to the foreman's own Consideration and Structure behavior than was the fact that he had or had not received the leadership training.

The third phase may be termed the "criterion phase," in which the relationships between Consideration and Structure and indices of foreman proficiency were examined. One finding was that production supervisors rated high in "proficiency" by plant management turned out to have leadership patterns high in Structure and low in Consideration. (This relationship was accentuated in departments scoring high on a third variable, "perceived pressure of deadlines.") On the other hand, this same pattern of high Structure and low Consideration was found to be related to high labor turnover, union grievances, worker absences and accidents, and low worker satisfaction. There was some indication that these relationships might differ in "nonproduction" departments. An interesting sidelight was that foremen with low Consideration and low Structure were more often bypassed by subordinates in the informal organizational structure. In any case, it was evident that "what is an effective supervisor" is a complex question, depending on the proficiency criterion emphasized, management values, type of work, and other situational variables.

The present study examines some of the questions left unanswered by this previous work.

PURPOSE

The present study focused on two main questions. First, what is the *form* of the relationship between leader behavior and indices of group behavior? Is it linear or curvilinear? As far as we know, no one has really examined this question. Rephrased, this question asks if there are critical levels of Consideration and/or Structure beyond which it does or does not make a difference in group behavior? Is an "average" amount of Structure better than a great deal or no Structure at all? Similarly, is there an optimum level of Consideration above and below which worker grievances and/or turnover rise sharply?

The second question concerns the interaction effects of different combinations of Consideration and Structure. Significant correlations have been found between each of these patterns and such indices as rated proficiency, grievances, turnover, departmental reputation, subordinate satisfactions, and so forth.[2] These studies present some evidence that scoring low on both dimensions is not desirable. They also indicate that some balance of Consideration and Structure may be optimal for satisfying both proficiency and morale criteria. The present study is a more intensive examination of possible optimum combinations of Consideration and Structure.

The present study investigates the relationships between foreman behavior and two primary indices of group behavior: labor grievances and employee turnover. Both of these may be considered as partial criteria of group effectiveness.

---

[2] Fleishman, Harris, and Burtt, *Leadership and Supervision;* A. W. Halpin, "The Leadership Behavior and Combat Performance of Airplane Commanders," *Journal of Abnormal and Social Psychology* 49 (1954): 19–22; J. K. Hemphill, "Leadership Behavior Associated with the Administrative Reputation of College Departments," *Journal of Educational Psychology* 46 (1955): 385–401; R. M. Stogdill and A. E. Coons, eds., *Leader Behavior: Its Description and Measurement* (Columbus, Ohio: Bureau of Business Research, Ohio State University, 1957).

PROCEDURE

Leader Behavior Measures

The study was conducted in a motor-truck manufacturing plant. Fifty-seven production foremen and their work groups took part in the study. They represented such work operations as stamping, assembly, body assembly, body paint, machinery, and export. At least three workers, drawn randomly from each foreman's department, described the leader behavior of their foreman by means of the *Supervisory Behavior Description Questionnaire*.[3] Each questionnaire was scored on Consideration and Structure, and a mean Consideration score and a mean Structure score was computed for each foreman. The correlation between Consideration and Structure among foremen in this plant was found to be $-.33$. The correlation between these scales is usually around zero,[4] but in this plant foremen who are high in Structure are somewhat more likely to be seen as lower in Consideration and vice versa. However, the relationship is not high.

Grievance Measures

Grievances were defined in terms of the number presented in writing and placed in company files. No data on grievances which were settled at lower levels (hence, without their becoming matters of company record) were considered. The frequency of grievances was equated for each foreman's work group by dividing the record for that group by the number of workers in that group. The reliability of these records, computed by correlating the records for odd and even weeks over an 11-month period and correcting by the Spearman-Brown formula, was .73. The entire 11-month record (for each foreman's work group) was used in the present analysis.

Turnover Measures

Turnover was figured as the number of workers who voluntarily left the employ of the company within the 11-month period. Again, the records for each foreman's group were equated by dividing the number who resigned by the number of workers in his work group. The nature of the records did not permit an analysis of the reasons which each worker

---

[3] Fleishman, "A Leader Behavior Description for Industry," in *Leader Behavior: Its Description and Measurement*, ed. Stogdill and Coons.
[4] Ibid.

FIGURE 27–1

Relation between Consideration and Grievance Rates

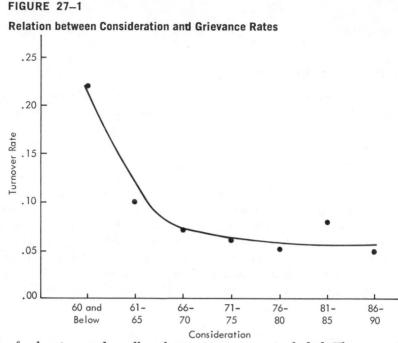

Consideration

gave for leaving, and so all such terminations are included. The corrected odd-even weeks reliability for this period was .59.

The reliabilities for the grievance and turnover measures are for the foremen's work groups and not for the individual worker. In the case of turnover, this reliability is quite high when one considers that different workers are involved in each time period. (Once a worker leaves, of course, he cannot contribute to turnover again.) The findings of stable grievance and turnover rates among groups under the same foremen is an important finding in its own right. The correlation between grievances and turnover is .37. This indicates that, while high grievance work groups tend to have higher turnover, the relationship is not very high. Each index is worth considering as an independent aspect of group behavior.

RESULTS

Leader Behavior and Grievances

Figure 27–1 plots the average employee-grievance rates for departments under foremen scoring at different levels of Consideration. From the curve fitted to these points it can be seen clearly that the relationship between the foremen's behavior and grievances from their work groups is negative and curvilinear. For most of the range increased Consideration goes with reduced grievance rates. However, increased Consideration

FIGURE 27–2

Relation between Structure and Grievance Rates

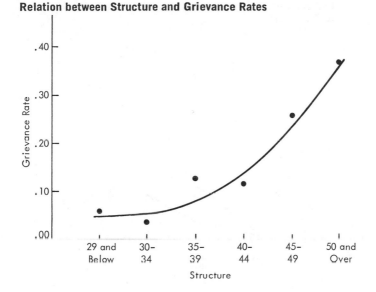

above a certain critical level (approximately 76 out of a possible 112) is not related to further decreases in grievances. Furthermore, the curve appears to be negatively accelerated. A given decrease in Consideration just below the critical point (76) is related to a small increase in grievances, but, as Consideration continues to drop, grievance rates rise sharply. Thus, a 5-point drop on the Consideration scale, just below a score of 76, is related to a small grievance increase, but a 5-point drop below 61 is related to a large rise in grievances. The correlation ratio (eta) represented by this curve is −.51.

Figure 27–2 plots grievances against the foremen's Structure scores. Here a similar curvilinear relationship is observed. In this case the correlation is positive (eta = .71). Below a certain level (approximately 36 out of a possible 80 on our scale) Structure is unrelated to grievances, but above this point increased Structure goes with increased grievances. Again we see that a given increase in Structure just above this critical level is accompanied by a small increase in grievances, but continued increases in Structure are associated with increasingly disproportionately large increases in grievance rates.

Both curves are hyperbolic rather than parabolic in form. Thus, it appears that for neither Consideration nor Structure is there an "optimum" point in the middle of the range below and above which grievances rise. Rather there seems to be a range within which increased Consideration or decreased Structure makes no difference. Of course, when one reaches these levels, grievances are already at a very low level and not

FIGURE 27–3

Combinations of Consideration and Structure Related to Grievances

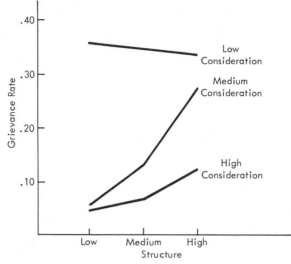

much improvement can be expected. However, the important point is that this low grievance level is reached before one gets to the extremely high end of the Consideration scale or to the extremely low end of the Structure scale. It is also clear that extremely high Structure and extremely low Consideration are most related to high grievances.

Different Combinations of Consideration and Structure Related to Grievances

The curves described establish that a general relationship exists between each of these leadership patterns and the frequency of employee grievances. But how do *different combinations* of Consideration and Structure relate to grievances? Some foremen score high on both dimensions, some score low on both, and so forth.

Figure 27–3 plots the relation between Structure (low, medium, and high) and grievances for groups of foremen who were either low, medium, or high Consideration. The curves show that grievances occur most frequently among groups whose foremen are low in Consideration, regardless of the amount of emphasis on Structure. The most interesting finding relates to the curve for the high Consideration foremen. This curve suggests that, for the high Consideration foremen, Structure could be increased without any appreciable increase in grievances. However, the reverse is not true; that is, foremen who were low in Consideration could not reduce grievances by easing up on Structure. For foremen average on Consideration, grievances were lowest where Structure was lowest and increased in an almost linear fashion as Structure increased. These data show a definite interaction between Consideration and Structure. Apparently, high Consideration can compensate for high Structure. But low Structure will not offset low Consideration.

Before we speculate further about these relationships, let us examine the results with employee turnover.

Leader Behavior and Turnover

Figures 27–4 and 27–5 plot the curves for the *Supervisory Behavior Description* scores of these foremen against the turnover criteria. Again, we see the curvilinear relationships. The correlation (eta) of Consideration and turnover is −.69; Structure and turnover correlate .63. As in the case with grievances, below a certain critical level of Consideration and above a certain level of Structure, turnover goes up. There is, however, an interesting difference in that the critical levels differ from those related to grievances. The flat portions of each of these curves are more extended and the rise in turnover beyond the point of inflection is steeper. The implication of this is quite sensible and indicates that "they gripe before they leave." In other words, a given increase in Structure (to approximately 39) or decrease in Consideration (to 66) may result in increased grievances, but not turnover. It takes higher Structure and lower Consideration before turnover occurs.

Different Combinations of Consideration and Structure Related to Turnover

Figure 27–6 plots the relation between Structure (low, medium, and high) and turnover for groups of foremen who were also either low, medium, or high on Consideration. As with grievances, the curves show that turnover is highest for the work groups whose foremen combine low Consideration with high Structure; however, the amount of Consideration is the dominant factor. The curves show that turnover is highest among those work groups whose foremen are low in Consideration, regardless of the amount of emphasis these same foremen show on Structure. There is little distinction between the work groups of foremen who show medium and high Consideration since both of these groups have low turnover among their workers. Furthermore, increased Structure does not seem related to increased turnover in these two groups.[5]

---

[5] This, of course, is consistent with our earlier finding that for increased turnover it takes a bigger drop in Consideration and a bigger increase in Structure to make a difference. Thus, our high and medium Consideration groups separate for grievances, but overlap for turnover.

FIGURE 27–4

Relation between Consideration and Turnover Rates

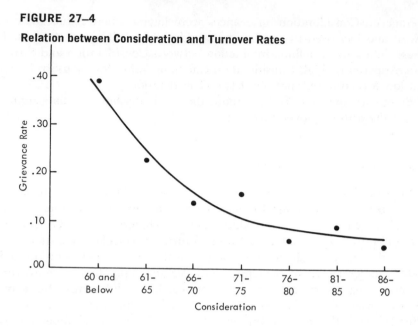

FIGURE 27–5

Relation between Structure and Turnover Rates

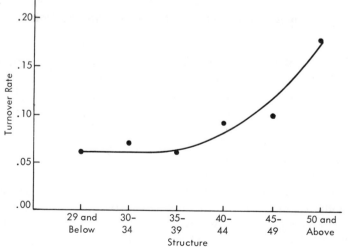

FIGURE 27–6

Combination of Consideration and Structure Related to Turnover

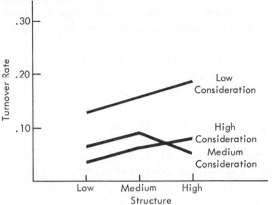

CONCLUSIONS

1. This study indicates that there are significant relationships between the leader behavior of foremen and the labor grievances and employee turnover in their work groups. In general, low Consideration and high Structure go with high grievances and turnover.

2. There appear to be certain critical levels beyond which increased Consideration or decreased Structure have no effect on grievance or turnover rates. Similarly grievances and turnover are shown to increase most markedly at the extreme ends of the Consideration (low end) and Structure (high end) scales. Thus, the relationship is curvilinear, not linear, and hyperbolic, not parabolic.

3. The critical points at which increased Structure and decreased Consideration begin to relate to group behavior is not the same for grievances and turnover. Increases in turnover do not occur until lower on the Consideration scale and higher on the Structure scale, as compared with increases in grievances. For example, if Consideration is steadily reduced, higher grievances appear before increased turnover occurs. It appears that there may be different "threshold levels" of Consideration and Structure related to grievances and turnover.

4. Other principal findings concern the interaction effects found between different combinations of Consideration and Structure. Taken in combination, Consideration is the dominant factor. For example, both grievances and turnover were highest in groups having low Consideration foremen, regardless of the degree of Structuring behavior shown by these same foremen.

5. Grievances and turnover were lowest for groups with foremen show-

ing medium to high Consideration together with low Structure. However, one of the most important results is the finding that high Consideration foremen could increase Structure with very little increase in grievances and no increase in turnover. High Consideration foremen had relatively low grievances and turnover, regardless of the amount of Structuring engaged in.

Thus, with regard to grievances and turnover, leader behavior characterized by low Consideration is more critical than behavior characterized by high Structure. Apparently, foremen can compensate for high Structure by increased Consideration, but low consideration foremen cannot compensate by decreasing their Structuring behavior.

One interpretation is that workers under foremen who establish a climate of mutual trust, rapport, and tolerance for two-way communication with their work groups are more likely to accept higher levels of Structure. This might be because they perceive this Structure differently from employees in "low Consideration" climates. Thus, under "low Consideration" climates, high Structure is seen as threatening and restrictive, but under "high Consideration" climates this same Structure is seen as supportive and helpful. A related interpretation is that foremen who establish such an atmosphere can more easily solve the problems resulting from high Structure. Thus, *grievances* may be solved at this level before they get into the official records. Similarly, *turnover* may reflect escape from a problem situation which cannot be resolved in the absence of mutual trust and two-way communication. In support of this interpretation, we do have evidence that leaders high in Consideration are also better at predicting subordinates' responses to problems.[6]

One has to be careful in making cause and effect inferences here. A possible limitation is that our descriptions of foreman behavior came from the workers themselves. Those workers with many grievances may view their foremen as low in Consideration simply because they have a lot of grievances. However, the descriptions of foreman behavior were obtained from workers drawn randomly from each foreman's group; the odds are against our receiving descriptions from very many workers contributing a disproportionate share of grievances. In the case of turnover, of course, our descriptions could not have been obtained from people who had left during the previous 11 months. Yet substantial correlations were obtained between foreman descriptions, supplied by currently employed workers, with the turnover rates of their work groups. Furthermore, we do have evidence that leader behavior over a year period tends to be quite stable. Test-retest correlations for Consideration, as well as for Structure, tend to be high even when different workers do the describ-

---

[6] E. A. Fleishman and J. A. Salter, "The Relation between the Leader's Behavior and His Empathy toward Subordinates," *Advanced Management,* March 1961, pp. 18–20.

ing on the retest.[7] Our present preference is to favor the interpretation that high turnover and grievances result, at least in part, from the leader behavior patterns described.

The nonlinear relations between leader behavior and our criteria of effectiveness have more general implications for leadership research. For one thing, it points up the need for a more careful examination of the *form* of such relationships before computing correlation coefficients. Some previously obtained correlations with leadership variables may be underestimates because of linearity assumptions. Similarly, some previous negative or contradictory results may be "explained" by the fact that *(a)* inappropriate coefficients were used, or *(b)* these studies were dealing with only the flat portions of these curves. If, for example, all the foremen in our study had scored over 76 on Consideration and under 36 on Structure, we would have concluded that there was no relation between these leadership patterns and grievances and turnover. Perhaps in comparing one study with another, we need to specify the range of leader behavior involved in each study.

There is, of course, a need to explore similar relationships with other criteria. There is no assurance that similar curvilinear patterns and interaction effects will hold for other indices (for example, group productivity). Even the direction of these relationships may vary with the criterion used. We have evidence,[8] for example, that Consideration and Structure may relate quite differently to another effectiveness criterion: management's perceptions of foreman proficiency. However, research along these lines may make it possible to specify the particular leadership patterns which most nearly "optimize" these various effectiveness criteria in industrial organizations.

28. PATTERNS IN MANAGEMENT [*]

Rensis Likert

Since 1947, the Institute for Social Research has been conducting a series of related studies [1] seeking to find what kinds of organizational structure and what principles and methods of leadership and management result in the highest productivity, least absence, lowest turnover, and the greatest

---

[7] Harris and Fleishman, "Human Relations Training."

[8] Fleishman, Harris, and Burtt, *Leadership and Supervision.*

[*] Condensed from *Developing Patterns in Management*, General Management Series no. 178 (American Management Association, 1955).

[1] Generous support from the Office of Naval Research, the Rockefeller Foundation, and the companies and agencies involved have made this research possible.

job satisfaction.[2] Studies have been conducted or are under way in a wide variety of organizations. These include one or more companies in such industries as the following: public utilities, insurance, automotive, railroad, electric appliances, heavy machinery, textiles, and petroleum.[3] Studies also have been made in government agencies.[4]

In general, the design of the studies has been to measure and examine the kinds of leadership and related variables being used by the best units in the organization in contrast to those being used by the poorest. In essence, these studies are providing management with a mirror by measuring and reporting what is working best in industry today.

Briefly stated, some of the findings which are relevant for this discussion follow.

Orientation of Supervision. When foremen are asked what they have found to be the best pattern of supervision to get results, a substantial proportion, usually a majority, will place primary emphasis on getting out production. By this they mean placing primary emphasis on seeing that workers are using the proper methods, are sticking to their work, and are getting a satisfactory volume of work done. Other supervisors, whom we have called employee-centered, report that they get the best results when they place primary emphasis on the human problems of their workers. The employee-centered supervisor endeavors to build a team of people who cooperate and work well together. He tries to place people together who are congenial. He not only trains people to do their present job well but tends to train them for the next higher job. He is interested in helping them with their problems on the job and off the job. He is friendly and supportive, rather than punitive and threatening.

---

[2] *A Program of Research on the Fundamental Problems of Organizing Human Behavior* (Ann Arbor: Institute for Social Research, University of Michigan, 1946).

[3] L. Coch and J. French, "Overcoming Resistance to Change," *Human Relations* 1 (1948): 512–32; R. Kahn and D. Katz, "Leadership Practices in Relation to Productivity and Morale," in *Group Dynamics Research and Theory*, ed. D. Cartwright and A. Zander (Evanston: Row, Peterson & Co., 1953); idem, "Human Organization and Worker Motivation," in *Industrial Productivity* (Industrial Relations Research Association, 1952); idem, "Some Recent Findings in Human Relations Research," in *Readings in Social Psychology*, ed. E. Swanson, T. Newcomb, and E. Hartley (New York: Henry Holt & Co., 1952); D. Katz et al., *Productivity, Supervision and Morale among Railroad Workers* (Ann Arbor: University of Michigan Press, 1951); D. Katz, N. Maccoby, and N. Morse, *Productivity, Supervision and Morale in an Office Situation, Part 1* (Ann Arbor: University of Michigan Press, 1950); F. Mann and H. Baumgartel, *Absences and Employee Attitudes in an Electric Power Company* (Institute for Social Research, 1953); idem, *The Supervisor's Concern with Costs in an Electric Power Company*, ibid.; F. Mann and J. Dent, *Appraisals of Supervisors and Attitudes of Their Employees in an Electric Power Company* (Institute for Social Research, 1954); N. Morse, *Satisfactions in the White-Collar Job* (Ann Arbor: University of Michigan Press, 1953); S. Seashore, *Group Cohesiveness in the Industrial Work Group* (Ann Arbor: University of Michigan Press, 1955).

[4] E. Jacobson and S. E. Seashore, "Communication Practices in Complex Organizations," *The Journal of Social Issues* 7, no. 3 (1951); D. Marvick, *Career Perspectives in a Bureaucratic Setting* (Ann Arbor: Institute of Public Administration, University of Michigan Press, 1954).

Higher levels of management, in discussing how they want their foremen to supervise, tend to place more emphasis on the production-centered approach as the best way to get results than do foremen.[5] Workers, on the other hand, tend to place less.

But which orientation yields the best results? A variety of studies in widely different industries show that supervisors who are getting the best production, the best motivation, and the highest levels of worker satisfaction are employee-centered appreciably more often than production-centered.[6] This is shown in Exhibit 28–1.

There is an important point to be added to this finding: Those employee-centered supervisors who get the best results tend to recognize that getting production is also one of their major responsibilities.

Closeness of Supervision. Related to orientation of supervision is closeness of supervision. Close supervision tends to be associated with lower productivity and more general supervision with higher productivity. This relationship, shown in Exhibit 28–2, holds for workers and supervisors.[7]

Low productivity, no doubt, at times leads to closer supervision, but it is clear also that it causes low productivity. In one of the companies involved in this research program it has been found that switching managers of high- and low-production divisions results in the high-production managers' raising the productivity of the low-production divisions faster than the former high-production divisions slip under the low-production managers. Supervisors, as they are shifted from job to job, tend to carry with them and to maintain their habitual attitudes toward the supervisory process and toward their subordinates.

Closeness of supervision is also related to the attitudes of workers toward their supervisors. Workers under foremen who supervise closely have a less favorable attitude toward their boss than do workers who are under foremen who supervise more generally.

Experiment Described

These results which have just been presented on closeness of supervision and on employee-centered supervision were among those found early in the series of studies conducted by the Institute. They led to an experiment which I should like to describe briefly.

As we have seen, the research findings indicate that close supervision results in lower productivity, less favorable attitudes, and less satisfaction on the part of the workers; while more general supervision achieves higher productivity, more favorable attitudes, and greater employee sat-

---

[5] E. A. Fleishman, "Leadership Climate, Human Relations Training, and Supervisory Behavior," *Personnel Psychology* 6, no. 3 (1953).

[6] D. Katz, N. Maccoby, and N. Morse, *Productivity, Supervision and Morale.*

[7] Ibid.

EXHIBIT 28–1

"Employee-Centered" Supervisors Are Higher Producers than "Production-Centered" Supervisors

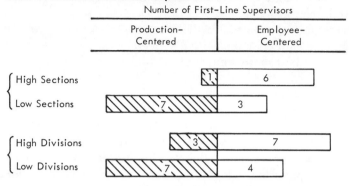

Number of First-Line Supervisors

	Production-Centered	Employee-Centered
High Sections	1	6
Low Sections	7	3
High Divisions	3	7
Low Divisions	7	4

EXHIBIT 28–2

Low-Production Section Heads Are More Closely Supervised than Are High-Production Heads

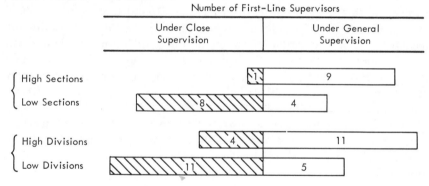

Number of First-Line Supervisors

	Under Close Supervision	Under General Supervision
High Sections	1	9
Low Sections	8	4
High Divisions	4	11
Low Divisions	11	5

isfaction. These results suggest that it should be possible to increase productivity in a particular situation by shifting the pattern of the supervision so as to make it more general. To test this we conducted an experiment involving 500 clerical employees.[8]

Very briefly, the experiment was as follows: Four parallel divisions were used, each organized the same as the others, each using the same technology and doing exactly the same kind of work with employees of comparable aptitude. In two divisions, the decision levels were pushed down, and more general supervision of the clerks and their supervisors was introduced. In addition, the managers, assistant managers, supervisors, and assistant supervisors of these two divisions were trained in group

[8] N. Morse, E. Reimer, and A. Tannenbaum, "Regulation and Control in Hierarchical Organizations," *The Journal of Social Issues* 7, no. 3 (1951).

methods of leadership.[9] The experimental changes in these two divisions will be called Program I.

In order to provide an effective experimental control on the changes in supervision which were introduced in Program I, the supervision in the other two divisions was modified so as to increase the closeness of supervision and move the decision levels upward. This will be called Program II. These changes were accomplished by a further extension of the scientific management approach. One of the major changes made was to have the jobs timed by the methods department and standard times computed. This showed that these divisions were overstaffed by about 30 percent. The general manager then ordered the managers of these two divisions to cut staff by 25 percent. This was to be done by transfers and by not replacing persons who left; no one, however, was to be dismissed.

Productivity in all four of the divisions depended upon the number of clerks involved. The work was something like a billing operation; there was just so much of it, but it had to be processed as it came along. Consequently, the only way in which productivity could be increased was to change the size of the work group. The four divisions were assigned to the experimental programs on a random basis, but in such a manner that a high- and low-productivity division was assigned to each program.

The experiment at the clerical level lasted for one year. Several months were devoted to planning prior to the experimental year, and there was a training period of approximately six months just prior to the experimental year. Productivity was measured continuously and computed weekly throughout the period. Employee and supervisory attitudes and related variables were measured just before and after the experimental year.

Productivity Reflected in Salary Costs. Exhibit 28–3 shows the changes in salary costs which reflect the changes in productivity that occurred. As will be observed, Program II, where there was an increase in the closeness of supervision, increased productivity by about 25 percent. This, it will be recalled, was a result of direct orders from the general manager to reduce staff by that amount.

Exhibit 28–3 shows, furthermore, that a significant increase in productivity was achieved in Program I, where supervision was modified so as to be less close. The increase in productivity in Program I was not so great as in Program II but, nevertheless, was a little more than 20 percent. One division in Program I increased its productivity by about the same amount as each of the two divisions in Program II. The other division in Program I, which historically had been the poorest of all of the divisions, did not do so well.

Productivity and Workers' Responsibility. Although both programs were alike in increasing productivity, they were significantly different in the other changes which occurred. The productivity increases in Program

---

[9] Methods developed by the National Training Laboratory in Group Development were drawn upon heavily in this training.

EXHIBIT 28–3

Change in Productivity

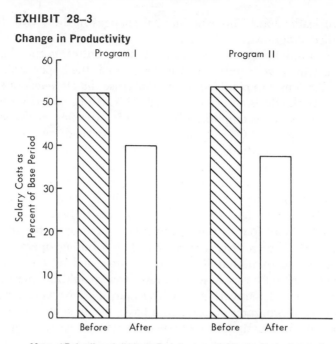

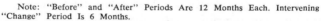

Note: "Before" and "After" Periods Are 12 Months Each. Intervening "Change" Period Is 6 Months.

II, where decision levels were moved up, were accompanied by shifts in an adverse direction in attitudes, interest, and involvement in the work and related matters. The opposite was true in Program I. Exhibit 28–4, for example, shows that when more general supervision is provided, as in Program I, the employees' feeling of responsibility to see that the work gets done is increased. In Program II, however, this responsibility decreased. In Program I, when the supervisor was away, the employees kept on working. When the supervisor was absent in Program II, the work tended to stop.

Effect of Employee Attitudes.   Exhibit 28–5 shows how the programs changed in regard to the workers' attitudes toward their superiors. In Program I all the shifts were favorable; in Program II all the shifts were unfavorable. One significant aspect of these changes in Program II was that the girls felt that their superiors were relying more on rank and authority to get the work done. In general, the shifts were greatest, both favorable in Program I and unfavorable in Program II, for those relationships which other studies have shown to be the most important in influencing behavior in the working situation. A number of other measures of attitudes toward superiors all showed similar shifts: favorable in Program I and unfavorable in Program II.

EXHIBIT 28–4

Employees' Feeling of Responsibility to See That Work Gets Done

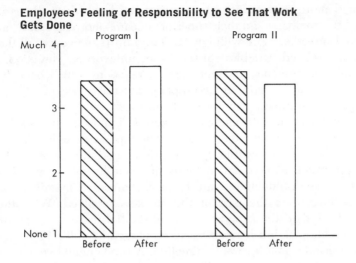

EXHIBIT 28–5

Satisfaction with Superiors as Representatives

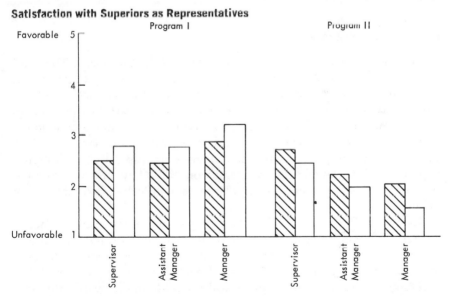

Fundamental Conclusion

This very brief description of this experiment, I hope, has made clear the pattern of results. Both experimental changes increased productivity substantially. In Program I this increase in productivity was accompanied by shifts in a favorable direction in attitudes, interests, and perceptions. The girls became more interested and involved in their work, they accepted more responsibility for getting the work done, their attitudes toward the company and their superiors became more favorable, and they accepted direction more willingly. In Program II, however, all these attitudes and related variables shifted in an unfavorable direction. All the hostilities, resentments, and unfavorable reactions which have been observed again and again to accompany extensive use of the scientific management approach manifested themselves.

This experiment with clerical workers is important because it shows that increases in productivity can be obtained with either favorable or unfavorable shifts in attitudes, perceptions, and similar variables. Further application of classical methods of scientific management substantially increased productivity, but it was accompanied by adverse attitudinal reactions upon the part of the workers involved. With the other approach used in the experiment, a substantial increase in productivity was also obtained. but here it was accompanied by shifts in attitudes and similar variables in a favorable direction. A fundamental conclusion from this experiment and other similar research is that direct pressure from one's superior for production tends to be resented, while group pressure from one's colleagues is not.[10]

Pressure for Production

Keeping in mind these results, let us look at another chart. The solid line in Exhibit 28–6 shows the relation between the amount of pressure a worker feels from his foreman for production and the productivity of the worker. Productivity is measured, and shown in the chart, as a percentage of standard; that is, jobs are timed, standards are set, and production is then expressed as a percentage of standard. As will be observed, the chart shows that greater pressure from the supervisor is associated with higher production. The differences in production from low pressure to high pressure are not great, but they are large enough to be important in any highly competitive industry.

The broken line in Exhibit 28–6 shows the relationship between amount of pressure the worker feels from his supervisor and his attitude toward his supervisor. In interpreting this curve, it is important to keep in mind that a worker's attitude toward his supervisor has a major influence upon all his other attitudes toward his work and his work situation, as well as his motivations toward his work. Little interest in production on the part of the supervisor, a laissez-faire point of view, is associated both with low production and with a less favorable attitude toward the supervisor. Workers who experience an average amount of pressure from their supervisors express the most favorable attitude toward them, while

---

[10] L. Coch and J. French, "Overcoming Resistance to Change."

EXHIBIT 28–6

The Relation of Productivity and Morale to Supervisor's Pressure for Production

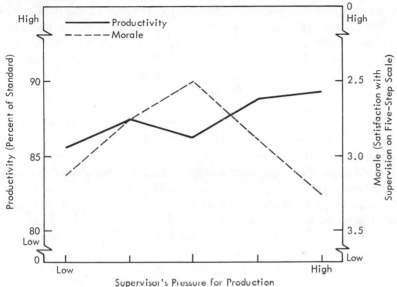

Supervisor's Pressure for Production

those workers who report feeling the greatest pressure from their supervisors have the least favorable attitude of all workers toward their supervisors. Direct pressure for production. here as in the clerical experiment, is associated with hostility, resentment, and unfavorable attitudes on the part of workers.

Exhibit 28–6 is based on several thousand workers and shows relationships which we have found also in other studies. In some situations the production curve drops slightly with high levels of pressure from the supervisor for production. But the general picture seems to be that relatively high pressure for production is associated with fairly good production but with relatively unfavorable attitudes.

High Cost

Available evidence indicates that a substantial proportion of workers generally are working under conditions like those shown in Exhibit 28–6. Only a fraction of all workers, of course, are working at present under high levels of pressure from their supervisors. But the probabilities are that when competition gets tough for a company, and costs must be cut, an attempt will be made to cut them by increasing the pressure for production. The accompanying consequences of this increased pressure are clear, as shown by Exhibit 28–6 and by the clerical experiment.

A similar situation exists with regard to decentralization. Decentralization is generally viewed as one way of pushing decisions down and providing more general supervision. But, when the decentralization involves basing the compensation of the man in charge of the decentralized unit largely on the earnings shown by this unit, increased pressure on subordinates often occurs. Substantial earnings over the short run can occur from supervising subordinates more closely and putting more pressure on them to increase production and earnings. But the adverse effects both on subordinates and on workers can be predicted. If current reports are correct, the staffs of some decentralized units are genuinely unhappy over the pressure which they are experiencing. Trained engineers as well as nonsupervisory employees are leaving, even for jobs that pay less.

Thus, though the scientific management approach has clearly demonstrated its capacity to get high production, this productivity is obtained at a serious cost. People will produce at relatively high levels when the techniques of production are efficient, the pressures for production are great, the controls and inspections are relatively tight, and the economic rewards and penalties are sufficiently large. But such production is accompanied by attitudes which tend to result in high scrap loss, lowered safety, higher absence and turnover, increased grievances and work stoppages, and the like. It also is accompanied by communication blocks and restrictions. All these developments tend to affect adversely the operation of any organization. Restricted communications, for example, tend to result in decisions based on misinformation or a lack of information.

Possible Advantages

There are important advantages to be gained if the resources of the scientific management approach and the human relations approach can be combined. These are illustrated schematically in Exhibit 28–7, which shows the relation between morale and production.

On the basis of a study I did in 1937.[11] I believed that morale and productivity were positively related; that the higher the morale, the higher the production. Substantial research findings since then have shown that this relationship is much too simple. In our different studies we have found a wide variety of relationships. Some units have low morale and low production; they would fall in Area A on the chart. Other units have fairly good morale and low production; these fall in Area B. Still others have fairly good production but low morale; these fall in Area C. Finally, other units have high morale and high production and fall in Area D on the chart.

Units with low morale and low production (Area A) tend to have super-

---

[11] R. Likert and J. Willits, *Morale and Agency Management* (Hartford: Life Insurance Agency Management Association, 1940).

EXHIBIT 28-7

Schematic Relationship between Morale and Productivity

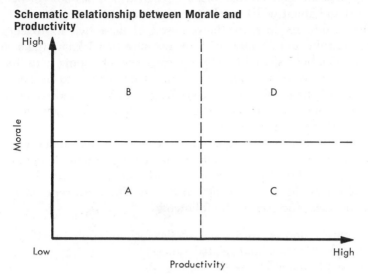

vision which is laissez-faire in character and in which the leadership function has been abandoned to all intents and purposes. Units which fall in Area B and have fairly good morale but poor production tend to have supervisors who try to keep people "happy." These supervisors are often found in companies in which human relations training programs have been introduced and emphasized.

Some supervisors in these companies interpret the training to mean that the company management wants them to keep employees happy; therefore, they work hard to do so. The morale of these workers is essentially complacent in character. The result is a nice "country club" atmosphere. Employees like it, and absence and turnover are low; but, since little production is felt to be expected, the workers produce relatively little.

Into Area C, of course. fall those units which have technically competent supervision that is pressing for production. Area D includes those units which have a kind of supervision which results in high production with high morale, high satisfactions, and high motivation. Here the nature of the morale can be characterized as "the will to achieve."

Integrated Approach

Most of us would agree, I believe, that the kind of supervision which we desire is that which is represented by Area D. It is my further belief that this kind of supervision represents an integration of the scientific management and human relations approach which has not yet been fully achieved and about which we know relatively little.

What will be required for the resources of these two approaches to be integrated fully and effectively? I am not sure that I know the answer to this question, but I should like to suggest a way of coping with it which I believe has real promise. Fundamentally, what I wish to propose is that the major resources of human relations research be focused upon what experience and research have shown to be the major weakness in the scientific management approach.

The tremendous contribution which scientific management and related management theories have made to increasing production and to improved organizational performance provides adequate evidence as to the great power of the basic concepts involved. These concepts include emphasis on such processes as the following:

1. The elimination of waste and inefficiency through functionalization, work simplification, and related processes
2. The establishment of specific work goals
3. The measurement of work accomplished and the continual examination of the extent to which the specified goals are being achieved
4. Coordinated and clear-cut channels of control, communication, and decision-making

Importance of Motivation

The critical weaknesses in the scientific management approach, of course, are the resentments, hostilities, and adverse motivational and attitudinal reactions which it tends to evoke. In my judgment, these hostilities and unfavorable attitudes stem from powerful motives which the scientific management approach has ignored in its overall conceptualization and in the day-to-day operating procedures which it has developed. Although the scientific management approach has ignored these powerful motives, it has not been able to avoid the substantial impact of their influence in daily operations.

The fundamental cause, therefore, of the adverse motivational reactions produced by the scientific management approach is the inadequate motivational assumption upon which it is based. It assumes, as classical management and economic theories do generally, that all persons are simple economic men.[12] More specifically, the underlying motivational assumption upon which scientific management is based is that it is only

---

[12] The gross inadequacy of this assumption with regard to the behavior of people as consumers has been amply demonstrated. See, for example, Katona, *Psychological Analysis of Economic Behavior* (New York: McGraw-Hill Book Co., 1951), or Klein et al., *Contributions of Survey Methods to Economics* (New York: Columbia University Press, 1954).

necessary to buy a man's time and he will then do willingly and effectively everything which he is ordered to do. Management textbooks emphasize authority and control as the foundation of administration. They either take for granted the power to control or hold that "the relationship of employer and employee in an enterprise is a contractual obligation entailing the right to command and the duty to obey." [13]

The critical weakness of the scientific management approach occurs at precisely the point where the human relations research approach has its greatest strength: motivation. The great power of human relations research findings is in the understanding and insight which they provide as to:

1. The character and magnitude of the powerful motivational forces which control human behavior in working situations
2. The manner in which these forces can be used so that they reinforce rather than conflict with one another

Modified Theory Called For

The fundamental problem, therefore, is to develop an organizational and management theory, and related supervisory and managerial practices for operating under this theory, which will make use of the tremendous resources of the scientific management concepts while fully utilizing in a positive and reinforcing manner the great power of all the major motivational forces which influence human behavior in working situations. To develop this organizational and management theory will be slow, complex, and difficult work. The motives upon which this modified theory should be based include:

1. All the economic motives
2. All the ego motives including the desires for status, recognition, approval, sense of importance and personal worth, and so forth
3. The desire for security
4. The desire for new experiences

Human relations research is yielding concepts which appear to be important tools in deriving a modified theory of management. For example, the research findings have clearly demonstrated that there is no set of specific supervisory practices which is the right or best way to supervise. A way of supervising which may yield the best results in one specific situation may produce poor results in a different situation.[14] The behavior of the superior is not the only variable which determines the subordinate's response. The subordinate's response is also determined by what he has

---

[13] J. D. Millett, *Management in the Public Service* (New York: McGraw-Hill Book Co., 1954); C. O'Donnell, "The Source of Managerial Authority," *Political Science Quarterly* 67 (1952): 573.

[14] D. Pelz, "Influence: A Key to Effective Leadership in the First Line Supervisor," *Personnel* 29 (1952).

learned to expect. Consequently, the response of the subordinate to the behavior of the supervisor will be influenced by the "culture" of the plant or organization and the expectations of the subordinate. To help superiors meet the problems created by this major finding, human relations research is providing evidence as to general principles which can serve as guides to the most appropriate way to supervise in a given situation. Moreover, it is also providing rapid and efficient methods of measuring what the culture and expectations are in any given plant or unit.

29. SPECIFIC LEADERSHIP BEHAVIORS THAT PROMOTE PROBLEM-SOLVING *

Norman R. F. Maier and Marshall Sashkin

WHEN THERE IS A CONFLICT BETWEEN TWO DECISIONS, one favored by the leader, the other by subordinates, the final decision can be a victory for one or the other, a compromise, or the generation of an integrative alternative. The outcome that results depends on the skill of the leader as well as the nature of the members. In a simulated problem situation previously studied,[1] the generation of an integrative alternative has been regarded as the best outcome because (a) it integrates the facts important to both sides of the controversy,[2] (b) it is associated with creativity,[3] and (c) it has the highest acceptance of all parties.[4] Conditions found to be favorable to the development of integrative solutions include the training of the leader in group decision[5] and instructing leaders to discuss problems of workers before raising his problem.[6] The most common approach of the leader, even after considerable training, is to try to persuade the workers to adopt

---

* From *Personnel Psychology* 24 (1971): 35–44.

[1] See N. R. F. Maier, *Principles of Human Relations* (New York: John Wiley & Sons, 1952).

[2] See N. R. F. Maier, "The Subordinate's Role in the Delegation Process," *Personnel Psychology* 21 (1968): 179–91; Maier and J. A. Thurber, "Innovative Problem-Solving by Outsiders: A Study of Individuals and Groups," *Personnel Psychology* 22 (1969): 237–50.

[3] See M. A. Colgrove, "Stimulating Creative Problem-Solving: Innovative Set," *Psychological Reports* 22 (1968): 1205–11.

[4] See N. R. F. Maier and L. R. Hoffman, "Acceptance and Quality of Solutions as Related to Leader's Attitudes toward Disagreement in Group Problem-Solving," *Journal of Applied Behavioral Science* 1 (1965): 373–86.

[5] See N. R. F. Maier, "An Experimental Test of the Effect of Training on Discussion Leadership," *Human Relations* 6 (1953): 161–73.

[6] See N. R. F. Maier and A. R. Solem, "Improving Solutions by Turning Choice Situations into Problems," *Personnel Psychology* 15 (1962): 151–57.

the solution he has in mind, as contrasted with the approach of posing a problem and requesting the workers' participation in finding a solution. The latter apparently is difficult for a leader to do. When he has a preferred solution in mind, there is a strong tendency for him to reveal a bias. It is also found that leaders usually fail to share data with the workers. This occurs even when they are requested to do so.[7]

Maier postulated that a problem-solving approach is more effective in resolving differences than a persuasion approach, and the sharing of data is essential to the problem-solving approach.[8] Thus, two specific behaviors of the leader seem to be conducive to developing innovative solutions: (1) the way the leader states the issue, and (2) the degree to which he shares any data that bear on the issue.

If training along general lines (not specifically requesting the above mentioned behaviors) increases these behaviors then the success of training can be related to specific acts. Further, if these specific acts are associated with Integrative solutions, which in turn are the product of problem-solving interactions, we have a basis for relating specific leadership acts with the problem-solving process. The purpose of this experiment is to test these relationships.

PROCEDURE

Problem Situation

The "Changing Work Procedure" case was used to set up the conflict between a foreman and three assembly workers.[9] The role play itself concerns the efforts of a factory foreman to get three workers to change their work procedure (a 3-step assembly job) in order to achieve an increase in productivity. The foreman has data from a time study that show each man is somewhat faster at some positions than others. One man tends to be a bottleneck on two of the positions. It is suggested that if the men stopped their hourly rotation and each worked on a fixed position, production would increase 20 percent. Since pay is based on a group piece rate, this seems like a reasonable request.

The roles of the workers reveal that the situation is boring and that they adopted the rotation to relieve monotony. They are given a hostile attitude toward time study and a feeling of distrust for management motives. Thus, the change suggested by the foreman is resisted because of the nature of the work and for emotional reasons (fear of rate cuts, and so forth, and hostility toward time study).

---

[7] Maier, "Subordinate's Role."

[8] See N. R. F. Maier, *Problem-Solving Discussions and Conferences* (New York: McGraw-Hill Book Co., 1963); Maier, *Problem-Solving and Creativity in Individuals and Groups* (Belmont, Calif.: Brooks/Cole, 1970).

[9] See Maier, *Principles of Human Relations.*

Subjects

A total of 424 university undergraduates (237 males and 187 females) participated in the experiment and were divided into 106 groups. Seventy-seven groups (153 males and 155 females) were subjects randomly assigned from a pool of all undergraduates in introductory psychology courses and were designated as the "Untrained" groups. The remaining 29 groups (84 males and 32 females) were students in undergraduate courses in industrial psychology and were designated as "trained," in that they had been exposed to the concept of group decision and had been involved in case discussion and role played in three cases involving conflict. The trained groups participated in the experiment about halfway through the term.[10] No training had been given with regard to the specific leadership behaviors investigated in this study.

Types of Data Collected

Following the role play, all Ss completed a brief questionnaire form. The form dealt with the type of solution reached, estimates of production, the foreman's discussion approach, and the sharing of data in the foreman's possession.

Solution Types

All group members wrote a brief description of the decision reached. These were classified as follows: (1) *Old Solutions.* This is the initial preference of the workers who want no change in their work procedure. This classification includes minor variations, such as a request for new time study, helping one another more, promises to try harder, and so forth. (2) *New Solutions.* This classification includes the initial preference of the foreman and requires each man to work only at his best position. This classification includes minor variations, such as a limited trial period, rest pauses, music, and so forth. (3) *Integrative Solutions.* These solutions satisfy the workers' needs by retaining a rotational system while also making use of the time-study data and therefore satisfying management. Integrative solutions are not obvious or clearly implicit in the role materials and must be generated. Examples include (*a*) Jack and Walt rotating while Steve (the bottleneck) remains on his best position, (*b*) all men rotating through all positions but spending more time on their best positions, (*c*) all men rotating between their two best positions, and (*d*) combinations of the above. (4) *Compromise Solutions.* An example of a com-

---

[10] First six chapters of N. R. F. Maier, *Psychology in Industry*, 3d ed. (Boston: Houghton-Mifflin, 1965).

promise would be to spend 2½ days a week on the Old method and 2½ days on the New. Of 108 groups tested, two reached compromise solutions and were not included in the data.

Workers' Production Estimates

The acceptance of those who must carry out the decision is a significant factor in its effectiveness. Acceptance was determined by obtaining a future production estimate from each worker. Workers reported whether production, under the decision adopted, would go down, remain the same, or go up. These responses were scored 1, 2, and 3, respectively, and group score was calculated by summing the scores of the three workers. These production estimates reflect workers' acceptance because the men have considerable control over their own productivity, regardless of the objective merits of the decision.

Foreman's Approach to the Discussion

To determine the degree to which the foreman was problem-oriented versus solution-oriented, workers were asked to check one of the following categories:

1. He tried to (a) persuade or (b) force us to adopt fixed positions.
2. He gave us a choice between working fixed positions or not changing.
3. He stated a problem in terms of (a) how to increase production or (b) how to use the time-study data.

The numbers one to three are the score values assigned to the responses. The higher the score, the greater the foreman's problem-orientation. Group scores were obtained by summing the responses of the three workers.

Foreman's Sharing of Time-Study Data

Behavior related to the sharing of the time-study data was determined from workers by asking them to classify the foreman's actions into one of the following three categories:

1. He did not share the time-study data, only reported conclusions.
2. He told us of, or we saw, some of the time-study data.
3. He showed us the time-study data table.

The numbers one to three are the score values assigned to the responses. Higher scores indicate a greater extent of data sharing. Group scores were obtained by summing the three workers' responses.

TABLE 29–1

Comparison of Trained and Untrained Leaders in Initiating Group Discussion

| | | Leader's Approach to the Group | | |
| | | Percent of Workers Reporting that the Foreman | | |
Group	N	Presented His Own Solution	Presented a Choice of Solutions	Presented a Problem
Untrained	231	42.4	25.5	32.0
Trained.	87	8.0	48.3	43.7
Total	318	33.0	31.8	35.2

Note: A Chi-square test comparing response distributions for trained versus untrained group members shows $x^2 = 35.3790$, 2 df, $p < .001$.

TABLE 29–2

Comparison of Trained and Untrained Leaders in Their Sharing of Data

Group	N	Did Not Share the Data	Shared Some of the Data	Shared All of the Data
Untrained	231	59.7	39.0	1.3
Trained.	87	42.5	29.7	29.7
Total	318	55.0	36.2	8.8

Note: A Chi-square test comparing response distribution for trained versus untrained group members shows $x^2 = 58.8742$, 2 df, $p < .001$.

RESULTS

The results of the behaviors of leaders of our trained and untrained samples are given in Tables 29–1 and 29–2. Table 29–1 shows the results pertaining to the method used in posing the discussion question. The frequency with which the three types of approaches were used is not only significantly different, but within the Trained groups, leaders are less inclined to persuade and more inclined to pose a problem, whereas for the Untrained groups the reverse holds.

Table 29–2 presents the data regarding the extent to which the data were shared with the group. Again, the results favor the Trained group in that the leaders of the Trained samples are more inclined to share the data than the leaders of the Untrained samples. The difference in the distributions of the three degrees of sharing is highly significant.

Table 29–3 shows the frequency with which the three different types of solutions were developed by the Trained and Untrained samples. As pre-

TABLE 29–3

Solutions Achieved by Trained versus Untrained Groups

		Type of Solution		
Group	N	Old (%)	New (%)	Integrative (%)
Untrained	77	20.8	66.2	13.0
Trained.	29	17.2	27.6	55.2
Total	106	19.8	55.7	24.5

Note: A Chi-square test comparing response distribution of trained versus untrained groups shows $x^2 = 21.0696$, 2 df, $p < .001$.

viously reported [11] training increases the frequency with which the integrative solutions are developed and the difference shown in Table 29–3 is significant.

It is clear that training has not made the leaders more permissive in the sense of letting the workers continue the "Old" method. This was a question raised in the 1953 study in which management personnel served as Ss. Rather, the Integrative solutions replaced the "New," indicating that leaders did not become either more permissive or more persuasive. Instead, the change in their behavior led to the generation of additional alternatives.

The fact that training increases the two samples of leader behavior investigated and also results in a higher proportion of Integrative solutions indicates some causal relationship. However, there may be additional changes in the leader's behavior that influence the effectiveness of the decision.

The measures of the acceptance of three types of solutions achieved are shown in Table 29–4. It will be recalled that the acceptance score for each group was based on each worker's judgment as to whether the solution adopted would cause production to (a) go down (b) remain the same, or (c) go up. The values assigned to these judgments were 1, 2, and 3, respectively, so that the lowest group score would be 3 and the highest, 9. It will be seen that the group scores for Integrative solutions were between eight and nine for both trained and untrained populations, and in each instance, these scores were significantly higher than for the Old or the New. In each comparison the acceptance score for the Trained population is higher than for the untrained, but only for New solutions does this difference reach acceptable significance ($p < .05$). Thus, even when solutions are matched, the value of the training is reflected by the better

[11] See Maier, "Experimental Test of the Effect of Training," 161–73.

TABLE 29–4

Acceptance Measures for Three Types of Solutions

| | | Mean Production Measure for Solution | | | | | Significance Level | |
| | | | | | | | Old vs. Integ. | New vs. Integ. |
Group	N	Old		New		Integrative		
Untrained	77	6.69	(16)	6.55*	(51)	8.50	(10)	$p < .001$	$p < .001$
Trained.	29	7.20	(5)	7.75*	(8)	8.88	(16)	$p < .001$	$p < .001$
Total	106	6.81	(21)	6.71	(59)	8.73	(26)	$p < .001$	$p < .001$

Note: Group scores may range from three to nine. The numbers in parentheses indicate frequency with which the type of solution was obtained. The significance levels for all comparisons are based on one-tailed t tests, as all comparisons are tests of directional predictions.

* $p < .05$.

TABLE 29–5

The Relationship between Leader Behaviors and Types of Solutions

| | | | Mean of Group Scores for | | | Significance Levels | |
| | | | | | Inte- | Old vs. | New vs. |
Variable	Group	N	Old	New	grative	Integ.	Integ.
Foreman's	Untrained	77	5.88[a]	5.39[b]	6.90[c]	$p < .10$	$p < .005$
Approach	Trained	29	7.20[a]	6.50[b]	7.31[c]	n.s.	n.s.
	Total	106	6.19	6.05	7.15	$p < .025$	$p < .005$
Foreman's	Untrained	77	3.56[d]	4.31[e]	5.00[f]	$p < .001$	$p < .02$
Sharing of Time-Study Data	Trained	29	5.00[d]	4.50[e]	6.31[f]	n.s.	n.s.
	Total	106	3.90	4.34	5.81	$p < .001$	$p < .001$

Note: For each variable, the group scores may range from three to nine. The actual ranges of group scores on each variable are identical with the potential ranges. The indicated significance levels are all based on one-tailed t tests, as all comparisons are tests of directional predictions. Similarly superscripted means are different at the following levels of confidence:

[a,f] $p < .10$.

[b,d] $p < .05$.

[c,e] n.s.

acceptance, particularly with regard to the obtaining of the change initially advocated by management.

Table 29–5 presents the ratings of the way the foreman initiated the discussion and the degree to which he shared the data. These ratings are given in relation to the type of solution achieved.

The top half of the table shows the measures of how the foreman posed the problem (a group score of three would indicate that all workers agreed that he posed his solution and tried to get it adopted, while a group score of nine would indicate that all workers agreed that he posed a problem rather than a solution). The third line shows that when Integrative solutions were reached, an average score of 7.15 was obtained. This value is significantly higher than the scores for either of the other two solution types. When the Untrained and Trained populations are examined separately (lines one and two) the behavior ratings associated with the Integrative solutions versus the Old or New are in the anticipated direction, but the differences for the Trained groups are not significant.

When solutions of the same type are compared (line one versus line two), the Trained groups rate the leader's approach higher than the Untrained groups, but an acceptable significance level ($p < .05$) was reached only for the comparison of "New" solutions.

The lower half of Table 29-5 shows the measures that indicate how the foreman handled the time-study data (a group score of three would indicate that the three workers agree he did not reveal the data and a group score of nine would indicate that the three workers agreed that he showed them all of the data). It will be seen that Integrative solutions are associated with the rating of 5.81 (last line) for the foreman's behavior. This value is significantly higher than those obtained in connection with the other two types of solutions.

New and Old types of solutions were not influenced significantly by the two measures of the foreman's behavior. Apparently, which of these solutions wins seems to depend on factors other than the two leadership behaviors investigated.

Comparisons of Untrained and Trained populations with regard to the sharing of data when solution types are equated (line four versus line five) reveal that within each solution type, the Trained groups have a higher score than the Untrained, but only with regard to the Old solution is the difference significant ($p < .05$).

The results clearly show that leader behaviors which promote problem-solving interaction are more likely to produce outcomes that not only are more acceptable, but which can be classified as both innovative and superior in quality.

DISCUSSION

When the leader of a group wishes to introduce a change, it is customary for him to describe the new idea and then find himself in the position of trying to persuade the members to adopt it. If the group is reluctant to go along with the change, we speak of "resistance to change." The leader's procedure associated with this approach to "change" is to present the solution and to supply factual evidence pointing to the merits of the change. This procedure is in direct opposition to the problem-solving approach in which a problem is posed and facts relevant to the problem are shared.

The results of this study reveal that posing the problem and sharing the factual information generates problem-solving behavior in the sense that ideas other than obvious alternatives are generated. Thus the appearance of Integrative solutions is associated with each of these leader behaviors.

Integrative solutions are superior in quality to either the alternative initially favored by management or that favored by the workers in the sense that they integrate the apparently contradictory facts marshalled by the conflicting parties. They also are the solutions most frequently generated by nonemotionally involved persons [12] and by persons found to be superior problem-solvers.[13]

In addition, the Integrative solutions attained significantly greater acceptance than the initially favored alternatives. Thus, from the point of view of solution quality and solution acceptance, the product of a problem-solving type of interaction is superior to the persuasion-type approach.

The results of this experiment also show the benefits of training that made the distinction between the leadership style in which the leader (a) poses a problem and the group generates the solution versus (b) poses a solution and persuades the group to adopt it. In our previous studies it was found that this complete change in behavior was difficult to achieve because the leader remains inclined to supply, suggest, or hint at a solution he knows about. Maier found that even after training, the predominant style of the leaders was still one of selling, but they seemed somewhat more inclined to listen and entertain objections.[14] The findings of the present study included more detailed measures of the leader's behavior and the analysis revealed that the leaders familiar with the concept of group decision were significantly more inclined to initiate group discussion with a problem-solving approach.

Similar conclusions can be drawn from the results bearing on the degree to which the leader shared the data with his group. Leaders of Trained groups did show a significant change in this respect, but there was still a general reluctance to share the data. It has been found that when the leader was instructed to share the data and obtain group participation, the leadership styles were no different than when he was instructed to introduce the change.[15] Individual differences in the leaders' perceptions of how to approach the introduction of change offset the effects of such instructions. The present study shows that the leader's behavior can be altered with training.

It is evident from the changes obtained that the training supplied to

---

[12] See Colgrove, "Stimulating Creative Problem-Solving"; Maier and Thurber, "Innovative Problem-Solving."

[13] See N. R. F. Maier and J. C. Janzen, "Are Good Problem-Solvers Also Creative?" *Psychological Reports* 24 (1969): 139–46.

[14] Maier, "Experimental Test of the Effect of Training."

[15] See Maier, "Subordinate's Role"; Maier and Thurber, "Innovative Problem-Solving."

our Trained groups was enough to produce significant changes. However, it will be recalled (Tables 29–1 and 29–2) that the leader behaviors, after training, still were considerably below the optimum. It is evident, therefore, that training must incorporate more skill practice if the full value of such training is to be materialized.

30. LEADER INFLUENCE AND PERFORMANCE *

John M. Ivancevich and James H. Donnelly

ONE OF THE MOST SCIENTIFICALLY STUDIED and controversial variables of the management process is leadership. There have been many different theories of leadership espoused by both practitioners and researchers. A number of situational theories of leadership began appearing in the behavioral science literature in the early 1900s.[1] The situational theories stress the importance of discussing leadership as a function of: (a) the personality characteristics of the leader, (b) the personality characteristics of the subordinates, (c) the performance expectations of the leader; (d) the performance requirements as perceived by subordinates, and (e) the organizational climate in which the leader and his subordinates must function.

Recently Katz and Kahn have suggested that a new concept of organizational leadership, described as incremental influence, is important and should be empirically investigated.[2] They refer to incremental influence in the following manner:

When we think of leadership in contrast to routine role performance, however, we become particularly interested in the kinds of individual behavior which go beyond required performance and realize more fully the potential of a given position for organizational influence. In other words, we consider the essence of organization leadership to be the influential increment over and above mechanical compliance with the routine directives of the organization . . .[3]

---

* From *Personnel Psychology* 23 (1970): 539–49.

[1] See R. Cattell, "New Concepts for Measuring Leadership in Terms of Group Syntality," *Human Relations* 4 (1951): 161–84; C. Gibb, "Leadership," in *Handbook of Social Psychology*, ed. G. Lindzey (Reading, Mass.: Addison-Wesley, 1954), pp. 120–48; R. M. Stogdill, *Individual Behavior and Group Achievement* (New York: Oxford University Press, 1959); B. M. Bass, *Leadership Psychology and Organizational Behavior* (New York: Harper & Row, 1960); and R. Likert, *New Patterns of Management* (New York: McGraw-Hill Book Co., 1961).

[2] D. Katz and R. L. Kahn, *The Social Psychology of Organizations* (New York: John Wiley & Sons, 1966).

[3] Ibid., p. 392.

The present study is an empirical investigation of the Katz and Kahn concept of leadership in a marketing department of a large business firm. More specifically, the study will analyze a number of performance correlates of the branch sales manager's incremental influence over salesmen. A recent investigation by Student found significant relationships between selected performance measures and incremental influence for first-line supervisors and hourly employees in a manufacturing plant.[4] Thus, it was assumed that a similar analysis could be conducted using managers and groups of white-collar employees.

Power Theory

In the social science literature, authority usually receives more attention than power since it is a more conspicuous phenomenon in everyday organizational life. There is, however, no shortage of classification systems which focus upon power.[5] The classification presentation which provided the best framework for the current study was the French and Raven typology.[6]

In the typology, French and Raven define power in terms of influence, and influence in terms of psychological change. They propose five bases of power by which an agent (leader), O, can exert influence over a person (subordinate), P. The strength of power O possesses in an organization is his maximum potential ability to control. The degree to which the leader, O, chooses to exercise his power is a personal matter.

The five sources of power are:

1. *Reward Power* based on the number of positive incentives which O is able to offer P. In order for O to use his reward power, he must be in control of resources that P values. It is also important for P to perceive O as possessing resources that he values. Thus, a leader may have a certain amount of power to increase the weekly wage of P but he is not perceived as possessing the ability to increase P's wage.
2. *Coercive Power* based on the absolute and perceived expectations that punishment will follow if one does not respond to the command and goals of O. In order for O to use coercive power to influence P, P must want to prevent O from carrying out punishment.

---

[4] K. R. Student, "Supervisory Influence and Work-Group Performance," *Journal of Applied Psychology* 52 (1968): 188–94.

[5] See R. Bierstedt, "An Analysis of Social Power," *American Sociological Review* 15 (1950): 730; H. A. Simon, "Authority," in *Research in Industrial Human Relations*, ed. C. M. Arensberg et al. (New York: Harper & Row, 1957); D. Cartwright, "Influence, Leadership, Control," in *Handbook of Organizations*, ed. J. G. March (Chicago: Rand McNally, 1965) pp. 1–47; and J. R. P. French, Jr. and B. H. Raven, "The Bases of Social Power," in *Studies in Social Power*, ed. D. Cartwright (Ann Arbor, Mich.: Institute for Social Research, 1959), pp. 150–67.

[6] Ibid.

3. *Legitimate Power* based on internalized values which dictate that O has a legitimate right to influence P and that P has an obligation to accept this influence.
4. *Referent Power* based on P's wanting to identify with O. This feeling of oneness is the desire of P and it may or may not be reciprocated by O. The identification of P with O can be sustained if P behaves, perceives, or believes as O does.
5. *Expert Power* based on O's possession of functional expertise. That is, the leader possesses some special knowledge which P perceives as being important. The experience, training, or displayed ability are some of the reasons for P's respect for O's expertise.

The five bases of power are instrumental in providing for the operationalization of the incremental influence leadership concept. The utilization of reward power, legitimate power, and coercive power in the organizational setting are related specifically to the leader's position in the organization hierarchy. The first line supervisor is at a lower organization level than the vice president of operations and, consequently, his reward power, legitimate power and coercive power bases would theoretically be significantly less than the vice president. Thus, the organization to a large extent specifies the amount of reward power, legitimate power and coercive power which can be exercised.

The amount and range of a leader's referent power and expert power is not dictated by the organizational system. These two categories of power are more closely associated with the technical, behavioral, and administrative skills of each individual leader. Thus, in the present study, referent power and expert power are identified as idiosyncratic concepts.

The five-classification typology of power can be reclassified into two distinct groupings of power: (1) the reward power, legitimate power, and coercive power bases which are affected by the formal organization system in general and the managerial hierarchy in particular; and (2) the referent power and expert power bases which are affected by the idiosyncrasies of each leader. Thus, it is reasonable to assume that referent power and expert power are conceptually different from reward power, legitimate power, and coercive power. Leadership based on referent power and expert power is conceived as being an increment in influence over and above the influence which is generated from possessing a position in the organizational hierarchy. Consequently, as stated by Student [7] the additive combination of referent power and expert power is a form of an operational definition and interpretation of incremental influence. This operational interpretation of referent power and expert power was used in the present study.

---

[7] Student, "Supervisory Influence and Work-Group Performance."

Related Research

This study relates the incremental influence concept to selected salesmen group performance measures. While the use of multiple performance criteria in studies of organizational job performance is becoming more common, it is still rare to find multidimensional investigations.[8] Leader influence will be related to eight performance measures, all of which are considered as being basically objective. It is not proposed that these eight variables represent all aspects of performance or are the only performance measures used in the company studied. They were selected from a roster of 14 measures because of their high degree of objectivity and their relevance to salesmen performance on the job.

March and Simon state that employees within an organization [9] must make two decisions: (1) to participate in an organization, and (2) to produce for an organization. The employee undertakes an inducement—contribution analysis—when making a participation related decision. If he perceives his contribution as being greater than the inducement to participate, he will not participate and may quit his job or stay away from the job by being absent. The decision of whether or not to produce is a function of the employee's reaction to motivational strategies of management, the employee's perception of the consequences of producing, and the goals of the employee.

The March and Simon discussion of decisions enabled the researchers to study the performance factors as measures of not participating (NP), or as production (P) measures.[10] A growing list of empirical research evidence suggests that incremental influence would relate to both (NP) and (P) performance measures.[11]

A research study by Fleishman, Harris and Burtt found a negative relationship between the concept referred to as consideration and absenteeism.[12] The consideration concept involves behavior which allows and fosters two-way communication, mutual trust, and rapport between the leader and his subordinates.

---

[8] See S. E. Seashore, B. P. Indik, and B. S. Georgopoulos, "Relationships among Criteria of Job Performance, *Journal of Applied Psychology* 44 (1960): 195–202.

[9] J. G. March and H. A. Simon, *Organizations* (New York: John Wiley & Sons, 1958).

[10] Ibid.

[11] See R. L. Kahn and D. Katz, "Leadership Practices in Relation to Productivity and Morale," in *Group Dynamics*, 2d ed., ed. D. Cartwright and A. Zander (Evanston, Ill.: Row, Peterson, 1960), pp. 554–70; Likert, *New Patterns of Management;* R. C. Day and R. L. Hamblin, "Some Effects of Close and Punitive Styles of Supervision," *American Journal of Sociology* 69 (1964): 499–510; F. C. Mann, "Toward an Understanding of the Leadership Role in Formal Organizations," in *Leadership and Productivity*, ed. R. Dubin et al. (San Francisco: Chandler, 1965), pp. 68–103; and Student, "Supervisory Influence and Work-Group Performance."

[12] E. A. Fleishman, E. F. Harris, and H. E. Burtt, *Leadership and Supervision in Industry* (Columbus, Ohio: Bureau of Educational Research, Ohio State University, 1955).

Fleishman and Harris investigated the relationship between leader consideration and turnover.[13] The main findings were that leaders with low consideration tend to have high turnover.

The research findings cited above, the concept of incremental influence, and the power classification system, led the authors to formulate two broadly stated propositions:

P_1: The incremental influence of leaders (that is, additive score of referent power and expert power) would be related to acceptable performance measures.

P_2: There would be a relationship between the referent power of leaders, P wanting to identify with O, and the not participating (NP) measures (that is, excused absenteeism, unexcused absenteeism and turnover).

METHOD

Research Site and Participants

This study employed data collected from a marketing organization of a large firm producing food products. The data were collected by a carefully pretested paper-and-pencil questionnaire and performance records. The attitude, opinion and perception measures were collected in one month, while the performance measures were collected over a 6-month period.

The sample consisted of 394 salesmen from 31 different sales branches of the company. These salesmen called on retail food outlets throughout the United States. Each sales branch manager supervised a group of salesmen in a geographical region. The unit of analysis for this study are the sales groups ($N = 31$) of 31 branch managers.

Measures of Leader Influence

The measures of leader influence utilized in this study were as follows:

Referent Power—A single-item rating by salesmen of the extent to which they comply with their branch manager's directives because he is a person they respect highly and they don't want to hurt him.

Expert Power—A single-item rating of the extent to which salesmen comply with their branch manager's directives because they respect his experience, training and overall astute judgment.

---

[13] E. A. Fleishman and R. F. Harris, "Patterns of Leadership Behavior Related to Employee Grievances and Turnover," *Personnel Psychology* 15 (1962): 43–56.

TABLE 30–1

Intercorrelation between Measures of Branch Manager Influence (N = 31)

Measure	1	2	3	4	5	6
1. Incremental Influence						
2. Referent Power	.76***					
3. Expert Power	.80***	.38*				
4. Reward Power	.49**	.37*	.39*			
5. Coercive Power	.25	.21	.18	.57**		
6. Legitimate Power	.29*	.44**	.32*	.19	.39**	

   * $p < .05$, two-tailed.
  ** $p < .01$, two-tailed.
 *** $p < .001$, two-tailed.

TABLE 30–2

Mean and Standard Deviation of Incremental Influence and Bases of Power (N = 31)

Measure	$\bar{X}$	σ
1. Incremental Influence	6.69	.98
2. Referent Power	2.98	.57
3. Expert Power	3.71	.51
4. Reward Power	3.01	.52
5. Coercive Power	2.69	.40
6. Legitimate Power	3.70	.54

Incremental Influence—The summing of the group mean for referent power and the group mean for expert power.

Reward Power—A single-item rating of the extent to which salesmen comply with their branch manager's directives because he can provide resources to those subordinates who cooperate with him and comply with directives.

Legitimate Power—A single-item rating of the extent to which salesmen comply with their branch manager's directives because the manager's position in the organization gives him a right to command salesmen.

Coercive Power—A single-item rating of the extent to which salesmen comply with their branch manager's directives because he can penalize or make the selling job difficult for those who do not cooperate with him.[14]

Each salesman assessed the six bases of power and incremental influence of their respective branch managers by ranking the six bases on a "1" most important factor to a "6" least important factor.

Table 30–1 presents the relationships between the six measures of branch manager influence over the salesmen, while Table 30–2 presents the means and standard deviations of incremental influence and the bases of power.

---

[14] J. G. Bachman, C. G. Smith, and J. A. Slesinger, "Control, Performance, and Satisfaction: An Analysis of Structural and Individual Effects," *Journal of Personality and Social Psychology* 4 (1966): 127–36.

TABLE 30–3

Salesmen Performance Measures

Performance Measures

1. Excused Absenteeism	(–)	The number of times an excused absence is granted, divided by the number of salesmen in the branch manager's group.
2. Unexcused Absenteeism	(–)	The number of times the salesmen are absent without an excuse, divided by the number of salesmen in the branch manager's group.
3. Turnover	(–)	The number of salesmen quitting and requesting transfers without the transfer involving advancement, potential monetary gain, or health reasons (for example, salesmen requesting transfer to Arizona for health purposes), divided by the number of men in the branch manager's group.
4. Market Potential Ratio	(+)	The total sales volume of the group, divided by the potential volume available to each group.
5. Number & Size of Orders	(+)	The addition of the total number of orders generated by the group, divided into the total sales volume for the group.
6. Efficiency Rating	(+)	The total number of orders taken by the salesmen groups divided by the total number of retail outlets called on by the salesmen groups.
7. Direct-Selling Costs	(+)	Adding the salesmen's expenses plus their compensation and dividing this by the total sales volume generated by the group. This figure is then measured against a budgeted amount allocated for selling expenses.
8. Route Density Factor	(+)	Adding the miles traveled by the group of salesmen and dividing the figure by the total number of retail outlets called on.

Note: A high score or ratio on any one of the eight salesmen group performance measures may indicate either acceptable or unacceptable performance, depending upon the specific measure. A "+" indicates that a high score represents acceptable performance, while a "−" indicates that a high score represents unacceptable performance.

Performance Measures from Historical Documentation

From a list of fourteen possible performance measures, the eight most objective measures (face validity) were utilized. These eight measures were tabulated weekly during a 24-week period from immediately preceding and following the administration of the leadership influence questionnaires. The measures used are summarized in Table 30–3.

Results

The first proposition suggested that high incremental influence (addition of referent power and expert power scores) would be related to acceptable performance measures. The results for this prediction are presented in Table 30–4.

TABLE 30–4

Relationships between Production Performance Measures and Branch Manager Power (N = 31)

Productivity Performance Measures	Incremental Influence	Referent Power	Expert Power	Reward Power	Coercive Power	Legitimate Power
	Salesmen Group Mean Perception of Their Branch Managers					
Market Potential Ratio	.23*	.25*	.21*	−.09	.14	.11
Number and Size of Orders	.34*	.19	−.02	.11	.08	.07
Efficiency Ratio.	.16	.21*	.16	.23*	−.12	−.16
Direct-Selling Costs	.26*	.10	.22*	−.04	.19	.13
Route Density Factor	.24*	.31*	.09	.12	.18	.01

* $P < .05$, one-tailed.

The predictions of the first proposition are generally supported by the findings. For four of the five production performance measures (market potential ratio, number and size of orders, direct-selling costs and route density factor), the predicted relationships are significant. There was, however, no significant relationship between incremental influence and the efficiency rating scores.

The second generally stated proposition suggested that measures of nonparticipation (that is, excused absenteeism, unexcused absenteeism and turnover) would be related to referent power. The results presented in Table 30–5 indicate that referent power is generally associated with excused and unexcused absenteeism, while no relationship between turnover and the bases of power were found.

Discussion

An analysis of the numerous theories of leadership leads one to conclude that the behavior and role of the leader is significantly affected by the leader's formal position in the organization hierarchy. The classic analysis of authority by Weber suggested that subordinates would comply with a leader's directive about performance because it is legitimate for the leader to command.[15] The extent to which subordinates adhere to the legitimacy concept of power determines the amount of incentives or punishment the leader must use to bring about agreement with performance directives.

---

[15] M. Weber, "The Essentials of Bureaucratic Organization: An Ideal-Type Contraction," in *A Reader in Bureaucracy*, ed. R. K. Merton et al. (Glencoe, Ill.: The Free Press, 1952), pp. 18–27.

TABLE 30–5

Relationships between Nonparticipating Performance Measures and Branch Manager Power (N = 31)

Nonparticipation Performance Measures	Salesmen Group Mean Perception of Their Branch Managers					
	Incremental Influence	Referent Power	Expert Power	Reward Power	Coercive Power	Legitimate Power
Excused Absenteeism.	−.32*	−.29*	−.29*	−.19	−.04	−.16
Unexcused Absenteeism	−.27*	−.22*	−.14	.10	.11	.04
Turnover	.03	.01	.04	−.07	.02	.06

* $P < .05$, one-tailed.

The rank orders of the mean scores in Table 30–2 indicated that legitimate power ranked second among the reasons for compliance with the directives of the branch manager. However, analysis of Tables 30–4 and 30–5 indicates that legitimate power as defined by French and Raven is not related to differences in the performance of the sales groups investigated.[16] This suggests that in the organizational setting of the study, attempts to bring about compliance with branch manager performance directive based upon the legitimate power of the manager may not be the most optimum.

The present findings indicate that a strategy that should be considered for bringing about compliance with leader directives is one which focuses upon the referent power and expert power concepts. This may necessitate having the leader work specifically on developing an understanding of his referent power and expert power among his subordinates. The most effective procedures for generating this desired perception among subordinates are not specifically known at present and further research is needed to uncover viable strategies.

Further examination of Tables 30–4 and 30–5 indicate that coercive power does not appear to be related statistically to the differences in the performance measures. The use of the managerial "stick" in the form of coercion is not a significant factor, at least with the group of salesmen studied. Whether this finding would hold with other groups of white-collar employees (for example, engineers, accountants, scientists, and so forth) must be tested in future research efforts.

It was assumed that incremental influence would be positively related to performance measures. As postulated, six of the eight performance measures relate to incremental influence. The two measures which showed no relationship were the efficiency rating and turnover. During the 24-week study period, turnover was not high and this may account for the

---

[16] French and Raven, "Bases of Social Power."

lack of any significant relationship. The lack of relationship between performance measures and the efficiency rating is not clear. The rating might be related to some factor which does not depend upon complying with the performance directives of the branch manager. For example, inaccurate recording of the total number of calls made may have led to not finding significant relationships.

The findings of this study generally agree with previous findings concerning the relationship between referent power and absences.[17] Thus, additional support for the belief that absences can be positively influenced (that is, decreased) via the referent power base is established for a white-collar group of subjects.

CONCLUSION

This study has been a needed first step (white-collar workers) in determining whether a qualitative distinction can be made between the French and Raven five bases of power. In one category is placed the organizationally determined reward power, coercive power and legitimate power; and in the other group would be the referent power and expert power concepts which have been added to equal incremental influence. Whether the incremental influence leadership concept has any operational and/or conceptual value for leaders at different management levels other than branch sales managers in organizations must be further investigated. The Student findings [18] and the present study results suggest that this concept can be applied equally well to blue-collar (manufacturing workers) or white-collar (salesmen) employees. Although the measures of performance for the manufacturing and salesmen subjects were different, they were generally objective and obtainable from company records. Applying the incremental influence and power framework to other leader-subordinate groupings depends primarily on employing understandable and operational performance measures.

---

[17] See Fleishman, Harris, and Burtt, *Leadership and Supervision in Industry;* and Fleishman and Harris, "Patterns of Leadership Behavior."

[18] Student, "Supervisory Influence and Work-group Performance."

31. USE OF LEADERSHIP POWERS IN INDUSTRY *

David Kipnis and Joseph Cosentino

STUDIES OF LEADERSHIP BEHAVIOR have focused mainly upon the identification of the dimensions of a leader's behavior and the consequence of variations in these dimensions for a subordinate's morale and productivity.[1] These studies have revealed the importance of leadership behavior as related to task direction and to maintaining the socioemotional well-being of subordinates. Less attention has been paid to the question of how leaders use the formal social powers associated with their organizational roles. Yet this question is of particular interest in industrial and military organizations. By virtue of their roles, formally appointed leaders control resources that are valued or required by subordinates. Among these resources are the control of sanctions, control of communication channels, and control of the direction of task performance. In essence these controls, or social powers, provide the means by which the formally appointed leader can exercise influence and thus have a central role in mediating the outcomes for subordinates.

Many questions can be raised concerning these powers. For example, does the amount of experience the individual has had as a supervisor relate to his use of the powers the organization allows him to control? In an unpublished doctoral dissertation by Schreiber it was found that when inexperienced leaders were given too much power, their behavior was disrupted.[2] What situational factors affect the use of social powers? Do supervisors directing large numbers of men use their powers in the same fashion as those directing fewer men? Does the personality of the supervisor influence the ways in which he uses the resources that he controls?

* From *Journal of Applied Psychology* 53, no. 6 (1969): 460–66. Copyright 1969 by the American Psychological Association. Reprinted by permission.

[1] R. F. Bales, "The Equilibrium Problem in Small Groups," in *Working Papers in the Theory of Action*, ed. T. Parsons, R. F. Bales, and E. A. Shills (Glencoe, Ill.: The Free Press, 1953); F. E. Fiedler, "The Contingency Model: A Theory of Leadership Effectiveness," in *Basic Studies in Social Psychology*, ed. H. Proshansky and B. Seidenberg (New York: Holt, Rinehart & Winston, 1965). E. A. Fleishman, "The Description of Supervisory Behavior," *Journal of Applied Psychology* 37 (1953): 1–6; and R. L. Kahn and D. Katz, "Leadership Practices in Relation to Productivity and Morale," in *Group Dynamics*, 2d ed., ed. D. Cartwright and A. Zander (Evanston, Ill.: Row, Peterson, 1960).

[2] Cited in L. F. Carter, "Leadership and Small Group Behavior" (Paper presented at the Second Conference on Social Psychology, University of Oklahoma, 1952).

Do overly aggressive supervisors use their coercive powers to induce compliance more frequently than less aggressive supervisors?

In essence we are asking if there is a psychology of the use of social powers within industry? With the exception of the important and systematic research that has derived from French and Raven's classification of social powers, there has not been much interest in this question.[3] Yet it is clear that one can distinguish between questions concerned with leadership style (that is, how the leader behaves with respect to decision making, consideration, task orientation, and so forth) and with leadership power. Several studies have reported that the influence of a leader over subordinates varied systematically with his control of resources, independently of his style of leadership.[4]

The purpose of the present study was to investigate one aspect of the relation between social power and supervisory behavior. The study investigated (a) the range of social powers available to supervisors when correcting subordinate behavior and (b) the situational and personal factors influencing the supervisors' use of these powers. The present research conducted in an industrial setting was a follow-up of a previously unpublished investigation of naval supervisors.[5] The military study found that a variety of personal and situational factors influenced the military supervisors' choice of corrective powers.

The following findings from the military study are relevant to the present research:

1. Military supervisors supervising large numbers of men relied upon their legal powers to punish by placing subordinates on report—a procedure often culminating in court-martial.
2. As the complexity of the problem increased, military supervisors (a) more frequently transferred subordinates to a different set of duties and (b) increased the number of corrective powers used.
3. There appeared to be a "treatment of choice" associated with problems presented by subordinates. Different powers were invoked by the supervisor according to the type of problem presented by the subordinate.
4. Experienced supervisors were more likely than inexperienced supervisors to correct directly a subordinate's behavior. Inexperienced supervisors either referred subordinates to someone else, or relied upon their

---

[3] J. R. P. French and B. Raven, "The Bases of Social Power," in *Studies in Social Power*, ed. D. Cartwright (Ann Arbor, Mich.: Research Center for Group Dynamics, 1959).

[4] D. Kipnis, "The Effects of Leadership Style and Leadership Power upon the Inducement of an Attitude Change," *Journal of Abnormal and Social Psychology* 58 (1958): 173–80; D. C. Pelz, "Leadership within a Hierarchical Organization," *Journal of Social Issues* 7 (1951): 49–55.

[5] D. Kipnis, W. P. Lane, and L. Frankfurt, *Leadership Problems and Practices of Petty Officers* (Washington, D.C.: Naval Personnel Research Activity Research Report 61–30, 1961).

legal powers. In a follow-up study on this last point, it was found that supervisors who lacked confidence in their leadership talents were more likely to use the latter forms of corrective powers.[6]

It was clear that the range of corrective powers reported by these military supervisors was not chosen because of whim or individual idiosyncracies. No supervisor mentioned physical coercion, fines of money, or excessive restrictions of personal liberties. The military supervisors' descriptions of their behavior were in fact descriptions of the constraints imposed upon them by the organizational structure. If the magnitude and variety of corrective powers permitted the supervisor were increased or decreased, it could be expected that the reports of the supervisors would be correspondingly altered.

METHOD

The same procedure used in the military study was used in this investigation. An open-ended questionnaire was administered to a sample of 184 supervisors from five different companies engaged in light manufacturing. The questionnaire was given on the first day of a supervisory training course. The questionnaire asked each supervisor to describe an incident that occurred within the past year in which a subordinate's behavior was below average. In addition, supervisors were asked to describe what was done about the incident by themselves or by others. Respondents were asked to give the following information concerning their subordinates: (a) number directly supervised, (b) union or nonunion members, and (c) hourly or salaried pay. In addition, they were asked how many years they had been a supervisor. This procedure provided a listing of the kinds of corrective powers available to the supervisors, as well as the frequency with which each of these corrective actions was used.

Usable returns were obtained from 131 supervisors. Of the remainder, 25 returns described incidents that happened to someone else and 28 described cases that involved female subordinates. It was decided to analyze only the male returns. The overwhelming majority of the supervisors (89 percent) were directing hourly paid, blue-collar workers. Hence the findings should not be generalized to salaried, white-collar samples.

The problems and actions taken by the supervisors were coded according to a classification system used in the naval study. This system was used directly with the industrial sample, with the addition of the category of man fired and the substitution of the category written warning for the category written report.

---

[6] D. Kipnis and W. P. Lane, "Self-Confidence and Leadership," *Journal of Applied Psychology* 46 (1962): 291–95.

The kinds of problems presented by subordinates were classified as follows:

1. *Attitude.* The subordinate showed a lack of interest in the company, work, or personal advancement.
2. *Discipline.* The subordinate failed to follow the rules of conduct prescribed by the company.
3. *Work.* The subordinate failed to maintain minimum standards in performing work.
4. *Appearance.* The subordinate failed to dress appropriately.

Corrective Actions

The ways in which the supervisors reported handling the problems were classified into eight categories. Since many supervisors reported taking more than one action, multiple coding was used. However, this multiple coding was used only between, and not within, categories.

1. *Verbal*:(a) Diagnostic talk—An attempt was made by the supervisor to find out the reasons for the subordinate's unacceptable behavior. (b) Corrective talk—The supervisor pointed out the consequences of the subordinate's substandard behavior, and/or discussed ways in which the subordinate could improve. There was no indication that the supervisor tried to find out why the subordinate was behaving as he did.
2. *Increased supervision*: (a) Extra instruction in the area of the subordinate's poor behavior was assigned, or the supervisor spent extra time with the subordinate, closely directing his work. (b) Inspection—Frequent checkups were made on the subordinate's performance.
3. *Situational change*: (a) Reassign—New or additional duties were assigned to the subordinate, or the subordinate was reassigned to a different task. The reassignment was not made for purposes of punishment. (b) Transfer—The subordinate was transferred to a different department or shift.
4. *Penalty*: (a) Reprimand—The subordinate was rebuked for his below-standard behavior. (b) Extra work—The supervisor assigned difficult or dirty work. (c) Reduced privileges—The subordinate was penalized by temporarily denying or reducing privileges.
5. *Refer*: The subordinate was referred to a superior, a peer, a specialist, or to the personnel office. The supervisor consulted with others as to what to do. Included here were two cases where the supervisor did nothing to correct performance.
6. *Written warning* (report for military): The subordinate was given an official written warning from the company advising him that his performance was unacceptable.
7. *Man fired*: The subordinate was discharged from the company.

TABLE 31–1

Subordinate Problems Reported by Supervisors

Problem of Subordinate	Industry[a] (%)	Military[b] (%)
Appearance	0	9
Attitude	8	7
Discipline.	27	14
Work	47	42
Work and attitude.	8	7
Work and discipline.	5	5
Work and appearance.	1	6
Other multiple combinations of problems	3	10
Totals	100	100
Totals		
Total work problems mentioned	62	67
Total discipline problems	36	24
Total attitude problems	18	23
Total appearance problems	2	23

[a] $N = 131.$
[b] $N = 146.$

8. *Example:* The supervisor acted as a model in the subordinate's problem area. This involved no direct attempts at instruction.

Outcomes

While not requested, some supervisors wrote on the questionnaire that the corrective actions taken had improved the subordinate's behavior and no further difficulty with the subordinate ensued. This information was coded in the following manner: (*a*) improvement—the actions taken corrected the behavior; and (*b*) not reported.

RESULTS

Table 31–1 shows the kinds of supervisory problems reported by the supervisors. For comparative purposes, the distribution of problems reported by the naval sample is also shown.

Examination of the totals in Table 31–1 shows that problems of appearance were mentioned more frequently by the military, while problems of discipline were mentioned less frequently. Two thirds of the problems mentioned by both industrial and military supervisors involved getting subordinates to do their work properly. Problems of motivation, as reflected in the incidence of attitudinal problems, were mentioned by up to 18 percent of the industrial sample and 23 percent of the military sample. These latter findings illustrate the well-known fact that socioemotional problems constitute an important aspect of supervision.

TABLE 31–2

Corrective Actions Taken by Supervisors

Action Taken By Supervisor	Industrial[a] (%)	Military[b] (%)	Comparison of Industrial Versus Military p[c]
Verbal			
Diagnostic talk	23	18	ns
Corrective talk	42	33	ns
Increased supervision			
Extra instruction	19	33	<.01
Inspection	7	10	ns
Situational change			
Reassign	3	18	<.01
Transfer	8	1	—d
Penalty			
Reprimand (verbal).	16	5	<.01
Extra work	0	9	—d
Reduced privileges	1	8	—d
Refer	15	15	ns
Written warning (report)	7	10	ns
Man fired (industry only)	8		
Set example	1	7	—d

[a] $N = 131$.
[b] $N = 146$.
[c] p values obtained through chi-square analyses in which the number of industrial and military supervisors stating they carried out the action were compared.
[d] Chi-square not computed because of small Ns involved.

Table 31–1 also indicated that most subordinates manifested one problem at a time to their supervisors. In 17 percent of the industrial descriptions and in 28 percent of the military descriptions, subordinates were described as manifesting two or more supervisory problems simultaneously. We shall return to this finding when we consider the relation between problem complexity and solutions attempted.

The corrective actions taken by the industrial sample are shown in Table 31–2. For purposes of comparison, the actions taken by military supervisors are shown also. It should be noted that the military classifications do not include the category man fired, since such a corrective action is not used in the military. Because 43 percent of the industrial supervisors and 51 percent of the military stated they used more than one corrective action, the total percentages shown in Table 31–2 exceed 100 percent.

Both industrial and military supervisors relied upon a wide variety of powers to correct performance. Many of the actions were based upon the supervisor's persuasive powers; others relied upon actual or verbal threats of punishment; others upon the expert knowledge of the supervisor; and still others upon the power of the supervisor to make changes in the work environment of the subordinate. Between 8–10 percent of both the industrial and military supervisors invoked higher administrative levels through the actual firing of the subordinate, or through the use of official warnings, or through formal reports. Finally, about 15 percent of both groups consulted with someone as to what to do about the problem, or referred the subordinate elsewhere. In essence, these listings represent the range of powers that the industrial and military organizations allowed their supervisors to use.

It may also be observed in Table 31–2 that industrial supervisors were less likely than military supervisors to attempt direct changes in their subordinates' behaviors. That is, significantly fewer industrial supervisors reported using extra instruction ($p < .01$), or changing the pattern of the subordinate's job duties in an attempt to correct performance ($p < .01$). In terms of direct punishments that did not involve formal proceedings, industrial supervisors more frequently relied upon reprimanding their subordinates ($p < .01$), whereas military supervisors used punishments that directly changed the subordinates' working conditions through extra work assignments or reduced privileges.

Relation between Problems and Actions

The first study found a "treatment of choice" associated with each problem encountered. To determine if this held in the present sample, the 109 supervisors who reported that their subordinates presented only a single problem were sorted into three problem areas of attitudes, discipline, and work. The distribution of corrective actions taken for each problem area was then determined.

Diagnostic talks were used more frequently in incidents involving attitudes or discipline than in incidents involving work (31 percent versus 15 percent, $p < .05$). Increased supervision was used more frequently in problems of work than in problems involving attitudes and discipline (45 percent versus 6 percent, $p < .01$). Finally 14 percent of the supervisors with discipline problems stated that the subordinate was fired, as compared to 0 percent of the supervisors with attitude problems and 3 percent of the supervisors with work problems. It appears that subordinates are most likely to be fired for breaking rules. These findings closely parallel the original military findings. In that study, poor work was associated with increased supervision, poor attitudes with diagnostic talks, discipline problems with official reports and/or diagnostic talks, and poor appearance with frequent inspections.

Another finding had to do with the complexity of the problems presented by the subordinate. In both studies, when the subordinate presented two or more problems simultaneously (for example, poor attitudes and poor work), supervisors changed the job environment of the subordinate. The action of transfer was reported by 18 percent of the industrial supervisors with complex problems and 5 percent of the industrial supervisors with simple problems ($p < .10$). In the military study, the action of reassignment was used by 39 percent of the supervisors reporting complex problems and 10 percent of the supervisors with simple problems ($p < .01$).

In addition to the specific kinds of actions used, problem complexity was also related to the number of corrective actions used by the supervisor. Two or more corrective actions were used by 38 percent of the industrial supervisors with simple problems and by 62 percent of the industrial supervisors with complex problems ($p < .05$). In the military study two or more corrective actions were reported by 41 percent of the supervisors with simple problems and 76 percent of the supervisors with complex problems ($p. < .01$).

Years of Experience as a Supervisor

The military study found that less experienced supervisors more frequently referred their subordinates to someone else. This finding was repeated in the present study. Twenty-seven percent of the supervisors ($N = 40$) with 2 years or less experience stated that they referred the subordinate's problem to someone else as compared to 7 percent of the industrial supervisors ($N = 30$) with 3–8 years of experience and 12 percent of the industrial supervisors ($N = 42$) with 9 or more years of experience ($p < .05$).[7] However, the present study found no evidence that inexperienced supervisors used official warnings as was true of inexperienced military supervisors.

Number of Men Supervised and Actions Taken

There is general agreement that the more men the supervisors are required to direct, the less able they are to give their men personal attention.[8] Support for this contention was found in the military study, in that military supervisors directing large numbers of men were less likely to use extra instruction and more likely to place subordinates on official report.

In the present study it was also found that as the number of men supervised increased, the use of official warnings increased. Seventeen percent of the supervisors ($N = 35$) directing 15 or more subordinates, 3 percent of those ($N = 36$) directing 7–14 subordinates, and 0 percent of those ($N = 40$) directing less than 7 subordinates used official warnings as a means of correcting subordinates' performances ($p < .01$, comparing 14 or less versus 15 or more). The use of extra instruction, however, was not

---

[7] Nineteen supervisors did not report their years of experience.

[8] E. Dale, *Planning and Developing the Company Organization Structure*, Research Report no. 20 (Washington, D.C.: American Management Association, 1959); D. Yoder, *Personnel Management and Industrial Relations* (New York: Prentice-Hall, 1956).

related to number of men supervised. There was no relation between years experience as a supervisor and number of men supervised.[9]

Union-Nonunion

There were only 12 supervisors of union members. While this number was too small for statistical analysis, inspection revealed that in comparison to nonunion members, supervisors were less likely to talk to union members, less likely to spend time with them in extra instruction, and more likely to reprimand them or to issue official warnings as preferred means of correcting performance.

Actions and Outcomes

The more corrective actions (excluding firings) the supervisor reported, the more likely he was to state that the subordinate's performance improved. Twenty-seven percent of the supervisors who used one corrective action and 52 percent of the supervisors who used two or more corrective actions stated that their subordinates' behavior improved ($p < .05$).

DISCUSSION

The findings point to the important role of corrective powers in supervisory decision-making and problem-solving behaviors. It appears that the range of corrective powers controlled by supervisors represents the range of potential solutions that they may try when correcting subordinate's performance. This problem-solving interpretation was suggested in the present study by the relationship between the kind and complexity of the problem presented by subordinates and the kind and number of corrective actions used by supervisors. For example, complex problems led to the supervisor's trying more corrective actions, and each kind of subordinate problem evoked a different corrective action. It would follow from this interpretation that as the range of corrective powers that is allowed the supervisor is increased or decreased by management, one could expect corresponding increases or decreases in the supervisors' abilities to correct subordinates' performance.

It was further found that industrial supervisors were less directive in their attempts to correct behavior than military supervisors. The military supervisor more often corrected subordinates' performance by changing their duties, increasing the amount of direct supervision, and by penalizing them by assigning extra work and/or invoking penalties. The industrial supervisor relied more on his persuasive powers through use of diagnostic talks, corrective talks, or verbal reprimands.

Does this mean that the industrial supervisor is more "tenderhearted,"

---

[9] Twenty supervisors did not report the number of men they supervised.

or does not have a tradition of using more direct forms of action? Even a cursory reading about the industrial management scene from the 1880s through the beginning of World War II would indicate that this is not the case. Prior to World War II the industrial supervisor was more likely to be the person allowed by management to have a major voice in hiring, firing, demotions, layoffs, wages, and the general regulating of the working conditions of his subordinates. A supervisor of that time was nicknamed aptly "bull of the woods." Since that time, however, supervisory powers have been reduced by union contracts, delegation of responsibilities to staff personnel, and broad charges in management philosophy. As a result of these recent events, industrial supervisors control a smaller range of corrective powers than do their military counterparts. This reduced control is believed reflected in the greater reliance of industrial supervisors, in the present sample, upon verbal persuasion rather than upon more direct attempts to influence subordinates.

Further questions concerned with leadership powers can be organized into three areas. The first is concerned with situational factors that influence the use of supervisory powers. The present study found differences between military and industrial organizations. Within each organization, span of control and kind of problem also influenced supervisor's corrective actions.

A second question is concerned with the supervisor's own response to his possession of social powers. An interesting study by Lange and Jacobs of the actual day-to-day behaviors that distinguish between effective and ineffective leaders used their powers to reward and punish inappropriately.[10] Instead of rewarding or punishing subordinates in terms of actual job performance, they used these sanctions to curry favor or to punish irrationally. Our research strongly suggests that inexperience and lack of confidence may make the supervisor reluctant to use the full range of powers that he controls.[11]

The third question that requires attention has to do with the subordinate's response to supervisory powers. Does reprimanding an employee do any good besides allowing the supervisor to "blow off steam"? Does reassigning the problem employee improve his performance? In what ways are the employee's self-esteem, ideological allegiances, and morale affected by reliance upon the various forms of power? Many students suggest that the possession of a broad complex of powers by a leader causes the subordinate to feel uneasy, distrustful, and reluctant to reveal weaknesses in himself to his supervisors.[12] These subordinate feelings in turn lead to dis-

---

[10] C. J. Lange and T. O. Jacobs, *Leadership in Army Infantry Platoons: Study II* (Fort Benning, Ga.: U.S. Army Infantry Research Unit, 1960).

[11] See Kipnis and Lane, "Self-Confidence and Leadership."

[12] See E. B. Hutchins and F. E. Fiedler, "Task Oriented and Quasi-Therapeutic Role Functions of the Leader in Small Military Groups," *Sociometry* 23 (1960): 393–406; M. Mulder, "Power and Satisfaction in Task-Oriented Groups," *Acta Psychologica*

tortions in upward communications and approach-avoidance conflicts over interactions with supervisors.[13] Thus it may prove that increasing the range of powers controlled by the supervisor will improve his problem-solving abilities, but at the expense of provoking more guarded and defensive behaviors among subordinates.

32. SITUATIONAL FACTORS RELATED TO LEADERSHIP EFFECTIVENESS *

Fred E. Fiedler

SHOULD A LEADER concentrate mainly on giving clear and concise directions or should he concern himself first with the feelings and the attitudes of his men, so that he can establish a true partnership with them? Should he be decisive and plan for his group, or should he encourage its members to think and work with him so that they will be self-motivated to perform their best? These questions represent in somewhat simplified terms today's major controversy in leadership training and management theory. The orthodox training doctrine, which has enjoyed unquestioned pre-eminence until relatively recent times, has held that the leader must be the brain of the group. He must plan, direct, coordinate, supervise, and evaluate work done by members of his group. The newer approach, evolved in the 1940s and known variously as human-relations oriented, nondirective, or group centered, has proposed that the leader's main function lies in enabling his men to become self-directing, and in developing an atmosphere which will permit group members to contribute most creatively and constructively to the task. This approach has led most recently to developments such as brainstorming and sensitivity training.

The issues which this controversy involves are by no means trivial. These two types of philosophies have determined in large measure the

---

16 (1959): 178–225; and L. G. Wispé and K. E. Lloyd, "Some Situational and Psychological Determinants of the Desire for Structured Interpersonal Relations," *Journal of Abnormal and Social Psychology* 51 (1955): 57–60.

[13] See G. D. Mellinger, "Interpersonal Trust as a Factor in Communication," *Journal of Abnormal and Social Psychology* 52 (1956): 304–9; W. H. Read, "Upward Communication in Industrial Hierarchies," *Human Relations* 15 (1962): 3–16.

training programs of industry, the military services, and government, and executive selection and development.

The seemingly simple question, asking which of two approaches is the more effective, has been surprisingly resistant to yielding a satisfactory answer. There have been studies supporting each of these two points of view, and many management theorists have come to the conclusion that different types of groups require different types of leadership. But this knowledge is not very helpful unless we can also specify the exact conditions under which each of these two leadership styles will work best.

LEADERSHIP ABILITIES AND STYLES

Intellectual abilities and technical competence play an important part in leadership, but within any given situation or supervisory level, differences in intelligence and ability tend to be small. The majority of top executives tend to fall into the superior intelligence group, and most shop foremen tend to have a high degree of technical knowledge of the work. Moreover, the relationship between intelligence and ability of a leader and the performance of his group tends to be small. Most research on leadership and supervision has concerned itself with personality and behavior which are related to the two major types of leadership styles.

The classical studies by K. Lewin and his associates comparing autocratic and democratic boys' groups set in motion a number of research programs in this area. Most of these studies have moved towards the use of personality and behavior for comparing task-centered and person-centered styles of leadership—autocratic versus democratic, structuring versus considerate, directive versus nondirective leadership.

The emphasis on these particular styles of leadership and attitudes is not too surprising. Leadership is essentially a relationship in which one person uses his power and influence in getting a number of people to work together and accomplish a common task. There are, after all, only a limited number of ways in which one person can get others to do his bidding. He can drive, order, or direct them, or he can guide, cajole, or get them involved in the task. The leader can devote himself to directing the task, or he can devote himself to seeing to it that his members become self-motivating and self-directing.

The research program on leadership effectiveness which we conducted under a contract from the United States Office of Naval Research was concerned with predicting group performance, and it used a measure related to two types of leadership. In a simple test an individual thinks of all the people with whom he has ever worked and then he is asked to describe the one person with whom he had most difficulty in working—his least preferred co-worker (LPC). The description is made on 20 items such as friendly or unfriendly, cooperative or uncooperative. The so-called LPC score is obtained by giving each of the 20 scale items a weight of one to eight points, with eight points indicating the favorable pole of the item, and totaling the points for the various items. Thus, a person with a high LPC score is one who describes his least preferred co-worker in relatively favorable, accepting terms; someone with a low score describes his least preferred co-worker in relatively unfavorable, rejecting terms. As previous studies have shown, leaders with high LPC scores tend to be permissive, nondirective, considerate in their reactions to group members, while leaders with low scores tend to be directive, managing, task controlling in their leadership behavior.

Our research program has involved a wide variety of groups, from basketball teams and surveying parties to military combat crews, open-hearth steel shops, small business concerns, and various laboratory and field experimental groups engaged in creative tasks. These studies have yielded high correlations between the LPC score of the leader and measures of actual group performance. However, in some studies the permissive, considerate leaders had the best performing groups while the managing, controlling, directive leaders had groups which yielded the best results in other cases.

MAJOR FACTORS AFFECTING LEADER INFLUENCE

In order to tell which style fits which situation, we need to categorize groups. Our research has shown that "it all depends" on the situation. After reviewing the results of all our work and the findings of other investigators, we have been able to isolate three major dimensions that seem to determine, to a large part, the kind of leadership style called for by different situations.

It is obviously a mistake to think that groups and teams are all alike and that each requires the same kind of leadership. We need some way of categorizing the group-task situation, or the job environment within which the leader has to operate. If leadership is indeed a process of influencing other people to work together effectively in a common task, then it surely matters how easy or difficult it is for the leader to exert his influence in a particular situation.

Leader-Member Relations. The factor that would seem most important in determining a man's leadership influence is the degree to which his group members trust and like him, and are willing to follow his guidance. The trusted and well-liked leader obviously does not require special rank or power in order to get things done. We can measure the leader-member relationship by the so-called sociometric nomination techniques that ask group members to name in their group the most influential person, or the man they would most like to have as a leader. It can also be measured by a group-atmosphere scale indicating the degree to which the leader feels accepted and comfortable in the group.

The Task Structure. The second important factor is the "task structure." By this term I mean the degree to which the task (*a*) is spelled out step by step for the group and, if so, the extent to which it can be done "by the numbers" or according to a detailed set of standard operating instructions, or (*b*) must be left nebulous and undefined. Vague and ambiguous or unstructured tasks make it difficult to exert leadership influence, because neither the leader nor his members know exactly what has to be done or how it is to be accomplished.

Why single out this aspect of the task rather than the innumerable other possible ways of describing it? Task groups are almost invariably components of a larger organization that assigns the task and has, therefore, a big stake in seeing it performed properly. However, the organization can control the quality of a group's performance only if the task is clearly spelled out and programmed or structured. When the task can be programmed or performed "by the numbers," the organization is able to back up the authority of the leader to the fullest; the man who fails to perform each step can be disciplined or fired. But in the case of ill-defined, vague, or unstructured tasks, the organization and the leader have very little control and direct power. By close supervision one can ensure, let us say, that a man will correctly operate a machine, but one cannot ensure that he will be creative.

It is therefore easier to be a leader in a structured task situation in which the work is spelled out than in an unstructured one which presents the leader and his group with a nebulous, poorly defined problem.

Position Power. Thirdly, there is the power of the leadership position, as distinct from any personal power the leader might have. Can he hire or fire and promote or demote? Is his appointment for life, or will it terminate at the pleasure of his group? It is obviously easier to be a leader when the position power is strong than when it is weak.

MODEL FOR ANALYSIS

When we now classify groups on the basis of these three dimensions, we get a classification system that can be represented as a cube; see Exhibit 32–1. As each group is high or low in each of the three dimensions, it will fall into one of the eight cells.

From examination of the cube, it seems clear that exerting leadership influence will be easier in a group in which the members like a powerful leader with a clearly defined job and where the job to be done is clearly laid out (Cell I); it will be difficult in a group where a leader is disliked, has little power, and has a highly ambiguous job (Cell 8).

In other words, it is easier to be the well-esteemed foreman of a construction crew working from a blueprint than it is to be the disliked chairman of a volunteer committee preparing a new policy.

I consider the leader-member relations the most important dimension, and the position-power dimension the least important, of the three. It is,

EXHIBIT 32–1

A Model for Classifying Group-Task Situations

for instance, quite possible for a man of low rank to lead a group of higher-ranking men in a structured task—as is done when enlisted men or junior officers conduct some standardized parts of the training programs for medical officers who enter the Army. But it is not so easy for a dis-respected manager to lead a creative, policy-formulating session well, even if he is the senior executive present.

VARYING REQUIREMENTS

By first sorting the eight cells according to leader-member relations, then task structure, and finally leader position power, we can now arrange them in order according to the favorableness of the environment for the leader. This sorting leads to an eight-step scale, as in Exhibit 32–2. This exhibit portrays the results of a series of studies of groups performing well but (*a*) in different situations and conditions, and (*b*) with leaders using different leadership styles. In explanation:

The *horizontal* axis shows the range of situations that the groups worked in, as described by the classification scheme used in Exhibit 32–1.

The *vertical* axis indicates the leadership style which was best in a

EXHIBIT 32–2

How the Style of Effective Leadership Varies with the Situation

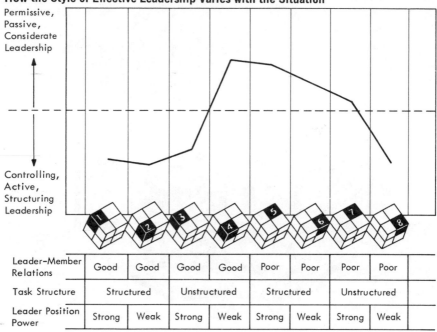

Leader–Member Relations	Good	Good	Good	Good	Poor	Poor	Poor	Poor	
Task Structure	Structured		Unstructured		Structured		Unstructured		
Leader Position Power	Strong	Weak	Strong	Weak	Strong	Weak	Strong	Weak	

certain situation, as shown by the correlation coefficient between the leader's LPC and his group's performance.

A positive correlation (falling above the midline) shows that the permissive, nondirective, and human-relations-oriented leaders performed best; a negative correlation (below the midline) shows that the task-controlling, managing leader performed best. For instance, leaders of effective groups in situation categories 1 and 2 had LPC-group performance correlations of −.40 to −.80, with the average between −.50 and −.60; whereas leaders of effective groups in situation categories 4 and 5 had LPC-group performance correlations of .20 to .80, with the average between .40 and .50.

Exhibit 32–2 shows that both the directive, managing, task-oriented leaders and the nondirective, human-relations-oriented leaders are successful under some conditions. Which leadership style is the best depends on the favorableness of the particular situation for the leader. In very favorable or in very unfavorable situations for getting a task accomplished by group effort, the autocratic, task-controlling, managing leadership works best. In situations intermediate in difficulty, the nondirective, permissive leader is more successful.

This corresponds well with our everyday experience. For instance:

Where the situation is very favorable, the group expects and wants the leader to give directions. We neither expect nor want the trusted airline pilot to turn to his crew and ask, "What do you think we ought to check before takeoff?"

If the disliked chairman of a volunteer committee asks his group what to do, he may be told that everybody ought to go home.

The well-liked chairman of a planning group or research team must be nondirective and permissive in order to get full participation from his members. The directive, managing leader will tend to be more critical and to cut discussion short; hence he will not get the full benefit of the potential contributions by his group members.

The varying requirements of leadership styles are readily apparent in organizations experiencing dramatic changes in operating procedures. For example:

The manager or supervisor of a routinely operating organization is expected to provide direction and supervision that the subordinates should follow. However, in a crisis the routine is no longer adequate, and the task becomes ambiguous and unstructured. The typical manager tends to respond in such instances by calling his principal assistants together for a conference. In other words, the effective leader changes his behavior from a directive to a permissive, nondirective style until the operation again reverts to routine conditions.

In the case of a research planning group, the human-relations-oriented and permissive leader provides a climate in which everybody is free to speak up, to suggest, and to criticize. Osborn's brainstorming method [1] in fact institutionalizes these procedures. However, after the research plan has been completed, the situation becomes highly structured. The director now prescribes the task in detail, and he specifies the means of accomplishing it. Woe betide the assistant who decides to be creative by changing the research instructions!

PRACTICAL TESTS

Remember that the ideas I have been describing emanate from studies of real-life situations; accordingly, as might be expected, they can be validated by organizational experience. Take, for instance, the dimension of leader-member relations described earlier. We have made three studies of situations in which the leader's position power was strong and the task relatively structured with clear-cut goals and standard operating procedures. In such groups as these the situation will be very favorable for the leader if he is accepted; it will be progressively unfavorable in proportion to how much a leader is disliked. What leadership styles succeed in these

---

[1] See Alex F. Osborn, *Applied Imagination* (New York: Charles Scribner's Sons, 1953).

EXHIBIT 32–3

How Effective Leadership Styles Vary Depending on Group Acceptance

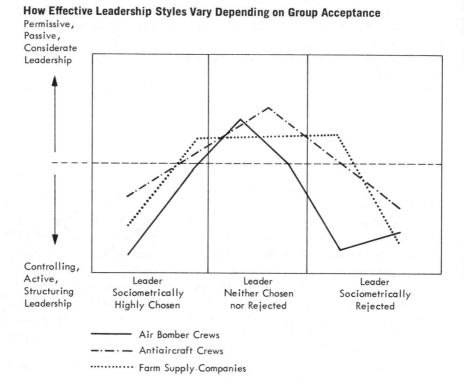

────── Air Bomber Crews

─·—·— Antiaircraft Crews

············ Farm Supply Companies

varying conditions? The studies confirm what our theory would lead us to expect:

The first set of data comes from a study of B-29 bomber crews in which the criterion was the accuracy of radar bombing. Six degrees of leader-member relations were identified, ranging from those in which the aircraft commander was the first choice of crew members and highly endorsed his radar observer and navigator (the key men in radar bombing) to those in which he was chosen by his crew but did not endorse his key men, and finally to crews in which the commander was rejected by his crew and rejected his key crew members. What leadership styles were effective? The results are plotted in Exhibit 32–3.

A study of antiaircraft crews compares the ten most chosen crew commanders, the ten most rejected ones, and ten of intermediate popularity. The criterion is the identification and "acquisition" of unidentified aircraft by the crew. The results shown in Exhibit 32–3 are similar to those for bomber-crew commanders.

Exhibit 32–3 also summarizes data for 32 small-farm supply companies. These were member companies of the same distribution system, each with its own board of directors and its own management. The performance of these highly comparable companies was measured in terms of percentage of company net income over a 3-year period. The first quarter of the line (going from left to right) depicts endorsement of the general manager by his board of directors and his staff of assistant managers; the second quarter, endorsement by his board but not his staff; the third quarter, endorsement by his staff but not his board; the fourth quarter, endorsement by neither.

As can be seen from the results of all three studies, the highly accepted and strongly rejected leaders perform best if they are controlling and managing, while the leaders in the intermediate acceptance range, who are neither rejected nor accepted, perform best if they are permissive and nondirective.

Now let us look at some research on organizations in another country:

Recently in Belgium a study was made of groups of mixed language and cultural composition. Such teams, which are becoming increasingly frequent as international business and governmental activities multiply, obviously present a difficult situation for the leader. He must not only deal with men who do not fully comprehend one another's language and meanings, but also cope with the typical antipathies, suspicions, and antagonisms dividing individuals of different cultures and nationalities.

At a Belgium naval-training center we tested 96 three-man groups, half of which were homogeneous in composition (all Flemish or all Walloon) and half heterogeneous (the leader differing from his men). Half of each of these had powerful leader positions (petty officers), and half had recruit leaders. Each group performed three tasks: one unstructured task (writing a recruiting letter) and two parallel structured tasks (finding the shortest route for ships through ten ports, and doing the same for twelve ports). After each task, leaders and group members described their reactions— including group-atmosphere ratings and the indication of leader-member relations.

The various task situations were then arranged in order, according to their favorableness for the leader. The most favorable situation was a homogeneous group, led by a well-liked and accepted petty officer, which worked on the structured task of routing a ship. The situation would be especially favorable toward the end of the experiment, after the leader had had time to get to know his members. The least favorable situation was that of an unpopular recruit leader of a heterogeneous group where the relatively unstructured task of writing a letter came up as soon as the group was formed.

There were six groups that fell into each of these situations or cells. A correlation was then computed for each set of six groups to determine which type of leadership style led to best team performance. The results, indicated in Exhibit 32–4, support the conclusions earlier described.

Of particular interest is the fact that the difficult heterogeneous groups

EXHIBIT 32–4

Effective Leadership Styles at Belgian Naval-Training Center

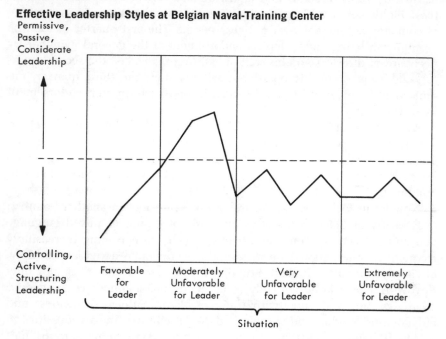

generally required controlling, task-oriented leadership for good performance. This fits the descriptions of successful leader behavior obtained from executives who have worked in international business organizations.

CONCLUSION

Provided our findings continue to be supported in the future, what do these results and the theory mean for executive selection and training? What implications do they have for the management of large organizations?

Selection and Training

Business and industry are now trying to attract an increasingly large share of exceptionally intelligent and technically well-trained men. Many of these are specialists whose talents are in critically short supply. Can industry really afford to select only those men who have a certain style of leadership in addition to their technical qualifications? The answer is likely to be negative, at least in the near future.

This being the case, can we then train the men selected in one leadership style or the other? This approach is always offered as a solution, and it does have merit. But we must recognize that training people is at best difficult, costly, and time-consuming. It is certainly easier to place people in a situation compatible with their natural leadership style than to force them to adapt to the demands of the job.

As another alternative, should executives learn to recognize or diagnose group-task situations so that they can place their subordinates, managers, and department heads in the jobs best suited to their leadership styles? Even this procedure has serious disadvantages. The organization may not always happen to have the place that fits the bright young man. The experienced executive may not want to be moved, or it may not be possible to transfer him.

Should the organization try to "engineer" the job to fit the man? This alternative is potentially the most feasible for management. As has been shown already, the type of leadership called for depends on the favorableness of the situation. The favorableness, in turn, is a product of several factors. These include leader-member relations, the homogeneity of the group, and the position power and degree to which the task is structured, as well as other, more obvious factors such as the leader's knowledge of his group, his familiarity with the task, and so forth.

It is clear that management can change the characteristic favorableness of the leadership situation; it can do so in most cases more easily than it can transfer the subordinate leader from one job to another or train him in a different style of interacting with his members.

Possibilities of Change

Although this type of organizational engineering has not been done systematically up to now, we can choose from several good possibilities for getting the job done:

1. *We can change the leader's position power.* Either we can give him subordinates of equal or nearly equal rank or we can give him men who are two or three ranks below him. We can either give him sole authority for the job or require that he consult with this group, or even obtain unanimous consent for all decisions. We can either punctiliously observe the channels of the organization to increase the leader's prestige or communicate directly with the men of his group as well as with him in person.

2. *We can change the task structure.* The tasks given to one leader may have to be clarified in detail, and he may have to be given precise operating instructions; another leader may have to be given more general problems that are only vaguely elucidated.

3. *We can change the leader-member relations.* The Belgian study referred to earlier demonstrates that changing the group composition changes the leader's relations with his men. We can increase or decrease the group's heterogeneity by introducing men with similar attitudes,

beliefs, and backgrounds, or by bringing in men different in training, culture, and language.

The foregoing are, of course, only examples of what could be done. The important point is that we now have a model and a set of principles that permit predictions of leadership effectiveness in interacting groups and allow us to take a look at the factors affecting team performance. This approach goes beyond the traditional notions of selection and training. It focuses on the more fruitful possibility of organizational engineering as a means of using leadership potentials in the management ranks.

Section Six

COMMUNICATION AND ORGANIZATIONAL BEHAVIOR

INTRODUCTION

IN THIS SECTION we continue our examination of social-psychological aspects of behavior in organizations. For convenience we have linked the areas of communication and organization behavior, although these can scarcely be separated from much of our previous discussion of leadership, motivation, and morale. All involve interpersonal relationships among individuals. However, in large organizations some problems take an additional emphasis and significance, and it is to these problems we now turn.

First of all, it may be well to define what an organization is. An organization can be thought of as the rational coordination of a number of people for the achievement of some common goal (or goals). This is achieved through division of labor and function, and through a hierarchy of authority and responsibility.[1] There are, of course, "formal" organizations, such as those outlined on an organization chart, and "informal" organizations, which arise spontaneously out of interactions among people. Both kinds of organizations exist within a single plant, as will be discussed in this section. Many important problems stem from the complex interaction of formal and informal organizations.

Organizations consist of various levels, functions, and subunits, structured into different systems of relationships. As we will see later, social

---

[1] For an elaboration of this definition, see E. H. Schein, *Organizational Psychology*, 2d ed. (Englewood Cliffs, N.J.: Prentice-Hall, 1970). See also, B. M. Bass, *Organizational Psychology* (Boston: Allyn and Bacon, 1965).

scientists have been questioning traditional models (for example, bureaucratic, hierarchical models) of organizational performance. And there is an increasing amount of research on properties of organizations related to performance and attitudes of individuals within these organizations.[2]

An important aspect of the behavior of individuals in organizations is the communication problem. This is the problem of the transmittal of information accurately and efficiently. More is involved here than factual information, since feelings and attitudes are also communicated. As the organization becomes more complex, so do problems of communication.[3]

The problem of organizational communication can be considered from several perspectives. First, there is the problem of *channels* of communication. This consists of the network of channels through which information flows. Some networks are more effective than others, and there are informal as well as formal communication channels. Davis,[4] for example, has described a method for studying organizational communication channels and has characterized such channels along a number of dimensions such as speed of transmission, degree of selectivity, and so forth. He has particularly emphasized the importance of investigating and understanding the operation of informal, "grapevine" communication channels in organizations and integration of such grapevine channels with the more formal communication activities of the organization. Seashore [5] provides a general discussion of the problems of organizational communication processes and points out that communications in organizations are significantly influenced by the nature of the people and the social systems within the organization, as well as by the particular organizational channels which happen to be used.

One question which might be asked is whether certain communication patterns or networks are more effective or more efficient than others in transmitting information. The first article in this section, "An Experimental Approach to Organizational Communication," by Bavelas and Barrett, approaches this "network problem" from the point of view of the small, task-oriented group. These authors point out that even small groups can differ in their commmunication patterns, and they investigate several different communication patterns in terms of their effect on group perfor-

---

[2] In particular, see L. W. Porter and E. E. Lawler, "Properties of Organizational Structure in Relation to Job Attitudes and Job Behavior," *Psychological Bulletin* 64 (1965): 23–51. The article reviews empirical studies on such variables as span of control, subunit size, total-organization size, tall/flat shape, centralized/decentralized shape, line/staff hierarchies.

[3] For a general discussion of problems of human communication and psychological research relevant thereto, see A. Chapanis, "Prelude to 2001: Explorations in Human Communication," *American Psychologist* 26 (1971): 949–61.

[4] K. Davis, "Management Communication and The Grapevine," *Harvard Business Review* 31 (1953): 43–49.

[5] S. Seashore, "Communication in Organizations," in *Management of the Urban Crisis*, edited by S. E. Seashore and R. J. McNeill (New York: Free Press, 1971).

mance. The article shows how these communication networks can be quantified and related to a variety of indices of "effectiveness." [6]

The important link between motivation and communication needs to be emphasized. Thus, subordinates may be reluctant to ask supervisors for help when they need it, if this is seen as a threatening admission of their inadequacy; and supervisors may hold back information which may reflect unfavorably on their competence. Even when communication apparently has taken place, what gets through depends on one's values, needs, and so forth. For example, one study asked executives to read a company case history and to identify its chief problem. Although each person read the same factual material, the particular problem identified (such as sales, human relations, or production) depended on the executive's own specialty.[7]

We return now to the basic problem of transmitting information from one individual to another. The article by Leavitt and Mueller, "Some Effects of Feedback on Communication," discusses this problem. The authors describe some experiments on the important variable of feedback and its relation to different criteria of communication effectiveness. The implications of these studies to supervisor-subordinate communication are especially relevant.

The remaining articles in this section take a broader view of human behavior and human problems in organizations. There have been many recent approaches to developing theories and models about organizational functioning. Some of these organizational theories have been useful in conceptualizing how organizations work. Others have been more concerned with the theoretician's ideas on how an organization *should* be constructed to achieve certain goals (for example, to maximize individual as well as organizational needs). Whatever the intent, there have been a number of alternatives proposed and no definite agreement on which model is best. It is important to note, however, that the generation of these theories leads to research which should allow tests to be made of the utility of the assumptions made by these different systems. In the next article, "Organizational Developments and the Fate of Bureaucracy," Bennis discusses the assumptions of traditional organizational systems, reviews the various organization theories which have been developed, and then makes forecasts about organizations of the future.[8]

---

[6] For a later review of studies of effectiveness of communication networks, see M. Shaw, "Communication Networks," in *Advances in Experimental Social Psychology*, vol. 1, edited by L. Berkowitz (New York: Academic Press, 1964).

[7] D. C. Dearborn and H. Simon, "Selective Perception: A Note on the Departmental Identifications of Executives," *Sociometry* 21 (1958).

[8] For a recent critical review of a number of these different approaches to organizational functioning, along with a comprehensive discussion of the relationships between organizational requirements and individual personality, see C. M. Lichtman and R. G. Hunt, "Personality and Organization Theory: A Review of Some Conceptual Literature," *Psychological Bulletin* 76 (1971): 271–94.

The next article, "Being Human and Being Organized," by Argyris, describes an organizational theory which has received considerable attention. Argyris contends that traditional organizational structures and systems are in conflict with certain basic individual needs (such as needs for independence and challenge). He calls for new approaches to maintaining organizational efficiency which have the effect of maximizing opportunities for individual freedom and development. It is interesting to compare these ideas with the notion of job enrichment (which we met earlier in the article by Herzberg in Section Four) and with the objectives of sensitivity training (which we also met earlier in the article by Dunnette and Campbell in Section Three). Both of these might be approaches to solving the dilemma of individual-organizational conflict posed by Argyris.[9]

One of the most critical issues in the study of organizations is the need for better methods of diagnosing organizational effectiveness. Adequate criteria of organizational effectiveness are obviously needed if we are to evaluate the consequences of various organizational changes, or if we are to evaluate the usefulness of the various organizational theories which have been proposed (see Article 35). Recent thinking suggests that traditional criteria have been too narrow in scope (for example, profits during a given period) and need to be expanded to include such variables as development of the potentials of organization members, attitude of employees, and flexibility of the organization to meet new problems. The next article, "Organizational Theory and Human Resource Accounting," by Likert and Bowers, reviews the work of the Institute for Social Research at the University of Michigan on this problem. Research is described which attempts to determine linkages between three sets of organizational variables: (1) causal variables, such as organizational structure or management style; (2) intervening variables, such as employee attitudes and effectiveness of organizational communication; and (3) end-result variables such as organizational efficiency and financial performance. The article stresses the need for accurate measurements of the value of the human resources of an organization, and the use of such measurements in evaluating the effectiveness of various organizational changes that might be implemented.

One relatively well-known and far-reaching program of organizational change is described in the next article, "Durability of Organizational Change," by Seashore and Bowers. This was essentially an attempt to change the management style of a garment manufacturing organization from a predominantly authoritarian management philosophy to a par-

---

[9] Argyris has suggested the use of sensitivity training as a technique for developing openness, trust, and more effective interpersonal communication among organizational members. See C. Argyris, *Management and Organizational Development: the Path from xa to yb* (New York: McGraw-Hill Book Co., 1971); idem, "T-Groups for Organizational Effectiveness," *Harvard Business Review* 42 (1964).

ticipative, employee-centered management philosophy, primarily based on the organizational theory of Likert.[10] The article describes the evidence for the changes in employee attitudes and performance that occurred as a result of the organizational intervention process and emphasizes the durability of the changes that occurred, over a period of approximately seven years. This research serves to strengthen the case for the value of participation and increasing employee independence and responsibility, as has been stressed in several other papers in this volume.

Another important aspect of an organization is the organizational climate, or predominant value system that pervades the organization.[11] A number of researchers have emphasized the need for studying organizational climates, particularly with a view toward identifying combinations of organizational climates and individual personalities which would be most compatible.[12] The next article by Andrews, "The Achievement Motive and Advancement in Two Types of Organizations," demonstrates how organizational climate and individual needs are related. In one type of organization, individuals who were primarily motivated by achievement needs were rewarded by advancement in the organization, whereas in another organization such individuals were typically ignored in favor of those with high needs for power and domination over others. Thus, the organizational climate is a powerful factor in determining the type of individual who will be successful within a particular organization.

SUGGESTED ADDITIONAL READINGS

Bass, B. M., and Deep, S. D. *Studies in Organizational Psychology*. Boston: Allyn and Bacon, 1972.

Forehand, G. A., and Gilmer, B. v.H. "Environmental Variation in Studies of Organizational Behavior." *Psychological Bulletin* 62 (1964): 361–82.

Ghorpade, J. *Assessment of Organizational Effectiveness: Issues, Analysis, Readings*. Pacific Palisades, Calif.: Goodyear Publishing Co., 1971.

Katz, D., and Kahn, R. L. *The Social Psychology of Organizations*. New York: John Wiley & Sons, 1966.

March, J. G., ed. *Handbook of Organizations*. Chicago: Rand McNally, 1965.

[10] R. Likert, *New Patterns of Management* (New York: McGraw-Hill Book Co., 1961); idem, *The Human Organization* (New York: McGraw-Hill Book Co., 1967).

[11] For a comprehensive treatment of problems in the conceptualization and identification of organizational climate variables, see R. Tagiuri and G. H. Litwin, *Organizational Climate: Explorations of a Concept* (Boston: Harvard University Graduate School of Business Administration, 1968).

[12] See, for example, B. M. Bass, "Interface between Personnel and Organizational Psychology," *Journal of Applied Psychology* 52 (1968): 81–88; G. A. Forehand, "On the Interaction of Persons and Organizations," in *Organizational Climate*, edited by R. Tagiuri and G. A. Litwin (Boston: Harvard University Graduate School of Business Administration, 1968), pp. 65–82; B. Schneider and C. J. Bartlett, "Individual Differences and Organizational Climate. I. The Research Plan and Questionnaire Development," *Personnel Psychology* 21 (1968): 323–34; idem, "Individual Differences and Organizational Climate," *The Industrial Psychologist* 7 (1969): 27–33.

March, J. G., and Simon, H. A. *Organizations.* New York: John Wiley & Sons, 1958.

Miller, E. J., and Rice, A. K. *Systems of Organization.* London: Tavistock, 1967.

Perrow, C. *Complex Organizations: A Critical Essay.* Glenview, Ill.: Scott, Foresman, 1970.

Pugh, D. S. "Modern Organizational Theory: A Psychological and Sociological Study." *Psychological Bulletin,* 66 (1966): 235–51.

Scott, W. G., and Mitchell, T. R. *Organization Theory: A Structural and Behavioral Analysis.* rev. ed., Homewood, Ill.: Richard D. Irwin, Inc., 1972.

33. AN EXPERIMENTAL APPROACH TO ORGANIZATIONAL COMMUNICATION [*]

Alex Bavelas and Dermot Barrett

COMMUNICATION AS A CRITICAL ASPECT of organization has been attracting more and more attention. If one may judge from articles and speeches, much of the current thinking on communication centers around categories of problems which arise in day-to-day operations—"getting management's point of view to the workers," "stimulating communication up the line as well as down," "obtaining better communication with the union," "establishing more effective communication within management, and especially with the foremen." Knowing how such questions usually arise, it is not surprising that their discussion invariably resolves itself into considerations of *content* and *technique*: on the one hand, analyses of what management ought to be saying to the worker, the union, the foreman; on the other hand, descriptions of devices which can best say it—bulletin boards, letters, films, public address systems, meetings, and so forth. In its extreme form this approach becomes one of searching for a specific remedy for a specific ill. Helpful and practical as this may be, it is doubtful that such activity can lead to the discovery and understanding of the basic principles of effective organizational communication. Breakdowns and other difficulties at some point of a communication system are often only superficially related to the local conditions which appear to have produced them. They may, rather, be cumulative effects of properties of the entire communication system taken as a whole. But what are these properties, if, indeed, they exist?

---

[*] From *Personnel* 27 (1951): 366–71.

FORMAL AND INFORMAL SYSTEMS

An organizational system of communication is usually created by the setting up of formal systems of responsibility and by explicit delegations of duties. These categories include statements, often implicitly, of the nature, content, and direction of the communication which is considered necessary for the performance of the group. Students of organization, however, have pointed out repeatedly that groups tend to depart from such formal statements and to create other channels of communication and dependence. In other words, informal organizational systems emerge. One may take the view that these changes are adaptations by the individuals involved in the direction of easier and more effective ways of working, or, perhaps, not working. It is no secret that informal groups are not always viewed by managers as favorable to the goals of the larger body. Also, it is by no means obvious that those informal groupings which evolve out of social and personality factors are likely to be more efficient (with respect to organizational tasks) than those set up formally by the managers. Altogether, if one considers how intimate the relations are between communication channels and control, it is not surprising that the managers of organizations would prefer explicit and orderly communication lines.

Is There "One Best Way?"

Unfortunately, there seems to be no organized body of knowledge out of which one can derive, for a given organization, an optimal communication system. Administrative thinking on this point commonly rests upon the assumption that the optimum system *can* be derived from a statement of the task to be performed. It is not difficult to show, however, that from a given set of specifications one may derive not a single communication pattern but a whole set of them, all logically adequate for the successful performance of the task in question. Which pattern from this set should be chosen? The choice, in practice, is usually made either in terms of a group of assumptions (often quite untenable) about human nature, or in terms of a personal bias on the part of the chooser. The seriousness of this situation is illustrated by the following example.

Let us assume that we have a group of five individuals who, in order to solve a problem, must share as quickly as possible the information each person possesses. Let us also assume that there are reasons which prevent them from meeting around a table, and that they must share this information by writing notes. To avoid the confusion and waste of time of each person writing a message to each of the others, a supervisor decides to set up channels in which the notes must go. He strikes upon the pattern shown in Figure 33–1.

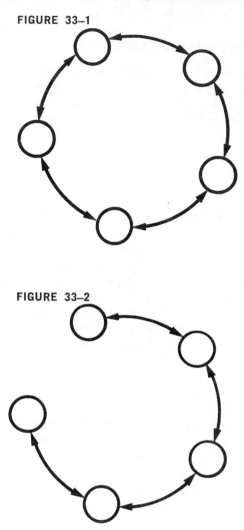

FIGURE 33–1

FIGURE 33–2

In this arrangement each individual can send to and receive messages from two others, one on his "left" and one on his "right." Experiments actually performed with this kind of situation show that the number of mistakes made by individuals working in such a "circle" pattern can be reduced by fully 60 percent by the simple measure of *removing one link*, thus making the pattern a "chain" as shown in Figure 33–2. The relevance of such a result to organization communication is obvious, simple though the example is. The sad truth, however, is that this phenomenon is not clearly derivable either from traditional "individual psychology" or from commonly held theories of group communication.

An Integral Process of Organization

Perhaps some headway can be made by approaching the general problem from a somewhat different direction. In the affairs of organizations, as well as in the affairs of men, chance always plays a part. However good a plan may be, however carefully prepared its execution, there is a point beyond which the probability of its success cannot be increased. With the firmest of intentions, agreements and promises may be impossible to carry out because of unforeseen events. Nevertheless, an organization whose functioning is too often interrupted by unforeseen events is looked upon with suspicion. Bad luck is an unhappy plea, and it may well be that the "unlucky" organization is more to be avoided than the simply incompetent one. On the other hand, few things about an organization are more admired and respected than the ability to "deliver" despite widely varying conditions and in the face of unusual difficulties.

In a very broad sense, it may be argued that the principal effort of organizational activities is the making of favorable conditions for the achievement of certain goals. In other words, an effort is made to increase, as much as the economics of the situation will permit, the probabilities of succeeding. This is the essence of the manager's job. The development of training and selection programs, the improvement of methods and the specification of techniques, the organization of research and development activities, the designation of responsibility and the delegation of duties— all these processes have one organizationally legitimate purpose: to increase the chances of organizational success. Upon this point rest almost all of the notions by which we are accustomed to evaluate organizations—in part or as a whole.

An organization is, in short, a social invention—a kind of "machine" for increasing certain sets of probabilities. (Which sets of probabilities are given to it to increase, which it chooses, how freely and by what means will not be discussed here. These problems, although they lie well within the scope of this subject, are outside the range of this paper. We will confine ourselves to a consideration of the process by which an accepted set of probabilities is optimized.) Probabilities of success are increased, however, only by taking relevant and appropriate actions. For the manager, these actions reduce in most instances to the gathering and evaluating of information in the form of reports, schedules, estimates, and so forth. It is entirely possible to view an organization as an elaborate system for gathering, evaluating, recombining, and disseminating information. It is not surprising, in these terms, that the effectiveness of an organization with respect to the achievement of its goals should be so closely related to its effectiveness in handling information. In an enterprise whose success hinges upon the coordination of the efforts of all its members, the managers depend completely upon the quality, the amount, and the rate

FIGURE 33–3

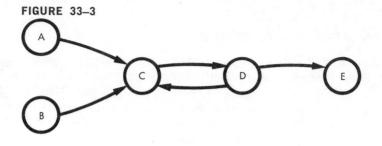

at which relevant information reaches them. The rest of the organization, in turn, depends upon the efficiency with which the managers can deal with this information and reach conclusions, decisions, etc. This line of reasoning leads us to the belief that communication is not a secondary or derived aspect of organization—a "helper" of the other and presumably more basic functions. Rather it is the essence of organized activity and is the basic process out of which all other functions derive. The goals an organization selects, the methods it applies, the effectiveness with which it improves its own procedures—all of these hinge upon the quality and availability of the information in the system.

Patterns of Communication

About two years ago a series of studies was begun whose purpose was to isolate and study certain general properties of information handling systems. The first phase of this research program [1] is directed at a basic property of all communication systems, that of connection or "who can talk to whom."

This property of connection can be conveniently expressed by diagrams. The meaning of the picture in Figure 33–3 is obvious. Individuals A and B can send messages to C but they can receive messages from no one; C and D can exchange messages; E can receive messages from D, but he can send messages to no one. The pattern shown in Figure 33–3, however, is only one of the many that are possible. A group of others is shown in Figure 33–4. An examination of these patterns will show that they fall into two classes, separated by a very important difference. Any pair of individuals in each of the patterns D, E, and F can exchange messages either directly or indirectly over some route. No pair of individuals in each of the patterns A, B, and C can exchange messages. Patterns like A, B, and C obviously make any coordination of thought or action virtually impossible; we will be concerned from this point on only with patterns like D, E, and F.

---

[1] These studies are supported jointly by the Rand Corporation and the Research Laboratory of Electronics at MIT.

FIGURE 33–4

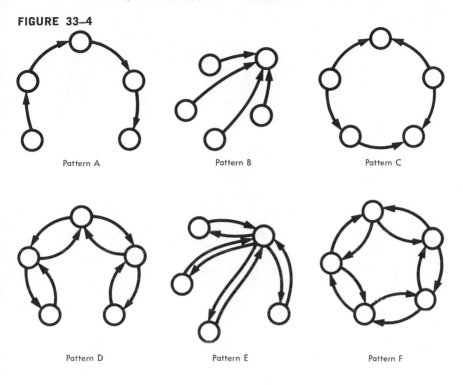

Pattern A   Pattern B   Pattern C

Pattern D   Pattern E   Pattern F

Since the individuals in any connected pattern like D, and E, and F can share ideas completely, should we expect that the effectiveness of individuals in performing group tasks or solving group problems would be the same in patterns D, E, and F except for differences in ability, knowledge, and personality? Should we expect differences in quality, and speed of performance? Is it likely that the individuals working in one pattern would show significantly better morale than the individuals working in a different pattern? Sidney Smith and Harold J. Leavitt conducted a series of experiments which yielded very definite answers to these questions.[2] An experimental design was used which made it possible to equate the difficulty of the tasks which the groups performed, and which permitted the canceling of individual differences by randomizing the assignment of subjects to patterns. Also, the experiment was repeated with different groups enough times to establish the consistency of the results. A brief summary of the findings is given in Figure 33–5. The use of qualitative terms in Figure 33–5 in place of the quantitative measurements which were actually made blurs the comparison somewhat, but it gives a fair picture of the way these patterns performed. Since the orginial experi-

---

[2] Harold J. Leavitt reports these experiments in detail in the *Journal of Abnormal and Social Psychology*, January 1951.

FIGURE 33–5

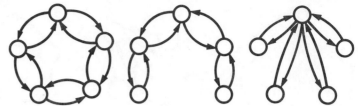

Speed	Slow	Fast	Fast
Accuracy	Poor	Good	Good
Organization	No Stable Form of Organization	Slowly Emerging but Stable Organization	Almost Immediate and Stable Organization
Emergence of Leader	None	Marked	Very Pronounced
Morale	Very Good	Poor	Very Poor

FIGURE 33–6

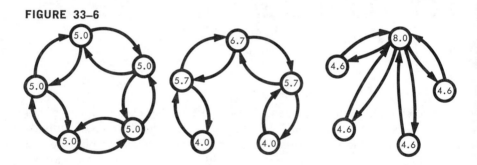

ments were done by Smith and Leavitt, this experiment has been re-peated with no change in the findings.

The question very properly arises here as to whether these findings can be "explained" in the sense of being related to the connection properties of the patterns themselves. The answer to this question is a qualified yes. Wtihout developing the mathematical analysis, which can be found in Leavitt's paper, the following statements can be made:

For any connected pattern, an *index of dispersion* can be calculated. Relative to this index, there can be calculated for *each position in each pattern* an *index of centrality* and an *index of peripherality*. The data suggest strongly that the rapidity with which organization emerges and the stability it displays are related to the gradient of the indices of centrality in the pattern. In Figure 33–6 these indices are given for each position. It should be added at this point that in the patterns in which

FIGURE 33–7

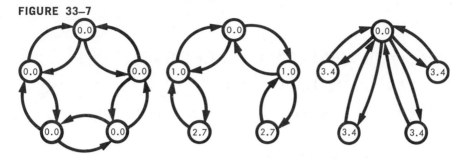

leadership emerged, the leader was invariably that person who occupied the position of highest centrality.

The index of peripherality appears to be related strongly to morale. In Figure 33–7 the indices of peripherality are given by position. Those individuals who occupied positions of low or zero peripherality showed in their actions as well as in self-ratings (made at the end of the experiments) that they were satisfied, in high spirits, and generally pleased with the work they had done. Those individuals who occupied positions of high peripherality invariably displayed either apathetic or destructive and uncooperative behavior during the group effort, and rated themselves as dissatisfied and critical of the group's operation.

A word of caution should be given concerning the slow, inaccurate, but happy "circle" pattern. Subsequent experiments by Sidney Smith indicate that this pattern possesses unusual abilities for adaptation to sudden and confusing changes of task—a quality lacking in the other two patterns.

A Promising Field for Research

Clearly, these experiments are only the beginning of a long story. The findings, although they promise much, settle nothing; but they do suggest that an experimental approach to certain aspects of organizational communication is possible and that, in all probability, it would be practically rewarding. As the characteristics of communication nets and their effects upon human performance *as they occur in the laboratory* become better understood, the need will grow for systematic studies of actual operating organizations. The job of mapping an existing net of communications even in a relatively small company is a complicated and difficult one, but it is not impossible. Some work is beginning on the development of field methods of observation. The importance of bridging the gap between the simple, directly controlled experiment and the very complex, indirectly controlled social situation cannot be overestimated.

34. SOME EFFECTS OF FEEDBACK ON COMMUNICATION *

Harold J. Leavitt and Ronald A. H. Mueller

THE EXPERIMENTS REPORTED HERE are concerned with the transmission of information from person A to person or persons B. Our problem deals with only one of the many relevant variables, the variable of feedback. The question becomes: how is the transmission of information from A to B influenced by the return of information from B to A? It is apparently taken for granted in industry, in the lecture hall, and in radio that it is both possible and efficient to transmit information from A to B without simultaneous feedback from B to A. On the other hand, the information theories of the cyberneticists and, to some extent, trial-and-error concepts in learning theory suggest that for A to hit successfully some target, B, requires that A be constantly informed of A's own progress. The servo-mechanism needs a sensory system that is capable of transmitting cues about the errors of its own motor system. The human being learning some motor skill apparently utilizes the same process. But when the human being (A) seeks to transmit information to another human being (B), A's own sensory system is hardly an adequate source of information *unless B* takes some action which will help A to keep informed of A's own progress. If A were trying to hit B with a brick, A's eyes combined with an inactive B would probably be adequate to permit A to hit his target after several trials. But if A seeks to hit B with information, he will probably be more successful if B helps to provide some cues which A's own sensory system cannot pick up directly. In other words, where communicaion between A and B is the goal, feedback, in the form of verbal or expressive language, should make for greater effectiveness.

If we take the human memory mechanism into account, we need not require that there be *contemporaneous* feedback between A and B. It may not even be necessary that there by any feedback from B_2 if feedback from a similar B_1 has already occurred. The practice sessions of the past may have provided enough feedback to permit one to hit his present target accurately. Language, for example, may be thought of as a tool originally learned with feedback, but currently useful in a multitude of

* From *Human Relations* 4 (1951): 401–10.

Readers familiar with the work of Professor Alex Bavelas will doubtless correctly recognize that many of the theoretical and experimental ideas in this research had their origins in his group. We are most grateful to Dr. Bavelas for both his direct and indirect help.

situations without simultaneous feedback to help us at least to get within range of our targets. But if the material to be communicated is relatively new and relatively precise, previously learned language may not be enough. Accurate transmission may require some additional contemporaneous feedback.

In addition to this hypothesis that contemporaneous feedback should increase the accuracy of transmission of information from A to B is the hypothesis that the completion of the AB circuit produces other effects on the AB relationship. Feedback from both A and B can increase the certainty of B that he is getting the intended information, and the certainty of A that he is getting it across. This increase in certainty, assuming motivated participants, should have some effect on feelings of frustration or achievement and, hence, on the feelings of hostility or security that pervade the relationship.

Our purpose, then, in these experiments is to try to test these hypotheses; to try to determine experimentally the effects of feedback (or the absence of feedback) on certain kinds of A-to-B communications.

EXPERIMENT I

What Are the Effects of Progressive Levels of Feedback?

We chose as our material-to-be-communicated in these experiments a series of geometric patterns. The patterns were all composed of six equal rectangular elements, but the relationships of the elements to one another differed from pattern to pattern (see Figure 34–1 for sample pattern). A's (the instructor's) job was to describe orally one of these abstract patterns to the members of his class as accurately as possible, accuracy to be measured from the students' reproductions of the described (but unseen) patterns.

Two instructors were used, and four groups of students (total student $N = 80$), with each instructor describing four patterns to each student group. There were four conditions of feedback. (1) *Zero feedback* in which instructors sat behind a movable blackboard to describe the patterns. No questions or noises were permitted from the students. (2) The *visible audience condition* in which students and instructor could see one another but no speaking by students was allowed. (3) A *yes-no condition* in which the visible audience was permitted to say only yes or no in response to questions from the instructor. And (4) A *free feedback situation* in which students were permitted to ask questions, interrupt, and so forth.

It was possible to have each instructor use each condition of feedback in a different order. (See Table 34–1.)

Besides reproducing the test patterns, students were asked to estimate their confidence in the correctness of their answers and, after the last

FIGURE 34-1

Sample of Problems Used in Experiment I

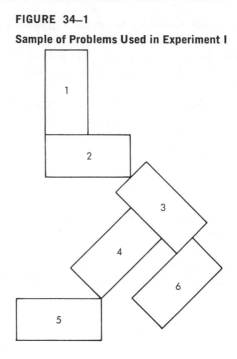

TABLE 34-1

Design of Experiment I

Pattern No.	1	2	3	4		5	6	7	8
Class 1:	zero	V-A	Y-N	free		zero	V-A	Y-N	free
		(Instructor X)					(Instructor Y)		
Class 2:	V-A	Y-N	free	zero		V-A	Y-N	free	zero
		(Instructor Y)					(Instructor X)		
Class 3:	Y-N	free	zero	V-A		Y-N	free	zero	V-A
		(Instructor X)					(Instructor Y)		
Class 4:	free	zero	V-A	Y-N		free	zero	V-A	Y-N
		(Instructor Y)					(Instructor X)		

pattern, to indicate the feedback condition they found most comfortable. We also timed the description of each pattern.

All students were given the same instructions at the beginning of the class period. They were told that the experiment was a test of their ability to understand instructions, and that they were to work as rapidly and as accurately as possible. Both instructors had had some previous experience in describing similar patterns, and both had participated in the construction of the test patterns.

Students' papers were scored for accuracy on a scale from 0 to 6. A particular rectangular element was scored correct if it bore the correct relationship to the preceding element. The first element was scored correct if it was correctly oriented on the page.

Results

1. *Accuracy.* The mean accuracy score for *all* patterns increased steadily from *zero* to *free feedback.* With *zero feedback* the mean was 4.7 out of a possible 6. The range of means for the eight different patterns given under this condition was 3.1 to 5.9. Under the *visible audience condition* the mean score was 5.3 with a range from 4.5 to 5.9. Under the *yes-no condition* the mean score was 5.5, the range 5.0 to 5.8. With *free feedback* the mean was 5.6 and the range 5.1 to 6.0.

2. *Confidence Level.* Students' estimates of their own accuracy correlated closely with actual accuracy. For all patterns the mean confidence levels were: *zero feedback,* 4.6; *visible audience,* 5.3; *yes-no,* 5.6; *free feedback,* 5.5. No effects of experience could be detected. There was a tendency to favor one instructor for the *free feedback situation* and the other for all others. These differences were slight and may indicate a differential skill on the part of the instructors in handling the different feedback conditions.

3. *Time.* The mean time required to give instructions under the four conditions were: *zero feedback,* 229 seconds; *visible audience,* 249 seconds; *yes-no,* 316 seconds; *free feedback,* 363 seconds. Any decrease in time with experience is once again obscured by differences in difficulty. No clear-cut differences between instructors were apparent.

4. *Other Observations.* Both instructors noticed some rather interesting behavior under certain conditions. When using *free feedback,* both found that on some occasions the students utilized their opportunities to speak by speaking aggressively and with hostility. There were comments like: (1) "That's impossible!" (2) "Are you purposely trying to foul us up?" (3) "You said left, it has to be right!" and so on. These comments even flowed on to students' papers, when they wrote beside their patterns such comments as: "The teacher made mistakes on this one, I didn't." These hostile reactions seemed to occur only when the *free feedback condition followed* other conditions. Both instructors noticed too that their *free feedback* experience stood them in good stead in the *zero feedback situations.* A student in the *free feedback situation* might say, "Oh, it looks like an L." In the next use of that pattern the instructors would find themselves saying, "It looks like an L."

Commentary

Although these data indicate that *free feedback* does yield more accurate results than the other conditions, some new questions arise. Can it not be argued that the *free feedback* method is more effective simply because it requires more time? Would the time required decrease if *free feedback* were used continuously? Does the *free feedback* method always put the teacher on the spot? Will he be attacked for his errors or lack of knowledge? Though *free feedback* may be helpful at first, is it of any use after the student and the teacher have had an opportunity to straighten out their language difficulties? Can the teacher improve just as much after a series of experiences without feedback as after a series with feedback? Can we show continuous improvement in the course of several trials without feedback,

EXPERIMENT II

Feedback versus No Feedback

In an attempt to answer some of these questions we designed another series of experiments that seemed to permit the most efficient use of our limited supply of instructors and students. The purpose of these experiments was to compare the two extreme conditions, *free feedback* and *zero feedback*, over a longer series of trials.

Method

Using eight new geometric patterns, all made up of six elements (see Figure 34–2), we selected ten instructors and ten separate groups of students, the groups ranging in size from 6 to 24. Five of the instructors were members of the English department at the institute, one taught German, one economics, and three psychology. Four of the classes were speech classes, six were general psychology. For three pairs of instructors the procedure was as follows:

Instructor *A* faced class *A* with four patterns in sequence and *zero feedback*. Then instructor *B* faced class *A* with four new patterns in sequence and *free feedback*. Instructor *A* then faced class *B* with his original four patterns and *free feedback*. Then instructor *B* faced class *B* with his original four patterns and *zero feedback*. For the other two pairs of instructors the procedure was reversed, instructor *A* beginning with *free feedback*.

We again asked for confidence levels, from both the students and instructors.

Results

1. *Overall.* The results of this experiment bear out the trend of the first. The mean student accuracy score for all *zero feedback* trials was 5.2 of a possible 6; the mean with *feedback* was 5.9. These means represent

FIGURE 34–2

Sample of Problems Used in Experiment II

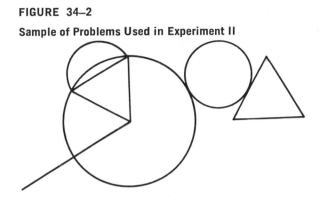

the students of ten instructors. The ranges for individual instructors were, with *zero feedback*, 3.8 to 5.8; with *free feedback*, 5.6 to 6.0. This difference between these means is significant at the 1 percent level.

In students' confidence in their results, the data again correlate closely with accuracy. The mean for *zero feedback* is 5.0 with a range from 3.5 to 5.7, while for *free feedback* the mean is 5.8 and the range 5.4 to 6.0. These differences are also significant.

In terms of time required to describe each pattern, *free feedback* remains a more time-consuming process. The average time for *zero feedback* is 166 seconds with a range from 60 to 273. For *free feedback* the average time is 284 seconds with a range of 193 to 423. These differences too are significant.

Finally in our measure of teacher confidence, means were 4.5 with *zero feedback* and 5.0 with *free feedback,* with respective ranges of 2.5 to 5.5 and 4.5 to 5.8. In all cases instructors were *less* confident than their students.

In every case individual instructors changed in the same direction as the means. Every instructor got better results with feedback than without, and every instructor took longer with feedback than without.

2. *Effects of Experience.* In Figure 34–3 are shown curves representing the changes in accuracy from pattern to pattern. Each instructor, you will recall, described four patterns in sequence under conditions of *zero feedback* and then *free feedback.*

From these accuracy curves one can see that *free feedback* starts at almost the maximum level and stays there. *Zero feedback* changes in the direction of greater accuracy from trial to trial.

As far as time (Figure 34–4) is concerned, the reverse is true. *Zero feedback* remains more or less constant, while *free feedback* time *declines progressively.*

There is at least one other way of analyzing the data that provides some rather interesting results. Our experimental design supplied us with

FIGURE 34–3

Accuracy (each point represents the mean of 10 groups)

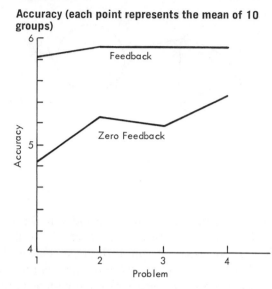

FIGURE 34–4

Time (each point represents the mean of 10 groups)

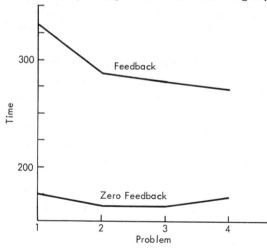

data for all combinations of (*a*) inexperienced (with these patterns) and experienced instructors. and (*b*) inexperienced and experienced classes, working (*c*) with and without feedback. The data broken down this way indicate that instructors' experience is the most significant factor present. Differences between experienced and inexperienced instructors are always greater than between experienced and inexperienced classes. This difference holds for *zero feedback* only, since with *free feedback* there are no perceptible differences among any of the different conditions.

3. *Other Observations.* One of our hypotheses in these experiments centered on the effects of feedback on the relationship between sender and receiver. We have no quantitative data that are relevant to this hypothesis, but we do have some observations that were astonishing in their consistency. These observations amounted to this. When an instructor faced a new class with *free feedback,* he got fairly rational feedback. That is, the students asked questions or asked for elaboration or repetition of a point. But when an instructor faced a class that had just been exposed to a *zero feedback* session, the instructor got an attack. The students asked lots of questions, but with barbs and implications about the instructor's (in) ability to do his job. The new instructor had innocently opened Pandora's box. This hostility did not last through more than one or two patterns, nor did it prevent the majority of students from expressing a preference for the *free feedback* method.

Commentary

In a sense these experiments demonstrate the obvious. When a receiver *B* is free to ask questions he can get a better understanding of what the sender *A* is trying to communicate. Moreover, with *free feedback* both the sender and the receiver can feel, correctly, more confident that they have respectively sent and received accurately. *Free feedback* requires more time, but there is some evidence that this time differential decreases with increased understanding between the sender and the receiver. Apparently the use of continuing *free feedback* could lead directly back into *zero feedback,* for once the common areas of misunderstanding have been clarified, contemporaneous feedback will no longer be necessary.

Apparently it is possible to improve communication skill with minimal feedback. The fourth *zero feedback* pattern is almost always more accurately sent than the first. This improvement can perhaps be thought of as a kind of personal feedback in which the instructor's own words are utilized to help him to increase his own effectiveness in the future. Much of it is no doubt empathic, the instructor imagining himself in the receiver's place and correcting his sending as a consequence. Some of the improvement, however, may come from feedback which our experimental barriers failed to block out; feedback in the form of noises. sighs, shuffling of chairs. We do not know from these experiments whether or not an instructor using *zero feedback* could eventually reach the *free feedback* level of accuracy and confidence, but it is clear that under our experimental conditions he can improve over his own original *zero feedback* level.

Besides the findings about the direct effects of feedback, the data raise some questions about indirect effects. We observed in both experiments that *free feedback* after *zero feedback* is accompanied by hostility. This hostility was apparently an effect of the *zero feedback* experience. It lasts only through one or two *free feedback* trials. Why should this be so? We believe that the mechanism centers around the notion of "certainty." In our attempts to satisfy our needs we must be as certain as possible that we are successful. Uncertainty is frustrating. Without feedback uncertainty is prevalent.

In the same vein we noted that instructors' confidence is lower than students' confidence. We suggest that the instructor can be satisfied only by knowing that the receiver is getting the proper information. But the receiver can be satisfied by comparing his own work with the sender's directions. The receiver then has more information available against which to check his own progress toward his goal. Hence he can be more certain of his progress. But the sender is not sure of what the receiver is receiving. He can get *some* information with feedback, but almost none but his own empathy without feedback. Hence his certainty and confidence are low. These differential feelings of certainty, adequacy, and hostility seem to us to be the most significant differentials between our *free feedback* and *zero feedback* systems.

SUMMARY AND CONCLUSIONS

Since the scope of this research has been limited by the utilization of one kind of problem, one kind of sender-receiver situation, and a relatively short series of experiences, our conclusions must be severely circumscribed.

To summarize, we found that, within narrow limits: (1) A completion of the circuit between sender and receiver (feedback) increases the accuracy with which information is transmitted. (2) Feedback also increases receiver and sender confidence in what they have accomplished. (3) The cost of feedback is time. But the difference in time between *free feedback* and *zero feedback* appears to decrease. (4) A sender and a receiver can improve without what we have defined as feedback experience. (5) *Free feedback* experience improves subsequent *zero feedback* trials measurably. (6) Sender experience contributes more than receiver experience to improved accuracy of communication. (7) *Zero feedback* engenders some hostility in the receiver that becomes clearly perceptible when the situation changes from *zero* to *free feedback*. This hostility is short-lived, lasting through only one or two *free feedback* trials. (8) *Zero feedback* engenders doubt in the sender.

These findings support the hypothesis that *free feedback* is an aid to accuracy in interpersonal communication. *Free feedback* seems to permit the participants to learn a mutual language, which language once learned may obviate the necessity for further feedback.

The findings also support the hypothesis that the presence or absence of feedback affects the sender-receiver relationship. *Zero feedback* is accompanied by low confidence and hostility; *free feedback* is accompanied by high confidence and amity.

35. ORGANIZATIONAL DEVELOPMENTS AND THE FATE OF BUREAUCRACY *

Warren G. Bennis

ORGANIZATIONS ARE COMPLEX, goal-seeking social units. In addition to the penultimate task of realizing goals, they must undertake two related tasks if they are to survive: (1) they must maintain the internal system and coordinate the "human side," and (2) they must adapt to and shape the external environment.

The means employed for the first task is a complicated system of social processes which somehow or other gets organizations and their participants to accommodate to their respective goals. This process of mutual compliance, where the two parties conform to and accommodate one another, is called *reciprocity*. The means for the second task has to do with the way the organization transacts and exchanges with its environment; this is called *adaptability*. The social arrangement developed to accomplish the tasks of reciprocity and adaptability in contemporary society is called *bureaucracy*.

Now is the time to challenge the conceptual and empirical foundations of bureaucracy. To jump to my conclusion first, I will argue that bureaucracy which has served us so well in the past, both as an "ideal type" and a practical form of organization, will not survive as the *dominant* form of human organization in the future. Social organizations behave like other organisms—they transform themselves through selective adaptation; and new shapes, patterns and models are emerging which promise basic changes. This argument is based on the assertion that the methods and social processes employed by bureaucracy to cope with its internal environment (reciprocity) and its external environment (adaptability) are hopelessly out of joint with contemporary realities. So within the next 25 to 50 years we shall all witness and participate in the end of bureaucracy.

The remainder of this paper elaborates this viewpoint. First, I shall take up the problem of linkage one: how organizations get men to comply, the problem of reciprocity. In this section I shall discuss how contemporary psychologists and students of organizational behavior at-

* Condensed from *Industrial Management Review* 7 (1966): 41–55. Parts of this article have been published in *Trans-Action*, July–August 1965.

tempt to resolve this issue. Then I shall discuss the second crucial linkage: adaptability. Finally, I shall sketch the conditions and structure for organizations of the future.

1. LINKAGE ONE: THE PROBLEM OF RECIPROCITY

The problem of reciprocity, like most human problems, has a long and venerable past. The modern version of this one goes back at least 160 years and was precipitated by a historical paradox: the twin births of modern individualism and modern industrialism. The one brought about a deep concern for the constitutional guarantees of personal rights and a passionate interest in individual emotions and growth. The other brought about increased rationalization and mechanization of organized activity. By coinciding, the growth of technology and enterprise tended to subvert the newly won individual freedoms and to subordinate them to the impersonal dictates of the work place. In its crudest form, the controversy is a conflict over priorities of criteria: the individual's needs, motives, goals, and growth versus the organization's goals and rights.

Enter Bureaucracy

Bureaucracy is a unique solution in that it links man's needs or organizational goals. It achieves this linkage through an influence structure based on *legal-rational* grounds instead of on the vagaries of personal power. The governed agree to obey through the rights of office and the power of reason; superiors rule because of their role incumbency and their technical (rational) competence. In short, bureaucracy is a machine of social influence which relies exclusively on reason and law. Weber once likened the bureaucratic mechanism to a judge *qua* computer: "Bureaucracy is like a modern judge who is a vending machine into which the pleadings are inserted together with the fee and which then disgorges the judgement together with its reasons mechanically derived from the code." [1]

The bureaucratic machine model was developed as a reaction against the personal subjugation, nepotism, cruelty, emotional vicissitudes, and subjective judgments which passed for managerial practices in the early days of the Industrial Revolution. For Weber, the true hope for man lay in his ability to rationalize, calculate, to use his head, as well as his hands and heart. Roles, institutionalized and reinforced by legal tradition, rather than personalities; rationality and predictability rather than irrationality and unanticipated consequences; impersonality rather than close personal

---

[1] R. Bendix, *Max Weber: An Intellectual Portrait* (New York: Doubleday & Co., 1960), p. 421.

relations; technical competence rather than arbitrary rule or iron whims—these are the main characteristics of bureaucracy.[2]

This is bureaucracy: the pyramidal organization which dominates so much of our thinking and planning related to organizational behavior, and which mediates the organization-individual dilemma through a rational system of role constraints.

Critiquing Bureaucracy

It does not take a great critical imagination to detect the flaws and problems in the bureaucratic model. We have all *experienced* them: bosses with less technical competence than their underlings; arbitrary and zany rules; an informal organization which subverts or replaces the formal apparatus; confusion and conflict among roles; and cruel treatment of subordinates based not on rational grounds but on quasi-legal, or worse, inhumane grounds.

Almost everybody else—certainly many students of organizational behavior—approaches bureaucracy with a chip on his shoulder. It has been attacked for many different reasons: for theoretical confusion and contradictions, for moral and ethical reasons, on practical grounds or for inefficiency, for methodological weaknesses, for containing too many implicit values, and for containing too few. The criticisms can be categorized as the following:

1. Bureaucracy does not adequately allow for the personal growth and the development of mature personalities.
2. It develops conformity and "group-think."
3. It does not take into account the "informal organization" and the emergent and unanticipated problems.
4. Its systems of control and authority are hopelessly outdated.
5. It has no adequate juridical process.
6. It does not possess adequate means for resolving differences and conflicts between ranks, and most particularly, between functional groups.

---

[2] For the sake of brevity, I simplify Weber's thinking more than I should. Most contemporary students of organizations would argue that bureaucracy must be viewed as a condition which can be dimensionalized and which can be found to vary empirically from firm to firm. The six dimensions most frequently cited are—
1. a division of labor based on functional specialization.
2. a well-defined hierarchy of authority.
3. a system of rules covering the rights and duties of the incumbents.
4. impersonality of interpersonal relations.
5. a system of procedures for dealing with work situations.
6. promotion and selection based on technical competence.
—R. H. Hall, "The Concept of Bureaucracy: an Empirical Assessment," *American Journal of Sociology,* 49 (1963): 33.

7. Communication and innovative ideas are thwarted or distorted due to hierarchical divisions.
8. The full human resources of bureaucracy are not utilized due to mistrust, fear of reprisals, and so forth.
9. It cannot assimilate the influx of new technology or scientists entering the organization.
10. It modifies the personality structure such that man becomes and reflects the dull, gray, conditioned "organization man."

Ten Approaches to the Problem

By way of introduction, I should say a few words about the ten approaches I will present and how I came to choose them. First of all, they are a diverse lot, with only one trait in common: an explicit recognition of the inescapable tension between individual and organizational goals. Aside from that, they approach the problem in a variety of ways using different value systems, theoretical and research traditions, and assigning divergent priorities to the centrality of the problem. Second of all, I have not—nor could I—include all the possible solutions or suggestions that are available. I have ignored, as well, those ubiquitous and important mechanisms of socialization which operate spontaneously and naturally in human organizations, such as reward systems, identification, etc. Nor have I cited the work of personnel psychology or human engineering, both of which are concerned with reducing the discrepancy between individual and organizational goals. Strictly speaking, I have selected for inclusion a number of recent, moderately well-known ideas, associated with a particular author.

The ten approaches can be grouped under five categories:

A. *Exchange theories*
    1. Barnard-Simon: inducement-contribution exchange
    2. H. Levinson: psychological contract
B. *Group theories*
    3. Mayo: the managerial elite
    4. Likert: the key role of the primary group and "linking pins" between groups
C. *Value theories*
    5. Argyris: interpersonal competence
    6. Blake and Mouton: the managerial grid
D. *Structural theory*
    7. Shepard: organic systems
E. *Situational theories*
    8. McGregor: management by objective
    9. Leavitt: management by task
    10. Thompson and Tuden: management by decision

Exchange Theories

1. The Barnard-Simon theory of exchange is an equilibrium model, very similar to an economic transaction, which specifies the conditions under which an organization can induce participation. On the one hand, there are inducements offered to the participants by the organization. These usually are wages, income, services. For each inducement there is a corresponding utility value. On the other hand, there are contribution utilities: these are the payments the participant makes to the organization, usually specified as work.

From this abstract generalization, predictions can be made concerning the participants' services by estimating the inducement-contributions balance. The greater the difference between inducements and contributions, the more satisfied—and the more compliant—the participant. In addition, a zero point on the utility scale can be derived which shows the point at which the individual is indifferent to leaving the organization as well as a point at which the participants' dissatisfactions cause search behavior and withdrawal from the organization.

2. The Levinson model of reciprocity is also an equilibrium model,[3] but the terms of the inducement-contribution ratio are converted into motivational units, usually of an unconscious kind. These units of exchange represent the psychological contract. According to Levinson, reciprocity is established by the participants and the organization through fulfilling the terms of the contract. The employees' contributions to the organization are energy, work, and commitment. The organization, for its part, provides a psychological anchor in times of rapid social change and a hedge against personal losses. In addition, the organization, through transference phenomena, provides the employees with defense mechanisms through social structure, an opportunity for growth and mastery, and a focal point for cathexis.

Group Theories

3. Elton Mayo challenged the fundamental basis of a society which was organized around archaic, economic hypotheses which grew out of an eighteenth-century, purely competitive model of society. Mayo referred to these as the Rabble Hypothesis: society consists of unorganized individuals, every individual acts in a manner calculated to secure his own self-interest, and man is logical. Mayo believed that management was blinded by the economic facts of life to the importance of association and human affiliation as a motivating force. Mayo and his associates were

---

[3] H. Levinson, "Reciprocation: The Relationship between Man and Organization" (Invited address at the Division of Industrial and Business Psychology, American Psychological Association, September 3, 1963).

really among the first to view industrial organization as a social system as well as an economic-technical system.

With this profound (now seemingly mundane) insight, Mayo saw the possibilities in using *cooperation* as an instrument to mediate the reciprocity dilemma. But in order to realize the norm of cooperation, a managerial elite, trained in the facts of social life, must take the responsibility. He wrote:

The administrator of the future must be able to understand the human-social facts for what they are, unfettered by his own emotions or prejudice. He cannot achieve this ability except by careful training—a training that must include knowledge of relevant technical skills, of the systematic order of operations, and of the organization of cooperation.[4]

Thus, success of the organization was based on the manager's ability to develop the effective organization of sustained cooperation.

4. The Likert theory of management also depends heavily on the importance of the cohesive, primary work group as a motivator:[5] to this extent it resembles the Mayo orientation. Yet, there are important differences at the *strategic* level. For Mayo, managerial elite was a necessity, while for Likert, cooperation between groups could be maintained through points of articulation which Likert refers to as "linking pins." Furthermore, in Likert's theory, decisions should be made at that point of the organizational social space where they are most relevant and where the data are available. Thus, the Likert solution entails a key role performing the linking-pin solution—rather than a managerial elite—and the use of the group to mediate the reciprocity dilemma.

Value Theories

5. Argyris starts from the position that the value system of bureaucracy itself has to be modified before individual growth and productivity can be attained.[6] He argues that bureaucratic values, which dominate organizational life, are basically impersonal values. These bureaucratic values lead to poor, shallow, and mistrustful relationships between members of the organization, or what Argyris calls "nonauthentic" relationships. These, in turn, reduce interpersonal competence, which leads to mistrust, intergroup conflict, rigidity, lowered problem-solving capacity, and eventually to a decrease in whatever criteria the organization uses to measure overall effectiveness. Managers brought up under this system of values are badly cast to play the intricate human roles now required of

---

[4] E. Mayo, *The Social Problems of an Industrial Civilization* (Cambridge, Mass.: Harvard University Press, 1945), p. 122.

[5] R. Likert, *New Patterns of Management* (New York: McGraw-Hill Book Co., 1961).

[6] C. Argyris, *Integrating the Individual and the Organization* (New York: John Wiley & Sons, 1964); idem, *Interpersonal Competence and Organizational Effectiveness* (Homewood, Ill.: The Dorsey Press, 1962); idem, *Personality and Organization* (New York: Harper & Bros., 1957). [Editors' note: Also see the next article in this section for Argyris' position on individual-organizational conflict.]

them. Their ineptitude and anxieties lead to systems of discord and defense which interfere with the effectiveness of the system.

Argyris' solution is to develop the interpersonal competence of the management group such that they can accept and instill new values, values which permit and reinforce the expression of feeling, of experimentalism, and the norms of individuality, trust, and concern.

6. Blake and Mouton have developed a solution for the reciprocity dilemma which is referred to as the managerial grid.[7] They conceptualize the organization-individual dilemma by dimensionalizing the problem along two axes. On the basis of this twofold analytic framework, it is possible to locate eight types of managerial styles. One dimension is "concern for people" and the other dimension is "concern for production." Management, according to Blake and Mouton, has to maximize both of these concerns, rather than one or the other. They call this desired state "team management." To arrive at this state, an elaborate system of *organizational training and development* is developed which encompasses both the linking-pin function and development of interpersonal competence.

Structural Theory

7. Shepard,[8] Burns and Stalker,[9] and others have attempted to replace the mechanical structure of bureaucracy with what they call an "organic" structure. Their structural approach presents a strong reaction against the idea of organizations as *mechanisms*, which, they claim, has given rise to false conceptions (such as static equilibria, frictional concepts like "resistance to change," and so forth) and, worse, false notions of social engineering and change such as "pushing social buttons," thinking of the organization *à la* Weber as a machine, and so forth. Organic systems are proposed as the natural alternative to mechanical systems. They emerge and adapt spontaneously to the needs of the internal and external systems rather than operate through programmed codes of behavior which are contained in formal role specifications of the mechanical structure. As in the Likert group theory, decisions are made at the point of greatest relevance, and roles and jobs devolve to the "natural" incumbent.

Situational Theories

A number of resolutions have been worked out which stress situational demands as a mediating factor. Three of the most significant of these are:

---

[7] R. R. Blake and J. S. Mouton, *The Managerial Grid* (Houston, Texas: Gulf Publishing Co., 1964).

[8] H. A. Shepard, "Changing Interpersonal and Intergroup Relationships in Organizations," in *Handbook of Organization*, ed. J. March (Chicago: Rand McNally, 1965).

[9] T. Burns and G. M. Stalker, *The Management of Innovation* (Chicago: Quadrangle Books, 1961).

8. Management by Objective, first noted by Drucker and further developed by McGregor,[10] attempts to link organizational goals to individual needs through the principle of "integration." It is a complicated process which entails a "working through" of the conflicts between individual objectives and organizational goals (almost in the psychotherapeutic sense) by the manager and his subordinates. The working through depends, to some extent, on the self-control and maturity of the individuals concerned and on a norm of collaboration between superiors and subordinates. Thus integration can be realized only if attention is kept both on the objectives of management and on the human processes which develop collaborative relationships between ranks.

9. Leavitt stresses the task constraints of the organization and the development of managerial practices which are appropriate to the task.[11] Thus he views the organization as a differentiated set of subsystems, rather than as a unified whole, which leads to the recognition that the organization must fit the task, rather than the other way around. In this way, he seriously challenges some of the other theories proposed above by asserting that in some parts of the system, highly authoritative (sponge theory) systems of management will have to be employed which understress participative norms and which resolve the organization-individual tension in favor of the system. At the same time, other parts of the system will apparently operate with close to minimum discrepancy between organizational goals and individual needs.

In a provocative article with Whisler, Leavitt suggests, keeping an eye on the computerized organizations of the future, that organizations will resemble not the pyramid, but a football (top management) which represents a ruling group very like Coleridge's idea of clerisy, a scholarly elite (trained in the arts of computers, mathematics, and statistics) balanced on the point of a church bell.[12] "Within the football," they write, "problems of coordination, individual autonomy, and group decision-making, and so on should arise more intensely than ever. We expect they will be dealt with quite independently of the bell portion of the company, with distinctly different methods of remuneration, control, and communication."

Thus, management-according-to-task will lead to a number of divergent forms of organization within the overall system. In the football and the church-bell resolution, for example, we can envision an organic head and a mechanical bottom.

10. Thompson and Tuden have developed a typology of organiza-

---

[10] D. McGregor, *The Human Side of Enterprise* (New York: McGraw-Hill Book Co., 1960).

[11] H. J. Leavitt, "Unhuman Organizations," in *Readings in Managerial Psychology*, ed. H. J. Leavitt and L. Pondy (Chicago: University of Chicago Press, 1964).

[12] H. J. Leavitt and T. L. Whisler, "Management in the 1980's," in *Readings in Managerial Psychology*.

TABLE 35–1

Beliefs about Causation	Preference about Possible Outcomes	
	Agreement	*Nonagreement*
Agreement	Computation in *bureaucratic* structure	Bargaining in *representative* structure
Nonagreement	Majority judgment in *collegial* structure	Inspiration in *"anomic"* structure

tional processes based on the types of decision issues called for.[13] They derive four types of organizational structures which appear appropriate to a particular decision issue. Along one dimension are beliefs about causation of decision and agreement versus nonagreement. Table 35–1 shows the relationships among the fourfold classification.

From this analytic classification, Thompson and Tuden derive four *strategies:* computation, compromise, judgment, and inspiration; and four organizational *structures* appropriate to the particular strategy. Where decisions are clear-cut, beliefs about causation and agreement about consequences are present, the bureaucratic structure is appropriate for the strategy of computation. Where there is agreement about outcomes but disagreement about causality, then majority judgment is required. Thompson and Tuden argue that a collegial structure, typical of the university and some voluntary organization, would be appropriate. Where there is agreement about causation but disagreement about causality, then majority judgment is required. Where there is agreement about causation but disagreement about outcomes of decision, then compromise through representative government—typical of government operations—would be appropriate.

Summary

Table 35–2 summarizes the major resolutions presented and the strategies implied to resolve the reciprocity issue.

These ten resolutions provide a perspective on revisions to the theory of bureaucracy. Some, like the Barnard-Simon model, are conservative, basically neo-Weberian in tone. Others, like the proposals of Argyris and Shepard, call for radical alterations in the value system or structure of bureaucracy. Still others, more moderate in tone, suggest a flexible arrangement based on situational demands. In all cases, they raise serious questions about the viability and nature of the bureaucratic mechanism.

---

[13] J. D. Thompson and A. Tuden, "Strategies and Processes of Organizational Decision," in *Comparative Studies in Administration*, ed. J. D. Thompson et al. (Pittsburgh: University of Pittsburgh Press, 1959), pp. 195–216.

TABLE 35–2

Ten Major Approaches to Resolving the Reciprocity Dilemma

Author	Resolution	Strategy
1. Barnard-Simon	Inducement-contribution	Economic incentives
2. Levinson	Psychological contract	Psychological reciprocity
3. Mayo	Organization of cooperation	Managerial elite
4. Likert	Group involvement	Linking pin and group development
5. Argyris	Value change	Interpersonal competence
6. Blake and Mouton	Team management	Group and organization development
7. Shepard	Organic structures	Group and organization development
8. McGregor	Management by objective	Integration through collaboration and self-control
9. Leavitt	Management by task	Task determines organizational arrangements
10. Thompson and Tuden	Organization by decision	Decision determines organizational arrangements

2. LINKAGE TWO: THE PROBLEM OF ADAPTABILITY

The capability of bureaucracy to succeed in its transactions and exchanges with its external environments has, until recently, gone unchallenged. For good reason: it was an ideal weapon to harness and routinize the human and mechanical energy which fueled the Industrial Revolution. It could also function in a highly competitive, fairly undifferentiated, and stable environment. The pyramidal structure of bureaucracy, where power was concentrated at the top—perhaps by one person or a group that had the knowledge and resources to control the entire enterprise— seemed perfect to "run a railroad." And undoubtedly for tasks like building railroads, for the routinized tasks of the 19th and early 20th centuries, bureaucracy was and is an eminently suitable social arrangement.

Now three new elements, already visible, promise to give new shape to American society and its organizational environments. They are: (1) the exponential growth of science, (2) the growth of intellectual technology, and (3) the growth of research and development activities.[14]

Science and technology have profoundly changed the shape and texture of the organizational environment in the following ways:

The rate of change is accelerating at an increasing rate. As Ellis Johnson said:

. . . in those large and complex organizations the once-reliable constants have now become "galloping variables" because of the impact of increasing complexity, trial and error must give way to an organized search for opportunities to make major shifts in the means of achieving organizational objectives.[15]

---

[14] D. Bell, "The Post-Industrial Society," in *Technology and Social Change,* ed. E. Ginzberg (New York: Columbia University Press, 1964), p. 44.

[15] E. A. Johnson, "Introduction," in *Operations Research for Management,* ed. McClosky and Tretethen (Baltimore: Johns Hopkins Press, 1954), p. xii.

The boundary position of the firm is changing. As A. T. M. Wilson has pointed out, the number and pattern of relations between the manager and eight areas of relevant social activity have become more active and complicated.[16] The eight areas are: government, distributors and consumers, shareholders, competitors, raw material and power suppliers, sources of employees (particularly managers), trade unions, and groups within the firms. Over the last 25 years, the rate of transactions with these eight social institutions has increased and their importance in conducting the enterprise has grown.

The causal texture of the environment has become turbulent. Emery and Trist, in an important paper, have conceptualized the field of forces surrounding the firm as a turbulent environment which contains the following characteristics: [17]

The environment is a field of forces which contains *causal* mechanisms and poses important choices for the firm.

The field is dynamic with increasing interdependencies among and between the eight social institutions specified above.

There is, among the institutions relating to the firm, a deepening interdependence between the economic and other facets of society. This means that economic organizations are increasingly enmeshed in legislation and public regulation.

There is increasing reliance on research and development to achieve competitive advantage and a concomitant change gradient which is continuously felt in the environmental field.

Finally, maximizing cooperation rather than competition between firms appears desirable because their fates may become basically positively correlated.

The upshot of all this is that the environmental texture of the firm, shaped by the growth of science and technology, has changed in just those ways which make the bureaucratic mechanism most problematical. Bureaucracy thrives under conditions of competition and certainty, where the environment is stable and, above all, predictable. The texture of the environment now holds in its turbulent and emergent field of forces causal mechanisms so rapidly changing and unpredictable that it poses insuperable problems for—and implies the end of—bureaucracy.

My argument so far can be summarized quickly. The first assault on bureaucracy arose from its incapacity to resolve the tension between individual and organizational goals. A number of resolutions emerged to mediate this conflict by supplementing the ethic of productivity with the ethic of personal growth and/or satisfaction. The second and more major

---

[16] A. T. M. Wilson, "The Manager and His World," *Industrial Management Review,* Fall 1961.

[17] F. E. Emory and E. L. Trist, "The Casual Texture of Organizational Environments" (Paper read at the International Congress of Psychology, Washington, D.C., September 1963).

shock to bureaucracy is caused by the scientific and technological revolution. It is the requirement of adaptability to the environment which leads to the predicted demise of bureaucracy as we know it.

Now, some students of organization have attempted to resolve this current dilemma, though not nearly in the same number or with the same vigor as they have the reciprocity issue. It is noteworthy that those who have made the attempt, like Burns, Stalker, Shepard, Leavitt, Argyris, and Simon, have been particularly attentive to—and have derived many of their ideas from—research and development organizations or professional associations, such as hospitals, universities, and the like. For the organizations of the future will undoubtedly resemble these, and will inherit their problems and attributes.

A FORECAST FOR ORGANIZATIONS OF THE FUTURE

A forecast falls somewhere between a prediction and a prophecy. It lacks the divine guidance of the latter and the empirical foundation of the former. But somewhere between inspiration and scientific certainty is a vision of the future of organizational life, which can be pieced together by detecting certain trends of the past and certain changes in the present that are on top of us. On this thin empirical ice, I want to set forth some of the conditions of organizational life in the next 25 to 50 years.

The Environment. As I mentioned before, the environment will be shifting and hold relative uncertainty due to the increase of research and development activities. The external environment will become increasingly differentiated, interdependent, and more salient to the firm. There will be greater interpenetration of the legal policy and economic factors, leading more and more to imperfect competition and other features of an oligopolistic and government-business controlled economy. (Telstar and similar operations, partnerships between industry and government, will become typical.) And because of the immensity and expense of the projects, there will be fewer identical units competing for the same buyers or sellers. In short, three main features of the environment will be: interdependence rather than competition, turbulent rather than steady competition. and large rather than small enterprises.

Aggregate Population Characteristics. We are living in what Peter Drucker calls the "educated society," and I think this feature is the most distinctive characteristic of our times. Within 15 years, two thirds of our population (living in metropolitan areas) will attend college. Adult education programs, not the least of which are the management development courses of such universities as MIT, Harvard, and Stanford, are expanding and adding intellectual breadth. All this, of course, is not just "nice" but necessary. For Secretary of Labor Wirtz recently pointed out that computers can do the work of most high-school graduates—more cheaply and effectively. Fifty years ago education used to be called nonwork and intellectuals on the payroll (and many staff) were considered "overhead." Today, the survival of the firm depends, more than ever before, on the proper exploitation of brain power.

One other characteristic of the population which will aid our understanding of organizations of the future is increasing job mobility. The lowered expense and ease of transportation, coupled with the very real needs of a dynamic environment, will change drastically the idea of "owning" a job—or "roots," for that matter. Participants will be shifted and will change from job to job and employer to employer with much less fuss than we are accustomed to.

Work-Relevant Values. The increased level of education and rate of mobility will bring about certain changes in the values the population will hold regarding work. People will tend to: (1) be more rational, be intellectually committed, and rely more heavily on forms of social influence which correspond to their value system; (2) be more "other-directed," and will rely on their temporary neighbors and workmates for companionships; and (3) require more involvement, participation, and autonomy in their pattern of work.

Tasks and Goals of the Firm. The tasks of the firm will be more technical, complicated, and unprogrammed. They will rely far more on intellectual power and the higher cognitive processes than on muscle power. They will be far too complicated for one man to comprehend, not to say control; they will call for the collaboration of professionals in a project organization.

Similarly, goals will become more differentiated and complicated, and oversimplified clichés, like "increasing profits" and "raising productivity," will be heard less than goals having to do with adaptive-innovative-creative capabilities. For one thing (as is true in universities and laboratories today), productivity cannot easily be quantified with the number of budgets produced, articles published, or number of patents. And hospitals have long ago given up the idea of using the number of patients discharged as an index of efficiency.

Finally, there will be an increase in goal conflict, more and more divergency and contradictoriness between and among effectiveness criteria. Just as in hospitals or universities today there is conflict between the goal of teaching and the goal of research, so there will be increased conflict among goals in organizations of the future. Part of the reason for this is implied in the fact that there will be more professionals in the organization. Professionals tend to identify as much with their professional organizations as with their employers. In fact, if universities can be used as a case in point, more and more of their income stems from outside professional sources, such as private or public foundations. Professionals tend not to make good "company men" and are divided in their loyalty between professional values and organizational demands.[18] This role conflict and ambiguity are both cause and consequence of the goal conflict.

   Organizational Structure.   Given the task structure, population characteristics, and features of environmental turbulence, the social structure in organizations of the future will take on some unique characteristics. First of all, the key word will be temporary: Organizations will become adaptive, rapidly changing *temporary systems*.[19] Second, they will be organized around *problems-to-be-solved*. Third, these problems will be solved by relative groups of *strangers* who represent a diverse set of professional skills. Fourth, given the requirements of coordinating the various projects, *articulating points or* "linking pin" personnel will be necessary who can speak the diverse languages of research and who can relay and mediate between various project groups. Fifth, the groups will be conducted on *organic* rather than on mechanical lines; they will emerge and adapt to the problems, and leadership and influence will fall to those who seem most able to solve the problems rather than to programmed role expectations. People will be differentiated, not according to rank or roles, but according to skills and training.

   Adaptive, temporary systems of diverse specialists solving problems, coordinated organically *via* articulating points, will gradually replace the theory and practice of bureaucracy. Though no catchy phrase comes to mind, it might be called an *organic-adaptive* structure.

   Motivation in Organic-Adaptive Structures.   The way organizations tie people into their systems so that they become effective units is the motivational basis of organizational behavior and its most pressing problem.[20] In fact, the first part of this paper on reciprocity explains how the theory and practice of bureaucracy fail to solve this problem. In the organic-adaptive structure, the reciprocity problem will be eased somewhat because individual and organizational goals should coincide more. This is made possible because organizations will provide more meaningful and satisfactory tasks. In short, the motivational problem will rely heavily on the satisfaction intrinsic to the task and to the participant's identification with his profession.

   There is another consequence which I find inescapable but which many will deplore. There will be a reduced commitment to work groups. These groups, as I have already mentioned, will be transient and changing. While skills in human interaction will become more important due to the necessity of collaboration in complex tasks, there will be a concomitant reduction in group cohesiveness. I would predict that in the organic-adap-

----

[18] A. W. Gouldner, "Cosmopolitans and Locals: Towards an Analysis of Latent Social Roles, I," *Administrative Science Quarterly* 2 (1957): 281–306.

[19] M. B. Miles, "On Temporary Systems," in *Innovation in Education,* ed. M. B. Miles (New York: Bureau of Publications, Teachers College, Columbia University, 1964), pp. 437–90.

[20] D. Katz, "The Motivational Basis of Organizational Behavior," *Behavioral Science* 9 (1964): 131–46.

tive system people will have to learn to develop quick and intense relationships on the job, and learn how to endure their loss.

In general, I do not agree with the Kerr et al emphasis on the "New Bohemianism" whereby leisure—not work—becomes the emotional-creative sphere of life,[21] or with Leavitt and Whisler, who hold similar views.[22] They assume a technological slowdown and leveling off, and a stabilizing of social mobility. This may be the society of the future, but long before then we will have the challenge of creating that push-button society and a corresponding need for service-type organizations of the organic-adaptive structure.

Jobs in the next century should become *more,* rather than less, involving; man is a problem-solving animal and the tasks of the future guarantee a full agenda of problems. In addition, the adaptive process itself may become captivating to many.

At the same time, I think the future I describe is far from a Utopian or necessarily a "happy" one. Coping with rapid change, living in temporary systems, setting up (in quick-step time) meaningful relations, then breaking them—all augur strains and tensions. Learning how to live with ambiguity and to be self-directing will be the task of education and the goal of maturity.

36. BEING HUMAN AND BEING ORGANIZED *

Chris Argyris

IT IS HARD TO IMAGINE being "civilized" without being "organized." Yet too much organization, or the wrong kind, can injure the individuals involved and through them can spoil an organization or a civilization. How can we design or "grow" organizations that maintain the right balance between individual needs on the one hand, and organizational requirements on the other?

The classical design for a formal organization has some very serious flaws. The nature of these flaws appears when we set side by side two pictures: first, a view of how human beings need to behave in our society in order to be healthy, productive, growing individuals; and second, how a

---

[21] C. Kerr et al., *Industrialism and Industrial Man* (Cambridge, Mass.: Harvard University Press, 1960).

[22] Leavitt and Whisler, "Management in the 1980's," in *Readings in Managerial Psychology.*

* From Trans-Action 1 (1964): 3–6. © July 1964 by Transaction, Inc., New Brunswick, New Jersey.

formal organization (a factory, business, or hospital) requires them to behave. Comparing these pictures, we see that the organization's requirements, as presented by "classical" descriptions, are sharply opposed to the individual's needs. We can, however, suggest some lines along which action and study might improve the "fit" between the human being and the nonhuman organization.

Picture of Health

There are certain lines along which the child becoming a man develops in our culture. We can discuss, as being most important, seven of these "developmental dimensions:"

1. From being passive as infants, humans grow toward activeness as adults.
2. From being dependent on others, an individual grows toward being relatively independent of others. He develops the ability to "stand on his own two feet" while at the same time acknowledging a healthy dependency. He does not react to others (his boss, for instance) in terms of patterns learned during childhood; thus, such independence is partly a matter of accurate perception of himself and those around him.
3. From only a few types of reaction or behavior, he develops many.
4. He moves from the shallow, brief, and erratic interests of his infancy to the intense, long-term, and coherent commitments of adulthood. He requires increasingly varied challenges; he wants his tasks to be not easy but hard, not simple but complex, not a collection of separate things but a variety of parts he can put together.
5. He begins to want long-term challenges that link his past and future, in place of the old brief and unconnected jobs which typically were engaged in by him as a child.
6. He begins wanting to go up the totem pole, instead of staying in the low place a child has.
7. He develops from being not very self-aware and impulsive to being both self-aware and self-controlled, and this lets him develop a sense of integrity and self-worth.

No one, of course, finishes his development along these seven lines. For one thing, if everyone became totally independent, incessantly active, and completely equal if not superior, society would be in a pretty difficult situation—sort of all fleas and no dog. One function of culture is to hold back, by our manners and morals, the self-expression of some individualists, so that others may also have a chance at self-development. Then too, people simply differ in needs and skills; not everybody wants to go into orbit, and some are too frail, too fat, or too stupid to be given the chance.

Admitting, then, that no one is ever through developing along these dimensions, we can still say that his self-actualization is the overall "profile" of how far he has developed along them. At this point we must add that in drawing this profile, not the surface appearance but the underlying meanings of a man's behavior are what have to be considered. For instance, an employee might seem to be always going against what management wants, so that people call him "independent," yet his contrariness may be due to his great need to be dependent on management, a need he dislikes to admit. The truly independent person is the one whose behavior is not mainly a reaction against the influence others have over him (though, of course, no person is totally independent). The best test of such independence is how fully the person will let other people be independent and active. Autocratic leaders may claim to like independent underlings, yet many studies have shown that autocratic leadership only makes both boss and underlings more dependence-ridden.

The Formal Organization

We turn now from the picture of a developing self to the organization. What are its properties, and what impact can we expect these to make on the human personality we have just viewed? What reactions can we expect from this impact?

To begin, the most basic feature of a formal organization is that it is "rational"—that is, it has been "designed," and its parts are purposefully related within this design; it has pattern and is shaped by human minds to accomplish particular rational objectives. For instance, jobs within it must be clearly defined (in terms of rank, salary, and duties) so that the organization can have logical training, promotion, and resignation or retirement policies.

But most experts on such organizations are not content to point to, as Herbert Simon does, this "rational design" they go on to say that this rationality, though an ideal that may have to be modified now and then, requires people in an organization to be very loyal to its formal structure if it is to work effectively. They have to "go by the rules." And the experts claim such design is "more human" in the long run than creating an organization haphazardly. It is senseless, cruel, wasteful, and inefficient, they argue, not to have a logical design. It is senseless to pay a man highly without clearly defining his position and its relation to the whole. It is cruel, because eventually people suffer when no structure exists. It is wasteful because without clearly predefined jobs it is impossible to plan a logical training or promotion or resignation or retirement policy. And it is inefficient because it allows the "personal touch" to dominate and this, in turn, is "playing politics."

In contrast to such experts, some human relations researchers have unfortunately given the impression that formal structures are bad, and that individual needs should come first in creating and running an organization. These latter men, however, are swinging (as recent analysis of their research has shown) to recognize that an extreme emphasis on the individual's needs is not a very tenable position either, and that organizational rules can be well worth keeping.

Principles of Design

What are the principles by which an organization is "rationally designed?" The traditionalists among experts in this field have singled out certain key assumptions about the best design for a formal organization. In our comments here these will be dealt with not as beyond question but only as the most useful and accurate so far offered. By accepting them to this extent, we can go on to look at the probable impact on human beings of an organization based on them.

As Gillespie suggests, these principles may be traced back to certain "principles of industrial economics," the most important of which is that "the concentration of effort on a limited field of endeavor increases quality and quantity of output." This principle leads to another: that the more similar the things that need doing, the more specialization will help to do them.

Specializing

The design-principle just mentioned carries three implications about human beings within organizations. First, that the human personality will behave more efficiently as the job gets more specialized. Second, that there can be found a one best way to define the job so it will be done faster. Third, that differences between human personalities may be ignored by transferring more skill and thought to machines.

But all these assumptions conflict sharply with the developmental needs or tendencies of human personality as a growing thing; a human being is always putting himself together, pushing himself into the future. How can we assume that this process can be choked off, or that the differences between individuals which result from the process can be ignored?

Besides, specialization requires a person to use only a few of his abilities, and the more specialized the task the simpler the ability involved. This goes directly counter to the human tendency to want more complex, more interesting jobs as he develops. Singing the same tune over and over is boring enough, but repeating the same note is absolutely maddening.

The Chain of Command

Mere efficiency of parts is not enough; an organization needs to have a pattern of parts, a chain of command. Thus, planners create "leadership," to control and coordinate. They assume that efficiency is increased by a fixed hierarchy of authority. The man at the top is given formal power to hire and fire, reward and penalize, so that employees will work for the organization's objectives.

The impact of this design-feature on human personality is clearly to make the individuals dependent on, passive and subordinate to, the leader. The results are obviously to lessen their self-control and shorten their time-perspective. It would seem, then, that the design-feature of hierarchic structure works against four of the growth lines, pushing individuals back from active toward passive, from equal toward subordinate, from self-controlled toward dependent, from being aware of long time-perspectives toward having only a short time-perspective. In all these four ways, the result is to move employees back from adulthood toward immaturity.

Planners have tried to cushion this impact in several ways. First, they see to it that those who perform well in the hierarchy are rewarded. But the trouble with this is that the reward ought to be psychological as well as material—and yet, because of the job-specialization which simplifies and does not satisfy a worker, few psychological rewards are possible. So the material reward has to seem more important, and has to be increased. To do this, however, means that one does nothing about the on-the-job situation that is causing the trouble, but instead pays the employee for the dissatisfaction he experiences. Obviously, management in doing this leaves an employee to feel that basic causes of dissatisfaction are built into industrial life, that the rewards received are wages for dissatisfaction, and that any satisfaction to be gained must be looked for outside the organization.

Other things are wrong with raising wages to make up for dissatisfaction. For it assumes that the worker can so split himself up that he can be quite satisfied with the anomalous situation we have just described him as being in. Second, it assumes he is mainly interested in what money can get. And third, it assumes he is best rewarded as an individual producer, without regard to the work group in which he belongs. This may well mean that a worker whose group informally sanctions holding production down will therefore have to choose between pleasing the boss and getting paid more, or pleasing his fellows and getting paid less.

Keeping Personalities Out

A second "solution" has been suggested by planners: to have very good bosses. The leaders, that is, should be objective, rational, and personify the reasonableness of the organizational structure. To do this means they keep from getting emotionally involved; as one executive states, "We must try to keep our personalities out of the job." Evaluating others, he sets aside his own feelings. And, of course, he must be loyal to the organization.

But this solution too violates some of the basic properties of personality. To split what one does from what one is, or to ask others to do it, is to violate one's self-integrity, and the same goes for the effort to keep personality out of the job. (As for impartiality, as May has pointed out, the best way to be impartial is to be as partial as one's needs require but stay aware of this partiality so as to "correct" for it at the moment of decision.)

One other solution has been offered: to encourage competition among employees, so as to get them to show initiative and creativity. Competing for promotions, this "rabble hypothesis" suggests, will increase the efficiency of the competitors.

Williams, however, conducting some controlled experiments, shows that this assumption is not necessarily valid for people placed in competitive situations. Deutsch supports Williams' results with extensive controlled research, and goes much further, suggesting that competitive situations make for so much tension that they lessen efficiency. Levy and Freedman confirm Deutsch's work and go on to relate competition to psychoneurosis.

Unity of Direction

We have looked at the design-features of job-specialization and hierarchic structure. A final principle of design is *unity of direction:* efficiency is supposed to increase if each administrative unit has a single activity planned and directed by a single leader. The implication is that this leader sets the goal, the conditions for meeting the goal, and the path toward it, for all his employees. If, because of job-specialization, the workers are not personally interested in the work-goal, then unity of direction creates the ideal conditions for psychological failure. For each individual basically (as we have said) aims at psychological success, which comes only when he defines his own goals, in relation to his personal needs and to the difficulties of reaching the goals.

Human Needs versus Organizational Requirements

What we have seen is that if we use the principles of formal organization as ideally defined, employees will be working in an environment where (1) they have little or no control over their workaday world; (2) they are expected to be passive, dependent, and subordinate; (3) they are expected to have a short time-perspective; (4) job-specialization asks them to perfect and value only a few of their simplest abilities; and (5) they are asked to produce under conditions (imposed by the principle of unity of direction) ideal for psychological failure.

Since behavior in these ways is more childish than adult, it appears that formal organizations are willing to pay high wages and provide adequate seniority if mature adults will, for eight hours a day, behave like children.

It is obvious that such behavior is incompatible with the human need to develop and "grow up." And it appears that the incongruency increases as (1) the employee is of greater maturity; (2) the formal structure is tightened in search of efficiency; (3) one goes down the line of command; (4) jobs become more mechanized.

That such incongruency will result in frustration, failure, short time-perspective and conflict hardly needs demonstration. How, in the face of all this, will the employee be able to maintain a sense of his own integrity? He will react in part like a turtle and in part like a porcupine: by leaving, by "ladder-climbing" within the organization, by such defense reactions as daydreaming, aggression, ambivalence, regression, projection, and so on; or by becoming apathetic toward the organization's makeup and goals. If this occurs, he will be apt to start "goldbricking" or even cheating. He may create informal groups who agree that it is right to be apathetic and uninvolved, and these informal groups may become formalized—instead of just gathering to gripe they will hold meetings and pass resolutions. Or he may take the view that money and "what's in it for me" have become the really important things about his work, and the "psychological rewards" are just malarkey. And he will end up by indoctrinating the new employees so that they will see the organization through the same mud-colored glasses as he does.

What to Do?

There is only one real way to improve the sad picture described above: by *decreasing* the dependency, decreasing the subordination, and decreasing the submissiveness expected of employees. It can be shown that making a job "bigger"—not more specialized and small—will help do these things; and that employee-centered (or democratic or participative) leadership also will improve the situation.

Yet, these remedies are limited, for they require employees who are already highly interested in the organization. And the situation which makes them needed is one in which employees are anything but interested. In such a situation, strongly directive leadership is almost necessary to get the apathetic employee to move at all. This, in its own turn, helps to create the very problem it is trying to solve!

An Unresolved Dilemma

The dilemma, then, is basic and is a continuing challenge to the social scientist and the leader in an organization. They may well begin their efforts to work for a solution—one in which the organization will be as efficient as possible, while the people in it will be as free and strongly developing as possible—by considering two facts. The first is that no organization can be maximally efficient that stunts its own vital parts. And the second is that our culture and each of its institutions, from family through nations and beyond, are one vast interlocking set of organizations.

37. ORGANIZATIONAL THEORY AND HUMAN RESOURCE ACCOUNTING *

Rensis Likert and David G. Bowers

ORGANIZATIONAL RESEARCH in business companies has the potential for making major and often unique theoretical contributions to the social sciences as well as helping to solve some of the most serious problems of present day society. To make these theoretical and practical contributions, however, more rapid progress must be made in organizational research and theory development than has occurred in the past two decades. The present researchers believe that we are on the verge of accelerating such progress, and in this article the reasons for this opinion will be indicated. Finally, examples of the unique and valuable contributions that organizational theory is likely to make in the next decade toward the solution of some of the grave social problems will be given.

Social scientists engaged in research on management and organizational performance initially expected to find a marked and consistent relationship between the management system of a leader, the attitudes and loyalties of his subordinates, and the productivity of his organization. A number of studies undertaken in the decade following World War II, including studies made at the Institute for Social Research, University of Michigan, have yielded many different relationships among these variables. In summarizing the relationships between the attitudes of employees and their productivity, various reviewers have concluded generally that the studies taken altogether show no simple, consistent, dependable relationship among the variables.[1]

These generally unexpected research findings raise an important ques-

---

* From *American Psychologist* 24 (1969): 585–92. Copyright 1969 by the American Psychological Association. Reprinted by permission.

[1] For example, see A. H. Brayfield and W. H. Crockett, "Employee Attitudes and Employee Performance," *Psychological Bulletin* 52 (1955): 396–424; R. Dubin et al., *Leadership and Productivity: Some Facts of Industrial Life* (San Francisco: Chandler, 1965); F. Herzberg et al., *Job Attitudes: Review of Research and Opinion* (Pittsburgh: Psychological Services of Pittsburgh, 1957); and D. C. Miller and W. H. Form, *Industrial Society: The Sociology of Work Organizations*, 2d ed. (New York: Harper & Row, 1964).

tion. What accounts for the failure to find consistent relationships among these variables?

The answer appears to be that the relations among these variables are so complex that taking measurements of these variables at one point in time in an organization or group of organizations and computing correlations among the variables is much too simple a research design to yield accurate knowledge and insights. This design ignores the influence of (a) many powerful conditioning or moderating variables and (b) the serious inaccuracies in the time-bound performance data. It yields, as surveys of the literature show, a confused and contradictory body of results.

Progressively, the nature of the variables causing these contradictory results is being discovered as well as their influence on the interrelationships among the leadership, motivational, and performance dimensions. The variables causing the contradictory results include; (a) the discrepancy between the leader's report of his behavior and his actual behavior; (b) the values, expectations, and skills of subordinates; (c) the manager's capacity to exercise influence upward; (d) the size of the unit or firm; (e) the kind of work being done; (f) time and changes over time; and (g) inaccurate or inadequate measurements of the criterion variables, such as productivity and earnings.

Data are available which indicate that, when one takes into consideration all of these variables that cause contradictory conclusions, especially the trends over time, the results are likely to show that there are consistent, dependable relationships among leadership, motivational, and performance variables.[2]

To test further this assumption, a series of related studies, referred to generally as the Inter-Company Longitudinal Studies, are being undertaken. A related program of research is being instituted for the development of human resource accounting, to provide far more accurate financial criteria. This involves developing the methodology to enable a firm (a) to estimate dollar investments made in building its human organization and (b) to estimate the present discounted productive value of that human organization.

Research Plan for the Longitudinal Studies

In this article, three broad classes of variables will be referred to, labeled, respectively—causal, intervening, and end-result. They can be defined briefly as follows:

1. The *causal* variables are independent variables that can be directly or purposely altered or changed by the organization and its management

---

[2] R. Likert, *The Human Organization: Its Management and Value* (New York: McGraw-Hill Book Co., 1967), chap. 5.

and that, in turn, determine the course of developments within an organization and the results achieved by that organization. "General business conditions," for example, although comprising independent variables, are *not* viewed as causal since the management of a particular enterprise ordinarily can do little about them. Causal variables include the structure of the organization and management's policies, decisions, business and leadership strategies, skills, and behavior.

2. The *intervening* variables reflect the internal state, health, and performance capabilities of the organization; for example, the loyalties, attitudes, motivations, performance goals, and perceptions of all members and their collective capacity for effective action, interaction, communication, and decision-making.

3. The *end-result* variables are the dependent variables that reflect the results achieved by that organization, such as its productivity, costs, scrap loss, growth, share of the market, and earnings.

Collection of periodic measurements from a set of business firms over about a 5-year period will be required to obtain sufficient data for testing hypotheses concerning the nature and magnitude of the interrelationships among the causal, intervening, and end-result variables. Present indications are that data over approximately the same span of time will be needed for the computations required to develop that phase of human resource accounting devoted to estimating the present and changing value of the human organization.

Planning for this project has been under way for more than two years. Pilot studies were started over a year ago. The activities to date have involved 20 organizational sites, including over 11,000 persons in eight different companies. Since February 1966, a machine-scored core questionnaire has been developed, computer programs have been created that are adequate to process the data in the form required for the major venture, and pilot efforts have been conducted in applying existing knowledge and current data to improve organizational capabilities and performance.

The following considerations illustrate the approach used in selecting research sites:

1. To study time lag effectively requires some variation in that lag. Enormous differences, on the other hand, would confound the analysis. Some variation, therefore, will be sought, but within reasonable limits. Factors that affect the time lag will be taken into account. Available evidence shows, for example, that the time lag between changes in the causal variables and performance differ with regard to: (*a*) *Size*—Lag time appears to be longer in larger organizations; (*b*) *Type of work*— Lag time may well be longer in repetitive, tightly engineered assembly manufacturing plants and probably is shorter in sales, research and development, and service industries; (*c*) *Organizational complexity*—

Complexity of organizational structure, as well as size, probably affects lag time. The cycle time is likely to be longer where events must cross many layers of hierarchy (tall organizations) and where operations are functionally different, yet interdependent in the long run.

2. Sites must be sufficiently autonomous in their operations to permit organizational improvement programs to succeed. It would not be desirable to include one section of a large installation that is highly dependent in its operation upon related components when these components are not also a part of the project.

3. Sites for which accurate, reliable performance records exist should be sought. The problems created by ambiguous and unreliable end-result performance criteria should be avoided. (This problem is discussed in greater detail in a subsequent section of this article.)

4. Sites with a history of unstable operation should be avoided, as, for example, those sites that experience recurring technical or market upheaval and those that are subject to rapid and frequent product and technological changes.

Data To Be Collected

Four distinct bodies of data are to be collected:

Questionnaire Data. Questionnaires will be administered at least once a year, initially by Institute of Social Research personnel. In addition, questionnaires will be administered in most firms on a sample basis more often than once a year. This additional query will obtain evidence concerning changes in relationships among the variables not adequately reflected in the annual measurements.

The instrument that will be employed contains a core of organizational measures covering both causal and intervening variables. This core consists of 18 indexes based on 48 multiple-choice items and reflects the theory of organization structure and functioning presented in *New Patterns of Management* and *The Human Organization*.[3] A much-simplified version of the concepts is shown as Figure 37–1.

The questionnaire includes, also, a supplement of approximately 70 additional items for diagnostic and research purposes, plus provision for optional specific items desired by each firm.

Performance Data. A major problem in this study is that of establishing criteria of performance comparable from one organization to another. Within any one firm, or perhaps among firms from the same industry, these measures may be more or less comparable. For comparisons across all firms and units, however, some broad conceptualization and data transformation of the performance variables of the kinds commonly en-

---

[3] R. Likert, *New Patterns of Management* (New York: McGraw-Hill Book Co., 1961): idem, *Human Organization*.

FIGURE 37–1

Schematic Relationships among Causal, Intervening, and End-Result Variables

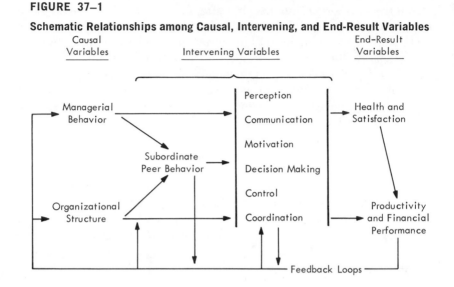

countered in organizational studies are clearly necessary. Performance is viewed in terms of an overall criterion of long-term profitability influenced by results in six subordinate areas: volume, efficiency, quality, development, attendance, and human costs (Table 37–1).

A major problem results from the fact that in any one of the six subordinate areas, there will be available in a particular firm only a partial representation of the total content. Measures in each area may be vastly different from one firm to another. It may be necessary, therefore, to transform all measures in some fashion to obtain criteria that are at least conceptually comparable from firm to firm. These analyses of the available end-result data will employ sophisticated methods and concepts of accounting and financial analysis. They also will make full use of recent research on performance criteria and organizational effectiveness carried out by Seashore and his colleagues.[4] The work employing accounting concepts will be directed by R. Lee Brummet, professor of accounting, Graduate School of Business Administration, the University of Michigan. It is probable that these analyses will increase the accuracy of the end-result data, making them more useful not only for research but also for operating purposes. As this occurs, there are likely to be some changes in the kinds of end-result measurements that are regularly compiled and made available for this project.

---

[4] S. E. Seashore, "Criteria of Organizational Effectiveness," *Michigan Business Review,* July 1965, p. 17; E. Yuchtman and S. E. Seashore, "A System Resource Approach to Organizational Effectiveness," *American Sociological Review* 32 (1967): 891–903.

TABLE 37–1

Categories of Subordinate Criteria Contributing to an Overall Criterion of Long-Term Profitability

Volume of Work	Efficiency	Quality	Attendance	Development	Human Costs
Volume of output	Production costs	Quality output	Absence Hours	Growth in volume	Accidents Physical
Market penetration	Waste	Rework ratio	worked per	Manpower	health
	Scrap	Accuracy	week	development	Psychological
	Down time	Customer	Turnover	Innovation	health
	Performance versus	returns			Tension
	Schedule	Customer complaints			Stress
	Performance versus	Repeat			Conflict
	Standard	business			Grievances
	Rate of	Rejection			Disciplinary
	earnings	rate			actions

Analyses of the Data

This project requires extensive and replicated analyses of large quantities of data. For this reason, a largely preprogrammed system of data processing and analysis is being used. Relationships will be computed among the causal, intervening, and end-result variables in the form of a correlation matrix for each time interval for which data are available. The computations will include all current questionnaire indexes, all questionnaire indexes from preceding measurements, and all performance criteria for an appropriate number of months. At the outset, this will be six months preceding and six months following the measurement point; later analyses will include a much greater number of months subsequent to the time of measurement of the causal and intervening variables. Correlations will be plotted as curves over time. By inspection, peaks can be located and the time intervals and the levels of maximum relationships observed.

Human Resource Accounting

The financial performance records of any firm and especially trends in the financial data will contain serious inadequacies and errors as long as human resources are ignored. These resources include the value of all such assets as a firm's human organization, its customer loyalty, shareholder loyalty, supplier loyalty, its reputation among the financial community, and its reputation in the community in which it has plants and offices.

The magnitude of these investments is revealed by the substantial sums paid for acquisitions and mergers in excess of the value of the physical assets. It also is revealed, as far as the value of the human organization is concerned, by the answers of company officers to the following question:

Assume that tomorrow morning every position in your firm is vacant, that all of the present jobs are there, all of the present plants, offices, equipment, patents, and all financial resources but no people. How long would it take and how much would it cost to hire personnel to fill all of the present jobs, to train them to their present level of competence, and to build them into the well-knit organization which now exists?

In response to this question the top management of several companies have estimated that it would take from two to ten times their annual payroll to cover the cost of rebuilding their human organization to the performance capabilities of their present staff. The most frequent estimates are from three to five times.

By using this procedure to obtain an estimate of the value of a firm's human organization, one can readily relate this estimate to earnings since payrolls usually exceed earnings by two- to tenfold. Computing an estimate for a typical firm by using conservative estimates, such as that the human organization is worth three times payroll and the payroll is about five times earnings, then the human organization of such a firm is worth about 15 times earnings (3×5). With this ratio of the value of the human organization to earnings, relatively minor fluctuations, for example, 10 percent, in the value of a firm's human organization can be equal to a substantial proportion of its annual earnings.

When the value of the other human resource assets are included, such as customer loyalty, supplier loyalty, shareholder loyalty, and financial reputation, even smaller fluctuations than 10 percent in all of the human resource assets can be equal to or exceed a typical year's earnings of a firm. When all forms of human resources are ignored in a firm's accounting reports, as at present, the stated earnings can show a favorable picture for several years when the actual assets and true value are steadily *decreasing* by a substantial fraction.

The development of human resource accounting is necessary to provide a firm with accurate financial reports to guide its decision. It also is needed to increase the validity of criteria measurements used in organizational research.

The methodology for all forms of human resource accounting will be developed. Initial efforts, however, are focused on developing accounting procedures for dealing with a firm's investment in its human organization. Presently the investigators are engaged in developing procedures for estimating the actual costs incurred in recruiting, selecting, training employees and familiarizing them with all aspects of their work, and in establishing effective working relations with others in the organization.

This work will enable a firm to estimate its investment in individuals and groups of individuals in the organization. Appropriate amortization assumptions have been developed to permit these investments to be written off over appropriate time spans.

Procedures for computing personnel replacement costs are being developed also. These procedures can provide another set of estimates that have relevance in personnel-planning accounting as well as providing the usual check on incurred cost estimates.

Firms already are deriving valuable insights into operating problems from these outlay and replacement cost measurements. Turnover figures, for example, often take on completely different meaning when expressed in these terms. The loss of a manager or engineer shortly after he has been given extensive training is quite different from the loss of a manager or engineer who is near retirement.

It is essential, however, for a firm to know not only its investment in human resources but to know as well the present productive capability of that human organization, that is, its present value to the firm. These value estimates cannot be made until reasonably accurate estimates of the relationships over a span of years among the causal, intervening, and end-result variables have been compiled. Data to permit these estimates are being obtained. Experimental calculations indicate that useful estimates can be derived from this approach.

Within five to ten years, procedures will be available for making reasonably accurate estimates of the trends in all of these various forms of a firm's human assets. The financial reports will then reflect, with reasonable accuracy, the financial state and changes of financial condition through time and not ignore, as at present, serious fluctuations in one third to one half of its assets. When these more accurate financial reports become available, the correlations between such causal variables as leadership style and such end-result variables as financial performance, even when measured at one point in time, will be much more likely to show consistent, dependable relationships than at present. Moreover, these more accurate and valid reports will encourage a company in its own self-interest to shift much more rapidly than now to the application of more complex and more effective management systems emerging from organizational research. These systems will provide more accurate data to a manager, enabling him to evaluate correctly any new development he undertakes.

Some Preliminary Results from Longitudinal Research

From the pilot studies started a couple of years ago, the second year of measurements are becoming available. The early data are confirming our expectations that measurements, over at least a few years time, are necessary to obtain correct estimates of the relationships that actually exist among the causal, intervening, and end-result variables. Some initial results will show the findings beginning to emerge.

In one continuous process plant, employing over 500 persons, measurements of the causal and intervening variables obtained in 1966 were related by work groups ($N = 40$ groups) to performance data for the same period of time. Three indexes of managerial behavior were used. The first index reflects the extent to which the manager is seen as being supportive and applying the principle of supportive relationships. This index is called "managerial support." The second refers to his efforts to use group problem-solving in dealing with work problems and to build his work group into a cohesive effective team; this is called "managerial interaction facilitation." The third reflects the manager's attempts to aid his subordinates on job problems and to provide the knowledge and technical resources they need for their work, and is labeled "managerial work facilitation."

These three measures of managerial behavior were related to monthly performance measurements for these 40 work groups for the four successive months just prior to and subsequent to the period when the causal variables were measured. The performance measurements were actual incurred costs, expressed as a percentage of the standard; the lower this ratio of costs, the better the performance. None of the 12 possible coefficients of correlation (three managerial variables related to performance for four separate months, or 3×4) was large enough to be statistically significant (for .05 level, $r = .31$).

When these measurements of managerial behavior, obtained in 1966, were related to monthly performance measured one year later, all 12 of the correlation coefficients were statistically significant. They varied from $-.48$ to $-.58$. These correlations should be negative, of course, since the better the managerial behavior is, the lower the costs should be. Clearly, in this case, managerial behavior is related to cost performance one year later but *not* at the time of the behavior assessment.

Similar results were obtained when the analysis was based on peer leadership within the work group. The same three leadership variables were used, but this time they dealt with the extent to which work-group members saw their own colleagues providing peer leadership in the form of support, interaction facilitation, and work facilitation. Using 1966 measurements of peer leadership, and again using performance data for four consecutive months in 1966, only 1 of the 12 possible correlations was significant. Peer support yielded $-.31$ correlation with performance in one of the four months.

The results again were quite different when the 1966 measures of peer leadership behavior, namely, peer support, peer work facilitation, and peer interaction facilitation, were related to performance results for four consecutive months one year later. All of the 12 possible correlations between the 1966 measurements of peer leadership and the 1967 measurements of performance are statistically significant. They range in magnitude from −.41 to −.59.

Comparable findings were obtained for five different indexes measuring intervening variables. These variables reflect the level of (a) work motivation; (b) communication, upward, downward, and lateral; (c) control, including managements' capacity to control work-group behavior; (d) interdepartmental coordination; and (e) decision making. The 1966 measurements of these variables when correlated with 1966 performance data for four consecutive months yielded only 2 statistically significant correlations out of a possible 20 (that is, 5 × 4). When the 1966 measurements of the five intervening variables were related to 1967 performance data, that is, one year later, all 20 of the correlation coefficients were significant and varied from −.37 to −.68. For the communication index, the correlations with the four monthly performance indexes were −.57, −.58, −.67, and −.68.

When measurements of the causal and intervening variables made in 1967 are related to performance data for four consecutive months in 1967, more of the correlations are statistically significant than for the 1966 data for both sets of measurements. Eight of 12 correlations relating managerial behavior to monthly measurements of performance, 4 of 12 peer correlations, and 17 of 20 correlations relating intervening variables to performance measurements are large enough to be statistically significant at the .05 level.

Nevertheless, the correlations between the 1966 measurements of causal and intervening variables and the performance data for one year later are quite consistently higher than the correlations between measurements of performance data and causal and intervening variables made at or near the same time in 1967. Thus, 12 of 12 correlations between the three measures of managerial behavior (support, work facilitation, and interaction facilitation) and four monthly measurements of performance are higher for the 1966–67 comparison than for the correlations based entirely on 1967 data. The same is true for 12 of 12 correlations dealing with peer leadership, and for 17 of 20 correlations relating intervening variables to performance data.

The results just reported are for a continuous process manufacturing plant. Yuchtman found similar results in data from sales organizations.[5] For example, he found that causal variables related to performance data measured at the same time yielded 10 significant correlations. When these same causal variables were related to performance data measured one year after the measurement of the causal variables, he obtained higher correlations generally and 14 instead of 10 significant correlations.

These results of the relationships over time among the causal, intervening, and end-result variables are, of course, consistent with theoretical

---

[5] E. Yuchtman, "A Study of Organizational Effectiveness" (Ph.D. diss., University of Michigan, 1966).

expectations. Data from other research sites involving other kinds of work and industries and for longer time periods soon will be available. The pattern that these results display will be extremely interesting.

Although the current findings correspond, in general, with expectations, it is important to add that often the relationships are appreciably more complex than expected and require the development and use of more elaborate analytical models than originally had been anticipated.

An example of these complex interrelationships involves the relationship between the capacity to exercise influence on decisions affecting a man's work and his productivity. Among scientists and engineers, the capacity to influence decisions concerning one's own work is associated with greater productivity.[6] But as Farris has shown, for engineering personnel, these relationships can be circular. Outstanding past performance increases the likelihood that a man can exert influence on decisions affecting his technical goals.[7] This relationship, which Farris found to be more marked than the converse, shows the pervasive influence of excellent performance. The high-performing engineer saw himself as being able to exert more influence on establishing the goals designated for him. He was more absorbed in his work, had more competent subordinates, and a better salary. These results make a great deal of sense. One would expect that individuals who have demonstrated greater capacity would have more influence on decisions and related activities both within their work group and in the organization generally. Effective group decision making enables every person to be heard, but the weight of each in the decision-making process is influenced appreciably by his demonstrated competence. This effect of a person's performance upon his capacity to exert influence is shown diagrammatically in Figure 37–1 by the feedback loops.

Applications of Organizational Theory and Principles of Organizational Change

The available and growing evidence justifies the view that further research very probably will demonstrate strong and consistent relationships among the causal, intervening, and end-result variables; that certain leadership styles and management systems consistently will be found more highly motivating and yielding better organizational performance than others.

If this proves to be the case, the emergence of more valid and effective organizational theory and improved management systems will have a widespread impact on all kinds of administration: education, hospital,

---

[6] D. C. Pelz and F. M. Andrews, *Scientists in Organizations: Productive Climates for Research and Development* (New York: John Wiley & Sons, 1966).

[7] G. F. Farris, "A Causal Analysis of Scientific Performance" (Ph.D. diss., University of Michigan, 1966).

business, and government. The application of improved management systems will lead to substantial improvement in organizational performance, accompanied by better physical and mental health and greater member satisfaction. The most important consequences, however, are likely to occur in fields other than administration.

To illustrate briefly, it is obvious that our society faces some extremely difficult and serious problems: deterioration of inner cities and urban riots; worldwide population exposion; student demonstrations and riots; social and economic development in the newer nations; conflicts among nations; and threats of nuclear and biological warfare.

In the past, nations have relied primarily on trial and error and "muddling through" to deal with these and other global problems. One can hope that the world's most enlightened leaders will turn soon to social science research for the solution of these problems.

If this were to occur tomorrow and if substantial funds were made available for the research, the progress initially would be slow. The nature of these serious problems is such that researching them is a very difficult task. The causes of the problems are extremely complex, the frequencies of the cause-and-effect cycles tend to be low (for example, urban riots or student demonstrations), and the cycles are of long duration. Another primary reason for the research being retarded and difficult is that the performance criteria available for evaluating any particular approach or solution to such major problems are usually inadequate or inaccurate. Studies designed to discover cause and effect relationships make progress more slowly and require vastly more data when the effects, that is, performance data, are inadequate, inaccurate, or "rare event" phenomena. Urban riots, for example, are rare events phenomena since they occur in any one city rather infrequently. When the performance criteria are inadequate or inaccurate, attempts to evaluate the effectiveness of any solution or strategy for dealing with the problem often yield unclear or contradictory relationships because of the "noise" or errors of measurement present. Under these conditions, starting de novo in research on a problem and gradually establishing cause and effect relationships is a slow process requiring a large number of observations to compensate for the errors in the performance criteria. On these kinds of problems, much faster progress can be made in the discovery and testing of new, more workable solutions if a relevant general theory or model can be applied and tested. All available fragmentary and relatively unreliable data can be used to evaluate such an overall theory and the strategies based on it. An effective valid theory can then be confirmed even though the performance criteria are spotty and at times contain errors.

Organizational research in business firms can provide the relevant general theory needed to accelerate the progress of research on these serious societal problems. There are two reasons for this being possible. First, the *fundamental* variables dealt with in business organizational research are essentially the same as those involved in these societal problems, namely, such variables as leadership, motivation, communication, interaction and the structure through which interactions occur, and conflict management. Second, organizational research in business establishments frequently can be undertaken in situations where there are (a) relatively accurate measurements of performance and (b) large populations of cause and effect cycles. Organizational research of this type, therefore, can provide the general theory and models for research and successful experimentation in seeking sound solutions to societal problems. In addition, the theory presently emerging from business organizational research can be used to derive potentially promising steps and strategies for dealing with these problems on an interim basis.

The theories from research in business companies can be used, for example, to suggest more effective organizational or institutional structure through which more constructive interactions can occur than is now the case. They can suggest programs for aiding leaders and other relevant persons to develop greater skill in establishing cooperative interaction and problem solving among conflicting parties. Another contribution would be the use of these theories to guide the building of appreciably more effective interaction-influence systems than presently exist. Effective multiple, overlapping, group interaction-influence systems are required to cope successfully with the kinds of problems suggested above.[8] These examples illustrate the immediate contributions that organizational research can be expected to make toward the solutions of serious societal problems.

If expectations are realized, or even partially realized, with regard to finding consistent dependable relationships among the causal, intervening, and end-result variables, one can expect, in the next decade, great progress in the development of appreciably more complex and powerful theories of organization and organizational change. These theories and related principles and procedures can contribute greatly toward the solution of any problems that involve conflict, interaction, or social organization. Business organizational research will then become, much more than at present, a source of general knowledge with wide applicability.

---

[8] Likert, *New Patterns of Management,* chap. 12; idem, *Human Organization,* chap. 10.

38. DURABILITY OF ORGANIZATIONAL CHANGE *

Stanley E. Seashore and David G. Bowers

THE AIM OF THIS ARTICLE is to add a modest footnote to the growing literature concerning planned change in the structure and function of formal organizations. The question asked is whether changes that have been planned, successfully introduced, and confirmed by measurements, over but a relatively short span of time, can survive as permanent features of the organization. Will such a changed organization become stabilized in its new state, or will it continue the direction and pace of change, or perhaps revert to its earlier state?

This report will include a brief review of an earlier effort to change an organization, a presentation of some new data about the present state of the organization, and some first speculations about the meaning of the data for the understanding of psychological and social phenomena in formal organizations.

BACKGROUND

The earlier events against which our new data are to be set are reported rather fully elsewhere.[1] A brief review of the essential facts will set the stage.

In late 1961 the Harwood company purchased its major competitor, the Weldon company. This brought under common ownership and general management two organizations remarkably similar in certain features and remarkably different in others. Both made and marketed similar products using equipment and manufacturing processes of a like kind; were of similar size in terms of business volume and number of employees; served similar and partially overlapping markets; were family-owned and owner-managed firms; and had similar histories of growth and enjoyed high reputation in the trade.

The differences between the two organizations are of particular interest. The Harwood company had earned some prominence and respect

---

* From *American Psychologist* 25 (1970): 227–33. Copyright 1970 by the American Psychological Association. Reprinted by permission.

[1] See A. J. Marrow, D. G. Bowers, and S. E. Seashore, *Management by Participation* (New York: Harper & Row, 1967).

for their efforts over many years to operate the organization as a participative system with high value given to individual and organizational development, as well as to effective performance. The Weldon company had for years been managed in a fashion that prevails in the garment industry, with a highly centralized, authoritarian philosophy with secondary concern for individual development and organizational maintenance. The two organizations were in 1962, rather extreme examples from the continuum vaguely defined by the terms authoritarian versus participative. Measurements in both firms in 1962 confirmed that the difference was not merely impressionistic, but was represented in quantitative assessments of the organizational processes for planning, coordination, communication, motivation, and work performance, and was represented as well in member attitudes. The two firms were also sharply contrasting in their performance in 1962, even though over a longer span of years their business accomplishments had been similar. In 1962 Weldon, in sharp contrast to Harwood, was losing money, experiencing high costs, generating many errors of strategy and work performance, suffering from member disaffection with consequent high absenteeism and high turnover. Weldon, despite its technical, fiscal, and market strengths, was near the point of disaster.

The new owners set out on a program to rebuild the Weldon enterprise according to the model of the Harwood company. The ultimate aim was to make the Weldon firm a viable and profitable economic unit within a short period of time. A rather strenuous and costly program was envisioned, including some modernization of the plant, improved layout and flow of work, improvements in records and production control methods, and product simplification, as well as changes in the human organization. The renewal program concerning the organization itself concerns us here.

The approach to organizational change can be characterized briefly in three respects: (a) the conception of the organizational characteristics to be sought; (b) the conception of processes for changing persons and organizational systems; and (c) the linking of the social system to the work system.

The guiding assumptions or "philosophy" on which the change program was based included elements such as the following:

1. It was assumed that employees would have to gain a realistic sense of security in their jobs and that this security would have to arise basically out of their own successful efforts to improve their organization and their performance, not out of some bargained assurances.
2. The introduction of substantial change in the work environment requires that employees have confidence in the technical competence and humane values of the managers and supervisors; this confidence

can be earned only if it is reciprocated by placing confidence in the employees.

3. In a situation of rapid change it is particularly necessary to use procedures of participation in the planning and control of the work and of the changes; such procedures are needed at all levels of the organization.

4. The rebuilding of an organization may require an input of technical resources and capital on a substantial scale—not unlike the investments required to rework a technology or control system of a factory.

5. Management involves skills and attitudes that can be defined, taught, and learned, and these skills and attitudes need not be confined to high rank staff; each member of the organization, at least in some limited degree, must learn to help manage his own work and that of others related to him.

6. Guidelines such as these are not readily understood and accepted unless they can be linked to concrete events and to the rational requirements of the work to be done and the problems to be solved.

The conception of change processes incorporated in the rebuilding of the Weldon organization emphasized the application of multiple and compatible change forces. The physical improvements in work resources and conditions were to be accompanied by informational clarity, enhanced motivation through rewards, and ample skill training and practice. That is, change was to be introduced simultaneously at the situational, cognitive, motivational, and behavioral levels so that each would support the others.

The linking of the social organization to the work system was to be accomplished through efforts, however limited, to design work places, work flows, information flows, and the like in a manner not merely compatible with but integral with the associated social organization and organizational processes.

The program of rebuilding the organization was carried out by the local management with substantial assistance and stimulation from the new owners and from a variety of consultants, including psychologists. The general planning and guidance of the program were influenced primarily by Alfred Marrow, board chairman of the Harwood Corporation and fellow of the Division of Industrial and Organizational Psychology of the American Psychological Association. The role of the Institute for Social Research was not that of change agent, but rather that of observing, recording, measuring, and analyzing the course of events and the change that resulted.

The change program was successful in important respects. Within two years there occurred improvements in employee satisfactions, motivations, and work performance. The organization took on characteristics of an adaptive, self-controlling, participative system. The firm as a business unit moved from a position of loss to one of profit. At the end of 1964, after two years of change effort, the factory was abandoned as a research site, the rate of input of capital and external manpower into the change program diminished substantially, and the factory and its organization were expected to settle down to something like a "normal" state.

EXPECTATIONS ABOUT CHANGE

From the start of this organizational change program there was a concern about the long-run consequences of the program, and there was uncertainty about the permanence of change. The following quotations from our earlier report illustrate the intentions, hopes, and doubts:

the whole organization, from the plant manager down to the production workers, were taken into an exercise in joint problem-solving through participative methods in groups, with a view toward making such procedures a normal part of the management of the plant.[2]

The refreezing of Weldon in a new and more effective state is not regarded as a permanent thing, but as another stage in the evolution and continuous adaptation of the organization. Some features of the conversion plan explicitly include the provision of built-in capacities for easier change in the future.[3]

Will the changes at Weldon last? The only evidence we have at the present time is that the change from a predominantly "authoritative" to a dominantly "consultative" type of management organization persisted for at least two years in the view of the managers and supervisors involved. Surely there exist forces toward a reversion to the old Weldon form of organizational life; it remains an uncertainty whether they will or will not win out over the new forces toward consolidation of change and further change of the intended kinds.[4]

In mid-1969, four and one-half years after the termination of the intensive change program, Dr. Bowers and I invited ourselves back to the Weldon plant for a follow-up measurement of the state of the organization. This remeasurement consisted of a one-day visit to the plant by a research assistant who administered questionnaires to managers, supervisors, and a sample of the employees.[5] In addition, certain information was abstracted from the firm's records, and the views of the plant manager were solicited as to changes that had taken place and possible reasons for change. We can turn directly to a few tables and figures representing the changes and the situation as of 1969.

---

[2] Ibid., p. 69.
[3] Ibid., p. 232.
[4] Ibid., p. 244.
[5] The assistance of Edith Wessner is acknowledged.

TABLE 38–1

Changes in Job Attitudes

Item	1962 %	1964 %	1969 %
Company better than most.	22	28	36
Own work satisfying	77	84	91
Satisfied with pay system	22	27	28
Company tries to maintain earnings	26	44	41
Satisfied with supervisor	64	54	54
Like fellow employees	85	86	85
Group cohesiveness	25	25	30
Plan to stay indefinitely	72	87	66
Expect future improvement in situation	23	31	43

RESULTS

First, we present some data from the production employees. Table 38–1 shows selected items from our questionnaire survey bearing on the issue of whether there has occurred a decline, a rise, or a stabilization of the attitudes, satisfactions, and optimism of the employees. The table shows the percentage of employees giving the two most favorable responses, of five offered, to each question. The columns represent the results in 1962 before the change program began, in 1964 at the conclusion of the formal change effort, and in 1969.

The general picture is one of the maintenance of earlier gains in the favorability of employee attitudes or the further improvement in attitudes. This observation holds for seven of the nine indicators. The remaining two deserve brief special comment.

Satisfaction with supervisors declined during the period of the active change program but has remained relatively high and constant since 1964. The initial decline is viewed as a consequence of the substantial change in the supervisors' role during the active change program. During that period, the supervisors acquired substantially more responsibility and authority as well as some new activities and duties that are thought to have removed the supervisors from a peerlike to a superior status relationship with the operators, which they retain now. This interpretation is, of course, speculative but made before the 1969 data were in hand.

The decline in the proportion of employees planning to stay on indefinitely is rather difficult to assess. The rise between 1962 and 1964 can be attributed to the improvement in pay and working conditions in that period. The subsequent decline is to be accounted for, partly, by the fact of recent production expansion and the presence on the payroll of a relatively larger number of turnover-prone short-service employees.

TABLE 38-2

Change in Task-Orientation Indicators

Item	1962 %	1964 %	1969 %
Company quick to improve methods	18	24	31
Company good at planning	22	26	35
Not delayed by poor services	76	79	90
Produce what rates call for.	44	67	53
Expect own productivity to improve	63	55	62
Peers approve of high producers.	58	58	66
Closeness of task supervision.	38	27	47
Desired closeness of supervision.	57	52	64
Mean productivity (% of standard)	87	114	?

One might also speculate that rising prosperity during the period might have increased the attractiveness of marriage, child bearing, or retirement for these female employees. In any case, the decline in the percentage committed to long job tenure appears to be at odds with the general rise in job satisfactions and in the marked rise in optimism about the future improvement in the Weldon situation. We should add that the decline in percentage committed to long tenure is confirmed by the fact of a moderate rise in actual turnover rates in recent months.

Table 38-2 shows a few selected items bearing on the question whether the rise in satisfactions and expectations is accompanied by some loss in productivity concerns and task orientation. The data, again, are from employee questionnaire responses (except for the last line) and show changes from 1962 to 1964, and then to 1969.

Five of the indicators reflect a rise in level of task orientation and production concern since the end of the formal change program. The remaining items are not negative, but merely indeterminate. There is clearly a rise in recent years in the percentage of employees who say the firm is quick to improve work methods, good at planning, provides services (maintenance, supplies, scheduling), who report that their peers approve of high producers, and who themselves desire frequent and ready access to supervisory help. Two sets of data require special comment.

The data on productivity, three lines in the table, should be considered as a set. The numbers show that the self-report of "Nearly always producing what the rates call for" rose substantially during the active change program, and this is confirmed by the actual productivity records of the firm as shown in the last line "Mean productivity against standard." During the same period, the percentage of employees expecting a further gain in their own productivity declined, as it should have considering that more employees were approaching the firm's hoped-for level of high productivity and earnings. By 1969 there was some decline in the percentage reporting high productivity and a corresponding rise in the percentage expecting a future rise in their productivity; this pair of related changes appears to reflect the presence on the staff of an increasing number of relatively new employees not yet up to the level of skill and performance they may reasonably expect to attain. There is a crucial item of missing data in the last line of the table; for technical reasons, we have not been able to calculate the current actual productivity rate in a form that allows confident comparisons with the earlier figures. Our best estimate is that productivity has been stable with a slight decline in recent months arising from the recent introduction of additional inexperienced employees.

Attention is also suggested to the pair of lines in Table 38–2 concerning closeness of supervision. At all three times of measurement, these production workers desired more close supervision than they actually experienced; these employees, unlike those in some other organizations, see their supervisors to be potentially helpful in improving productivity and increasing piece-rate earnings. The decline in experienced closeness of supervision during the period 1962–64 matches other evidence to be presented later that during this period there was a substantial change in the supervisors' role that diverted the supervisors from immediate floor supervision and left a temporary partial shortage of this service to production workers. The figures show that by 1969 this supervisory deficit had been recouped and more. This sustains our general view that during the years following the Weldon change program there has been not a decline in concern for task performance among employees and in the organizational system generally but rather a further gain in task orientation.

The change in supervisory behavior mentioned earlier is shown in Figure 38–1. We attempted at the three points in time to measure the extent to which supervisors, in the view of employees, engaged in behaviors we categorize as "supportive," "goal emphasizing," and "work facilitating." (Two additional dimensions of leader behavior that we now use in describing organizations are not represented here because they were not yet identified in 1962; we chose to continue use of the initial measurement methods rather than to update them.)

Figure 38–1 shows that the amount of supervisory supportiveness experienced by employees remained constant during the 1962–64 period and has risen slightly since then. Goal emphasis and work facilitation both dropped during the active change program, for reasons mentioned earlier, and have since risen above their 1962 levels. These data sustain our belief that the Weldon organization since 1964 has increased its

FIGURE 38–1

Change in Three Dimensions of Supervisory Leadership Behavior

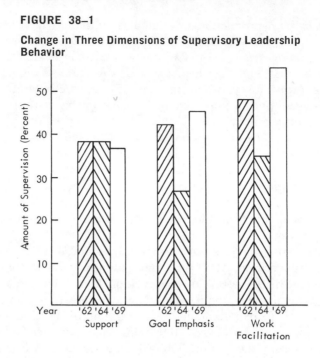

expression of concern for production goals and its provision of conditions for effective work performance, and at no cost of declining concern for employee attitudes and satisfactions.

One more set of data from the employees is pertinent here, namely, their description of the amount and hierarchical distribution of control in the Weldon organization. One of the explicit aims of the change program was that of increasing the total amount of control and of altering the distribution of control so that lower rank people—supervisors and operators—would have some added degree of control. This was accomplished during the change program period to a very limited and nonsignificant degree. Subsequent changes have been in the direction intended and more substantial in degree. The data are shown in Figure 38–2. In 1969, compared with the earlier periods, there is more control being exercised in total, with a notable increment in the case of the headquarters staff, a further small decline for the local plant management, and increments for the supervisors and for the employees. There appears to have been a change of modest degree, more or less as hoped for, and there has clearly not been a reversion to the original condition of concentrated control in the hands of the plant manager.

We turn now to some indicators of the state of the Weldon organization from the views of the supervisors and managers. The data presented in Figure 38–3 are derived from Likert's assessment instrument "Profile

FIGURE 38–2

Change in Amount and Hierarchical Distribution of Control

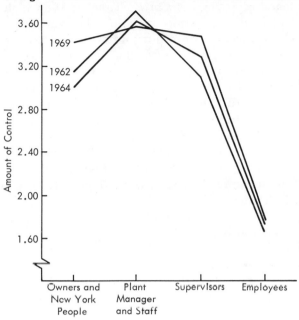

FIGURE 38–3

Change in Profile of Organizational Characteristics

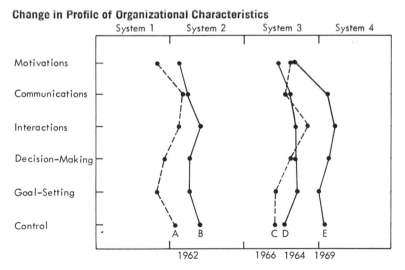

of Organizational and Performance Characteristics." [6] Most readers will have some acquaintance with this instrument and the theory and research data that it expresses, but a brief characterization might be helpful. The instrument used is a 43-item graphic-scale rating form that allows the respondent to describe his own organization as it presently functions and as he ideally would like it to function. The items are so chosen and arranged that the respondent may report a syndrome of organizational characteristics that locates the organization on a scale ranging from "authoritative" to "participative." Likert discerns four regions of this scale, named Systems 1, 2, 3, and 4, with word labels ranging from "Authoritarian" through "Benevolent Authoritarian" and "Consultative" to "Participative." The conception is analogous to McGregor's "Theory X" and "Theory Y" scale, and also to Blake's two-dimensioned matrix. To put it somewhat disrespectfully, the bad guys are thought to have and to prefer System 1 organizations while good guys aspire to and approach the System 4 state. The results for Weldon, 1962, 1964, and 1969 are represented in Figure 38–3.

At the left of the field are two graph lines showing the state of the Weldon organization in 1962, first as rated by the Institute for Social Research research team from interview protocols and observations, and next and somewhat more favorably as rated by the supervisors and managers on the scene. Weldon at that time was described to be autocratic—in some respects rather harshly autocratic and in some respects more benevolently autocratic. The state of the organization in 1964 and in 1966 is represented in the next two lines. These data are from supervisors and managers; they indicate a pattern of change that is substantial in magnitude and wholly compatible with the intentions embodied in the Weldon change program. There was no regression toward the earlier state during the 1964–66 period. The right-hand line represents the results of our 1969 assessment; it shows that in the view of the managers and supervisors at Weldon, the organization has progressed still further toward their ideal of a participative organizational system.

A final remark should be made about measured changes in Weldon before we turn to a consideration of the meaning of these data. Some readers will be interested in business outcomes as well as in the attitudes and behavior of the members of the organization. Briefly, Weldon moved from a position of substantial capital loss in 1962 to substantial return on investment in 1964; this direction of change in profitability has continued through 1968, the last year of record. Employee earnings which rose substantially between 1962 and 1964 have been sustained at a relatively high level. During the period since 1964 there have been substantial gains in efficiency and volume for the factory as a whole. New

---

[6] R. Likert, *New Patterns of Management* (New York: McGraw-Hill Book Co., 1961); idem, *The Human Organization* (New York: McGraw-Hill Book Co., 1967).

products and work methods have been introduced. By such business indicators, Weldon is a successful organization.

DURABLE CHANGE

The evidence we must weigh, although somewhat mixed and with a few contrary elements, appears to sustain the conclusion that the Weldon organization, far from reverting to its prior condition, has during recent years made additional progress toward the organizational goals envisioned by the owners and managers in 1962, and envisioned as well by supervisors and production employees at a somewhat later time. This outcome invites speculations about the psychological and social forces that are at work.

We confess a brief regret that there was not an opposite outcome, for we are rather better equipped with ideas about organizational stability and regression than we are with ideas about organizational change and continuing development. For example, before the data became available, we were prepared to make some remarks about the "Hawthorne effect" —about the superficiality and transient quality of organizational and behavioral changes induced under conditions of external attention and pressure; but it boggles the mind to think of a "Hawthorne effect" persisting for over eight years among people half of whom were not on the scene at the time of the original change. Similarly, we were prepared to make wise remarks about cultural forces, habits, and the natural predilection of managers for nonparticipative methods; these we thought would help explain a reversion to the prevailing conditions in organizations. We were prepared to assert that in the absence of contrary environmental forces, external influences, and purposive continuing change efforts of a vigorous kind, an organization would migrate back to some more primitive form of organizational life.

Clearly we need to appeal to other ideas than these. We are, all of us, ill prepared to do so. Two recent and fairly comprehensive reviews of organizational change strategies [7] say nothing about the permanence of continuation of change processes, except for a remark by Shepard that "change in the direction of collaboration-consensus patterns [participative patterns] . . . facilitates growth, change and adaptation to new environmental challenges and opportunities." [8]

A first explanatory idea rests on the possibility that the heavy investment of external talent, money, and effort that characterized the original change period at Weldon has been continued during the subsequent

[7] H. J. Leavitt, "Applied Organizational Change in Industry," in *Handbook of Organizations,* ed. J. G. March (Chicago: Rand-McNally, 1965); H. A. Shepard, "Changing Interpersonal and Intergroup Relationships in Organizations," in *Handbook of Organizations,* ed. J. G. March (Chicago: Rand-McNally, 1965).

[8] Shepard, "Changing Interpersonal and Intergroup Relationships," p. 1141.

years. We are assured that this is not the case. There has indeed been some additional use of external consultants, but at a modest rate that is considered normal and permanent. There has indeed been further improvement and change in the work system and the production facilities, but at no more than a permanently sustainable rate. There has indeed been a continuation of certain organizational activities introduced as part of the original change program, but these are regarded as normal operating procedure and not as special change efforts. Economic conditions have been favorable to the firm, but they were also favorable at the distressed time preceding the change of ownership in 1962.

We believe that there are three other lines of explanation that do bear scrutiny. These thoughts about the Weldon experience are not offered with any sense of great insight or of conceptual innovation. They are offered only as suggestions for lines of inquiry and emphasis in future organizational research. The first concerns the provision of "lock-in" devices that make difficult the reversal of the original change.

It was mentioned earlier that the original change program contained some notions of seeking mutually reinforcing change action across the psychological, organizational, and technological domains. A central idea was to make structural changes in the organization that matched the work system and that did not violate reasonable assumptions about the values and motives of individual members. For example, the revitalized piece-rate pay system was viewed to be viable only if sustained by the provision of assured services that allowed high earnings, a revision of the record and information flow system that assured instant supervisory response to low earnings, and a moderating of the prior job assignment system so that a production employee could become skilled in the work assigned. The idea of systemic consistency is surely an elementary one, no more than common sense—a habit of thought for those who have learned to view the factory as a total system in which all elements are interdependent. The interdependence of elements tends to preserve, to enhance, and to "lock in" the central characteristics of the system and thus to prevent retrogression.

A second factor in Weldon's continuation of intended change might lie in the earlier legitimation of concern about organizational processes. This is speculative, for we have no ready way to assess the extent to which there was implanted the habit of deliberate and self-conscious examination of the potential side effects of the many policy and operating decisions, usually technical or economic in origin, that arise daily. One of the fragmenting features of many organizations is the tendency to isolate problems, to treat them as if they could be optimally resolved without reference to their broader context. An organization habituated at all levels to think about, discuss openly, and to weigh properly the full range of elements in the organizational system might well have unusual capacities for self-maintenance and self-development.

A third possible explanation of the maintenance of the changes at Weldon and their further development under conditions of limited continuing external influence might lie in the inherent merit of the participative organizational model. Could it be that people who have experienced a taste of it get hooked, know what they want, and lend their effort to maintaining it? A glance at the newspaper headlines on almost any day will suggest that some of our fellow citizens do not like what they are experiencing in formal organizations and have thoughts of having something better, by force if necessary.

39. THE ACHIEVEMENT MOTIVE
AND ADVANCEMENT IN TWO
TYPES OF ORGANIZATIONS *

John D. W. Andrews

RECENTLY MCCLELLAND, in *The Achieving Society*, has demonstrated a positive relationship between strong national achievement concerns, as coded from children's readers and other cultural products, and rapid economic development.[1] He has also shown that this connection is mediated by socialization practices and adult occupational choice. That is, parents in achievement-oriented societies are more apt to value achievement and to use child-raising practices which are known to produce strong need for achievement (n Achievement). High n Achievement members of such societies, as they grow up, tend to choose business occupations as the most satisfying to their liking for moderate risk, ample feedback about results, and personal responsibility for decisions. These findings constitute the outlines of a causal sequence leading to a high level of national economic productivity.

The present study is directed toward clarifying the link between individual n Achievement and broader social processes, through an investigation of how executives with various motive patterns advance in various types of firms. Most businessmen do not contribute to national economic productivity through strictly individual activity, but rather through participation in and leadership of business organizations. One may extend McClelland's position to argue that a successful firm works well because it is organized to provide an effective channel for the economically productive efforts of its achievement-oriented members, and that a predomi-

* From *Journal of Personality and Social Psychology* 6, no. 2 (1967): 163–68. Copyright 1967 by the American Psychological Association. Reprinted by permission.
[1] D. C. McClelland, *The Achieving Society* (Princeton, N.J.: Van Nostrand, 1961).

nance of such firms should add up to a rapid rate of national economic growth.

It is well established that individuals with strong n Achievement work hard and effectively at tasks which provide the opportunity for attaining a personal standard of excellence.[2] Further, since businesses generally provide many opportunities for this sort of achievement, and benefit from it, it is to be expected that executives with high n Achievement will advance most rapidly (as indicated by promotions and raises) in their organizations.

This simple prediction is complicated, however, by the fact that such advancement is not solely a function of the individual's performance, but depends on the values and judgments of his superiors in the firm; and, while business in general may be favorable to achievement, it seems probable that firms vary somewhat in the singlemindedness with which they reward executive productiveness. This is particularly likely in a country such as Mexico, the site of the present study, where the dominant values differ as follows from the achievement-linked orientations of the United States: concern with "lineal" (older-younger) relationships, rather than with peer relationships or individual activity; preference for "being" rather than "doing"; fatalism rather than subjugation of nature; and present rather than future time orientation.[3] These different value orientations will probably dictate in part the kinds of executive behaviors that are rewarded by advancement and thus the kinds of concerns it is useful for executives to develop in a given firm. Also, those who advance most rapidly are apt to be men who already share the firm's central values, and who should then use their increased influence in ways that will further strengthen those values.

The foregoing are the basic considerations that have generated these hypotheses:

1. When individual executives are tested for motivational concerns (such as n Achievement), the executive group of a given firm will have high scores on the motive that parallels the orientation of the firm as a whole.
2. Advancement in the firm will be a joint function of individuals' motive patterns, on the one hand, and dominant firm values, on the other. That is, rapid advancement (as measured by job status, promotions, and raises) is predicted in those cases where there is congruence between individual motive scores and dominant firm orientation. Less rapid advancement should occur when such congruence is absent.

---

[2] See J. W. Atkinson, *Motives in Fantasy, Action, and Society* (Princeton, N.J.: Van Nostrand, 1958), chap. 19; McClelland, *Achieving Society,* chap. 6; and McClelland et al., *The Achievement Motive* (New York: Appleton-Century-Crofts, 1953), chap. 8.

[3] F. Kluckhohn and F. Strodtbeck, *Variations in Value Orientations* (Evanston, Ill.: Row, Peterson, 1961).

METHOD

Firm Selection

The first step in the study was selection of two firms that would provide a clear-cut contrast in value orientations. It was specified that one firm should be highly achievement oriented, progressive and expansive in its policies, and economically successful. The other firm should be less achievement oriented, more conservative and traditional, and less successful economically. It became apparent very early that the second firm selected to be low on these criteria was strongly oriented toward power relationships. For this reason, the firms will be referred to subsequently as Firm A (achievement) and Firm P (power).

The selection of firms was made by Elliott Danzig,[4] an industrial psychologist working in Mexico, from among nine of his client organizations. He was provided with two descriptions of "pure" firm types, elaborations of the characterizations given above, and asked to match them as closely as possible. While his judgments are of an informal, nonquantitative type, they are based on several years intimate acquaintance with the firms and are documented with specific observations; hence, they seem adequate for distinguishing the relative positions of the two organizations on the dimension specified.

Danzig's descriptions of the two firms are as follows:

Firm A. This is an American subsidiary, and prior to the study the parent company sent a new president (an American) to reorganize it. He gave the firm a thorough shaking up. New services and departments were instituted, including an Industrial Relations Department, Advance Planning Department, the launching of new products, and so forth. Production rose 40 percent in one of their four plants, actually to 115 percent of rated capacity, simply as a result of changes designed to make better use of managerial talent. The profits of the company began to rise about a year after the new president's arrival and, interrupted by the recent recession, have again hit record levels (1962). Productivity per employee has gone up. The company is doing well against its competitors in Mexico and is planning a move into a new area of production and marketing as well.

The success of the company is based in considerable part on a vigorous and continuing effort, initiated by the head of the firm, to get the right men in the right jobs. The new president undertook a thorough employee evaluation program as soon as he arrived, making extensive use of psychological testing and freely shifting men around so as to best use their

---

[4] Gratitude is due him for making available the data analyzed in this study, for his collaboration, and for his thoughtful suggestions about the investigation.

capabilities. This man does not hesitate to advance a junior executive to high responsibility, if he seems able to handle it, or to fire an incompetent; his concern with evaluation is such that he has worked out his own point system for combining psychological evaluations into a single score which is used as a minimum criterion for consideration. He also shows considerable diplomatic skill in making men feel pleased with the changes that are made. He has actively urged the employment of Mexicans in high positions, even to the point of moving out Americans, and Mexicans can now look forward to just recognition of their capabilities.

The result of these policies is an atmosphere which provides many opportunities for achievement. Clearly visible to employees, most of whom are Mexican, is the fact that talent and effort are rewarded by increased position and opportunity to act. Many people respond to this challenge, and those who do not are replaced or advised of the fact and given help, if possible, through the counseling service. This company is a good example of the achievement-oriented business firm.

Firm P. This all-Mexican firm has a number of features which place it at the relatively nonentrepreneurial end of the scale. While in a relatively expansive area of economy, its early lead based on a large initial investment has been dwindling as the competition moves up. There has been only one expansion of operations in the past few years, partly because of discriminatory restrictions by the mayor of Mexico City. It has been argued by persons who know the firm and the city that a resourceful firm could find ways to circumvent such restrictions.

The internal environment of the company presents a picture consistent with the above. The firm is headed by a man who is generally very unpredictable. He runs his economic empire, playing the grand patron, rather like a feudalistic hacienda. All employees, good or bad, are considered the responsibility of the company, but an executive is quite likely to get a dressing down at one of the boss' command-performance gatherings for his staff.

This pattern has its effects throughout the organization. It produces insecurity and anxiety, an atmosphere in which an executive can never be sure of what the results of his decisions or attempts at creative ventures are going to be. This leads to timidity and a concern for hanging on to one's job rather than doing it well. Responsibility for getting a job done is not clearly given, and such is the fear of unpredictable consequences that few are willing to take the risk of making full use of the decision-making scope they do have. A further consequence of this is that people choose their subordinates with an eye to getting those who will not challenge their positions. They tend to prefer easily dominated yes-men who will not make their own work look poor by being too conspicuously productive.

Work in the company suffers from the effects of this entangling paternalism. There is reluctance to give rational, constructive criticism, with the result that employees get very little feedback about the quality of their work. Similarly, there is hesitation about firing an incompetent person, toward whom a paternal responsibility is apt to be felt. Thus Firm P shows few achievement-oriented characteristics and is more strongly oriented around issues of dominance and dependence.

In view of the strong dominance-submission or lineal power orientation present in Firm P, it was decided to study TAT-measured n Power as well as n Achievement, thus producing a symmetry that has made it possible to test the relationship between two types of motives and two types of firm orientations. The parallel between the description of Firm P and TAT themes scorable for n Power seems to have reasonably good face validity and is strengthened by the use of a stimulus picture that is very sensitive to superior-subordinate or lineal relationships (see discussion under Measurements section below).

Subjects

Subjects were selected as follows. All Mexican executives on whom complete data were available were included in the study, a sampling that reflects the nearly all Mexican composition of the firms. (Firm A had a few Americans.) Since the subjects were tested because of management referral for evaluation, they were probably not a random sample of the total executive group; their rate of promotion, for example, was somewhat higher in each firm than that for the total group. Also, there is no way of ruling out the possibility that executives were selected for testing by somewhat different means in the two firms; one such difference, in proportions of upper- and lower-level men, has been controlled for in the data analysis pertaining to Hypothesis 1 (Tables 39–1 and 39–2). It seems unlikely, however, that different proportions of certain types of individuals in the samples from the two firms could account for differences in the association between variables *within* a single firm, and, since it is these associations that are predicted in Hypothesis 2, it does not seem probable that they are artifactual products of such sampling variations.

Measurements

The variables discussed in the main hypotheses were operationalized via the following measures:

1. Individual strength of n Achievement and n Power was coded by the author in the standard manner from TAT stories obtained orally by clinical psychologists two to four years prior to the present study.[5] All scoring was completed before the relation of other variables was examined. Three TAT pictures were used, the only three from a large set

---

[5] See manuals in Atkinson, *Motives in Fantasy, Action, and Society.*

TABLE 39–1

Mean n Achievement Scores Classified According to Firm (A and P) and Job Level (I and II)

	Job Level I			Job Level II		
Firm	N	M	SD	N	M	SD
A	9	7.00	4.69	17	2.59	3.35
P	21	2.05	3.42	9	4.29	3.68
Difference (A − P)		+4.95[b]			−1.70[a]	

[a] $t = 1.16$, $p > .10$ (1-tailed test).
[b] $t = 2.86$, $p < .005$ (1-tailed test).

TABLE 39–2

Mean n Power Scores Classified According to Firm (A and P) and Job Level (I and II)

	Job Level I			Job Level II		
Firm	N	M	SD	N	M	SD
A	9	0.44	0.83	17	1.29	1.57
P	21	2.05	1.99	9	0.89	0.99
Difference (A − P)		−1.61[b]			+0.40[a]	

[a] $t = .79$, $p > .20$ (1-tailed test).
[b] $t = 3.13$, $p < .005$ (1-tailed test).

which had been given to all subjects. These were: (a) a man in a white shirt sitting at what might be a draftsman's worktable with a small, unclear photo (possibly of his family) placed on it, (b) a nearly naked man climbing or hanging on a rope,[6] (c) heads of two men, older and younger, close together.[7] Virtually all of the power imagery was elicited by this last card, and this was entirely concerned with themes of fatherlike guidance, instruction, or domination of a younger man. This lineal power theme must be distinguished from other kinds of power situations (for example, one in which peer influence is the theme) and is especially suitable for the purposes of this study. This is true, first, because of its relevance to the superior-subordinate relations which are very important in a

---

[6] See H. A. Murray, *Thematic Apperception Test Manual* (Cambridge: Harvard University Press, 1943), card 17 BM.

[7] Ibid., card 7BM.

business firm; and second, because of its congruence with the lineal, paternalistic pattern which is believed to characterize Firm P and Mexico in general as well.[8]

2. The variable of individual success in the firm was measured in three ways. The first measure was an estimate of job-status level at the time of the study; this was a measure of success since it presumably represents the outcome of an executive's efforts at advancement over an extended period. Job status was classified into two categories: Level I, major executives, decision-makers in the firm; and Level II, minor executives, concerned primarily with decision implementation. These estimates were made on the basis of descriptions of the formal organization, such as organizational charts. It will be noted that since achievement-related behavior (taking moderate risks and responsibility, seeking feedback) centers on decision-making and its consequences, Level I should contain all jobs for which n Achievement is a crucial personality characteristic. The second measure of success was the number of promotions received in the four years prior to the time of the study (1958–1962), and the third was the number of raises received in the same time period. Data on this last variable were, unfortunately, unavailable for Firm A.

It will be seen that firm values and evaluation criteria are considered to have been relatively constant over the 4-year period 1958–1962. Similarly, motive strength was measured as of the early part of that period (1958–1960) and is assumed to have been fairly stable over the same time span. Thus the motive measures and the measures of firm orientation are the independent variables of this study, while the indexes of success, which are obtained either as totals over the 4-year period (promotions, raises) or at the end of the period (job status), are subsequent in time and are the dependent variables.

RESULTS

Tables 39–1 and 39–2 are pertinent to testing Hypothesis 1; they present comparisons of mean n Achievement and n Power scores for the two firms, cross classified according to job level. An analysis of variance performed on these data shows that overall firm differences (main row effects) are not statistically reliable, though they are in the right direction. The interaction effects are considerably stronger ($p < .10$), and comparison of the cell means indicates that for both n Achievement and n Power the firm differences are in the predicted direction and highly significant statistically, for the Level I subjects, with a much weaker trend in the opposite direction for the Level II group. In a sense, this finding

---

[8] Kluckhohn and Strodtbeck, *Variations in Value Orientations;* O. Lewis, *The Children of Sanchez* (New York: Random House, 1961).

TABLE 39–3

Correlations, Biserial (r_{bis}) and Pearsonian (r), in Firms A and P between Motive Score (n Achievement and n Power) and Three Measures of Advancement (job level, frequency of promotions, frequency of raises)

Motive	Job Level: I or II[a]		Promoted: Yes or No[a]		No. Raises	
	N	r_{bis}	N	r_{bis}	N	r
Firm A						
n Achievement[b].	26	+.64**	24	+.43***	21	+.36*
n Power[b].	26	−.39**	24	+.11	21	−.20
Firm P						
n Achievement[b].	30	−.37**	30	0.00		
n Power[b].	30	+.38**	30	+.34**		

a Used as dichotomous variable in calculation of r_{bis}.
b Used as continuous variable in calculation of r_{bis}.
* $p < .10$ (1-tailed test).
** $p < .05$ (1-tailed test).
*** $p < .01$ (1-tailed test).

anticipates the results concerning the relationship between motive strength and job level and shows that the two questions cannot be completely separated. If we expect that individuals whose motives are congruent with the firm's orientation will gravitate toward the top, then it is appropriate to test the hypothesis concerning mean motive score differences between firms by focusing on executives who do reach the top, that is, the Level I group. In these terms Tables 39–1 and 39–2 confirm Hypothesis I, since among Level I subjects Firm A is markedly higher in n Achievement and lower in n Power than Firm P.

Table 39–3 presents the relationship between motive strength and the three indexes of success, separately for Firms A and P. As predicted in Hypothesis 2, the correlations are significantly positive between n Achievement and all measures of success in Firm A, and between n Power and all measures of success in Firm P. Further, in three of five instances the nondominant motive is negatively correlated with measures of success, a finding which emphasizes even more strongly the differences between the two firms. In short, these data give firm support to the main hypotheses of the study.

DISCUSSION

The findings reported above show that the patterns of status and advancement in Firms A and P can reasonably be interpreted as the outcome of a mutual adjustment process between men with different motivational concerns, on the one hand, and firms with varying organizational values, on the other. In Firm A, the activities leading to job effectiveness and to advancement appear to coincide, a state of affairs which probably makes for economy of concern and effort among its executives. In Firm P, on the other hand, considerable conflict seems evident: while achievement concern may, as in Firm A, produce good job performance, it is, if anything, a negative factor in advancement; the latter requires a very different orientation to lineal power. In view of this tension between two basic goals of Firm P's executives, it is not surprising that the company as a whole should be less productive economically than Firm A.

The generally opposite relationships of the two motives to advancement in *both* companies emphasize the antagonism of the achievement and lineal power orientations per se. This conclusion is similar to the findings that in the sphere of parent-child relations authoritarianism (especially on the father's part) inhibits n Achievement in the son, since such control is incompatible with the encouragement of independence that fosters achievement concerns.[9] In organization life, too, it appears, the two orientations conflict and have sharply different effects as far as the encouragement of achievement is concerned.

These results, while confirming the importance of n Achievement for business activity, make it necessary to qualify the proposition that business is always achievement oriented and always attractive to high n Achievement individuals.[10] Clearly, this is much less true in Firm P than in Firm A. It seems likely that achievement-oriented businesses like Firm A will be more prevalent in high n Achievement nations, with the result that individual n Achievement is effectively channeled into economic productivity. In countries where other values predominate, however, business firms will probably partake of such values and be less purely achievement oriented (as is true of Firm P in Mexico); in such cases, whatever achievement concern exists in the country will be used ineffectively or deflected into other lines of activity, and business will be less productive as a result.

Finally, it should be noted that the correlations between advancement and motive score (Table 39–3) constitute a refined and objectified version of the informal company descriptions with which the study began. Such correlations not only confirm the original judgments; they are also important new facts about the firms, being indexes of implicit or de facto organizational values. Such indexes, having been given preliminary construct validation in the present study, can subsequently be used in various new ways. One may, for example, compare them with what a firm's managers *say* they use as standards for advancement, or, again, with the "culture" of the firm, as coded from its documents in a way similar to that used by McClelland with children's readers at the national level.[11]

---

[9] McClelland, *Achieving Society.*
[10] Ibid.
[11] Ibid.

It should also be possible to group firms according to type of product, degree of economic success, nationality, or any other characteristic, and then compare the relations between personality and advancement that predominate within different groups. Finally, one might study changes in such correlations, for example, to assess the effects of a change in structure or in management policy.

Section Seven

FATIGUE, ACCIDENTS, AND CONDITIONS OF WORK

INTRODUCTION

THIS SECTION is concerned with certain characteristics and environmental aspects of the job which may reduce or impair work efficiency and, thereby, work output. The question here is: "What factors are related to *work decrement or facilitation* on the job, and how can we modify the conditions of work to minimize decrement and worker injuries?"

Even when everyone is highly motivated, it is clear that continuous activity or work, in certain tasks, leads to reduction in the ability to perform adequately. The term "fatigue" is frequently used to describe this phenomenon. There has been much controversy about the usefulness of this term, since there appears to be no single process which can be termed "fatigue." It has been shown that feelings of tiredness, physiological indications (for example, decreased sugar and increased lactic acid in the blood), and work decrement may or may not occur in the same individuals at the same time. The article by McFarland, "Fatigue in Industry: Understanding Fatigue in Modern Life," outlines some of the problems in the study of fatigue, describes some recent advances in the identification and measurement of fatigue, and presents a current view of this complex problem.

Monotony, or boredom, is another on-the-job phenomenon which may lead to performance deterioration. It is often difficult to distinguish between monotony and the feelings of tiredness associated with fatigue. Both are unpleasant and result from continuous work. However, monot-

439

ony seems more a function of work which presents no challenge to the individual. In fact, many of the principles of motivation described earlier in Section Four (for example, job enrichment) apply to the problem of reducing "monotony."

One of the important things about monotony is that it is, in large measure, dependent on the individual's perception of his job. This is demonstrated in the article by Smith, entitled "The Prediction of Individual Differences in Susceptibility to Industrial Monotony." This article shows that some workers find one job boring, while other workers do not. But what are some of the characteristics of people that make some of them more likely than others to find a given job monotonous? Are they likely to be more intelligent, more ambitious, more extroverted, younger, and so on? The article by Smith presents considerable evidence on these questions.

Another related problem is the effects of shift and nightwork on human functioning. Recent trends in our society have intensified, rather than reduced, the need to evaluate these effects. Examples of operations requiring round-the-clock work are the manning of national defense systems, the monitoring of automated factories, and the use of atomic reactors. In "Shift Work and Human Efficiency," Bloom describes some of the research on the sleep-wakefulness cycle and suggests how the scheduling of shift work might be improved.

In recent years organizations have been experimenting with a number of variations in work schedules, such as the 4-day work week and individualized hours of work. Of particular interest is the impact of these variations on employee productivity, attitudes toward work, use of leisure time, and on life styles in general. Research on these problems is just beginning. The next article, "Worker Adjustment to the 4-Day Work Week," by Nord and Costigan, investigated the pattern of employee responses to introduction of a 4-day week in a pharmaceutical company. They found that employee reactions were generally positive and that absenteeism declined after introduction of the new work schedule. They also found that the change in working hours had far-reaching effects on employee's home life and leisure patterns, and that the effects of the 4-day week may be different for men and women as well as for employees of different age groups. Obviously this is an area that will receive greater research attention in future years.

There has been a renewed interest in the problem of identifying optimum schedules of sequencing work and rest, particularly in our space program.[1] As small crews begin to make longer space voyages, the optimum scheduling and allocation of work-rest and sleep periods becomes critical, especially since alertness and proficiency must be maintained at

---

[1] J. T. Ray, O. E. Martin, Jr., and E. A. Alluisi, *Human Performance as a Function of the Work-Rest Cycle* (National Academy of Sciences, National Research Council Publication 882, 1961).

high levels. Psychological research has also been concerned with the effects of various environmental conditions on job proficiency. The important environmental factors which have been investigated include the effects of noise, lighting, temperature, ventilation and, more recently, vibration, isolation, stress, and g-forces (positive, negative, and zero). Although we can be confident that extremes in these conditions affect human performance, we need to know the extent of these effects, the "critical levels" at which an increase in temperature, noise, and so forth, begin to affect performance, and we need to know if some skills are more affected than others. Of course, in the new military and space environments in which people will work, we need to know much about human tolerance and limitations under strange and extreme environmental changes. In many cases, entire "environmental systems" are being developed for man to take with him.

Psychologists have played important roles in our space programs—through their jobs in industries concerned with these programs, with NASA itself, and with private and governmental laboratories doing research for these programs. Many of these contributions involve the development of methods for selecting and training the astronauts, for assessing their performance, and for the design of effective displays and control systems. Many studies are concerned with fatigue, working conditions, and task performance in the space environment. Grether[2] has summarized some of the environmental variables which have been examined including the effects of weightlessness, acceleration and deceleration, severe confinement, isolation, stress, and vibration. It should be pointed out that space is only one of the more unusual environments which recently have come under study. There is, for example, great interest in the jobs that man can perform in undersea and high-altitude environments.[3]

It is important to point out that sometimes researchers have to *simulate* environmental conditions in order to study their effects more precisely under controlled conditions. Thus, much research on atmospheric conditions, temperature, and so forth, is carried out in especially constructed instrumented chambers, and factors such as acceleration and deceleration may be programmed for a huge human centrifuge. In some cases, it is necessary to develop such simulations because it is *not possible* at the time to work in the actual environment. As Grether has pointed out, and as the later, more extensive flights in the Gemini, Apollo, and Skylab series have shown, the predictions made from such simulations to later performance in the space program have been quite accurate, indeed.

---

[2] W. F. Grether, "Psychology and the Space Frontier," *American Psychologist* 17 (1962): 102–8.

[3] For an excellent survey of some recent research on the effects of unusual environments on human performance, see N. W. Heimstra and A. L. McDonald, *Psychology and Contemporary Problems* (Monterey, Calif.: Brooks/Cole, 1973), chap. 4.

The information developed from these programs will tell us a great deal about conditions under which productive work can be carried out in such future environments.

A word is in order regarding the relation of environmental factors to different skills. It should be pointed out that there is considerable evidence that different skills (for example, computation, manual dexterity, memory) are affected differently by the same environmental (heat, noise, stress) condition. Some skills do not show much deterioration if an individual goes without sleep, or is subjected to stress, extreme heat, or cold.[4] Other skills deteriorate more quickly. This points up the need for precise task descriptions and the use of multiple-performance measures in such research, in order to facilitate prediction of these effects to new tasks requiring similar skills.[5]

This is an appropriate place to comment on the increasing interest in the effects of drugs and alcohol on human task performance. The increased use of prescription and other drugs makes it important for us to know how different drugs and dosages affect different skills. It has already been shown that the magnitude of such effects depend on the specific type of human performance involved,[6] and some drugs have been shown to facilitate performance or to keep performance from deteriorating over time.[7] The effects of alcohol, which have become of great concern in industry, are to depress performance, even in small doses. But the magnitude of this effect also depends on the type of task being performed.[8]

The last two articles in this section are concerned with on-the-job accidents and industrial safety. A recent report of the National Safety Council[9] indicated that the number of fatalities from accidents in 1971 was 115,000 and the number of disabling injuries was 11,200,000. The largest proportion of these accidents were motor vehicle (54,700 deaths and 2,000,000 injuries) and home (27,500 deaths and 4,200,000 injuries). But accidents at work accounted for 14,200 fatalities and 2,300,000 disabling injuries. The National Safety Council estimates that such work-related accidents resulted in an economic loss of $9.3 billion

---

[4] Strong motivation in many of these studies undoubtedly plays a critical role. It is remarkable how resistant to deterioration many skills are, when individuals are determined to do their best.

[5] For a discussion of this problem, see E. A. Fleishman, "The Development of a Performance Taxonomy for Describing Human Tasks," *Journal of Applied Psychology* 51 (1967): 1–10.

[6] E. A. Fleishman, "On the Relation between Abilities, Learning, and Human Performance," *American Psychologist* 27 (1972): 1017–1032.

[7] W. J. Baker and G. C. Theologus, "Effects of Caffeine on Visual Monitoring," *Journal of Applied Psychology* 56 (1972): 422–27; W. J. Baker, A. M. Geist, and E. A. Fleishman, *Effects of Cylert on Physiological, Physical Proficiency, and Psychomotor Performance Measures* (Washington: American Institutes for Research, 1967).

[8] J. Levine, G. Greenbaum, and E. Notkin, *The Effect of Alcohol on Human Performance: A Classification and Integration of Research Findings* (Washington: American Institutes for Research, 1973).

[9] National Safety Council, *Accident Facts* (Chicago: National Safety Council, 1972).

in 1971, with an average cost to industry of \$120 per worker. Further, an estimated 245,000,000 man-days were lost to industry in 1971 as a result of work-related accidents. Certainly these figures point up the tremendous need to learn more about the causes of accidents in order to reduce their frequency and severity.

The problem of accident causation is a complex one. Some accidents are attributable to situational factors, some to mechanical failures, some to human elements, and some to chance factors. Even the mechanical or engineering aspects are not independent of human elements. Thus, some workers will circumvent the best-designed mechanical safety devices. And, in the next section, we will see how psychologists are developing principles by which machines can be designed to minimize the human errors made in operating them.

It is frequently reported that a small proportion of workers are responsible for a large proportion of the accidents in particular jobs. This has led to the notion of "accident proneness" as a trait which is more pronounced in some individuals than in others. It is erroneous, however, to designate as "accident-prone" individuals who have a large proportion of accidents over a certain time period. One needs to demonstrate that it is the *same* employees who consistently have the most accidents over different time periods. The demonstration of such a correlation over different time periods is essential for identifying accident proneness.

Of course, a big factor in accidents is the fact that job hazards increase the liability of workers on certain jobs to have more accidents than workers on other jobs. If correlations in accident rates over two time periods are calculated on a sample of workers chosen from a number of such different jobs we may get a significant correlation. But much of this relationship is due to situational factors common to these workers over time and not necessarily to personal traits of the individuals. This situation makes it necessary to "partial out" differences in job hazards in estimating accident proneness. In "The Phenomenon of Accident Proneness," Arbous and Kerrich describe some of the problems in identifying the probable contributions of these "personal factors" to industrial accidents. They clarify the important distinction between "accident proneness" and "accident liability" and discuss some statistical and clinical approaches in dealing with the analysis and reduction of accidents.

A number of different approaches have been tried in the effort to reduce industrial accidents, including personnel selection, training, clinical, and engineering approaches. While all of these may make some contribution to reducing accidents, it is also important to consider the motivational aspects of this problem. The reward system within a particular department or plant is undoubtedly critical. If management uses incentives for volume or speed of output and not for safety, it is unlikely that simple verbal appeals or safety publicity campaigns will reduce accidents. Thus, if a foreman knows he will be reprimanded for not meeting certain production goals, unless safety behavior is made an important component of his evaluation, he is less likely to enforce safety regulations which may slow up production. The final article by Kerr, "Complimentary Theories of Safety Psychology," touches on this problem and serves as a summary and an attempted resolution of much of the evidence on accident behavior. Kerr emphasizes situational or "industrial climate" factors as major determinants of accidents, and this leads to some recommendations for better control of the accident problem.

SUGGESTED ADDITIONAL READINGS

Appley, M. and Trumbull, R.   *Psychological Stress.* New York: Appleton-Century-Crofts, 1967.

Broadbent, D.   "Effects of Noise on Behavior." In *Handbook of Noise Control,* edited by C. M. Harris. New York: McGraw-Hill Book Co., 1957.

Broadbent, D. E., and Little, E. A. J.   "Effects of Noise Reduction in a Work Situation." *Occupational Psychology* 34 (1960): 133–40.

Burns, N. M., Chambers, R. M., and Hendler, E., eds.   *Unusual Environments and Human Behavior.* New York: Free Press, 1963.

Dubin, R.   "Work and Leisure: Institutional Perspectives." In *Work and Leisure in the Year 2001,* edited by M. D. Dunnette. Belmont, Calif.: Wadsworth, 1973.

Fleishman, E. A.   *Structure and Measurement of Physical Fitness.* Englewood Cliffs, N.J.: Prentice Hall, 1964.

Glickman, A. S., and Brown, Z. H.   *Changing schedules of work: Patterns and implications.* Washington: American Institutes for Research, 1973.

Hadden, W., Suchman, E. A., and Klein, D.   *Accident Research.* New York: Harper & Row, 1964.

Kleitman, N.   *Sleep and Wakefulness.* Chicago: University of Chicago Press, 1963.

Kryter, K. D.   *The Effects of Noise on Man.* New York: Academic Press, 1970.

Miller, J. M. and Uhr, L.   *Drugs and Behavior.* New York: Wiley, 1960.

Myers, T. I.   *Psychobiological Factors Associated with Monotony Tolerance.* Washington, D.C.: American Institutes for Research, 1972.

Myers, T. I.   "Tolerance for Sensory and Perceptual Deprivation." In *Sensory Deprivation: Fifteen Years of Research,* edited by J. P. Zubek, pp. 289–332. New York: Appleton-Century-Crofts, 1969.

Shaw, L., and Sichel, H. S.   *Accident Proneness.* New York: Pergamon Press, 1971.

Tinker, M. A.   "Illumination Standards for Effective and Comfortable Vision." *Journal of Consulting Pschology* 3 (1939): 11–20.

Uhrbrock, R. S.   "Music on the Job: Its Influence on Worker Morale and Production." *Personnel Psychology* 14 (1961): 9–38.

40. FATIGUE IN INDUSTRY:
UNDERSTANDING FATIGUE
IN MODERN LIFE *

R. A. McFarland

ONE OF THE MOST PERPLEXING PROBLEMS in modern life concerns our lack of understanding and control of what is called fatigue. There is probably no single word in our vocabulary which has been less adequately described or understood, yet few people would deny personal acquaintance with it. Definitions of the nature of fatigue are almost as numerous as the articles that have been written about it, since each depends largely upon the interests or technical background of the author.

The many different interpretations of fatigue have been caused by the fact that the word does not have a specific scientific meaning. In medical terms it is not a distinct clinical entity. It refers, generally speaking, to a group of phenomena associated with impairment, or loss, of efficiency and skill, and the development of anxiety, frustration, or boredom. In common usage, it is not unlike the word 'unconscious' which has become a convenient category used to classify certain phenomena that are not clearly understood, yet are none the less real.

Earlier workers were primarily concerned with muscular work on fatigue of nervous fibres. Their points of view can be classified according to whether they emphasized a reduced work output; physiological changes in body functions and the production of chemical products of fatigue; or a feeling of tiredness. These early studies of muscular fatigue are not directly related to many of the highly skilled tasks encountered in our modern life which require complex, coordinated and accurately timed activities. Deterioration of a skill in such workers is therefore very different from loss in ability to lift a weight repeatedly.

The kind of fatigue caused by hard muscular work is best called acute. It results in a loss of efficiency, which is temporary, and is relieved by rest. Chronic fatigue, on the other hand, with which we will be primarily concerned, is not relieved by rest or sleep, and is cumulative in its effects. It is largely a psychological or psychiatric problem characterized by boredom, loss of initiative and progressive anxiety, but it is nevertheless very real to those who suffer from it. It is often puzzling to the physician because there is usually no physical cause. In a few cases there may be an

* From *Ergonomics* 14, no. 1 (1971): 1–10.

organic basis ranging from simple anemia to the onset of a neuromuscular disease. In the medical treatment of chronic fatigue, the results have generally been poor. There is now some evidence, however, both subjective and objective, that certain salts of potassium and magnesium are beneficial in their effects on this condition.

One of the most widely accepted current explanations is that fatigue is an outcome of conflict and frustration within the individual. It is manifested in its extreme or chronic forms as a well-developed anxiety neurosis. To limit fatigue to any single cause, however, may be misleading, as will be brought out below.

Physiological Factors in Fatigue

For many years, physiologists, in various laboratory experiments, have attempted to localize fatigue in certain parts of the body, such as the muscles or the nervous system. The muscular fatigue found in treadmill studies, however, does not resemble the fatigue of modern life, because the muscles are used in very different ways. Similarly, laboratory studies of isolated nerve fibres are equally inconclusive except for special circumstances such as the important role of oxidation in the efficient functioning of the nervous tissue.

Other physiologists have attempted to associate fatigue with the accumulation of toxic substances, such as lactic acid, in the blood. As an explanation of fatigue, however, lactic acid is much more restricted than at first believed. That it is not the only factor is demonstrated by the fact that many track records are broken by athletes even after running several heats and accumulating large amounts of lactate in their blood. Furthermore, many industrial workers doing heavy work, as well as miners at high altitudes, have normal values of blood lactate.

Another physiological approach to fatigue relates to the exhaustion of energy reserves. Experiments indicate that in very exhausting work, as in a marathon race, ingesting glucose definitely helps to maintain efficiency. In severe exercise on a bicycle ergometer, very low blood-sugar levels resulted in complete exhaustion and sensory impairment in human subjects. However, these effects were rapidly counteracted by ingesting glucose, and the subjects could then continue their severe exercise for an hour or more. Those who are in poor physical condition have low energy reserves and a reduced capacity for transforming energy, and they, as well as the athlete, may also benefit from glucose or some other readily utilizable fuel taken between meals.

However, it is hard to explain how sugar might counteract the effects of fatigue in mental performance, since it is known that the metabolic cost of mental work is very slight indeed. In carefully controlled experiments years ago, Benedict and Benedict found that sustained mental effort for several hours required only the number of calories in half a peanut! [1] Other experiments have shown that in mental work it is not the nervous system that increases oxygen consumption, but rather it is owing largely to the increased muscular tension associated with sustained attention.

In general, fatigue cannot be considered a simple physiological condition resulting from sustained activity. Furthermore, if one thinks of the body as a whole, fatigue cannot be defined solely in terms of biochemical changes in the muscles or nerves, or by the exhaustion of energy reserves. If one is placed under stress, however, various forms of exhaustion and fatigue may result. Emotion or prolonged effort may influence adversely. Also a person's adaptation, and mental performance, and skill may deteriorate. It appears to be more relevant therefore to consider the role of psychological variables.

Psychological Aspects of Fatigue

Quite possibly those psychologists who have stressed the role of higher nervous functions as opposed to neuro-muscular ones may be on the right track. They have shown experimentally that mental functions show a loss of efficiency through simple and prolonged repetition of arithmetical or color-naming tests. This loss appears as a mental lapse or blocking during which the individual finds it impossible to carry on the activity without frequent errors. As he tires, the lapses are longer and the errors more frequent.

Fatigue also has an emotional component which, though not easily measured, must be taken into consideration. Although a person can readily adjust to temporary conflicts, there seems to be a cumulative ill effect from prolonged emotional stress and mental effort which is often designated as fatigue.

The interesting concept of skill fatigue developed by Bartlett has helped to explain the deterioration of performance in pilots.[2] In the Cambridge "Cockpit Studies," a large group of RAF pilots were studied under simulated flying conditions in a standard spitfire cockpit with full controls and instruments. The pilots "flew" for at least two hours, some continuing until exhaustion after six to seven hours. Although piloting errors due to the misuse of the controls decreased steadily throughout the experiments, this improvement was more than offset by a deterioration in accuracy of timing and skill.

---

[1] F. G. Benedict and Cornelia G. Benedict, *Mental Effort in Relation to Gaseous Exchange, Heart Rate, and Mechanics of Respiration,* Carnegie Institution of Washington Publication 446 (Washington, D.C., 1933), p. 83.

[2] F. C. Bartlett, "The Bearing of Experimental Psychology upon Human Skilled Performance," *British Journal of Industrial Psychology* 8 (1951): 209–17.

As the subjects became more fatigued, they were willing to accept lower and lower standards of accuracy and performance. Furthermore, they failed to interpret the various instrument readings as being part of a single integrated system, but paid attention to one or the other of them as individual, isolated instruments. As fatigue increased, the pilots' range of attention decreased, and forgetting or ignoring the more distant instruments was common. Possibly the most significant finding was the general tendency for a sudden increase in errors at the end of a flight. A tired airman, it seems, has an almost irresistible tendency to relax when he nears the airport.

In skill fatigue, then, the "standards" accepted and followed by the central nervous system unwittingly deteriorate. Although a person may think he is doing better work, actually his performance is getting poorer and poorer. At first, it is more likely that he will do the right things at the wrong time, but if accurate timing is important, gross errors will finally begin to appear.

Fatigue Resulting from Stress

In understanding the relationship of the stresses of our modern environment to fatigue, the contributions of physiologists such as Cannon and Selye are very helpful. Cannon has described the ways in which the body maintains a physiologic constancy or steadiness under conditions which might be expected to prove profoundly disturbing, frustrating and fatiguing.[3] Selye as an example of the modern trend, has worked out detailed observations concerning specific nervous and humoral alterations reflecting the general adaptation of the organism to stress.

The working hypothesis that has resulted from these kinds of studies is that measurable substances in the blood and urine indicate glandular activities of the body in response to stress. Thus, chronic fatigue resulting from stress, can, in fact, have an underlying physical basis. Interestingly enough, chronic fatigue can also apparently contribute to some of the other ailments so characteristic of our modern life, such as mental illness, peptic ulcers, and certain aspects of heart disease such as high blood pressure.

We also know that anxiety and fatigue are related. Whether they are causally related is not necessarily important, since the existence of either state may react on and intensify the other. Even the normal person has latent anxieties which may be accentuated if he becomes fatigued. The neurotic individual, on the other hand, is fatigued in proportion to the extent of his anxieties.

---

[3] W. B. Cannon, *The Wisdom of the Body* (New York: W. W. Norton & Co., 1932).

Psychophysiological Concepts of Fatigue

In recent years there have been many advances in our understanding of what happens in the central nervous system when we are tired. One relates to the electrical rhythms or patterns from the brain that can be observed on electroencephalograms. Some years ago a physiologist implanted electrodes in the brain of a cat.[4] He observed that the electrical stimulation of certain parts of the brain, specifically the *medial thalmus,* seemed to make the animal lethargic and sleepy. Later workers using similar techniques showed that this suppressive action can also take place in the cerebral cortex, the seat of all our conscious processes.

This inhibitory system in the brain, however, is matched by what one might call an activating system based in the reticular formation. As Grandjean has stated, a person's ability to perform "is dependent on the degree of activity of the two systems: if the inhibitory system dominates, the organism is in a stage of fatigue; while if the activating system has the upper hand, the organism is ready to step up performance."[5] This tends to explain situations that are familiar to all of us, such as the fatigue or tiredness that occurs in monotonous or boring situations, and the sudden change, or awakening, that takes place when something new and interesting or unexpected happens.

Fatigue and Poor Performance

In the past, most of the studies relating to the effects of environmental stresses such as loud noise, hot and cold temperatures, and changes in work cycles on fatigue, have shown but little impairment. In laboratory studies the subjects tend to compensate for the subtle effects of noise and temperature on performance by trying harder. Also, the measures of fatigue in industry are often difficult to appraise except by an increase in accidents. Recently, experimental psychologists have devised new techniques of measurement. By progressively increasing the complexity of the tests, or by superimposing one task upon another, a percentage decrement in performance (known to be present, but hard to measure) is finally revealed. What is needed to prevent the masking of fatigue is a combined measure of both speed and accuracy. With the development of information theory, a nonarbitrary way of combining measures of speed and accuracy in a simple "rate-of-information-transmission" measure is available.[6]

---

[4] See W. R. Hess, "Stammganglien-Reizversuche," *Ber. ges Physiol.* 42 (1927): 554–55.

[5] E. Grandjean, "Fatigue: Its Physiological and Psychological Significance," *Ergonomics* 11 (1968): 427–36.

[6] See R. A. McFarland, "The Effects of Altitude on Pilot Performance," in *Proceedings of XVII International Congress on Aviation and Space Medicine,* ed. B. Hannisdahl and C. W. Sem-Jacobsen (Oslo: Universitetsforlaget, 1969), pp. 96–108.

Two avenues of approach have been developed to detect and scale increased effort in performance tests. One is concerned with the spare mental capacity for a central task in relation to a peripheral task at the same time. The other area relates to physiological measures such as arousal and tenseness. A number of techniques for measuring not only muscular tenseness, but also central nervous system activity, and even specific components of neural reaction to signals have been developed. Some of these measures appear promising for the study of the deleterious effects of fatigue.

Industrial Fatigue, Productivity, and Work Schedules

Fatigue appears to be a chief factor limiting a person's output. Various studies have shown that when the working day is lengthened, hourly productivity goes down, and when the number of hours worked is reduced, hourly performance increases. Thus long working days and overtime are relatively inefficient since production does not appear to be maintained at the earlier high rate. It should be pointed out, however, that these findings can only be verified where the individual has some control over his work rate. On an assembly line a worker cannot make voluntary adjustments, and must maintain the scheduled pace. Nevertheless, extended working hours in these situations will result in fatigue with a consequentially greater likelihood of accidental errors, and illness.

There is some evidence that eight hours of work a day in the United States, where the work is fairly intensive, is the maximum that should be permitted for optimum productivity. For easier work or where it is possible to schedule several relaxing breaks over the course of the work day, longer hours may well be permissible.

On the Continent, in the transition to a 5- from a 6-day week, Grandjean notes that a drop in the number of hours worked is not matched by a proportionate drop in worker productivity, since most personnel slightly increased their hourly output.[7] However, when the same number of hours are worked in a 5-day week as in the former 6-day week, that is, a 9- to 9¾-hour working day, the results are much less desirable, and many European industrial physicians believe that a 5-day week is only advantageous when the daily working hours do not exceed 8½ hours.

Similar trends were also noted during the Battle of Britain, when factories began working 24 hours a day, 7 days a week. At first there was an increase in output, but after a few months, absenteeism and sickness increased, and employees often arrived late for work. Sunday work was discontinued without reducing production. One factory, after reducing the hours, set a new record for one week's production. It was concluded that increased hours of work above an optimum number, which varies

---

[7] Grandjean, "Fatigue: Its Physiological and Psychological Significance."

slightly with different industries, do not increase production proportionately and may even result in a decrease. From these and many other similar observations, it may be inferred that fatigue and recovery are normal cyclical phenomena to be accepted as a part of life. Only when recovery from physical effort is not completed in 24 hours do we need to be concerned.

The time of day at which work is carried out is also related to fatigue. In most studies dealing with this topic one of the commonly used criteria is work output, and where this has been related to work shift, consistently slightly higher outputs have been recorded for the day shifts. Similarly, in an exhaustive industrial study of 62,000 errors made in hourly readings of different measuring instruments, the greatest incidence of error was found during the night shift with the peak at about 3:00 A.M. The general explanations advanced for these differences in industrial perfromance are: the human circadian, or day–night system; the incompatibility of the socio-temporal enivronment of the night-shift worker; and from the interaction of these, impairment of health.

Preliminary studies have been conducted of the physiological and psychological reactions of subjects who were flown on long west–east, east–west and north–south jet flights. These assessments were made before the flight, after arrival at the distant destination, and after return. Significant physiological changes were found after both the east–west and west–east flights which involved primary shifts in circadian periodicity, but not after the north–south flight. An impairment of psychological performance was noted on the east–west, but not the west–east or north–south flights. The only finding in common to all three flights was an increase in subjective fatigue.

It is interesting to note that this subjective fatigue, or feelings of tiredness, persisted as long as the body temperatures remained elevated, in most cases for a day or two following the flights. One practical result of these studies relates to the fact that several large international companies now give their personnel an extra day off to recuperate after crossing several time zones in jet flights. This policy is also followed for some U.S. government officials.

Operational Fatigue in Aircrews

Since fear and apprehension, as well as boredom, can give rise to fatigue, we might expect to find fatigue present to some extent in commercial aviation. The author served as medical adviser to PAA in the opening of air routes in the Pacific in 1936–37, and in the Atlantic in 1939, as well as in South America and Africa. It had been anticipated that flying fatigue would be pronounced, and the government regulatory bodies therefore required frequent layovers of the air crews. Contrary to expectations, however, few cases of operational fatigue were observed.

This was due to the fact that the operating and engineering departments did everything possible to train the men for their duties, and to provide equipment which was reliable as possible. In this way fear and apprehension were apparently allayed and, in addition, comfortable living facilities, including athletics, were provided for the pilots on the ground. In fact, the only evidence of fatigue that the author was able to identify was in Hawaii, where an excess of "relaxation" occurred on some occasions! [8]

Fatigue Resulting from Excessive Leisure and Boredom

In modern life the way in which we adjust to leisure time is an excellent example of the kinds of problems our modern technology is creating as well as solving. In the days of Socrates and Plato the "end-aim" of life was leisure for the exercise of man's highest faculties. They had slaves to do their chores and we have machines. Yet ours is a work-centered, and for some a work-compulsive society, and it is probably unrealistic to expect that free time resulting from reduced working hours will be used creatively or productively in the sense of the Greeks. The minds of men must be exercised, and if there are no problems we usually create them, even artificial ones. For us, idleness often brings uneasiness, a feeling of lack of purpose and, eventually, fatigue.

Conclusion

Since fatigue in its many forms can result from a variety of causes acting singly or in combination, it is difficult to give clear-cut rules or principles for its control or prevention. Each case must be evaluated according to its own peculiar characteristics. Nevertheless, a few rather general remarks can be made.

For the individual suffering from chronic fatigue, the most logical first step would be an examination by a physician to determine whether or not any organic basis for the condition exists. Where it does not, attention must be directed towards finding the most likely cause, or causes, among the major ones outlined in this article, and making the necessary changes in one's life and schedule of living. Easier said than done, admittedly, but then, there is no sure cure, or cures, for chronic fatigue which will work equally well for different people.

A few recommendations of general applicability would include: adequate, though not excessive, sleep; the establishment of a daily work-rest cycle acceptable to the individual; the elimination, in so far as possible, of conditions resulting in excessive stress, anxiety, or boredom; the institution of a definite, adhered-to schedule of physical exercise or sports, com-

---

[8] R. A. McFarland, *Human Factors in Air Transportation: Occupational Health and Safety* (New York: McGraw-Hill Book Co., 1953).

patible with the individual's capabilities; the possible use of stimulants or medications—but only under a physician's direction.

For the organizational control of fatigue, as in industry, the coordinated efforts of the medical and administrative departments are needed. The medical department should be concerned with the maintenance of fitness through adequate physical and mental hygiene program, and in industries where it is appropriate with the selection of emotionally stable and fatigue-resistant personnel. They should also, in conjunction with the engineering or industrial safety departments, see that harmful excesses of environmental variables such as noise, vibration, temperature, and so forth, are removed or controlled. In addition, all equipment used by the worker, and his work task, should be designed with optimum efficiency, safety, and comfort in mind. Finally, those in charge of administration can contribute most by seeing that work schedules, working conditions, and personnel relations are all maintained at levels consistent with the interests and well-being of the employee, as well as of the company.

41. THE PREDICTION OF INDIVIDUAL DIFFERENCES IN SUSCEPTIBILITY TO INDUSTRIAL MONOTONY *

Patricia Cain Smith

MOST MODERN INDUSTRIAL JOBS are repetitive and alleged to be uncreative. Observers of the industrial scene have been greatly concerned about the consequent feelings of monotony and boredom by the workers. Superficially, it would seem that repetition in work would be a *cause* of boredom, that work which appeared repetitive to the observer would necessarily be accompanied by boredom, and work with apparent variety by absence of boredom. Industrial investigations established very early, however, that jobs with all the appearance of being repetitive were not always considered monotonous by the workers.[1] Investigations of clerical workers,

---

* From *Journal of Applied Psychology* 39, no. 5 (1955): 322–29. Copyright 1955 by the American Psychological Association. Reprinted by permission.

[1] P. S. Florence, *Economics of Fatigue and Unrest and the Efficiency of Labor in English and American Industry* (New York: Henry Holt & Co., 1924); Chen-Nan Li, "A Summer in the Ford Works," *Personnel Journal* 7 (1928): 18–32; H. Münsterberg, *Psychology and Industrial Efficiency* (Cambridge: Houghton Mifflin Co., 1913), pp. 195–98; S. Wyatt, J. N. Langdon, and F. G. L. Stock, *Fatigue and Boredom in Repetitive Work*, Industrial Health Research Board, Report no. 77 (London, 1937).

schoolteachers, and professional workers, on the other hand, have repeatedly indicated that many persons find each of these more varied kinds of work boring. (For summaries of these studies, see Hoppock and Robinson [2] or Viteles.[3])

An observer of a job may classify it as repetitive solely on the basis of the observed frequency of repetition of the task. This type of classification does not take into account the perceptions of the worker. Repetition for the worker depends upon what he perceives in the task, and his perceptions are not subject to immediate scrutiny by an observer. For instance, if a worker perceives variety in the minute changes of detail or in the social situation around him, the job is for him one in which there is variety. Repetition as defined by externally observable frequency of occurrence cannot be stated as a valid *cause* of monotony. Repetition is rather one characteristic of the task as perceived by the worker—one aspect of the experience of monotony.

These considerations enable us to define our terms, at least in a general way. For the purposes of this discussion, we shall use the terms monotony and boredom interchangeably to designate the experience which arises from the continued performance of an activity which is perceived as either uniform or repetitive, and which also induces a desire for change or variety. This definition, obviously, restricts monotony to the experience of the individual. It has frequently been suggested or assumed that there are individual differences in susceptibility to such experiences.[4] This study was undertaken to investigate factors in the individual which might predispose him to experiences of boredom.

Procedure

The research was conducted in a small knitwear mill in northern Pennsylvania. Most operators in the plant, and all included in this study, were paid by piece rate. The active support of both the plant manager and the business agent of the union was a major factor in securing the confidence of the workers.

Although feelings of boredom are most directly assessed by verbal reports of the workers, we conducted a preliminary study in an attempt to obtain more objective supplementary criteria. As reported previously,[5] we found, however, that such indirect indicators of boredom as talking, fre-

---

[2] R. Hoppock and H. A. Robinson, "Job Satisfaction Researches of 1950," *Occupations* 29 (1951): 575–78.

[3] M. S. Viteles, *Motivation and Morale in Industry* (New York: W. W. Norton & Co., 1953).

[4] O. Lipmann, "The Human Factor in Production," *Personnel Journal* 7 (1928): 94–95; Münsterberg, *Psychology and Industrial Efficiency;* Wyatt, Langdon, and Stock, *Fatigue and Boredom in Repetitive Work.*

[5] P. C. Smith, "The Curve of Output as a Criterion of Boredom," *Journal of Applied Psychology* 37 (1953): 69–74.

quency of rest pauses, average working speed, and the shape and variability of the output curve were both unreliable and invalid in this situation. Verbal report was the only available criterion.

Detailed interviews with a number of workers laid the groundwork for the main study, orienting the investigator and aiding the union and management in "selling" the workers on the desirability of the study. The subjects of the main study were 72 women workers, all engaged in light, repetitive work. We included only sewing-machine operators who had been on the job three months or more, and who remained continuously on the same task throughout each working day. The questionnaire form was used rather than interviews, both because it permitted contact with a larger number of workers and because any later application of the findings would be much more practical if information could be gathered in paper-and-pencil form. All questions were pretested and, when necessary, revised before administration to the main group. Questionnaires were unsigned.

Some criterion questions concerning the experience of monotony were adapted from the much-quoted studies of Wyatt, Langdon, and Stock [6]; others were suggested by the interviews. Included were such obvious terms as "Do you often get bored with your work?," "Is your job too monotonous?," "Would you like to change from one type of work to another from time to time if the pay remained the same?" and some similar multiple-choice and completion items. The frequencies of choice of answers to each question were compared for the entire group, by the chi-square technique, and a weighted criterion score was devised on the basis of those items most closely agreeing with each other. Subjects were then separated into three approximately equal groups—the nonsusceptible, the susceptible, and an intermediate group of workers. This criterion seemed superior to the criteria used by most previous investigators, who relied either upon shape of the productive curve or on answers to questions about preference for regularity in daily habits outside the work situation.[7] Table 41–1 shows the criterion questions.

The worker who does not suffer from monotony when doing repetitive work has been portrayed in the literature as an inferior, insensitive sort of person—placid, extraverted, happy,[8] unable to daydream,[9] uncreative,[10]

---

[6] Wyatt, Langdon, and Stock, *Fatigue and Boredom in Repetitive Work.*

[7] R. E. Dunford, "A Study of Monotony Types" (Master's thesis, Ohio State University, 1925); Wyatt, Langdon, and Stock, *Fatigue and Boredom in Repetitive Work;* Münsterberg, *Psychologay and Industrial Efficiency;* L. A. Thompson, Jr., "Measuring Susceptibility to Monotony," *Personnel Journal* 8 (1929): 172–97.

[8] R. N. McMurry, "Efficiency, Work-Satisfaction and Neurotic Tendency, A Study of Bank Employees," *Personnel Journal* 11 (1932): 201–10; Thompson, "Measuring Susceptibility to Monotony"; Wyatt, Langdon, and Stock, *Fatigue and Boredom in Repetitive Work.*

[9] Ibid.

[10] H. Wunderlich, "Die Einwerkung Einförmiger, Zwangsläüfiger Arbeit auf die Persönlichkeitsstruktur," *Schr. Psychol. Berufseignung* 31 (1925): 49–50.

TABLE 41–1

Criterion Questions and Weighting of Each

Question	Answer	Weight
Do you often get bored with your work?	Yes	1
	?	0
	No	−1
Is your job too monotonous?	Yes	2
	?	0
	No	−2
Would you like to change from one type of work to another from time to time, if the pay remained the same?	Yes	1
	?	0
	No	−1
Would you like to be a forelady?		−
What time of day seems most boring to you?		
Choice of any hour from 7:00 A.M. to 3:00 P.M.		1
Choice of hour from 3:00 P.M. to 4:00 P.M.		0
Choice of any hour outside of working hours.		0
How well do you like the work that you do?		
I think that it is extremely monotonous.		1
I think that it is very monotonous.		1
I think that it is pretty monotonous.		1
I think that it is not very interesting.		0
I think that it is pretty interesting.		−1
I think that it is very interesting.		−1
I think that it is fascinating.		−1
Is there anything about the work which you particularly dislike?		
It is too monotonous.		10
Other responses.		0

and, above all, unintelligent.[11] Such portrayals in textbooks and in journals are distinguished more for their literary than for their scientific value. Nevertheless, they furnished us with a number of hypotheses concerning characteristics related to susceptibility to monotony. Further hypotheses were formulated during the preliminary interviewing and observational periods. Questions designed to test each of these hypotheses were included in the questionnaire, and answers to each question were compared for the three criterion groups. Significance of relationships was tested by the chi-square test.

All three criterion groups were included in every analysis. Where the response categories were "Yes,?, No," the "?" response was, in most cases,

---

[11] I. Burnett, *An Experimental Investigation into Repetitive Work*, Industrial Fatigue Research Board, Report no. 30 (London, 1925). W. W. Kornhauser, "Some Business Applications of a Mental Alertness Test," *Journal of Personnel Research* 2 (1922): 103–21; M. S. Viteles, "Selecting Cashiers and Predicting Length of Service," *Journal of Personnel Research* 2 (1924): 467–73; Wunderlich, "Die Einwerkung Einförmiger"; S. Wyatt, "Experimental Study of a Repetitive Process," *British Journal of Psychology* 3 (1927): 192–209; S. Wyatt, J. A. Fraser, and F. G. L. Stock, *The Effects of Monotony in Work*, Industrial Fatigue Research Board, Report no. 56 (London, 1929); Wyatt, Langdon, and Stock, *Fatigue and Boredom in Repetitive Work*.

chosen too infrequently to make the chi-square technique applicable. The interpretation of such responses is ambiguous, moreover, meaning for various respondents, "I don't know," "Sometimes one, sometimes the other." "I don't understand the question," "I don't wish to answer the question," or "The question does not apply to me." Usually these responses were omitted from the analysis. In a few cases, indicated in the tables, the "?" response was chosen sufficiently often to bring the predicted frequencies up to five. In these instances, as in all questions with multiple-response categories, the significance was first tested for all responses. Responses were then grouped into two categories for purposes of comparability. An additional p value is therefore reported in each case for a 3×2 chi-square table. Yates' correction for continuity was applied throughout.

Table 41-2 shows the questions, the most frequently chosen answers for each of the three groups, and the level of significance for each, for all those relationships found to be significant at the 5 percent level or better and to differentiate between the extreme groups.

Hypotheses and Results

Hypothesis I. Younger workers are more susceptible to monotony than older ones. Age was compared with answers to the criterion questions. The results showed that workers under 20 were significantly more susceptible and those over 35 significantly less so, although no relationship obtained between 20 and 35. Three other kinds of personal-history items were investigated—marital status, number of children, and number of years of experience at this or similar work—but trends in these proved to disappear when age was held constant. Age, then, is a correlate of susceptibility in this group.

Hypothesis II. Susceptible workers are more ambitious, either for themselves or for their children. No item in this list discriminated among the groups. Level of aspiration seemed not to be related to feelings of monotony in this sample.

Hypothesis III. The susceptible worker does not daydream. It has been suggested that the nonsusceptible worker does not feel the monotony because he daydreams. This hypothesis was rejected by this study, the answers showing an insignificant tendency (8 percent level) in the other direction. The monotony-susceptible workers tended to daydream more, both in and out of the plant.

Hypothesis IV. The susceptible worker is likely to be extroverted. This suggestion is related to the preceding one, the extrovert presumably needing more stimulation from his environment. However, none of the personality-questionnaire items, intended to measure introversion-extroversion, was related to the criterion in this study.

Hypothesis V. The susceptible worker will be more restless in his

TABLE 41–2

Summary of Items Significantly Related to Monotony Susceptibility (answers to questions and p values derived from the chi-square test of significance of relationships—all p's based on 3 × 2 tables unless otherwise indicated.)

| | | Answers Chosen Most Frequently by | | | |
		Monot. Susc.	Middle Group	Non-susc.	p
Question	*Answer*				
How old are you?	Under 20	X			
	20–24				.03*
	25–29				
	30–34				
	35 and over			X	
	Under 25	X			.02
	25 and over			X	
How long have you been doing the same work?	Less than 3 mo.			X	
	3–6 mo.	X			.05†
	6 mo. and over			X	
Do you like to daydream at your work around the house?	Yes	X			
	?			X	.03*
	No				
	Yes	X			.02‡
	?			X	
Do you especially like to have a definite schedule of home duties so that you can do them at the same time every day?	Yes			X	
	No	X			.03
If you had an evening to spend as you liked, what would you *usually* rather do? (CHECK AS MANY AS YOU LIKE)					
Knit§					
Sew				X	.0003‖
Visit friends				X	.07‖
Go to the movies				X	.27‖
Listen to the radio				X	.06‖
Go downtown		X			.36‖
Read			X		.08‖
Dance		X			.08‖
Drive around in the car			X		.19‖
Something else you would like to do very much. (If so, what?_____)				X#	.0006‖
More than average number checked				X	
Average number or fewer checked		X			.09
When you are working around the house, what job do you prefer? (CHECK AS MANY AS YOU LIKE)					
Washing dishes				X	.11‖
Dusting				X	.08‖
Cleaning drawers				X	.02‖
Washing clothes				X	.01‖
Scrubbing floors				X	.006‖
Cooking				X	.35‖
Drying dishes				X	.32‖
Cleaning rugs				X	.32‖
Washing windows				X	.01‖
Ironing				X	.04‖
Making beds				X	.03‖
Mending				X	.01‖
Something else around the house which you like to do very much. (If so, what?_____)				X#	.13‖
More than average number checked				X	
Average number or fewer checked		X			.02

* p based on more than two response categories.
† Trend disappeared when records of workers only between ages of 20 and 25 were analyzed.
‡ "No" was infrequently chosen and omitted from analysis.
§ Item checked by only three workers.
‖ Analyzed with response checked vs. not checked.
These were almost all quiet domestic activities.

TABLE 41–2 (Continued)

Question	Answer	Monot. Susc.	Middle Group	Non-susc.	p
Do you often quarrel with anyone in your home?	Yes	X			.002
	No			X	
Are you anxious to get away from home?	Yes	X			.005
	No			X	
Do you often quarrel with your mother?	Yes	X			.03
	No			X	
Do you often quarrel with your father?	Yes	X			.04
	No			X	
Have you had any other job, either in the mill or elsewhere, which you prefer to the one you have now?	Yes	X			
	No			X	.0002
Is there anything about the work which you particularly dislike? (If so, what?_____)	Yes	X			
	No			X	.002
What part of the day do you enjoy more, the part of the day you spend in the mill?				X	.002
the part of the day you spend away from the mill?		X			
How good do you feel that your job is? Check the opinion which is most like yours. (CHECK ONLY ONE)					
a. I would not stay on my job for a minute if I could get something else. It is very unpleasant work.		X			
b. I would really prefer something else, but it is all right here.		X			
c. I like this job about as well as any job which pays the same.					.003
d. I like this job better than most jobs I know about.			X		
e. I wouldn't take another job unless it paid a good deal more.			X		
f. I feel that it is the ideal job for me.			X		
Responses a, b, and c		X			.002
Responses d, e, and f				X	
Do you know of any job you would rather have than the one you have, even if the pay were the same?	Yes	X			
	No			X	.007
Is there anything that could be done to make your job more pleasant? (If so, what?_____)	Yes	X			
	No			X	.008
Do you like it (the work) better or worse than when you started?	Better			X	
	Worse	X			.02

daily habits and in his leisure-time activities. Two kinds of questions were included to investigate this possibility.

First, questions concerning preference for definite schedules of home duties, walking the same way to school (or work) every day, of preferring to stay home during vacations, and so forth, had been used as *criterion* questions in several earlier studies.[12] The relationship of feelings of boredom at work to preference for variety in other situations had not been proved, and hence such questions scarcely seemed satisfactory as criteria.

---

[12] Münsterberg, *Psychology and Industrial Efficiency;* Thomson, "Measuring Susceptibility to Monotony."

Preference for regularity might prove to be a general trait, however, so several such questions were included in the questionnaire. The results were in the direction of the hypothesis for eight of the ten questions, two being indeterminate. A total of all these items was related to the criterion at the 2 percent level.

Secondly, leisure-time preferences were investigated by two check-lists of recreational and housework activities, constructed on the basis of the preliminary interviews. All but 4 of the 21 activities were checked more frequently by the nonsusceptible group, these 17 including all the housework items and all of the recreational activities which could be performed sitting down, with the exception of reading and driving around in the car, which were checked more frequently by the middle group. The susceptible group, in contrast, preferred dancing or going downtown (which in this community meant window shopping). The total number of the items checked was related to the criterion at the 1 percent level. Since most of these activities were settled and routine, we must consider the hypothesis quite tenable that susceptible workers are more likely to be restless outside the plant than less susceptible workers.

These two groups of items proved not to be significantly related to each other when responses for workers in a restricted age range (20–35) were compared, although each group was still significantly related to the criterion. Differences in living arrangements and personal circumstances may make it possible for workers to develop preferences for irregularity in only limited portions of their lives, or preferences may actually be expressions of two separate traits.

Hypothesis VI. The susceptible worker will be less satisfied with his personal, home, and plant situation in aspects not directly concerned with uniformity or repetitiveness.

Questions concerning personal adjustment included a number from various personality questionnaires, designed to measure so-called neurotic tendencies. Most of these items showed no significant relationship to the criterion. The few differentiating items referred not to neuroticism in general, but to feelings of persistent depression and discouragement, and seemed to concern contentment more than tendency to show other neurotic symptoms. The distribution of obtained chi squares does not deviate from chance expectancy sufficiently to be sure that the relationships between these items and the criterion is not merely fortuitous. The consistency of kind of item, however, is encouraging. To a certain extent, then, the discontented persons in this group also found their work monotonous. This finding is probably related to the results concerning more frequent daydreaming in the susceptible group.

Questions concerning home life showed clear-cut relationships to the criterion. All but one of these items discriminated at better than the .05 level of significance, and the total of all at the .0002 level. Home adjustment is a close correlate of susceptibility in this sample.

General work adjustment, similarly, appeared to be closely related to complaints of monotony. Nine of the 11 questions concerning working conditions and work attitudes showed significant relationships at the 10 percent level or below, the median of the 11 being below the 1 percent level. For the total group, and also for the group with ages between 20 and 35, relationships among home-, personal-, and work-adjustment total scores were compared. All were statistically significant (p less than 5 percent level). (Extremely unfavorable comments concerning factory conditions and supervision occurred frequently in all criterion groups. Differences in frankness do not, therefore, account for the relationships found among the various kinds of dissatisfaction.) The overlapping was very great here; either feelings of monotony color all of the attitudes of the workers toward their families, personal lives, and work, or these feelings are a reflection of a general dissatisfaction.

Hypothesis VII. The monotony-susceptible workers are more intelligent than the others. Because of the correlation between intelligence and educational level in such groups, and because information concerning educational level could be readily obtained without sacrificing anonymity, educational background was compared with reported monotony for the entire group. Education ranged from fourth grade to two years of college. No significant relationship appeared with the criterion,[13] although there was a slight tendency toward higher educational levels in the nonsusceptible group.

Hypothesis VIII. Feelings of monotony are not merely a function of the task performed, but are related to other more general factors in the individual worker. This hypothesis, of course, underlies the others, and is clearly tenable in view of the number of personal correlates demonstrated in this sample.

In summary, four kinds of items were to a significant degree negatively related to reports of monotony in this group:

1. Age, which was related to the other personal-history items and to some extent to the adjustment or contentment score.
2. Preference for regularity in daily routine.
3. Lack of restlessness as expressed in preference for inactive leisure-time activities.
4. Satisfaction in personal, home, and factory life.

For the homogeneous group (20–35), combined scores for these last three groups of items concerning preference for regularity, restlessness,

---

[13] In an attempt to assess intelligence more directly, a group test was given to workers from the extreme categories. Turnover, transfer, and desire to retain anonymity reduced the groups to 8 susceptible and 13 nonsusceptible workers, too few, of course, for drawing of broad generalizations. The median and mean, however, were *higher* for the nonsusceptible than for the susceptible groups, confirming the results obtained with education.

and satisfaction proved to have no significant correction with one another, when tested by the chi-square test ($p's = .52, .43,$ and $.19$). A combined weighted score of these factors clearly separated the criterion groups. Still better separation was achieved by the use of minimum cutting scores based on a pattern analysis.

Discussion

Cross validation, with employees tested before employment, is obviously necessary in a study of this kind, despite the relative specificity of the predictions, to establish generality of relationships and direction of causation. Direct repetition of this study so far has been impossible. Confirmation of the results has, however, come from several sources.

First of all, the negative finding concerning intelligence has considerable support. One early study, that of Thompson, found a slight inverse relationship between intelligence and susceptibility to uniformity.[14] Even the classic study of Wyatt et al. reported such small differences between the most and least bored groups that in only four of the ten comparisons were they statistically significant.[15] Other studies were based on turnover, rather than job satisfaction, and results might well be attributable to more able persons securing better jobs than less able.[16] More recently, Heron has reported results consistent with those of the present study, using male unskilled workers in England.[17] His criterion of job adjustment (a special rating by supervisors) proved, when age and experience were partialled out, not to be predicted by "General Mental Ability." The relationship between intelligence and boredom is by no means established.

The positive findings concerning preferences. personality characteristics, and age have received support from several sources. Five studies have been completed by the writer, using women workers in garment factories in various sections of the country, and comparing answers at the time of employment with later absences and with length of service. Results have been very consistent for age at time of employment, it being negatively related to absences and positively related to subsequent length of service up to the age of 45. Preference for regularity and lack of restlessness items predicted only absence rate, and only in the two studies in which the towns had populations of over 25,000. The satisfaction items predicted both absence and length of service in all situations, but to highly variable extents, possibly reflecting differences in the tendencies of

---

[14] Thompson, "Measuring Susceptibility to Monotony."

[15] Wyatt, Langdon, and Stock, *Fatigue and Boredom in Repetitive Work.*

[16] Kornhauser, "Some Business Applications of a Mental Alertness Test."

[17] A. Heron, "A Psychological Study of Vocational Adjustment," *Journal of Applied Psychology* 36 (1952): 385–87.

applicants in various situations to fake such items. Even this degree of consistency is encouraging, however.

Other investigators have reported supporting evidence concerning the generality of the traits involved. Pierce, using college students, showed a relationship between poor scores on a modification of the home adjustment items and flexibility as measured by Luchins' *Einstellung* test.[18] Bews similarly for college students showed a relationship of poor home-adjustment scores to susceptibility to satiation in laboratory tasks.[19] Heron's results are remarkably consistent.[20] In addition to the negative finding concerning intelligence, he reported a positive relationship between job maladjustment and "Emotional Instability" (which included "Many Worries"), but *no* relationship with "Neurotic Extraversion" ("Hysteric Tendency"). A fourth factor, "Speed of Approach," not directly comparable to any in the present study, showed low predictive value.

The picture which emerges from these studies of the personality of the person who is satisfied doing repetitive work is one of contentment with the existing state of affairs, placidity, and perhaps rigidity. His satisfaction would seem to be more a matter of close contact with and acceptance of reality than of stupidity or insensitivity.

Since the preference for uniformity in work extends into daily habits outside the work situation, is related to lack of conflict or rebellion in the home, and is correlated with contentment both in the factory and out, feelings of monotony seem to be symptomatic of other discontent and restlessness rather than specific to any particular task.

Summary and Conclusions

Responses to questions concerning feelings of monotony and boredom on the job were compared, for a group of 72 women, with answers to other questions designed to test hypotheses derived primarily from accounts of previous writers concerning the personal characteristics associated with susceptibility to monotony. Four hypotheses were not supported in this study: that the susceptible worker is more ambitious, tends not to daydream, is extroverted, and is more intelligent. Three remained tenable: that the susceptible worker is likely to be young, restless in his daily habits and leisure-time activities, and less satisfied with personal, home, and plant situations in aspects not directly concerned with uniformity or repetitiveness.

---

[18] I. R. Pierce, "A Study of Rigid Behavior and Its Relationship to Concrete and Abstract Thinking" (Ph.D. diss., Cornell University, 1950).

[19] B. Bews, "An Experimental Investigation of the Concept of Psychical Satiation" (Master's thesis, Cornell University, 1951).

[20] Heron, "A Psychological Study of Vocational Adjustment."

On the basis of this and confirming evidence, an eighth hypothesis was considered tenable: that feelings of monotony are not merely a function of the task performed, but are related to more general factors in the individual worker. It was suggested that satisfaction with repetitive work does not necessarily reflect insensitivity and stupidity, as the more romantic textbooks seem to imply.

42. SHIFT WORK AND HUMAN EFFICIENCY *

Wallace Bloom

SINCE THE END OF WORLD WAR II, the need for shift workers has been rapidly expanding, both in the services and in industry. Our national defense now requires constant operational manning of missile bases, air-warning nets, communication facilities, base-security systems, and the like. And in industry, and particularly the chemical, metallurgical, and atomic industries, modern technology poses the same necessity for round-the-clock, 7-day-a-week operations.

Finding the most effective way of scheduling and assigning shift work is a problem with a direct bearing, therefore, on both our national security and our continued economic progress. Thus far, however, the attempts to solve it seem to have given insufficient attention to one of its most important aspects—the effects of shift work upon the biological rhythm of workers.

By habitually observing socially determined schedules specifying the hours for work, play, meals, and sleep, man has developed a diurnal rhythm—that is, a regularly recurring day-night variation in the chemical constituents of the blood and in the activity of the liver, kidneys, and endocrine glands. It should be emphasized that this is not something with which we are born—it is induced by our observance of a particular pattern of sleep and activity. As our rhythm attains a degree of autonomy, it makes it easier for us to stay awake during certain hours of the day and harder for us to do so at other times.

Our diurnal rhythm also imposes a corresponding periodic character on our efficiency. This was shown as far back as 1906 in the tests of sensory activity, motor activity, and simple mental activity carried out by Marsh.[1] More recently, on the basis of a 20-year study of Munich industries, Lehman established a positive relation between efficiency and

* From "Shift Work and the Sleep-Wakefulness Cycle," *Personnel* 38 (1961): 24–31.
[1] H. D. Marsh, *The Diurnal Course of Efficiency,* Archives of Philosophy, Psychology, and Scientific Methods no. 7 (New York: Columbia University Press, 1906), p. 95.

the amount of adrenaline in the blood.[2] and Kleitman, the recognized authority on sleep and wakefulness, has demonstrated that there is a marked inverse relation between reaction time and body temperature.[3] Reaction time is a good measure of alertness, while body temperature, which fluctuates through a range of about 2° F each day, provides an accurate reflection of the rhythmic metabolic changes, for it reaches its low point between 2:00 and 5:00 A.M. and its high point in midafternoon. According to Kleitman's findings, we are most alert at the high point of our daily temperature curve and least alert at the low point.

But a particular temperature curve, like the rhythm of which it is an index, will eventually be altered if the day-night schedule that originally established it is replaced by a new one. As Kleitman points out:

If [a man] remains awake during the entire night, both temperature and performance fall below their drowsiness levels, reaching minima between 2:00 A.M. and 4:00 A.M., when it is hardest to keep awake. Then there begins an upswing which crosses the drowsiness level at the usual getting-up time. . . . The curve can be shifted, inverted, distorted, shortened, or lengthened, by following a new schedule of activities for a certain number of weeks.[4]

The fixity of any individual's temperature curve is thus a simple measure of the degree to which he has adapted to a particular time cycle. When he is suddenly subjected to a new 24-hour schedule—as happens when a worker is assigned to a new shift—we can expect that his temperature curve will change, with the high point moving toward his activity period. This assumption has been confirmed by studies of the physiological effects of long-distance flights. The results are of course the same whether the new time schedule is imposed by shift rotation or by geographical change.

When the Rhythm Is Disrupted

Until the adjustment has been completed, the individual will suffer a discrepancy between his accustomed sleep-wakefulness cycle and the one required by his new environment. Strughold has called this discrepancy "incomplete time or cycle adaptation." [5]

The effect of this discrepancy on shift workers, and particularly on

---

[2] G. Lehman, "Diurnal Rhythm in Relation to Working Capacity," *Acta Medica Scandanavica* 145, suppl. 278, pp. 108–9.

[3] N. Kleitman, *Sleep and Wakefulness* (Chicago: University of Chicago Press, 1939), p. 220.

[4] Kleitman, "The Sleep-Wakefulness Cycle of Submarine Personnel," *Human Factors in Undersea Warfare* (Washington, D.C.: U.S. Department of the Navy, 1949), pp. 329–30.

[5] H. Strughold, *The Physiological Day-Night Cycle in Global Flights* (Randolph Field, Tex.: USAF School of Aviation Medicine, 1952), p. 2.

rotating-shift workers, should perhaps be spelled out here. As we have seen, efficiency is directly related to diurnal rhythm. The worker suffering incomplete time adaptation therefore undergoes not only some physical discomfort but a loss in efficiency, for his body and mind are most ready to perform well at hours when he is off duty, or at only a few of his on-duty hours. Thus shift rotation, which at first glance seems so eminently fair because it provides for the equal sharing of the inconvenience of night work, imposes a physiological hardship on all the workers every time the shifts are changed and may lead to a general decrease in efficiency.

How long incomplete time adaptation persists has not yet been determined, but it is known that a flight across the Atlantic, which occasions a gain or loss of five hours, generally requires an adjustment period of a week or more. A change to a work shift six hours earlier or later than one's previous shift, even if it is preceded by a 24-hour rest period, must therefore impose an incomplete-adaptation period of at least several days. At all events, it seems certain that rotating the shifts at whatever time interval is most convenient administratively does not result in optimal performance and that many companies rotate their shifts too frequently for the adaptive powers of the employees concerned.

Besides the length of the adaptation period, several questions about the adaptation process itself are worthy of further study. Does the adaptation proceed at a constant, gradual rate—say, one hour or two hours each day? Or is it irregular or even spasmodic—with no change occurring for the first several days and an abrupt change thereafter? Are there setbacks in the course of the adaptation—that is, reversions toward the original cycle? Research must provide the answers to these questions if management is to improve its shift scheduling to secure the highest possible degree of alertness on the part of the workers.

What we already know about the sleep-wakefulness cycle, however, affords a basis for several improvements upon current practice. The following suggestions will illustrate how the findings of physiological research might be applied by industry:

1. *Selection of Individuals for Rotating Shifts.* It has been established that people vary in their ability to modify their diurnal rhythms. Some can adjust to a 6-hour change in about a week; others find the adaptation very difficult. Kleitman and a companion once experimented with living an artificial 6-day week. After six weeks, Kleitman was still experiencing seven temperature cycles a week, while his partner had changed to six.

"Since an individual's curve of performance follows his body-temperature curve," he recommended, "considerations of efficiency in doing work, in addition to purely humanitarian reasons, demand that the services concerned employ for night duty, or other abnormal shifts, only individuals who are capable of shifting or inverting their body temperatures on short notice." [6]

The problem of adaptation is doubly severe under shift rotation, for the workers involved must adapt both to the rotation itself and to night work. Companies that use this system should therefore carry out tests of the candidates' adaptability to these changes. The tests could take the form of measuring their temperatures after an experimental 6- or 8-hour change in shifts or a change to night hours. When the men have spent a week or ten days on the new shift, the adaptability of their temperature curves can then be determined.

2. *Special Training and Conditioning for Shift Work.* Training programs for shift workers should include sessions at which physicians explain the diurnal rhythm and what happens in shift changes and during night work. The workers should also be told how they can best arrange their time-off activities for easing the adjustment to the new hours and getting to sleep during daylight hours. During the training period, the company should institute a gradual transition to the time schedule on which they will be working—by shifting their schedule one hour each day, for instance.

3. *Fixed Shifts Instead of Rotating Shifts.* Companies now using rotating shifts should review their scheduling problem to determine whether fixed shifts can be substituted. If they do decide to switch, they should explain all the reasons for their decision to the men involved.

The advantages of such a change were demonstrated in 1956 by an overseas military communications center. Partly on the advice of this writer but primarily because of a personnel shortage, the center abandoned its rotating 4-shift schedule in favor of a fixed schedule of three shifts—from midnight to 7:30 A.M., from 7:30 to 4:30 P.M. (including time for a noon meal), and from 4:30 to midnight. The results proved beneficial in a number of ways. Performance improved as the men became familiar with the variations in work load peculiar to their shift. They grew accustomed to eating at the same time every day, and they no longer had to look at a calendar to ascertain which hours and days they were scheduled to work.

When some men were transferred and had to be replaced, the senior workers were given the option of changing their shifts. Most of them turned it down. The new men, though they did not like the system at first, soon adjusted to the schedule and fitted in well. Even those who had been accustomed to rotating shifts at their previous stations and were greatly upset by the new arranegment when they first arrived liked it better after a while.

The use of fixed shifts at this center also eased the manpower shortage:

---

[6] Kleitman, *Sleep and Wakefulness*, p. 267.

whereas 39 men had formerly been assigned to each shift to allow for rotation, the fixed shifts managed with from 33 to 39 men, according to the work load. The responsibility for setting the days-off schedule was given to the shift supervisors, and most men got two successive days off each week.

4. *Fewer Shift Rotations.* If rotating shifts prove unavoidable, the changes should be made infrequently. Rotating the assignments once a month rather than once a week (as many companies now do) would reduce the number of drastic physiological adjustments required of the workers from 52 to 12 a year. Since it takes air travelers at least a week to adjust to a 6-hour change, we can expect that workers whose hours have been similarly altered are still suffering incomplete time adjustment on the third day of their new shift, when, in many companies, they once again have to change their working hours. The crews of transoceanic planes, Strughold recommended, should not be subjected to this change too often; and if they are regularly flying back and forth, they should be allowed to maintain the diurnal cycle of their home continent.

5. *Longer Rest Periods between Shift Changes.* Shift schedules should also be arranged to allow a maximum of time off between changes. With a reduction in the number of shift changes, it might be possible to allow workers as many as three days off.

6. *Shorter Time for the Graveyard Shift.* Since the early-morning shift (from midnight onwards, say) is the period when it is most difficult to keep alert, shortening it would probably improve efficiency, as well as reduce the stress on the workers. A company with a 4-shift cycle could cut the graveyard shift down to five hours by simply adding 20 minutes to each of the other three shifts.

7. *More Attention to Personnel Problems.* Even with the aid of selection tests, no company can expect that it will assign to shift work only those employees who can make a healthy adjustment to it. Diagnostic interviews should therefore be held with shift workers who have accidents or show an above-average number of sick reports so that those with psychological difficulties can be weeded out.

These recommendations, derived as they are from the findings of physiological research, may perhaps seem somewhat unrelated to the practical requirements of a company that cannot confine its operations to a 1-shift, 5-day week. They are supported, however, by the findings of numerous studies of the effects of shift work, and particularly of shift rotation and night work, on the workers involved. Some of the more pertinent of these findings may be summarized.

In a survey of shift-work patterns among 50 large American companies in 1951, the National Industrial Conference Board found that fixed shifts were more usual than rotating shifts on a 5-day operation with two or three shifts and that among companies with a rotating-shift system the rotation was generally on a weekly or fortnightly basis.[7] Some companies, the study found, added an extra (and versatile) man to each crew, so that it could work throughout the week while individual members still had regular days off. With seven men for every six jobs, say, there could be one man off each day, the extra man filling in for him; the latter, of course, would also get one day off a week.

Research on Shift Work

The effects of various shift-work patterns have been studied in a number of countries, and from several points of view. Among American studies, two should be mentioned here. The first was concerned with the effects on a group of women workers of a change from a single 9-hour shift to two alternating 6-hour shifts. Under the new system, some of the women, who worked in the morning for one week and in the afternoon for the next, reported difficulty in adjusting their habits of eating and sleeping. The second study found that workers whose shifts were changed found it even harder to adjust to the change in mealtimes than to get enough sleep. Of the workers questioned, 62 percent complained of this difficulty, and 35 percent said the adjustment took them more than four days.

In Sweden, researchers found many instances of failure to adjust to changing shifts. The shift workers, they pointed out, were being forced to live in a different time sequence from that of their community and of the many people to whom they were intimately related. In a study of errors made in entering figures in the ledgers of a large Swedish gas works under a rotating 3-shift system, it was found that a very high number of errors occurred around 3:00 A.M. (The night shift ran from 10:00 P.M. to 6:00 A.M.) The number of errors did not vary significantly either by season or by day of the week. Moreover, the same variation in errors appeared on the last night of the week as on the first, indicating that the plant's weekly rotation system was not allowing the workers enough time to change the general pattern of their diurnal rhythm.[8]

Reviewing the findings of German research, Pierach reported one study that found ulcers eight times more common among shift workers than among day workers and another that found them four times more common.[9] Of the 170 shift workers covered by still another study he mentioned, half gave up shift work because of ulcers. Only about 50 percent

[7] See H. P. Northrup, *Shift Problems and Practices*, Studies in Personnel Policy, no. 118 (New York: National Industrial Conference Board).

[8] B. Bjerner et al., "Diurnal Variation in Mental Performance," *British Journal of Industrial Medicine*, April 1955, pp. 103–10. (Also reviewed in *National Safety News*, September 1955, pp. 55–56.)

[9] See A. Pierach, "Biological Rhythm-Effects of Night Work and Shift Changes on the Health of Workers," *Acta Medica Scandanavica* 152, suppl. 307.

of night workers can change to day work in one week, Pierach maintained, also noting that the loss of man-days through illness was greater in a 3-shift than in a 2-shift activity. During World War II, some industries in Bavaria instituted a rotation system called the flying shift change, under which the crews worked for 12 hours and then had 24 hours off. This practice, however, had adverse effects on the workers' health.

A negative report on another scheduling system, the split shift, comes from a paper on the experience of the British munitions industries during World War I. This system, under which a crew might work from 6:00 to 10:00 A.M. and then from 2:00 to 6:00 P.M., was very unpopular with workers, says the bulletin.

Finally, Japanese researchers have reported that officers engaged in coastal navigation lost sleep under a shift system and suffered chronic fatigue.

Research on Night Work

Having to be awake during the usual hours for sleep poses a number of special problems, whether the workers involved are on a fixed night shift or are serving night duty on a rotating shift.

Perhaps the most obvious of these is the difficulty of getting enough sleep during the daytime. Of the workers questioned in a study by Maier, 42 percent said that when they were on the night shift they did not sleep enough by day, and 75 percent said they got less than eight hours' sleep a day.[10]

Of the night workers covered in a German study reviewed by Pierach, slightly less than half reported getting more than five hours' sleep a day. The workers also complained of sleepiness, headaches, and a loss of ability to concentrate. Errors and accidents were more frequent during night work than during day work, the same study found. Some other effects of night work have also been reported by Pierach. A study of nurses on a night shift found that they suffered loss of appetite (as demonstrated by weight) and digestive interruptions, and that there was too much acid in their small intestines. Doctors have recommended that an ulcer patient be removed from night shifts. And, of the night workers studies in one investigation, 25 percent eventually gave up night work.

Similar data have been supplied by two studies of British industry. One cites as the main objection to night work the inability of workers to obtain adequate sleep by day. This problem may be attributable to the disruption of the workers' ordinary habits, the paper suggests, or its causes may be social—noises and disturbances, or the responsibility of caring for one's children. The workers studied said they were often tempted to curtail their period of sleep in order to join the family midday

---

[10] N. R. F. Maier, *Psychology in Industry*, 2d ed. (Boston: Houghton Mifflin Co., 1955), p. 450.

meal or to obtain some recreation. The study of munitions industries mentioned above found that it was difficult for night workers to consume substantial food at an unfamiliar meal hour and that their digestion was likely to be upset.

Further word on the sleep problem has come from some investigators in the United States who point out that the night worker's sleep is likely to be disturbed by the presence of daylight and the extra noise and heat of the daytime. Their studies have convinced them that work should never be scheduled for the nighttime.

Since loss of sleep has been found to be so prevalent among night workers, its physiological effects deserve further mention.

In 1951, research psychologists at Tufts College conducted an experimental study of the effects of loss of sleep on subjective feelings.[11] As might be expected, of the 415 college undergraduates who participated, those who slept between eight and nine hours each day felt much better than those who slept only six hours. Subjects who went without sleep for long periods of time reported that feelings of sleepiness came in waves, reaching their peak between 3:00 and 6:00 A.M. The subjects also felt irritable and noted that their ability to carry out tasks requiring attention and effort had decreased. The 17 subjects who remained awake for 100 hours were restless as well, and complained of headaches. They did not recover until they had lived and slept normally for one week.

In a study of the effects of loss of sleep and rest on air crews, McFarland found that loss of sleep had marked effects on performance on mental tests requiring prolonged effort and continuous attention.[12] The most striking changes were loss of memory, hallucinations, heightened irritability, and wide fluctuations in emotional state.

The correlation between loss of sleep and loss of efficiency at tasks requiring continuous attention has been confirmed by other studies, though it is also known that short tasks may be performed with little diminution of efficiency over a considerable time. In general, the quality of work suffers more than the quantity.

The Need to Respect Rhythm

To sum up, then, most shift workers experience serious inconveniences of two kinds: disruption of their normal diurnal body rhythms and, largely as a result of this disrupiton, loss of sleep resulting in fatigue. The effects of fatigue are cumulative and, to make matters worse, frequently

---

[11] Tufts College: Institute for Applied Experimental Psychology, *Handbook of Human Engineering Data* (Port Washington, N.Y.: Special Devices Center, Office of Naval Research), part 7, chap. 2, sec. 1, Data T, pp. 1–6.

[12] R. A. McFarland, *Human Factors in Air Transportation* (New York: McGraw-Hill Book Co., Inc., 1953), p. 343.

show no obvious sign, so that a man's performance may be severely impaired without his being aware of it.

The need to respect the normal diurnal rhythm has been forcefully expressed by Pierach: "No organ or organ system is exempt from the 24-hour rhythm in its function. . . . Rhythm heals; continued activities contrary to rhythm make one weak and sick." [13]

For centuries now, men have studied the ebb and flow of the oceans and have used the knowledge thus gained to schedule the comings and goings of ships with a high degree of exactitude. By comparison, we still have much to learn about the tides within the human body—and what little we do know is still not being used to schedule the activities of men to best advantage. It is to be hoped that with further research and experimentation we shall ultimately be able to design shift-work schedules that will insure maximum efficiency and a minimum of personal hardship.

43. WORKER ADJUSTMENT TO THE FOUR-DAY WEEK *

Walter R. Nord and Robert Costigan

THE FOUR-DAY WORK WEEK has been, and most probably will continue to be, introduced in many organizations. This change may have profound effects on the lives of the individuals. While considerable speculation and anecdotal information have been published, to date there is little reliable empirical evidence about the effects of the four-day week on workers.

The only major empirical study that could be found was reported by Steele and Poor.[1] Their data showed that workers overwhelmingly saw the change as beneficial for their lives at work and at home. However, because Steele and Poor's study was primarily descriptive and cross-sectional and the authors did not state how long various parts of their population had been on the four-day week, inferences concerning individual adjustment over time were not possible.

The present exploratory research was designed to provide longitudinal data on the responses of people to the four-day work week. Since it was

---

[13] Pierach, "Biological Rhythm-Effects of Night Work," p. 159.

* From "Worker Adjustment to the Four-Day Week: A Longitudinal Study, *Journal of Applied Psychology* 58 (1973): 60–66. Copyright 1973 by the American Psychological Association. Reprinted by permission.

[1] J. L. Steele and R. Poor, "Work and Leisure: the Reactions of People at 4-Day Firms," in *4 Days, 40 Hours,* ed. R. Poor (Cambridge, Mass.: Burk and Poor, 1970).

expected that reactions to the four-day week would change over time, the design called for repeated measurements in the same plant.

METHOD

Subjects

The data were collected from employees of a nonunionized medium-sized St. Louis-based pharmaceutical company that had recently changed from a workweek of five 8-hour days to four 9½-hour days.[2] The plant employed approximately 100 members of each sex whose average age was in the late 40s. The employees were described by management as a closely knit group; many of the workers were related to each other. Only foremen, group leaders, and lower-level employees who were working in the plant for at least 10 of the 12 months covered by the survey, and were employed there at the time of both the first and third administrations of the questionnaire, were included in the analysis. From this pool, 131, 126, and 111 useable questionnaires were received for surveys I, II, and III respectively. For most analyses all the Ss were included; however, for several analyses only those 59 Ss who responded to all measurements were included.

The plant itself was highly automated. Many jobs were heavily machine paced and consisted of monitoring machinery.

Procedure

A questionnaire was designed to elicit information on demographic factors, attitudes towards the 4-day week, and changes in work and home life resulting from the new work schedule. The questions were mainly open-ended, although some closed and scaled items were used. The questionnaire was distributed with each person's paycheck at three different times. The first administration was July 7, 1971, six weeks after the initial trial period had begun; the second administration was August 24, 1971; the final administration was May 25, 1972, approximately one year after the initial trial period had begun. The same questionnaire was used each time except for changes in time references and the addition of a question after each survey.

Interviews with the personnel and other managers were used to supplement the questionnaire data, but, except in interpreting the absenteeism data, are given little attention in this report.

---

[2] While initially the change was on a trial basis, there was every indication that it would be permanent if it was successful. Approximately three months after the beginning of the trial period, it was formally announced that the change would be permanent.

TABLE 43–1

**Open-Ended Questions and Coding Categories
(major categories and elements for coding)**

Dichotomous Coding Categories	*Elements*
1. What plans (if any) have you made for the 3-day weekend?	
1a. Plans versus no plans	1a. Plans listed or not
1b. Type of plan—task or recreational	1b. *Task*—shopping, doctor's appointments, work around house, moonlighting, special work projects *Recreational*—sports, rest and relaxation, visit relatives and socialize, travel
2. In the last ___ weeks, have you noticed anything different about your job? If yes, please describe.	
2. Job changes—favorable versus unfavorable to company goals.	2. *Favorable to company goals*—More work done, higher employee morale, more relaxed at work, employees busier, better continuity of projects, less absenteeism, better adjusted *Unfavorable to company goals*—Less work done, greater fatigue, lower employee morale.
3. In the last ___ week have you noticed anything different about the plant (or office)? If yes, please describe.	
3. Changes in plant—favorable versus unfavorable to company goals.	3. *Favorable to company goals*—More work done, higher employee morale, more relaxed at work, employees busier, better continuity of projects, less absenteeism, better adjusted *Unfavorable to company goals*—Less work done, greater fatigue, lower employee morale
4. In the last ___ weeks, have you noticed anything different about your home life? If yes, please describe.	
4. Changes in personal life—favorable versus unfavorable to self.	4. *Favorable to self*—more time with family and friends, more rest and relaxation, get more done at home, other happiness feelings, moonlighting, better adjusted. *Unfavorable to self*—Less time with family and friends, problems—for example, meals, housekeeping, more tired after work, emotional problems, spend more money.

Analysis

Responses to the closed-end items were simply recorded. The open-ended responses were coded into the categories listed in Table 43–1. The coded and closed-end items for each survey were cross tabulated. Only the cross tabulations which were relevant to the effects of the four-day week were run; such relationships as age versus sex or age versus number of children were not considered.

To measure overall attitudes, Ss were asked to check one of five statements which best described their feelings about the old and new workweeks. Two statements favored the four-day week, one was neutral, and two favored the five-day week. For purposes of analysis, the two favorable statements were interpreted as showing favorable overall attitudes to the four-day week; the other three were interpreted as showing less favorable attitudes.

Information was also collected about the Ss themselves. The demographic variables of sex, age, marital status, and children living at home were dichotomized into age groups of 40 and under versus 41 and over, married versus not married, and one or more children living at home versus none living at home. In addition, data on the average number of hours of sleep and weight were included for analysis.

Finally, the jobs were classified as high- or low-paced. High-paced jobs were ones where the worker's pace was determined primarily by an assembly line or a machine; these jobs were mainly in shipping and receiving, processing, and packaging. Low-paced jobs included office, janitorial, maintenance, and cafeteria personnel.

RESULTS

Overall Attitudes Toward the 4-day Week

For all three surveys, overall attitudes toward the 4-day week were very favorable: 81 percent highly favorable to 19 percent less favorable attitudes. The percentages remained nearly constant for all three surveys.

Attitude and Pace. Table 43–2 shows the frequency of responses for attitude toward the four day week for individuals under high- and low-paced jobs. It can be seen that in all three periods, workers favored the four day week for both types of jobs. While no significant association between job pace and attitudes was found 6 or 13 weeks after initiation, after one year attitudes of workers on low-paced jobs tended to be less favorable towards the four-day week than those of workers on high-paced jobs ($\chi^2 = 4.21$, p <.05). To further explore the correlates of attitudes and job pace, χ^2 and/or Fisher exact probabilities were calculated for the relationship of pace with perceived changes in home life, in the job, and in the plant for each survey. None of these tests reached statistical significance.

Overall Attitude and Selected Demographic Variables. The results of cross tabulations of attitude with age, sex, marital status, and children living at home were subjected to χ^2 analysis for each of the three surveys.

TABLE 43–2

Cross Tabulations of Attitude Toward Four-day Week and Job-Pace over Time

Favorableness of Attitude	Time Since Initiation					
	6 Weeks		13 Weeks		1 Year*	
	Low	High	Low	High	Low	High
Low-paced jobs	12	46	13	51	14	39
High-paced jobs	10	54	8	45	6	49

* $x^2 = 4.21$, p $< .05$

No significant associations between attitudes and these demographic factors appeared for any of the three periods.

Overall Attitudes and Specific Attitudinal Dimensions. To determine what specific attitudes might account for differences in overall attitudes, all of the variables in Table 43–1 were tested for their association with overall attitudes. x^2 analysis was used to test the association between workers' overall attitudes and the number of specific plans. These data, summarized in Table 43–3, indicated that people without plans held less favorable overall attitudes toward the new workweek than people with plans both six weeks and one year after the change. . . . While many people without plans were still favorable to the four-day week, a large majority of those who held less favorable attitudes did not mention any plans for the three-day weekend. The mention of plans was also positively associated with favorableness of the reported changes in home life six weeks after initiation of the four-day week. ($x^2 = 5.28$, p $< .05$).

Further analysis revealed that type of plans people had (recreational-versus task-oriented) were not related to their attitudes after 6 and 13 weeks. However, a year after initiation, people with recreational-oriented plans were apt to show less favorable attitudes toward the four-day week (Fisher exact test, p $< .001$).

The association of overall attitudes with changes in job and plant were tested for each period using Fisher exact tests. No significant associations were found between attitudes and perceived changes at any time period. However, after both 13 weeks and 1 year, workers who perceived the changes as favorable to company goals held more favorable attitudes towards the four-day week (p $= .0006$ and p $= .0036$ respectively).

Specific Attitudes over Time

In order to see what specific changes occurred over time, the proportions of the number of reports of perceived changes in job, plant, home life, and the number of plans to the total number of Ss in each survey

TABLE 43–3

Frequency of Attitudes towards the Four-Day Week versus the Presence or Absence of Plans for the Three-Day Weekend (by time period)

| | Time Since Initiation | | | | | |
| | 6 Weeks** | | 13 Weeks | | 1 Year* | |
Plans	Yes	No	Yes	No	Yes	No
Favorable attitude	62	44	51	50	43	42
Unfavorable attitude	2	21	8	14	4	16

* $x^2 = 6.12$, p = .01
** $x^2 = 18.74$, p < .001

TABLE 43–4

Proportions of Reports of Changes to Total Number of Respondents (by time period)

| | Time Since Initiation of 4-day Week | | |
Type of Change	6 Weeks (N = 131)	13 Weeks (N = 126)	1 Year (N = 111)
Plant	.13	.13	.16
Job	.20	.24	.32
Home life	.48	.37*	.35***
Plans	.79	.68	.83**

* Different from p_1, p < .05
** Different from p_2, p < .05
*** Different from p_1, p < .01

were calculated. The results presented in Table 43–4, showed a significant tendency for people to perceive more changes in their home life after 6 weeks than after 13 weeks ($Z = 2.22$, $p < .05$) and after one year ($Z = 2.66$, $p < .01$). Moreover, they reported fewer plans after 13 weeks than after one year ($Z = 2.55$, $p < .05$). Similarly, they reported making fewer plans after 13 weeks than after 6 weeks ($Z = 1.82$, $p < .07$). Also they perceived more job changes over time; after one year more job changes resulting from the new work week were reported than after 6 weeks ($Z = 1.93$, $p < .06$). Thus, over the period of one year, Ss tended to report proportionately fewer changes in home life but slightly more in job life.

The data were tested for qualitative changes overtime. Tests of proportions compared the three periods on changes in plant, changes in job, changes in home life, plans versus no plans, and type of plans. No significant differences in proportions between time periods were found for changes in plant, changes in job, plans versus no plans, and types of

TABLE 43–5

Frequency and Proportions of Responses Indicating Effects on Home Life over Time

| | Time Since Initiation | | | | | |
| | 6 Weeks | | 13 Weeks | | 1 Year | |
Effect on Home Life	Number of Responses	%	Number of Responses	%	Number of Responses	%
Favorable to personal life	63	63	47	66	29	45
Unfavorable to personal life	36	37	24	34	35	55
Total.	99	100	71	100	64	100

* Proportions differed significantly from 6 and 13 weeks, p < .05.

plans. However, as shown in Table 43–5, whereas 6 and 13 weeks after initiation 63 percent and 66 percent of the effects on home life were seen as favorable, after one year only 45 percent were seen as favorable. The differences between first two and the third periods were both statistically significant (Z = 2.13, 2.12; p < .05 respectively). For the most part these differences were due to workers reporting few favorable effects after one year.

Personal Factors and the 4-day Week

Data on the personal variables of hours of sleep and weight were collected after all three periods. For each dependent variable, an analysis of variance for repeated measures was performed on the 59 Ss who answered these questions in all three surveys. While no statistically significant weight changes were found, after one year on the four-day week workers averaged 6.72 hours of sleep per night as compared to 7.05 hours per night on the five day week and 6.98 and 7.02 hours per night after 6 and 13 weeks on the four-day week. This main effect was statistically significant (F = 2.95, df = 3/171). Most of this effect was due to a decline in the hours of sleep reported after one year on the 4-day week.

Demographic Factors. The appropriate test of association was run for age versus changes in home life, types of plans, changes in job, and changes in plant on the data from each time period. Of the 12 tests, only the relationship between worker's age and the type of plans they made reached an acceptable level of significanec. As shown in Table 43–6, 13 weeks and one year after initiation older workers tended to make more task plans and younger workers made more recreational-oriented ones.

The appropriate tests of association of sex of worker versus changes perceived in plant, home life, plans, and job were run for each survey.

TABLE 43-6

Frequencies of Type of Plans for Three-Day Weekend versus Age (by time period)

	Time Since Initiation of 4-day Week					
	After 6 Weeks		After 13 Weeks*		After 1 Year**	
Age	40 and Under	41+	40 and Under	41+	40 and Under	41+
Recreational plans	30	29	35	25	30	22
Task-oriented plans	19	26	9	17	12	28

* $x^2 = 4.08$, $p < .05$
** $x^2 = 6.99$, $p < .01$

TABLE 43-7

Frequencies of Responses after One Year for Sex versus Changes in Job, Plans, and Changes In Home Life

	Changes in Job*		Plans**		Changes in Home Life***	
Sex	Favorable to Company Goals	Un-favorable to Company Goals	Recre-ational	Task	Favorable to Personal Life	Un-favorable to Personal Life
Male	14	10	29	23	13	16
Female	10	1	14	26	25	10

* $p = .05$ (Fisher Exact Probability Test)
** $x^2 = 3.83$, $p = .05$
*** $x^2 = 4.65$, $p < .05$

Of the 12 tests, 3 reached acceptable levels of significance; all 3 of these relationships appeared in the third survey. As shown in Table 43-7, after one year females, more than males, saw the change to the four-day week as resulting in changes on their job which are more favorable to the company and changes in their home life which are more favorable to them. Moreover, females made more task-oriented plans and males made more recreational-oriented plans. Again, these relationships reached statistical significance only after one year.

The appropriate test of association was run for marital status versus home life and plans for all three surveys. None of these relationships were statistically significant.

In the surveys conducted 13 weeks and one year after the change, information on the number of children living at home was collected. The appropriate test for association was run on children living at home (none, or one or more) versus plans and home life. Of the four tests only one relationship reached significance. One year after the change people with one or more children living at home more frequently felt the four-day week had unfavorable consequences on their personal life ($\chi^2 = 4.66$, df = 1, p < .05) than did people with no children living at home.

Absenteeism

The average hours of absenteeism per day for the 5 months prior to and the 16 months following the introduction of the four-day week are reported in Table 43–8. In order to control for the partial confounding of the change in the length of the workweek with normal seasonal variation, two sets of comparisons were made.

First, the January–May 1971 period (prior to the 4-day week) was compared with both the June–September 1971 period (the first four months following new workweek) and the January–May 1972 period. Secondly, the June–September 1971 period was compared with the October–December 1971 and June–September 1972 periods. As the footnote to Table 43–8 implies, the periods were not directly comparable due to a 10 percent reduction in the work force. However, even if a full 10 percent was subtracted from the figures for the earlier periods, absenteeism after initiation would still be less than it was before.

The January–May 1971 figure minus 10 percent is about 42.7 compared to 37.7 for the comparable 1972 period and 40.5 for the June–Sept. period of 1971. Similarly, the June–September 1971 figures minus 10 percent is about 34.6 compared to 30.2 for the comparable 1972 period, although the October–December period would appear to be the same or slightly higher than that of the preintroduction period.

Thus, when seasonal factors and changes in the number of employees are controlled for, the four-day week was associated with a decrease in absenteeism of over 10 percent. Moreover, when a comparison of the four-month period immediately following the introduction of four-day week was made with the comparable period one year later, the level of absenteeism was approximately 10 percent lower for the latter period.

TABLE 43–8

Hours of Absenteeism per Workday [1]

	Period		
	January–May	*June–September*	*October–December*
1971	47.4	40.5	44.5
1972	37.7	30.2	(not available)

[1] During the 21-month period, employment declined approximately 10 percent. Thus, the early 1971 figures are based on slightly more people than the later 1971 and the 1972 figures.

DISCUSSION

The results of this study must be interpreted cautiously for several reasons. The data were collected from only one plant for one year. Secondly, the differences between some of the periods were confounded with seasonal variations and other uncontrolled forces. Finally, the effect of repeated questioning is unknown. Given these limitations, this exploratory study still revealed several trends to direct future research. In particular, employees had consistently positive attitudes towards the four-day week. They saw the change as favorable to company goals and as having little effect on their individual work environment throughout the research period. The perceived favorableness of the effects on home life varied over time. One year after the change, the effects of the four-day week on home life were perceived as significantly less positive than at first.

In addition to these findings, several possibly significant patterns emerged. First, most reports of unfavorable changes were home- rather than work-related. For all three surveys only 37 responses indicating unfavorable changes in job and changes unfavorable to company goals were reported. By contrast, the corresponding number of unfavorable changes in home life was 95. Moreover, the proportion of negative changes on home life increased significantly over time; no similar changes occurred on work-related responses. Although the data on absenteeism were confounded with decreases in employment and seasonal factors, absenteeism 12 to 16 months after the introduction of the 4-day week was approximately 10 percent less than the four-month period immediately following the change.

Perhaps the most important implication of the present study for future research concerns the observed tendency for few significant patterns of response to occur soon after the change, but a larger number of patterns to become apparent over the period of one year. While a certain number of statistically significant results were to be expected as a function of the number of tests run, the tendency for significant results to appear after one year, but not after 6 or 13 weeks suggests that many of the effects of the four-day week may be stronger over time. Thus, studies of the 4-day week may yield sharply different results depending on how long after the change they are conducted. Individual adjustments to changes which affect established daily routines may take some time to develop into new stable patterns.

The specific content of some of the relationships which emerged over time also merit further investigation. First, the fact that after both six weeks and one year, workers who reported making plans to use the three-day weekend were significantly more likely to perceive the new work week favorably draws attention to social-psychological problems of leisure. While the findings in this study could be due to such factors as personality characteristics, if they are replicated in other research, organizations may find counseling in use of leisure to be a useful step. Further support for this argument came from the tendency for the reported effects on home life to become more negative over time. Perhaps, when the novelty of the change subsided, some individuals, particularly the roughly 20 percent who had not made any plans, found the larger block of leisure time less attractive than at first.

The data also suggested that age and sex may be related to plans to use leisure time. Since younger and male workers were more apt to make recreational-oriented plans than were older and female workers, and females were more apt to see the influence on home life as being more favorable, perhaps females experienced interrole conflict between their job outside the home and their role of homemaker. Their new full day of "leisure" permitted them to catch up on house work which the social norms of our society still require of women. Their new leisure time was more structured and they felt better about their performance of one of their major social roles. Males, by contrast, may have had fewer tasks required by their nonwork roles. They made more recreational plans but did not feel the increment in satisfaction from a reduction in interrole conflict that females might have experienced. If future research replicates these findings, and our sex roles do not change radically, it may well be that the four-day week will be of greater benefit for females than for males.

44. THE PHENOMENON OF ACCIDENT PRONENESS *

A. G. Arbous and J. E. Kerrich

PEOPLE FIRST STUMBLED ON THE IDEA of "accident proneness" when it was observed that. in most work groups studied, a minority were responsible for the majority of accidents. This spectacular observation led the unwary in the past to formulate the concept of accident proneness as a means of explanation.

It is a difficult matter to define what is meant by this term and evolve a sensible measure of whatever it indicates. Apparently it was meant to define some personal trait as opposed to some characteristic of the environment, which predisposed some to have more accidents than others in work conditions where the risk of hazard was equal to all. The term would appear to imply, moreover, that it is possible either (a) to differentiate clearly between two classes of people—those who are accident

---

* Extracted and adapted from *Industrial Medicine and Surgery* 22 (1953): 141–48.

prone and those who are not, or (b) at least to be able to rank the group in terms of the severity of their proneness to accident.

Even today, after the trenchant comments of writers like Mintz and Blum,[1] the fallacy of this line of argument, based on the distribution of accidents in a single period of observation, does not appear to have penetrated the mind of the layman, or even of many specialists working in the field of accident prevention. It is appropriate, therefore, in our study of this phenomenon that we should drive this point home by considering from an actual example the extent to which the accident-proneness concept enables one to differentiate between persons with the hope of producing beneficial results.

The implied advantage of this theory is that after having spotted who the accident-prone cases are in a group, their removal from the group should result in a decrease in the relative frequency of accidents sustained by the remainder. This objective is laudable and obvious. If it cannot be achieved, there is little point in our clinging to the concept of proneness.

The fallacy of this line of reasoning is strikingly revealed by reference to an example from Adelstein's data, covering the records of 104 shunters with three years' service.[2] He reports the effect of removing cases with a high accident record in the first year of service as follows:

TABLE 44–1

The Accident Rates for the Shunters Who Joined in 1944 and Shunted for Three Years

	1st Year	2nd Year	3rd Year
Mean accident rate for 104 men. 557		.355	.317
After removing 10 men with highest rate in			
1st year, i.e., 94 remaining men. 393		.361	.329

In this case the annual accident rate in the second and third years actually went up a trifle after the removal of the ten men who had had most accidents during the first year. Clearly, evidence of this type indicates that our conception of the term accident proneness stands in need of a critical examination from first principles.

What is meant by the term accident proneness? Farmer and Chambers state: "The fact that one of the factors connected with accident liability has been found to be a peculiarity of the individual allows us to differentiate between 'accident proneness' and 'accident liability.' (Accident proneness' is a narrower term than 'accident liability' and means a

---

[1] A. Mintz and M. L. Blum, "A Re-examination of the Accident-Proneness Concept," *Journal of Applied Psychology* 33 (1949): 195–211.

[2] A. M. Adelstein (Ph.D. diss. on the accident rates of railway operatives, University of Witwatersrand, South Africa, 1951).

personal idiosyncrasy predisposing the individual who possesses it in a marked degree to a relatively high accident rate. 'Accident liability' includes all the factors determining accident rate: 'accident-proneness' refers only to those that are personal."[3] From the above it is obvious that environmental factors plus the personal factor of accident proneness in the individual determine the accident liability of individuals in any given situation. It is, however, concerning the latter that confusion has arisen. This term is widely used in current literature and yet it is scarcely ever well defined.

It is frequently suggested that "inherent accident proneness" is a stable invariable attribute of the individual (in much the same way as we regard his general mental ability, manual dexterity, and so forth) and that accident liability depends on: (a) inherent accident proneness; (b) variations in personal health, age, experience, fatigue, and so forth; (c) the risks inherent in the environmental situation. It is of vital importance whether accident proneness is a stable or variable attribute, for surely there would be little point in attempting to devise means of measuring or assessing an unstable phenomenon. The general belief today is that accident proneness is a fairly stable attribute. However, of equal importance is the question as to whether it is a general or specific factor. Thus it is conceivable that A may be more prone than B in situation X, but B more prone than A in situation Y. On the other hand, it may well be that no matter what the situation is, A will always be more prone than B, although the liabilities of both will have changed by the same amount owing to the different risks in the situation itself. This latter view is one which is quite generally held, and the accident-prone individual is regarded as one who has many accidents at home, at work, on the public highways, and is in fact a sort of "calamity Joe" who is always "coming unstuck." There is, however, no proof for either of these two hypotheses, and some pertinent comments have been made in this regard by Brown and Ghiselli.[4] Again the matter is an important one for prediction and accident prevention policies.

It is clear from the above that the term *accident proneness* should be clearly defined before we attempt to make any practical use of it. A clear conception of its meaning can only be obtained by a close scrutiny of our existing knowledge and the methods of analysis which have given rise to it.

The Prediction of Accident Proneness

Considerable advantages would be gained if techniques could be discovered which would predict the accident proneness of individuals (if

---

[3] E. Farmer and E. G. Chambers, *Tests for Accident Proneness,* Industrial Health Research Board, Report no. 68 (London, 1933).

[4] C. W. Brown and E. E. Ghiselli, "Accident Proneness among Street Car Motormen and Motor Coach Operators," *Journal of Applied Psychology* 32 (1948): 20–23.

such a phenomenon exists) in a given situation, before they had actually entered that situation and incurred accidents. These are clearly stated by Farmer and Chambers in their successive attempts to do so.[5] The authors are also careful to point out that:

Care must be taken not to make accident incidence *per se* a measure of accident proneness, for this is to adopt the position of those who say that accidents are due to carelessness and when asked to define carelessness, do so in such a way as to leave little doubt that by carelessness they mean having an undue number of accidents. "Accident proneness" implies the possession of those qualities which have been found from independent research to lead to an undue number of accidents. If the term is used in this way a person can be said to be accident prone without any knowledge of the number of accidents he has sustained, for this statement will merely mean that he is more likely than others in equal conditions of exposure to sustain accidents. Such a knowledge would make it possible to warn certain people against entering dangerous occupations, so that although they were accident prone in a relatively high degree, they might go through life with very few accidents.[6]

Be this as it may, the fact remains that the discovery of these "qualities" can only be achieved by measuring the validity with which certain tests can predict some criterion of accident proneness in a given group. This criterion can only be the number of accidents sustained by the respective individuals in that group. Moreover, whether or not "accident proneness" really does exist, we should be happy if we could predict the *number of accidents* a person is likely to have. Hence, a good fit with some theoretical bivariate distribution is of considerable importance quite apart from what the parameters happen to signify. And this is the obvious line of approach which the investigators take. A further point must be made in this connection. Prediction only becomes feasible when the criterion of the attribute to be predicted is itself reliable and stable. If an individual's accident record in the same set of circumstances is an unstable reflection of his "inherent accident proneness," then prediction of proneness by this means must be a shaky affair. The correlations between the incidence of accident shown earlier in this study indicate quite clearly that there is very little consistency in the records of individuals from period to period. It is not surprising, therefore, that all attempts to predict accident proneness using accident records as a criterion or measure of this have so far failed rather lamentably.

What is surprising is that the investigators should have persisted in the face of these insurmountable difficulties before establishing a more stable criterion of proneness.

---

[5] Farmer and Chambers, *Tests for Accident Proneness; A Study of Accident Proneness among Motor Drivers,* Industrial Health Research Board, Report no. 84 (London, 1939); *The Psychological Study of Individual Differences in Accident Rates,* Report no. 38 (London, 1926); and *A Study of Personal Qualities in Accident Proneness and Proficiency,* Industrial Health Research Board, Report no. 55 (London, 1929).

[6] Ibid.

Having been unsuccessful in their first and second attempts, the investigators proceed to a third and a fourth, and the reader is amazed to find the latter report opening with what can only be regarded as a statement of creed, in view of the absence of any intervening research findings which could alter the position as stated by them above: "Previous statistical investigations have shown that industrial workers exposed to equal risks were unequal in their liability to sustain accidents, and that this unequal liability was a relatively stable phenomenon, manifesting itself in different periods of exposure and in different kinds of accidents." [7]

Furthermore, the stability of their own criterion in this particular case (as reflected by correlations between accidents in successive periods) was only of the order of .18 to .33.

It is not surprising, therefore, that despite the one or two refinements introduced in the constitution of groups tested, these latest attempts should have yielded only inconclusive results. Surely if the efficiency with which the criterion can predict itself is only of the order of .3, then it is a fond hope to expect that any test which can only measure part of the criterion will have a predicting efficiency as great as or greater than .3.

Had the above research findings been more positive, they would have warranted fairly detailed consideration in this study. As it is, a summary of the main conclusions will suffice. The student who is interested in making further attempts on this problem, is however, strongly advised to study the original works if only to acquaint himself with the type of difficulty to be encountered and the pitfalls to avoid. These will be largely concerned with: (a) the selection of appropriate experimental groups, and the control of such influences as age, experience, and environmental factors; (b) the definition of events which are to be regarded as accidents, and the completeness and accuracy of these data; (c) the stability or consistency of accident records in successive periods as a measure or criterion of personal accident proneness; (d) the adequacy of existing instruments of statistical analysis, and the precautions which must be taken against the use of techniques which are suspect, to say the least, when applied to frequency distributions associated with accident data. The techniques usually applied in psychological research are, for the most part, dependent upon the normal distributions and correlation surfaces. Accidents, on the other hand, are a discrete variable and yield J-shaped or negative binominal distributions. This fact alone alters the whole meaning and predicting efficiency of the ordinary product-moment correlation coefficient.

If the incidence of accidents in successive exposure periods is as unstable as previous research findings have shown it to be, then surely one can hope for little efficiency in one's predicting techniques. There is, of course, the final hope that if more attention is given to the defini-

---

[7] Farmer and Chambers, *A Study of Accident Proneness among Motor Drivers.*

tion of accidents to be included in the study, this deficiency may be overcome. The unreliability of the criterion may in some measure be due to the fact that accident data are not uniform, and that by merely including for study all accidents (from existing records), irrespective of causes or the manner in which they occurred, one is in effect collecting a hotchpotch of events which are by no means homogeneous or representative of the phenomenon of proneness. The result may be similar to that of mixing measures of height and weight or scores from test A and test B in the same distribution.

This point might well be elaborated for the consideration of future research workers. It is felt that in most previous research scant attention has been paid to the definition of what constitutes an accident. It is appropriate that the following questions should be asked and answered: (1) What are the phenomena that are being studied? What is our variable? What constitutes our total statistical population of events? (2) If it is not possible to record the total population of events in any given set of circumstances, what sample can we hope to study? (3) How is this sample selected, and is it representative of the whole?

What Constitutes an Accident?

An accident might justifiably be defined in the following manner: In a chain of events, each of which is planned or controlled, there occurs an unplanned event, which, being the result of some nonadjustive act on the part of the individual (variously caused), may or may not result in injury. This is an accident.

There are certain aspects of this definition which need emphasizing. Firstly, it is the occurrence of the unplanned or unpredicted event which constitutes the accident. Secondly, this event is due to some nonadjustive act on the part of the individual concerned. Thirdly, the resulting injury is a consequence of this unplanned event, and does not itself constitute the accident—it follows afterwards. From this it follows that our statistical population of events is the sum total of all unplanned incidents in the given environmental circumstances and in the given population of individuals. By definition also, there will exclude all events which can definitely be attributed to the influence of mechanical or impersonal causes—for example, the case of a bus driver being stung by a hornet, inherent defects in the machine, and so forth. This naturally implies a strict investigation of all accidents in order to establish the factor of personal causation. This will also serve the purpose of debiting the correct individual for the responsibility of the accident. Thus if A drops a brick and it falls on B's head, the former has the "unplanned event" and the latter the injury; who has the accident? The answer surely is A and not B, who is usually debited with this in the register.

By definition all the following must be regarded as constituting our population of accidents:

1. *Errors, Slips, and Near Accidents.* Here we can be almost sure that data in respect of these would be incomplete, even with the most rigorous supervision. It might be profitable, however, to set up experimentally controlled conditions in a laboratory, equating the environmental circumstances for all subjects, and undertake the study of errors in some series of test situations. This might well throw some light on the proneness of individuals to this type of "accident," which could perhaps be related to accidents in the industrial situation.

2. *Accidents Producing Minor Injuries.* Only under highly controlled conditions could one be sure of amassing data which were complete and accurate, and which did not merely reflect a tendency on the part of some to report these incidents.

3. *Accidents Producing Major Injuries.* Here one could be reasonably sure of collecting all the data. The difficulty is, of course, that incapacity usually means a subsequent period of nonexposure which may be of considerable length and may even result in the removal of the individual from the work situation.

4. *Accidents Resulting in Death.* Here one is virtually certain of the data, but these occurences are inevitably followed by subsequent nonexposure.

This self-elimination of many of our cases (and unfortunately they are the very ones whom one is interested in studying) has a serious effect upon subsequent statistical analysis.

Thus under normal circumstances (that is, excluding those subject to the highest degree of control and supervision) one can only be reasonably sure of collecting and including *complete* data on major accidents. This means that we get a selected sample of our total population of "unplanned events" (or accidents) for study, *and this sample is selected purely in terms of subsequent injury.* Now if the resulting injury is determined *by chance,* this would mean that we should get a random or representative sample of our total population of events. This would be extremely fortunate, for any conclusions arrived at on the basis of this sample would then be applicable to the total population of events. If, on the other hand, the resulting injury were not chance determined, but were in some way a function of the manner in which the unplanned event originally occurred, then we should be left with a selected sample, and statistical results could no longer be applied to the parent population from which these events came. It might be justifiable to argue that in any case one is only interested in studying major accidents and not the minor which have trivial consequences. This may well be so, but it must then be conceded that one is no longer studying accidents but merely the incidence of injury resulting from accidents, which may have nothing to do with personal liability.

Under the circumstances where one is studying accidents causing major injury only, it would appear that there are two *"liabilities"* to be considered: (a) the liability of the individual to have an unplanned event or accident in a given environment, and (b) the liability of this event to result in subsequent injury in a given environment—resulting in its being recorded.

It is conceivable, therefore, that if injury were not chance determined, the following results may be obtained, where e represents unplanned events without injury, (e) represents unplanned events with major injury, and the suffix indicates the type of accident:

Individual A—e_1, e_1, e_3, (e_7), e_9, e_{12}, $e_3 = 1$ reported major accident

Individual B—e_1, (e_7), (e_7), $(e_4) = 3$ reported major accidents

In the records, B would obviously be considered more accident prone than A, but this would not be a reflection of his proneness to unplanned events (slips or near accidents), since B has only four, whereas A has eight. It would rather be a reflection of the liability of such events as he had to result in injury. This may well be determined by factors beyond his control, and the study of the (e)'s would give little indication of the individual's susceptibility to (e)'s.

It is appreciated that the development of this theme of the "double liabilities" tends to lead to a state of confusion where one feels that the problem slips one's mental grasp. This is not because the argument itself is confusing, but rather because we have not yet devised techniques of analysis which will enable us to disentangle the skeins of a confused and intricate pattern of events.

The Analysis of Accident Liability

The above considerations might well lead one into a state of despondency and frustrated resignation were it not for the fact that a different approach to the problem seems possible. This approach may not enable us to analyze accident liability in terms of universal principles, laws of distribution, and so forth, with reference to human behavior in general, but it may well enable us to reduce the incidence of accidents in our community by enhancing our knowledge of the mechanisms at work in causing individuals to have accidents. And surely this is the ultimate objective of all this work. This approach has been clearly explained by Viteles [8] in his reference to the accident reduction programs of the Cleveland Railway Company.[9] Viteles' introductory comments to these studies are worth considering:

The psychological study of accidents in the manufacturing industry has been largely confined to a statistical study of factors influencing accident suscepti-

---

[8] M. S. Viteles, *Industrial Psychology* (New York: W. W. Norton & Co., 1932).

[9] Metropolitan Life Insurance Co., *The Accident-Prone Employee* (New York, 1930).

bility. Such statistical studies are of questionable significance in arriving at a knowledge of the causes of accidents. . . . They suffer from serious limitations as practical aids in the reduction of accidents.

In the first place the statistical approach is oriented from the viewpoint of discovering relations existing in a group of individuals, and not from the point of view of the adjustment of the single individual who has become involved in or is susceptible to accidents. . . . The function of the statistical approach and of statistical investigations in preventing accidents attributable to the human factor may be described as that of investigatory *group* tendencies. In contrast with this is the *clinical approach*—the functions of which are to determine the relationship existing among a number of factors which have played or may play a part in the case of the individual who becomes involved in accidents and to develop a program for the prevention of additional accidents on his part.

Another limitation of the statistical viewpoint in accident prevention is its emphasis upon isolated aspects of individual personality, in contrast with the concern, in the clinical approach, for the total personality of the accident-prone individual. . . . It is undoubtedly true that a detailed examination of each stone tells much about the *structure* of a mosaic, but the contribution of each to the value of the whole flows from the *integration* of the various parts, and can only be fully determined through an examination of the whole, and of the interrelationships among the parts in the whole.

The aim of the clinical approach is to examine the whole individual, and from an examination of the whole to arrive at a knowledge of the significance of the various aspects of his personality—the relative importance of each sector of his personality in a given situation. The application of the clinical approach in the analysis of accident causes involves a complete study of the individual involved in accidents—it makes the individual the point of departure, and provides for a thorough examination of every factor—physical, mental, social, and economic, and of those extraneous to the individual—which may have played a part in the accident in which he has been involved.

The diagnosis of accident proneness is being followed by special treatment, and treatment based on an exact knowledge of the factors which are responsible for the accident record in the case of the particular individual. Treatment takes the form, not of mass education, or the more drastic measure of termination, but most frequently that of systematic instruction designed to efface faulty habits . . . medical treatment, discipline, encouragement and supervisory follow-up. . . . It recognizes that there are many different causes of accidents and that they may combine in different patterns in different individuals.

The knowledge of the factors which play a part in the case of a single individual is obtained by an experimental study of the individual. This includes psychological examination, close observation of operation details, a review of his relationship with supervising officers and fellow workers, and possibly a detailed study of the home circumstances.

The case study of each accident-prone motorman in the Cleveland Railway Company involved: (1) A careful examination under normal operating conditions of: (*a*) general operation, (*b*) motoring habits, (*c*) mental factors, (*d*) physical factors. (2) Analysis of previous and current years accident record. (3) Personal interview. (4) Decision as to primary causes of accident proneness. (5) Preparation of report of case recommending treatment based upon findings. (6) Treatment and follow-up.

The most significant finding of the Cleveland study is that in no two cases were the causes of accident proneness exactly similar. In most instances, several causes existed, although in each case, one of these was found to be of primary importance. The percentage distribution of primary causes of accident proneness among the 50 men is given in Table 44–2.

TABLE 44–2

Distribution of Primary Causes of Accident Proneness among Motormen of the Cleveland Railway Company

Primary Causes	%
Faulty attitude	14
Failure to recognize potential hazard	12
Faulty judgment of speed and distance	12
Impulsiveness	10
Irresponsibility	8
Failure to keep attention constant	8
Nervousness and fear	6
Defective vision	4
Organic disease	4
Slow reaction	4
High blood pressure	2
Senility	2
Worry and depression	2
Fatigability	2
Improper distribution of attention	2
Inexperience	2
Miscellaneous	6

As a result of this application of the clinical method in the study and treatment of motor drivers, the combined rate of accidents on the part of the motormen involved in the study dropped from 1.31 per 1,000 miles in 1928 to .75 in 1929—equivalent to a reduction of 42.7 percent.

Viteles quotes the experiences of the accident clinics run on similar lines at the Milwaukee Railways & Light Company (under the direction of Dr. Bingham and illustrates the value of these techniques by stating that:

As a result . . . the actual net savings in cost of injuries and damages in 1929 as compared with 1928 amounted to 300,670. Collision accidents on bus lines and street railways have been reduced more than 35 percent since the work was started in 1927. . . . The figures for 1931, as compared with those for 1926, show a 58 percent reduction in collision of surface cars with trolleys; 54.4 percent with pedestrians; 71.3 percent with other surface cars; 36.8 percent in boarding and alighting accidents; and 23.6 percent in all other accidents. . . . Associated with these economic returns are enormous social benefits in reducing the suffering and the general social maladjustment associated with personal injury resulting from accidents.[10]

Spectacular though these results are, their achievement should not pass without certain comment:

1. The application of these procedures can be an expensive business where one spends a considerable time on individual cases. In the case of railway accidents, where the consequences are very severe on account of the large insurance and damages claims, and so forth, the proposition becomes an economic one. It is doubtful, however, whether many industries could be persuaded to adopt similar measures when, owing to the lesser consequences of accidents, the economic gains would not necessarily show a profit in the financial statement, even though the social and indirect gains might be equally great.

2. These results do not necessarily constitute a validation of the clinical procedures used nor of the diagnoses made in individual cases. This can only be achieved by their application to (a) an experimental and (b) a control group, as was done in the Hawthorne Experiment of the Western Electric Company. The point is, of course, that the results may be just as "screwy" as they were found to be in this classic experiment, namely, the accident rates in the control group (receiving no treatment) may also go down, not because of any measures being adopted in their own case, but principally because they were being applied in the case of another group. This might indicate that individuals were responding, not so much to the "shrewdness" of diagnosis, as to the new interest being taken in them by management—to the new psychological atmosphere prevailing in the works. It is conceivable that the diagnoses may not have been directly responsible for the results. These may have been due primarily to management's interest in the situation. Employees were taken into management's confidence. Their problems were discussed with them in a sympathetic manner which enabled them to understand them better; this probably created a new attitude of mind on the part of the workers to the problem of accidents, and encouraged them to think of safety in new terms, and to regard their work habits in a new light. They were thus able to see the significance of causes and relationships which had probably never occurred to them before, and to heed these in the everyday work situation. It is possible that this new mental approach pervaded the whole work group as the result of clinical studies, and may well have been the more general and underlying factor responsible for the spectacular results achieved. The natural rejoinder to these comments is: "Does it matter, as long as the results are forthcoming, and the whole business is a paying proposition?" This point is readily conceded, but the truth of the matter

---

[10] W. V. Bingham, *Personality and Public Accidents—The Study of Accident-Prone Drivers* (Transactions of the 17th Annual Safety Congress, New York, 1928).

is of fundamental interest to the investigator. It may well be that the accident clinicians on these railways were not really so much gaining knowledge concerning the direct relationship between personal factors and accidents as learning what Roethlisberger has called "new social skills." If this is so, then the development of these is of the utmost importance. It may be possible in the future, therefore, to define these techniques along new lines, and make them more of an economic proposition to the average industrial plant.

3. The third point to be emphasized here is the fact that the term "accident proneness" is now no longer used in the original sense. It is now defined on the basis of a *clinical* and not a *statistical* diagnosis, and, as such, is largely a term of convenience, rather than of precise mathematical definition. This loss of precision is perhaps more than compensated for by the advantages of a new approach "which places special emphasis on the individual . . . and recognizes the great variety of individual differences. In dealing with each motorman, truck driver, or automobilist, he is recognized not as one of the mass, but as a distinct personality." [11]

45. COMPLEMENTARY THEORIES OF SAFETY PSYCHOLOGY [*]

Willard Kerr

PROBABLY THE MOST UNIVERSALLY IGNORED AREA of safety psychology is that pertaining to the psychological climate of the work place. A devotion to safety gadgets on the one hand and concern for the alleged proneness factors within the accident repeater on the other hand have led to the almost total neglect of the situational factors which help shape work personality and help manufacture accident-free or accident-liable employees.

Many investigators have shown that becoming a safe worker is a typical learning function.[1] The decline in accidents from date of employment in the typical job is a representative learning curve. But like other learning curves, the decline in error performance can be obstructed by a multitude of other factors. It now appears that a chief obstruction to the rapid decline in error performance is defective psychological climate. This conclusion, to be supported in this paper, stands in sharp contrast to past emphasis upon the accident-proneness theory.

---

[11] Ibid.

[*] From *Journal of Social Psychology* 45 (1957): 3–9.

[1] R. H. Van Zelst, "The Effect of Age and Experience upon Accident Rate," *Journal of Applied Psychology* 38 (1954): 313–17.

The Accident-Proneness Theory

Before presenting the crucial evidence on this theory, the term "accident proneness" should be defined. *Accident proneness* is a constitutional (that is, permanent) tendency within the organism to engage in unsafe behavior within some stated field of vocational activity. A temporary tendency to have accidents is not proneness; it is liability. And proneness is not general; that is, its referrent to an activity field must be limited to be meaningful, for, obviously, *everyone* is "accident prone" in a general sense because there are potential tasks that no human being can perform without accident (for example, climb the outside walls of the Empire State Building to the top with one's bare hands).

Professors Mintz and Blum and Maritz have shown that the accident-proneness theory has been explaining entirely too much of the industrial accident rate.[2] The research of Cobb, Johnson, Whitlock and Crannell, Forbes, Farmer and Chambers, and Harris point toward the same conclusion.[3] Mintz and Blum showed that the frequency of "repeater" accidents approximates a pure-chance (Poisson) distribution. Maritz then suggested that the final crucial test of variance in the industrial accident rate accounted for by proneness is the correlation between one's accidents experienced over two different periods of accident exposure—such as the last two years and the next two years. Ghiselli and Brown have collated 18 such coefficients from the literature,[4] and the present author has computed their median; it is .38. This typical value suggests that only about 15 percent of the variance in individual accidents is accounted for by variance in individual accident proneness; furthermore, this even may be spuriously high because such coefficients are contaminated by the correlation of the worker's-position hazard with the consistency of his accidents over split time periods. In fact, it is almost certain that much, if not most, of this 15 percent of potential variance due to accident proneness actually is due to environmental factors (temperature differences,

---

[2] A. Mintz and M. L. Blum, "A Re-examination of the Accident-Proneness Concept," *Journal of Applied Psychology* 33 (1949): 195–211; J. S. Maritz, "On the Validity of Inferences Drawn from the Fitting of Poisson and Negative Binomial Distributions to Observed Accident Data," *Psychological Bulletin* 47 (1950): 434–43.

[3] P. W. Cobb, unpublished reports to Highway Research Board, Washington, D.C., 1938–39, summarized in H. M. Johnson, "The Detection and Treatment of Accident-Prone Drivers," *Psychological Bulletin* 43 (1946): 489–532; J. B. Whitlock and C. W. Crannell, "An Analysis of Certain Factors in Serious Accidents in a Large Steel Plant," *Journal of Applied Psychology* 33 (1949): 494–98; T. W. Forbes, "The Normal Automobile Driver as a Traffic Problem," *Journal of General Psychology* 20 (1939): 471–74; E. Farmer and E. G. Chambers, *A Study of Personal Qualities in Accident Proneness and Proficiency*, Industrial Health Research Board, Report no. 55 (London, 1929); and F. J. Harris, "A Comparison of the Personality Characteristics of Accident and Non-accident Industrial Population" (abstract), *American Psychologist* 4 (1949): 279.

[4] E. E. Ghiselli and C. W. Brown, *Personnel and Industrial Psychology* (New York: McGraw-Hill Book Co., 1948).

fumes, congestion-space-threat differences, and so forth) left uncontrolled and hence correlated with each other in the 18 coefficients cited.

Even allowing the unreasonable assumption that these 18 coefficients were not influenced by fatigue and stress differences in different job locations, the 15 percent of variance in accidents "accounted for" by proneness still leaves 85 percent of the variance in accident rates unaccounted for.

It is interesting that an earlier study of automobile drivers by Forbes arrived independently at the similar conclusion that the accident repeater contributes not more than 3 or 4 percent to the accident problem.[5] Both Johnson and Thorndike, who later surveyed the entire research literature on automobile safety, likewise found that such constitutional factors as basic aptitudes yielded negligible relationships with accident records.[6] Relevant, also, is the fact that Hunt, Wittson, and Burton computed the psychiatric discharge rate at naval induction stations and subsequently during World War II to vary between 4 and 9 percent (such dischargees were, of course, those individuals regarded as "prone" to behavior unsafe to themselves and/or their country).[7]

Two situational or climatic theories may explain the remaining non-chance variance.

The Goals-Freedom-Alertness Theory

Plainly, both management and union training activities, policies, and leaderships are responsible for some interference with the normal decline of error performance.

In stating this theory now, we hold that *great freedom to set reasonably attainable goals is accompanied typically by high-quality work performance*. This theory regards an accident merely as a low-quality work behavior—a "scrappage" that happens to a person instead of to a thing. Raising the level of quality involves raising the level of alertness; such high alertness cannot be sustained except within a rewarding psychological climate. The more rich, therefore, the climate in diverse (economic and noneconomic) reward opportunities, the higher the level of alertness—and the higher the level of work quality. Obviously the rewards system must be geared to support high-quality work behavior.

In business practice some training interferes by too much "telling what to do and what not to do" and too little encouragement to the new worker to do his own thinking and "stand on his own feet." Union leadership

---

[5] Forbes, "Normal Automobile Drivers."

[6] Johnson, "Detection and Treatment of Accident-Prone Drivers"; R. L. Thorndike, "The Human Factor in Accidents," *USAF School of Aviation Medical Reports* (Randolph Field Texas, February 1951).

[7] W. A. Hunt, C. L. Wittson, and H. W. Burton, "Further Validation of Naval Neuropsychiatric Screening," *Journal of Consulting Psychology* 14 (1950): 485–88.

likewise often is guilty of too much propagandizing and not enough "asking" in relations with new workers. Such initial climate for the new worker is less conducive to alertness than to a relatively unmotivated, resigned, passive conformity to the apparently already structured total situation.

Accidents, of course, show that the total situation is *not* firmly structured and from them the worker gradually accepts more self-responsibility in order to survive. But an accident is an expensive teaching device. Furthermore. if it occurs in a climate in which the employee is expected to supply his energy but not his opinions or ideas, the accident is misunderstood as a foreign intruder which does not belong in the scheme of events. In such circumstances, it rarely occurs to management, union, or worker that an accident is made necessary and inevitable in order to teach the employee his own individuality and essential personal dignity.

Even the teaching efficiency of the accident itself is interfered with, however, if most aspects of the total psychological climate in effect deny that the individual's own mental content is important.

If the climate encourages the individual to set up long-term and short-term goals with reasonable probability of attainment, the *Gestalt* of the work situation seems less fixed and the worker feels himself to be a significant participant. Significant participation makes for habits of alertness, problem-raising, and problem-solving. The psychological work environment must reward the worker emotionally for being alert, for seeking to contribute constructive suggestions, for passing a tip to a co-worker on how best to do something or how not to get hurt, and for achievement out of the ordinary. The worker must feel free to exercise influence over his environment.

Considerable evidence supports this theory. Factory departments with more movement of personnel among departments, that is, intracompany transfer mobility, have fewer accidents; [8] the same is true of departments with greater promotion probability for the typical employee (r is $-.40$).[9] Departments with the best suggestion records (rewarded) tend to have fewer accidents.[10] Additional evidence of the influence of the stimulating individual climate on safety is found in the tendency toward fewer accidents in individual-type than in crew-type jobs at the International Harvester Works.[11] In individual-type work, the employee rarely is uncertain about his responsibility for consequences; he better knows his immediate work goals. Another interesting bit of evidence is that in two different studies the factory departments with incentive pay systems, although problem departments in regards to monotony, lower job prestige,

---

[8] W. A. Kerr, "Accident Proneness of Factory Departments," *Journal of Applied Psychology* 34 (1950): 167–70.

[9] Ibid.

[10] Ibid.

[11] V. Keenan, W. A. Kerr, and W. E. Sherman, "Psychological Climate and Accidents in an Automotive Plant," *Journal of Applied Psychology* 35 (1951): 108–11.

and lower promotion probability, still have no more accidents than departments without incentive pay systems.[12] This seems in such defiance of expectations as to suggest that incentive pay systems restrict accidents by encouraging greater individual initiative and alertness.

Accidents are more frequent in jobs of lower-rated prestige; [13] one interpretation of this finding is that climatically the job must seem worthy enough to the worker to sustain his euphoria level. This interpretation is supported by the finding of Hersey that out of 400 accidents which were studied clinically, more than half took place when the worker was in a worried, apprehensive, or some other low emotional state.[14]

This individual goals-freedom-alertness theory suggests the climatic need for providing emotional reward opportunities for alertness—such as special economic incentives, prestige-building honors, extra privileges, machine and work-space decoration contest participation, and representation on special committees and councils. These rewards held as attainable goals by workers in relatively "dead end" jobs should operate to raise the average level of alertness, not just to hazards but to everything.

The Adjustment-Stress Theory

The individual goals-opportunity-alertness theory of safety seems to cover much of the variance not covered by the proneness theory, but some variance still remains and it appears necessary to verbalize a third theory. Probably almost all of the remaining variance can be explained by a third theory—*an adjustment-stress theory*. It holds that *unusual, negative, distracting stress upon the organism increases its liability to accident or to other low-quality behavior*. This too is a climatic theory, because environment is internal as well as external, and this theory refers to distractive negative stresses imposed upon the individual organism either by internal environment (such as disease organisms, alcohol, or toxic items) or by external environment (such as temperature excesses, poor illumination, excessive noise level, excessive physical work strain). Its stresses are different from those experienced by the accident prone; their stresses result from a *constitutional* inadequacy. Ordinary adjustment stress is *not* the result of constitutional inadequacy but of temporary conditions.

What often appears at first to be constitutional accident proneness may be shown very clearly upon more careful examination to be the operation of *temporary* stress factors. The most sobering example of this is found in the curve of accident rates of successive age groups of industrial workers.[15] This curve shows high rates in the first ten years of the

---

[12] Ibid.; W. A. Kerr, "Accident Proneness of Factory Departments."

[13] Ibid.

[14] R. B. Hersey, "Emotional Factors in Accidents," *Personnel Journal* 15 (1936): 59–65.

[15] W. A. Kerr, "Psychological Climate and Safety" (Address given at the Midwest Safety Show, National Safety Council, Chicago, May 4, 1950).

work life and a secondary increase in rates between the ages of 40 and 55. These age periods also are the great stress periods in the typical work life; that is suggested by the fact that the accident-rate curve and the turnover-rate curve superimpose almost perfectly upon each other when plotted through successive age groups of the industrial population.[16] The alleged proneness within the young accident repeater is largely dissipated when one considers that most of the stress is environmental, and associated with adjustment to work discipline, attaining self-sufficiency away from parental ties, courtship, marriage, assumption of family economic responsibilities, and the struggle for a foothold on a vocational ladder that seems to lead somewhere worthwhile. Another set of obvious stress explanations comes to mind to account for the "middle-age boom" in accident rate.

Temporary stress factors which already have been found significantly correlated with accident rates include employee age,[17] work-place temperature,[18] illumination,[19] mean-rated comfort of the shop (r is $-.70$),[20] degree of operational congestion,[21] obvious danger factor threateningly present,[22] manual effort involved in job (r is $.47$),[23] weight of parts handled,[24] frequency of parts handled,[25] alcohol consumption,[26] and influence of disease organisms.[27]

Complementary Limitations and Interpretations

It seems wise to emphasize that both of these new theories of safety complement each other as well as existing proneness theory. In the goals-freedom-alertness theory it must be recognized that (a) even under an optimal opportunity climate, individuals who lack the characteristics necessary for the work probably will continue to have accidents; (b) excessive physical stresses can cause accidents in any psychological climate; and (c) psychological stresses relative to adjustment to changing

---

[16] H. D. Kitson, "A Critical Age as a Factor in Labor Turnover," *Journal of Industrial Hygiene* 4 (1922): 199–203.

[17] W. A. Kerr, "Psychological Climate and Safety."

[18] J. W. Griffith, "The Time Factor in a Psychological Analysis of Accidents" (Master's thesis, Illinois Institute of Technology, June 1950).

[19] II. M. Vernon, T. Bedford, and C. G. Warner, *A Study of Absenteeism in Certain Scottish Collieries,* Industrial Health Research Board, Report no. 62 (London, 1931).

[20] V. Keenan, W. A. Kerr, and W. E. Sherman, "Psychological Climate and Accidents."

[21] Ibid.

[22] Ibid.

[23] Ibid.

[24] Ibid.

[25] Ibid.

[26] H. M. Vernon, *Accidents and Their Prevention* (New York: Macmillan, 1937).

[27] E. M. Newbold, *A Contribution to the Study of the Human Factor in the Causation of Accidents,* Industrial Fatigue Research Board, Report no. 34 (London, 1919).

life aspirations, family and marital affairs, and so forth, still will carry over into the work-place psychological climate and cause accidents.

In the adjustment-stress theory it must be admitted that individual differences do exist in ability to withstand what ordinarily would be stress-inducing situations. Yet, such individual differences account for less than one fifth of the variance in individual accident rates; therefore, the limitations on the accident-proneness theory appear to be much more severe than those on the adjustment-stress theory. The fact is that both employer judgment and job-applicant judgment operate to prevent the operation of any great amount of accident proneness. While all of us are accident prone for one task or another, we don't ordinarily apply for or allow ourselves to be engaged in such tasks—and we probably couldn't get hired for such tasks if we tried.

On the basis of the evidence summarized and the author's own estimates, the variance in accident rates among industrial personnel probably distributes in terms of theoretical causation according to the following pattern:

Accident proneness	1% to 15%
Individual goals-opportunity-alertness	30% to 40%
Adjustment stress	45% to 60%
Total Variance	100%

Constructive thinking about the individual goals-opportunity climate and about adjust stresses should assist industry to escape the defeatism of the overly emphasized proneness theory and better understand and control accidents.

Section Eight

ENGINEERING

PSYCHOLOGY

INTRODUCTION

THE GROWING AWARENESS that man and machines function in relation to each other has led to a branch of applied science known as "engineering psychology." This field deals with ways of designing machines, operations, and work environments so that they match human capacities and limitations.[1] Various other terms have been used, more or less interchangeably, to label this field, including *human engineering, human factors engineering, applied experimental psychology, biomechanics, biotechnology,* and *ergonomics.*

Much of the recent research in this field grew out of military necessity, since the development of increasingly complex weapon and support systems required better information on the human capacities needed to perform them. Today, engineering psychology is prominent in many diverse fields in industry. Psychologists contribute to the design of household appliances, radar scopes, artificial limbs, telephone sets, electronic computers, semiautomatic post office equipment, jet-aircraft cockpits, and numerous other industrial machines.

---

[1] For a more comprehensive discussion of these fields, see E. J. McCormick, *Human Factors Engineering.* 3d ed. (New York: McGraw-Hill Book Co., 1970); W. C. Howell and I. L. Goldstein, *Engineering Psychology: Current Perspectives in Research* (New York: Appleton-Century-Crofts, 1971). For shorter discussions for the general reader, see A. Chapanis, *Man-Machine Engineering* (Belmont, Calif.: Wadsworth, 1965); and Chapter 14 in R. M. Gagné and E. A. Fleishman, *Psychology and Human Performance* (New York: Holt, Rinehart & Winston, 1959).

In this section we shall look at man as a component link in man-machine systems. A man-machine system can be defined as an operating combination of one or more men with one or more equipment components, which interact to bring about some common desired outcome. In its simplest form, a man-machine system can be a man using a simple tool. In intermediate forms, it can represent a person driving a truck or operating an industrial machine or a telephone switchboard. In highly complex form, a man-machine system is represented by a missile launch crew, a city telephone system, the air-traffic-control system of the United States, or the worldwide space-vehicle tracking system.

This section will discuss the man-machine systems concept and the role of the psychologist in this area. We will then turn to the problems of allocating functions in these systems to men and machines. Following this, we will focus on certain aspects of man as he is used in a system, as a processor of visual information and as a monitor and decision-maker. Finally, we will review how the psychologist develops models to help him cope with some of the more complex problems of man-machine interaction.

In the first article in this section, by Taylor, "Psychology and the Design of Man-Machine Systems," we get a good introduction to *man-machine systems concepts*. Taylor's article represents the "new look" in engineering psychology with its emphasis on man as "an organic data transmission and processing link" inserted between the mechanical or electronic displays and controls of a machine. Here we encounter the notions of man as an information channel, a multipurpose computer, and a feedback control system. This article also describes the role of the engineering psychologist in basic research, in designing machines, and in evaluating man-machine systems.

In planning a complex man-machine system, there are many decisions about the functions to be performed by different parts of the system. Of particular concern are the parts to be assigned to the human and machine components. There has been much discussion, for example, of whether man or devices can better be utilized in landing a space capsule or in making early explorations of planets. Much, of course, depends on the state of technology at the time; for example, a few years ago it would have been out of the question to design a bank accounting system in which checks are sorted and printed automatically by machine. Changing technology means reevaluating the roles of the human and machine components. In the next article, "On the Allocation of Functions between Men and Machines," Chapanis discusses the issues involved in dividing up system functions and reviews some of the relative advantages of man and machine components for particular functions.[2]

---

[2] For a discussion which focuses on the allocation of functions between men and computers, see W. Edwards, "Men and Computers," in *Psychological Principles in*

The next two articles deal with specific research representative of "display" and "information processing" problems in equipment design. The term "display" refers to various means of providing information to people. A whole set of visual display problems is represented in the area of instrument and dial design. What is the optimum way to display visual information so that it can be processed effectively by the human operator? The article by Graham, entitled "The Speed and Accuracy of Reading Horizontal, Vertical, and Circular Scales," illustrates one such problem.

In recent years there has been an increasing requirement for the human operator in systems to do more "monitoring," requiring sustained vigilance or attention. This requirement has been intensified with the increased automation and computer control in systems. The human operator often scans instruments, dials, scopes, and other displays watching for malfunction indications, warnings, or signals requiring decisions to be made. This has led to an active field of research on "vigilance" and decision-making problems. The article by Adams, Stenson, and Humes, "Monitoring of Complex Visual Displays—Some Vigilance and Decision-Making Problems," reviews this area of research and describes a study investigating some of the conditions which may affect performances of this type. The article also discusses how such research contributes to more general psychological theories about human performance and how such theories are tested. Finally, the article discusses the implications of laboratory findings for the use of human operators in semiautomatic man-machine systems.

The concluding article in this section, by Chapanis, is entitled "Men, Machines, and Models." The author discusses what models are, provides many examples of models in research and development activities, points out their advantages and disadvantages, and evaluates their contribution to engineering psychology.

SUGGESTED ADDITIONAL READINGS

Bennett, E., Degan, J., and Spiegel, J. *Human Factors in Technology* (New York: McGraw-Hill, 1963).

Davis, H. L., ed. "Human Factors in Industry—II," *Human Factors* 15 (1973): 193–268.

DeGreene, K. B. *Systems Psychology.* New York: McGraw-Hill Book Co., 1970.

Fitts, P. M., Schipper, L., Kidd, J. S., Shelly, M., and Kraft, C. "Some Concepts and Methods for the Conduct of Man-Machine System Research in a Laboratory Setting," in E. A. Fleishman (ed.), *Studies in Personnel and Industrial Psychology,* rev. ed. (Homewood, Ill.: Dorsey Press, 1967).

System Development, edited by R. M. Gagné (New York: Holt, Rinehart & Winston, 1962); J. C. R. Licklider, "Man-Computer Symbiosis," *IRE Transactions on Human Factors in Electronics* 1 (1960): 4–11.

Gagné, R. M., ed.   *Psychological Principles in System Development* (New York: Holt, Rinehart and Winston, 1962).

Grether, W.   "Engineering Psychology in the United States." *American Psychologist* 23 (1968): 743–51.

Howell, W. C., and Goldstein, I. L. "Engineering Psychology Today: Some Observations from the Ivory Tower." *Organizational Behavior and Human Performance* 5 (1970): 159–69.

Howell, W. C., Johnston, W. A., and Goldstein, I. L.   "Complex Monitoring and Its Relation to the Classical Problem of Vigilance." *Organizational Behavior and Human Performance* 1 (1966): 129–57.

Parsons, H. M.   *Man-Machine Systems Experiments* (Baltimore: John Hopkins Press, 1972).

Parsons, H. M.   "Environmental Design." *Human Factors* 14 (1972): 369–482.

Van Cott, H. P., and Kinkade, R. C., eds.   *Human Engineering Guide to Equipment Design*, rev. ed. (Washington: Government Printing Office, 1972).

46. PSYCHOLOGY AND THE DESIGN OF MAN-MACHINE SYSTEMS *

Franklin V. Taylor

PSYCHOLOGISTS HAVE BEEN HELPING ENGINEERS design machines for more than 15 years. It all began during World War II with the rapid development of radars, sonars, aircraft control systems, and other similar devices. Previous to this time, the only role played by psychologists relative to military mechanisms was that of doing research and giving advice on the selection and training of the operators. However, very early in the war, it became apparent that these Procrustean attempts to fit the man to the machine were not enough. Regardless of how much he could be stretched by training or pared down through selection, there were still many military equipments which the man just could not be moulded to fit. They required of him too many hands, too many feet, or in the case of some of the more complex devices, too many heads.

Sometimes they called for the operator to see targets which were close to invisible, or to understand speech in the presence of deafening noise, to track simultaneously in three coordinates with the two hands, to solve in analogue form complex differential equations, or to consider large amounts of information and to reach life-and-death decisions in split

* Selected portions from "Psychology and the Design of Machines," *American Psychologist* 12 (1957): 249–56. Copyright 1957 by the American Psychological Association. Reprinted by permission.

seconds and with no hope of another try. Of course the man often failed in one or another of these tasks. As a result, bombs and bullets often missed their mark, planes crashed, friendly ships were fired upon and sunk. Whales were depth-charged.

Because of these "human errors," as they were called, psychologists were asked to help the engineers produce machines which required less of the man and which, at the same time, exploited his special abilities. The story of what happened is sufficiently well known not to require any lengthy retelling here. In brief, the psychologists went to work, and with the help of anatomists, physiologists, and, of course, engineers they started a new interdiscipline aimed at better machine design and called variously human engineering, biomechanics, psychotechnology, or engineering psychology. The new field has developed rapidly in the 17 or 19 years of its existence.

It seems fitting, now that engineering psychology has been recognized as a viable entity, that we examine this new field to find out just what it is that psychology is doing for the design of machines.

Central to engineering psychology is the concept of the *man-machine system*. Human engineers have for some time now looked upon the man and the machine which he operated as interacting parts of one overall system. In Figure 46–1 is shown a paradigm of the concept. This may be viewed as a radar device, a pilot-aircraft control system, a submarine-diving control station, the captain's station on the bridge of his ship, or, in fact, any man-machine system at all.

In essence, it represents the human operator as an organic data transmission and processing link inserted between the mechanical or electronic displays and controls of a machine. An input of some type is transformed by the mechanisms into a signal which appears on a display. Perhaps it is shown as a pointer reading, a pattern of lights, or a pip on a cathode-ray tube. However it appears, the presented information is read by the operator, processed mentally, and transformed into control responses. Switches are thrown, buttons are pushed, or force is applied to a joy stick. The control signal, after transformation by the mechanisms, becomes the system output, and in some devices it acts upon the displays as well. These latter are called "closed-loop" systems in contrast to "open-loop" systems wherein the displays do not reflect the human's response.

When the man and the machine are considered in this fashion, it immediately becomes obvious that, in order to design properly the mechanical components, the characteristics of the man and his role in the system must be taken into full account. Human engiineering seeks to do this and to provide as much assistance to the system designer as possible. Specifically, the psychologist tries to help his engineering colleague in three different ways. First of all, he studies the psychology of the human as a system component. Second, he assists the engineer in experimentally evaluating prototype man-machine systems. Finally, he teams up with

FIGURE 46–1

The Man-Machine System

Man

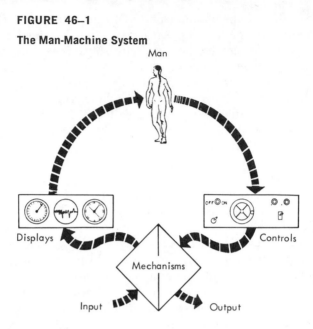

Displays

Controls

Mechanisms

Input   Output

engineers to participate actively in the design of machines. Each of these human engineering functions will be described in turn, beginning with the last and the least scientific activity.

Human Engineering Technology

Human engineering is not only a science, it is also a technology; it not only tries to find out things about the interaction of men and machines, it builds the latter. And, surprisingly enough, it is not just the engineers who do the building. There are psychologists also, renegades to be sure but psychologists nevertheless, who are taking an active hand in the design of systems. It is true that with some their apostasy is venial, having progressed only to the stage of writing human engineering handbooks; but with others the defection is more serious, it having developed to the stage where they can spend anything up to full time in systems planning and design with only a twinge or two of longing for the serenity of the research laboratory and the comfort of statistics.

The aim of the human engineering technologist is to apply the knowledge of human behavior, which he and others have gained, to the structuring of machines. He seeks to translate scientific findings into electronic circuits and "black boxes" which in specific situations will compensate for the human's limitations or complement his abilities. Specifically, the practicing engineering psychologist works on an engineering team and participates in the design of man-machine systems. Using procedural analysis techniques, drawing upon his psychological knowledge and attitudes, and employing his common sense and creative ability, the human engineer proceeds to contribute to system development at three levels of complexity.

At the simplest, he designs individual displays, controls, or display-control relationships. At a somewhat more complex level, the human engineering technologist contributes to the design of consoles and instrument panels. At the highest level of complexity, he assists in structuring large systems composed of many mechanical elements and frequently several human beings. In this capacity he helps to determine what information must flow through the system, how it must be processed, how many men are required, what tasks they will perform, and what type of information each one will need. In short, the engineering psychologist helps at this level to determine the configuration of the system.

Human engineering technology is much more extensively practiced by psychologists than is generally recognized by those who are not closely identified with the field. The specific nature of each accomplishment and the difficulty of assigning individual credit for team effort conspire with security and proprietary considerations to keep the lay and psychological public in almost complete ignorance of the technological products of human engineering. However, literally hundreds of devices and systems have been affected to a greater or lesser extent during the last ten years by the efforts of engineering psychologists. Every major type of military equipment has received some attention, as have also certain nonmilitary products such as aircraft instruments and cabins, flight control towers, artificial limbs, semiautomatic post-office sorting equipment, telephone sets, theodolites, experimental equipment for the earth-satellite program, control panels for an atomic reactor, and numerous industrial machines.

Man-Machine Systems Evaluation

The second way in which the engineering psychologist assists in the design of machines is by taking part in systems evaluations. Like human engineering technology, evaluation studies require a sizeable effort yet receive scarcely any publicity. Evaluations have been performed on headphones, range finders, gunsights, fire-control and missile-control systems, radar sets, information-plotting systems, combat-information centers, aircraft control towers, and numerous assorted display and control components. In some instances, the experiments have been carried out in the laboratory with the system inputs being simulated. In other cases, the tests are conducted in the field. But in both situations, the attendant complexities and difficulties of statistical control make this necessary variety of research as trying as any in which psychologists are likely to participate.

The reason that psychologists were called upon in the first place to assist in these evaluations was that they possessed methods for dealing with human variability. In contrast, the engineers generally had worked only with time-stationary components and, therefore, found themselves at somewhat of a loss when they were called upon to assess the performance of devices which were being operated by men.

Engineering Properties of the Man

The third and final way in which psychologists help in the design of machines is through studying, by conventional means, the behavior of the man as a machine operator. They have undertaken to study selected aspects of the behavior of the man as a system component. The intent here is to provide the engineers or the technologically oriented psychologists with information concerning certain of the characteristics of the man in order that the properties of the machine may be made to harmonize with them. This class of responses may be characterized in a number of different ways:

1. First off, as was pointed out at the very beginning, the human in a man-machine system can be considered as an information transmission and processing link between the displays and the controls of the machine. When so viewed, his behavior consists of reading off information, transforming it mentally, and emitting it as action on the controls. Thus, the performance may be described as of the type in which the operator's responses image in some way the pattern or sequence of certain of the input events. For example, the S signals when a tone comes on and withholds his response when he hears nothing, or he presses one key when he sees a red light and a different key when he sees a green one, he perceives the range and bearinf of a radar target and identifies its location verbally, he moves a cursor to follow the motion of a target image. In all these cases, the essential interest in the behavior focuses upon the correlation in space and time between events in a restricted and predefined stimulus "space" and corresponding events in preselected response "space."

2. Another way to characterize the behaviors studied in engineering psychology is to indicate that they are voluntary and task-directed or purposive. The operator of a man-machine system is always consciously trying to perform some task. Perhaps it is to follow on a keyboard the successive spatial positions of a signal light, perhaps to see a visual target imbedded in "noise" and to signal its position, possibly it is to watch a bank of displays in order to determine malfunction and to take action where necessary. In all cases, the operator is voluntarily trying to accomplish something specific; he is not just free associating, or living.

3. A third characteristic of the human operator's behavior emerges as a corollary of voluntary control. The class of human responses of interest to the engineering psychologist involves chiefly the striate muscles. Because

it is through the action of this type of effector that men speak and apply force to levers and handwheels, it is these muscles which play the dominant role in the human's control of machines.

4. Finally, practical considerations dictate that vision and audition be the sense modalities most often supplying the input to the human transmission channel. Because of the nature and location of the eyes and ears and because of their high informational capacity, they are ideal noncontact transducers for signal energies emitted by the mechanical or electronic displays of machines.

These four characteristics define some of the human reactions investigated in engineering psychology. The concepts and models of orthodox psychology are beginning to be replaced by physical and mathematical constructs and engineering models. We have already encountered the notion of the man as an information channel. Systems psychologists also view him as a multipurpose computer and as a feedback control system. The virtue of these engineering models is that they furnish ready-made a mathematics which has already proved itself of value when applied to the inanimate portions of the man-machine system and which may turn out to be useful for the human element as well. In addition, they provide the behavioral scientist with a new set of system-inspired hypothetical constructs and concepts which may redirect his research and stimulate entirely novel lines of inquiry.

Whereas orthodox psychology still speaks in a construct language consisting of terms like stimulus, response, sensation, perception, attention, anticipation, and expectancy, the new "hardware" school is rapidly developing a concept argot which, although quite unintelligible to outsiders, is providing considerable inspiration to the initiates. Human behavior for this psychological avant-garde is a matter of inputs, outputs, storage, coding, transfer functions, and bandpass.

And this is far more than a matter of language. The research itself is changing. Questions about human behavior are now being asked experimentally which were literally inconceivable a few years ago. Yet they are the very questions to which engineers desire answers. How stationary and linear is the man? What frequencies can he pass and how many bits per second can he transmit under a variety of different conditions? How does the human's gain change with different system dynamics? How well can he perform as a single integrator, or double integrator, or triple integrator? How effectively can he act as the surrogate for different computer functions? These are some of the experimental questions which engineering psychologists are beginning to ask and which, no doubt, will be asked with increasing frequency as the new field develops.

It is probably not too much to expect that one day soon we will have a completely revised textbook of human engineering, perhaps entitled *The Engineering Properties of the Man,* which will present to engineers in a form which is useful to them the system-relevant facts of psychology as then known. Instead of conventional chapter headings like "Seeing," "Hearing," "Speaking," "Moving," and "Working," it might contain such rubrics as "Mechanical Properties of the Man," "Transduction," "Informational Capacity and Bandwidth," "Linear Properties of the Man" (including analogue addition, integration, differentiation, and multiplication by constants), and "Nonlinear Properties of the Man" (including, it must be confessed, most everything else). Such a treatise, when it is written, will certainly be welcomed by the system designer, and he will waste no time in putting the information to use.

47. ON THE ALLOCATION OF FUNCTIONS BETWEEN MEN AND MACHINES *

Alphonse Chapanis

NUMEROUS WRITERS AGREE that one of the first and most important problems in man-machine system design has to do with the allocation of functions between men and machines.[1] This problem can be viewed from several points of view and there is a considerable amount of uncertainty about how allocation decisions can best be approached.[2] In this paper I shall try to do four things: (1) describe the nature of the allocation problem, (2) say something about the approaches that have been taken to this problem in the past, (3) give you a few of my views on the contemporary status of the problem, and (4) suggest a strategy for dealing with it.

---

* From *Occupational Psychology* 39 (1965): 1–11.

[1] H. E. Bamford, Jr., "Human Factors in Man-Machine Systems," *Human Factors* 1, no. 4 (1959): 55–59; A. Chapanis, "Le Facteur humaine dans la construction des systemes," in *L'Automation: Aspects Psychologiques et Sociaux*, Studia Psychologica, ed. A. Chapanis et al. (Louvain: Publications Universitaires, 1960), pp. 7–38; Chapanis, "Human Engineering," in *Operations Research and Systems Engineering*, ed. C. D. Flagle, W. H. Huggins, and R. H. Roy (Baltimore, Md.: Johns Hopkins Press, 1960), chap. 19, pp. 534–82; idem, "On Some Relations between Human-Engineering Operations Research and Systems Engineering," in *Systems: Research and Design*, ed. D. P. Eckman (New York: John Wiley & Sons, 1961), chap. 8, pp. 124–66; R. M. Gagné, ed., *Psychological Principles in System Development* (New York: Holt, Rinehart, & Winston, 1962); 1963; C. T. Morgan et al., *Human Engineering Guide to Equipment Design* (New York: John Wiley & Sons, 1963); and H. W. Sinaiko and E. P. Buckley, "Human Factors in the Design of Systems," in *Selected Papers on Human Factors in the Design and Use of Control Systems*, ed. H. W. Sinaiko (New York: Dover Publications, 1961), paper 1, pp. 1–14.

[2] P. M. Fitts, "Functions of Man in Complex Systems," *Aerospace Engineering* 21, no. 1 (1962): 34–39; N. Jordan, "Allocations of Functions between Man and Machines in Automated Systems," *Journal of Applied Psychology* 47 (1963): 161–65.

The Nature of the Problem

Industrial engineers and operations researchers use the words "allocation model," "allocation problem," or "assignment problem" to refer to those situations in which they want to combine activities and resources so as to maximize the effectiveness of a system.[3] The kind of allocation problem with which we are concerned is a special case of this more general one. However, you will not find our problem discussed in textbooks of industrial engineering or operations research because our problem has no neat mathematical model and no elegant mathematical solution.

The nature of our allocation problem can be described very simply. In planning any man-machine system, an engineer can usually think of many alternative ways of designing it.[4] These alternative designs may vary in a number of respects. For example, the designer may use different numbers and sizes of machine units. He may design one very large machine or several smaller ones to do exactly the same thing. Or he may use different kinds of linkages—mechanical, hydraulic, or electrical—between various parts of the system. Also among the things which a designer may vary is the number of people in a system and the functions which these people perform.

Let's take a specific example. Think of an industrial engineer who is designing a system to handle checking accounts in a bank. He could, conceivably, design the system in such a way that virtually all of the functions were performed by people. Tellers would receive the checks, sort them into their proper accounts, enter the amount of each check into the appropriate ledgers by hand, compute the bank balances by mental arithmetic or with the help of a simple device like an abacus, prepare monthly statements by hand, and mail off monthly statements to account holders. There are, in fact, some banks in the world which still operate in essentially this way.

A somewhat more complex type of system might provide the clerk with machines (for example, adding machines) to assist him in his computations, although he might still make entries and do all other operations by hand. Still more complex would be a system in which machines not only assisted the clerk in making his computations but printed out the bank balances on the appropriate forms. Next we might consider a system in which all of the accounts and all of the checks carry an identifying number such that the numbers are read and sorted by machine into the appropriate accounts. Further we might consider a system in which the checks are not only sorted into accounts automatically, but in which

---

[3] C. W. Churchman, R. L. Ackoff, and E. L. Arnoff, *Introduction to Operations Research* (New York: John Wiley & Sons, 1957).

[4] See Chapanis, "On Some Relations between Human-Engineering Operations Research and Systems Engineering."

balances are computed automatically by machine, the amounts of the checks and balances are printed out on the appropriate statements, and the statements are addressed and mailed out to the account holder, all by machine.

Each of these alternatives is realistic and workable. Further, I have discussed them in an order which represents increasing amounts of machine participation and decreasing amounts of human participation in the system as a whole. Incidentally, although I have mentioned only five different systems here, some engineers distinguish as many as ten different levels of automaticity in man-machine systems.[5] The important thing to notice, however, is that the functions which human operators perform in each of these systems is different.

When we ask about the allocation of functions between men and machines we are asking essentially: What functions of the system should be assigned to men and what to machines? Or, what kinds of things can and should human operators be doing in a man-machine system? These are fundamental questions about man-machine system design. They are important because decisions about the allocation of functions influence all of the later design thinking about the system. In fact, some decisions about the allocation of functions should ideally be made before the first blueprints are drawn and before the first components are built.

Earlier Conceptions of the Man-Machine Allocation Problem

If we look at what various writers have said about the way in which functions should be allocated to men and machines, we find little of direct and immediate help. Usually one finds a general discussion of the kinds of things that people do in man-machine systems and statements about some general characteristics of man as a component in man-machine systems. Often, too, one finds some general statements about the kinds of things people can do better than machines and vice versa (see Table 47–1 for an example).

Comparisons such as these serve a useful function, but only in the most elementary kind of way. I think they are useful primarily in directing our thinking towards man-machine problems and in reminding us, in general terms, of some of the characteristics that men and machines have as systems components. But when we come face to face with the practical realities of assigning functions in a genuine man-machine system, we find such general statements of almost no help at all. Why is this the case? The answer, I think, lies in the following:

1. *General man-machine comparisons are frequently wrong.* Like most general statements, the ones that compare men and machines are wrong,

---

[5] G. H. Amber and P. S. Amber, "A Yardstick for Automation," *Instruments and Automation* 30 (1957): 677.

TABLE 47–1

A Highly Abbreviated List of the Relative Advantages and Disadvantages of Men and Machines

Men	Machines
Able to handle low probability alternatives, that is, unexpected events.	Difficult to program. Difficult to anticipate all possible events and so virtually impossible to program for all such contingencies.
Able to perceive, that is, to make use of spatial and temporal redundancies and so to organize many small bits of information into meaningful and related "wholes."	Zero, or very limited, ability to perceive. "Organization" has to be elaborately programmed, which is difficult to do because of the many alternative ways organization can be formed from elements.
Possess alternative modes of operation. Can accomplish same or similar results by alternative means if primary means fail or are damaged.	Alternative modes of operation limited. May break down completely when partial injury or damage occurs. Not able to regenerate or heal.
Limited channel capacity, that is, there is a maximum amount of information that can be handled per unit time, and this is small.	Channel capacity can be made almost as large as desired.
Performance subject to decrement over fairly short time periods because of fatigue, boredom, and distraction.	Behavior decrements only over relatively long periods of time.
Comparatively slow and poor computers.	Excellent and very rapid computers.
Flexible; can change programming easily and frequently. Very large number of programs possible.	Relatively inflexible. Flexibility in kind and number of programs can be achieved only at a great price.

Source: A. Chapanis, "Human Engineering" in *Operations Research and Systems Engineering*, ed. C. D. Flagle, W. H. Huggins, and R. H. Roy (Baltimore, Md.: Johns Hopkins Press, 1960), chap. 19, pp. 534–82.

or at least misleading, in particular instances. Consider, for example, the statement that machines surpass people in computational ability. In general, I think most of us would probably agree with this. The giant digital computers with which we are all familiar clearly do fantastic computational feats at speeds which are incredibly fast by mortal standards. Yet does this mean that we should always use a digital computer, or any kind of a machine, when there are computations to be done in a system? Not at all. Many kinds of computations in man-machine systems are still most logically and sensibly done "in one's head." For still other kinds of computations, the most sensible implements to provide are a pencil and a pad of paper. I think it also correct to say that digital computers are not likely to supplant an engineer and his slide rule for many kinds of tasks.

Numerous exceptions of this same character can be found to all of the general statements contained in Table 47–1. To sum up, then, when we come to apply general rules about human or machine characteristics to particular functions in real man-machine systems, we often find that the rules are wrong or misleading.

2. *It is not always important to decide on a component which can do a particular job better.* The second reason why general statements such as those in Table 47–1 are often not useful in practical situations is that the systems engineer is not necessarily concerned with which component is the better of the two for a particular function. He may often be interested only in the question: Is the component good enough to do the job? Let me illustrate this point with the following example.

There are in the United States a large number of superhighways— highways which have from 4 to 12 lanes engineered with carefully designed curves, grades, and crossings so that they may carry a large volume of traffic (up to 10,000 vehicles per hour) at average speeds of 60 or more miles per hour. Some of these highways are toll roads—that is, the motorist must pay a fee or charge every time he travels on them. There are two principal methods used to collect these tolls. One method makes use of human toll collectors who accept money from the motorist, make change if necessary, deposit the money into a collection box or register, and signal the motorist that he may proceed. The other method makes use of a machine. The motorist drives up to a collection bin and drops his money into the machine. The coins may be in any combination whatsoever that adds up to the required toll. The machine counts the money, and if the correct amount has been received, it switches a signal from red to green to tell the motorist that he may proceed. After the motorist has passed over a treadle, the machine resets its own cycle for the next automobile.

If you compare the two components—the human versus the machine toll collector—you find that the human can do the job much better in certain respects. Not only can he make change (which the machine does not do), but he can take care of more automobiles per hour than the machine can. But does this mean that for the system as a whole we should use only human toll collectors? Not at all. Even though human toll collectors are better, the machines do the job well enough. In fact, from the standpoint of the operation of the system as a whole, the machines have enough other advantages to make up for their deficiencies.

3. *General comparisons between men and machines give no considera- tion to tradeoffs.* The last sentence above suggests the third reason why general statements about men and machines are often of little help. In the practical business of designing systems, the engineer always has to con- sider tradeoffs—the values of using a particular kind of component versus the costs of using that component. Incidentally, I use the word "costs" here in its most general sense to refer to all the disadvantages that come with a particular component. The cost-value problem is perhaps illus-

trated most easily in the field of space exploration. Suppose that we are considering a vehicle to do scientific studies on the surface of the moon. I think most of you would agree that we can plan to do many more kinds of experiments with our space vehicle if we have a well-trained astronaut on board than if we do not. A human is generally much more flexible, that is, he can do many more different kinds of things, than a machine. This advantage, however, carries with it a terrific penalty, and that penalty is weight. To enable the astronaut to live we have to provide him with a carefully controlled artificial environment, food, water, and all other things necessary for his survival. This means that much of the weight of the space vehicle is taken up with materials which serve no purpose other than to keep the astronaut alive.

In such a situation, one question the systems engineer wants to know is this: Is it better to design a vehicle which contains a human operator and less equipment, or is it better to design a vehicle which has no human operator and more equipment aboard? Comparisons such as those given in Table 47–1 unfortunately never help us to solve these tradeoff problems.

Some Current Views on the Division of Functions Between Men and Machines

I should like now to summarize for you a few of my thoughts about the problem of assigning funitions to men and machines. In particular I want to make three generalizations which do not seem to have been expressed before.

1. *The allocation of functions in man-machine systems is determined in part by social, economic, and political values.* The first general statement I should like to propose is that decisions about the assignment of functions in man-machine systems are always influenced to some extent by social, economic, and political values. These are usually unstated and implicit. Unfortunately, we in the United States often forget about these hidden assumptions because we know, or think we know, what our own social and economic values are. Let me see if I can illustrate what I mean by a simple example.

Imagine that we are considering the design of a mail-handling system for a new post office. The question arises whether the mail should be sorted and canceled by people or automatically by machine. The proper answer to this question depends on a great many things, among them the cost of human labor, the attitudes and stereotypes which labor has to monotonous and repetitive work, the value to the national economy of having these operations done by people instead of by machines, the availability of the machines and spare parts, the availability of skilled maintenance technicians to service the machines and keep them operating, the volume of mail that is normally handled by the post office, the attitudes of the citizens towards postal services and government work, and so on. Given certain conditions, I think it is quite possible that we might decide to have these jobs done by people; given other conditions, we would undoubtedly conclude that these jobs should be done automatically. In any event, it is fairly clear that postal and communications systems which work well in some countries are not at all appropriate for other countries at the present time.[6]

In its broadest terms, then, I am suggesting that man-machine systems are not entirely culture free. Failure to recognize this fact can lead a systems designer into making some serious errors.

2. *Assignment functions must be continually reevaluated.* The second generalization I want to make is that assignment decisions are not fixed and immutable. These decisions are always made at some point in time, and relative to a particular state of development of engineering art. Not so many years ago it would have been completely meaningless to consider the possibility that we should use a machine to "read" numbers on checks and sort the checks automatically into their proper accounts. Today this question is not meaningless, because we do, in fact, have machines which can do precisely that. On the other hand, it is trivial to ask today whether we could use a machine to read the addresses on letters and sort the letters automatically according to their destinations. There simply aren't machines available to read all of the kinds of handwriting that people use. Twenty years from now, however, this might no longer be a meaningless question. There is much work in progress on machines to read handwriting and I am confident that these efforts will eventually be successful enough to merit serious consideration.

Designing a system is something like writing a book. Unless you draw a line in time and work against that deadline, you will never complete either job. This continual reevaluation means, to paraphrase a common adage, that a human engineer's work is never done.

3. *Many of the difficulties experienced in making allocation decisions arise from engineering uncertainties.* Those of us who are in the human sciences often feel insecure and apologetic about our own science and subject matter. We often feel that it is our ignorance about human behavior which is responsible for the difficulties we have in making decisions about man-machine system design. If you have ever worked closely with systems engineers, however, you soon come to realize that there is much uncertainty on the machine side of the equation as well. In the first place, there is no such thing as *a* system design process, precise and specifiable.[7] Instead, systems designers often proceed with much trial

---

[6] The International Bank for Reconstruction and Development, *The Economic Development of Tanganyika* (Baltimore, Md.: Johns Hopkins Press, 1961), and *The Economic Development of Uganda* (Baltimore, Md.: Johns Hopkins Press, 1962).

[7] A. Kossiakoff, "The Systems Engineering Process," in *Operations Research and Systems Engineering*, ed. C. D. Flagle, W. H. Huggins, and R. H. Roy (Baltimore, Md.:

and error, just as anyone else does. In addition, although I realize it is dangerous to make a generalization about this point, I have the feeling that engineers are sometimes overly optimistic in their predictions about what they can do with their machines. As a result, the final products frequently fall short of what had been anticipated for them.

For these and other reasons, one usually finds that allocation decisions are not fixed even for a single system. Instead, we find the engineers making a series of approximations, modifications, and changes during the development of the system as they discover that certain things can or cannot be done with the machine components. These, in turn, require a continual reexamination of the roles which the men and machines are to play in the system.

A Strategy for Making Allocation Decisions

Finally, I want to say a few words about what I consider to be the best strategy for making decisions about the division of labor between men and machines in systems. Let me say at the outset that I shall not give you any simple method for making these decisions infallibly because I do not believe that any such method exists. Rather I think that the best I can do is to give you a general approach to the problem.

1. *Prepare a complete and detailed system specification.* The first step consists of preparing a complete and detailed specification of the system.[8] We need to know precisely what the system is supposed to do, the environment in which it will operate, the inputs it will receive, the operations it will perform on these inputs, and the outputs it is supposed to produce. We also need to know in detail all of the constraints—engineering, environmental, economic, and social—under which it must be constructed and operated.

2. *Analyze and list system functions.* The second step is to prepare a detailed list of the functions which the system is to perform. Perhaps the greatest error committed in this area is that psychologists are too fond of vague and general descriptive names which are of little use in practical work. Take the term "decision-making," for example. Psychologists use this term to refer to a broad spectrum of human behaviors. What a subject does in a choice-reaction experiment is referred to as decision-making. Similarly, what an industrialist does when he tries to decide manufacturing strategies is also called decision-making. Yet these are vastly different orders of complexity. A machine can often do the former, but seldom the latter. Other vague terms that are often used in this work

Johns Hopkins Press, 1960), chap. 5, pp. 82–118; J. M. Salzer, "Evolutionary Design of Complex Systems," in *Systems: Research and Design,* ed. D. P. Eckman (New York: John Wiley & Sons, 1961), chap. 10, pp. 197–215.

   [8] Chapanis, "Human Engineering."

are: sensing, perceiving, monitoring, shunting, short-term memory, scanning, coding, and so on.

The key to success here is that our list of systems functions must be highly specific and operational in character. It must describe the particular things that need to be done. As an example, take a mail-handling system for a post office. What are the functions that need to be performed? They are such things as:

a) Letters and cards must be sorted into certain size ranges.

b) Letters and cards within a size category must be stacked with the postage stamps oriented in a particular direction.

c) Mail must be checked to insure that it is carrying sufficient postage.

d) Stamps must be canceled.

And so on.

3. *Make tentative assignments for each function.* The next step consists of assigning each of the jobs to be done to a man or machine, or, what is much more common, to some combination of a man and a machine. These decisions are made in terms of assignments that will be best for the operation of the system as a whole, given all of the constraints under which it must be constructed and operated.

With a detailed list of functions before us, assignment problems become much easier. Sometimes, in fact, they are immediately obvious. Consider, for example, the function of checking the mail to see that it has the correct postage. This has to be a human function in part. No one knows how to build a machine to read the values of postage attached to an envelope.

Sometimes, of course, assignment decisions have to be made simply on the basis of our best judgment of what a man or a machine can or cannot do, or on the basis of our experience with similar systems which have been constructed in the past.

Finally, some decisions may have to wait for experimental evidence or the results of other types of studies to assist us in our decisions. It is unfortunate that the kind of information the human engineer or the system engineer needs for these decisions is seldom to be found in textbooks of psychology. An example of the kind of data the engineer needs is shown in Figure 47–1. This comes again from the field of space exploration. It compares the reliability of completely automatic systems of different levels of redundancy against a double redundant system in which one of the components is a well-trained man. Notice how much more reliable the system is when we have a man provide the redundancy in the system. This is due, of course, to the flexibility which man brings to the system, but the important thing to notice is that the vague word *flexibility* has been translated here into a highly meaningful, systems-relevant criterion.

4. *Evaluate the sum total of functions which have been assigned to man.* After individual tasks have been allocated to men and machines or

FIGURE 47–1

The Reliability of a Double Redundant Navigation System in Which One of the Redundant Components Is a Man (Dashed Line) as Compared with the Reliability of Systems with Various Orders of Redundancy in Which All Components Are Machines (Solid Lines)

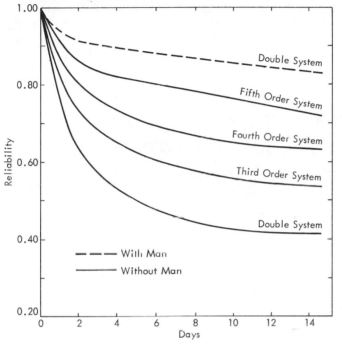

Source: M. A. Grodsky, "Risk and Reliability," *Aerospace Engineering* 21, no. 1 (1962), 28–33.

to some combination of them, the sum total of the human functions must be carefully assessed to see that they make up a job which is interesting, motivating, and challenging to the human operator. Men, unlike machines, work best at some medium level of difficulty. If the job is too difficult, a man may give up in despair or break down under the strain of trying to do it. On the other hand, it is not good to design a system in such a way that the human operator does nothing more than push a button occasionally. Under these circumstances. the operator soon realizes that he is being used inefficiently and he may become indifferent or inattentive, go to sleep, or even actively rebel against the system. This means that individual functions which might be done better by machine should sometimes be assigned to human operators solely for the purpose of making the job complex enough to match the human operator's psychological needs.

Conclusion

Let me conclude now with one more observation: The reason this is both such a difficult and such a challenging problem is that we are dealing here with integrated human behavior, with all its nuances, richness, variety, and complexity. In the final analysis, these are not problems of man versus machine, but rather of man versus man—man the user and operator of machines versus man the designer of them.

48. THE SPEED AND ACCURACY OF READING HORIZONTAL, VERTICAL, AND CIRCULAR SCALES *

Norah E. Graham

A SERIES OF EXPERIMENTS has been designed to compare the human response to numerical information displayed on horizontal, vertical, and circular scales. It has already been shown that if an operator has to control a moving pointer on a scale by turning a knob, then speed and accuracy are greatest when the horizontal scale is used.[1] This suggests that clockwise rotation of the control knob is naturally associated with pointer movement from left to right when the control is vertically below the display. The principal value of this work lies, therefore, in the information which it gives about display-control relations: the subjects could have ignored all the scale markings except the one on which the pointer was to be kept. The comparison of the three types of display is not complete without some measure of the speed and accuracy of making scale readings and this is the purpose of the experiments described here.

Method

The subjects (Ss) read the scales from a projected cinefilm. Horizontal, vertical, and circular scales, identical to those used in the previous experi-

* From *Journal of Applied Psychology* 40 (1956): 228–32. Copyright 1956 by the American Psychological Association. Reprinted by permission.

[1] N. E. Graham, I. G. Baxter, and R. C. Browne, "Manual Tracking in Response to the Display of Horizontal, Vertical, and Circular Scales," *British Journal of Psychology* 42 (1951): 155–63; N. E. Graham, "Manual Tracking on a Horizontal Scale and in the Four Quadrants of a Circular Scale," *British Journal of Psychology* 43 (1952): 70–77.

FIGURE 48–1

Horizontal, Vertical, and Circular Scales

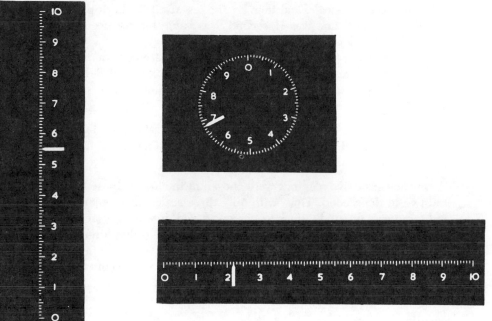

ments (Figure 48–1) were drawn in white ink on black paper. The pointer, which was cut out of aluminum foil and painted white, was placed opposite the appropriate number as each scale was photographed. A 16-mm. cinecamera was used and the timing regulated by the successive-frame exposure technique. The camera was fitted with an accurate frame counter worked from the shutter shaft so that each frame was counted as it was exposed. The speed of projection was 24 frames per second, so that, for example, a setting which the Ss were to see for ½ second was exposed for 12 frames. Each exposure was followed by eight seconds of black spacing which allowed Ss to write down the scale reading. The word "READY" then appeared on the screen. for two seconds, to prepare Ss for the next scale.

The projected circular scale was 5.1 in. in diameter and the horizontal and vertical scales were 16 inches in length. The intervals between scale markings were therefore the same on all three displays. The scales were viewed from a distance of 40 inches and appeared approximately at eye level. The angle subtended at the eye by the image of a scale on the screen was comparable to that subtended by the displays in the tracking experiments.

The film started with one example of each scale, which remained on the screen for ten seconds; the correct reading appearing alongside the scale after the first five seconds. This was followed by nine practice readings, three on each scale, and then by the test itself. In both practice and test, the exposure time was ½ second, this value having been chosen as the result of a pilot experiment.

When choosing the test numbers, the scales were considered as being made up of five major segments—0–2, 2–4, 4–6, 6–8, and 8–10—and on each scale two readings were chosen in each segment. The subdivisions within the major segments were divided into two groups:

1. .1, .4, .6, and .9, all of which are next to an extra-long graduation mark
2. .2, .3, .7, and .8, all of which are two subdivisions away from such a well-defined scale marking

On each scale five readings were chosen in the first of these two groups and five in the second. Thus, with only three scales, five major segments, and two types of subdivisions to be considered, it was only necessary for each subject to make $3 \times 5 \times 2 = 30$ readings in order for a complete analysis of the results to be possible.

Sixty male university sutdents, all studying some branch of engineering, acted as Ss.

Results

The Ss' responses were scored as follows: (a) Correct readings scored 0, (b) readings in error by ±0.1 scale units scored 1, and (c) all other errors and omissions scored 2.

The resulting distribution of scores was approximately normal. Marked improvement in performance occurred during the practice exposures, but the scores obtained during the experiment proper show no systematic improvement.

The error score for each segment of the three scales is shown in Table 48–1. The high incidence of mistakes at the ends of the scale is very noticeable. This is to be expected on the linear scales, as it may take longer to find the pointer in these positions, but it is surprising to find a similar trend on the circular scale.

It was also found that the position on the scale in which the pointer lies has more effect on the accuracy of reading on one type of scale than on another. This is due to the very high error at the top of the vertical scale. Many more mistakes were made between eight and ten on this scale than in any other region of the three displays.

It was also shown that the errors are significantly greater on the vertical scale than on the horizontal or the circular scale, but the difference between the latter two may be attributed to chance.

Another significant variable is the unit or section of the scale in which the pointer lies. In this case the t test shows that the liability to make

TABLE 48–1

The Total Error Score for Each Segment of the Three Displays

Major Segment	Scale			Total Error
	Horizontal	Vertical	Circular	
0–2	80	72	78	230
2–4	33	58	38	129
4–6	44	48	40	132
6–8	18	64	41	123
8–10	53	123	64	240
Total error	228	365	261	854

mistakes is significantly greater at the ends of the scales in sections 0–2 and 8–10 than in the three middle sections, 2–4, 4–6, and 6–8.

A more detailed analysis of the results showed that the position of the subdivision within the major segment (that is, the tenths) had no significant effect on the accuracy of reading. The total error score for the group of readings ending in .1, .4, .6, or .9 was 457, while the total score for those ending in .2, .3, .7, or .8 was 397.

When compared with the residual variance the differences between Ss are highly significant. The best S read 29 out of the 30 scales correctly, while the poorest made 21 mistakes.

Table 48–2 shows the frequency with which different types of error occurred on the three scales. The number of correct readings was greatest on the horizontal scale, and even if the readers had been allowed a margin of error of ±0.1 scale units, this display would still have ranked first in order of accuracy. Readings on the circular scale, on the other hand, were nearly always correct to within 0.2 scale units and only one reading on this display was missed altogether.

When the direction of the errors is taken into account, it is seen that there is a tendency to overestimate a reading by 0.1 or 0.2 scale units on the circular scale. This was particularly true of the four readings 0.2, 8.6, 1.4, and 4.6. For example, 11 Ss read 1.4 as 1.6 and 13 read it as 1.5. Only four Ss underestimated and called it 1.3. Or again, 8.6 was read as 8.8 by 9 Ss, and as 8.7 by 17 Ss, whereas only 2 mistook it for 8.5. This accounts for the high error score at the extremities of the circular scale, particularly between 0 and 2, though it does not explain it. Such a tendency to overestimate is not peculiar to the circular scale, however. On the vertical scale errors of +0.1 occur much more frequently than those of −0.1.

DISCUSSION

The gross errors of +1.0 scale unit which occurred in the present experiment were all associated with readings in the second half of a

TABLE 48–2

The Frequency with Which Errors of Different Magnitude Were Made on Each Scale

	Horizontal		*Vertical*		*Circular*	
	Number	*%*	*Number*	*%*	*Number*	*%*
Correct readings.	413	69.0	324	54.0	390	65.0
Errors						
+1.0	4	1.0	3	1.2	2	0.3
−1.0	2		4		0	
+0.2	6	2.0	8	2.6	34	6.0
−0.2	6		8		2	
+0.1 . . . . ∴	66	24.3	110	31.2	102	26.7
−0.1	80		77		58	
Other errors	11	3.7	23	11.0	11	2.0
Missed readings	12		43		1	
Total	600	100.0	600	100.0	600	100.0

numbered division. Kappauf remarks that under these conditions the scale number read is apt to be that nearest to the pointer.[2] The tendency noted by the same author to "round out" readings, particularly in the first numbered interval of scales which start at zero, is not apparent in the present experiment, presumably because of instructions to record the zero in such cases; it may, however, occur in practical situations. Vernon considers that gross mistakes are also liable to occur near the zero on circular scales,[3] but the present results confirm the finding of Sleight that gross errors at the ends of a scale are less frequent on scales without a clearly defined break.[4]

The mistakes which do happen at the ends of the circular scale are principally local, that is to say, of less than one numbered scale division. Local errors in any part of the scale display a tendency to overestimation. This was also noted by Sleight and seems to have no obvious explanation.

Sleight attributes the differences between the scales used in his experiment to the variation in their "effective" area: the larger the area to be scanned, the less accurate the reading. Such an explanation does not account, however, for the difference between the horizontal and vertical scales, which he also found to be significant, and which the present work suggests is the more important difference. From a physiological point of view, an explanation can be based on the shape of the visual field and the mechanics of eye movements. Objects that subtend an angle of more than

---

[2] W. E. Kappauf, "A Discussion of Scale-Reading Habits," USAF WADC Technical Report no. 6569, 1951.

[3] M. D. Vernon, "Scale and Dial Reading," Flying Personnel Research Committee Report no. 668, 1946.

[4] R. B. Sleight, "The Effect of Instrument Dial Shape on Legibility," *Journal of Applied Psychology* 32 (1948): 170–88.

½° at the eye can be detected if they lie within a field whose boundaries are approximately 100° to the right or left of the point of fixation, 70° above it, and 80° below it. The width of the visual field is thus considerably greater than its height, which is one factor that might favor the reading of horizontal scales. This is simply another way of saying that the eyes are set in the head in a horizontal line. The linear displays as they appeared in this experiment subtended an angle of approximately 10° at the eye. No difficulty should have been experienced, therefore, in finding the pointer even at the top of the vertical scale. The region of foveal vision, however, only subtends an angle of about 3° at the eye and, in order to read the scale, it is necessary to focus on the pointer itself. During very short exposures the accuracy of reading therefore depends upon the speed with which eye movements can be made. Scanning along a horizontal line is a relatively simple action involving the use of the lateral and medial recti muscles only. Raising or lowering the eyes, on the other hand, involves the joint action of the superior and inferior recti and the inferior and superior obliques. According to Duke-Elder, it has been shown by photographic studies that the eyes can follow lines in the horizontal plane more easily than in any other.[5] It has been found, moreover, that horizontal eye movements are the most rapid and vertical ones the slowest. When the fact that people are accustomed, when reading, to scanning along a horizontal line is added to this evidence, it is not difficult to explain the superiority of the horizontal scale.

Summary

1. The speed and accuracy of reading comparable horizontal, vertical, and circular scales has been studied by means of a film. Pictures of the scales were flashed on a screen at 10-second intervals, the exposure time being ½ second.

2. The vertical scale is clearly less easy to read than either of the other two displays, particular difficulty being experienced near its ends.

3. The success of the circular scale may be attributed to the fact that it presents a smaller area to be scanned. The shape of the visual field and the relative ease of moving the eyes from side to side, rather than up and down, are thought to account for the greater accuracy on the horizontal scale.

---

[5] W. S. Duke-Elder, *Textbook of Ophthalmology* (London: Kimpton, 1932).

49. MONITORING OF COMPLEX VISUAL DISPLAYS—SOME VIGILANCE AND DECISION-MAKING PROBLEMS *

Jack A. Adams, Herbert H. Stenson, and John M. Humes

INTRODUCTION

THE ADVENT OF AUTOMATIC CONTROL and computing subsystems in modern semiautomatic man-machine systems has meant changes in response emphasis for the human operator. In older systems, the operator had little assistance from machines in displaying, monitoring, controlling, computing, and decision-making, and his task was often one of relatively high work load where all of these response classes were required in generous amounts. The rise of automatic subsystems has not necessarily eliminated any of these response classes for the operator, but it has shifted their emphasis in two basic ways:

1. There is an increasing requirement on monitoring behavior that demands sustained vigilance, or attention. With digital computers and automatic control devices assuming much of the routine responding, the operator must be alert for signals commanding his assigned response classes that will serve as inputs to the system. The concern for system performance at this time is the relatively long-term monitoring conditions under which human vigilance may deteriorate.

2. A greater proportion of operator response is involved in decision-making functions than ever before. This does not imply that simpler responding has been eliminated, but only that it occupies a reduced status in the daily job routine. Many simple response classes must be retained at high strength in the operator's repertoire as redundancy elements to enhance system reliability because, when automatic subsystems malfunction, the operator can play the vital role of inserting manual inputs as substitutes for the normally automatic ones. Lusser has emphasized that the tremendous complexity of equipment has created grave problems for system reliability,[1] and Westbrook has been

---

* From "Monitoring of Complex Visual Displays—II. Effects of Visual Load and Response Complexity on Human Vigilance," *Human Factors* 3 (1961): 213–21.
    [1] R. Lusser, *The Notorious Unreliability of Complex Equipment* (Redstone Arsenal: Research and Development Division, 1956).

among those developing the view that the human operator as a versatile redundant component can give a significant increment to reliability.[2] Man has other virtues as a system element, but in many ways we can justify him for reliability reasons alone.

The human operator is not going to be a good decision-maker, or a redundant subsystem, if he cannot accurately and speedily detect the signals that command his responses. Thus, the contribution of the human operator to system performance becomes importantly dependent upon his vigilance under conditions of prolonged monitoring when the automatic subsystems are doing most of the work. And, because monitoring activities in semiautomatic systems now occupy a substantial portion of the operator's time, the determiners of monitoring behavior become an important topic for research. Most experiments on vigilance reveal man as a poor monitor by demonstrating decrement in response proficiency as observation time becomes longer.

The impetus for these experiments that show vigilance decrement primarily came out of World War II problems of monitoring radarscope where the operator had to detect the occurrence of a small, transient, raw radar return, and the emphasis on this class of signals has persisted in vigilance research. However, we cannot assume that the results of such experiments are generalizable to the tasks of present and future systems. The tasks for human operators in semiautomatic systems have new variables that may have new influences on the development of vigilance decrement. There are three prominent classes of new variables:

1. *Symbolic stimuli.* Information from a digital computer is commonly presented as alphanumeric characters and specialized symbols that often will persist for some time on the display, or perhaps persist indefinitely until a response is made to them. They are not the transient, near threshold signals that have dominated most vigilance research so far.
2. *Load.* Conrad uses the term "load" to mean the number of stimulus sources that can present critical signals for response.[3] Rather than watch a single display element like a radarscope, the monitoring operator must now scan a number of stimulus sources. Any one of the sources may exhibit a critical change for detection and response.
3. *Response complexity.* The increasing emphasis on decision-making responses has been mentioned above.

It is evident that the issue for system design and use is these new operator variables with an unknown influence on monitoring behavior. Frankmann and Adams have pointed out that the occasional vigilance

---

[2] C. B. Westbrook, "The Pilot's Role in Space Flight," USAF Wright Air Development Center Technical Note 59–31, 1959.

[3] R. Conrad, "Some Effects on Performance of Changes in Perceptual Load," *Journal of Experimental Psychology* 49 (1955): 313.

experiment that has used a complex task with multiple stimulus sources has failed to show vigilance decrement,[4] and this is a puzzling finding because of the commonplace decrement found for simple tasks. Studies by Hoffman and Mead, Broadbent, Howland, Jerison and Wallis, Jerison and Wing, and Loeb and Jeantheau all failed to find decrement in tasks where more than one stimulus source was monitored.[5] Adams and Boulter found a very slight decrement but for one measure only.[6] Investigators have most often used tasks which gave them a decrement and have failed to exploit the scientific understanding that might arise in the study of tasks that do not induce decrement at all.

Findings for complex vigilance tasks may seemingly be at odds with those for simple vigilance tasks, but the inconsistencies are resolved when viewed in terms of the *activationist hypothesis* that relates alertness to the stimulation level of the task. The basis for this hypothesis is the provocative physiological research on the ascending reticular activating system which has been reviewed by Hebb, Lindsley, Malmo, and Samuels, and has been related to the vigilance literature by Frankmann and Adams, Broadbent, and Scott.[7] This hypothesis emphasizes that a stimulus enroute to its cortical area not only travels its traditional sensory pathway (cue function) but also travels along collateral pathways through the reticular formation and terminates in diffuse, nonspecific cortical firings (arousal function). Scott has most explicitly documented the implications of stimulus arousal for vigilance, and he has emphasized the performance

[4] Judith P. Frankmann and J. A. Adams, "Theories of Vigilance," *Psychological Bulletin* 58 (1961).

[5] A. C. Hoffman and L. C. Mead, *The Performance of Trained Subjects on a Complex Task of Four Hours' Duration* (Washington, D.C.: U.S. Department of Commerce, 1946; D. E. Broadbent, *The Twenty Dials Test under Quiet Conditions* (Cambridge: Medical Research Council, Applied Psychology Research Unit, APU 130/50, 1950); D. Howland, "An Investigation of the Performance of the Human Monitor," USAF WADC Technical Note 57–43, 1958; H. G. Jerison and R. A. Wallis, "Experiments on Vigilance: One-Clock and Three-Clock Monitoring," USAF WADC Technical Report 57–206, 1957; H. G. Jerison and S. Wing, "Differential Effects of Noise and Fatigue on a Complex Vigilance Task," USAF WADC Technical Report 57–14, 1957; and M. Loeb and G. Jeantheau, "The Influence of Noxious Environmental Stimuli on Vigilance," *Journal of Applied Psychology* 42 (1958): 47.

[6] J. A. Adams and L. R. Boulter, "Monitoring of Complex Visual Displays: I. Effects of Response Complexity and Intersignal Interval on Vigilant Behavior When Visual Load Is Moderate," USAF Command and Control Development Division Technical Note AFCCDD–TN–60–63, 1960.

[7] D. O. Hebb, "Drives and the C.N.S. [Conceptual Nervous System]," *Psychological Review* 62 (1955): 243; D. B. Lindsley, "Psychophysiology and Motivation," in *Nebraska Symposium on Motivation*, ed. M. R. Jones (Lincoln; University of Nebraska Press, 1957); R. B. Malmo, "Activation: A Neuropsychological Dimension," *Psychological Review* 66 (1959): 367; I. Samuels, "Reticular Mechanisms and Behavior," *Psychological Bulletin* 56 (1959); Frankmann and Adams, "Theories of Vigilance"; D. E. Broadbent, *Perception and Communication* (New York: Pergamon Press, 1958); and T. H. Scott, *Literature Review of the Intellectual Effects of Perceptual Isolation*, Defense Research Board Report HR66 (Ottawa: Department of National Defense, 1957).

deterioration that occurs in repetitive tasks with a uniform sensory environment.[8] He concluded that loss of efficiency is a function of sensory uniformity, and the more unchanging the stimuli, the sooner deterioration occurs. Furthermore, Scott holds that the human operator undergoes a period of "sensory habituation" to the arousal properties of stimuli. A gradual loss of alertness develops through continued exposure to uniform stimuli. Under conditions of severe isolation over extended periods, more pronounced behavioral changes such as hallucinations appear, as in the well-known McGill studies of sensory deprivation.

The failure of decrement to appear for complex vigilance tasks is consistent with the activationist hypothesis presumably because of the heightened stimulation of the complex display, the increased response-produced stimulation from the head and eye movements of visual scanning, and the added sources of internal stimulation if choice and decision are involved in the responding. An explanation of these findings in terms of a work-inhibition construct like Hull's I_R conforms less well because, if anything, the increased response activity in a complex task should produce more, not less, decrement.[9] A similar strain is placed on a work-inhibition view for the well-known findings of Deese and Ormond and of Jenkins, where vigilance decrement was least when signal rate was the highest.[10] More responses per unit of time bettered performance, not worsened it, as work notions would imply. Even the recovery benefits of rest for vigilance decrement that have been found by Mackworth and Adams, which seem to fit the work-inhibition hypothesis so comfortably, can just as well be explained by the activationist hypothesis in terms of changes in stimulation that accompany the casual rest period administered in psychological experiments.[11]

Perhaps the difficulty with the activationist hypothesis, at this time, is that it explains too much. The core of the hypothesis is stimulation, but the hypothesis is loosely expressed and gives no operational definition of stimulation, either in terms of environmental or response-produced stimuli. The potential explanatory power of the hypothesis is large, but research needs to clarify the operations that define the amount and the variation in environmental and response-produced stimulation that are relevant for human alertness. Until we give explicit definition to the

---

[8] Ibid.

[9] C. L. Hull, *Principles of Behavior* (New York: Appleton-Century Co., 1943).

[10] J. Deese and E. Ormond, "Studies of Detectability during Continuous Visual Search," USAF WADC Technical Report 53–8, 1953; H. M. Jenkins, "The Effect of Signal Rate on Performance in Visual Monitoring," *American Journal of Psychology* 71 (1958).

[11] N. H. Mackworth, *Researches on the Measurement of Human Performance*, Medical Research Council Special Report Series No. 268 (London: Her Majesty's Stationery Office, 1950); J. A. Adams, "Vigilance in the Detection of Low-Intensity Visual Stimuli," *Journal of Experimental Psychology* 52 (1956): 204.

sources of stimulation, and relate them to measures of alertness, we cannot accept or reject this scientific hypothesis or predict vigilance decrement in new tasks.

METHOD

Purpose

The purpose of this experiment was to provide data on the monitoring behavior of the human operator in semiautomatic man-machine systems, and to provide a first approximation of the defining operations for environmental and response-produced stimulation for the activationist hypothesis. On the environmental side, stimulation level was defined by the number of visual stimulus sources to be monitored. Response-produced stimulation was manipulated in terms of response complexity. Three hours of continuous visual monitoring were required in a simulated air-defense surveillance task.

Stimulus Display

The subject sat in a sound-treated room, illuminated by broad-band blue lighting, and viewed a phosphorescent screen of 22-inch diameter in the wall of the room, on which the display was rear-projected. Six or 36 symbols were the stimulus sources in the projected display.

Figure 49–1 is an example of the display for six stimulus sources. The subject's task over the 3-hour monitoring period was to detect the change of a G to an F and report it with a simple or complex response by pressing one or more buttons on a panel located by his right hand. The symbol marked F 675 in Figure 49–1 is an event to be reported. The critical F signal persisted for 20 seconds before reverting to G. The 3-hour period was divided into nine 20-minute trials for scoring purposes, and the mean intersignal interval on a trial was 280 seconds. There were four signals on a 20-minute trial and the randomly assigned intersignal intervals were 100, 220, 340 and 460 seconds. These four intervals were randomly assigned for each trial.

The task simulated a semiautomatic air-defense system where a computer would periodically display symbolic information about aircraft to the operator. An animated 35-mm. strip film simulated a 1,000-mile surveillance area, with aircraft programmed for speeds of either 450, 900, or 1,800 knots. Once initiated, an aircraft symbol was programmed linearly in the direction indicated by the arrow attached to the symbol and at a rate proportional to one of the three speeds. The three speeds were always equally divided among the symbols on the display. When a symbol reached the edge of the screen it was removed and immediately

FIGURE 49-1

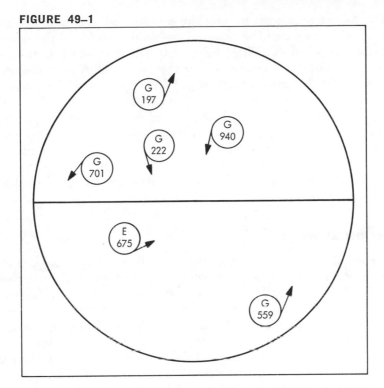

The vigilance display with a moderate visual load of six symbols. Symbol 675 with the G changed to F for 20 seconds is an event to be detected and reported. The display looked the same for 36 symbols except that it was visually crowded. (Not drawn to scale.)

replaced by another at a different place on the screen, thereby always keeping visual load constant for a subject. The method was to project a frame of film on the phosphorescent screen in front of the subject for three seconds, and then remove the image for one second with a shutter mechanism—thus allowing the symbols to go into a brief phosphorescent decay state on the screen. During the 1-second off period the next frame was advanced. When the shutter was raised and a new film frame was presented, a critical change for detection was or was not present. This task, then, represented a strip-film simulation of a computerized system where the computer drum was periodically read and its data flashed on a display in front of the operator.

Apparatus

A modified DuKane strip-film projector, Model 576–39A, was used. Automatic presentation of the film for three hours was by a cam-timing device which controlled a solenoid-operated shutter and the film-advance mechanism.

The subject responded by pressing a button on a 41-button response panel at his right hand. The experimenter on the outside of the room and a repeater panel of 41 telltale lights that indicated which buttons were pressed. In addition, response latency was measured. A photoelectric-cell system activated a timer when a signal first appeared on the screen, and the timer was stopped when the subject pressed any one of the buttons. Between responses the subject kept his hand in a standard rest position. If the subject moved his hand from this control position, a light appeared on the experimenter's panel and the intercom system was used to inform the subject that his hand must be kept in the proper position. This technique was an experimental control for error in response latency measures ascribable to the distance of the hand movement.

Experimental Design

We investigated two values of visual load, 6 and 36 symbols as stimulus sources, and 2 values of response complexity, Detection (D) and Evaluation (E). Four independent groups of 15 subjects each were employed. Each group received one of the four combinations of load and response complexity, and their designations were 6-D, 6-E, 36-D, and 36-E. Response complexity was defined in terms of the number of choices involved in evaluating the signal change and reporting it. A subject in the Detection condition merely had to detect the change and press the button labeled F on his response panel. In the Evaluation condition, however, a subject had to detect the signal change and then make a 4-choice evaluation of the symbol on the display and indicate his decision by first pressing either button A, B, C, or D, and then following it with the buttons for F and the three numbers of the symbol. The subject had to decide whether the symbol whose G had changed to F ended in an odd or an even number, and whether the symbol was above or below the horizontal line across the center of the display. For example, the subject might be required to respond by pressing buttons DF 675.

Each subject was given a 3-hour practice session on a day preceding his criterion session. The purpose of the practice session was to provide thorough learning so that changes in the scores of the subsequent criterion session reflected changes in the vigilance state of a subject, not learning effects. To promote learning during the practice session, the subject was given complete knowledge of errors over the intercom system. A different film was used for the practice session than for the criterion session. The visual load and the condition of response complexity were the same in both sessions, but the mean signal rate was 1 minute in the practice session and 1/5 minute in the criterion session. Analysis of these practice data indicated that the training goal was accomplished because the mean response latency curve for each group was at its asymptote by the end of the practice session.

TABLE 49–1

Percent of Signals Receiving Correct Response over the 3-Hour Observation Period

	Blocks of Three Trials			
Group	*1–3*	*4–6*	*6–9*	*Total*
6-D	98.9	100.0	98.9	99.3
6-E	93.3	97.2	95.0	95.2
36-D	96.3	96.7	96.7	96.6
36-E	89.7	88.8	88.8	89.1

No knowledge of results was given in the criterion session because this was a source of stimulation outside those of interest for the experiment. A subject's cigarettes, matches, and watch were taken from him before each session.

Subjects

The 60 subjects were male university undergraduate students. They were paid for their participation.

RESULTS

Table 49–1 shows the percent of signals correctly detected by each group. The typical vigilance experiment almost always uses percent correct as the basic performance measure, and ordinarily decrement appears as a function of observation time. In contrast, it will be noted that none of the four groups shows a decrement effect during the 3-hour period. This finding confirms an earlier one by Adams and Boulter using the same apparatus.[12] Differences in the overall level of percent correct are seen in Table 49–1, but they are associated with the level of visual load and response complexity, not trials.

The failure of percent correct to change as a function of observation time does not mean that changes in vigilance did not take place. Our measurement of response latency recognized that deterioration of response speed might occur even though the subject made a correct response. The mean latency for all correct responses by a subject on a trial was used as his basic score for analysis, and a plot of group means is shown in Figure 49–2. As might be expected, the more demanding search task under high visual-load conditions results in Groups 36-D and 36-E performing at a poorer level than Groups 6-D and 6-E with a moderate

---

[12] Adams and Boulter, "Monitoring of Complex Visual Displays."

FIGURE 49–2

Mean Response Latency as a Function of Trials (3-Hour Observation Time) for Each of the Four Groups

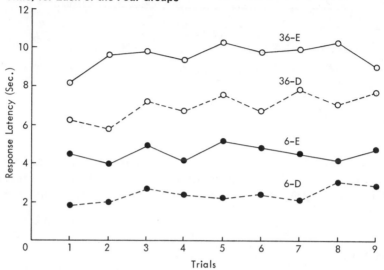

visual load. Also, the two Evaluation response conditions exhibited poorer performance than simple Detection responding. Vigilance decrement in response latency over trials was a slight effect, when it was discernible at all.

DISCUSSION AND CONCLUSIONS

The traditional vigilance measure of percent correct failed to show decrement over three hours when the complex visual task had multiple stimulus sources and the critical signals were nontransient. Whatever differences were found in percent correct were associated with the overall difficulty of an experimental condition, not observation time. Response efficiency as a function of visual stimulus load is consistent with the work of Conrad, and the longer latency for more complex decision responding is a straightforward expectation.[13]

The effects of waning vigilance, as revealed in an increase of response latency over three hours, was associated only with the simple Detection response, not the Evaluation decision responding. This same finding emerged in an earlier study by Adams and Boulter, and is corroborated here.[14] It appears that response-produced stimulation, at least of a central kind, is significant for alertness states. Lindsley has discussed evidence for cortical firings exerting a descending or feedback stimulation on the

---

[13] R. Conrad, "Some Effects on Performance."
[14] Adams and Boulter, "Monitoring of Complex Visual Displays."

reticular formation, and this may be the mediational basis of added alerting properties in decision-making that is absent in simple detection responding.[15]

The hypothesis associated with visual load as a source of environmental simulation for attentiveness was not sustained. It was hypothesized that 36 stimulus sources would provide a much higher level of environmental stimulation than 6 sources, and decrement should be less. But decrement was found to be differentially associated with the response-complexity variable, not load. There are three likely explanations:

1. The moderate visual load was sufficient stimulation for good alertness, and increasing it makes no further difference.
2. External, environmental stimulation is far less important for vigilance than response-produced stimulation. We appear to be on increasingly safe grounds in ascribing high alertness to *some* source of stimulation, but we will not have careful statements of the empirial laws of vigilance until the sources of stimulation are identified and properly weighted as determinants of monitoring behavior.
3. The *amount* of stimulation may be of far less significance for maintaining alertness than the *variety* of stimulation. Increasing the visual load from 6 to 36 increases the amount, but it may not increase the variety of environmental stimuli. Earlier findings suggest that variety in stimulation may be critical.

With all of these definitional problems for the activationist hypothesis, it is evident that much research remains to be done. Increasingly, vigilance findings are emerging which cannot be explained by fatigue-like hypotheses. While no one at present is suggesting that views of effector fatigue are inappropriate explanations for all decremental phenomena and should be displaced by the activationist hypothesis, there are findings such as those reported here where work-decrement views appear to be strained in their application.

Implications for Semiautomatic Man-Machine Systems

It is commonly heard that the human operator in complex semiautomatic systems will be confronted with serious vigilance problems because automatic controls and computer subsystems are doing most of the responding, and deterioration in his monitoring behavior will degrade performance of the overall system. Such judgments at worst are based on causal observations, and at best on tenuous generalizations from research on simple vigilance tasks that have their roots in World War II systems. Many times the state of our scientific knowledge in engineering psychology leaves no choice but to generalize from experiments on simple tasks to the behavioral demands of complex tasks that are common in contempo-

---

[15] Lindsley, "Psychophysiology and Motivation."

rary and future semiautomatic systems. Generalizations from simple tasks to complex ones may be good or bad. depending on whether a complex task has new variables or interactions not present in simpler situations. Adams and Xhignesse have pointed out that the adequacy of generalizations from simple to complex tasks is an empirical matter for research, and the experiment reported here, as well as others on complex tasks with multiple sources, shows that generalizations from simple to complex vigilance tasks cannot be made uncritically.[16] Our experiment does not support the gloomy predictions about man as a poor monitor in semiautomatic systems. We found no decrement in percent of signals correctly detected, and the small decrement in response latency that did occur for two out of four groups probably would not be considered operationally significant for most systems. There is something about complex tasks that is favorable for human vigilance.

The activationist hypothesis is favored for explaining vigilance data from complex tasks, but we have indicated that the hypothesis has many loose ends. As research better delineates the activationist hypothesis, we may eventually develop the capabilities to unify the findings for simple and complex vigilance tasks, to predict monitoring behavior for different types of tasks, and to design tasks that will keep human alertness high for relatively long periods. Designing for vigilance may require that the human operator be given certain types and number of stimulus sources, or that the distribution of responses between man and machines allocate to man the number and type of responses that will keep him alert even though machines may be able to handle them with ease. There may be more to optimizing system performance than simply assigning a response item to a subsystem that is unoccupied at the moment.

50. MEN, MACHINES, AND MODELS *

Alphonse Chapanis

THE HISTORY OF PSYCHOLOGY is a tortuous, winding road stretching back through thousands of years in time. If we look back along it we can make out many instructive features about the road itself, the signs along it, and the terrain and climate through which it has brought us to this present

---

[16] J. A. Adams and L. V. Xhignesse, "Some Determinants of Two-Dimensional Visual Tracking Behavior," *Journal of Experimental Psychology* 69 (1960): 391.

* Extracted from "Men, Machines, and Models," *American Psychologist* 16 (1961): 113–31. Based on the Presidential Address delivered to the Society of Engineering Psychologists at the 68th Annual Convention of the American Psychological Association, Chicago, Ill., September 5, 1960. Copyright 1961 b; the American Psychological Association. Reprinted by permission.

moment. One thing which interests me greatly is that the highway which we call the history of psychology is littered with the wrecks of discarded models.

Aristotle, that venerable philosopher to whom we trace so much of our ancestry, made eloquent use of physical and mechanical analogies over two thousand years ago. See, for example, how he explains our ability to remember:

> Evidently we must regard this . . . as similar to a painting. For an active stimulus stamps on the soul a sort of imprint of the sensation, analogous to stamping with a seal ring. For this reason, too, persons who are deeply moved by passion or by ardor of youth do not remember, just as if the effort and the seal were applied to running water. In other persons, because of their worn-out condition, like old buildings, or because of the hardness of their receptive principle, no impression is made.[1]

Although it would not serve my purpose to review with you the history of mechanistic models which have been applied to the human organism, it is interesting to see how persistently and regularly they keep reappearing. For example, Descartes, inspired perhaps by the hydraulically operated moving figures which were then in vogue in some of the public gardens, wrote in 1650:

> It is to be observed that the machine of our bodies is so constructed that all the changes which occur in the motion of the spirits may cause them to open certain pores of the brain rather than others, and, reciprocally, that when any one of these pores is opened in the least degree more or less than is usual by the action of the nerves which serve the senses, this changes somewhat the motion of the spirits, and causes them to be conducted into the muscles which serve to move the body in the way in which it is commonly moved on occasion of such action; so that all the movements which we make without our will contributing thereto . . . depend only on the conformation of our limbs and the course which the spirits, excited by the heat of the heart, naturally follow in the brain, in the nerves, and in the muscles, in the same way that the movement of a watch is produced by the force solely of its mainspring and the form of its wheels. . . .[2]

This was followed almost exactly a century later (1748) by LaMettrie's *L'Homme Machine,* a title which in turn was reincarnated exactly two centuries later in an edition of Carlson and Johnson's *The Machinery of the Body.*[3]

There appears to be a certain pattern in all this activity. Like Descartes, modelists seem to be inspired by the latest physical theories and playthings of the times. Newton's mechanics brought forth models of man

---

[1] W. A. Hammond, *Aristotle's Psychology* (New York: Macmillan Co., 1902), p. 199.

[2] B. Rand, *The Classical Psychologist* (New York: Houghton Mifflin Co., 1912), pp. 172 f.

[3] A. J. Carlson and V. Johnson, *The Machinery of the Body,* 3d ed. (Chicago: University of Chicago Press, 1948).

which treated him simply as a machine made up of levers and similar linkages. Watt's steam engine and the development of thermodynamics produced models of man which viewed him as nothing but a complicated heat engine. When servomechanisms mushroomed during World War II we heard that man is nothing but a servosystem. Somewhat more recently communication theory has been translated into models which purport to show that man is only an information-handling system.

The Contemporary Status of Psychological Models. By and large, the very old models of man have been tried, found wanting, and long since discarded. They are, to be sure, resurrected and discussed from time to time by the historians of psychology, but in the light of contemporary knowledge they usually appear quaint, naive, and amusing. Even some of the newer models of man have been under test long enough so that they are also beginning to lose some of their original aura and enchantment. The servomodel, for example, about which there was so much written only a decade or two ago, now appears to be headed toward its proper position as a greatly oversimplified, inadequate description of certain restricted aspects of man's behavior. When the model of man as an information-handling system first hit psychology, everyone was measuring everything in bits. In today's scientific market, it is becoming apparent that the information model was greatly overvalued.

Despite this sobering history it seems to me that models are flourishing as never before in psychology. Everyone is constructing models of all sorts of things in experimental psychology. Indeed, it is almost as though there was a special form of magic attached to the word "model." Things which ten years ago would have been identified with more ordinary words like hypothesis, theory, hunch, and empirical equation are now very often called models simply because it is the thing to do.

Physical analogies are now even firmly implanted in our everyday speech. We say that a person may, at various times, be "all wound up," "tight as a drum," or "breathing fire." His "thread of life" is to some extent dependent on "the wheel of fortune." He works in a "pyramidal organization" and finds himself protected by the "checks and balances of the American Constitution." That such models carry over even into the arts is attested by the title of a recent Broadway hit, *I Am a Camera.*

Engineering psychology is characterized by the paucity of its models and by its almost complete avoidance of model building as a method for the solution of its problems. Perhaps it is this state of affairs which led Conover to say recently that in his opinion one of the "most critical problems in human factors today" is the development of a "truly useful mathematical model of human behavior . . . that can be utilized in the analysis of man-machine systems." [4]

---

[4] C. W. Simon, "Human Factors Research Problems," *Human Factors Society Bulletin* 2 (1959): 16–17.

This divergence in methods of attacking man-machine problems is so striking that it constitutes another important reason for us to look closely at models in general. Are we overlooking an important technique? What are models, anyway? Exactly what functions do they serve? What are some of the dangers involved in their use? These are some of the questions which have motivated me to write about "Men, Machines, and Models." When I have finished I hope that I may have helped you to formulate your own answers to these questions.

What Exactly Are Models?

As a point of departure, let us see if we can find a satisfactory definition of the word "model." Usually when you have the problem of arriving at a precise definition, you turn to a dictionary for help. In this case, unfortunately, that ordinarily reliable standard of English expression turns out to be of singularly little help. *Webster's Unabridged Dictionary* (second edition), for example. gives 15 definitions of the word model, none of which seems particularly consonant with the kind of model we mean when we speak of a "man-machine model." Among other things, *Webster's* says that a model may be:

A person who poses.
A copy, as "She is the *model* of her mother."
A woman who displays costumes to customers.
The original pattern according to which other items are made.
A tool used in molding cornices.
The curvature in the back and belly of such musical instruments as the violin.
An example to be imitated, as a *model wife*.
A miniature representation of a thing.

Of these possibilities, only the last one mentioned above seems to approximate the sense in which we have used the word model so far. Even in this case, however, it appears that the dictionary definition implies rather concrete *miniature* representations, such as model airplanes, model ships, and the like, rather than the symbolic representations to which the word model is often attached these days.

Another standard reference source, the 1959 *Encyclopaedia Britannica*, contributes little more of value to us. The article on "Models and Model-making" in that work discusses such things as burial models; toys; models in the motion picture industry; models for teaching and recognition training; models of airplanes for wind tunnel tests; and models of factories for testing layouts, lines of flow, and operating efficiency.

Perhaps the most important conclusion to be drawn from this brief excursion into documentation is that the scientific and engineering models with which we are concerned have a very special meaning, a meaning which has not yet found its way into the common English language.

If we turn to the model builders themselves for help in this definitional problem, we find ourselves no less confused. Models, we find from reading the literature, come in a bewildering variety. There are mechanical models, true models, adequate models, distorted models, dissimilar models, static models, dynamic models, structural models, iconic models, analog models, symbolic models, material models, formal models, mathematical models, and analytic models—just to name a few. Some authors avoid the problem. Underwood, for example, starts his discussion of models by saying frankly: "I am not going to state a specific definition. . . ." [5] Other more philosophical writers have, frankly, left me floundering in a maelstrom of polysyllabic and largely incomprehensible words. For this reason I have abandoned all prior definitions of the word model in favor of one which makes sense to me. It is this:

Models are analogies.

Scientific or engineering models are representations, or likenesses, of certain aspects of complex events, structures, or systems, made by using symbols or objects which in some way resemble the thing being modeled.

It seems to me that this definition divests the word of much of the magic which seems to have become attached to it recently, and exposes at once the basic strengths and weaknesses of models. It suggests some of the reasons why models are useful in scientific and engineering work, but at the same time hints at some of the dangers and fallacies involved in their construction and use. But first, some amplifying remarks about kinds of models.

On the Basic Kinds of Models. One can find almost as many classifications of models as there are model builders. In an attempt to get at essentials again I would assert that there are only two basic kinds of models: replica models and symbolic models. Although the distinction between the two kinds of models is not always sharp, it is generally possible to classify models as one or the other.

The essential thing about replica models is that they look like the thing being modeled in some respect. I use the words "look like" here in a very loose sense to convey the general idea of a pictorial representation. A globe is a replica model of the earth because, in some respects, it looks like the earth. A model of an atomic submarine is a replica model because it looks like the real thing. Replica models are material models; they are, in short, tangible. Very often a replica model is made with a change in spatial or temporal scale. A replica model of the earth is smaller than the earth itself; a replica model of the atomic structure of uranium, on the other hand, is larger.

Symbolic models are intangible in the sense that they make use of ideas, concepts, and abstract symbols to represent the objects being

---

[5] B. J. Underwood, *Psychological Research* (New York: Appleton-Century-Crofts, 1957), p. 257.

FIGURE 50–1

A Symbolic Model of a Closed-Loop Tracking System

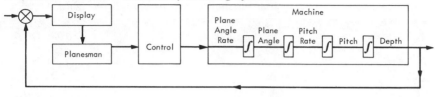

modeled. The model of man in a closed-loop tracking system (Figure 50–1) is a symbolic model. The model does not look at all like the real thing. Instead, lines and arrows are used to symbolize, by analogy, the flow of information from one element in the system to another. The major elements of the system are symbolized by blocks, and the movement of the vehicle itself (a submarine in this case) through a fluid medium is symbolized by mathematical symbols, integral signs. As should be apparent, mathematical models form a subclass of symbolic models.

Models may, of course, be mixed, that is, combine both replica and symbolic features. As a model of the earth, a globe is a replica model to the extent that it is spherical in shape and that the land and water masses are correctly scaled on the surface of the model. But a globe contains symbolic features because, for example, color codes are used to represent the depths of the oceans and the heights of land masses.

Some Things That Are and Are Not Models. With these definitions before us, we can see that some things which are not called models in human engineering work could properly be so classified. Many types of displays, for example, clearly fall in this category. Figure 50–2 shows the gas recovery and fractionating unit in a modern oil refinery, and Figure 50–3 the graphic panel in the control house from which the operation of the entire refinery unit is monitored and controlled. This graphic panel is a true *visual display* in the human engineering sense of the word, but it is also a *model* in our present sense of the word. The panel models or represents the major pieces of equipment in the refinery unit, the direction of flow of hydrocarbons in the interconnecting pipes, and state (temperature, pressure, and rate of flow) of the process at various points. Although the panel contains both replica and symbolic features, the latter predominate.

Some other things which we find commonly in human engineering work are mock-ups, simulators, mannikins, and training devices. All are properly models, according to my way of thinking. That these essential identities are recognized in some other places is shown by the following quotation, which I have extracted from Paragraph 3.4.5 of Signal Corps Technical Requirement SCL-1787A, "Human Factors Engineering for Signal Corps Systems and Equipment" (13 April 1959): "Mock-ups shall

FIGURE 50–2

The Gas Recovery and Fractionating Unit in a Modern Oil Refinery (The operation is controlled automatically by instruments in the control house, lower right.)

be employed wherever essential to detail a human task or work-space layout. Mock-ups may vary from mathematic models to simple drawings of appropriate scale to three-dimensional simulators. . . ."

On Models versus Theories.   There is also, it seems to me, much confusion between models and things which a short while ago were more often referred to as generalizations, hypotheses, and theories. In part this situation probably arises because the word theory has so many different connotations.[6] Still there is an essential difference between theory and model, and it is well to keep this distinction in mind.

A model is an analogy and no one expects an analogy to be completely accurate. When we use an electronic computer as a model for the brain, we obviously do not mean that our heads are full of transistors, wires,

---

[6] See, for example, the fine discussion on this question by E. G. Boring, "The Role of Theory in Experimental Psychology," *American Journal of Psychology* 66 (1953): 169–84.

FIGURE 50-3

The Major Pieces of Equipment in the Refinery Illustrated in Figure 50-2 Are Represented on This Graphic Panel in the Control House

Courtesy of the Humble Oil and Refining Company.

soldered connections, and magnetic cores. Nor do we believe for a moment that nerve impulses in the brain travel with the speed of electrical impulses in the computer. Neither do we grant that nerve spikes look like or have the manufactured precision of electrical potentials emanating from a power supply. With a model it is not even important that any of these conditions be true, for a model can tolerate a considerable amount of slop. It is only an analogy, a statement that in some ways the thing modeled behaves "like this." Modeling is playing a kind of child's game— a grown-up sophisticated version of a child's game, to be sure, but a game nevertheless. The game is called "make believe."

Theory, on the other hand, is a conceptual system which attempts to describe the real thing. The basic elements, or pieces, of a theory are actually supposed to be there in the thing about which you are theorizing and they are supposed to behave the way the theory says. Whereas a model can tolerate some facts which are clearly not in accord with it, facts which do not agree with theory are fatal to the theory.

What Good Are Models?

Enough now of definition. What good are models? Models, I think, serve a number of useful functions.

Models describe and help us to understand complex systems or events. First and foremost, models describe complex systems or events in simple terms so that we can more easily understand them. They do this essentially by replacing intricate and complex systems with simpler and more familiar analogies. In this role models are indispensable teaching-aids at every level of instruction from the nursery school through the university. In fact, this use of models is so commonplace and so well accepted that we can easily lose sight of it in any systematic treatment of the subject. Let us look quickly at a few examples.

The precise timing and sequence of events which transpire inside an internal combustion engine can be slowed down in a model so that its action becomes readily comprehensible. The movement of the planets in the skies can be speeded up in a model so that years or even centuries are compressed within reach of the human memory span. Models of the human body help the student to see the intricate organization and arrangement of our internal organs. Models of the earth help the student visualize and understand geodetic relationships with a clarity which mere words or symbols cannot hope to match.

We must not get the idea, however, that models are useful only in describing tangible structures and systems. They can also be used to describe theories, concepts, and ideas. A first-rate example of such an application is Broadbent's mechanical model for human attention.[7]

The model consists merely of a Y-shaped tube (Figure 50–4), mounted vertically, and a set of small balls. Each ball has a number so that it can be readily identified. The Y tube has a narrow stem which will just take only one ball, though the branches are wider. At the junction of the stem and branches is a hinged flap which normally hangs straight downward, but which can be pivoted about its upper edge so as to close off either branch of the Y.

In this model the balls represent information from various stimuli. The branching arms represent different sensory channels. For example, one arm might be the eyes, the other the ears. Or one might be one ear, the other the other ear. The bottom of the Y represents a response output, so

---

[7] D. E. Broadbent, "Effects of Noises of High and Low Pitch on Behavior," Medical Research Council Applied Psychology Research Unit Report no. APU 222/54, 1954. Broadbent actually described two models: one for human attention; the other for immediate memory, the latter being a somewhat more complex version of the former. Since both serve the same function, I shall discuss only one of them.

FIGURE 50–4

Broadbent's Model of Human Attention

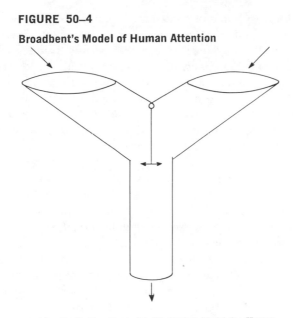

After D. E. Broadbent, "A Mechanical Model for Human Attention and Immediate Memory," *Psychological Review* 64 (1957), 205–15.

that the process of dropping a ball into the arms and observing its emergence at the bottom is analogous to that of delivering a stimulus to some sense organ and observing a response.

The action of this model is, in some ways, analogous to the reception and processing of information from various sense channels. For example, if two balls are dropped simultaneously, one into each of the two branches of the Y, they will jam in the junction and neither will go through. This is similar to what sometimes happens when competing pieces of information arrive simultaneously over two different channels.[8] If, in the model, the hinged flap is used to close off one of the two arms before the balls are dropped, the ball entering the other branch will get through readily. This is roughly comparable to the effect of set introduced by prior instructions in experiments on multichannel listening. To continue, if the two balls are not dropped simultaneously, the first to arrive at the junction will usually push the flap over and emerge successfully. This is similar to what happens when messages do not arrive simultaneously in studies of multichannel listening.[9]

Some of the other experimental findings which can be simulated in this

---

[8] D. E. Broadbent, "Listening to One of Two Synchronous Messages," *Journal of Experimental Psychology* 44 (1952): 51–55; E. C. Poulton, "Two-Channel Listening," *Journal of Experimental Psychology* 46 (1953): 91–96.

[9] W. Spieth, J. F. Curtis, and J. C. Webster, "Responding to One of Two Simultaneous Messages," *Journal of the Acoustics Society of America* 26 (1954): 391–96.

model are the reception and processing of stimuli of different intensities,[10] the reception of information over previously quiet versus previously active channels,[11] the effects of random versus systematic patterns of presentation,[12] and the effects of various speed and load stresses.[13]

Let us summarize now what this model does. First, because it is such a simple mechanical analog it helps us understand Broadbent's theoretical views on information processing.[14] Second, it is a convenient mnemonic device for recalling and integrating the results of a number of related experiments. It is, in short, a kind of crutch to help us understand and to lead us gently into a more formal, rigorous theory of human information processing. Broadbent himself claims no more for the model than this.

Models help us learn complex skills. Closely allied to the above is the use of models, or training devices, for teaching specific skills. Models for this purpose range from extremely simple ones (aircraft silhouettes for recognition training) through enormously complex, full-scale models of submarines, control rooms, aircraft cockpits, or control consoles like those shown in Figure 50–3. The brevity of this section should not be taken to mean that this use of models is relatively unimportant, but rather that it is too well known to merit any extended discussion.

Models provide the framework within which experiments are done. The third role of models is particularly pertinent to engineering psychologists because so much of our research originates from, and is motivated by, real-world problems. What do we do when we do an experiment in engineering psychology? We observe some aspect of man-machine interaction in the real world which looks intriguing and for which we would like to have an empirical answer. We abstract from the real-world situation those variables, independent and dependent, which seem relevant, and design an experiment accordingly.[15] Sometimes we may even say that we "simulate" the real world in the laboratory; at other times we

---

[10] D. E. Berlyne, "Stimulus Intensity and Attention in Relation to Learning Theory," *Quarterly Journal of Experimental Psychology* 2 (1950): 71–75; D. E. Broadbent, "Effects of Noises of High and Low Pitch on Behavior," Medical Research Council Applied Psychology Research Unit Report no. APU 222/54, 1954.

[11] R. Hyman, "Stimulus Information as a Determinant of Reaction Time," *Journal of Experimental Psychology* 45 (1953): 188–96; E. C. Poulton, "Listening to Overlapping Calls," *Journal of Experimental Psychology* 52 (1956): 334–39.

[12] J. C. Webster and P. O. Thompson, "Some Audio Considerations in Air Control Towers," *Journal of the Audio Engineering Society* 1 (1953): 171–75.

[13] R. Conrad, "Speed and Load Stress in a Sensori-Motor Skill," *British Journal of Industrial Medicine* 8 (1951): 1–7; J. F. Mackworth and N. H. Mackworth, "The Overlapping of Signals for Decisions," *American Journal of Psychology* 69 (1956): 26–47.

[14] In essence, Broadbent feels that the human perceptual system has such a limited capacity that a selective operation is to make efficient use of the nervous system by selecting inputs which have much in common, that is, inputs which contribute little new information. The way in which selections are made depends in part on the organism and in part on the input (physical intensity, earliness in time, absence of recent inputs to the channel, rate and patterns of arrivals, and so on.)

[15] A. Rosenblueth and N. Wiener, "The Role of Models in Science," *Philosophy and Science* 12 (1945): 316–21.

FIGURE 50–5

A Symbolic Model of a Communication System

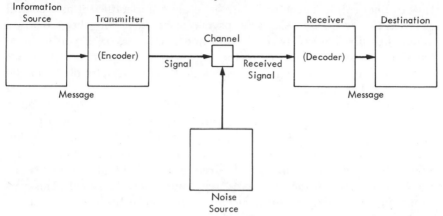

may say that we use "simulators" in our laboratory experiment. What-ever we say, however, there can be no doubt about one thing: our ex-perimental situation is a model of the real world. To a considerable extent the generality of our experimental findings depends on the fidelity of the model we have made of the real world.

Experiments as models differ from most other kinds of models in at least one important respect. The conclusions drawn from most ordinary models are arrived at by mathematical argument, by the application of formal rules of logic, or by somewhat less rigorous forms of reasoning. The conclusions are *deduced* from the basic concepts, assumptions, rela-tionships, and principles built into the model. It is a tautological tech-nique, because we can get out of the model only what we have already put into it. The conclusions follow inexorably from, and contain no more information than, what we have already put into the model. I like to think of it as something like asking a multiple-choice question. The answer you get is already contained in the question.

When we use experiments as models, however, we interrogate nature for her conclusions. We ask an open-ended question and the answers we can get are almost unlimited in variety.

Models help us to see new relationships. Consider the impact of the information model on psychology (Figure 50–5). Why has this model had such an influence on contemporary psychology? Is it because we have never had a model like this before? Not at all. Go back to some old textbooks in psychology, before communication theory was born, and you will find diagrams like the one in Figure 50–5. To be sure you will have to cross out the words in Figure 50–5, and substitute words like stimulus, receptor, nerve cell, effector, and response. But the diagram, the model, is an old one in psychology. Psychologists have been concerned about the way our sense cells encode information for thousands of years. Although they did not call it "encoding," they have always identified it as a central problem in psychology. Similarly, psychologists have long been worried about the correlation between stimuli and responses, or, if you want to translate this into faddish terms, the information transmitted from input to output. No, I think we have to conclude that the novelty of the model is not what has made it so important.

The real reason for the impact of this model on psychology is that it made us see some old problems in new ways. When information theory was developed and applied to switching networks and to communication systems, it turned out that there was something called channel capacity which described the amount of error-free information that could be transmitted over a wire, the air waves, or along a carrier signal. This was something which happened in machines. But since the human operator could be squeezed into the same pattern, an interesting question immediately popped into a lot of heads: "Maybe this channel capacity which we find in machines—maybe there's something like that in people too." And, as you know, this idea has generated a lot of informative research. The idea of the measure of information itself, the idea that information was somehow related to the number of possible alternatives, the concept of redundancy—all these came with the model when we borrowed it from the engineers and draped it around our own shoulders.

Models help us predict when experiments are impossible. Another important use of models is to enable the engineer or investigator to make predictions about complex events when experimentation is either difficult or impossible. This may happen for any of a number of reasons. Sometimes the events are so complicated that it would be prohibitively expensive to conduct an experiment. A good example would be attempts to test alternative methods of organizing a manufacturing plant. To use rigorous methods of controlled experimentation for such a problem might well exhaust the financial resources of the company.

Models assist in engineering design. Models are also extremely useful in many other types of practical design problems. In studying the efficient arrangement of men and machines in specialized work areas (Figure 50–6), models and mock-ups help the designer visualize how the final ensemble will look. Such three-dimensional models are much more powerful than drawings or symbolic representations. Many serious design errors are detected by three-dimensional models even after blueprints and plans have been thoroughly checked and approved.

Models amuse us. To evaluate properly the role of models in scientific and engineering work, the final thing we must do is to recognize clearly that one of the reasons why scientists and engineers spend so much time with them is that they are fun. They are fun to design, fun to build, and fun to look at.

FIGURE 50–6

A Replica Model of a Radar Installation Used to Study the Arrangement of Men and Machines

Some Dangers in the Use of Models

For all of their usefulness, models are subject to some extremely important sources of error. Indeed, we should even go further than this and say: *Because* models are so useful in engineering and scientific work it is especially important that we recognize clearly what their limitations are. Only in this way can we avoid being trapped or misled into danger-ous and fallacious conclusions. Models have so many limitations that it is difficult to know how to classify them. For purposes of exposition, how-ever, I have assembled them under the following headings:

Models invite overgeneralization. In my opinion the worst error com-mitted in the name of models is to forget that at best a model represents only a *part*—and usually only a small part—of the thing being modeled. There is an almost universal tendency to suppose that a model, once it is built or formulated, is more than it is.. This shows up in many ways. In certain superficial ways the behavior of an electronic digital computer is something like that of the brain. Once we admit so much, the next step is easy. We forget that this is only an analogy and we lapse quickly into calling the computer a "brain." The next step is equally easy. Now we find ourselves saying, and, I am afraid, believing, that the computer *is* a brain. This is just so much rubbish! A computer is no more a brain than the Palomar telescope is an eye, or a bulldozer a muscle.

Models of the human operator can be convenient and useful. But we must remember that any replica or symbolic model of the human operator is at best a coarse and crude approximation of the real thing. The only reasonably accurate model of a human operator is another human operator. Even then everything we have learned as psychologists warns us that one person is not a good model for another unless the two are identical twins.

It is a difficult thing not to be wafted into a distorted world of illusion and hallucination by the heady and intoxicating fragrance of that magic word—model. My antidote is a simple one. Whenever anyone uses the word *model*, I replace it with the word *analogy*. The result is something like a breath of fresh air, or a cold shower, or some strong black coffee, in clearing the murky cobwebs from the discussion. Try it.

The relationships between variables may be incorrect. Another reason why models may be in error follows directly from what I have said above. It is that one or more of the functional relationships assumed to hold between critical variables in the model may be incorrect, that is, relationships in the model may not conform to those which actually exist in the object or event being modeled. This danger is one to which models of man are, I think, particularly prone. It is easy to be misled about the way variables are connected in human behavior, even when logic and common sense seem to be on your side.[16]

Models are too often not validated. Another very serious criticism which can be leveled against many models is that they are not validated, or. if attempts are made to validate them, the procedures used are scientifically valueless. This is not so much a criticism of the models themselves as it is a criticism of the model builders. I am sometimes frankly appalled by the faith which some model builders have in their own powers of analytical and synthetic reasoning when it comes to making models of human behavior. Those of us who have been in the business of human engineering for any length of time can point to any number of instances of poor human engineering design which originated in somebody's carefully reasoned, logical analysis of a work situation. I will state my bias on this score in no uncertain terms: I will gladly exchange 100 well-informed guesses at any time for the results of one carefully executed experiment.

---

[16] A. Chapanis, *Research Techniques in Human Engineering* (Baltimore, Md.: Johns Hopkins Press, 1959), p. 5 f.

Even when we find model builders attempting to make some validation of their models, we sometimes find them using as scientific evidence the crudest form of observations collected under completely uncontrolled conditions. It is as though the Hawthorne experiments had never occurred! [17] Let us take one real example. Once upon a time the problem of traffic delays at toll booths was tackled by some operations-research people. They constructed a mathematical model, added it, multiplied it, integrated it, differentiated it, and came out with some conclusions about how the toll booths should be manned and operated. Then came the critical part. Is the model any good? Let us take the author's own words: "The only way to find out was to try it. If it worked continuously for a week, it should be able to work indefinitely." They installed the new system at a toll-collecting site and measured traffic flow and some other things for one week. Although the operation of the new system did not conform entirely to expectations, there is no doubt that during that week conditions were better than they had been previously. So say the authors: ". . . there is a good deal of satisfaction in seeing the validity of so much work actually established." [18] Please understand me. The authors may well have been correct. Their system may indeed have been better. But you will have to agree that this kind of test is *not* a model of scientific inference.

Model building diverts useful energy into nonproductive activity. My final criticism of model building is that the modeler often becomes so intrigued with the formulation of his models that he constructs them for essentially trivial problems. Having at one's disposal a large electronic computing machine, for example, invites one to try out all kinds of things, because computers are such fun to play with. Considering the state of knowledge within psychology, however, the easiest problems to build models for are essentially unimportant problems. If it gives the modeler pleasure, I suppose we should not complain. But it does seem to me sometimes to be such a waste of talent.

So where do we stand now on the question of models? Should we as engineering psychologists model ourselves after our colleagues in operations research? I leave the answer for each of you to decide for himself. My mind is made up.

---

[17] See F. J. Roethlisberger and W. J. Dickson, *Management and the Worker* (Cambridge, Mass.: Harvard University Press, 1939); and especially A. Chapanis, *Research Techniques in Human Engineering* (Baltimore, Md.: Johns Hopkins Press, 1959), pp. 73 f.

[18] C. W. Churchman, R. L. Ackoff, and E. L. Arnoff, *Introduction to Operations Research* (New York: John Wiley & Sons, 1957).

Section Nine
CONSUMER PSYCHOLOGY

INTRODUCTION

In the previous sections we have been discussing human behavior primarily with respect to problems within the working environment. The focus has been on the behavior of two groups of people—employees and managers—and the factors related to their job performance and their roles as producers. The success of an organization, however, is also dependent on the behavior of a third group of people—the consumers of the products and services produced by the enterprise. Ultimately, the organization's profitability and growth depends on the acceptance and marketability of these products and services. The psychologist also has an important role in research related to the welfare and protection of the consumer.

In this section, we will examine how the psychologist applies scientific methods in the effort to understand factors affecting the behavior of individuals in their roles as consumers. The concern here is with human factors in the marketing. distribution, and sales aspects of the enterprise. In particular, we will look at such problems as consumer preferences and attitudes, product testing, advertising effectiveness, and product packaging and pricing.

There are a number of other aspects of the field, such as public opinion polling and sampling methods,[1] techniques of questionnaire construc-

---

[1] See, for example, M. J. Slonim, *Sampling* (New York: Simon and Schuster, 1960); F. J. Stephan and P. J. McCarthy, *Sampling Opinions* (New York: John Wiley & Sons, 1963).

tion and interviewing,[2] and analysis of buying behavior and selling.[3] Also, a comprehensive understanding of consumer behavior should include contributions from a number of disciplines such as sociology and economics [4] as well as from psychology. However, we have chosen to emphasize as the theme of this section, what is, perhaps, the major contribution of psychology to this field—the application of experimental methods in consumer research.

The first article, "Potential Contributions of the Consumer-Oriented Psychologist," by Perloff, serves as an introduction to the field, reviews some historical background, and describes the range of problems of interest to psychologists who study consumer behavior. The article stresses the important role of the industrial psychologist in meshing industry's distribution objectives with consumer needs. In particular, the article discusses the kinds of problems in which the consumer-oriented industrial psychologist might become more involved in the light of current social and technological trends in our society.

When a manufacturer develops a new product, it is important for him to make accurate predictions about its acceptability by consumers who will eventually make decisions about buying or using the product. Moreover, it is desirable to do this as early as possible during the product's development. Marketing a product and waiting for consumer reaction is obviously an expensive and hazardous process. There are of course questions about the size of the potential market, the segment of the population most likely to use the product, aspects of the product that should be changed or emphasized, factors increasing the product's acceptance, and so forth. We will examine some techniques which have been developed to answer such questions.

The Quartermaster Food and Container Institute of the Armed Forces has conducted extensive laboratory and field studies on the acceptance of different foods. Many of the techniques developed there are applicable to a variety of problems in the manufacturing and distribution of consumer goods. Much of this research is carried out in specially built food-acceptance laboratories, with individual booths for each subject. The article by Peryam and Haynes, "Prediction of Food Preferences by Laboratory Methods," describes this program, discusses some issues in such laboratory research, and presents some research illustrating the utility of a laboratory approach.

---

[2] S. L. Payne, *The Art of Asking Questions* (Princeton, N.J.: Princeton University Press, 1951); R. L. Kahn and C. T. Cannell, *The Dynamics of Interviewing* (New York: John Wiley & Sons, 1957); R. L. Gorden, *Interviewing Strategy. Techniques and Tactics* (Homewood, Ill.: Dorsey Press, 1969).

[3] H. C. Cash and W. J. E. Crissy, *The Psychology of Selling*. 4 vols. (New York: Personnel Development Association, 1957–58).

[4] G. Katona, *The Powerful Consumer: Psychological Studies of the American Economy* (New York: McGraw-Hill Book Co., 1960).

Another frequently used method of determining consumer preferences is the consumer panel. Such panels are used for a variety of purposes, including testing reactions to TV programs, testing advertising copy, getting opinions about various products and packages, and taste testing of products. Sometimes such panels are brought together as a group for one or more sessions; sometimes they never meet but are on call for testing a product in their homes; and sometimes they are contacted by telephone or respond by mail. In the case of some TV program analyses, a nation-wide panel may keep diaries of viewing hours or have their dial-setting behavior recorded on small devices attached to the set. The validity of certain of these panels is certainly dependent on many factors, including their representativeness and their ability to make the required discrimina-tions, and on the motivation of panel members. Nevertheless carefully selected panels may be useful for a number of purposes. The article by Fleishman, "An Experimental Consumer Panel Technique," represents an attempt to combine the panel technique with experimental methods. The approach used was one which used behavioral measures of actual brand usage, along with attitudinal preference measures. Another feature of the approach was that it was conducted with consumers in the field, rather than in the laboratory, and that it allowed for the *formation* of prefer ences over a more extended period.

The previous two articles have illustrated the use of rating measures and behavioral measures as indicators of consumer reactions. Another class of measures which has received attention in this field may be termed psychophysiological measures. The assumption here is that meas-ures of autonomic nervous system and circulatory activity such as blood pressure, heart rate, and galvanic skin response are responsive to stimuli which arouse the subject emotionally. (Such effects are, of course, the basis of various "lie detector" tests.) Consequently products and ads with different strengths of appeal may produce measurable variations in such indices. If this were true perhaps a more objective index related to the interest value of an advertisement or package design might be identified. While some positive results have been obtained in which such measures have been evaluated,[5] problems of instrumentation and the difficulty of controlling experimental conditions have not made these procedures feas-ible. And while some relations were established, the methods were not reliable enough to allow the kind of differentiation between stimuli (packages, ads, and so forth) necessary. It has also been difficult to dif-ferentiate pleasant and unpleasant arousal. However, there has recently appeared a new measure which is receiving increasing attention. In "Pu-pil Dilation as a Measure of Consumer Response," Krugman describes work with the pupil response as an index of the interest value of stimuli

---

[5] G. Eckstrand and A. R. Gilliland, "The Psychogalvanometric Method for Measur-ing the Effectiveness of Advertising," *Journal of Applied Psychology* 32 (1948): 415–25.

and shows how this index has been used to predict sales and product preferences.[6]

The next article deals with the problem of evaluating advertising effectiveness.[7] The enormous quantity of money spent annually on advertising has intensified the demand for research assurance that such money is being well spent. A number of different approaches to evaluation of advertising effectiveness have been tried, including recall or recognition methods and liking or preference methods. One type of study investigated changes in product images as a function of an advertising campaign.[8] Other approaches which have been used include eye movement photography and paired-comparison methods to determine which of several advertisements to which an individual has been briefly exposed are most preferred for subsequent viewing.[9] Recently, the use of operant conditioning techniques to determine the "reinforcement value" of various advertisements has received widespread attention as a possible method for determining attention-value and effectiveness of advertisements. In this approach, the subject is required to engage in some activity, such as pumping a foot pedal, in order to receive desired reinforcements. Thus, the rate at which an individual is willing to engage in such activity in order to receive various possible reinforcing stimuli (such as printed advertisements or commercial messages) is taken as an indication of the value or effectiveness of these advertisements. The article by Winters and Wallace, "Operant Conditioning Techniques in Advertising Research," reviews a number of studies which have been conducted using this approach to evaluating advertising effectiveness and concludes that this is a promising method for use in advertising research.

An interesting contribution of experimental psychology to consumer research has been in the application of "psychophysical methods" to a variety of consumer problems. These methods, such as paired comparisons, constant stimulus methods, and scaling techniques, were originally used to determine sensory thresholds to stimuli and to stimulus differences. Companies have used such methods to determine discrimination thresholds for perfumes in soap, syrup in colas, menthol in cigarettes, and so forth. Such information can be very important in *product development* and in the scaling of psychological or perceived properties of products,

---

[6] For a recent review of research on pupil dilation and a somewhat critical evaluation of this method in marketing research, see R. D. Blackwell, J. S. Hensel, and B. Sternthal, "Pupil Dilation: What Does It Measure?" *Journal of Advertising Research* 10 (1970): 4, 15–18.

[7] For a general discussion of this area, see D. B. Lucas and S. H. Britt, *Measuring Advertising Effectiveness* (New York: McGraw-Hill Book Co., 1963); J. J. Wheatley, *Measuring Advertising Effectiveness* (Homewood, Ill.: Richard D. Irwin, Inc., 1969).

[8] W. D. Wells, F. J. Goi, and S. Seader, "A Change in Product Image," *Journal of Applied Psychology* 42 (1958): 120–21.

[9] J. Tiffin and D. M. Winick, "A Comparison of Two Methods of Measuring the Attention-Drawing Power of Magazine Advertisements," *Journal of Applied Psychology* 38 (1954): 272–75.

where it is not possible to use a physical scale such as inches, grams, or foot-candles. Sometimes such "perceptual scales" are actually used in *quality control* of products as a substitute for chemical or physical analysis. Thus, many companies obtain scale values of product qualities as a standard part of their quality control procedure. Sometimes such consumer judgments are used to *match* products off the production line (such as batches of whiskey) against a standard sample of the product. If the match is not within certain limits a check is made on the production process. Such matches also can be made against other brands on the market.[10]

The last article in this section is concerned with the problem of determining the most effective way of presenting weight and price information to consumers in order to enable them to make the most rational purchasing decisions. The growing interest in consumerism in our society has led to an increasing concern by consumer psychologists in studying and understanding factors which lead to rational consumer choices in the marketplace. Thus, recent emphasis on "truth-in-packaging" and "truth-in-lending," for example, raises a number of questions about the most effective method for presenting information about products or services to the consumer. One psychologist [11] investigated the extent to which consumers are actually deceived by packaging practices which present consumers with packages of similar size but which differ in net contents. He found that while consumers were indeed deceived by such packaging practices, they were also subsequently more dissatisfied with packages which contained lesser amounts of the product, suggesting that such deceptive packaging practices may actually tend to lower sales of such products. Other studies by Friedman [12] were concerned with investigating the extent to which consumers were actually able to determine unit prices of various supermarket products as a function of several different methods of presenting price information. His studies concluded that there is considerable confusion in making rational choices of most economical packages of supermarket products, and that dual-pricing practices currently being adopted by many supermarkets would yield substantial reduction in difficulty for rational consumer decision-making. The article by Gatewood and Perloff, "An Experimental Investi-

---

[10] For a description of how such a "yardstick" for a perceived taste quality of a product was developed, and how it was used in product development, see E. A. Fleishman, "The Perceived Menthol Intensity of Different Brands of Menthol Cigarettes," in *Studies in Personnel and Industrial Psychology*, rev. ed., edited by E. A. Fleishman (Homewood, Ill.: Dorsey Press, 1967), 795–801.

[11] J. C. Naylor, "Deceptive Packaging: Are the Deceivers Being Deceived?" *Journal of Applied Psychology* 46 (1962): 393–98.

[12] M. P. Friedman, "Consumer Confusion in the Selection of Supermarket Products," *Journal of Applied Psychology* 50 (1966): 529–34; idem, "Consumer Price Comparisons of Retail Products: The Role of Packaging and Pricing Practices and the Implications for Consumer Legislation," *Journal of Applied Psychology* 56 (1972): 439–46.

gation of Three Methods of Providing Weight and Price Information to Consumers." provides experimental evidence that providing consumers with unit price information produces a significant increase in accuracy of consumer choices while significantly reducing the time required to make such choices, as compared with conventional pricing practices and with use of computational aids by consumers.

SUGGESTED ADDITIONAL READINGS

Aaker, D. A., and Day, G. S.   *Consumerism: Search for the Consumer Interest.* New York: Free Press, 1971.

Britt, S. H., ed.   *Psychological Experiments in Consumer Behavior.* New York: John Wiley & Sons, 1970.

Engel, J. F., Kollat, D. T., and Blackwell, R. D.   *Consumer Behavior.* New York: Holt, Rinehart & Winston, 1968.

Holloway, R. J., Mittelstaedt, R. A., and Venkatesan, M.   *Consumer Behavior: Contemporary Research in Action.* New York: Houghton Mifflin, 1971.

Hughes, G. D.   *Attitude Measurement for Marketing Strategies.* Glenview, Ill.: Scott, Foresman and Co., 1971.

Jacoby, J., Olson, J. C., and Haddoch, R. A.   "Price, Brand Name, and Product Composition Characteristics as Determinants of Perceived Quality." *Journal of Applied Psychology* 55 (1971): 570–579.

Kassarjian, H. H.   "Personality and Consumer Behavior: A Review. *Journal of Marketing Research* 8 (1971): 409–18.

Kassarjian, H. H., and Robertson, T. S., eds.   *Perspectives in Consumer Behavior.* Glenview, Ill.: Scott, Foresman and Co., 1968.

Kollat, D. T., Engel, J. F., and Blackwell, R. D.   "Current Problems in Consumer Behavior Research. *Journal of Marketing Research.* 7 (1970): 327–32.

Robertson, T. S.   *Consumer Behavior.* Glenview, Ill.: Scott, Foresman and Co., 1970.

51. POTENTIAL CONTRIBUTIONS OF THE CONSUMER-ORIENTED PSYCHOLOGIST *

Robert Perloff

THE ACTIVITIES OR OPERATIONS of industry are, simply put, (1) manufacturing or production and (2) distribution and sales. Industrial or applied psychologists have concerned themselves generally with the manufacturing function, including the selection of workers and their training, the adaptation of machines and equipment to the limitations and abilities of their human operators, and the fusion of social and organizational processes with the objectives of business and industry.

These activities, however, are concerned with what goes on behind the counter, with the people who make the product, with how it should be made, with the social and organizational fabric interlacing worker with work.

But what about the public, that body of individuals that is tied in more explicitly with the distribution and sales functions? In the next decade or two, how can we marshal our technological resources to keep pace with, and ourselves add to the state of knowledge of distributing and consuming goods and services, while at the same time benefiting the public? It is to this objective—the industrial psychologist's concern with the consumption function and with the public at large—that this article is addressed.

In particular, we will seek first to trace the contribution that industrial or applied psychologists have made in helping to mesh industry's distribution objectives with the consumer's goals for obtaining production information more efficiently and meaningfully. Next, we will try to sketch the marketing-consumption-behavioral areas where it would be reasonable for behavioral scientists, the business establishment, and the public to expect applied psychologists to be navigating in the next 10 or 15 years.

THE HERITAGE OF CONSUMER PSYCHOLOGY

Contrary to the opinions held by many well-informed people, both inside and beyond the psychological community, consumer-oriented industrial psychologists began to ply their wares in the first quarter of the

---

* From *Business and Society* 4 (1964): 28–34.

20th century, very often paralleling their interests in, and researches among, the allegedly more traditional problems in personnel selection, training, testing, rating methodology, and job satisfaction.

Among the earlier psychologists writing in this field are such men as Hollingworth, Scott, and Starch, discussing the orthodox topics of attention, motivation (the nature of appeals in advertising), and the psychological factors indigenous to successful selling practices.[1] Among the more recent mid-century psychologists engaged in integrating and communicating the substance and method of psychology as it relates to consumer behavior are Hattwick, Hepner, and Lucas and Britt, covering a potpourri of topics, including the mechanical factors present in good and bad advertisements, the nature and interests of media audiences, geographical differences associated with consumer tastes and preferences, techniques for pretesting advertising communications, and understanding individual differences peculiar to the consumption of such nonadvertising products as program content among the broadcast media and the stories, features, and news presentations in newspapers and magazines.[2]

While this dichotomy might well be arbitrary, it would appear as though the industrially or consumer-oriented applied psychologist has interpreted the fundamentals of psychology and himself conducted research in two domains: (1) substantive or clearly behavioral, and (2) technique or methodological.

THE SUBSTANTIVE OR BEHAVIORAL DOMAIN

The substantive or behavioral domain spans the gamut from the significant contributions made by Paterson and Tinker in charting the kinds of typography that attracts attention, is easily read, and is well remembered; [3] through the voluminous and programmatic research conducted by Katona, where the psychological variables of attitude, confidence, level of aspiration, and others, are identified, measured, and integrated into grand economic forecasting schemes; [4] and the clinically oriented approach symbolized as well by Dichter [5] as by any other practitioner, the approach that is commonly designated motivation re-

---

[1] H. L. Hollingworth, *Advertising and Selling* (New York: Appleton, 1913); W. D. Scott, *The Psychology of Advertising* (Boston: Small, Maynard, 1908); and D. Starch, *Principles of Advertising* (Chicago: A. W. Shaw, 1923).

[2] M. S. Hattwick, *How to Use Psychology for Better Advertising* (Englewood Cliffs, N.J.: Prentice-Hall, 1950); H. W. Hepner, *Modern Marketing: Dynamics and Management* 3d ed. (New York: McGraw-Hill Book Co., 1955); and D. B. Lucas and S. H. Britt, *Advertising Psychology and Research* (New York: McGraw-Hill Book Co., 1950).

[3] D. G. Paterson and M. A. Tinker, *How to Make Type Readable* (New York: Harper & Row, 1940).

[4] G. Katona, *The Powerful Consumer: Psychological Studies of the American Economy* (New York: McGraw-Hill Book Co., 1960).

[5] E. Dichter, "Psychology in Market Research," *Harvard Business Review* 25 (1947): 432–43.

search, utilizing projective techniques, depth interviewing, and psychoanalytically slanted efforts to understand the "real" reasons underlying the individual's seemingly inscrutable behavior.

In this rubric, too, should be included the multitude of distinct and continuous studies sponsored by government agencies such as the U.S. Army's Quartermaster Research and Engineering Command in Natick, Massachusetts, by the handful of academicians engaged in this kind of research, and by manufacturers, advertising agencies, and the advertising media. Many of these research enterprises deal with might be called man-product systems, that is, the achievement of some harmony of product development and package design with the consumer's sensory and esthetic tastes, or with problems involving buying intentions, or with demographic factors describing the various audiences of communications media. Studies like these have been of incalculable value for determining the psychological characteristics of purchasers and markets, production schedules, inventory controls, guides in the matter of reader or viewer interests, and parameters of audition, gustation, olfaction, and vision relevant to consumer behavior.

Therefore, it would seem to be fairly evident that industrial psychology's heritage substantively or behaviorally is more than an adequate springboard for continuing to make contributions in the decades ahead.

TECHNIQUE OR METHODOLOGICAL DOMAIN

The technique or methodological contributions of the psychologist to consumer understanding and betterment have been patently enormous. We include here questionnaire and instrument construction,[6] identification and content of interviewer bias, scaling techniques, and a veritable storehouse of apparatus, including the tachistoscope and eye cameras.[7]

In the last dozen years, too, scores of applications have been made of now standard psychometric developments such as the semantic differential used for measuring product and corporate images,[8] and factor analytic as well as other data reduction techniques directed at probing for basic dimensions and the underlying structures oftentimes obscured by the prodigal multitudes of intercorrelations and other statistical indices.

Even if the industrial psychologist were not to add to these and other available tools and techniques, he would probably have a sufficiently versatile portfolio of techniques and methodologies with which to investi-

---

[6] A. B. Blankenship, *Consumer & Opinion Research* (New York: Harper & Row, 1943); H. H. Remmers, *Introduction to Opinion and Attitude Measurement* (New York: Harper & Row, 1954).

[7] J. S. Karslake, "The Purdue Eye Camera: A Practical Apparatus for Studying the Attention Value of Advertisements," *Journal of Applied Psychology* 24 (1950): 417–40.

[8] C. E. Osgood, G. J. Suci, and P. Tannenbaum, *The Measurement of Meaning* (Urbana: University of Illinois Press, 1957).

gate hundreds of new and important questions concerning the consumer and his marketplace behavior.

DIRECTIONS FOR CONSUMER PSYCHOLOGY

Where might this heritage of consumer behavior research and methodological achievements logically lead the industrial psychologist? There are three platforms from which one can proceed to help assure for industrial psychology a profitable berth in industry, a respected acceptance by society and consumers, and perhaps even an honored niche in the family of science. These platforms or new directions are. (1) the scientific and technological, (2) the social and psychological, and (3) the consumer qua consumer.

The Scientific-Technological Direction

First, let us look at the scientific and technological milieu and its implications for the industrial psychologist's contributions to his employer and the public, via consumer-oriented channels. For example:

a) Advances in hardware-telemetering devices. For example: If a man's physiological changes during an orbital flight are recorded instrumentally on earth, it is possible certainly to record practically the full spectrum of physiological measures of individuals while they are watching television or reading the newspaper, while listening to an experimental sterephonic recording of Bach, while driving an automobile over a treacherously safe turnpike, or while scanning the canned goods on the shelves of supermarkets. Hence we are no longer justified in making that once comfortable retreat from our responsibilities by saying that consumer behaviors during the process of consumption are incapable of being observed.

In a word, we are now able to allow the experimental subject, say a consumer, to behave more or less naturally, in his consumer habitat or environment, shaving with a new or an experimental electric shaver or being swooshed in a rocket-like elevator to the heights of a new skyscraper—while in the researcher's control room, possibly miles away, the consumer's pulse rate, galvanic skin response, and photographic and other records are being stored. Here is a vast new field of research and service opening up, making possible more valid behavioral influences because implicit in our observations are the operations and behaviors of people as they are manifest in life, not in the artificial and frequently distorted confines of the laboratory.

b) Advances from within psychology, programmed learning. Beyond the implications of programmed learning for industrial training, what is its relevance for the grand area of communications, including advertising and public relations communications, between industry and its various publics? There is mounting evidence, within educational institutions and industrial training programs alike, that information presented systematically, a frame at a time, utilizing the benefits of reinforcement, and allowing the individual to proceed in accordance with his own abilities and readiness to learn, is absorbed and retained with a degree of efficiency equal to or exceeding that achieved using more conventional methods. With appropriate modification. there is no reason, other than indolence, why we cannot program for consumers how to assemble home phonographic systems, or how to maintain in proper working order power mowers (along with keeping intact the individual's fingers and toes while operating the mower), or how to repair punctured plastic kiddie pools.

Programmed instruction is no panacea for the learning process, nor should it be used necessarily in helping the individual learn *all* that needs to be learned, but on the other hand it would be irresponsible for the consumer-directed industrial psychologist to overlook its potentialities for communications with and making more lasting impressions upon the consumer and the public.

c) *Advances in medical science, such as longevity.* There are many things that senior citizens can do with their time besides buying cottages in Florida or subscribing to bigger and better hospital or insurance plans, or feeding the pigeons in the park. Many older people, for instance, are willing and able to eat candy, to buy chic dresses or modish sports jackets, or even to do some skin diving. However, it seems that, like people, psychologists in industry defer to certain antediluvian stereotypes among which is the myth regarding the older person's passivity or frailty or his insufficiency of esthetic and physiological appetites. When we think about this, not to mention look at the data, we are immediately struck by how ridiculous is our exclusion of the older person from these consumer behaviors. It would seem to be apparent, then, that a contribution, not only to the public, but obviously to the marketing interests of industry as well, can and should be made in the direction of considering actively the senior citizen as a consumer for most products and services typically directed to those of us who are less "senior" agewise. Specifically, what I am proposing is that advertising or promotional literature be directed explicitly to the aged as well as to other groups and, too, that wherever this is practicable, products be designed in such a way as to be attractive to and consumable by the aged. Moreover, a munificent byproduct of a more explicit consideration of the older person as a consumer would be his reawakened interest in useful and relaxing ways of spending his time.

The Social-Psychological Direction

Next, let us examine suggestively the social and psychological platform or milieu, and its implications for the industrial psychologist's contributions to his employer and the public, again via consumer-oriented channels.

a) First, the matter of tastes, standards, or values. As our tastes and preferences change, as mores take on new dimensions, the public's needs will assume new forms and it perceptions of industry and its products will become more or less favorable as the way that industry and its products become more or less similar to the modes of the day. I am suggesting, to be concrete, that if beards no longer appear to be viewed as peculiar or affected, then any policies against beards, either in the company's advertising or promotional literature, or in its hiring practices, should be recognized as prejudices to be eradicated. One may say that beards and such matters are trivia over which we should not be concerned. In themselves, perhaps, they may be trivia, but I suspect that they are symptomatic of the moods of the times through which we travel and that some sensitivity to these moods could bring us a step closer in our understanding of the people who make the product and those who buy it and use it. The matter of taste—what people consider to be in good taste or what might be considered offensive—should be explored by the psychologist in industry to a far greater extent than this subject is being probed currently.

To industry, the benefits of such investigations are obvious and possibly staggering. To the public, the benefits of such investigations include principally, not only learning more about this particular component of behavior, but also the results of such studies should direct us to change our characterizations of ourselves and of our products, to be less irritating and more palatable to the public. For instance, in some very preliminary work we are doing there are some emerging suggestions in the data that with respect to taste, males find the advertising of female products more distasteful than they do of male products—and the same thing appears to be true for females; that advertisements featuring human ailments such as itching and hemorrhoids appears to be more offensive to people not afflicted with these conditions than to those who are afflicted; and that claims or representations that insult the intelligence, rather than those that are merely whimsical, may be viewed with more than innocuous disdain.

b) Next, what are the effects on industry's distribution and sales of such sweeping changes in our society as, to name but two, (1) the larger proportion of people attending college, and (2) early marriages? Assuming that there is some positive correlation between education and behavior, industry should begin representing itself more rationally to its publics. Perhaps the policies of a company could be explained in its various pieces of literature more critically and less superficially. The second illustration, early marriages, is rife with implications for the psychologist in industry. One very obvious implication is in the realm of plant-community relations—say in housing, schools, parks, and zoning ordinances. Without going further, the point here is that if industry is unable to anticipate social and psychological changes such as these, it should at least keep up with them.

c) *Next, the problem of disaster management.* In many communities the plant or building occupied by a company or institution is the only large, solid structure, or structures, around for miles. What happens in case of some catastrophe—natural, nuclear, or otherwise? Is there a plan? Do people know where to go? what to do? Is there a procedure for medical aid, for sustenance, for rebuilding? Pessimistic or fatalistic as one might be, the optimal strategy is to have a plan and some sufficiently large shelter to accommodate the employees at least, or perhaps even the entire community if provisions for the community are not available in the municipality.

Now what does the psychologist have to do with disasters? Just this. Modest as he might claim his facts to be, certainly he knows more than others in the organization about the conditions that make for apathy and the conditions needed to transform apathy to action. Moreover, his interest and research in attitude change, leadership, group processes, and allied problems should equip him as well as other scientists to prepare for and handle problems like these. Indeed, the excessively modest psychologist, and perhaps even his skeptical boss, would be well advised to examine the impressive compendium of research findings explicated by Steiner and Berelson.[9]

The Consumer Qua Consumer Direction

It is true, regrettably, that in the half century of industrial psychology's existence, the great preponderance of the industrial psychologist's time, energy, and research product has been directed explicitly to the problems to which *management* has invited his attention. This is true, certainly, for the industrial psychologist's ancient infatuation with personnel research—selection, training, job analysis, performance evaluation, and worker morale; but it is perhaps more disturbingly and nakedly manifest for the industrial psychologist concerned with consumer research in general and advertising research in particular. This is not to say that the psychologist has not benefited the makers or the consumers of the nation's goods. It is axiomatic, for instance, that the worker who is fit for his job or whose performance is accurately assayed is a happier person. Similarly, the consumer whose attention is directed to a new product is, presumably, a more satisfied individual. *Implicitly,* then, it can be safely claimed that the individual in our society has been helped, albeit indirectly, by the industrial psychologist's efforts.

---

[9] G. A. Steiner and B. Berelson, *Human Behavior: An Inventory of Scientific Findings* (New York: Harcourt, Brace & World, 1964).

Consumer benefits like these, however, would doubtlessly be multiplied if the psychologist should seek *directly and explicitly* to serve the consumer's needs, to study the consumer qua consumer, as it were, not as an individual whose attention and purchasing behavior are coveted to serve ends, the propriety and the economic value of these ends notwithstanding, determined by advertising and the mass media.

What I would like to propose, therefore, is that a relatively new frontier the industrial psychologist might scout would be that in which he seeks to study the consumer for the sake of understanding consumer behavior because consumer behavior is scientifically important on the one hand, and is relevant to helping the consumer derive greater satisfaction and pleasure from the products and services he consumes, on the other.

If the industrial psychologist were to adopt this posture, I daresay that many positive outcomes would likely appear. For one, the consumer would be better educated, better informed, with respect to the items he desires. He would be more critical, more judicious, more efficient in selecting, using, and maintaining his articles of consumption. He might well cut fewer fingers in opening cans, lose his temper less often as a consequence of automatically reaching in the store for one product but inadvertently taking another with inexcusably similar shape and design, place in the closet fewer "educational" games because of inscrutable and therefore psychologically threatening directions, and perhaps, above all, make wiser decisions in spending his dollars, decisions harmonious more with his needs and life style than exclusively deferent to the goals of advertisers and the mass media.

THE CONSUMER RENAISSANCE

How might this consumer renaissance come about? Industrial psychologists could pursue with vigor and purpose employment or consulting opportunities with consumer "protection" organizations, including the product testing groups and publications, and government agencies. With regard to government agencies, it is entirely likely that a new era of employment opportunity for the psychologist when President Johnson created the position of a special presidential assistant for consumer affairs.

Industrial psychologists might become more receptive to, and inquisitive about, opportunities for employment with or consulting for the labor unions, where they could possibly perform research directed at understanding more systematically, and communicating this understanding to the union member for his betterment as a consumer, the parameters of preferential and other consumer behavior.

Because consumption is so broad a concept it must and indeed does encompass many possibly surprising "products" and "services," including leisure time activities, travel, museum peregrinations, tours through cities being visited, and the like. What is being suggested here is that these ways of spending time and money could well be exposed to scholarly examination undertaken as much to understand better the whims and foibles of homo sapiens as to help man ensconce himself in the interstices of the changing technology and social structure characterizing the autumn of the 20th century.

In conclusion, I have tried to sketch a few of the kinds of contributions the consumer-oriented industrial psychologist has the capacity to make, stemming from the technological and the social frameworks in which he will be operating in the years ahead. Although these contributions may require some innovative behavior, even risks here and there, the outcomes should be of immense value not only to industry, but rewarding to the industrial psychologist as a scientist and a man.

52. PREDICTION OF FOOD PREFERENCES BY LABORATORY METHODS *

David R. Peryam and John G. Haynes

PREDICTION OF THE ACCEPTABILITY OF FOODS to potential consumers has become an important problem to the food industries in recent years, and is perhaps even more important in planning military feeding. The success of a commercial product may depend on the preferences of a loyal minority, but military rations must take into account those of the entire population of servicemen. The final criterion of the acceptability of foods must be that of consumption, but there are techniques of assessing acceptability besides the obviously valid one of recording eating behavior in the normal situation. The most common, the most efficient, and probably the most reliable is to measure the verbally expressed affective responses of a sample of consumers, and from these measurements establish the positions of various food items on some continuum from which acceptance behavior may be inferred.

Before this method can be used effectively, certain questions must be answered. What task should be set for the consumer subjects? What kind of experimental situations will call forth responses which are valid for predicting acceptance? Such problems are particularly important to the armed services. Military consumers are a fairly homogeneous group, but the conditions under which rations are used vary widely. Many military

* From "Prediction of Soldier's Food Preferences by Laboratory Methods," *Journal of Applied Psychology* 41 (1957): 2–6. Copyright 1957 by the American Psychological Association. Reprinted by permission.

feeding situations are totally inaccessible for conducting tests on foods, and others offer varying degrees of difficulty. The various types of pre-testing that are used by the Quartermaster Corps may be conveniently classified according to whether testing is done in "artificial" or "natural" situations. The "artificial" situations include (a) laboratory testing under controlled conditions using civilian subjects and (b) soldier-consumer panel testing at military posts using laboratory-like procedures. The "natural" situations include (a) normal mess-hall feeding, (b) planned test exercises where rations are used by selected groups of soldiers, and (c) regular field maneuvers where rations are used under nontest conditions.

The relative value of these approaches will depend upon the criteria by which they are judged. If one demands experimental control, or is particularly concerned about economy of testing, the "artificial" situations have the advantage. However, if attention is concentrated primarily on test validity, the "natural" situations are superior, sincce one is entitled to assume that results become more valid as the test situation more closely approximates the actual conditions of consumption, granting, of course, that the test population is always a good sample of the population of interest. The laboratory method is the one most used by the Quarter-master Corps. Important decisions as to the selection or rejection of items are frequently made on the basis of laboratory results alone. How-ever, there has been a tendency to distrust laboratory results and to require additional testing in the field. It became apparent that the lack of knowledge of the true value of the various types of pretesting, and of relationships among them, was retarding the ration-development program and making it unduly expensive. The experiment reported here represented the initial phase of a program of research planned to remedy the situation.

The test subject variable was selected for first investigation since it represented one of the most obvious differences between laboratory tests and any field test conducted with service personnel. The problem may be stated as follows: How well do the relative preference ratings of foods by groups of soldiers correspond with ratings by groups of civilians when the test situations are made to correspond as closely as possible? Referring to the classification scheme above, this represented comparison of the laboratory and soldier-consumer panel situations.

PROCEDURE

The laboratory tests were conducted at the Quartermaster Food and Container Institute in the food-acceptance laboratory, which is especially built for running sensory tests on foods. It is secluded, air-conditioned, and comfortable. Test subjects sit in panel booths separated from the food preparation room. Soldier-consumer panel tests were run at Fort Lee,

Virginia, in a dining hall which was made available between regular meals for that purpose.

The 12 test foods (see Table 52–3) were selected so that distinctly different types would be reprsented and so that their preference ratings, as established in previous laboratory tests, would cover a wide range. Food materials for the two locations were drawn from a common source and methods of preparation were controlled to assure identity. Other controllable physical factors, such as the holding time before serving and the size of samples, were standardized at the two test locations. Time of testing in relation to regular mealtimes was made comparable.

Preference was measured by means of a 9-interval rating scale, commonly known as the "hedonic scale," which was developed at the Quartermaster Food and Container Institute in 1949 [1] and has been used extensively with satisfactory results.[2] The questionnaire used at Fort Lee was headed by these instructions:

We want to find out how well certain foods are liked by Army men. You will be served three samples of food, one after another. As soon as you finish each, show how much you liked or disliked it by marking on the scale underneath the name of that food. Then have a drink of water and wait for the next sample. Please do not talk about the foods during the test. It is important to have each man give his own answers—peoples' likes and dislikes are expected to be different.

Three vertically oriented scales were arranged across the page below the instructions. Each was about five inches long with nine equally spaced intervals labeled with the following phrases, reading from top to bottom: "like extremely," "like very much," "like moderately," "like slightly," "neither like nor dislike," "dislike slightly," "dislike moderately," "dislike very much," "dislike extremely." The appropriate food name was rubber-stamped above each scale prior to testing. The form used at the institute was identical except that the instructions were omitted since most of the institute subjects were already familiar with the method. New subjects were given oral instructions. None of the Fort Lee subjects had ever participated in a test of this kind before.

It was not feasible to serve all 12 foods to one person at a single sitting. Experience has shown that if the number of foods is not strictly limited, the ratings of those served later may be affected, usually showing a decrement. Therefore, only three foods were presented to each subject in each test session, so that four sessions were required to test one replication

---

[1] D. R. Peryam and N. F. Girardot, "Advanced Taste Test Method," *Food Engineering* 194 (1952): 48–61.

[2] D. R. Peryam, "Field Testing of Armed Forces Rations," in *Food Acceptance Testing Methodology: A Symposium*, ed. D. R. Peryam, F. J. Pilgrim, and M. S. Peterson (Washington, D.C.: National Research Council, Advisory Board on Quartermaster Research and Development, 1954), pp. 75–85; K. R. Wood and D. R. Peryam, "Preliminary Analysis of Five Food Preference Surveys," *Food Technology* 6 (1953): 248–49.

of the 12 foods. Combinations of foods were established for four replications in such a way that no two foods appeared together more than once. Four replicates were run at Fort Lee, but only replicates one and two at the institute.

Forty persons participated in each session at the institute. They were selected each time from a pool of approximately 600 employees of the Chicago Quartermaster Depot by a standard procedure designed to obtain widespread participation. Most test subjects participated in only one session and none in more than two. Fifty soldiers participated in each Fort Lee session, each group being drawn from a different company. Selection within companies was not random since a small number of men were always unavailable for administrative reasons. Thus, there was not strict assurance that the groups were representative of the Army; on the other hand, no reason was known why their food preferences should have differed from those of the Army in general.

The institute test subjects came to the laboratory in small groups. Each was given a questionnaire, with additional verbal instructions for those people who were new. They were seated in the panel booths and the three test items were presented one at a time in random order. At Fort Lee all 50 men were brought into the dining hall at the same time. They were seated two at a table, where places had been prepared with questionnaires, water, and necessary utensils, and were briefed by the test monitor before beginning the test. Again, the food items were served one at a time in random order.

RESULTS AND DISCUSSION

The index of preference used here was that derived by assigning the values one to nine to the scale categories, beginning at the "dislike extremely" end, and taking the mean of the resulting distribution of values. The mean rating and standard deviation were obtained for each food in each replicate. Thus there were six sets of ratings—four from Fort Lee and two from the institute.

Product-moment correlations between sets of ratings for the 12 foods were obtained for all possible pairings of individual laboratory and field replicates and also between sets of ratings obtained by combining ratings from the individual replicates. These correlations, which are predictive validity coefficients in light of the purpose of the experiment, are shown in Table 52–1. (All of the correlations are positive.) Minimum validity is represented by the eight correlations grouped together in the upper left-hand corner of the table which were derived from the sets of ratings from single replicates. The remaining correlations all involve combinations of ratings from more than one replicate and demonstrate the expected improvement with increased length of test.

The correlation between averages of the 200 field ratings and 80

TABLE 52–1

Correlations between Field and Laboratory Mean Ratings for Single Replicates and Mean Ratings Based on Combined Replicates (N = 50 for field replicate; N = 40 for laboratory replicate; all correlations positive)

		Field	*Labora-tory Repli-cate 1*	*Labora-tory Repli-cate 2*	*Labora-tory Repli-cates 1 & 2*
Single replicate	1	.88	.88	.90
	2	.92	.92	.95
	3	.84	.78	.87
	4	.80	.82	.83
Combined replicates	1 & 2	.91	.89	.92
	3 & 4	.99	.85	.86
	1, 2, 3 & 4	.86	.86	.92

Note: Average (Fisher's hyperbolic arc-tangent transformation method) of eight correlations between single replicates is .86.

laboratory ratings was +.92. An equation expressing the relaitonship may be written as follows:

$$Y \text{ (field)} = 1.23 \ X \text{ (lab)} - 2.30.$$

The assumption of linearity may be an oversimplification, subject to change on the basis of more extensive investigation; however, it seemed most appropriate for the present data. A scatter diagram of the data did not justify any other assumption.

The above equation suggests that the two groups of subjects were responding differently in ways that affected both level of rating and units of discrimination. The grand mean over all foods for the laboratory was 6.43 as compared to 5.61 for the field, while the respective ranges of means were 4.81 and 5.82 (Table 52–3). It is apparent that the soldiers responded to the low-preference foods with more frequent and intense "dislike." The soldiers' comments written on the questionnaires gave further evidence of this tendency to respond more strongly and with fewer inhibitions than the typical laboratory subject, and suggested the possibility of differences in attitude toward the test situation as well as differences in attitude toward the foods. In spite of this, however, the high correlation shows that differences between foods produced differences in evaluation behavior that were proportional for the two groups of subjects.

Although secondary to validity in this experiment, test reliability was also considered. The "intralocation" correlations between sets of ratings provided a single estimate of laboratory reliability and six estimates of field reliability (Table 52–2). It was expected a priori that the laboratory

TABLE 52–2

Intercorrelations among the Four Field Replicates
(N = 50; all correlations are positive)

	Replicate 1	Replicate 2	Replicate 3
Replicate 2. 95		–	–
Replicate 3. 94	.92		–
Replicate 4. 96	.80	.91	

Note: Average (Fisher's hyperbolic arc-tangent transformation method) is .93.

results would be more reliable because of better control in the laboratory situation. The laboratory correlation was .84 while the average field correlation was .93; however, only one intralaboratory correlation was obtained and this figure may not have been generally representative. The Spearman-Brown prophecy formula shows that to obtain a reliability comparable to that in the field, the number of laboratory subjects would have to be increased only from 40 to 120, that is, considerably fewer than the 200 actually used in the field.[3]

Another aspect of reliability is presented in Table 52–3 which gives the standard error of the mean (SE_m) for each food. Two figures are shown for the laboratory. Column 2 gives the actual value obtained from the distribution of 80 laboratory ratings and Column 3 projects this figure to $N = 200$, assuming no change in variance. For 10 of the 12 foods the projected laboratory SE_m is lower than the field SE_m, which indicates that a laboratory retest should reproduce its numerical indices more accurately than a field retest. This further suggests that the field reliability coefficients were higher because of the larger N and the greater range of the scale utilized in the field and not because the rating of each food was more precisely located on the scale.

Since the results reported here were based on the testing of only a small number of foods selected from the hundreds of items which may be of concern in military feeding, the possible effects of selection bias should be considered. The fact that the foods were not randomly selected detracts from the general applicability of the findings. Consumers tend to like, rather than dislike, the great majority of items that are available for use in military as well as civilian feeding. In the present experiment the test foods were selected to cover a wide range of preference; hence, there was considerably more loading with low-preference foods than would have been the case had the items been randomly selected. At the same time, use of the wider range of the scale should have improved the correlation. However, another factor in the present experiment would have tended to

[3] H. Gulliksen, *Theory of Mental Tests* (New York: John Wiley & Sons, 1950).

TABLE 52–3

Mean Preference Ratings and Standard Errors of the Mean for Laboratory and Field

	Laboratory*			Field**		
	Actual		Projected			Differ-
Food	$\bar{X}$	SEm	SE$_m$***	$\bar{X}$	SEm	ences****
Peaches.	8.43	.066	.042	8.23	.047	.005
Salmon	8.08	.091	.058	7.12	.111	.053
Corn	7.14	.144	.091	7.38	.086	−.005
Corned beef	7.02	.159	.100	6.02	.144	.044
Ham and eggs	6.88	.175	.111	6.40	.140	.029
Bread	6.75	.154	.097	6.50	.139	.042
Carrots	6.66	.177	.088	4.54	.164	.076
Sauerkraut	6.31	.236	.149	6.18	.151	.002
Cheese bar	5.69	.223	.141	3.48	.156	.015
Milk	5.46	.186	.118	4.68	.178	.060
Cabbage	5.15	.252	.159	4.26	.168	.009
Meat bar	3.62	.230	.145	2.46	.130	−.015
Grand mean	6.43			5.61		
Range of means	4.81			5.82		

* Combined data for two laboratory replicates, $N = 80$.
** Combined data for four field replicates, $N = 200$.
*** Projected to $N = 200$, assuming no change in variance.
**** Field SE_m minus projected laboratory SE_m.

lower, rather than raise the correlation, if we may assume that the probability of finding differences between laboratory and field would increase as the group of test foods became more heterogeneous. The attempt was made to maximize heterogeneity by selecting foods to cover a wide range of food types so that there was greater opportunity for differences to appear than would be the case with random selection of test foods.

Some further limitations on the significance of these results for the ration-testing program should be noted. First, neither group of test subjects was a random sample of a well-defined population. They were merely typical of what might be expected on a continuing basis in the two test situations. Further, only certain ones of the many possible sources of variation between types of pretests were allowed to operate, for example, quite a number of factors which would affect preferences in normal mess-hall feeding may have been entirely disregarded. However, this was deliberately accepted in designing the experiment. The intent was to compare two practical test situations where the two types of subjects could be reached, controlling only in regard to those factors which could be considered incidental, such as the rating scale, the number and combination of samples, and the food materials and their preparation and serving. Test subjects, test location, and certain conditions inseparable from test location varied independently. Under these conditions, representing what is normally attainable, good correlation was established. This both supports the inference that soldiers' food preferences are the same as those of the civilian population and demonstrates the practical equivalence of the two test procedures. The "intra-" and "intersituation" correlations were of the same order, which suggests that any noncorrespondence between test results is just as likely to have been due to unreliability of the basic method as to differences between the subjects or the situations.

These results have very satisfactory implications for the methods of food acceptance evaluation currently being used by the Quartermaster Corps. It has been shown that laboratory ratings for a series of foods will accurately predict relaitve preferences as established by the soldier-consumer panel method. The fact that the validity of neither method for predicting actual food acceptance has been established does not detract from the importance of the finding. It represents significant progress toward rationalization and integration of methods for the pretesting of rations and serves as a sound basis for eliminating much expensive and unnecessary field testing.

CONCLUSIONS

The primary conclusion was a practical and specific one, namely, that pretesting of rations in the institute laboratory may be considered equivalent to pretesting by the soldier-consumer panel method. Corollary conclusions were: (a) both laboratory and field preference ratings have satisfactory reliability and (b) the hedonic scale method is adequate for evaluating food preferences under varying conditions.

53. AN EXPERIMENTAL CONSUMER PANEL TECHNIQUE *

Edwin A. Fleishman

EXPERIMENTAL INVESTIGATIONS of product preferences are often confined to the laboratory situation with a restricted sample or to simple spot tests made in conjunction with consumer surveys. Previous experiments of these types have been made with shaving creams,[1] breads,[2] cigarettes,[3] and cola drinks.[4] In an experiment by the writer, preferences for a product were allowed to develop over a period of time.[5] The study reported here was a further attempt to obtain a larger sample of behavior regarding consumer preferences than usually results from traditional techniques. Moreover, the experimental investigation was conducted at the consumer level, using a panel of families selected from a cross section of a large metropolitan city. The products investigated included six well-known brands of bottled beer.

THE PROBLEM

The purpose of the study was to observe the formation of beer preferences during a 7-day period, under conditions in which all means for identifying the beers except actual brand names were available to the subjects.

---

* From *Journal of Applied Psychology* 35 (1951): 133–35. Copyright 1951 by the American Psychological Association. Reprinted by permission.
    [1] H. Schlosberg, "A Well-Controlled Method of Evaluating Consumers' Goods," *Journal of Applied Psychology* 25 (1941): 401–7.
    [2] D. Katz, "A Study of the Taste of Bread," *Human Factors* 16 (1937): 241–46.
    [3] S. Chase, "Blindfolded You Know the Difference," *New Republic* 55 (1928): 296–98; and R. W. Husband and J. Godfrey, "An Experimental Study of Cigarette Brand Identification," *Journal of Applied Psychology* 18 (1934): 220–23.
    [4] J. G. Jenkins, "An Application of Psychological Techniques to Market Research," *Psychological Bulletin* 33 (1936): 33, 726; N. H. Pronko, and J. W. Bowles, Jr., "Identification of Cola Beverages: First Study," *Journal of Applied Psychology* 32 (1948): 304–12; idem, "Identification of Cola Beverages: A Further Study," ibid., pp. 559–64; idem, "Identification of Cola Beverages: A Final Study," *Journal of Applied Psychology* 33 (1949): 605–8; and N. H. Pronko and D. T. Herman, "Identification of Cola Beverages: Postscript," *Journal of Applied Psychology* 34 (1950): 68–69.
    [5] E. A. Fleishman. "An Experimental Study of Cigarette Preference" (Paper read at the Eastern Psychological Association, Springfield, Mass., April 1949).

THE METHOD

The procedure included: (1) the selection of an unbiased panel of 20 families, (2) supplying them with unlabeled bottles of beer for a seven day period, and (3) observing and recording their preferences during that time.

The Consumer Panel. The panel of beer consumers included families living in different sections of the city. The same proportion of families from each of the four socio-economic groups was included in the sample as is found in the general beer-drinking population of that city.[6] Fifteen percent of the families were Black. In the sample were beer drinkers whose expressed preferences included many different brands. The number of families whose previous preferences included each of the brands in the study was equated.

An important factor in selecting the families (as in all panel techniques) was their availability and their willingness to cooperate. This had been determined during a previous survey by the writer involving 250 respondents. The families within the classifications mentioned above were then selected randomly. The potential subjects were reinterviewed to assure their cooperation and their understanding of the study.

Procedure. The experiment lasted for seven days, during which time the families drank as many bottles of beer as they wanted. The study was conducted during the hot summer months when consumption was at a maximum.

The experimental bottles of beer were provided the families each morning. Each day each home received 48 bottles of beer in blank cases. Included were eight bottles of each of six different brands from which they could choose during the rest of the day. The bottles contained no labels or brand names. Instead, the tops on the bottles of each brand were painted with different colors. Thus, the tops of one brand might all be painted red, the tops of a second brand might all be green, and so on. All beers of the same brand would have tops of the same color on any one day. The subjects were told that the colors would be reassigned to the brands by random selection from day to day. Thus, a brand might or might not have the same color top from one day to the next. The subjects had to make a new set of choices each day as to what they "liked" or "didn't like." The subjects were not told which six brands were included in the experiment. All the bottles were of the same size, shape, and color. The subjects could not distinguish between the brands on the basis of beer

---

[6] E. A. Fleishman. "An Evaluation of Consumers' Beer Preferences," 1949. This study found that the "A" socio-economic group consumed 4.2 percent of the beer sold in this city, the "B" group consumed 7.3 percent, the "C" group 38.1 percent, and the lowest group, "D," consumed 50.4 percent. The panel contained approximately these ratios of families within each socio-economic group. Thus, of the 20 families selected, one was from the "A" group, two from the "B" group, seven from the "C" group, and the remaining ten from the "D" group.

TABLE 53-1

**Absolute and Relative Frequency with Which
Bottles of Each Brand of Beer Were Consumed
During the Seven Day Period**

Brands	Number of Bottles Consumed	Percentage of Total
A...........	625	18.4
B...........	613	17.9
C...........	591	17.4
D...........	566	16.6
E...........	514	15.1
F...........	497	14.6
Total.........	3406	

color. During the study they drank no beer except that provided by the experimenter.

The subjects kept records of the brands they drank (according to the top color) on the check form provided each day. They also expressed their preferences for that day on the space provided on the form. Each day the remaining bottles, bottle caps, and empties were collected, the forms checked against the bottles returned, and the home provided with the next day's supply.

The subjects were provided with more than they needed so that they could have an unrestricted choice of brands. On the weekend they were provided with 12 of each brand instead of the customary 8. During the course of the study frequent follow-up calls were made to insure that instructions were being followed and that there were no misunderstandings. The families were also provided with a set of printed instructions.

The study operated on the basic assumption that the people would drink more of what they liked and tend to avoid more of brands they disliked. Since the colors on the six brands were changed from day to day, a new set of decisions was made each day. The data offer two indices of preference. One includes the differences between the brands in the number of bottles of each consumed during the seven day period. The other is represented in the day by day tabulation of the brands (according to top color) named as preferred by the individuals in the study.

RESULTS

The results show that there were significant differences between brands in the number of bottles of each consumed by the panel of consumers. Table 53–1 presents the total number of bottles of each brand consumed during the 7-day period and the percentage of the total this represents for each brand.

The chi square based on Table 53–1 was 16.7 which is significant be-

TABLE 53–2

**Percentage of Times Each
Brand Was Named as
"Liked Best" during the
Course of the Study**

Brands	Percentage "Liked Best"
A	23.2
C	21.4
B	18.7
D	17.1
E	11.9
F	7.7

yond the .01 level. In other words, there appeared to be real differences in preference for beers, even when the brand names were not known. A more complex analysis, which involved successive elimination of different brands and combinations of brands from the analysis revealed that the majority of the variation was a result of the avoidance of Brands E and F. The differences between the number of bottles of Brands A, B, and C consumed were not significant. Brand D was not prepared significantly more than the last two brands and was not avoided significantly less than the leading three brands in the study.

In addition to drinking most of what they liked, all subjects were requested to write in on the daily record sheet they received, the color of the top on the brand they liked best that day. The number preferring each "color" was tabulated under the appropriate brand each day. Table 53–2 summarizes the proportion of times each brand was named as preferred over the remaining five during the seven days. In all, 327 choices were made.

The relationship between expressed preference and the amount of each brand actually consumed is shown to be high.

An analysis of the day to day variation in the number of bottles of each brand consumed daily yielded a chi square which was not significant (chi square $= 22.4$, d.f. $= 25$, P$>$.05). Thus, although there were significant differences between brands in the total number of bottles of each consumed, there was little shift from day to day in the brands preferred and avoided. The trend was generally maintained through the week. The two avoided brands were consistently avoided, and the brand high each day generally varied among the three preferred brands.

An analysis of differences in preference between the families in the panel, however, showed wide interfamily differences in the number of bottles of each brand consumed. Thus, every brand was preferred by some family during the study. However, more of the families formed preferences for Brands A, B, and C, than for the other brands.

It was also found that preferences formed were for the most part unstable and most subjects did not actually pick out the same brands from day to day. In other words, the individuals contributing to the total number of bottles consumed of a particular brand during the week, differed from day to day. Thus, although more of the subjects liked Brands A, B, or C, more of the time and avoided Brands E and F more of the time, individual preferences generally tended to shift from day to day.

The relationship between previous brand preferences and preferences formed during the experiment was also investigated. The percentage of times Brand A drinkers said they liked Brand A during the study, the percentage of Brand B drinkers who named Brand B (by colored top, of course), and so on, was as follows: Brand A drinkers, 56.3 percent; Brand D drinkers, 45.2 percent; Brand C drinkers, 28.9 percent; Brand B drinkers, 26.3 percent; and Brand F drinkers, 12.5 percent. Thus, users of Brands A and D seemed more apt to form preferences for their old brands when the brand names were not known than did users of other brands. The percentage of times drinkers of Brands B, C, and F picked their own brands are within the limits of chance expectancy.

SUMMARY

A panel of consumers was selected from a large city and their preferences for brands of beer investigated through the use of an experimental technique.

1. The study showed that there were real differences in preferences for beers even when the brand names were not known.
2. Of the beers investigated, three were generally preferred, one occupied a position just below the leaders, and two were more generally avoided. This was on the basis of the total number of bottles consumed during the study.
3. The preferences expressed by the subjects during the study were in agreement with the amount actually consumed.
4. The general trend in preference for the families in the study generally prevailed for the group from day to day.
5, Preferences expressed by the individuals in the study generally proved to be unstable and shifted from one brand to the next. However, more people preferred three of the brands and avoided two others more of the time.
6. However, previous users of two of the brands seemed better able to form preferences for their old brands when the brand names were not known than users of the other brands.
7. The study indicates that important information may be gained using experimental techniques at the consumer level. The fruitfulness of the approach to problems of consumer research should increase with more refined techniques and research projects of longer duration.

54. PUPIL DILATION AS A MEASURE OF CONSUMER RESPONSE *

Herbert E. Krugman

In 1960, Hess and Polt reported finding a relationship between pupil dilation and the interest value of visual stimuli.[1] Since then, studies utilizing measurement of changes in pupil diameter have been conducted on problems involving the evaluation of advertising materials, packages and products. These studies have led to a growing conviction that in many areas of human behavior one might make better predictions of behavior from pupil responses than from verbal or opinion data. The purpose of this report is to provide a brief review of the concepts involved, method of measurement, measurement goals, problems of data collection, two recently completed validation studies, and some objectives for the future.

CONCEPT

Hess and Polt reported that "Increases in the size of the pupil of the eye have been found to accompany the viewing of emotionally toned or interesting visual stimuli." A technique for recording such changes was developed so that the factor of adjustment to light was eliminated as a measurement problem. While the pupil is capable of changes from about 2 to 8 mm. in response to light, or an areal increase of 16 fold, the variation in pupil diameters involved in studies of interest is usually well within ±10 percent and often within ±2 percent.

The "plus or minus" quality referred to here is an operational function of the method of measurement (to be described). However, it does raise the question of what kinds of stimuli create measurable dilations and what kinds create measurable contractions.

Apparently there are two broad categories of affect-arousing or interest-producing stimuli that create dilations. The first category involves pleasant stimuli; the second involves stimuli that evoke fear, anxiety, or shock. Contractions, on the other hand, are associated with stimuli that lack the power to interest or arouse the viewer. While stimuli that evoke fear, anxiety, or shock are usually absent in commercial objects and

---

* From "Some Applications of Pupil Measurement," *Journal of Marketing Research* 1 (1966): 15–19.

[1] E. H. Hess and J. M. Polt, "Pupil Size as Related to Interest Value of Visual Stimuli," *Science* 132 (1960): 349–50.

symbols, the meaning of stimuli must be considered before one can infer that a dilation indicates pleasurably toned interest.[2] Airline, insurance, and drug advertising, for example, might be ruled ineligible for measurement of pupil response because a dilation might represent anxiety rather than pleasurably toned interest. In the case of such questionable stimuli one might have to consider the circumstances, inquire of the respondents, and exercise a degree of judgment before deciding that dilation represented a favorable response. While such problems are in fact quite rare in the commercial environment, their possibility must be noted.

METHOD

To conduct pupil dilation studies in the manner developed by Hess and Polt, three work stages are required.[3] First, the material to be tested is prepared in 35-mm. slide form and each stimulus slide is matched for reflected illumination with a neutral control slide containing nothing but the numbers one through five. Each study usually accommodates ten stimuli, or a total of ten pairs of stimulus and control slides.

In preparing stimulus slides it may be necessary to reduce light/dark contrasts within a picture. Modification of the stimulus to reduce light/dark contrasts may diminish somewhat the aesthetic value of pictures, but this has not yet seemed to present a problem.

The subject looks at each slide for ten seconds while his left eye is photographed at the rate of two photographs per second. While looking at each control slide, the pupil diameter is primarily a function of the light value of the slide.[4] As the matched (for light value) stimulus slide comes on, the pupil diameter may increase (as a function of greater interest) or it may decrease (as a function of lesser interest). It is this increase or decrease which is measured for each pair of control and stimulus slides.

The films are developed and each negative is projected onto a special scoring table large enough for the pupil to be measured with a ruler. The basic measure is the percent increase or decrease in the average pupil diameter for the 20 photographs taken while viewing a stimulus slide, in comparison with the average pupil diameter for the 20 photographs taken while viewing the control slide.

---

[2] Presumably we are concerned here with the parasympathetic branch of the autonomic nervous system (vegetative functions) whereby the pupil may be dilated via inhibition (the lay term might be "relaxation") of that system and a weakening of control of the sphincter muscle in the iris; one would hope to eliminate the role of the sympathetic branch (fight, flight, and so forth) whereby the pupil may be dilated via stimulation of the system and a contraction of the dilator muscle in the iris.

[3] For further details of the method see E. H. Hess and J. M. Polt, "Pupil Size in Relation to Mental Activity During Simple Problem Solving," *Science* 143 (1964): 1190–92.

[4] The control slide probably has some interest in its own right or as a signal to anticipate something of interest. Contraction may involve disappointment. Rotation of stimuli is, therefore, quite important.

MEASUREMENT GOALS

Early studies were concerned primarily with measuring the pleasurably toned interest or "appeal" of individual ads, packages, or product designs.[5] To this was added before-and-after measurement in which responses to a photo of the product were measured twice. Between exposures to the photo of the product, different respondents were exposed to different information (that is, different ads, paragraphs of copy, and so forth) to see which information was more persuasive or which added more appeal to the product (which, along with awareness, is the goal of advertising).[6]

Television commercials have also been inserted as "in-between" stimuli for before-and-after studies. In this indirect manner, animate stimuli were evaluated for the first time. Equipment has since been developed to take direct measures of response to animate stimuli, so that pretesting of television commercials, television programs, and motion pictures can be considered as possible applications of pupil research.

DATA COLLECTION

Conventional measures usually require the subject as he views stimuli, (1) to decide whether he likes or dislikes the stimuli, (2) to decide how he will tell this, and (3) to tell it. These three operations or units of response are absent in pupil measurement. Pupil measurement therefore circumvents language and translation problems in cross-cultural opinion and attitude surveys.

Subjects who participate in pupil-measurement studies look at slides with the assumption that questions will be asked when the slides have all been shown. To fulfill this expectation, and also to interrelate pupil with verbal data, an interview is always conducted. The camera is quiet though visible and few subjects comment about it. Those who ask are answered frankly.

VALIDATION

A number of studies suggested the usefulness of pupil measurement as a predictor of behavior. In the case of products, pupil response was found

---

[5] By-product data obtainable from pupil photographs include where subjects are looking during the period of exposure. Thus, dilation or contraction can be traced approximately to parts of a stimulus. In addition, a persistently ascending or descending response can be identified, if such occurs during the period of exposure.

[6] This may circumvent the problem of an anxious response to airline, insurance, or drug *advertising*, that is, instead of measuring response to the ad itself the emphasis is on shifts in the nonanxious product appeal.

to be related to sales data for watches, while in the case of ads, pupil response was found to be related to (split-run) coupons returns.[7] These studies, however, were confined to pairs of stimuli. To evaluate the extent of the relationship, or to determine whether pupil response was perhaps more predictive of sales than were other measures, it became desirable to compare an array of pupil responses and an array of verbal responses (for example, ratings) from the same subjects against a similar array of sales data. Two such studies were conducted and are reported here. They involved greeting cards and sterling silver patterns.

Greeting Cards

Ten humorous greeting cards (four friendship and six birthday) were chosen by a cooperating manufacturer to represent wide ranges in sales performance. Each card was photographed with the first and third sides of the four-sided (foldover) card showing on the slide. This eliminated the surprise element of "turning the page" and, in one card, of a mechanical pop-out device. More recently developed equipment permits a film presentation of realistic card handling and card opening.

Camera equipment was installed in a rented store in the Roosevelt Field Shopping Center (Garden City, Long Island) during January 1964, and 23 male and 26 female subjects were recruited from among passing shoppers.[8] Immediately after pupil measurement, interview data were obtained on order of recall, and then with the actual cards shown, on "card liked best" and "card liked least." The data were given to the manufacturer who then provided rank-order information on sales. Results are shown in Table 54–1.

Although the pupil response correlated approximately .40 for both sets of cards, because of the small number of cases neither correlation is statistically significant. The correlation of pupil response with sales rank would possibly have been higher if the testing procedure had not required removal of the pop-out spring from "Hi!" before photographing.

It may also be worth noting that, in the case of the larger group (birthday cards), the correlation between pupil response and sales was numerically larger than that between verbal rank and sales, but also that pupil response was *negatively* correlated with verbal rank (rho = − .60).[9]

---

[7] Conducted and to be published by F. J. Van Bortel of the Chicago office of Marplan.

[8] Actually, a total of 57 subjects was tested, but records for 8 had to be discarded because of incomplete or blurred photographic plates.

[9] The agreement between sales and pupil response is relatively independent of the influence of verbal rating, as determined by the Kendall partial-rank correlation coefficient. With verbal rating partialled out, the Kendall coefficient increased +.04, a negligible change. For details of this test, see S. Siegel, *Nonparametric Statistics* (New York: McGraw Hill Book Co., 1956), pp. 223–29.

TABLE 54–1

Comparison of Sales, Pupil Responses, and Verbal Ratings for Greeting Cards

| | | Pupil Response | | |
Title of Card	Sales Rank	Rank	Percent Change	Verbal Rank
Friendship)[a]				
Hi	1	3	− .1	2
Awkward Age	2	1	+1.7	3
Dolce Vita	3	2	+1.0	1
You're Nice	4	4	− .2	4
Birthday)[b]				
Old as Hills	1	1	+2.9	4
Elephant	2	6	− .1	2
Swiss Cheese	3	2	+2.7	5
Cane	4	4	+1.7	1
Witch	5	3	+1.8	6
Horn	6	5	+ .4	3

[a] Rank-order coefficient: Sales rank with Pupil rank = +.40
      Sales rank with Verbal rank = +.40
      Neither value is significant.
[b] Rank-order coefficient: Sales rank with Pupil rank = +.37
      Sales rank with Verbal rank = +.09
      Neither value is significant.

Sterling Silver Patterns

A cooperating retailer (Georg Jensen, Inc.) selected ten sterling silver patterns to represent a wide range in sales performance. These patterns are an exclusive line identified with the retailer. Each pattern was represented by a single place setting consisting of knife, fork, and spoon, and was photographed on a blue velvet background.

Camera equipment was installed in an alcove at the rear of Jensen's Fifth Avenue store during February 1964, and 39 female subjects were recruited from among those shoppers entering the silverware section to examine this category of merchandise. Immediately after pupil measurement, respondents were shown the ten actual place settings and were asked to rank them in order of liking, that is, 1 high to 10 low. As it happened, the 39 subjects included 13 who reported that they were actually shopping for sterling and 26 who were only browsing. The data were given to the retailer who then provided retail sales data for the completed year of 1962. It must be noted, however, that these 1962 data represent a combination of sales of flatware (primarily) and serving pieces and are not available on a separate basis. However, to supplement these data, Table 54–2 includes some retailer comments which appear relevant.

For both the shoppers and the browsers, the correlation between sales history and pupil response was numerically larger than the correlation

TABLE 54-2

Comparison of Sales, Pupil Responses and Verbal Ratings for Silverware

Pattern[c]	Sales[a] Rank	Shoppers[b]			Browsers		
		Pupil Rank	Percent Change	Verbal Rank	Pupil Rank	Percent Change	Verbal Rank
Acorn.	1	5	+ .5	8	1	+1.0	2
Acanthus.	2	1	+2.3	6.5	3	+ .2	4.5
Cactus	3	7	− .9	3	6	− .1	3
Cypress	4	3	+1.7	4	5	0.0	7
Continental	5	2	+2.1	2	2	+ .6	4.5
Pyramid	6	10	−2.6	1	8	−1.4	1
Blossom	7	9	−2.2	10	10	−3.7	10
Caravel	8	4	+ .8	9	4	+ .1	9
Argo	9.5	6	− .1	6.5	7	− .9	8
Nordic	9.5	8	−1.4	5	9	−2.2	6

^a The following rank-order correlations were obtained:
Sales rank with shoppers' pupil rank = +.43
Sales rank with shoppers' verbal rank = +.14
Sales rank with browsers' pupil rank = +.66 (p = .05)
Sales rank with browsers' verbal rank = +.60 (p = .05)

^b The shoppers' percent change in pupil dilation was more favorable than the browsers' that is, larger +% of smaller −%, for seven of the ten patterns, suggesting greater interest in silverware in general on the part of the shoppers. A one-tail test of this hypothesis shows that t = 1.84, df = 9, p = .05.

^c Retailer's comments:

Acorn	"This gets the bulk of our advertising by far"
Acanthus	
Cactus	
Cypress	"Sells better out of town"
Continental	"Only pattern that doubled its volume in recent years—will be advertised next year"
Pyramid	"What the public thinks is tasteful but isn't"
Blossom	
Caravel	"A 'designer's design'—not expected to sell in the USA"
Argo	"Introduced in 1963 and not doing well"
Nordic	"Discontinued years ago—didn't sell"

between sales and verbal ratings (the difference was not statistically significant, however).[10]

It is interesting to note that the pupil response and verbal rating differed sharply for "Pyramid," with the pupil response in "agreement," with sales. "Pyramid" received the highest verbal rating from both shoppers and browsers, but ranked tenth and eighth, respectively, in pupil response. Apparently the public showed better taste than their verbal ratings would indicate.

Logically, we would expect that shoppers (who are actually planning to purchase silver) would be more "interested" in sterling than browsers. The results of the pupil response, that is, shoppers having larger percent increases and smaller percent decreases in pupil size, support this expecta-

---

[10] A more precise test of interpretations of this order might be to compare the predictive power of pupil and verbal data against the later sales behavior of the same group, that is, even though it may be practical to use pupil data on small groups to predict something about larger groups, the interpretations underlying these predictions would in most cases require special testing.

TABLE 54-3

Analysis of Variance Summary

Source of Variation	Sum of Squares	d.f.	Mean Square	F
Sex	17,987.72	1	17,987.72	2.78
Error I	304,064.39	47	6,469.46	
Greeting cards.	57,157.72	9	6,350.86	5.29[a]
Sex x cards.	46,848.62	9	5,205.40	4.33[a]
Error II	508,264.86	423	1,201.57	

[a] p = .01

tion. This finding, which was statistically significant, adds suggestive, though not definitive, indication of validity.

RELIABILITY

The results of the studies reported in this paper, as well as the accumulating results from a variety of similar studies, encourage the belief that pupil response is a promising new tool for study of consumer behavior.

However, because the magnitude of changes in pupil diameter are relatively small, the question of reliability of measurement becomes important. For example, in view of the relatively small range of pupil response (from approximately −2 percent to +3 percent in the studies reported in this paper), are the responses to these stimuli really significantly different, or are they simply within the range of random fluctuation? Furthermore, is there any real agreement from subject to subject? We shall present what data are available bearing on these two questions.

SIGNIFICANCE OF STIMULUS EFFECTS

An analysis of variance was performed at the time the pupil response data were collected for the greeting cards. This analysis was designed to evaluate the effects attributable to sex stimuli (the greeting cards), and interaction of sex and stimuli. The results are presented in Table 54-3.

The results presented in Table 54-3 may be interpreted as follows:

1. On the whole, male and female subjects do not differ significantly in their pupil responses to greeting cards.
2. The various greeting cards *do* evoke significantly different pupil responses.
3. Male and female subjects *do* differ significantly in their pupil responses to certain greeting cards.

In other words, the differences in pupil response, though numerically small, are real.

TABLE 54-4

Intersubject Consistency

Stimulus	Shoppers	W	P
Greeting cards	Total (49)	.11	<.001
Sterling silver	Shoppers (13)	.19	<.01
Sterling silver	Browsers (26)	.11	<.005

INTERSUBJECT CONSISTENCY

In Tables 54-1 and 54-2, pupil responses were averaged for all subjects, then ranked for comparison with sales rank data. The question remains, to what extent do pupil response rankings agree from subject to subject? To answer this question, Kendall's coefficient of concordance (W) was computed with the results shown in Table 54-4.

For each of the groups, the odds are better than a thousand to one that the consistency of pupil response ranking was not due simply to chance. In short, the answer to the question is that pupil response rankings do agree significantly from subject to subject. Furthermore, in the case of the greeting card study, the average pupil response rank of cards for male subjects correlated +.77 (p. = .01) with the average pupil response rank of cards for female subjects. For shoppers and browsers in the sterling silver study, the correlation was +.81 (p = .01).

THE FUTURE

In general, the results of our experience with measurement of pupil response indicate that this is a sensitive and reliable technique with considerable promise for study of the interest-arousing characteristics of visual stimuli. The impact of the environment is often difficult to determine from conscious impressions verbally reported. For a variety of reasons, people may not be practiced or competent to accurately verbalize their feeling in certain areas of living. Pupil measurement seems to provide a powerful new tool for the study of these areas.

55. OPERANT CONDITIONING TECHNIQUES IN ADVERTISING RESEARCH *

Lewis C. Winters and Wallace H. Wallace

THIS PAPER is a literature review of the use of operant conditioning techniques in advertising research, and it describes the types of operant conditioning techniques available and discusses what they measure. Emphasis is placed on studies of the reliability and validity of such techniques in measuring advertising effectiveness.

There are several terms which are used throughout. Since the terms have been borrowed from the operant conditioning field, definitions are given for the most frequently used terms:

Operant Conditioning. An operant is some unit of behavior, such as a press on a foot pedal, the movement of a switch, or some other "voluntary" response. The process of controlling the subject's operant behavior is referred to as operant conditioning.

Reinforcement. An event which will control the process of conditioning by changing the rate of occurrence of behavior which it follows—that is, change the probability of occurrence of the operant. A positive reinforcement will increase the probability of the occurrence of the operant. A negative reinforcement will decrease it.

Conjugate Reinforcement. In conjugate reinforcement, the intensity of continuously available reinforcing stimuli varies directly and immediately with the rate of response.[1] For example, the rate of pressing a foot pedal could be used to control the brightness of a television screen.

In advertising research, one key question is: How reinforcing are the various images on the TV screen or in the pages of a magazine? It is assumed that the more positively reinforcing they are, the more a person will make them available. If their availability to him depends on the rate of his operant responding, there is in that rate an index of the reinforcement of the material.

In practical terms, the rate of responding is of direct interest to most advertisers. For example, if consumers watch one commercial more actively than another, this can be important information for an advertiser's decisions.

---

* Reprinted from "On Operant Conditioning Techniques," *Journal of Advertising Research* 10 (1970): 39–45. © Copyright 1970, by the Advertising Research Foundation.
[1] See O. R. Lindsley, "A Behavioral Measure on Television Reviewing," *Journal of Advertising Research* 2 (1962): 2–12.

CONPAAD. CONPAAD is a machine used to provide an index of the reinforcement power of various stimulus materials. The word "CONPAAD" stands for Conjugately Programmed Analysis of Advertising. All CONPAAD studies to date have used the rate of pressing a foot pedal as the operant response.

Simultaneous versus Segmented

One major distinction found in operant conditioning systems is in terms of the way stimuli are presented to the respondent. In one system, the respondent has two stimuli simultaneously presented. and measurements are made to determine which stimulus produces the highest rate of responding. An example of simultaneous presentation would be two television shows being run concurrently with the respondent able to see and hear either or both, depending on how he pumps two pedals—one controlling one show and one controlling the other.

In a sequential system, stimuli are presented one after the other. This is like the situation when a person watches a show at home with one commercial inserted early and one later in the show. Typically, studies using the sequential system have imbedded commercials in a show of some type. Studies using the CONPAAD device have used the sequential system.

Proportional versus On-Off Availability

Proportional availability means the faster the rate of response, the brighter the video and/or the louder the audio of an advertisement. A rate of response of 25 percent on a foot pedal yields 25 percent brightness and/or loudness; a rate of 50 percent yields 50 percent, and so forth. With an on-off system, the response is strong enough to produce full presentation (100 percent) of the stimulus or it produces just the minimal "threshold" stimulus—one or the other.

The use of percent of rate of responding has a specific meaning in these cases. The maximum rate of response is determined for each subject. The actual rate is measured by counting the number of foot presses during a particular time segment of a commercial. The percent of rate of responding is the actual rate divided by the maximum rate.

Early studies applying operant conditioning techniques to advertising research used the sequential, on-off system.[2] Later studies have used a sequential, proportional system.[3]

---

[2] P. E. Nathan and W. H. Wallace, "An Operant Behavioral Measure of TV Commercial Effectiveness," *Journal of Advertising Research* 5, no. 4 (1965): 13–20; L. C. Winters and W. H. Wallace, "Operant Behavioral Measures of the Effect of Advertising Content and Placement" (Speech presented at American Psychological Association Convention, Chicago, 1965).

[3] L. C. Winters and N. Love, "Correlating Preliminary and Finished Versions of Television Commercials on an Operant Behavioral Measure" (Speech presented at American Psychological Association Convention, Washington, D.C., 1967).

Approach versus Avoidance Systems

In approach systems, the response increases the intensity of, or makes available, the reinforcing stimulus; the subject is given the choice of approaching—making the stimulus available, or more intense—or not. In avoidance systems, two stimuli are available. One is the presumably positively reinforcing stimulus (for example, the show), the other is a noxious stimulus (for example, static). The subject's response serves to decrease the intensity of, or remove the noxious stimulus. Here the subject chooses between avoiding the noxious stimulus or not.

In most advertising research using operant conditioning, the approach system has been used. However, avoidance conditions (for example, static, picture out of focus, and so forth) may provide as much, if not more, discrimination between advertisements. Future research on avoidance system is proposed.

Operant Conditioning Studies

In the typical operant conditioning study conducted in the academic laboratory, the purpose of the research is almost diametrically opposed to that in advertising. The usual academic researcher has a rat in a box pressing a lever for a pellet of food. The experimenter manipulates the reinforcement to determine the effect on the rat's behavior. Most of the manipulations center around providing different schedules of reinforcement—for example, rewarding the rat for every correct response versus rewarding him after every fifth correct response. The crucial aspect is that the reinforcement, be it a pellet of food or a drink of milk, is discrete, usually unchanging in magnitude. The focus is on the subject's behavior, not on the quality of the reinforcement.

In the typical advertising research study, the human respondent makes a response which controls whether or not a segment of a television show or commercial, a print ad, or a radio commercial stays on or fades. Here the subject's behavior is of concern only insofar as it indicates the reinforcing quality of the stimulus.

The experimenter infers from the changes in rate of response the degree to which these types of stimuli represent a changing magnitude of reinforcement for the respondent. This raises the basic question as to whether or not response rates vary as a function of the properties of the stimuli—that is, does a more interesting (positively reinforcing) stimulus produce a higher rate of operant responses to make it available? The section on validity directs itself to this basic question.

The assumptions made by users of operant techniques are shown graphically in Figure 55–1, which uses the CONPAAD technique as an illustration.

The rate of responding in Time 1 can be either high or low. If it is

FIGURE 55–1

Schematic Representation of CONPAAD System for Commercial Testing

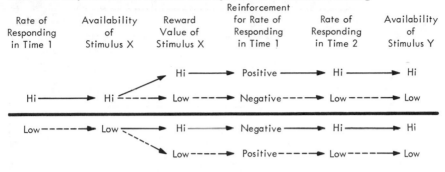

high, then Stimulus X will be highly available (for example, bright or audible). If Stimulus X (for example, a few frames of a television commercial) was highly rewarding, the high rate of responding will be positively reinforced and maintained. Thus, the picture remains bright and the sound remains loud. As a result, Stimulus Y (for example, the next few frames) will be more readily available.

If, however, Stimulus X was low in reward value, then the high rate of responding will be negatively reinforced and the rate of responding in Time 2 will be decreased and Stimulus Y will not be as available. The possibilities are also diagrammed for the case where response rate is initially low. In general, "the reinforcing" stimuli are joint (conjugate), and each is available to the extent that its immediate predecessor was rewarding. Under this system, presumably, the advertisement with the most highly rewarding stimuli will receive the highest overall rate of operant responding.

One important aspect of the advertising research application of operant conditioning is its emphasis on continuous stimuli. Television shows and commercials, narrative stories, and radio commercials cannot be broken into discrete chunks without losing continuity. Most animal studies use episodic material—for example, one response or one chunk of food.

An emphasis on continuous materials does not prevent conjugate measures from being broken into meaningful segments during analysis of "whole" data. Analyses of commercials for research purposes, in fact, should be moment by moment to enable diagnostic evaluation. In practice, data for commercials have later been broken into 10- or 20-second segments, and the reinforcement value of each segment has been plotted.

Operant Conditioning and Advertising Effectiveness

Reliability. Over the past few years, several studies have indicated that CONPAAD yields very reliable data. One early study with a sc-

TABLE 55–1

CONPAAD Correlation Coefficients

	Group		
Group	II	III	IV
I	.26	.74*	.80**
II		−.28	.43
III			.28

* $p < .02$.
** $p < .01$.

quential, on-off system tested six campaigns for sweaters. In each campaign, three ads were used. Each ad featured a different sweater, but the same sweaters were used in all the campaigns with different copy and backgrounds. Although the campaigns varied in effectiveness overall, the rank order of those three sweaters was the same in all six campaigns.

Another study tested the same respondents on the same commercials two different times. The test-retest correlation was +.85 ($p < .02$).

Wolf, Newman, and Winters recently reported on four sequential, proportional studies, in which the same ads were shown to four different groups of people.[4] The correlations between groups tended to be high if the groups were similar in age and sex, and low if they were dissimilar. Table 55–1 contains the correlations between the groups in these studies.

The highest correlation (+.80) was between Groups I and IV. Group I had 192 men. Group IV had 96 respondents, 70 percent of which were men. The next highest correlation (+.74) was between Groups I and III. Group III had 9 respondents—all men between 18 and 65. By contrast, the lowest correlations were between Group II and Group I, and Group II and Group III. Group II contained 96 women in their 20s.

Validity.   There are several ways for assessing the validity of an operant conditioning measure of advertising effectiveness. An example of recent studies from psychological literature illustrate their applicability. Lipsitt, Pederson, and Delucia have shown the possible range of ages that can be used with operant conditioning.[5] Infants, all about one year old, had to press a panel to increase the intensity of light on a clown picture. The infants learned to press the panel to maintain the light, but when the experimenter turned out the light for good, the infants stopped pressing. In the jargon of psychology, their response extinguished.

Lovitt has applied operant conditioning techniques to auditory ma-

[4] A. Wolf, D. Z. Newman, and L. C. Winters, "Measures of Interest as Related to Ad Lib Readership," *Journal of Advertising Research* 9 (1969): 40–45.

[5] L. P. Lipsitt, L. J. Pederson, and C. A. Delucia, "Conjugate Reinforcement of Operant Responding in Infants," *Psychonomic Science* 4 (1966): 66–68.

terial.[6] His study is significant in that he gave respondents a choice between two simultaneous stories; he used a simultaneous, on-off situation.

Also of importance to an analysis of validity is the fact that five of seven 12-year-olds gave the same operant switch-pressing score as they did verbal preference score for the two stories. Lovitt argues that the operant response is superior because it also gives a quantifiable measure for different segments of the story while the verbal measure was for overall preference.

Brock and Balloun had college undergraduates press a button to eliminate static on tape recorded messages.[7] They found that smokers pressed more than nonsmokers to remove static if the message disputed any link between smoking and cancer. Also, students having higher church attendance and recourse to prayer pressed less to clarify an anti-Christian message.

Brock and Balloun illustrated the usefulness of operant conditioning in an avoidance situation. It is also an example of how advertising researchers can develop their own criterion measures without having to make outrageous assumptions. That is, there is good face validity to the assumption that a church goer is less interested in anti-Christian messages.

A study of the construct validity of CONPAAD utilized high- and low-information commercials. Berlyne, Byrne and Clore, and Sieber and Lanzetta all suggest that individuals prefer more information than less (up to the point of overload).[8]

Therefore, if two commercials on the same topic are made, the one with greater information should be more reinforcing and, hence, receive a higher score on CONPAAD. A test of this prediction was made for two coffee commercials.[9] The results showed a greater response to the higher information commercial ($p < .05$).

Another study was based on extinction theory. Extinction theory states that when a reinforcing stimulus is removed, the responses will slow down and eventually terminate. It could be expected that consumers would eventually extinguish or satiate to a message which contained little or no information. In the study, a commercial was created which consisted primarily of numbers running backwards (10, 9, 8, 7, 6, 5, 4, 3) and repeated six times.

---

[6] T. C. Lovitt, "Free-Operant Preference for One of Two Stories: A Methodological Note," *Journal of Educational Psychology* 58 (1967): 84–87.

[7] T. C. Brocks and J. L. Balloun, "Behavioral Receptivity to Dissonant Information," *Journal of Personality and Social Psychology* 6 (1967): 412–28.

[8] D. E. Berlyne, *Conflict, Arousal, and Curiosity* (New York: McGraw-Hill Book Co., 1960); D. Byrne and G. L. Clore, "Effectance Arousal and Attraction," *Journal of Personality and Social Psychology* 6 (1967): 1–18; and J. E. Sieber and J. T. Lanzetta, "Conflict and Conceptual Structure as Determinants of Decision-Making Behavior," *Journal of Personality* 32 (1964): 622–41.

[9] Winters and Wallace, "Operant Behavioral Measures."

This number commercial was in the context of a regular TV show. Response rates were plotted over time to this pseudo-commercial. Respondents' scores showed a steady decline, and 95 percent of the respondents reached the criterion of complete extinction.

Sales data have also been used to assess predictive validity. However, one problem arises here: getting a reliable difference between advertisements on a sales measure. But such differences have been found on a coupon redemption test for a low-priced product.

These commercials were tested on CONPAAD and the results were confounded by the interest level of the show they were in—following an "exciting" spot there was no difference in the commercials.[10] Only when the two followed a "dull" part of the show did the "good" commercial "win." Byrne and Clore have shown that when there is a very high arousal level, there is less discrimination.[11] The exciting spot was from a show which depicted a subway knifing. It may be that such material aroused people so much that they failed to discriminate between surrounding stimuli.

In another sales study, two commercials for the same detergent were compared.[12] Table 55–2 shows that on the sales (coupon) test, Commercial 1 for the product sold more of the product than did Commercial 2; Commercial 1 also was superior ($p < .05$) to Commercial 2 in the sales test. Table 55–2 also shows that in the operant conditioning test, Commercial 1 for the product had a higher rate of pressing than did Commercial 2. Both the audio and video are significant at $p < .10$.

Predictive validity studies on print ads include recent studies by Wolf, Newman, and Winters.[13] These studies had in common the insertion of editorial and advertising materials in an abbreviated version of a popular women's magazine. Since the material in each article was of the same length, the reader's response of interest in these studies was the amount of time she kept the material on a screen in front of her.

Independent readership data were gathered on the editorial material. Telephone interviews were conducted with a random sample of 200 women on the subscription list of the magazine containing the articles. These interviews were completed several days after the receipt of the magazine. The criterion for CONPAAD to predict was the percentage of women having read the entire article.

The format of all the articles was identical, and each article was one page in length. In the first CONPAAD study, 14 articles were studied. The articles were placed in various positions of a mock slide magazine.

---

[10] Ibid.

[11] Byrne and Clore, "Effectance Arousal and Attraction."

[12] D. Z. Newman and W. H. Wallace, "Validation of an Operant Conditioning Technique Through Induced Sales Data" (Speech presented at Eastern Psychological Association, Boston, 1967).

[13] Wolf, Newman, and Winters, "Operant Measures of Interest."

TABLE 55-2

Sales Data Compared to CONPAAD Data for the Same Commercials

Sales Test Data

Commercial	Percent Redeeming Coupon
1	33
2	21
Control	24

Operant Responding Data

Commercial	Audio Rate Score	Video Rate Score
1	79%	79%
2	74%	74%

The articles were rotated for position to balance for potential position biases. Ninety-six undergraduate females from the University of Pennsylvania served as respondents in the first study. The rank-order correlation (rho) between the field readership survey and CONPAAD was +.78 (p < .01).

The other two studies utilized 6 of the original 14 articles. Two articles from approximately high-, medium-, and low-field readership were selected. One of these studies (II) used 48 females from 18 to 55 years old. The other (III) used 96 females (mothers of very young children) under the age of 25. This latter study employed a sequential, proportional system. The other two studies employed sequential, on-off systems.

In Study II, the overall rank-order correlation of the CONPAAD time scores and field readership for the six articles was rho = +.77 (p < .02). The comparable correlation in Study III was rho = +.66 (p < .05). Actually, the lower correlation for Study III was understandable from a hindsight analysis. The overall correlation would have been perfect had one article not been included. This article was concerned with mortgages, a topic which was found to be quite uninteresting according to field readership and the two other CONPAAD studies. However, Study III employed all young mothers—a group who might be predicted to show more than average interest in the topic of mortgages.

Future Directions

Academic circles have become interested in conceptual problems related to CONPAAD. A central problem revolves around the relationship of response rates and magnitude of reinforcement. Professor Skinner said that the two were directly and perfectly related.[14] Neuringer reviews some of the experiments on the problem.[15] To summarize them briefly, the relationship of response rates to magnitude of reinforcement clearly holds for only some situations. These situations seem to involve choice.

For example, Neuringer presented pigeons with two buttons, spatially separated. The pigeons had to choose which button to peck. This choice dictated how much food they would receive for pecking this button an additional specified number of times. Neuringer found that the rate of response in choosing the button was proportional to the magnitude of reinforcement (food). However, the rate of pecking was not positively related to the magnitude of reinforcement once the choice situation had been removed. The application of this to CONPAAD suggests that the CONPAAD respondent must always be in a continuous choice situation.

Neuringer's study involved a *spatial* choice. Shimp has shown that when a *temporal* choice exists, there is also a positive relationship between rate of response and reinforcement value.[16]

Extrapolating from pigeons to humans contains dangers, but it also can provide ideas. It can suggest answers to many problems besetting the use of CONPAAD-like devices.

One problem, for example, was that more discrimination was found in print-ad studies than in television studies. Figure 55–2 shows the distribution of scores for early sequential, proportional CONPAAD studies. It should be noted that there is much more spread in the scores for the print studies. Even though only 15 commercials are represented in Figure 55–2, the range is very representative of scores using that system.

The increased role of choice may provide a partial answer to this difference between commercials and print ads. The print-ad situation provides a number of choices with the respondent in control of the situation. The reason is that with print ads, the respondent keeps the ad (35-mm slide) on the screen for as long as he presses. Once he stops pressing, he loses it and the next slide comes on. He has the choice of staying with the present page (slide) or turning the page (changing slides) and doing so at his own rate.

This can be contrasted with the television situation. With commercials, the respondent has a choice between commercial (or show) and sitting placidly in a semi-darkened room—not very much of a choice.

Recently, respondents have been provided with more spatial choices, just as at home. The consumer at home can watch TV, read a newspaper, talk to someone, pet the dog, get a snack, and so forth. To partially repro-

---

[14] B. F. Skinner, *The Behavior of Organisms, an Experimental Analysis* (New York: Appleton-Century-Crofts, 1938).

[15] A. Neuringer, "Effects of Reinforcement Magnitude on Choice and Rate of Responding," *Journal of Experimental Analysis of Behavior* 10 (1967): 417–24.

[16] C. P. Shimp, "The Reinforcement of Short Interresponse Times," *Journal of Experimental Analysis of Behavior* 10 (1967): 425–34.

FIGURE 55–2

The Distribution of CONPAAD Scores for Print Ads and Commercials

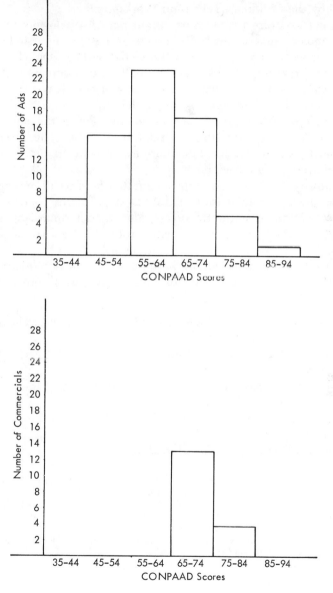

duce these choices, current studies utilize a slide projector continuously presenting different slides as well as the TV show with commercials. A similar system has been used for the evaluation of Sesame Street "commercials" by the Children's Television Workshop.[17]

Repeating exposure to the same commercial is analogous to Shimp's temporal choice situation mentioned above. In essence, repeated exposure allows for a wearout measure with the CONPAAD system. In practice, the respondent watches a TV show with the same commercial spliced into it four or five times. What becomes crucial here is not so much the rate at which the commercial is responded to the first time, but the change or slope of the rates from one presentation to the next. Preliminary research has indicated that the relative slope of a commercial from first to fourth exposure in one, 20-minute experiment predicted attention-interest wearout in later months.[18]

Grass and Wallace have recently shown that field recall measures over time also correlate with these CONPAAD slope scores collected in the laboratory.[19] Work is currently being done to determine the stimulus characteristics which are associated with various CONPAAD slope scores.

To conclude, operant conditioning, although a relatively new technique has rapidly found a place in the battery of advertising research techniques. Where does operant conditioning advertising research stand today?

1. There is a body of data which says it is a reliable and valid measure of attention or interest.
2. By building choice into the stimulus situation, the sensitivity of this measure seems to have been enhanced.
3. Recently CONPAAD scores have been used to predict the wearout of attention and recall of television commercials.
4. It is not a panacea. It may measure interest but not necessarily predict attitude change, for example.
5. Questions still remain for future research.

---

[17] G. S. Lesser, "Designing Program for Broadcast Television" (Speech presented at American Psychological Association, Washington, D. C., 1969).

[18] R. C. Grass, L. C. Winters, and W. H. Wallace, "Generation and Satiation of Attention during an Advertising Campaign" (Speech presented at American Psychological Association, Washington, D.C., 1969).

[19] R. C. Grass and W. H. Wallace, "Satiation Effects on TV Commercials," *Journal of Advertising Research* 9 (1969): 3–8.

56. AN EXPERIMENTAL INVESTIGATION OF THREE METHODS OF PROVIDING WEIGHT AND PRICE INFORMATION TO CONSUMERS *

Robert D. Gatewood and Robert Perloff

TRUTH IN THE PACKAGING and the pricing of products in the American marketplace has been a subject of public controversy in recent years. despite the 1966 "Fair Packaging and Labeling Act." The basic issue in this controversy is alleged consumer confusion in the determination of price comparisons. The 1966 law was designed to reduce this confusion by *(a)* regulating the location, the print size, and the statement of net contents; *(b)* directing the establishment of standard definition of such terms as "serving" and "small," "medium" and "large" sizes; and *(c)* empowering certain agencies, in extreme conditions, to establish the net weights of packages and number of sizes to be offered for a product group.

Recently, several consumer advocates have criticized the effectiveness of this law on the grounds that price comparisons are no easier for the consumers to accurately make now than before enactment. The Consumer Federation of America has said, "Truth in packaging . . . is one of the best non-laws in the books."[1] Also, Virginia Knauer, presidential adviser on consumer affairs, has stated, "We don't think the labeling on products has adequate or clear information. We think something should be done about the Fair Packaging and Labeling Act."[2]

The most frequently proposed alternatives are *(a)* to equip consumers with small devices which, when given total price and weight, would yield price per unit and *(b)* to require retailers to clearly mark the price per unit on each item. Grocers argue that devices such as in *a* above are extremely easy to use, have universal application, and require neither additional change in the law nor great expense to implement. The second

---

* From *Journal of Applied Psychology* 57 (1973): 81–85. Copyright 1973 by the American Psychological Association. Reprinted by permission.
[1] S. E. Cohan, "Packaging Law Is on Book, but Ills It Aimed to Cure Are Still Troublesome," *Advertising Age* 40 (1969): 10.
[2] "Mrs. Knauer Twits Commerce, Says It Fails to Cut Package Proliferation," *Advertising Age* 40 (1969): 1.

alternative (in *b* above) is favored by many consumer advocates as being more effective in providing necessary information to consumers for making price comparisons. Grocers, in general, have opposed this alternative. *Advertising Age* has written, ". . . supermarket managers and suppliers complain that such a regulation will cause them to double their labor force, raise prices, or go out of business altogether." [3]

In the present article, an attempt is made to evaluate the consumer's ability to process weight and price information in making price comparisons under the foregoing two methods as well as under the present supermarket method. It would seem critical to collect such information prior to implementation of one of these methods nationally.

Previous research in this area is extremely limited. A survey of the psychological literature indicates only one experimental investigation prior to the passage of the 1966 act. Friedman directed 33 young homemakers, each having completed at least one year of college, to select the most economical (largest quantity for the price) package for each of 20 supermarket products. [4] Of the 660 purchased, 284 (43 percent) were purchased for more than the lowest price, indicating that these subjects could not adequately process this information.

The research reported in the present article tested the following hypotheses:

1. Consumers are significantly more accurate in choosing the most economical package from a product group when price-per-unit information is directly available for this product group than when the information is not available.
2. The time required for consumers to choose the most economical package is significantly less when price-per-unit information is directly available than when it is not directly available.
3. There is no significant difference in accuracy of consumer choice of most economical packages between the following two experimental conditions: *(a)* current display methods and *(b)* current display methods with the addition of a computational aid.
4. There is no significant difference in time required to arrive at decisions of most economical package between the two conditions stated in Hypothesis 3.
5. The number of sizes of packages within a product group is significantly negatively correlated with the number of correct choices of most economical package for the two experimental conditions: *(a)* current display methods and *(b)* current display methods with the addition of a computational aid. For the condition of price-per-unit information, the correlation will not be significant.

---

[3] "Grocers Moan, but New York Moves on Unit Prices," *Advertising Age* 40 (1969): 3.
[4] M. P. Friedman, "Consumer Confusion in the Selection of Supermarket Products," *Journal of Applied Psychology* 50 (1966): 529–34.

METHOD

A simulated supermarket situation was set up to collect data for this research, using samples of nine food products as experimental items. The simulation was meant to be representative of the shopping situation that a consumer is confronted with in a supermarket. Therefore, the nine product groups and the items within each were samples drawn from a single supermarket. This supermarket was a member of a large chain that was judged to stock approximately the same products, sizes, and brands as other members of the chain.

The nine product groups chosen for experimentation were randomly selected from the nonperishable items carried by the supermarket. Specifically, the sampling was random selection from within each size within a product group.

Seventy-five volunteer subjects participated in this investigation, 64 of whom were women; 60 of the 75 subjects had completed at least one year of college; 48 were between 20 and 29 years of age, 17 were between 30 and 39. and 10 were 40 years or older.

Subjects were assigned randomly to the three treatment conditions, 25 to each. Each subject performed the experimental task individually. When volunteers reported for the experiment, all were told that their task was to choose the "most economical package" for each of the nine product groups; this was defined as using the information available on the food packages (weight, servings, strength, and so forth) to choose that package which gave the most quantity for the money, or the "best buy." All food packages used in the simulaiton were numbered. To indicate his choices of most economical packages, a subject was asked to write only the numbers of the packages of his choice on the answer sheet he was provided.

In Treatment A, the subjects were presented with the same information as in a supermarket. That is, the packages were presented with the net weight and/or the number of servings on the label and the total price stamped on the package. Quantity and price were displayed in the same manner for Treatment B. However, the subjects in this condition were asked to make use of a computational aid to assist them in making decisions. The device requires the consumer to match the total price of the package (recorded on the outer circle of the device) with the net weight of the package (recorded on the movable inside wheel of the device); the cost per ounce of the package is then shown in a box in the center of the wheel. All subjects in Treatment B were instructed in the use of this device and trained to a criterion of three successful price-per-unit computations. For Treatment C, subjects were presented with quantity and price as in Treatment A and, in addition, with cost-per-ounce of net weight of the package. This method of presenting information is commonly referred to as "unit pricing." This information was calculated and printed on small slips of paper which were placed under each package.

A major question in any simulation experiment concerns the fidelity of the simulation and whether the subject behavior elicited under the simulated conditions is representative of the behavior under actual conditions. To estimate the representativeness of the experimental behavior of the subjects, 12 additional subjects were asked to complete the experimental task in the supermarket from which the food items were purchased. It was possible to have subjects "shop" under Conditions A and B in an actual supermarket because these conditions did not require any change in the normal method of presentation of information by the supermarket. Twelve additional subjects therefore were asked to complete the same experimental task, six for each of these two treatments, as were the subjects in the simulation constituting this experiment.

RESULTS

Single-factor analyses of variance were performed comparing the three treatment conditions on accuracy of choice of most economical and total time required to make all nine choices.

The scoring key was determined for all product groups, except one, by dividing the net weight of each package into the total price of the package, yielding cost per ounce. For these eight product groups, the correct answer was the package having the lowest price per ounce. For one product group, instant potatoes, the most economical package was determined by dividing the number of ounces of potatoes made by the contents into the total price of the package; it was this cost per ounce that was the correct choice, and not the cost per net weight. Information regarding the number of servings and size of servings (defined on all packages as 4 ounces) was conspicuously displayed in all packages and assumed to be accurate. It should be noted that subjects were instructed that the most economical package should be determined from information presented on the package and could be in terms of net weight, servings, or in any other conventional measure.

The mean number of correct choices for each of the three treatments was A, 5.72 ($\sigma = 1.31$); B, 5.96 ($\sigma = 1.57$; and C, 8.04 ($\sigma = .45$). An analysis of variance showed that these differences were significant beyond the .01 level. The Newman-Keuls test for probing the nature of the differences between treatment means following a significant overall effect indicated the differences between Treatment Groups A and C and B and C to be significant ($p < .01$). The difference between Treatment Groups A and B was not significant.

The mean number of minutes spent in making the nine choices for each

TABLE 56–1

Correlation Coefficients between Number of Sizes, Number of Unique Size-Price Combinations, and Number of Accurate Choices

Treatment	Correlation Between Number of Sizes and Correct Choices	Correlation Between Number of Unique Size-Price Combinations and Correct Choices
A.	.50*	.48*
B.	.40*	.45*
C.	.04	.03

* $p < .05$.

treatment was A, 23.93 ($\sigma = 10.00$); B, 31.72 ($\sigma = 9.57$); and C, 3.60 ($\sigma = 1.11$). These differences were also statistically significant beyond the .01 level. Newman-Keuls analyses indicated all differences among the three treatment groups to be significant ($p < .01$) with the subjects in Treatment C requiring significantly less time to make the nine decisions than those of the other two treatments. Similarly, the subjects in Treatment A required significantly less time than did those in Treatment B.

Analyses were performed to estimate a relationship between the number of sizes within a product group and the accuracy of choice of most economical package. Also, the number of unique size-price combinations or distinct choices within each product group was determined and related to accuracy of choice. This number of unique combinations was, in general, different from the number of sizes for each product group. This was a result of the same-sized, but different brand, packages having different prices within a product group.

Correlation analyses were performed between the number of sizes and number of correct choices and between the number of unique size-price combinations and number of correct choices for each of the three experimental conditions. For Conditions A and B, all computed coefficients were significant; for Condition C, neither of the coefficients was significant. Table 56–1 summarizes the results. Finally, data gathered from the 12 subjects performing the experiment in the supermarket were summarized. Table 56–2 presents the mean number of correct choices and the mean time spent in making the nine choices for these subjects, together with the same information for corresponding groups in the simulation.

Although analyses of variance or t tests to test the differences between the in-store subjects and the simulation subjects on the two measures were not performed because of large discrepancies in sample size, it would appear, nevertheless, that the pattern of data obtained for the in-store subjects parallels those engaged in larger experiments.

TABLE 56–2

Data Comparing Performance of In-Store Subjects and Simulation Subjects for Treatments A and B

	Treatment A				Treatment B			
	In-store Condition[a]		Simulation Condition[b]		In-store Condition[a]		Simulation Condition[b]	
Item	$\bar{X}$	σ	$\bar{X}$	σ	$\bar{X}$	σ	$\bar{X}$	σ
No. of correct choices........	5.07	.82	5.72	1.31	5.34	1.29	5.96	1.57
No. of minutes to make nine choices........	27.83	11.27	23.93	10.00	35.12	11.76	31.72	9.57

[a] $n = 6$.
[b] $n = 25$.

DISCUSSION

The results of experimentation offer support to those that favor unit prices as a method of presenting information to consumers about weight and price of supermarket items.

The first hypothesis, that consumers are significantly more accurate in their choices of "most economical" when receiving unit-price information, was supported. A review of individual scores leads to two interesting observations. First, the variability in individual scores is considerably less for those in the unit-pricing treatment than in the other two. For each of these two treatments, scores ranged from two correct to eight correct. In the unit-pricing condition the range was from seven to nine correct, indicating that all subjects were able to process this information adequately. This would seem to be a highly desirable end product of an information system. A second observation is that even when unit-pricing information is presented, further education on economical purchasing is needed. Only 3 of the 25 subjects accurately chose the economical package of instant potatoes, despite instruction that "most economical" could be judged in terms of information in addition to price per unit. Apparently, subjects developed a set that price per unit of net weight was always the most economical. Therefore even with unit pricing for most goods, it would seem necessary to inform consumers that they should be cognizant of factors such as strength of solution (bleach, artificial sweeteners) or one-ply or two-ply construction (tissues), when determining economy of purchase. The computational aid did not improve the accuracy of consumer choices when compared with choices made under present supermarket methods of presenting information, supporting Hypothesis 3. This device was designed to make price-per-ounce calculations faster and more accurate for consumers. However, this calculation is only one part of the information a consumer must process before making a decision; he must still keep account of the price per unit for each package and make a judgment based on this information. This apparently is a difficult task, leading to errors of choice. A possibility for error is also introduced in the manipulatory aspects of the device. If the consumer inadvertently matches the wrong numbers on the device, he will naturally receive the wrong information. There would seem to be numerous possible occasions to commit such inadvertent mistakes, including misreading information on the package, misreading the entries on the aid, and accidentally moving the wheel on the aid.

The second hypothesis, that significantly less time is required for consumers to choose the most economical package when unit-pricing information is presented, was also supported.

Inspection of individual scores indicate very little variability in the time needed to make the nine decisions under unit pricing. For this treatment, all subjects completed the task in from 2 to 4 minutes. For Treatment A, the range was from 11 to 56 minutes and for Treatment B, from 23 to 60 minutes. This is an important observation. Speed in processing information would also seem to be a desirable end product of a pricing system.

Hypothesis 4, that there is no difference in time required to arrive at decisions under the two conditions other than the unit-pricing condition, was not supported. Obviously, the time required to manipulate the computational device for each calculation added greatly to the total shopping time.

Hypothesis 5, that the number of sizes of packages within a product group is inversely correlated to accuracy of choice for Treatments A and B, but not correlated for Treatment C, was not supported. For Treatments A and B, significant positive correlations were found between the number of correct choices and the number of sizes and also between the number of correct choices and the number of unique size-price combinations. These findings are significant in that one thrust of present governmental work to aid consumers in making price comparisons is to reduce the number of sizes within a product group. Correlations found in this study, of course, are based on limited data and therefore are not definitive; but they indicate that such a strategy may not be appropriate.

A few observations on the representativeness of the simulation seem to be appropriate. For this experiment, there are two points of comparison. The first is comparing the performance of the subjects in Treatment A with that of subjects in the previously reported study. In the study conducted by Friedman, subjects performed the experimental task in actual supermarkets, with an accuracy rate of 57 percent.[5] The accuracy

---

[5] Ibid.

rate for comparable subjects in the present experimentation was 63 percent, suggesting the comparability of the simulation with higher fidelity experimentation. A second comparison can be made between the performance of the simulation subjects and those that made their choices in the store (Table 56–2). For both treatments, performance differences were small, further supporting the contention of representativeness.

Indexes

NAME INDEX

SUBJECT INDEX

This book is set in 10 and 9 point Caledonia, leaded 2 points. Section numbers are 24 point Caledonia italic and section titles are 18 point Caledonia. Reading numbers and titles are 14 point Caledonia. The size of the type page is 27 × 46½ picas.